MARQUEE SERIES

Microsoft® Office 2016

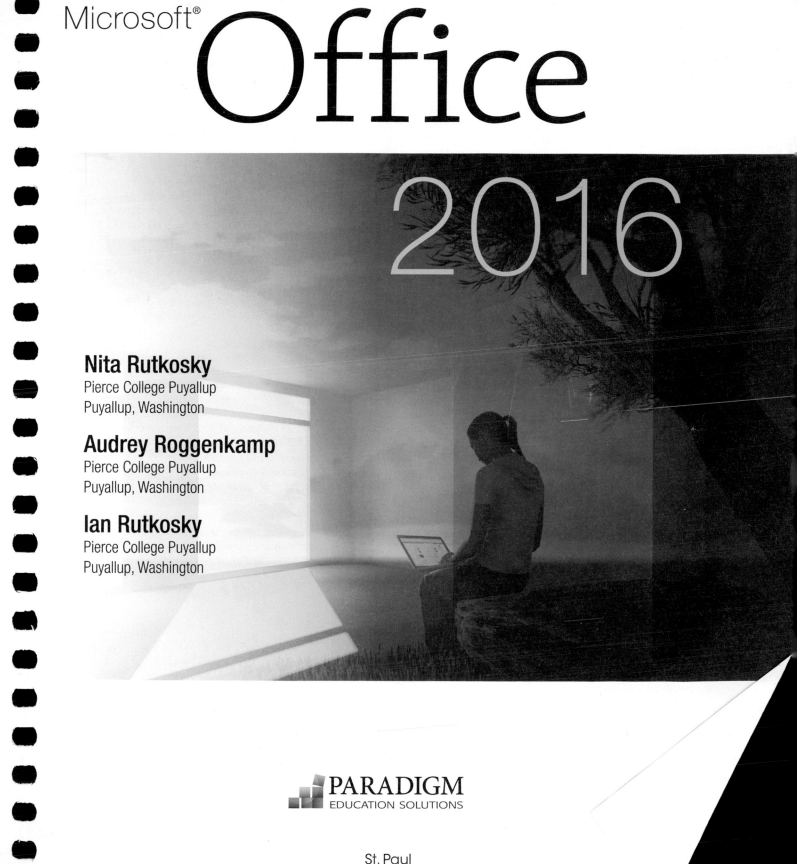

Nita Rutkosky
Pierce College Puyallup
Puyallup, Washington

Audrey Roggenkamp
Pierce College Puyallup
Puyallup, Washington

Ian Rutkosky
Pierce College Puyallup
Puyallup, Washington

PARADIGM
EDUCATION SOLUTIONS

St. Paul

Senior Vice President	Linda Hein
Editor in Chief	Christine Hurney
Director of Production	Timothy W. Larson
Production Editors	Rachel Kats, Jen Weaverling
Cover and Text Designer	Valerie King
Copy Editor	Sarah Kearin
Senior Design and Production Specialist	Jaana Bykonich
Assistant Developmental Editors	Mamie Clark, Katie Werdick
Testers	Desiree Carvel; Ann E. Mills, Ivy Tech Community College of Indiana, Indianapolis, IN
Instructional Support Writer	Brienna McWade
Indexer	Terry Casey
Vice President Information Technology	Chuck Bratton
Digital Projects Manager	Tom Modl
Vice President Sales and Marketing	Scott Burns
Director of Marketing	Lara Weber McLellan

Care has been taken to verify the accuracy of information presented in this book. However, the authors, editors, and publisher cannot accept responsibility for Web, email, newsgroup, or chat room subject matter or content, or for consequences from application of the information in this book, and make no warranty, expressed or implied, with respect to its content.

Trademarks: Microsoft is a trademark or registered trademark of Microsoft Corporation in the United States and/or other countries. Some of the product names and company names included in this book have been used for identification purposes only and may be trademarks or registered trade names of their respective manufacturers and sellers. The authors, editors, and publisher disclaim any affiliation, association, or connection with, or sponsorship or endorsement by, such owners.

Cover Photo Credits: © whitehoune/Shutterstock.com; © Photobank gallery/Shutterstock.com.

Information Technology Essentials Photo Credits: Page ITE-1: Image 1, © Photobank/Shutterstock.com and Image 2, © iStockphoto.com/Whitehoune, page 8 (header); Page ITE-2: (top) © iStockphoto.com/Andrew Parfenov, (middle) © iStockphoto.com/Neustockimages, (bottom) courtesy of Epson America, Inc.; Page ITE-3: (top) © iStockphoto.com/darren wise, (bottom left) © iStockphoto.com/Oleksiy Mark, (bottom right) courtesy of Motorola; Page ITE-4: (top) courtesy of McKesson Provider Technologies, (middle) courtesy of SanDisk Corporation, (bottom) courtesy of Intel Corporation; Page ITE-5: (top) courtesy of ASUSTeK Computer Inc., (bottom) © Alexey Rotanov / Shutterstock; Page ITE-6: (top) courtesy of Logitech, (middle) courtesy of Western Digital Corp., (bottom) courtesy of Verbatim Americas LLC.; Page ITE-8: (top) used with permission from Microsoft Corporation; Page ITE-11: (bottom left) © iStockphoto.com/killerb10, (bottom right) courtesy of Intuit Inc.; Page ITE-12: (top) courtesy of Opera Software APA; Page ITE-16 (middle) © iStockphoto.com/nolimitpictures, (bottom) © iStockphoto.com/Sebastien Cote; Page ITE-25 (top) © iStockphoto.com/MHJ.

We have made every effort to trace the ownership of all copyrighted material and to secure permission from copyright holders. In the event of any question arising as to the use of any material, we will be pleased to make the necessary corrections in future printings. Thanks are due to the aforementioned authors, publishers, and agents for permission to use the materials indicated.

ISBN 978-0-76386-675-4 (print)
ISBN 978-0-76386-677-8 (digital)

© 2017 by Paradigm Publishing, Inc.
875 Montreal Way
St. Paul, MN 55102
Email: educate@emcp.com
Website: ParadigmCollege.com

Printed in the United States of America

24 23 22 21 20 19 18 17 16   2 3 4 5 6 7 8 9 10 11 12

Contents

Contents   **v**

Preface

Marquee Series, Microsoft Office 2016 prepares students to work with Microsoft Office 2016 in a business office or for personal use. Incorporating an accelerated, step-by-step, project-based approach, this text builds student competency in Word, Excel, Access, and PowerPoint 2016.

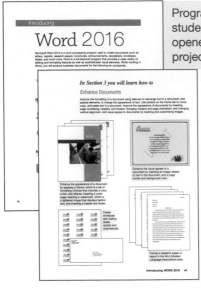

Program openers provide an overview of the software's best uses and give students a preview of the software features and workplace applications. The openers also provide an overview and visual representation of some of the projects that students will complete.

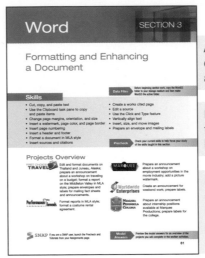

Accessed through the ebook, data files for each section are available for download.

Precheck quizzes allow students to check their current skills before starting section work.

Each program section begins with a list of skills and an overview and model answer preview of the projects completed in that section.

Students with SNAP access are encouraged to launch the Precheck quiz and section tutorials from their Assignments page.

Activities begin with a short explanation of the application's features followed by streamlined, point-and-click instruction that pares reading to a minimum.

In Brief—Bare-bones summaries of major commands and features provide instant review and a quick reference of the steps required to accomplish a task.

Magenta color highlights text to be typed.

Screen captures visually reinforce activity steps.

In Addition—Sidebars offer extra information on key features and subfeatures.

Interactive tutorials provide guided training and measured practice.

Check Your Work—Accessed through the ebook, locked PDFs allow students to confirm that they have completed the activity correctly.

Integrating Programs—Activities devoted to integrating information among Microsoft Office 2016 programs highlight the benefits of using the Office suite. Projects include copying, exporting, linking, and embedding data. Students learn how to manage data efficiently in the business office or for personal use.

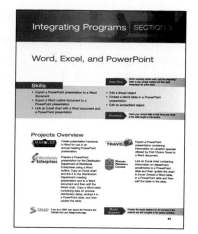

Workbook eBook

Section study tools and assessement activities are provided in the *Workbook* ebook, which students can link to directly from their student ebook or their SNAP Assignments page.

Study Tools—A PowerPoint presentation with audio support and In Brief step lists help students further develop and review section skills.

Knowledge Check—Objective completion exercises allow students to assess their comprehension and recall of program features, terminology, and functions.

Recheck—A concept quiz for each section enables students to check how their skills have improved after completing section work.

Skills Exercise—Additional activities, performed live in the application, are available to SNAP users. SNAP will automatically score student work and provide detailed feedback.

Skills Review—Completing these hands-on exercises reinforces learning of key features and skills. Instructions include some guidance, but less than is provided within the section activities.

Skills Assessment—Framed within a workplace project perspective, these assessments evaluate the ability to apply section skills and concepts in solving realistic problems. They require the demonstration of program skills and decision-making, which may include additional research or an Individual Challenge.

Marquee Challenge—Culminating assessments test mastery of program features and their problem-solving abilities.

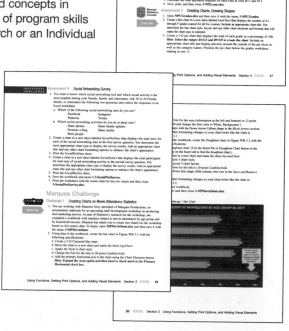

SNAP Training and Assessment

SNAP is a web-based training and assessment program and learning management system (LMS) for learning Microsoft Office 2016. SNAP is comprised of rich content, a sophisticated grade book, and robust scheduling and analytics tools. SNAP courseware supports the *Marquee Series* content and delivers live-in-the-application assessments for students to demonstrate their skills mastery. Interactive tutorials increase skills-focused moments with guided training and measured practice. SNAP provides automatic scoring and detailed feedback on the many activities, exercises, and quizzes to help identify areas where additional support is needed, evaluating student performance both at an individual and course level. The *Marquee Series* SNAP course content is also available to export into any LMS system that supports LTI tools.

Paradigm Education Solutions provides technical support for SNAP through 24-7 chat at ParadigmCollege.com. In addition, an online User Guide and other SNAP training tools for using SNAP are available.

Student eBook and *Workbook* eBook

The student ebook and *Workbook* ebook provide access to the *Marquee Series* content from any device (desktop, tablet, and smartphone) anywhere, through a live Internet connection. The versitile ebook platform features dynamic navigation tools including a linked table of contents and the ability to jump to specific pages, search for terms, bookmark, highlight, and take notes. The ebooks offer live links to the interactive content and resources that support the print textbook, including the student data files, Precheck and Recheck quizzes, interactive tutorials, and PowerPoint presentations with audio support. The *Workbook* ebook also provides end-of-section Knowledge Check, Skills Review, Skills Assessment, and Marquee Challenge activities.

Instructor eResources

All instructor resources are available digitally through a web-based ebook on the Paradigm Bookshelf. The instructor materials include:

- Planning resources, such as lesson plans, teaching hints, and sample course syllabi

- Presentation resources, such as PowerPoint slide shows with lecture notes

- Assessment resources, including live and annotated PDF model answers for section work and workbook activities, rubrics for evaluating student work, and section-based exam banks

Information Technology Essentials

The Information Processing Cycle

Computers process information in the same way that humans make decisions. We use our eyes and ears to *input* facts and data into our brains. We use our brains to *process* that data and organize it into information. The resulting *output* is a thought or decision that we can display or present by drawing it, writing it, or making a video or audio recording of it. If we decide to keep the results for future use, we can *store* the paper or recording in a file cabinet.

As shown in Figure 1, the information processing cycle can be divided into four segments: input, processing, output, and storage. It relies on computer hardware to mimic the human thought process. The term *hardware* refers to the devices you can physically see and touch in and on the computer.

Input

Input involves getting data into the computer so that it can be processed. Some commonly used input devices are described in the following sections.

Keyboard Designed based on the layout of keys on a typewriter, the keyboard is primarily used for typing text. Although numbers are found in a row above the letters, most PC keyboards also include a calculator-style number pad for the convenience of bookkeepers, accountants, and others who frequently work with numbers.

Twelve keys labeled F1 through F12, as well as several other named keys, can be programmed to perform special functions in software applications. For example, the F1 key usually displays a help window where you might type a request for instructions on how to print what has just been typed. The Home key might move the cursor to the left side of a line in one program, but to the upper left corner of the page in another. (The cursor, also known as the insertion point, is the flashing bar, dash, or other symbol that indicates where the next character you type will appear on the screen.)

Figure 1 The Information Processing Cycle

A keyboard and mouse are examples of common input devices.

Mouse A mouse is a pointing device used for issuing commands and selecting text or files for processing. Moving the mouse on the desktop causes a pointer to move on the screen. If you point to the File tab in the top left corner of the Microsoft Word screen, for example, and then click the left mouse button, the backstage area will appear, allowing you to click the *Open* option if you want to access a file you have previously saved.

If you want to delete several words or lines of text in a file, you can point to the beginning of the first word, hold down the left mouse button, drag the mouse to highlight the text, and then press the Delete key to remove the text from the document.

Most tablets, such as the iPad, utilize a touchscreen as the main mode of user input. Touchscreens have advanced and allow multiple fingers or thumbs to be used simultaneously on the screen.

Touchpad Most laptop computers provide a touchpad instead of a mouse as a pointing device. To use a touchpad, move your index finger across the pad to position the cursor and then use your thumb to press the buttons at the bottom of the pad.

Touchscreen A touchscreen allows you to select items and input commands by physically touching a specific area of the monitor. Most smartphones and tablets utilize touchscreen technology. Touchscreens are also used at information kiosks to provide an easy way to select items of interest, without the necessity of a keyboard. Servers at restaurants use touchscreens to place orders since they are much easier to clean than keyboards and can be used with only one hand.

A scanner is a tool to input either pictures or text.

Scanner A scanner works like a photocopier to transfer pictures or text into a computer. If you don't have a digital camera, you can scan hard copies of your photos into a PC and then organize or enhance them with photo-editing software.

Digitizing Pen and Drawing Tablet Although a mouse can be used for drawing designs and pictures, it is very clumsy. Better detail can be achieved with a digitizing pen and drawing tablet. Some tablets and laptop computers now accept "handwritten" input with a digitizing pen called a stylus.

Tablet PCs are useful for writing notes by hand when in a meeting or on the road.

Engineers, architects, and designers often use a sophisticated type of graphics tablet to make precise drawings such as those used in building construction and the manufacture of circuit boards for computers. Such graphics tablets are made up of hundreds of tiny intersecting wires that form an electronic matrix embedded in the tablet surface. A stylus or crosshair cursor activates these intersection points, which collectively represent the image.

Joystick A joystick (named after the control stick used to fly fighter jets) is an input device consisting of a small box with a vertical stick that, when pushed in a certain direction, moves the cursor on the screen. Most often used to control fast-moving images in computer games, joysticks can also be used by people who have difficulty using a mouse.

Digital Camera Digital cameras can be used to transfer pictures and videos onto a computer. A webcam is a popular example of a video camera that can be used in combination with headphones and a microphone to communicate with people all over the world. Many computers, including all smartphones, now come with built-in cameras and microphones to make this type of communication easier.

A joystick is an input device used to move objects on a computer screen and is a common input device for computer gaming.

Microphone With a microphone you can add a "sound bite" to a computerized slide presentation or speak to a friend over the Internet. Microphones can stand on a desk or be worn as part of a headset.

Bar Code Reader Bar code readers are used for entering the Universal Product Code (UPC) found on items in grocery and retail stores. They also are used to track medication administration in hospitals.

A digital camera captures images in a digital format and often contains an output device for viewing those images.

A webcam is a digital camera that can be controlled remotely over the Internet.

Dual Purpose Devices Although usually thought of as storage devices, compact discs (CDs), digital video discs (DVDs), flash drives, and hard drives all allow you to enter data into a computer quickly and easily.

Processing

A computer's central function is to process data. Processing can involve calculating numbers, editing text, modifying pictures, and

A bar code reader scans a UPC. The resulting input can be used to check a patient's identity and medication requirements.

other information management tasks. The central processing unit (CPU) is the brain of the computer that handles those tasks. The rate at which the CPU can process data is known as the *clock speed*.

Processors Most IBM-compatible PCs use a central processing unit made by Intel or AMD. These CPUs process data at clock speeds from 2.0 to 4.0 gigahertz (GHz). (One gigahertz equals one billion cycles per second.) The first Apple Macintosh computers ran on Motorola 68000 processors, but Macs now use Intel processors and can run IBM-compatible PC operating systems.

Many CPUs include multiple processors on a single chip. These dual-core or quad-core processors can process multiple instructions simultaneously for better performance. Some CPUs have six processors in one. Single-core processors use a technique called

Flash drives are small, easy-to-handle, portable storage devices that many people use to carry important data with them wherever they go.

multitasking, in which one processor switches between programs so quickly that the user doesn't perceive any interruption, but both programs are actually running more slowly than they would with two separate processors or with one dual-core processor.

Memory Chips Memory chips are the hardware that provides the workspace for the data and instructions the computer is processing. The user workspace is called *random access memory (RAM)* because the CPU has quick and easy access to it. Having a large amount of RAM is like having a large work table where you can spread out books, papers, pencils, a calculator, and other tools you need to do your work. RAM is considered volatile or temporary storage because it disappears completely when the power to the computer is shut off.

The amount of RAM a personal computer needs depends on the operating system it runs. A Windows 10 or Windows 8.1 system requires at least 1 gigabyte (GB). A gigabyte equals about one billion bytes.

A processor chip (a CPU) performs the calculations in a computer.

Read only memory (ROM) is sometimes confused with RAM due to the similarity of their names, but ROM is nonvolatile and contains the getting-started instructions that the PC needs when the power is first turned on. As its name implies, ROM can only be used as programmed by the PC manufacturer. You can't make any changes to it; you can only cause its contents to be "read" into the computer.

The motherboard is a container for the computer's CPU and RAM, and contains slots for adding expansion cards. Figure 2 shows a typical motherboard layout.

Figure 2 Motherboard Layout

Output

Output is processed data that can be used immediately or stored for later use. Output may be produced in either hard copy or soft copy, or in both forms. Hard copy is a permanent version of output, such as a letter printed on paper using a printer. Soft copy is a temporary version of output and includes any output that cannot be physically handled. Soft copy output devices include monitors and speakers.

Monitor A monitor is a screen used for displaying graphics and text. Although older cathode ray tube (CRT) monitors are still in use, new PCs are sold with flat screen, liquid crystal display (LCD) or light-emitting diode (LED) monitors. In an LCD monitor, liquid crystals are sandwiched between two sheets of material. Electric current passing through the crystals causes them to twist. This twisting effect blocks some light waves and allows other light waves to pass through, creating images on the screen. In an LED monitor, the LCD method of light transmission is enhanced by positioning red, green, and blue LEDs behind the liquid crystals. An LED monitor provides a more vibrant, colorful display than an LCD monitor.

Flat screen, LCD monitors are the most commonly used output devices.

Printer Printers provide hard copy printouts on paper. Several printing technologies are available, including ink-jet, which squirts liquid ink onto the paper, and laser, which fuses powdered toner to the paper.

Speakers and Headphones Speakers and headphones provide audio output in stereo or surround sound for movies, radio programs, streaming video, online learning courses, and telephone calls.

Computer speakers provide sound output.

Storage

The storage portion of the information processing cycle involves recording output so that it will be available after the computer has been shut off and RAM has been erased.

Output can be stored for future use on hard drives, CDs, DVDs, and flash drives. A *drive* is a PC device that can read and write data onto the surface of a round platter (disk) as it spins. Hard disk platters are made of metal; compact and digital video discs are made of plastic. Flash drives and solid-state hard drives store data in nonvolatile RAM; they have no moving parts, but they provide the same function as conventional drives.

Hard drives contain a stack of metal platters (disks), a drive motor, and read/write heads that are positioned to access the top and bottom of each platter. Hard drive capacities vary; an average desktop PC might have a hard drive that holds 500 GB.

Data CDs are made of the same material that is used for music CDs. In fact, you can play your favorite music CDs using the CD drive of your PC. CDs can hold about 700 MB of data. DVDs can hold from 4 GB to 8 GB,

Portable external hard drives are available in a variety of sizes, styles, and colors.

This flash drive storage device has a USB connector that fits into a standard USB port.

depending on whether they can record on one or two layers. Blu-ray discs are used both for high-definition video and for data; a Blu-ray disc can hold 25 GB to 50 GB.

The flash drives on the market today can hold from 128 megabytes to 256 gigabytes of data on a printed circuit board inside a protective plastic case. They are the size and shape of a person's thumb. Some drives even provide fingerprint authorization. Flash drives connect directly to a USB port and thus do not require the installation of any device driver programs to support them.

System Unit Ports

Ports are the sockets that the input, output, and storage devices plug into (see Figure 3). In the early days of personal computing, serial, parallel, and printer cables and ports were found on all PCs. Today, most external, or *peripheral*, devices use Universal Serial Bus (USB) cables and ports. USB cables and connector plugs are smaller, thinner, and more durable. They transmit data at up to 5 gigabits per second (Gbps) for a USB 3.0 port. As many as 127 devices can be connected to a computer host at once through a daisy-chain-style connection setup.

USB hubs provide extra connection options for computers with only one or two USB ports. You can even make backup copies of your data to an external hard drive connected to your computer via the USB port on your keyboard.

Exploring Technology　1

Identify the processor, clock speed, and amount of random access memory (RAM) in a computer you often use. *Hint: On a computer running Windows 10 or 8.1, right-click the Start button and then click* System *at the pop-up menu. In either operating system, if the Control Panel is displayed using Classic view, double-click the System icon.*

Exploring Technology　2

Identify the hardware you have on your computer and categorize each piece as input, output, or both.

Figure 3 System Unit Ports

LAN port　USB ports　microphone connection　speaker connection　video port

Computer Software

Software refers to the operating instructions and applications that allow computers to process the numbers, pictures, sounds, and text we enter into them. We can touch the disc that contains the software, but not the lines of programming code that make up the software.

Personal Computer Operating Systems

The original personal computer operating system, MS-DOS (Disk Operating System), used a command-line interface, which meant that commands were typed into a text prompt and the computer returned text output to the monitor. Today, most operating systems use Graphical User Interfaces (GUIs), in which a mouse is used to manipulate graphic objects such as icons and windows on-screen.

If a PC has an older CPU with a clock speed that is too slow, or if it does not have enough RAM, the PC will run slowly or it won't be able to run the operating system at all. Windows 10 and Windows 8.1 require, at a minimum, a CPU that runs at 1 GHz and has 1 GB of RAM.

The operating system for Apple Macintosh computers is Mac OS. The tenth version of the Mac operating system is called Mac OS X. Since its initial introduction in 2001, several updates to this operating system have been released, each one with a different code name. El Capitan (version 10.11) was released in September 2015. Previous versions included Yosemite, Mavericks, Mountain Lion, Lion, and Snow Leopard.

The Windows 10 operating system requires a CPU that runs at 1 GHz.

The Mac OS X operating system can run on IBM-compatible PCs.

Applications

Applications allow someone with no technical knowledge of how a PC works to use a computer to balance his or her checkbook or to insert a photograph into a personalized greeting card, print it out, and send it to a friend. Thousands of software applications are available to empower users to perform these and other tasks, ranging from mundane to amazing. This section presents the most common types of computer applications on the market today.

Word Processing Word processing software was originally designed as a replacement for the typewriter. Now a word processing program such as Microsoft Word can support photos and drawings; mathematical calculations; text in table format; text of varying sizes, shapes, and colors; and even sound bites.

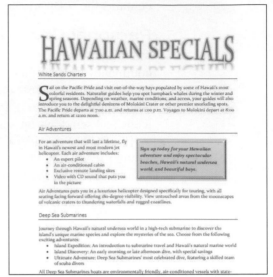

Microsoft Word is a word processing program with several formatting features that can be applied to words, lines, paragraphs, pages, or entire documents.

Spreadsheet Spreadsheet software such as Microsoft Excel can be used for both simple and complex calculations. Current versions can also support graphics and perform some database tasks, such as sorting. A series of keystrokes or clicks used to perform a task can be saved as a macro and programmed to run at the press of a key.

Because formulas are used to create calculations, you can ask, "If I spend only $2 per day on coffee instead of $5, how much money will I save per month?" When you replace one value with another, the program will automatically recalculate your budget.

Database Database software such as Microsoft Access is designed to keep track of information. It allows you to arrange data alphabetically, numerically, or chronologically, or you can filter the data to display only those items that match your criteria, such as the names of customers who spent more than $500 at your online music store last year. Database software can easily do simple calculations, such as showing monthly subtotals and an annual total for each of your customers, but complex math is usually best left to spreadsheet software.

An Excel spreadsheet can calculate elements of a sales report, such as quarterly total sales, and display them in a chart.

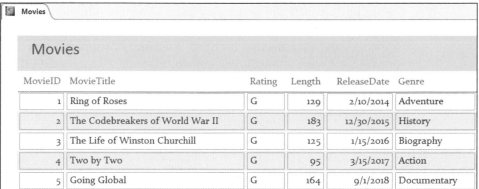

Information can be entered into an Access database by using a form designed for that purpose.

An Access database report is a selection of data in a database. The user chooses which types of information should be included in the report, and the database automatically finds and organizes the corresponding data.

Presentation Presentation software such as Microsoft PowerPoint allows users to create slide shows that can be viewed on a computer monitor or projected onto a large screen. Slide shows can include clip art, graphs and charts, photos, drawings, video clips, sound, and text. Features such as arrows and boxes that "fly" into the screen and slide transition effects can add interest and emphasis to the content of a presentation.

PowerPoint can combine text, graphics, sounds, and videos.

Audio, Video, and Photo Editing Photo-editing software is used for organizing, retouching, and editing photographs and videos. Programs such as PaintShop Pro and Photo Elements allow you to edit photographs by cropping, removing the red-eye effect, or by making more advanced changes such as putting one person's head on another person's body. You can also create your own slide shows with background audio and then email the results to friends and family or copy them to the cloud and display them on your TV.

Video-editing software such as Adobe Premiere can be used to edit video clips to remove the shots you took of your feet when you forgot to stop recording, or to add music, or to rearrange the scenes to create a more logical flow—or a more creative one. You can also edit the audio tracks. With some relatively inexpensive products, you can fine-tune the sound and achieve a professional level of quality.

The Internet provides many options for uploading and sharing videos, music, and photos. YouTube is a popular website that allows users to watch and post videos. Many emerging new musicians use the website SoundCloud to upload their latest tracks and share them with the community. Websites such as Imgur and Photobucket are useful for uploading and sharing images.

Graphics and Drawing Applications such as Adobe Photoshop, Adobe Illustrator, Microsoft Paint, and Corel PaintShow Pro are popular software packages that provide the tools to design graphical images that can be used for web pages, posters, marketing brochures, and greeting cards. Visio is a graphics application that focuses more on technical and business drawings, flow charts, and organizational charts to illustrate complex processes. Visio is vector graphics–based, meaning that it uses points, lines, curves, and geometric shapes to create images. Raster-based graphics programs use groups of pixels (picture elements) to make an image.

A digitized pen and tablet may seem to be a requirement for using drawing applications, but you can do amazing things with a mouse by, for example, picking a circle from a group of shapes and then making it larger or smaller or turning it into an oval. Free graphics and drawing software applications include Inkscape, Skencil, and GIMP.

Suites Software applications are often bundled into packages called *suites*. Widely used versions of the Microsoft Office suite contain the word processing application, Word; the spreadsheet application, Excel; the database application, Access; and the presentation application, PowerPoint.

Paint is a basic image-editing program included with Windows.

Adobe Photoshop is a high-end image-editing program used by graphics professionals.

Money management software enables users to manage their money by helping them pay bills, balance checkbooks, keep track of income and expenses, maintain investment records, and more.

Smartphones include PIM software that tracks appointments and stores contact information.

Money Management Quicken and Microsoft Money are two software applications with an interface that resembles a checkbook. Users can not only write and print checks, but also track their spending habits, create a budget, generate cash flow reports, download their credit card charges, and keep track of their savings and investments.

TurboTax and TaxCut are income-tax preparation programs that prompt you to enter your tax information and then print duplicates of the state and federal forms with your data on the appropriate lines. They also let you file your tax returns electronically and direct your refund to your bank account.

Personal Information Management Microsoft Outlook and Lotus Organizer are examples of personal information management (PIM) programs that keep track of your to-do list, address book, and personal calendar. Many PIMs also contain a scheduler with an alarm to alert you of a meeting, whether it occurs daily, weekly, or only once. Smartphones and tablets can synchronize with your computer's PIM program so you can carry your information everywhere you go.

Collaboration Businesses often need several people to collaborate on a project. Collaborative software or groupware, such as IBM Notes, Adobe Connect, and Microsoft Office SharePoint, provides a way to keep track of who has made or suggested changes to documents or plans and to distribute everything electronically. A calendar feature allows

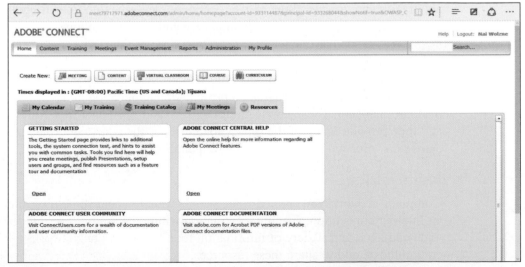

Collaboration software (groupware) can help team members stay connected.

users to schedule meetings at times when others are free. Both email and instant messaging (IM) functions are used, providing real-time communication among team members wherever they are in the world. SharePoint allows direct editing of documents through Word, Excel, or PowerPoint and also provides controlled access to shared documents via the web.

Gaming Computer games have come a long way since the Solitaire program included in the first versions of Windows. Today's games contain high-quality 3D animations, sound, and action that are very realistic. Role playing, action, sports, and fantasy games are just a small part of a fast-growing industry. You can even play games over the Internet with people in other cities and countries.

Some games, especially those that include realistic simulations, require a lot of computing power. You will need a fast CPU, plenty of RAM, and a dedicated video card for the best performance.

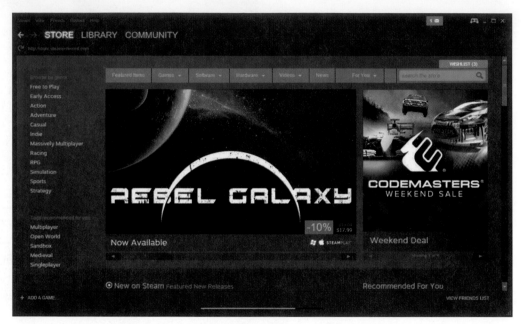

Electronic distribution through services like Steam allow gamers to access thousands of video games that can be downloaded and installed ontheir computers.

Open Source Open source software is the general term for applications that are provided completely free of charge, with no license fees or restrictions and no copyrights to worry about. You can download the software, copy it, and give it to your friends. The programming source code is also provided without charge and anyone is allowed to modify and improve it. Linux is a popular open source operating system. For further details about open source software, go to www.opensource.org.

OpenOffice is a suite of applications that is considered open source and includes a word processor, a spreadsheet program, a presentation application, a drawing application, and a database manager. These applications can save and open data files from Microsoft Office, and they provide many of the same capabilities as the equivalent retail products. OpenOffice can be downloaded for free from www.openoffice.org.

Networks

Computer networks are created when people want to share something such as a printer, an Internet connection, specific information within the confines of their business, or the wide and abundant variety of information found on the web. Networks allow computers to communicate and to share these resources.

Local Area Networks

The Local Area Network (LAN) illustrated in Figure 4 consists of several computers that are physically connected to one another via a central hub called a *switch*. The network also includes a server (a computer that manages the network) and a shared printer. Most LANs are not stand-alone systems; they connect to the Internet as well, so users can take advantage of online resources such as the web and email.

Wide Area Networks

A company might have several LANs, each in a different location or branch office, and these LANs can be connected to one another to form Wide Area Networks (WANs), as shown in Figure 5. The key difference between a LAN and a WAN is that in a WAN, the company does not own all the pathways between the computers. The data has to go out in "public" to reach its destination, whether that is via a leased optic line or the Internet. Leaving the protected local area carries security risks but also provides connectivity benefits.

Figure 4 Local Area Network

Figure 5 Wide Area Network

Large companies lease dedicated telephone lines (T1 or T3 lines) or satellite connections to connect their LANs. Many smaller companies find it more affordable to connect their branch offices via the existing Internet infrastructure.

Network Components

Computer networks require specialized hardware and software designed to share information and for other collaborative functions. The various components are explained in this section.

Clients Clients are the computer workstations where end users run the various applications necessary for them to do their jobs. In a client-server network, clients request information from the servers. Figure 6 shows an example of a client-server architecture. In this type of network structure, the networking paths allow a client computer to send information to a server, which can then relay the information back to that client computer or to another client on the same network. In this network, devices such as network hard drives and printers can be shared resources, available through their respective servers. In addition, the file server can provide access to a shared hard disk.

Figure 6 Client-Server Architecture

Servers Servers are data providers that are often larger and more powerful computers than clients. They house the network operating system software that organizes data sharing among the end users' PCs. They can hold large databases of information that users access to compile the reports that keep their organizations running smoothly. Servers might also be used as the storage location for everything every user creates, so that everyone else has easy access to it.

For small networks, the same computer can function as both client and server in a peer-to-peer network where all computers are equal and each one is both data requester and data provider (see Figure 7).

Figure 7 Peer-to-Peer Architecture

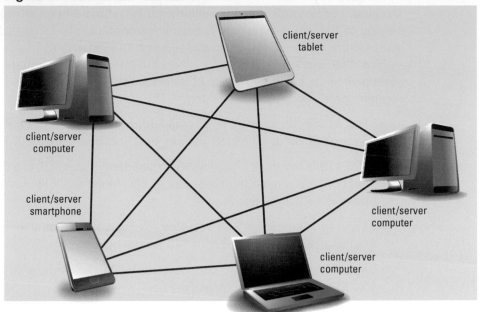

Switches and Routers Within a LAN, all the computers and other network-enabled devices (such as printers) must have a way of communicating with one another. Switches and routers serve as central hubs for that communication.

A switch is a box into which each computer connects via a cable. A switch that connects devices via radio frequency (RF) rather than via cables is called a *wireless access point*. A router is a more sophisticated version of a switch. A router can pass data from one LAN to another and throughout the Internet. Routers can be wired, wireless, or both.

Connectivity The PCs that make up a network have to be connected to each other in some way. The original method of connecting PCs used physical cables containing several strands of wire. The latest method is wireless and uses radio frequencies to carry data over short distances from a PC to a switch or router. All the devices are often located in the same room, but the signals are strong enough to penetrate the walls in homes and offices.

The most commonly used type of network cable is unshielded twisted pair cable (UTP). UTP cable is rated by category, and higher categories are needed for faster networks. Standard home networks use Cat 5 or Cat 5e cables; for business use, Cat 6 cable is the norm. Cat 7 and Cat 7a are the newest cable standards that provide up to 10 gigabits per second.

Wireless connections are used where cables are difficult to install or where the users are mobile or not close to a switch or router. Commonly called Wi-Fi, these connections are known by their technical 802.11 protocol specifications.

A switch provides a central connection place for cables from multiple computers.

A router enables you to join two or more networks, or to join your LAN to the Internet.

Protocols A *protocol* is a generally accepted agreement on how to behave in a certain situation. For example, in many countries it is considered proper protocol to stand during the playing of the national anthem. Computer protocols are international agreements on how to manufacture hardware and software, and how to send data from one computer to another.

Now that wireless connectivity is becoming more common in the home computer market, more people are becoming aware of its associated technical labels. The following is a list of common protocols:

- 802.11ac is the current Wi-Fi standard. It has a maximum data rate of 1,300 Mbps and a range of about 70 meters indoors or 250 meters outdoors.

- 802.11n is the most common Wi-Fi standard; many 802.11n devices are still in use today. It has a maximum data rate of 450 Mbps and a range of about 70 meters indoors or 250 meters outdoors.

- 802.11g is an earlier Wi-Fi standard. It has a maximum data rate of 54 Mbps and a range of 38 meters indoors or 140 meters outdoors.

- 802.11b and 802.11a are now obsolete Wi-Fi standards, with maximum data rates of 54 Mbps and 11 Mbps, respectively.

- TCP/IP (Transmission Control Protocol/Internet Protocol) defines the rules for sending and receiving data between network devices. Each device has a unique IP address, which is a series of four numbers between 0 and 255, separated by periods, like this: 192.168.0.1.

- HTTP (HyperText Transfer Protocol) defines the rules for sending and receiving web pages (hypertext) on the Internet. For example, you might see http://ParadigmCollege/myschool.edu on the uniform resource locator (URL) or Address line of your Internet browser. Figure 8 shows how data travels across the Internet.

Figure 8 Internet Infrastructure
Data moves across the Internet by traveling through a collection of physical devices.

http://www.senate.gov/

Step 1
You issue a request for information from the US Senate's home page.

Step 2
Your request is sent from your computer across a telecommunications medium such as a wireless tower, telephone lines, cable lines, or satellite.

Step 6
Your request arrives at the US Senate's web server. The information is sent back to your Internet address.

Step 3
Your request passes through one or more routers.

Step 5
Your request passes through one or more national ISPs.

Step 4
Your request passes through your local Internet Service Provider's (ISP's) computer. The address you entered is converted to an IP address, which is a series of numbers that uniquely identifies the location of the web page.

- HTTPS (HyperText Transfer Protocol Secure Sockets) encrypts data before sending it over the web. You can see the letters *https* on the URL line when you reach a web page asking for your credit card number or when you are paying your bills online, such as https://emcp/mybank.com/myaccount.

- POP3 is the current version of Post Office Protocol for receiving email. POP is a store-and-forward system in which your email waits on the mail server until you pick it up via an email application such as Outlook; then it forwards it to that application.

- SMTP (Simple Mail Transfer Protocol) enables you to send email. The message is transferred to the recipient's mail server on the Internet, where it waits for the user to pick it up via his or her email application.

- FTP (File Transfer Protocol) provides an efficient, fast way to transfer files between computers. It is commonly used for files that are too large for email attachments and for large repositories of files.

HTTPS is a protocol that protects your personal data. Note the padlock at the left side of the Address bar and the website name in green at the top of the screen.

Connectors and Ports Wired network connections commonly use RJ-45 connectors. These are similar to telephone connectors (which are RJ-11 or RJ-14) but they use eight wires instead of the usual 2 or 4. An RJ-45 connector is slightly wider than its telephone counterpart.

Exploring Technology 5

If you have Windows 10, display the Start menu, type **network**, and then click *View network connections* in the list that appears. A list of the computers and other devices in your LAN appears. Open the Network and Sharing Center and explore the icons and links there to learn more about your network. What protocols are installed? What is your connection speed?

Exploring Technology 6

Ask your instructor if your school has wireless connectivity. If yes, find out where wireless is active and then go to that area to see if you can locate the wireless access point(s) (antennas) that are installed. For example, if the school cafeteria has wireless connectivity, you may be able to see the hardware that provides the access to the Internet mounted on the ceiling or walls.

The Internet

The Internet is a global network of computers that allows data of all types and formats to be passed freely from one computer to another (see Figure 9). The web, email, and FTP are different parts of the Internet.

Figure 9 The Internet Network
Communications systems include computer hardware and communications software that allow computer users to exchange data around the house or around the world.

World Wide Web

The World Wide Web is a collection of hypertext files containing graphics, audio, and video that can be accessed on the Internet. The web is only a part of the Internet, albeit a very large part.

Electronic Mail

Electronic mail (email) uses its own protocols (such as SMTP and POP3) to route a message between computers on the Internet and hold it at a destination mail server until the recipient picks it up.

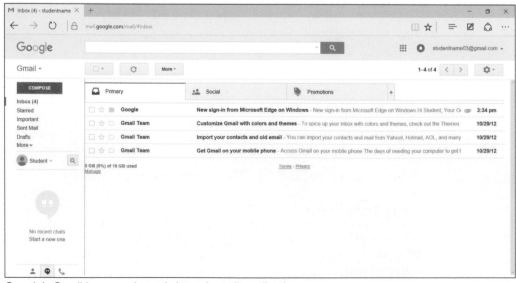

Google's Gmail is a popular web-based email application.

File Transfer Protocol

Like email and the web, File Transfer Protocol (FTP) is an information workspace on the Internet. It was originally used for exchanging data between incompatible mainframe systems, such as those made by IBM and those made by UNIVAC, but is now used to transfer files. A FTP server can be accessed through a web browser or a dedicated FTP application such as FileZilla.

FileZilla is a commonly used application for transferring files through an FTP site.

Web 2.0

When the World Wide Web became popular in the mid 90's, content hosted on websites was relatively static and created by publishers. Users didn't have much of a chance to interact and be active members in creating and managing the content. Websites were only updated when the content creators felt the need to do so.

As the infrastruture of the Internet grew and became more capable of delivering users more bandwidth and speed, the way users interacted with the World Wide Web changed. Websites began allowing users to interact more and add content to websites. For example, the video-sharing website YouTube relies entirely upon users uploading videos and providing feedback in the form of comments. A service such as YouTube would have not been viable in the past because of the bandwidth requirements for watching a video on the Internet. A few key elements of Web 2.0 are mass user participation, user created and shared content, social connectivity, and web-integrated applications.

Social Networking With the advent of Web 2.0, social networking websites became very popular. Facebook and MySpace were the pioneers of social networking, which consists of users creating and maintaining a profile with which other users can view and interact. When Facebook and MySpace were first introduced, they had very limited features that expanded over time. MySpace's popularity waned as Facebook became an

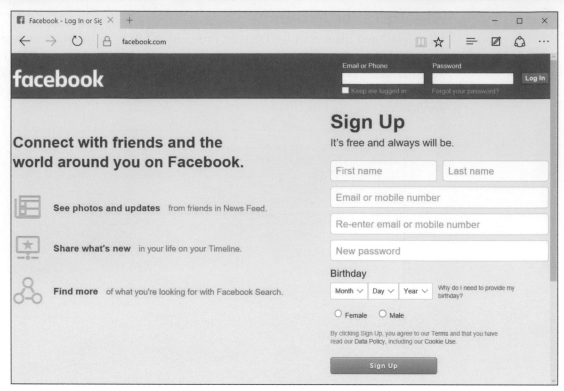

Facebook is currently the most commonly used social networking website.

easier-to-use, more streamlined platform. Facebook allows users to interact with their friends and families by sharing pictures, videos, stories, hyperlinks, event information and so on.

Currently, the most widely used social networking sites are Facebook, Twitter, and LinkedIn. Other social networking sites tend to be based on certain interests. For example, Pinterest is a social networking website that allows users to share ideas through media, primarily pictures. Users can go on Pinterest and find an activity or craft another user has "pinned" on his or her profile.

Media Sharing Increased bandwidth and user interaction led to websites being designed to provide users a place to share media such as pictures, music, and videos. These websites generate money by providing users a platform to share their media and then placing advertisements on the website. Imgur, Tumblr, SoundCloud, and YouTube are all examples of media-sharing websites. While these websites allow you to upload media, you must be the rightful owner of the media in order to share it online. Websites like YouTube will take down any content that contains copyrighted materials.

Since so much user-created media is available on the Internet, finding specific content can be difficult. Fortunately, there are websites dedicated to providing you with links and information to find content. For example, the website Reddit allows users to post links to pictures, videos, music, articles, and so on in an online bulletin board system. Once a link to content has been posted on Reddit, every user can either "up vote" or "down vote" the post. This voting system allows users to control the content that other users may or may not see.

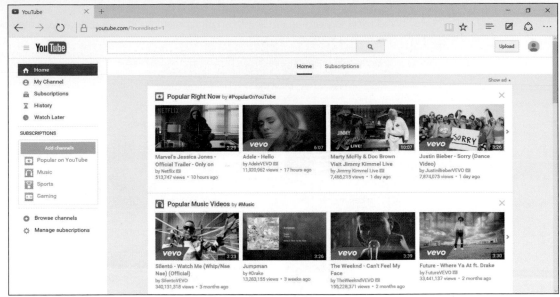
YouTube is the most commonly used video-sharing website.

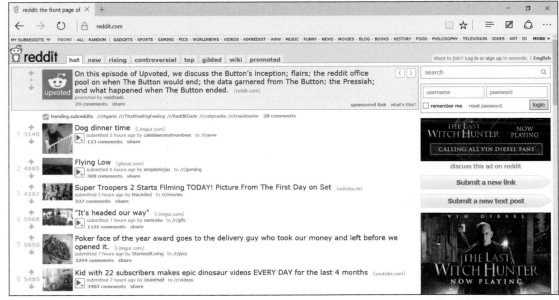
Reddit is a website where users post links to content and other users can vote on it.

Security Issues

Malware is a term describing computer programs that have malicious intent. Viruses, spyware, ransomware, worms, and adware programs all fall into this category.

Viruses

A computer virus is a string of code written to hurt others by damaging or destroying their computer files or making their computer experience difficult. Viruses are stored in executable (program) files; when the program runs, the virus code executes, causing damage and copying the virus into the computer's memory, where it infects other programs (see Figure 10). A virus is typically spread via an email attachment. Some viruses send themselves out via automatically generated emails to everyone in your address book.

Figure 10 How a Virus Attacks
When you forward an email with an attachment such as a picture, you may be spreading a damaging virus.

The receiver opens the attachment (with a virus) and is infected. The person then sends an email with attachment to another person, infecting that person when the attachment is opened.

email infected by virus

The receiver does not open the attachment, deletes the email, and is not infected.

email infected by virus

Spyware

Spyware tracks your activity as you surf the Internet and reports it to companies that want to sell you their products—or steal your identity. Spyware takes advantage of cookies, the small files that websites put on your computer to remember who you are on your next visit.

Ransomware

Ransomware is malicious code that takes control of either your computer or files on your computer and restricts access to them until a ransom is paid to the attacker.

Worms

A worm is a self-replicating computer program that distributes itself via a network, as shown in Figure 11. Unlike a virus, it does not necessarily attach itself to another file. Worms are usually designed to damage a network, in many cases by simply clogging up the network's bandwidth and slowing its performance.

Figure 11 How a Worm Attacks
A worm reproduces itself and attacks all the computers on a network.

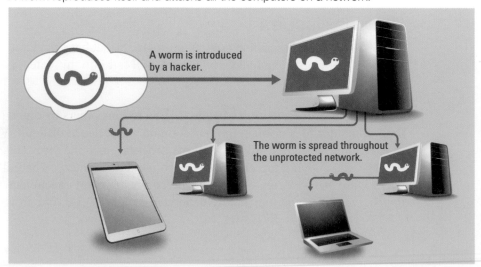

A worm is introduced by a hacker.

The worm is spread throughout the unprotected network.

Figure 12 How a Trojan Attacks
A Trojan pretends to be a useful program but instead opens your system to hackers.

Step 1
A hacker introduces
a Trojan virus.

Step 2
The Trojan virus
opens a "back door."

Step 3
The hacker gains access to the
computer through the "back door."

hacker

Trojan

Named after the infamous Trojan horse of the Greek legend, a Trojan is malware that masquerades as a useful program. When you run the program, you let the Trojan into your system (see Figure 12). Trojans open a "back door" to your system for malicious hackers.

Adware

Adware looks at files on your computer and then sends pop-up advertisements that try to sell you products and services. Although annoying, adware is not usually destructive, but it can slow down your processor and Internet speed significantly.

Privacy Threats and Information Theft

Spyware programs can steal your personal information and tell it or sell it to other people who might be able to impersonate you and take money from your bank account or charge large purchases to your credit card.

Phishing is a method of convincing people to reveal their passwords, credit card numbers, social security numbers, and other private or confidential information. Phishers pretend to

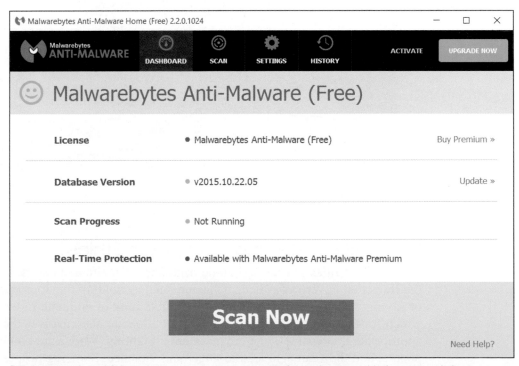

Products such as Malwarebytes scan your computer for malware and help prevent it from downloading in the first place.

be representatives of the victim's bank or a government agency by sending official-looking emails with obscure links back to websites that look exactly like the real website. The information they gather is then used in schemes involving identity theft that allow them to gain access to the victim's bank account, which they empty of its funds.

Protection Software

Several computer programs are available to protect against virus attacks and the installation of spyware or adware on your computer. Some examples of anti-virus applications are McAfee VirusScan and BitDefender AntiVirus. Spybot Search & Destroy, SpySweeper, AdAware, and Spyware Detector are used for spyware and adware. Windows 10 and Windows 8.1 include an anti-spyware program called Windows Defender.

To minimize infection, always update your computer with the latest security patches as they become available. Keep your protection software up to date by downloading the latest "signature" files of known viruses.

Exploring Technology 7

Explore the programs on your computer and identify what protection software is installed. Verify that the protection software is up-to-date and active while you are working, and that a regular scan of all files takes place.

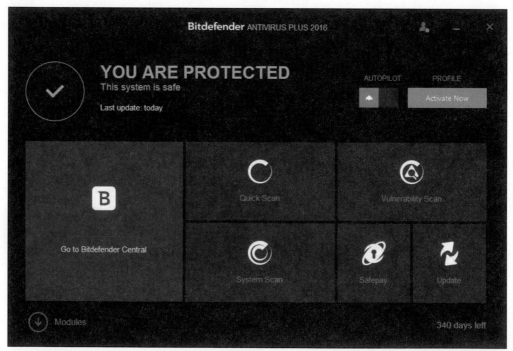

The installation of an antivirus software program such as Bitdefender AntiVirus Plus is essential for computers connected to the Internet. Keeping these virus definitions up to date will significantly help in the fight against viruses.

Email Etiquette and Computer Ethics

Two types of rules govern and guide behavior: etiquette and ethics. *Etiquette* refers to the rules that govern courteous behavior, such as holding the door open for someone, or saying "please" and "thank you." We often think of etiquette in terms of knowing which fork to use in a fancy restaurant, but etiquette also involves the rules for language appropriate in a businesslike environment. "Fighting words" are embarrassing to some people, and they can also lead to anger and violence. Showing proper etiquette is a way of showing a person respect. If you show disrespect to someone, that is not proper etiquette.

When applied to computer communication, improper etiquette can result in serious misunderstandings or ill will among coworkers. It can even lead to the loss of a lucrative business contract or even a job.

Ethics are the moral principles that govern behavior. In the news, we often see reports about corporate executives who have been charged or convicted of funneling company money into their own personal bank accounts. Politicians are accused of taking bribes from lobbyists in return for a favorable vote on a piece of legislation that will be profitable for the lobbyist's organization. Taxpayers claim tax deductions they are not entitled to. Students submit reports that were written by someone else. People offer to copy the latest music CD or software program they just purchased and give it to their friends. Where do you stand on these ethical issues?

Both etiquette and ethics have direct application to computers, especially in relation to email and copyright issues.

Email Etiquette

Everyone—friends, relatives, schoolmates, coworkers, employers, teachers, businesses, government officials, and sales and marketing departments—is sending email these days. Speedy communication with other people all over the world can be fun, exciting, and productive. However, it can also cause problems. What you write in an email message can hurt someone's feelings, be misinterpreted, or be accidentally sent to the wrong person. You can cause yourself embarrassment or even get yourself fired.

Here are 10 rules of email etiquette. You might want to add a few of your own.

Ethics are the rules we use to determine what is right and wrong, and these rules help guide our choices and actions, both in our personal and business lives.

1. Be brief and to the point. Emails are supposed to be a fast way to communicate. Don't slow down the process.
2. Don't use ALL CAPITAL letters. It looks and feels like you're shouting or angry.
3. Remember to attach the attachment. Mentioning what you are "attaching" in any type of email is a good idea. Get in the habit of stopping as soon as you type the phrase "I am attaching…" and immediately clicking the button for attaching the file.
4. Use spell check (even if you're a great speller). Using the spelling check feature only takes a few seconds and it shows that you care about quality. But watch out! It is easy to click "Change" instead of "Ignore" and change a person's name to a common word and that, whether humorous or not, is an embarrassing mistake.
5. Reread what you wrote from the perspective of the receiver. Ask yourself how the recipient is likely to interpret your words. Did you leave out or misspell a word that completely changes the meaning?
6. Double-check the address in the *To* box. Confirm that you clicked the correct name in your address list. Once you click the Send button, there is *no* way to stop the message or undo an address mistake.
7. Watch your language. Profanity can come back to haunt you.
8. Assume your email will be read by *lots* of other people. Emails are often forwarded so others can take action or to inform a supervisor. Avoid cute or friendly asides and comments that you only want a close friend to see.

9. Always put something in the *Subject* line. A well-written subject will help the receiver decide where to file your message and whether to read it now or wait until later.

10. Privacy does not exist in emails, especially those in a corporate environment. The email administrator can potentially see the contents of any email. Company policy may allow checking emails to ensure that no company secrets are exposed, or to stop harassing or abusive email.

Software Piracy and Copyright Infringement

When you install a software application, you must accept the license agreement that describes the legal contract between the user (you) and the software developer. If you do not accept the agreement, the installation process will stop. By accepting the agreement, you agree to everything it says. The contract often covers the number of people who may use the program at the same time. That would usually be one person, but organizations can purchase agreements that cover a specific number of users.

Most software is copyrighted, with the exception of open source software, mentioned earlier. Copyright laws in the United States and most (but not all) other countries state that authors, music composers, TV show and movie creators, artists, and publishers own the works they create and distribute and that no one is allowed to use or copy their work without specific permission. Software license agreements might specify that you can make one backup copy, but you cannot give that copy to a friend. The same rules apply to all copyrighted material including music CDs, DVDs, and songs available on the web. Infringing on a copyright is illegal, and this law is enforced.

Warning: This computer program is protected by copyright law and international treaties. Unauthorized reproduction or distribution of this program, or any portion of it, may result in severe civil and criminal penalties, and will be prosecuted to the maximum extent possible under the law.

OK

Software manufacturers usually obtain a copyright that prohibits the illegal copying and distribution of software. Warnings such as this one are designed to remind users of the copyright law.

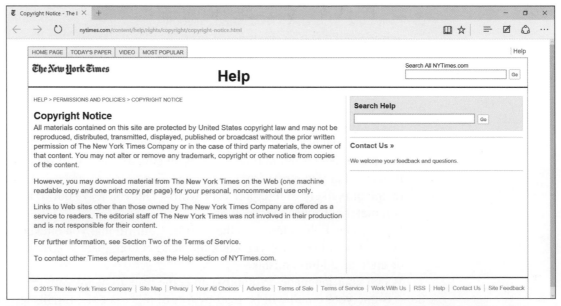

The copyright notice on *The New York Times* web page reminds visitors that the content of the site is copyrighted.

Formerly known as the Software Publishers Association, the Software & Information Industry Association (SIIA, www.siia.net) encourages people who witness software piracy to inform them so that they can investigate the situation. Once they gather enough evidence, they will contact the organization's executives, ask them to prove they have enough licenses, and encourage them to purchase the software legally. In most cases the pressure works, but if necessary, the SIIA may take legal action.

Software piracy is a felony, but even if it were not, other compelling reasons exist for why you should not copy programs, music, or DVDs. For one, doing so hurts the people who spend a lot of time and money creating products for your enjoyment. They do research. They buy computers, musical instruments, or video cameras. They pay money for studio time to record their songs, and then more money to advertise them and ship them to music stores. They may sell their creations to publishing companies who agree to pay them royalties based on sales. Will you send money to your favorite band every time you give a friend a copy of their latest CD? If graphic artists and musicians can't pay their expenses and cover the cost of making the songs, movies, computer games, and other software you enjoy, how can an individual artist, or even a large company, continue to create more?

Exploring Technology 8

Check to see who is the registered user of each of the applications on your computer by running it and watching for the name on the startup screen. If it isn't registered to your organization, your department, or yourself, ask a supervisor why not. Your action could actually help save your organization from costly litigation and potential fines.

Exploring Technology 9

Navigate to www.riaa.com and click the Report Piracy tab. Read about what you can do to help stop software piracy.

Exploring Technology 10

Use your word processor to write the explanation you will use when you decline to give or receive an unauthorized copy of a music CD, software program, DVD, or any other copyrighted material.

Glossary

802.11 protocol a protocol for wireless LAN technology that specifies an over-the-air interface between the wireless client device and a server, or between two wireless devices, approved by the IEEE in 1997; also called *Wi-Fi*

802.11ac protocol approved in January 2014, this protocol for wireless LAN technology is built on 802.11n but has approximately three times the transfer rate

802.11g protocol approved in June 2003, this protocol for wireless LAN technology operates in the same frequency range as 802.11b but with transfer rates similar to 802.11a

802.11n protocol this protocol for wireless LAN technology provides for speeds of up to 150 Mbps at a range of up to 250 meters (820 feet)

adware software that tracks the websites that a user visits to collect information for marketing or advertising

bar code reader an electronic device that uses photo technology to read the lines in a bar code; the lines and spaces contain symbols that the computer translates into information

cathode ray tube (CRT) monitor a large, sealed glass tube housed in a plastic case; used with older desktop computers

central processing unit (CPU) the part of a computer that interprets and carries out instructions that operate the computer and manage the computer's devices and resources; consists of components, each of which performs specific functions; also called the *microprocessor* or *processor*

client a smaller computer, terminal, or workstation capable of sending data to and from a larger computer (host computer) in a network

client-server architecture a type of network architecture in which a personal computer, workstation, or terminal (called a *client*) is used to send information or a request to another computer (called a *server*) that then relays the information back to the user's client computer or to another computer (another client)

collaboration software programs that enable people at separate computer workstations to collaborate on a single document or project; also called *groupware*

compact disc (CD) a plastic disc 4.75 inches in diameter and about 1/20th of an inch thick; uses laser technologies to store information and data

connectivity refers to the ability to link with other programs and devices

copyright the legal protection of an individual's or business's original work, such as software applications, music, and books, that prohibits others from duplicating or illegally using such work or products; an artist or author whose work is copyrighted has the right to charge others for its use

database a computer application in which data is organized and stored in a way that allows for specific data to be accessed, retrieved, and used

digital camera a type of camera that records and stores images, including people, scenery, documents, and products, in a digitized form that can be entered into and stored by a computer

digital versatile disc (DVD) an extremely high-capacity optical disc; also called a *digital video disc (DVD)*

digitizing the process of converting analog information to digital information; sometimes referred to as "going digital"

digitizing pen an electronic pen device, resembling a standard writing pen, used with a drawing tablet to simulate drawing on paper

drawing tablet a tablet with wires under the surface that, when used with a digitizing pen, allows the user to create and capture drawings that can be entered and stored on a computer

dual-core processor a central processing unit (CPU) chip that contains two complete processors along with their cache memory

electronic mail (email) a text, voice, or video message sent or received remotely or over a computer network, or the system by which such a message is sent

ethics rules used to determine the right and wrong things to do

etiquette rules governing courteous behavior

File Transfer Protocol (FTP) a transmission standard that enables a user to send and receive large files, such as reports, over the Internet

flash drive storage device with a USB connector

gigabyte unit of memory equal to 1,073,741,824 bytes

graphical user interface (GUI) a computer interface that enables a user to control the computer and launch commands by pointing and clicking at graphical objects such as windows, icons, and menu items

graphics computer-generated pictures produced on a computer screen, paper, or film, ranging from a simple line or bar chart to a detailed, colorful image or picture; also called *graphical images*

graphics tablet a flat tablet used with a pen-like stylus or a crosshair cursor to capture an image; the user grasps a stylus or crosshair cursor and traces an image or drawing placed on the tablet surface

hard copy a permanent, tangible version of output, such as a letter printed on paper

hard drive a device for reading and writing to the magnetic storage medium known as a hard disk; consists of one or more rigid metal platters (disks) mounted on a metal shaft in a container that contains an access mechanism

Hypertext Transfer Protocol (HTTP) the communications standard used to transfer documents on the World Wide Web

information processing cycle a cycle during which a computer enters, processes, outputs, and/or stores information

ink-jet printer a nonimpact printer that forms images by spraying thousands of tiny droplets of electrically charged ink onto a page; the printed images are in dot-matrix format, but of a higher quality than images printed by dot-matrix printers

input data that is entered into a computer or other device, or the act of capturing such data

input device any hardware component that enables a computer user to enter data and programs into a computer system; keyboards, point-and-click devices, and scanners are among the more popular input devices, and a desktop or laptop computer system may include one or more input devices

Internet a worldwide network of computers linked together via communications software and media for the purpose of sharing information; the largest and best-known network in the world; also called *the Net*

Internet service provider (ISP) an organization that has a permanent connection to the Internet and provides temporary access to individuals and others for free or for a fee

joystick an input device (named after the control lever used to fly fighter planes) consisting of a small box with a vertical lever that, when pushed in a certain direction, moves the cursor correspondingly on the screen; often used for computer games

keyboard an electronically controlled hardware component used to enter alphanumeric data (letters, numbers, and special characters)

laser printer a nonimpact printer that produces output of exceptional quality using a technology similar to that of photocopy machines

light emitting diode (LED) a small light that is used in an LCD to improve color and image appearance

liquid crystal display (LCD) a display device in which liquid crystals are sandwiched between two sheets of material

local area network (LAN) a computer network physically confined to a relatively small geographical area, such as a single building or a college campus

malware malicious software

megabyte a unit of memory that stores approximately 1 million bytes

memory a chip-based data storage system in which each bit of data is represented by a binary on/off state; a series of 1s and 0s

monitor the screen, or display device, on which computer output appears

motherboard the main circuit board inside a personal computer to which other circuit boards can be connected; contains electrical pathways, called *traces*, etched onto it that allow data to move from one component to another

mouse an input device that, when moved about on a flat surface, causes a pointer on the screen to move in the same direction

multitasking the ability of an operating system to run more than one software program at a time; the use of different areas in Windows RAM makes this possible

network a group of two or more computers, software, and other devices that is connected by one or more communications media

nonvolatile storage that retains its data even when there is no power being supplied to it; a hard disk and a flash drive are both nonvolatile

open-source software software whose programming code is owned by the original developer but made available for free to the general public, who is encouraged to experiment with the software, make improvements, and share the improvements with the user community

operating system (OS) a type of software that creates a user interface and supports the workings of computer devices and software programs that perform specific jobs

output information that is written or displayed as a result of computer processing; also the act of writing or displaying such data

peer-to-peer architecture a network design in which each computer or workstation comprising the network has equivalent capabilities and responsibilities

personal information manager (PIM) software software that helps users organize contact information, appointments, tasks, and notes

phishing an activity characterized by attempts to fraudulently acquire another person's sensitive information, such as a credit card number

Photo-editing software an application that allows users to create and modify images and output them in one of the various image file formats.

port a plug-in slot on a computer to which you can connect a device, such as a printer or, in the case of accessing the Internet, a telephone line; also called an *interface*

Post Office Protocol (POP) server a special type of server that holds email messages until they are accessed and read by their recipients

presentation software an application that allows a user to create a presentation of slides

printer the most common type of hard-copy output device that produces output in a permanent form

processing the manipulation of data by the computer's electrical circuits

processor the part of a computer that interprets and carries out instructions that operate the computer and manages the computer's devices and resources; consists of components, each of which performs specific functions; also called the *central processing unit (CPU)*

protocol a set of rules and procedures for exchanging information between network devices and computers

quad-core processor a CPU that contains four complete processors in a single chip

random access memory (RAM) a computer chip or group of chips containing the temporary, or volatile, memory in which programs and data are stored while being used by a computer

read-only memory (ROM) a computer chip on the motherboard of a computer containing permanent, or nonvolatile, memory that stores instructions

router a hardware device that connects two or more networks

scanner a light-sensing electronic device that can read and capture printed text and images, such as photographs and drawings, and convert them into a digital form a computer can understand; once scanned, the text or image can be displayed on the screen, edited, printed, stored on a disk, inserted into another document, or sent as an attachment to an email message; also called an *optical scanner*

server a computer and its associated storage devices that users access remotely over a network

Simple Mail Transfer Protocol (SMTP) a communications protocol installed on the ISP's or online service's mail server that determines how each message is to be routed through the Internet and then sends the message

soft copy a temporary version of output, typically the display of data on a computer screen

software programs containing instructions that direct the operation of the computer system and the written documentation that explains how to use the programs; types include system software and application software

software piracy the act of copying or using a piece of software without the legal right to do so

software suite a combination of application programs (usually integrated) bundled as a single package; may contain applications such as word processing, spreadsheet, database, and other programs

spreadsheet software a productivity program that provides a user with a means of organizing, calculating, and presenting financial, statistical, and other numeric information; used to manipulate numbers electronically instead of using a pencil and paper

spyware software that tracks the activity of Internet users for the benefit of a third party

stylus a sharp, pointed instrument used for writing or marking on a graphics tablet or other device

switch a small hardware device that joins multiple computers together within one local area network (LAN)

T1 line a high-speed telephone line that allows for both voice and data transmission and can carry data at a speed of 1.544 megabits per second

touchpad an input device that enables a user to enter data and make selections by moving a finger across the pad; also called a *track pad*

touchscreen an input device that allows the user to choose options by pressing a finger (or fingers) on the appropriate part of the screen

Transmission Control Protocol/Internet Protocol (TCP/IP) protocol that governs how packets are constructed and sent over the Internet to their destination

Universal Product Code (UPC) a type of code printed on products and packages consisting of lines and spaces that a computer translates into a number; the computer then uses this number to find information about the product or package, such as its name and price, in a computerized database

Universal Serial Bus (USB) port a type of port that is widely used for connecting high-speed modems, scanners, and digital cameras to a computer; a single USB port can accommodate several peripheral devices connected together in sequence

video-editing software software that allows users to edit sound and video and output it in various digital formats

virus a program that is designed to harm computer systems and/or any users, typically sent via email

volatile storage that loses its data when power is lost; the RAM on a motherboard is volatile, for example

webcam a digital video camera that captures real-time video for transmission to others via a web server or an instant messaging tool

wide area network (WAN) a network that spans a large geographical area

Windows a Microsoft-developed GUI operating system for personal computers

word processing software a type of computer application that allows the user to create, edit, manipulate, format, store, and print a variety of documents, including letters, memos, announcements, and brochures

World Wide Web (www) a global system of linked computer networks that allows users to jump from one site to another by way of programmed links on web pages; also called *the web*

worm a program that actively transmits copies of itself over the Internet, using up resources and causing other problems; also called a *software worm*

Workbook

The *Workbook* ebook includes study tools and an assessment activity. These resources are designed to help you further develop and demonstrate mastery of the concepts learned in this section.

Adjusting Monitor Settings, Copying Data Files, and Changing View Options

Skills

- Set monitor resolution
- Modify DPI settings
- Copy files from OneDrive

- Copy files from a network location
- Change view options
- Display file extensions

The Microsoft Office product line has evolved over time, becoming available on Apple computers, tablets, phones, and through the Internet. This textbook and the accompanying ebook were written using a typical personal computer (tower/box, monitor, keyboard and mouse) or laptop. While you may be able to perform some of the activities in this textbook on a different operating system or tablet, not all of the steps will work as written and may jeopardize any work you may be required to turn in to your instructor. If you do not have access to a compatible computer, explore what options you have at your institution such as where and when you can use a computer lab.

One of the evolutions of the Microsoft Office product is that it is now offered in a subscription-based plan called Microsoft Office 365. An advantage of having a Microsoft Office 365 subscription is that it includes and incorporates new features or versions as they are released, as long as your subscription is active. For example, when Microsoft released Office 2016, any Office 365 users with the Office 2013 version were automatically upgraded. This new direction Microsoft is taking may impact section activities and assessments. For example, new features and tweaks may alter how some of the steps are completed. The ebook will contain the most up-to-date material and will be updated as new features become available.

In Activity 1 you will customize your monitor settings so that what you see on the screen matches the images in this textbook. In Activity 2 you will obtain the data files you will be using throughout this textbook from OneDrive. Activity 3 includes instructions on how to change the view settings so that your view of files in a FIle Explorer window matches the images in this textbook.

Before beginning projects in this textbook, you may need to customize your monitor's settings and turn on the display of file extensions. Projects in the sections in this textbook assume that the monitor display is set at 1600 x 900 pixels, the DPI is set at 125%, and that the display of file extensions is turned on. Adjusting a monitor's display settings is important because the ribbon in the Microsoft Office applications adjusts to the screen resolution setting of your computer monitor. A monitor set at a high resolution will have the ability to show more buttons in the ribbon than a monitor set to a low resolution. The illustrations in this textbook were created with a screen resolution display set at 1600 × 900 pixels. In Figure GS1 at the bottom of the page, the Word ribbon is shown three ways: at a lower screen resolution (1366 × 768 pixels), at the screen resolution featured throughout this textbook, and at a higher screen resolution (1920 × 1080 pixels). Note the variances in the ribbon in all three examples.

What You Will Do   Adjust the monitor settings for your machine to match the settings used to create the images in the textbook. If using a lab computer, check with your instructor before attempting this activity.

1 Right-click a blank area of the desktop and then click the *Display settings* option at the shortcut menu.

2 At the Settings window with the *Display* option selected, scroll down and click the <u>Advanced display settings</u> hyperlink.

3 Scroll down and look at the current setting displayed in the *Resolution* option box. For example, your screen may be currently set at 1920 × 1080. If your screen is already set to 1600 × 900, skip ahead to Step 7.

> Screen resolution is set in pixels. Pixel is the abbreviation of picture element and refers to a single dot or point on the display monitor. Changing the screen resolution to a higher number of pixels means that more information can be seen on the screen as items are scaled to a smaller size.

Figure GS1 Word Ribbon at Various Screen Resolutions

1366 x 768 Screen Resolution

1600 x 900 Screen Resolution

1920 x 1080 Screen Resolution

4 Click the *Resolution* option box and then click the 1600 × 900 option. If necessary, check with your instructor for alternate instructions. ***Note: Depending on the privileges you are given on a school machine, you may not be able to complete these steps.***

> If the machine you are using has more than one monitor, make sure the proper monitor is selected. (The active monitor displays as a blue rectangle.)

5 Click the Apply button.

6 Click the Keep changes button at the message box asking if you want to keep the display settings.

> Some monitor settings will render the computer unusable because objects on the desktop or in a window will become inaccessible and hidden. In this case, Windows will automatically revert the settings to the previous configuration after 30 seconds.

7 Click the Back button.

8 At the Settings window with the *Display* option active, look at the percentage in which the size of text, apps, and other items currently display (also known as the DPI setting). For example, items on your screen may display at 100%. If the percentage is 125%, skip to Step 12.

> As the resolution on monitors has increased, text, application windows, buttons, options, and so on start to appear smaller and smaller on the screen. To counter this, Windows allows you to increase the size of these objects by changing the DPI setting. The computers used to create the images in this textbook uses the 125% DPI setting, which slightly increases the size of text, applications, buttons, and options.

9 Click and hold down the left mouse button on the button on the slider bar below the text *Change the size of text, apps, and other items*, drag the slider button until *125%* displays, and then release the mouse button.

10 Click the Apply button.

11 At the message indicating that you must sign out of your computer, click the Sign out later button.

12 Click the Close button.

Activity 2 Retrieving and Copying Data Files

While working through the activities in this book, you will often be using data files as starting points. These files need to be obtained from OneDrive or other locations such as your school's network drive. All of the files required to complete the bookwork are provided through OneDrive, which you can access through links in the textbook's ebook. Make sure you have Internet access before trying to retrieve the data files from OneDrive. Ask your instructor if alternate locations are available for retrieving the files, such as a network drive or online resource such as Angel, BlackBoard, or Canvas. Retrieving data files from an alternate location will require different steps, so check with your instructor for additional steps or tasks to complete.

What You Will Do In order to complete the activities in this textbook, you will need to obtain the data files from OneDrive. Make sure you have access to OneDrive or an alternate location containing the files.

1 Insert your USB flash drive into an available USB port.

2 Navigate to this textbook's ebook. If you are a SNAP user, navigate to the ebook by clicking the textbook ebook link on your Assignments page. If you are not a SNAP user, launch your browser, go to https://paradigm.bookshelf.emcp.com, log in, and then click the textbook ebook thumbnail. *Note: The steps in this activity assume you are using the Microsoft Edge browser. If you are using a different browser, the following steps may vary.*

3 Navigate to the ebook page that corresponds to this textbook page.

4 Click the Ancillary Links button in the menu. The menu of buttons may be at the top of the window or along the side of the window, depending on the size of the window.

Data Files ▶ 5 At the Ancillary Links dialog box that appears, click the Data Files: All Files hyperlink.

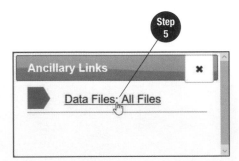

6 Click the Download hyperlink at the top of the window.

> A zip file containing the student data files will automatically begin downloading from the OneDrive website.

7 Click the Open button in the message box saying that the DataFiles.zip has finished downloading.

8 Right-click the *ExcelS2* folder in the Content pane.

9 Click the *Copy* option at the shortcut menu.

10 Click your USB flash drive that displays in the Navigation pane at the left side of the File Explorer window.

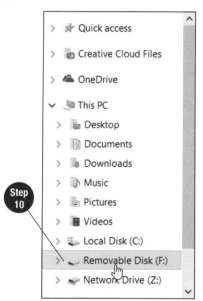

11 Click the Home tab and then click the Paste button in the Clipboard group.

12 Close the File Explorer window by clicking the Close button in the upper right corner of the window.

You can change the view of the File Explorer window to show the contents of your current location (drive or folder) in various formats, including icons, tiles, or a list, among others. With the Content pane in Details view, you can click the column headings to change how the contents are sorted and whether they are sorted in ascending or descending order. You can customize a window's environment by using buttons and options on the File Explorer View tab. You can also change how panes are displayed, how content is arranged in the Content pane, how content is sorted, and which features are hidden.

What You Will Do Before getting started with the textbook material, you need to adjust the view settings so that items in the File Explorer window appear the same as the images in the textbook.

1 Click the File Explorer button on the taskbar.

> By default, a File Explorer window opens at the Quick access location, which contains frequently-used folders such as Desktop, Documents, Downloads, Pictures and so on. It also displays recently used files at the bottom of the Content pane.

2 Click the drive letter representing your storage medium in the Navigation pane.

3 Double-click the *ExcelS2* folder in the Content pane.

4 Click the View tab below the Title bar.

5 Click the *Large icons* option in the Layout group.

> After you click an option on the View tab, the View tab collapses to provide more space in the File Explorer window.

6 Click the View tab.

7 Click the *Details* option in the Layout group.

8 With files now displayed in Details view, click the *Name* column heading to sort the list in descending order by name.

9 Click the *Name* column heading again to restore the list to ascending order by name.

10 Click the View tab and then click the *File name extensions* check box in the Show/hide group to insert a check mark. ***Note: If the check box appears with a check mark in it, then file extensions are already turned on—skip this step.***

Inserting a check mark in a check box makes the option active. The files in the File Explorer window will now display any files with a file extension.

11 Close the File Explorer window by clicking the Close button in the upper right corner of the window.

In Addition

Changing the Default View for All Folders

You can set a view to display by default for all folders of a similar type (such as all disk drive folders or all documents folders). To do this, change the current view to the desired view for the type of folder that you want to set. Next, click the Options button on the View tab and

then click the View tab at the Folder Options dialog box. Click the Apply to Folders button in the Folder views section and then click OK. Click Yes at the Folder Views message asking if you want all folders of this type to match this folder's view settings.

MARQUEE SERIES

Microsoft® Word 2016

Nita Rutkosky
Pierce College at Puyallup
Puyallup, Washington

Audrey Roggenkamp
Pierce College at Puyallup
Puyallup, Washington

Ian Rutkosky
Pierce College at Puyallup
Puyallup, Washington

PARADIGM
EDUCATION SOLUTIONS
St. Paul

Senior Vice President	Linda Hein
Editor in Chief	Christine Hurney
Director of Production	Timothy W. Larson
Production Editors	Rachel Kats, Jen Weaverling
Cover and Text Designer	Valerie King
Copy Editor	Sarah Kearin
Senior Design and Production Specialist	Jaana Bykonich
Assistant Developmental Editors	Mamie Clark, Katie Werdick
Testers	Desiree Carvel; Ann E. Mills, Ivy Tech Community College of Indiana, Indianapolis, IN
Instructional Support Writer	Brienna McWade
Indexer	Terry Casey
Vice President Information Technology	Chuck Bratton
Digital Projects Manager	Tom Modl
Vice President Sales and Marketing	Scott Burns
Director of Marketing	Lara Weber McLellan

ISBN 978-0-76386-699-0 (text)
ISBN 978-0-76386-700-3 (digital)

© 2017 by Paradigm Publishing, Inc.
875 Montreal Way
St. Paul, MN 55102
Email: educate@emcp.com
Website: ParadigmCollege.com

Contents

Word 2016

Microsoft Word 2016 is a word processing program used to create documents such as letters, reports, research papers, brochures, announcements, newsletters, envelopes, labels, and much more. Word is a full-featured program that provides a wide variety of editing and formatting features as well as sophisticated visual elements. While working in Word, you will produce business documents for the following six companies.

First Choice Travel is a travel center offering a full range of traveling services from booking flights, hotel reservations, and rental cars to offering travel seminars.

The Waterfront Bistro offers fine dining for lunch and dinner and also offers banquet facilities, a wine cellar, and catering services.

Worldwide Enterprises is a national and international distributor of products for a variety of companies and is the exclusive movie distribution agent for Marquee Productions.

Marquee Productions is involved in all aspects of creating movies from script writing and development to filming. The company produces documentaries, biographies, as well as historical and action movies.

Performance Threads maintains an inventory of rental costumes and also researches, designs, and sews special-order and custom-made costumes.

The mission of the Niagara Peninsula College Theatre Arts Division is to offer a curriculum designed to provide students with a thorough exposure to all aspects of the theatre arts.

In Section 1 you will learn how to

Create and Edit Documents

Use Microsoft Word to create, edit, and format a variety of business documents and use Word's powerful editing and formatting features to produce well-written and visually appealing documents. Some powerful editing features include checking the spelling and grammar in a document and using Thesaurus to find appropriate synonyms for words; using AutoCorrect to improve the efficiency of entering information in a document; and creating a document using a predesigned template.

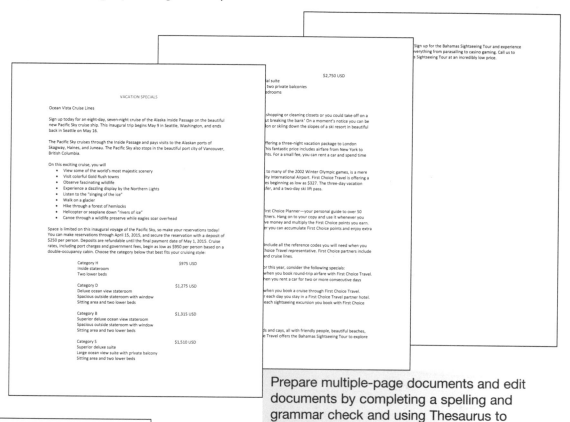

Prepare multiple-page documents and edit documents by completing a spelling and grammar check and using Thesaurus to find appropriate synonyms for words.

Download online templates from and create a variety of documents including letters, faxes, certificates, or awards.

In Section 2 you will learn how to

Format Characters and Paragraphs in Documents

Word contains a number of commands and procedures that affect how the document appears when printed. The appearance of a document in the document screen and how it looks when printed is called the *format*. Formatting can include such tasks as changing the font; aligning and indenting text; changing line and paragraph spacing; setting tabs; and inserting elements such as bullets, numbers, symbols, and special characters. The readability of a document can be improved by setting text in tabbed columns and by formatting using styles.

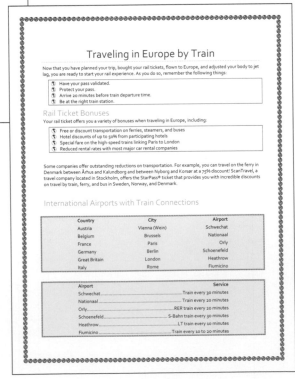

OSLO, NORWAY

History

The founding of Oslo took place in the turbulent period between the *Viking Age* and Norway's *Catholic Middle Ages*. Many remnants and ruins from ancient Oslo can be found in Memorial Park. The city has a fascinating, interesting, and dramatic history.

Oslo's population was substantially reduced during the time of the Black Death in 1348, which claimed over fifty percent of the inhabitants. This epidemic also had political consequences for Norway, which was reduced to a province of Denmark. During this period, Copenhagen was the actual capital of Norway. Oslo was also greatly affected by the Lutheran Protestant Reformation of 1537, with religious conflicts, political separation from the Catholic Church, and the foundation of a Protestant National Church. Many ruins of churches and monasteries bear witness to this process.

Oslo was completely destroyed by fire in 1624. Following intense renewal and advanced city planning in the spirit of the Renaissance, a completely new city was created and named Christiania. In 1814 Norway was united with Sweden, and Christiania experienced strong economic and political growth. In 1905 the union with Sweden was dissolved and Norway gained its independence. The original name of Oslo was reinstated in 1924.

Population

Oslo is the capital of Norway and has more than 500,000 inhabitants. Approximately 900,000 people live in the Greater Oslo area, representing twenty percent of the total population of Norway.

Commerce and Industry

The working population of Oslo distributed according to occupation includes: industry, 16%; building and construction, 6%; transport, 9%; trade, services, and tourism, 69%.

Apply font formatting such as changing the font, font size, and font color. Apply paragraph formatting such as changing alignment, indentations, and line spacing.

Traveling in Europe by Train

Now that you have planned your trip, bought your rail tickets, flown to Europe, and adjusted your body to jet lag, you are ready to start your rail experience. As you do so, remember the following things:

- Have your pass validated.
- Protect your pass.
- Arrive 20 minutes before train departure time.
- Be at the right train station.

Rail Ticket Bonuses

Your rail ticket offers you a variety of bonuses when traveling in Europe, including:

- Free or discount transportation on ferries, steamers, and buses
- Hotel discounts of up to 50% from participating hotels
- Special fare on the high-speed trains linking Paris to London
- Reduced rental rates with most major car rental companies

Some companies offer outstanding reductions on transportation. For example, you can travel on the ferry in Denmark between Århus and Kalundborg and between Nyborg and Korsør at a 75% discount! ScanTravel, a travel company located in Stockholm, offers the StarPass® ticket that provides you with incredible discounts on travel by train, ferry, and bus in Sweden, Norway, and Denmark.

International Airports with Train Connections

Country	City	Airport
Austria	Vienna (Wein)	Schwechat
Belgium	Brussels	Nationaal
France	Paris	Orly
Germany	Berlin	Schoenefeld
Great Britain	London	Heathrow
Italy	Rome	Fiumicino

Airport	Service
Schwechat	Train every 30 minutes
Nationaal	Train every 20 minutes
Orly	RER train every 20 minutes
Schoenefeld	S-Bahn train every 30 minutes
Heathrow	LT train every 20 minutes
Fiumicino	Train every 10 to 20 minutes

Apply formatting such as inserting bullets and special characters, setting text in tabbed columns, applying paragraph shading and lines, and inserting a page border. Use style sets to apply predesigned formatting such as bolding and centering text, changing fonts, and applying border lines to headings.

In Section 3 you will learn how to

Enhance Documents

Improve the formatting of a document using features to rearrange text in a document, add special elements, or change the appearance of text. Use buttons on the Home tab to move, copy, and paste text in a document. Improve the appearance of documents by inserting page numbering, headers, and footers; changing margins and page orientation; and changing vertical alignment. Add visual appeal to documents by inserting and customizing images.

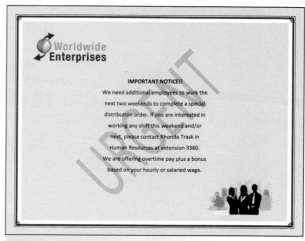

Enhance the visual appeal of a document by inserting an image related to text in the document, and a page border and background color.

Enhance the appearance of a document by applying a theme, which is a set of formatting choices that includes a color, a font, and effects; inserting a cover page; inserting a watermark, which is a lightened image that displays behind text; and inserting a header and footer.

Create envelopes and mailing labels quickly and automatically.

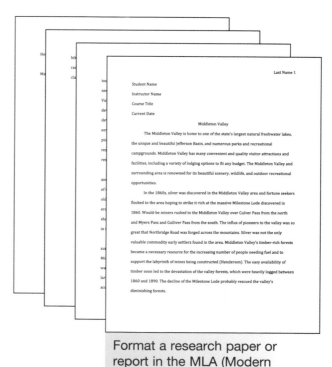

Format a research paper or report in the MLA (Modern Language Association) style.

In Section 4 you will learn how to

Apply Special Features

Word contains special formatting features that can be applied to a document to enhance the visual display of text. For example, add visual appeal to a document with the WordArt and drop cap features and by inserting shapes. Use the SmartArt feature to create visual representations of data such as organizational charts and graphics, and use the Tables feature to create, modify, and format data in columns and rows. Improve the ease with which others can read and understand text by setting it in columns. Insert hyperlinks in a Word document that will link to another file or a location on the Internet and save a Word document in the PDF file format.

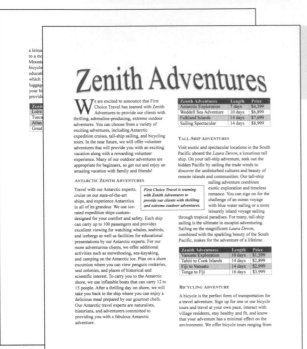

Use Word's special features to enhance a document with WordArt text, a drop cap, and a built-in text box. Improve the readability of a document by setting text in columns.

Insert columnar data in a table and format the table to make the data easier to read and understand.

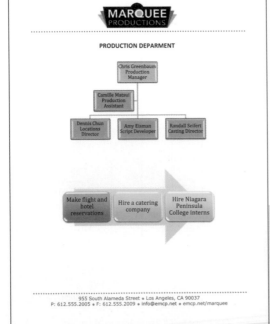

Use Word's SmartArt feature to illustrate hierarchical data in an organizational chart or create a graphic to show data processes, cycles, or relationships or present data in a matrix or pyramid.

Word

Creating and Editing a Document

Data Files   Before beginning section work, copy the WordS1 folder to your storage medium and then make WordS1 the active folder.

Skills

- Create, save, and print a document
- Close a document and close Word
- Move the insertion point
- Insert and delete text
- Scroll in a document
- Select, replace, and delete text
- Use Undo and Redo
- Check the spelling and grammar in a document
- Use AutoCorrect
- Use the Thesaurus
- Change document views
- Hide and show white space

- Change the display percentage
- Navigate and find text using the Navigation pane
- Find and replace text
- Use the Tell Me feature
- Use the Help feature
- Review and print a document
- Create a document using a template
- Create, rename, and delete a folder
- Copy and paste a document
- Save a document in a different format

Precheck   Check your current skills to help focus your study of the skills taught in this section.

Projects Overview

Prepare a document describing a special vacation package and edit and format two documents describing various vacation specials offered by First Choice Travel.

Customize a sample employee incentive agreement and prepare a fax cover page for the agreement.

Use a letter template to prepare one letter to First Choice Travel regarding a movie site and another to the manager of The Waterfront Bistro requesting catering information.

Edit a letter to Marquee Productions regarding costuming for a film.

Write a letter to Josh Hart at Marquee Productions explaining the catering services offered by The Waterfront Bistro and then prepare a fax sheet for the letter.

SNAP   If you are a SNAP user, launch the Precheck and Tutorials from your Assignments page.

Model Answers   Preview the model answers for an overview of the projects you will complete in the section activities.

Microsoft Word is a word processing program you can use to create, save, edit, and print documents. To create a document in Word, open the Word program and then click the *Blank document* template. This opens a blank document with the insertion point positioned at the beginning of the document. The document screen contains a variety of features for working with a document, such as the Title bar, Quick Access Toolbar, ribbon, and Status bar. Type text in a document and press the Enter key, and the insertion point moves down to the next line with extra spacing above the line. If you want to create a new line without including the extra spacing, use the New Line command: Shift + Enter. When entering text, Word includes an AutoCorrect feature that will automatically correct certain words that are entered incorrectly. After creating a document, save the document so it is available for future use. Save a document at the Save As dialog box.

FIRST CHOICE TRAVEL

What You Will Do   As an employee of First Choice Travel, you have been asked to create a short document containing information on a travel package. You will save and then print the document so you can send it to other employees for review.

Tutorial
Opening a Blank Document

Tutorial
Exploring the Word Screen

Tutorial
Entering Text

Tutorial
Undoing an AutoCorrect Correction

Tutorial
Saving with a New Name

Tutorial
Printing a Document

① At the Windows 10 desktop, click the Start button and then click the Word 2016 tile.

Depending on your system configuration, these steps may vary.

② At the Word 2016 opening screen, click the *Blank document* template.

③ At the blank Word document, identify the various features by comparing your screen with the one shown in Figure 1.1.

Refer to Table 1.1 for a description of the screen features.

Figure 1.1 Word Document Screen

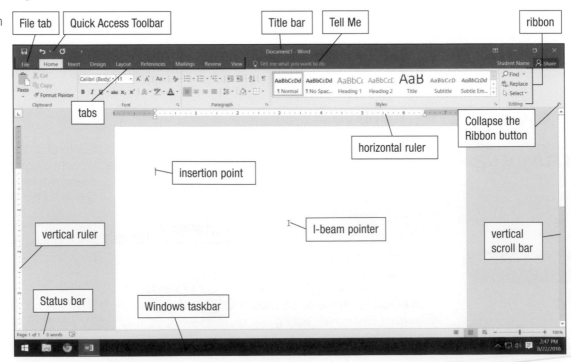

Table 1.1 Screen Features and Descriptions

Feature	Description
Collapse the Ribbon button	when clicked, removes the ribbon from the screen (redisplay the ribbon by clicking a tab [except the File tab] and then clicking the Pin the ribbon button [previously the Collapse the Ribbon button)
File tab	when clicked, displays the backstage area that contains options for working with and managing documents
horizontal ruler	used to set margins, indents, and tabs
I-beam pointer	used to move the insertion point or to select text
insertion point	indicates location of next character entered at the keyboard
Quick Access Toolbar	contains buttons for commonly used commands
ribbon	area containing tabs with options and buttons divided into groups
Status bar	displays number of pages and words, view buttons, and Zoom slider bar
tabs	contain commands and buttons organized into groups
Tell Me	used to look up a feature and provide options for using the feature
Title bar	displays document name followed by program name
vertical ruler	used to set top and bottom margins
vertical scroll bar	used to view various parts of the document beyond the screen
Windows taskbar	divided into three sections—the Start button, the task buttons area, and the notification area

4 Type Moment's Notice Travel Package as shown in Figure 1.2 and then press the Enter key.

> Pressing the Enter key begins a new paragraph in the document.

5 Type First Choice Travel, hold down the Shift key, press the Enter key, and then release the Shift key.

> Shift + Enter is the New Line command. Use this command to keep lines of text within the same paragraph, which creates less space between one line and the next.

6 Type Los Angeles Office and then press the Enter key.

7 Type the remainder of the text shown in Figure 1.2.

> Type the text as shown. When you type *adn* and then press the spacebar, the AutoCorrect feature will automatically correct it to *and*. When you type *teh* and then press the spacebar, AutoCorrect corrects it to *the*. Do not press the Enter key to end a line of text within a paragraph. Word will automatically wrap text to the next line.

8 Click the File tab to display the backstage area.

> The File tab is located in the upper left corner of the screen at the left side of the Home tab.

Figure 1.2 Steps 4–7

Moment's Notice Travel Package

First Choice Travel
Los Angeles Office

Are you spontaneous adn enjoy doing something on a moment's notice? If this describes you, then you will be interested in the First Choice Travel Moment's Notice Travel Package. For teh low price of $599 you can fly from New York to London for a four-day stay. The catch to this incredible deal is that you must make your reservation within the next week and complete your London stay within 30 days.

---

9 Click the *Save As* option.

10 At the Save As backstage area, click the *Browse* option.

If you are saving to your OneDrive, click the *OneDrive - Personal* option. Click the desired folder in the right panel, click in the *File name* text box at the Save As dialog box, type the desired document name, and then press the Enter key.

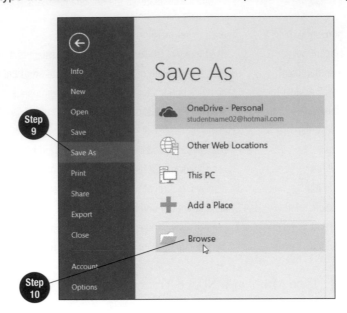

11 At the Save As dialog box, click the drive in the Navigation pane that contains your storage medium.

Press the F12 function key to display the Save As dialog box without displaying the Save As backstage area.

12 Double-click the *WordS1* folder in the Content pane.

13 Click in the *File name* text box, type 1-FCTTravelPkg, and then press the Enter key (or click the Save button).

Word automatically adds the file extension *.docx* to the end of a document name.

14 Print the document by clicking the File tab, clicking the *Print* option, and then clicking the Print button at the Print backstage area.

When you click the File tab, the backstage area displays with options for working with and managing documents. Refer to Table 1.2 for descriptions of the options and information you will find in each option's backstage area.

**Save Document
to Removable Disk**
1. Press F12.
2. In Navigation pane at
   Save As dialog box,
   click drive containing
   removable disk.
3. Double-click folder in
   Content pane.
4. Click in *File name* text
   box.
5. Type document name.
6. Press Enter.

Print Document
1. Click File tab.
2. Click *Print* option.
3. Click Print button.

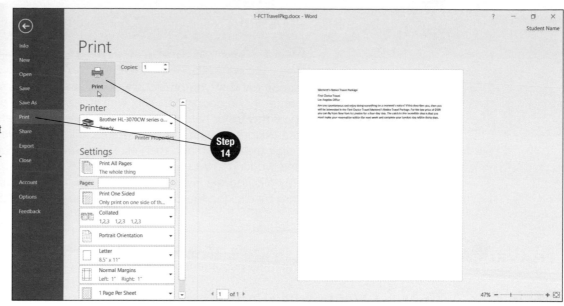

Table 1.2 Backstage Area Options

Option	Information
Info	permissions, possible issues with sharing the document, document versions, properties (for example, number of pages, number of words), date created, date last modified, date last printed, author
New	available templates such as Blank document as well as online templates
Open	options for opening documents; list of recently opened documents
Save	saves previously saved document or displays Save As backstage area with options and locations for saving a document
Save As	options and locations for saving a document
Print	number of copies, printer, settings (for example, one-sided pages, letter size, normal margins, one page per sheet)
Share	share document with specific people; share document using email, present document online, and share as a blog post
Export	export document as PDF or XPS document; change file type
Close	close currently open document
Account	user information, connected services, product information
Options	Word Options dialog box with options for customizing Word
Feedback	opens window with options for providing feedback to Microsoft on Microsoft products

Check Your Work Compare your work to the model answer to ensure that you have completed the activity correctly.

In Addition

Understanding Default Document Formatting

A Word document is based on a template that applies default formatting. Default formatting refers to formatting automatically applied by Word. Some of the default formats include 11-point Calibri as the font, line spacing of 1.08, and 8 points of spacing after each paragraph (added when you press the Enter key). You will learn more about fonts and paragraph spacing in Section 2.

Correcting Errors

Word contains a spelling feature that inserts wavy red lines below words it cannot find in the Spelling dictionary. You can edit these words or leave them as written. The wavy red lines do not print.

Activity 1.2	# Saving and Closing a Document; Closing Word

As you are working in a document that you previously saved and named, consider saving any new information you enter in the document. This way, if the power is disrupted or some other issue occurs with the software or hardware, you have the most recent version of your document saved. To save a document with the same name, click the Save button on the Quick Access Toolbar or click the File tab and then click the *Save* option at the backstage area. When you are finished working in Word, close any open documents and then close Word. Close a document by clicking the File tab and then clicking the *Close* option at the backstage area. Close Word by clicking the Close button in the upper right corner of the screen.

What You Will Do   Your supervisor has asked you to include additional information in the Moment's Notice Travel Package document you created.

Tutorial
Saving with the Same Name

Tutorial
Closing a Document and Closing Word

1 With **1-FCTTravelPkg.docx** open, make sure the insertion point is positioned at the end of the paragraph and then press the Enter key.

2 Type 3588 Ventura Boulevard.

3 Press Shift + Enter and then type Los Angeles, CA 90102.

Moment's Notice Travel Package

First Choice Travel
Los Angeles Office

Are you spontaneous and enjoy doi
will be interested in the First Choice
you can fly from New York to Londo   **Step 2**
must make your reservation within

3588 Ventura Boulevard
Los Angeles, CA 90102   **Step 3**

4 Save the document with the added text by clicking the Save button 🖫 on the Quick Access Toolbar.

Step 4

5 Add additional text to the document by pressing Shift + Enter and then typing 213-555-7800.

6 Save the document with the added text by clicking the File tab and then clicking the *Save* option at the backstage area.

If you are working in a document that has not been saved, clicking the Save button on the Quick Access Toolbar or clicking the File tab and then clicking the *Save* option will cause the Save As backstage area to display.

7 Close the document by clicking the File tab and then clicking the *Close* option at the backstage area.

8 Close Word by clicking the Close button in the upper right corner of the screen.

Check Your Work Compare your work to the model answer to ensure that you have completed the activity correctly.

In Addition

Naming a Document

Document names created in Word and other applications in the Office suite can be up to 255 characters in length, including the drive letter, folder names, server name, and spaces. File names cannot include any of the characters in the table at the right.

Symbol Name	Symbol
forward slash	/
backslash	\
greater-than symbol	>
less-than symbol	<
asterisk	*
question mark	?
quotation mark	"
colon	:
pipe symbol	|

Activity 1.3   Opening and Editing a Document

An existing document can be opened from the *Recent* option list at the Open backstage area, from a folder in OneDrive, or from the computer's hard drive or removable disk. In this activity, you will open a document from the WordS1 folder on your USB flash drive. (If you saved your student data files in a location or folder other than a USB flash drive, check with your instructor for specific steps.) After you create a document, you will often want to make changes to it. These changes may include adding text, called *inserting*, or removing text, called *deleting*. Before inserting or deleting text, position the insertion point at the desired location using the keyboard or the mouse. Use the Backspace key or Delete key on the keyboard to delete text.

What You Will Do   First Choice Travel marketing staff members have reviewed your document on vacation specials and recommended a few changes. You need to create a revised version.

Tutorial
Opening a Document from a Removable Disk

Tutorial
Moving the Insertion Point and Inserting and Deleting Text

1 At the blank Word screen, click the File tab.

> This displays the Open backstage area. If you have a document open and click the File tab, you will need to click the *Open* option to display the Open backstage area.

2 At the Open backstage area, click the *Browse* option.

3 In the Navigation pane of the Open dialog box, click the drive where your USB flash drive is located (such as *Removable Disk (F:)*).

> Press Ctrl + F12 to display the Open dialog box without displaying the Open backstage area.

4 Double-click the *WordS1* folder in the Content pane.

5 Double-click ***FCTVacSpecials.docx*** in the Content pane.

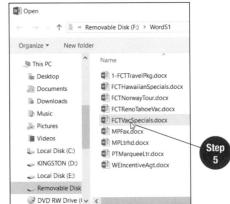

6 With the document open, click the File tab and then click the *Save As* option.

7 At the Save As backstage area, click the *Browse* option. (This should display the Save As dialog box with the WordS1 folder active on your storage medium.)

8 At the Save As dialog box, press the Home key to move the insertion point to the beginning of the file name in the *File name* text box, type 1-, and then press the Enter key. (The document name in the *File name* text box should display as **1-FCTVacSpecials.docx**.)

> Pressing the Home key saves you from having to type the entire document name. To open the Save As dialog box without displaying the Save As backstage area, press F12.

9 Position the mouse pointer at the beginning of the second paragraph and then click the left mouse button.

> This moves the insertion point to the location of the mouse pointer.

In Brief

Open Document from Removable Disk
1. Press Ctrl + F12.
2. In Navigation pane, click drive containing removable disk.
3. Double-click folder in Content pane.
4. Double-click document.

10 Press the Up, Down, Left, and Right arrow keys located to the right of the regular keys on the keyboard.

Use the information shown in Table 1.3 to practice moving the insertion point.

11 Press Ctrl + Home to move the insertion point to the beginning of the document.

12 Click at the beginning of the paragraph that begins *Sign up today for* and then type Ocean Vista Cruise Lines announces the inaugural voyage of the Pacific Sky ocean liner. Press the spacebar after typing the period.

By default, text you type is inserted in the document and existing text is moved to the right.

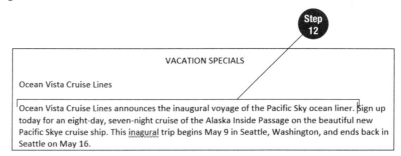

Step 12

VACATION SPECIALS

Ocean Vista Cruise Lines

Ocean Vista Cruise Lines announces the inaugural voyage of the Pacific Sky ocean liner. Sign up today for an eight-day, seven-night cruise of the Alaska Inside Passage on the beautiful new Pacific Skye cruise ship. This inagural trip begins May 9 in Seattle, Washington, and ends back in Seattle on May 16.

13 Press Ctrl + End to move the insertion point to the end of the document and then click anywhere in the last sentence in the document (the sentence that begins *Let First Choice Travel take*).

14 Press the Backspace key until the insertion point is positioned at the left margin and then press the Delete key until you have deleted the remainder of the sentence.

Pressing the Backspace key deletes any characters to the left of the insertion point. Press the Delete key to delete any characters to the right of the insertion point.

15 Click the Save button on the Quick Access Toolbar.

Clicking the Save button saves the document with the same name (**1-FCTVacSpecials.docx**).

Table 1.3 Insertion Point Keyboard Commands

Press	To move insertion point
End	to end of line
Home	to beginning of line
Page Up	up one screen
Page Down	down one screen
Ctrl + Home	to beginning of document
Ctrl + End	to end of document

Check Your Work Compare your work to the model answer to ensure that you have completed the activity correctly.

In Addition

Adding Buttons to the Quick Access Toolbar

You can add to the Quick Access Toolbar buttons that represent commonly used features. For example, you might want to add the Open button to save steps when opening a document or the Quick Print button to save steps when printing a document. To add a button to the Quick Access Toolbar, click the Customize Quick Access Toolbar button at the right side of the toolbar and then click the desired button name at the drop-down list.

In addition to moving the insertion point to a specific location, you can use the mouse to move the display of text in the document screen. Use the mouse with the vertical scroll bar to scroll through text in a document. The vertical scroll bar displays toward the right side of the screen. Scrolling in a document changes the text displayed but does not move the insertion point. Previously, you learned to delete text by pressing the Backspace key or the Delete key. You can also select text and then delete it, replace it with other text, or apply formatting to it. If you make a change to text, such as deleting it, and then change your mind, use the Undo and/or Redo buttons on the Quick Access Toolbar.

What You Will Do   The assistant manager, Jordan Keyes, has reviewed the document and asked you to make a few changes.

Tutorial
Scrolling

Tutorial
Selecting, Replacing, and Deleting Text

Tutorial
Using Undo and Redo

1   With **1-FCTVacSpecials.docx** open, press Ctrl + Home to move the insertion point to the beginning of the document.

2   Position the mouse pointer on the down scroll arrow on the vertical scroll bar and then click the left mouse button several times.

> This scrolls down the lines of text in the document. Scrolling changes the display of text but does not move the insertion point.

3   Position the mouse pointer on the vertical scroll bar below the scroll box and then click the left mouse button two times.

> The scroll box on the vertical scroll bar indicates the location of the text in the document screen in relation to the remainder of the document. Clicking below the scroll box on the vertical scroll bar scrolls down one screen of text at a time.

4   Position the mouse pointer on the scroll box on the vertical scroll bar, click and hold down the left mouse button, drag the scroll box to the top of the vertical scroll bar, and then release the mouse button.

5   Position the mouse pointer anywhere in the word *Behold* (located immediately after the first bullet) and then double-click the left mouse button to select it.

> Selected text displays with a gray background. You can also drag through text with the mouse to select it. When you select text, the Mini toolbar displays. You will learn more about the Mini toolbar in Activity 2.1.

On this exciting cruise, you will
- Behold some of the worlds most m
- Visit colorful Gold Rush towns
- Observe fascinating wildlife
- Experience a dazzling display by the

6   Type View.

> When you type *View*, it replaces *Behold*.

7   Move the insertion point to the beginning of the word *Glacier* (located in the second paragraph under the *Ocean Vista Cruise Lines* heading) and then press the F8 function key on the keyboard. Press the Right Arrow key until the words *Glacier Bay and* are selected.

> Pressing the F8 function key turns on Extend mode. Use the insertion point movement keys to select text in Extend mode.

The Pacific Skye cruises through Glacier Bay and the Inside ports of Skagway, Haines, and Juneau. The Pacific Skye also Vancouver, British Columbia.

8 Press the Delete key.

9 Hold down the Ctrl key, click anywhere in the first sentence of the second paragraph (begins with *Ocean Vista Cruise Lines announces*), and then release the Ctrl key.

> Holding down the Ctrl key while clicking the mouse button selects the entire sentence.

10 Press the Delete key to delete the selected sentence.

11 Click the Undo button on the Quick Access Toolbar.

> When you click the Undo button, the deleted sentence reappears. Clicking the Undo button reverses the last command or deletes the last entry you typed. Click the arrow at the right side of the Undo button and a drop-down list displays the changes made to the document since it was opened. Click an action to undo it and any actions listed above it in the drop-down list.

12 Click the Redo button 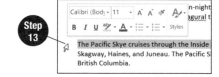 on the Quick Access Toolbar.

> Clicking the Redo button deletes the selected sentence. If you click the Undo button and then decide you do not want to reverse the original action, click the Redo button.

13 Position the mouse pointer between the left edge of the page and the first line of text in the second paragraph until the pointer turns into an arrow pointing up and to the right (instead of the left) and then click the left mouse button.

> The space between the left edge of the page and the text is referred to as the **selection bar**. Use the selection bar to select specific amounts of text. Refer to Table 1.4 for more information on selecting text.

14 Deselect the text by clicking in the document.

> Deselecting cancels the selection of text.

15 Save the document by clicking the Save button on the Quick Access Toolbar.

Table 1.4 Selecting with the Mouse

To select	Complete these steps using the mouse
a word	Double-click the word.
a line of text	Click in the selection bar to the left of the line.
multiple lines of text	Drag in the selection bar to the left of the lines.
a sentence	Hold down the Ctrl key and then click anywhere in the sentence.
a paragraph	Double-click in the selection bar next to the paragraph or triple-click anywhere in the paragraph.
multiple paragraphs	Drag in the selection bar.
an entire document	Triple-click in the selection bar.

Check Your Work Compare your work to the model answer to ensure that you have completed the activity correctly.

In Addition

Resuming Reading or Editing a Document

When you work in a multiple-page document and then close the document, Word remembers where the insertion point was last positioned. When you reopen the document, Word displays a Welcome Back message at the right side of the screen near the vertical scroll bar.

The message tells you that you can pick up where you left off and identifies the page where your insertion point was last located. Click the message and the insertion point is positioned at the top of that page.

Use Word's spelling checker to find and correct misspelled words and find duplicated words (such as *and and*). The spelling checker compares words in your document with words in its dictionary. If a match is found, the word is passed over. If no match is found for the word, the spelling checker stops, selects the word, and offers replacements. The grammar checker will search a document for grammar, punctuation, and word usage errors. The spelling checker and the grammar checker can help you create a well-written document but these features do not replace the need for proofreading.

What You Will Do   Continuing with the editing process, you are ready to check the spelling and grammar in the First Choice Travel vacation specials document.

Tutorial
Checking Spelling and Grammar

1 With **1-FCTVacSpecials.docx** open, press Ctrl + Home to move the insertion point to the beginning of the document.

2 Click the Review tab and then click the Spelling & Grammar button in the Proofing group.

> When you click the Spelling & Grammar button, Word selects the first misspelled word and displays the Spelling task pane at the right side of the screen with options for correcting the error, ignoring the error, or adding the word to the spelling dictionary. It also contains a brief definition of the selected word in the list box. If a grammar error is selected, the Grammar task pane displays.

3 When the word *inagural* is selected in the document and *inaugural* is selected in the list box in the Spelling task pane, click the Change button in the pane.

> Refer to Table 1.5 for an explanation of the buttons in the Spelling task pane and Grammar task pane.

4 When the word *worlds* is selected in the document and *world's* is selected in the list box in the Grammar task pane, click the Change button.

5 When the word *Your* is selected in the document and *You* is selected in the list box in the Grammar task pane, click the Change button.

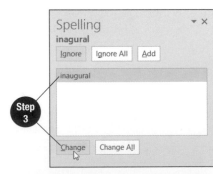

In Brief

Check Spelling and Grammar
1. Click Review tab.
2. Click Spelling & Grammar button.
3. Ignore or change as needed.
4. Click OK.

6 When the word *the* is selected (this word occurs twice), click the Delete button in the Spelling task pane.

7 When the word *of* is selected in the document and *off* is selected in the list box in the Grammar task pane, click the Change button.

8 When the word *utah* is selected in the document and *Utah* is selected in the list box in the Spelling task pane, click the Change button.

9 Click OK at the message box telling you the spelling and grammar check is complete.

10 Click the Save button on the Quick Access Toolbar to save the changes made to the document.

Table 1.5 Spelling Task Pane and Grammar Task Pane Buttons

Button	Function
Ignore	during spell checking, skips that occurrence of the word; in grammar checking, leaves currently selected text as written
Ignore All	during spell checking, skips that occurrence and all other occurrences of the word in the document
Add	adds selected word to the main spelling check dictionary
Delete	deletes the currently selected word(s)
Change	replaces selected word in sentence with selected word in list box
Change All	replaces selected word in sentence with selected word in list box and all other occurrences of the word

Check Your Work Compare your work to the model answer to ensure that you have completed the activity correctly.

In Addition

Changing Spelling Options

Control spelling and grammar checking options at the Word Options dialog box with the *Proofing* option selected. Display this dialog box by clicking the File tab and then clicking *Options*. At the Word Options dialog box, click *Proofing* in the left panel of the dialog box. With options in the dialog box, you can tell the spelling checker to ignore certain types of text, create custom dictionaries, show readability statistics, and hide spelling and/or grammar errors in the document.

Editing While Checking Spelling and Grammar

When checking a document, you can temporarily leave the Spelling task pane or Grammar task pane by clicking in the document. To resume the spelling and grammar check, click the Resume button in the Spelling task pane or Grammar task pane.

The AutoCorrect feature automatically detects and corrects some typographical errors, misspelled words, and incorrect capitalization. In addition to correcting errors, you can use the AutoCorrect feature to insert frequently used text. Use the Thesaurus to find synonyms, antonyms, and related terms for a particular word.

What You Will Do   You need to insert additional text in the First Choice Travel vacation specials document. To speed up the process, you will add an entry to AutoCorrect. You will also use the Thesaurus to find synonyms for specific words in the document.

Tutorial
Adding and Deleting
an AutoCorrect Entry

Tutorial
Using the Thesaurus

1 With **1-FCTVacSpecials.docx** open, click the File tab and then click *Options*.

2 At the Word Options dialog box, click *Proofing* in the left panel and then click the AutoCorrect Options button in the *AutoCorrect options* section.

3 At the AutoCorrect dialog box, type bst in the *Replace* text box and then press the Tab key.

4 Type Bahamas Sightseeing Tour in the *With* text box and then click the Add button.

5 Click OK to close the AutoCorrect dialog box.

6 Click OK to close the Word Options dialog box.

7 Press Ctrl + End to move the insertion point to the end of the document, make sure the insertion point is positioned a double space below the last bulleted item, and then type the text shown in Figure 1.3. (Type the text exactly as shown. AutoCorrect will correct *bst* to *Bahamas Sightseeing Tour* when you press the Enter key or the spacebar.)

Figure 1.3 Step 7

bst

The Bahamas consist of over 700 islands and cays, all with friendly people, beautiful beaches, and magnificent dive spots. First Choice Travel offers the bst to explore these exciting and breathtaking islands. Sign up for the bst and experience the bustling city of Nassau, which offers everything from parasailing to casino gaming. Call us to discover how you can join the bst at an incredibly low price.

In Brief

Add AutoCorrect Entry
1. Click File tab.
2. Click *Options*.
3. Click *Proofing*.
4. Click AutoCorrect Options button.
5. Type text in *Replace* text box.
6. Type text in *With* text box.
7. Click Add button.
8. Click OK.
9. Click OK.

Use Thesaurus
1. Click in word.
2. Click Review tab.
3. Click Thesaurus button.
4. Right-click word in Thesaurus task pane list box.
5. Click *Insert*.

8 Click anywhere in the word *breathtaking* (located in the second sentence in the paragraph you just typed), click the Review tab, and then click the Thesaurus button in the Proofing group.

9 At the Thesaurus task pane, right-click the word *spectacular* in the task pane list box and then click *Insert* at the drop-down list.

> You can also hover the mouse pointer over the desired word in the task pane list box, click the arrow that displays at the right side of the word, and then click *Insert* at the drop-down list.

10 Close the Thesaurus task pane by clicking the Close button ⊠ in the upper right corner of the task pane.

11 Position the mouse pointer on the word *bustling* (located in the third sentence in the paragraph you just typed) and then click the right mouse button. At the shortcut menu that displays, point to *Synonyms* and then click *lively* at the side menu.

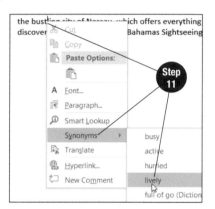

12 Click the Save button to save the document with the same name.

13 Click the File tab and then click *Options*. At the Word Options dialog box, click *Proofing* in the left panel and then click the AutoCorrect Options button.

14 At the AutoCorrect dialog box, type bst in the *Replace* text box.

> This selects *bst* and *Bahamas Sightseeing Tour* in the list box.

15 Click the Delete button and then click OK to close the dialog box.

16 Click OK to close the Word Options dialog box.

Check Your Work Compare your work to the model answer to ensure that you have completed the activity correctly.

In Addition

Using the Thesaurus Task Pane

Depending on the word you are looking up, the words in the Thesaurus task pane list box may display followed by *(n.)* for *noun*, *(v.)* for *verb*, *(adj.)* for *adjective*, or *(adv.)* for *adverb*. Click a word in the list box and a definition of the word displays below the list box. (You may need to install a dictionary before you will see a definition. To install a dictionary, click the Get a Dictionary hyperlink. At the Dictionaries pane, click the desired dictionary and then click the Download button.)

Changing Document Views;
Hiding and Showing White Space

By default, a document displays in Print Layout view. This view displays the document on the screen as it will appear when printed. Other views are available, such as Read Mode, Web Layout, Outline, or Draft. Change views with buttons in the view area on the Status bar or with options in the Views group on the View tab. Change to Draft view and the document displays in a format for efficient editing and formatting. The Read Mode displays a document in a format for easy viewing and reading. Change to Web Layout view to display a document as it would appear as a web page. In Print Layout view, a page displays as it will appear when printed, including the white space at the top and bottom of the page representing the document's margins. To save space on the screen, the white space can be removed using the Hide White Space icon. Redisplay white space using the Show White Space icon.

What You Will Do   Several people will be reviewing the First Choice Travel vacation specials document on-screen, so you decide to experiment with various views to determine the best one for on-screen reviewing.

Tutorial
Changing Document
Views

Tutorial
Hiding and Showing
White Space

1 With **1-FCTVacSpecials.docx** open, press Ctrl + Home to move the insertion point to the beginning of the document.

2 Change to Draft view by clicking the View tab and then clicking the Draft button ▤ in the Views group.

Change to Draft view to display the document in a format designed for efficient editing and formatting. In Draft view, margins and other features such as headers and footers do not display.

3 Change to Web Layout view by clicking the Web Layout button ▤ in the view area on the Status bar (see Figure 1.4).

Change to Web Layout view to display the document as it would appear as a web page.

4 Change to Read Mode by clicking the Read Mode button ▤ in the Views group.

Read Mode displays a document for easy viewing and reading. You can also display a document in Read Mode by clicking the Read Mode button in the view area of the Status bar.

5 Display the next two pages on the screen by clicking the Next button (right-pointing triangle in a circle) that displays at the right side of the screen.

Figure 1.4 View Buttons in View Area on Status Bar

Print Layout button

Read Mode button   Web Layout button

6 Display previous pages by clicking the Previous button (left-pointing triangle in a circle) that displays at the left side of the screen.

7 Continue navigating in Read Mode using the keyboard commands shown in Table 1.6.

8 Return to Print Layout view by pressing the Esc key.

Pressing the Esc key displays the document in Print Layout view. You can also return to Print Layout view by clicking the View tab and then clicking *Edit Document* at the drop-down list.

9 To save space on the screen, remove the white space that displays at the top and bottom of each page as well as the gray space between pages. To do this, position the mouse pointer on the gray space above the page until the pointer turns into the hide white space icon and then double-click the left mouse button.

10 Scroll through the document and then redisplay the white and gray space at the top and bottom of each page. To do this, position the mouse pointer on the gray line at the top of the page until the pointer turns into a show white space icon and then double-click the left mouse button.

Table 1.6 Navigating in Read Mode

Press this key	To complete this action
Page Down or spacebar	Move to next page or section.
Page Up or Backspace key	Move to previous page or section.
Right Arrow	Move to next page.
Left Arrow	Move to previous page.
Home	Move to first page in document.
End	Move to last page in document.
Esc	Return to previous view.

In Addition

Zooming In on an Object in Read Mode

If your document contains an object such as an image, shape, SmartArt, or table, you can zoom in on the object in Read Mode by double-clicking the object. The object appears larger on the screen and a button containing a diagonally pointing arrow displays just outside the upper right corner of it. Click this button to zoom in even more on the object. Click once outside the object to return it to its original size.

Activity 1.8   Changing the Display Percentage

By default, a document displays at 100%. This display percentage can be changed with the Zoom slider bar located at the right side of the Status bar and with options in the Zoom group on the View tab. To change display percentage with the Zoom slider bar, drag the button on the bar to increase or decrease the percentage, or click the Zoom Out button to decrease the display percentage or the Zoom In button to increase the percentage. Use buttons in the Zoom group on the View tab to return to the 100% display percentage, display one page or multiple pages, expand the document across the screen, and display the Zoom dialog box.

What You Will Do   Several people will be reviewing the First Choice Travel vacation specials document on the screen so you decide to experiment with various views and zoom percentages to determine the best view for on-screen reviewing.

Tutorial

Changing the Display Percentage

1. With **1-FCTVacSpecials.docx** open, press Ctrl + Home to move the insertion point to the beginning of the document.

2. Click the Zoom Out button ⊟ at the left side of the Zoom slider bar to decrease the display percentage to 90%.

   > Figure 1.5 identifies the Zoom slider bar along with Zoom Out and Zoom In buttons.

3. Click the Zoom In button ⊞ at the right side of the Zoom slider bar to increase the display percentage to 100%.

4. Position the mouse pointer on the Zoom slider button on the Zoom slider bar, click and hold down the left mouse button, drag to the right to increase the display percentage, drag left to decrease the percentage, and then release the mouse button.

5. Click the View tab.

6. Click the 100% button in the Zoom group to return to the default display percentage of 100%.

7. Click the One Page button in the Zoom group to display just the first page on the screen.

8. Click the Multiple Pages button in the Zoom group to display all of the pages on the screen.

9. Click the Zoom button in the Zoom group to display the Zoom dialog box.

   > You can also display the Zoom dialog box by clicking the Zoom level button (the percentage that displays at the right side of the Zoom slider bar).

In Brief

Display Zoom Dialog Box
1. Click View tab.
2. Click Zoom button.

10 Click the *75%* option in the *Zoom to* section of the dialog box.

11 Click OK to close the Zoom dialog box.

The document displays at 75%.

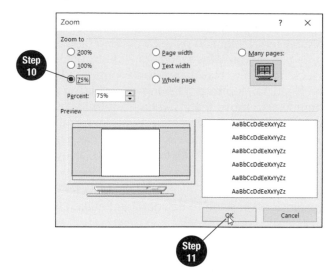

12 Click the 100% button in the Zoom group to return to the default display percentage.

Figure 1.5 Zoom Slider Bar

In Addition

Working with Windows

The Window group on the View tab contains a number of buttons for working with windows. Click the New Window button to open a new window containing the same document. This is useful if you want to view a portion of the document while editing in another location. If more than one document is open, the documents can be arranged so that a portion of each is visible. To do this, click the Arrange All button in the Window group. Click the Split button in the Window group to split the open document in two with a split bar and another horizontal ruler. Splitting a window is useful if you want to view different parts of a document at one time. Compare the contents of two documents by opening both documents and then clicking the View Side by Side button in the Window group. Both documents display on the screen arranged side by side. By default, synchronous scrolling is active, which means that scrolling in one document results in the same scrolling in the other document. Turn off synchronous scrolling by clicking the Synchronous Scrolling button.

Use the Navigation pane to browse in a document or search for specific text or items. Display the Navigation pane by clicking the Find button in the Editing group on the Home tab or by clicking the *Navigation Pane* check box in the Show group on the View tab to insert a check mark. The Navigation pane contains three tabs—Headings, Pages, and Results. Click the Headings tab to display in the Navigation pane thumbnails of each page. Click a page thumbnail to move the insertion point to that page. Search for text by clicking in the search text box and then typing the desired text. With the Pages tab active, each occurrence of the search text is highlighted in the pages. Click the Results tab to display each occurrence of the search text along with the text that displays before and after each occurrence.

What You Will Do   Review the First Choice Travel vacation specials document by using the Navigation pane to navigate and search for specific text in the document.

Tutorial
Navigating Using the
Navigation Pane

Tutorial
Finding Text

1   With **1-FCTVacSpecials.docx** open, display the Navigation pane by clicking the View tab and then clicking the *Navigation Pane* check box to insert a check mark.

You can also display the Navigation pane by clicking the Find button in the Editing group on the Home tab.

2   Click the Pages tab in the Navigation pane.

Clicking the Pages tab displays thumbnails of each page in the Navigation pane.

3   Click the page 2 thumbnail in the Navigation pane.

Clicking the page 2 thumbnail moves the insertion point to the beginning of page 2.

In Brief

Display Navigation Pane
1. Click View tab.
2. Click *Navigation Pane* check box.
OR
1. Click Home tab.
2. Click Find button.

4 Click the page 1 thumbnail in the Navigation pane.

5 Click in the search text box in the Navigation pane (contains the text *Search document*) and then type Pacific Skye.

After you type *Pacific Skye*, each occurrence of the text is highlighted in the document.

6 Click the Next Search Result button in the Navigation pane (displays as a down arrow) to select the next occurrence of *Pacific Skye*. Click the button again to select the next occurrence.

You can click the Previous Search Result button (displays as an up arrow) to display the previous occurrence of the search text.

7 Click the Results tab to display in the Navigation pane each occurrence of the search text *Pacific Skye* along with the text that displays before and after each occurrence.

8 Select the first occurrence of *Pacific Skye* in the document by clicking the first item in the Navigation pane.

9 Click the X at the right side of the search text box.

Clicking this button ends the current search, removes the search text in the Navigation pane, and selects the current search result in the document.

10 Close the Navigation pane by clicking the Close button in the upper right corner of the pane.

You can also close the Navigation pane by clicking the *Navigation Pane* check box in the Show group on the View tab to remove the check mark.

In Addition

Displaying Ribbon Options

Control how much of the ribbon displays on screen with the Ribbon Display Options button in the upper right corner of the screen. Click this button and a drop-down list displays with options for hiding the ribbon, showing only the tabs, or showing tabs and commands. You can also turn off the display of the ribbon by clicking the Collapse the Ribbon button located above the vertical scroll bar or with the keyboard shortcut Ctrl + F1. Redisplay the ribbon by double-clicking any tab or by pressing Ctrl + F1.

Activity 1.10 Finding and Replacing Text

In the previous activity you used the Navigation pane to find all occurrences of specific text in the document. If you want to find text and then replace it with other text, use options at the Find and Replace dialog box with the Replace tab selected. Display this dialog box by clicking the Replace button in the Editing group on the Home tab.

What You Will Do   As you review the vacation specials document, you discover that the name of the ship is spelled incorrectly and that the ship's cabins are divided into categories rather than classes. You decide to use the Find and Replace feature to correct these errors.

Tutorial

Finding and Replacing Text

1 With **1-FCTVacSpecials.docx** open, press Ctrl + Home to move the insertion point to the beginning of the document.

2 The name of the ship is the *Pacific Sky*, not the *Pacific Skye*. To change the name, display the Find and Replace dialog box by clicking the Home tab and then clicking the Replace button in the Editing group.

3 At the Find and Replace dialog box with the Replace tab selected, type Skye in the *Find what* text box and then press the Tab key.

> Pressing the Tab key moves the insertion point to the *Replace with* text box. You can also click in the *Replace with* text box.

4 Type Sky in the *Replace with* text box.

5 Click the Replace All button at the bottom of the dialog box.

> Clicking the Replace All button replaces all occurrences of the text in the document. If you want control over what is replaced in a document, click the Replace button to replace text or click the Find Next button to move to the next occurrence of the text.

6 At the message telling you that four replacements were made, click OK.

7 Click the Close button to close the Find and Replace dialog box.

8 The word *class* is used to designate cabins, when it should instead be *category*. To make this change, click the Replace button in the Editing group on the Home tab.

9 At the Find and Replace dialog box with the Replace tab selected, type class.

> When you open the Replace dialog box, *Skye* is automatically selected in the *Find what* text box. When you begin typing *class*, the selected text is automatically deleted.

10 Press the Tab key and then type category in the *Replace with* text box.

> When you type the find text and the replace text in all lowercase letters, Word will find and replace all occurrences regardless of the capitalization. For example, Word will find *Class* in the document and replace it with *Category*.

11 Click the Replace All button.

Find and Replace Text
1. Click Replace button.
2. Type find text.
3. Press Tab key.
4. Type replace text.
5. Click Replace or Replace All button.
6. Click OK.
7. Click Close button.

12 At the message telling you that six replacements were made, click OK.

13 Click the Close button to close the Find and Replace dialog box.

14 Click the Save button on the Quick Access Toolbar to save the document.

Check Your Work Compare your work to the model answer to ensure that you have completed the activity correctly.

In Addition

Exploring Options at the Expanded Find and Replace Dialog Box

The Find and Replace dialog box contains a variety of check boxes with options you can choose for completing a find and replace. To display these options, click the More button located at the bottom of the dialog box. This causes the Find and Replace dialog box to expand as shown at the right. The options are described in the table below.

Option	Action
Match case	Exactly match the case of the search text. For example, if you search for *Book*, Word will stop at *Book* but not *book* or *BOOK*.
Find whole words only	Find a whole word, not a part of a word. For example, if you search for *her* and did not select *Find whole words only*, Word would stop at t*her*e, *her*e, *her*s, and so on.
Use wildcards	Search for wildcards, special characters, or special search operators.
Sounds like	Match words that sound alike but are spelled differently, such as *know* and *no*.
Find all word forms	Find all forms of the word entered in the *Find what* text box. For example, if you enter *hold*, Word will stop at *held* and *holding*.
Match prefix	Find only those words that begin with the letters in the *Find what* text box. For example, if you enter *per*, Word will stop at words such as *perform* and *perfect* but will skip over words such as *super* and *hyperlink*.
Match suffix	Find only those words that end with the letters in the *Find what* text box. For example, if you enter *ly*, Word will stop at words such as *accurately* and *quietly* but skip over words such as *catalyst* and *lyre*.
Ignore punctuation characters	Ignore punctuation within characters. For example, if you enter *US* in the *Find what* text box, Word will stop at *U.S.*
Ignore white-space characters	Ignore spaces between letters. For example, if you enter *F B I* in the *Find what* text box, Word will stop at *FBI*.

Word includes the Tell Me feature, which provides information and guidance on how to complete a function. To use Tell Me, click in the *Tell Me* text box on the ribbon to the right of the View tab and then type the function for which you want help. As you type, a drop-down list displays with options that are refined as you continue typing, a feature referred to as *word-wheeling*. The drop-down list displays options for completing the function, displaying information on the function from sources on the web, or displaying information on the function in the Word Help window. When you first click in the *Tell Me* text box, the drop-down list will contain the last five functions you entered.

What You Will Do   To enhance the appearance of the document, you decide to use the Tell Me feature to change the font color of the title *VACATION SPECIALS*. You will also use the Tell Me feature to access the Word Help window and find articles on AutoCorrect.

Tutorial
Using the Tell Me Feature

1 With **1-FCTVacSpecials.docx** open, select the title *VACATION SPECIALS* by positioning the mouse pointer in the title and then triple-clicking the left mouse button.

2 Click in the *Tell Me* text box.

The *Tell Me* text box is located on the ribbon to the right of the View tab and contains the text *Tell me what you want to do*. When you click in the text box, the last five functions entered will display in a drop-down list.

3 Type font color in the *Tell Me* text box.

A drop-down list displays with options such as *Font Color, Font Size, Border Color, Text Highlight Color,* and *Font*.

4 Position the mouse pointer on the *Font Color* option in the drop-down list.

5 At the side menu that displays, click the *Blue* color option in the *Standard Colors* section.

The Blue font color is applied to the selected title. The Tell Me feature guided you through the process of applying font color without you having to learn how to apply font color using a button on the ribbon or an option at a dialog box.

6 The Tell Me feature also includes access to the Word Help window. To display the Word Help window with information on AutoCorrect, click in the *Tell Me* text box and then type AutoCorrect.

7 At the drop-down list, click *Get Help on "AutoCorrect"*.

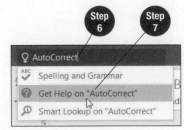

The Word Help window opens with articles on AutoCorrect.

In Brief

Use Tell Me Feature
1. Click in *Tell Me* text box.
2. Type function.
3. Click option at drop-down list.

8 At the Word Help window, click the first hyperlink in the window list box.

Clicking the hyperlink opens the article in the Word Help window.

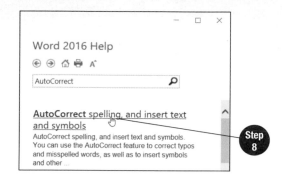

9 The Word Help window contains five buttons for navigating and managing the window. Click the Back button (contains a left-pointing arrow) in the Word Help window to display the previous window.

10 Click the Forward button (contains a right-pointing arrow) to redisplay the article on AutoCorrect.

11 Click the Use Large Text button to increase the size of text in the window.

Print information on a topic or feature by clicking the Print button and then clicking the Print button at the Print dialog box.

12 Click the Home button to return to the home screen of the Word Help window.

13 Close the Word Help window by clicking the Close button in the upper right corner of the window.

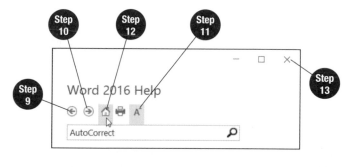

Check Your Work Compare your work to the model answer to ensure that you have completed the activity correctly.

In Addition

Accessing Smart Lookup

Using the Smart Lookup feature, you can access information on a function from a variety of sources on the web such as Wikipedia, Bing, and the Oxford dictionary. The Tell Me feature is one way to access Smart Lookup. To use Tell Me for Smart Lookup, click in the *Tell Me* text box, type the function on which you want to display information, and then click the *Smart Lookup* option in the drop-down list. Clicking the *Smart Lookup* option displays the Smart Lookup task pane at the right side of the screen with information on the function from a variety of locations on the Internet. Smart Lookup can also be accessed with the Smart Lookup button in the Insights group on the Review tab or by selecting text about which you want additional information, right-clicking the selected text, and then clicking *Smart Lookup* at the shortcut menu.

Activity 1.12 Using the Help Feature; Previewing and Printing

The Word Help window can be opened through the Tell Me feature or by pressing the F1 function key on the keyboard. You can also open the Word Help window directly from dialog boxes or the backstage area. Display a dialog box and then click the Help button in the upper right corner and the Word Help window displays with specific information related to the dialog box. Display the backstage area and then click the Help button in the upper right corner of the screen and the Word Help window displays with information related to the specific backstage area. The Print backstage area provides options for previewing the document before printing, indicating the number of copies, specifying the pages for printing, and customizing the document.

What You Will Do   You are ready to print the First Choice Travel vacation specials document, but first you want to learn more about printing a document. You decide to experiment with the Help feature in a dialog box and backstage area and then use Help to learn about printing.

Tutorial
Using the Help Feature

Tutorial
Previewing
and Printing

1   With **1-FCTVacSpecials.docx** open, press Ctrl + Home to move the insertion point to the beginning of the document.

2   Click the Font group dialog box launcher 🔲 to display the Font dialog box.

> The Font group dialog box launcher is located in the lower right corner of the Font group and displays as a small button containing a diagonal arrow.

3   Click the Help button in the upper right corner of the dialog box.

4   Look at the information that displays in the Word Help window and then close the window by clicking the Close button in the upper right corner of the window.

5   Close the Font dialog box by clicking the Close button in the upper right corner of the dialog box.

6   Click the File tab to display the backstage area.

7   Click the Help button in the upper right corner of the backstage area.

8   Look at the information that displays in the Word Help window and then close the window by clicking the Close button.

9   Click the Back button in the backstage area to return to the document.

10 Press the F1 function key to display the Word Help window.

11 Click in the Word Help window search text box, type print, and then press the Enter key.

12 Click a hyperlink in the Word Help window list box that pertains to printing a document.

13 Read the information and then close the window by clicking the Close button.

14 Click the File tab and then click the *Print* option to display the Print backstage area.

> At the Print backstage area, your document displays at the right side of the screen as it will appear when printed. The left side of the Print backstage area displays three

categories—*Print*, *Printer*, and *Settings*. Click the Print button in the *Print* category to send the document to the printer. Specify the number of copies you want printed with the *Copies* measurement box in the *Print* category. Use the gallery in the *Printer* category to specify the desired printer. The *Settings* category contains a number of galleries, each with options for specifying how you want your document printed.

15 Click twice on the Zoom In button at the right side of the Zoom slider bar.

Click the Zoom In button to increase the size of the page or click the Zoom Out button to decrease the size of the page.

16 Click the Next Page button located below and to the left of the preview page to display the next page in the document.

17 Click the Zoom to Page button located at the right side of the Zoom slider bar.

18 Print only page 2 of the document by clicking in the *Pages* text box (in the *Settings* category), typing 2, and then clicking the Print button.

19 Move the insertion point to any character in page 3 and then print page 3. Begin by clicking the File tab and then clicking the *Print* option.

20 At the Print backstage area, click the top gallery in the *Settings* category and then click *Print Current Page* at the drop-down list.

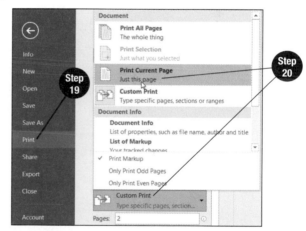

21 Click the Print button.

22 Save and then close **1-FCTVacSpecials.docx**.

Check Your Work Compare your work to the model answer to ensure that you have completed the activity correctly.

In Addition

Specifying Pages to Print

Identify a specific page, multiple pages, and/or a range of pages for printing at the Print backstage area. Print specific pages by clicking in the *Pages* text box and then typing the page numbers of the pages you want printed. To print specific multiple pages, use a comma to indicate *and* and use a hyphen to indicate *through*. For example, to print pages 2 and 5, type **2,5** in the *Pages* text box. To print pages 6 through 10, type **6-10**. You can enter both commas and hyphens when specifying page numbers.

Getting Help on a Button

When you hover the mouse pointer over certain buttons, the ScreenTip that displays includes a Help icon and the text *Tell me more*. Click this hyperlinked text and the Word Help window opens with information about the button feature. You can also hover the mouse pointer over a button and then press F1 to display the Word Help window with information about the button feature.

Word includes a number of template documents formatted for specific uses. Each Word document is based on a template document, with the Normal template as the default. With Word templates (and Microsoft online templates), you can easily create a variety of documents, such as letters, reports, and awards, with specialized formatting. Display available templates by clicking the File tab and then clicking the *New* option. At the New backstage area, click in the search text box, type a category, and then press the Enter key. Word displays templates matching the category. Click the desired template and then click the Create button. You must be connected to the Internet to download online templates.

What You Will Do　You are the projects coordinator for Marquee Productions, a movie production company. The company's travel agency is First Choice Travel, and you need the agency to make flight and hotel reservations for personnel involved in filming a movie in and around Toronto. You decide to use a letter template to help you format the letter.

Tutorial

Creating a Document
Using a Template

1　Click the File tab and then click the *New* option.

2　At the New backstage area, click in the search text box (contains the text *Search for online templates*), type business letter equity theme, and then press the Enter key.

3　Click the first *Letter (Equity theme)* template in the backstage area.

4　Click the Create button.

5　At the letter document, click the *[Pick the date]* placeholder and then type the current date. (Your date will automatically change to numbers when you click outside the placeholder.)

6　If necessary, select the name that displays below the date and then type your first and last names.

7　Click the *[Type the sender company name]* placeholder and then type Marquee Productions.

8　Click the *[Type the sender company address]* placeholder, type 955 South Alameda Street, press the Enter key, and then type Los Angeles, CA 90037.

9　Click the *[Type the recipient name]* placeholder and then type Ms. Melissa Gehring.

10　Press the Enter key and then type First Choice Travel.

In Brief

**Create Document
Using Template**
1. Click File tab.
2. Click *New* option.
3. Click template.
4. Click Create button.

11 Click the *[Type the recipient address]* placeholder, type 3588 Ventura Boulevard, press the Enter key, and then type Los Angeles, CA 90102.

12 Click the *[Type the salutation]* placeholder and then type Dear Ms. Gehring:.

13 Click anywhere in the three paragraphs of text in the body of the letter and then type the text shown in Figure 1.6.

> **Dear Ms. Gehring:**
>
> Marquee Productions will be filming a movie in and around the Toronto area from July 9 through August 31, 2018. I would like scheduling and pricing information for flights from Los Angeles to Toronto, as well as information on lodging.
>
> Approximately 45 people from our company will need flight reservations and hotel rooms. Please locate the best group rates and let me know the approximate costs. I would like to finalize preparations by the end of the month.

Step 13

14 Click the *[Type the closing]* placeholder and then type Sincerely,.

15 Make sure your first and last names display below *Sincerely*. If not, select the current name below *Sincerely* and then type your first and last names.

16 Click the *[Type the sender title]* placeholder and then type Projects Coordinator.

17 Click the Save button on the Quick Access Toolbar.

18 At the Save As backstage area, navigate to the *WordS1* folder on your storage medium.

19 At the Save As dialog box with the WordS1 folder active, type 1-MPLtrtoFCT in the *File name* text box and then press the Enter key (or click the Save button).

20 Print the letter by clicking the File tab, clicking the *Print* option, and then clicking the Print button.

21 Close the document by clicking the File tab and then clicking the *Close* option.

Figure 1.6 Step 13

> Marquee Productions will be filming a movie in and around the Toronto area from July 9 through August 31, 2018. I would like scheduling and pricing information for flights from Los Angeles to Toronto, as well as information on lodging.
>
> Approximately 45 people from our company will need flight reservations and hotel rooms. Please locate the best group rates and let me know the approximate costs. I would like to finalize preparations by the end of the month.

Check Your Work | Compare your work to the model answer to ensure that you have completed the activity correctly.

In Addition

Specifying a Template Category

When you search for online templates at the New backstage area, a *Category* list box displays at the right side of the screen. The list box displays the category and the number of templates that fit within the category. Click the desired category in the list box, and only templates matching that category will display in the New backstage area.

Managing Folders and Documents; Saving in a Different Format

As you continue working with documents, consider document management tasks such as creating a folder and copying, moving, and deleting documents. You can complete many document management tasks related to one or more documents at the Open dialog box or Save As dialog box. By default, Word saves a file as a Word document and adds the extension .docx to the name. With the *Save as type* option at the Save As dialog box, you can save a document in a different format such as rich text or an earlier version of Word, or as a web page or plain text file.

What You Will Do Since First Choice Travel will be communicating with Marquee Productions, you decide to create a folder into which you will insert Marquee Productions documents. You will also save a document in an older version of Word.

Tutorial
Managing Folders

Tutorial
Managing Documents

Tutorial
Saving in a Different Format

1. Click the File tab.

2. At the Open backstage area, click the *Browse* option.

3. At the Open dialog box, navigate to the WordS1 folder on your storage medium.

4. Click the New folder button.

5. Type Marquee and then press the Enter key.

6. Click the document *MPFax.docx* in the Open dialog box Content pane, hold down the Ctrl key, click *1-FCTVacSpecials.docx*, and then release the Ctrl key.

   Use the Ctrl key to select nonadjacent documents. Use the Shift key to select adjacent documents.

7. Right-click either of the selected documents and then click *Copy* at the shortcut menu.

8. Double-click the *Marquee* folder.

   Folders display in the Open dialog box Content pane before documents. Folders display preceded by a file folder icon and documents display preceded by a document icon.

9. Position the mouse pointer in a white portion of the Open dialog box Content pane, click the right mouse button, and then click *Paste* at the shortcut menu.

   The copied documents are inserted in the Marquee folder.

10. You need to send **1-FCTVacSpecials.docx** to a colleague who uses Word 2003, so you need to save the document in that format. At the Open dialog box with the Marquee folder active, double-click *1-FCTVacSpecials.docx*.

11. Click the File tab and then click the *Save As* option.

12 At the Save As backstage area, click the *Browse* option.

13 At the Save As dialog box, make sure WordS1 is the active folder and then type 1-FCTVacSpecialsWd2003 in the *File name* text box.

14 Click the *Save as type* option box and then click *Word 97-2003 Document (*.doc)* at the drop-down list.

15 Click the Save button in the lower right corner of the dialog box.

> If a compatibility checker message displays, click the Continue button.

16 Close the document.

17 Press Ctrl + F12 to display the Open dialog box. If the WordS1 folder on your storage medium is not already the active folder, navigate to the WordS1 folder.

18 At the Open dialog box, rename the Marquee folder by right-clicking the folder name and then clicking *Rename* at the shortcut menu.

19 Type MarqueeProductions and then press the Enter key.

> The new folder name replaces the original folder name. You can also rename a folder by clicking the Organize button, clicking *Rename* at the drop-down list, and then typing the new folder name.

20 Delete the MarqueeProductions folder by first clicking the folder to select it.

21 Click the Organize button and then click *Delete* at the drop-down list.

22 At the message asking if you are sure you want to delete the folder and all of its contents, click the Yes button.

23 Close the Open dialog box.

24 Close Word by clicking the Close button in the upper right corner of the screen.

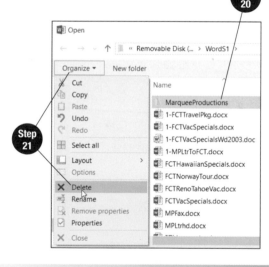

Check Your Work — Compare your work to the model answer to ensure that you have completed the activity correctly.

In Addition

Editing a PDF File in Word

PDF stands for Portable Document Format and is a common format for sharing files. A PDF file can be opened and edited in Word. When you open a PDF file, Word converts the file to a .docx file and the data in the file may not display in the exact format as in the PDF file. Converting a PDF file to a Word document works best with text-based documents.

Features Summary

Feature	Ribbon Tab, Group	Button	Quick Access Toolbar	File Tab Option	Keyboard Shortcut
AutoCorrect dialog box				*Options, Proofing, AutoCorrect Options*	
close document				*Close*	Ctrl + F4
close Word		✕			Alt + F4
collapse or redisplay ribbon		⤒			Ctrl + F1
Draft view	View, Views	▤			
Extend mode					F8
Help					F1
hide white space		⯅⯆			
Move insertion point to end of document					Ctrl + End
Move insertion point to start of document					Ctrl + Home
Navigation pane	View, Show				Ctrl + F
New backstage area				*New*	
New Line command					Shift + Enter
Open backstage area				*Open*	Ctrl + O
Open dialog box					Ctrl + F12
Print backstage area				*Print*	Ctrl + P
Print Layout view	View, Views	▤			
Read Mode	View, Views	📖			
redo (repeat) an action			↷		Ctrl + Y
replace text	Home, Editing	ᵃᵇ⤳ac			
Save As backstage area				*Save* OR *Save As*	
Save As dialog box					F12
save document		💾		*Save*	Ctrl + S
show white space		⯆⯅			
Spelling & Grammar	Review, Proofing	ABC✓			F7
Tell Me feature	*Tell Me* text box				Alt + Q
Thesaurus	Review, Proofing	📖			Shift + F7
undo an action			↶ ▾		Ctrl + Z
Word Options dialog box				*Options*	

Word

Formatting Characters and Paragraphs

Data Files Before beginning section work, copy the WordS2 folder to your storage medium and then make WordS2 the active folder.

Skills

- Apply fonts and font effects
- Apply formatting with Format Painter
- Repeat a command
- Align text in paragraphs
- Indent text
- Change line spacing
- Change paragraph spacing
- Find and replace formatting
- Create bulleted and numbered lists
- Insert symbols
- Insert special characters
- Set tabs and tabs with leaders
- Apply borders and shading to text
- Apply a page border
- Apply styles and style sets
- Apply themes

Precheck Check your current skills to help focus your study of the skills taught in this section.

Projects Overview

Edit and format documents on Oslo, Norway, and Petersburg, Alaska; format a document on traveling by train in Europe; and format documents on vacation packages in Oregon and Nevada and cross-country skiing vacation packages.

Prepare a letter to the chair of the Theatre Arts Division at Niagara Peninsula College requesting 20 theatre interns.

Prepare a movie distribution schedule.

SNAP If you are a SNAP user, launch the Precheck and Tutorials from your Assignments page.

Model Answers Preview the model answers for an overview of the projects you will complete in the section activities.

Apply character formatting to text with buttons in the Font group on the Home tab. Formatting a document changes how the document displays and prints. The top row of the Font group contains options and buttons for changing the font and font size of text as well as changing text case and clearing formatting. The bottom row contains buttons for applying formatting to text such as bold, italics, underlining, strikethrough, subscript, superscript, text effects, highlighting, and font color. Microsoft Word has taken some commonly used commands and placed them on the Mini toolbar. When you select text, the Mini toolbar displays above the selected text. The Mini toolbar disappears when you move the mouse pointer away from it.

What You Will Do   You have been asked to improve the appearance of a document on Oslo, Norway, by applying a different font and various font effects to the text.

Tutorial
Applying Font Formatting Using the Font Group

Tutorial
Applying Font Formatting Using the Mini Toolbar

Tutorial
Highlighting Text

1 Open **FCTOslo.docx** and then save it with the name **2-FCTOslo**.

2 Select the words *Oslo, Norway* and then click the Bold button B in the Font group on the Home tab.

3 With *Oslo, Norway* still selected, click the Change Case button Aa ⁻ in the Font group and then click *UPPERCASE* at the drop-down list.

> Use options at the Change Case drop-down list to specify the case of selected text.

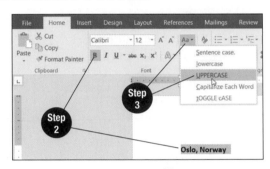

4 With *OSLO, NORWAY* still selected, click the Text Effects and Typography button A ⁻ and then click the *Fill - White, Outline - Accent 1, Shadow* option at the drop-down gallery (fourth column, first row).

5 Select *History* and then click the Underline button U ⁻ in the Font group.

6 Select and then underline the remaining headings: *Population*; *Commerce and Industry*; *Climate*; *Holiday, Sport, and Leisure*; and *Sightseeing Tours*.

7 Select the words *Viking Age* in the first paragraph below the *History* heading and then click the Italic button *I* on the Mini toolbar above the selected text.

> The Mini toolbar displays above selected text. The toolbar disappears when you move the mouse pointer away from it.

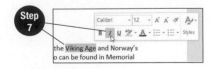

8 Select the words *Catholic Middle Ages* in the first paragraph and then click the Italic button on the Mini toolbar.

9 Select the entire document by clicking the Select button in the Editing group on the Home tab and then clicking *Select All* at the drop-down list.

10 Click the *Font* option box arrow in the Font group. Hover the mouse pointer over various typefaces in the drop-down gallery and notice how the text in the document reflects the selected font.

> This feature is referred to as *live preview*. It provides you with an opportunity to see how the document will appear with text formatting applied before you actually apply it.

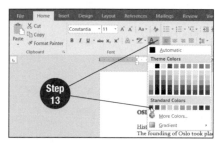

11 Scroll down the gallery and then click *Constantia*.

12 Click the *Font Size* option box arrow and then click *11* in the drop-down gallery.

13 Click the Font Color button arrow and then click the *Dark Red* color option (first option in the *Standard Colors* section).

14 Deselect the text by clicking anywhere in the document.

15 You want to identify specific text for review by colleagues so you decide to highlight the text. To do this, click the Text Highlight Color button arrow in the Font group and then click the *Yellow* color option at the drop-down list. Select the first sentence in the second paragraph (the sentence that begins *Oslo's population was substantially reduced*).

> When you click the Text Highlight Color button, the mouse pointer displays with a highlighter pen attached. Highlighting stays on until you click the Text Highlight Color button again.

16 Select the first sentence in the *Population* paragraph to highlight it and then click the Text Highlight Color button to turn it off.

17 Remove the text highlighting by pressing Ctrl + A (this selects the entire document), clicking the Text Highlight Color button arrow, and then clicking *No Color* at the drop-down list.

18 Save **2-FCTOslo.docx**.

Check Your Work Compare your work to the model answer to ensure that you have completed the activity correctly.

In Addition

Using Typefaces

A typeface is a set of characters with a common design and shape. It can be decorative or plain and either monospaced or proportional. Word refers to typeface as *fonts*. A monospaced typeface allots the same amount of horizontal space for each character, while a proportional typeface allots a varying amount of space for each character. Proportional typefaces are divided into two main categories: *serif* and *sans serif*. A serif is a small line at the end of a character stroke. Consider using a serif typeface for text-intensive documents because the serifs help move the reader's eyes across the page. Use a sans serif typeface for headings, headlines, and advertisements.

Using the Font Dialog Box and Format Painter; Repeating a Command

In addition to buttons in the Font group, you can apply font formatting with options at the Font dialog box. Display the Font dialog box by clicking the Font group dialog box launcher. With options at this dialog box, you can change the font, font size, and font style; change the font color; choose an underline style; and apply formatting effects. Once you apply formatting to text, you can copy that formatting to different locations in the document using the Format Painter. If you apply formatting to text in a document and then want to repeat the formatting for other text, use the Repeat command. Repeat a command by pressing the F4 function key or Ctrl + Y.

FIRST CHOICE TRAVEL

What You Will Do   The changes you made to the Oslo document have enhanced the readability and appearance of the text. Now you will turn your attention to the headings.

Tutorial
Applying Font Formatting Using the Font Dialog Box

Tutorial
Formatting with Format Painter

Tutorial
Repeating the Last Command

1. With **2-FCTOslo.docx** open, press Ctrl + Home to move the insertion point to the beginning of the document and then select the entire document by pressing Ctrl + A.

2. Click the Font group dialog box launcher.

3. At the Font dialog box, click *Cambria* in the *Font* list box (you will need to scroll up the list box to display this option) and then click *12* in the *Size* list box.

4. Click the *Font color* option box arrow and then click the *Dark Blue* color option (ninth option in the *Standard Colors* section).

5. Click OK to close the dialog box.

6. Select the heading *History* and then click the Font group dialog box launcher.

7. Click *Candara* in the *Font* list box (you will need to scroll down the list box to display this option), click *Bold* in the *Font style* list box, and then click *14* in the *Size* list box (you will need to scroll down the list box to display this option).

8. Click the *Underline style* option box arrow and then click *(none)* at the drop-down list.

9. Click OK to close the dialog box.

10. Click anywhere in the heading *History* and then double-click the Format Painter button in the Clipboard group on the Home tab.

> When Format Painter is active, the mouse pointer displays with a paintbrush attached. Click the Format Painter button to apply formatting to one location only. Double-click the Format Painter button to apply formatting to more than one location.

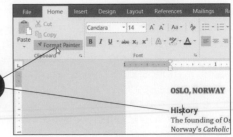

In Brief

**Applying Font
Formatting at Font
Dialog Box**
1. Click Font group dialog
   box launcher.
2. Choose options in
   dialog box.
3. Click OK.

**Apply Formatting
with Format Painter**
1. Apply formatting.
2. Double-click Format
   Painter button.
3. Select text.
4. Click Format Painter
   button to turn it off.

11 Select the title *OSLO, NORWAY*.

> With Format Painter active, selecting text applies formatting. Selecting the title removed the text effect and applied the same formatting that you applied to the *History* heading.

12 Scroll down the document and then click anywhere in the word *Population*.

> When using Format Painter, apply formatting to a single word by clicking anywhere in the word. To apply formatting to more than one word at a time, select the text.

13 Select individually each of the headings: *Commerce and Industry*; *Climate*; *Holiday, Sport, and Leisure*; and *Sightseeing Tours*.

14 Click the Format Painter button to turn off Format Painter.

15 Select the last sentence in the document (the sentence that begins *All tours by boat*) and then click the Font group dialog box launcher.

16 At the Font dialog box, click the *Small caps* check box in the *Effects* section to insert a check mark.

17 Click OK to close the dialog box.

18 Select the text *Tour 1: Mini Cruise* and then press F4.

> Pressing F4 repeats the previous command and applies the small caps effect to the selected text.

19 Select the text *Tour 2: Fjord Cruise* and then press F4. Select the text *Tour 3: Fjord Cruise with Dinner* and then press F4. Select the text *Tour 4: Selected Oslo Sightseeing* and then press F4.

> You can also repeat a command with the keyboard shortcut Ctrl + Y.

20 Press Ctrl + Home to move the insertion point to the beginning of the document, select the heading *OSLO, NORWAY,* and then change the font size to 16 points.

21 Save **2-FCTOslo.docx**.

Check Your Work Compare your work to the model answer to ensure that you have completed the activity correctly.

In Addition

Using Font Keyboard Shortcuts

Along with buttons in the Font group and the Font dialog box, you can apply character formatting with the following keyboard shortcuts:

Font Group Button	Keyboard Shortcut	Font Group Button	Keyboard Shortcut
Font	Ctrl + Shift + F	Bold	Ctrl + B
Font Size	Ctrl + Shift + P	Italic	Ctrl + I
Increase Font Size	Ctrl + Shift + >	Underline	Ctrl + U
Decrease Font Size	Ctrl + Shift + <	Subscript	Ctrl + =
Change Case	Shift + F3	Superscript	Ctrl + Shift + +

Paragraphs of text in a document are aligned at the left margin by default. This default alignment can be changed to center, right, or justified. Change paragraph alignment with buttons in the Paragraph group on the Home tab, with the *Alignment* option at the Paragraph dialog box, or with keyboard shortcuts. Text alignment can be changed before you type a paragraph or you can change the alignment of an existing paragraph or group of paragraphs.

What You Will Do   You will improve the appearance of the Oslo document by changing the text alignment of specific paragraphs in the document.

Tutorial

Changing Paragraph
Alignment

1 With **2-FCTOslo.docx** open, position the insertion point anywhere in the title *OSLO, NORWAY.*

2 Click the Center button in the Paragraph group on the Home tab.

3 Select from the middle of the first paragraph of text below the *History* heading to somewhere in the middle of the third paragraph of text.

Entire paragraphs do not have to be selected to change the alignment, only a portion of each paragraph.

4 Click the Justify button in the Paragraph group.

5 Press Ctrl + End to move the insertion point to the end of the document.

6 Click the Align Right button in the Paragraph group.

7 Type your first and last names, press Shift + Enter key, and then type First Choice Travel.

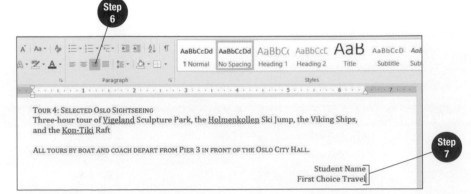

8 Click any character in the sentence above your first and last names (the sentence that begins ALL TOURS BY BOAT AND COACH...).

9 Click the Paragraph group dialog box launcher.

Clicking the Paragraph group dialog box launcher displays the Paragraph dialog box with the Indents and Spacing tab selected. Use the *Alignment* option box in the *General* section to change text alignment in the document.

10 At the Paragraph dialog box, click the *Alignment* option box arrow.

11 Click the *Centered* option at the drop-down list.

The *Alignment* option box at the Paragraph dialog box provides another method for changing paragraph alignment.

12 Click OK to close the Paragraph dialog box and apply center alignment to the sentence.

13 Move the insertion point to the beginning of the document.

14 Select the three paragraphs of text below the *History* heading.

15 Click the Align Left button ☰ in the Paragraph group and then deselect the text.

16 Save **2-FCTOslo.docx**.

Check Your Work Compare your work to the model answer to ensure that you have completed the activity correctly.

In Addition

Aligning Text with Keyboard Shortcuts
Align text with the following keyboard shortcuts:

Alignment	Keyboard Shortcut
Left	Ctrl + L
Center	Ctrl + E
Right	Ctrl + R
Justified	Ctrl + J

A paragraph of text in a document can be indented. For example, you can indent the first line of text in a paragraph, all lines of text in a paragraph, or the second and subsequent lines of a paragraph (called a *hanging indent*). Several methods are available for indenting text, including buttons in the Paragraph group on the Home tab and the Layout tab, markers on the horizontal ruler, options at the Paragraph dialog box with the Indents and Spacing tab selected, and keyboard shortcuts.

What You Will Do   You will improve the appearance of the Oslo document by changing the indent of specific paragraphs of text.

Tutorial
Indenting Text

1. Select the three paragraphs of text below the *History* heading.

2. Position the mouse pointer on the Left Indent marker on the horizontal ruler, click and hold down the left mouse button, drag the marker to the 0.5-inch mark on the ruler, and then release the mouse button.

   If the horizontal ruler is not visible, click the View tab and then click the *Ruler* check box in the Show group to insert a check mark. The ruler indent markers are shown in Figure 2.1. To precisely position a marker on the ruler, hold down the Alt key while dragging the marker.

3. Position the mouse pointer on the First Line Indent marker on the horizontal ruler, click and hold down the left mouse button, drag the marker to the 1-inch mark on the ruler, and then release the mouse button.

4. Position the mouse pointer on the Right Indent marker on the ruler, click and hold down the left mouse button, drag the marker to the 6-inch mark on the ruler, and then release the mouse button.

5. Click anywhere in the paragraph below the *Population* heading and then click the Layout tab.

6. In the *Indent* section of the Paragraph group, click in the *Left* measurement box and then type 0.5.

7. Click the *Right* measurement box up arrow until *0.5"* displays.

8 Click anywhere in the paragraph below the *Commerce and Industry* heading.

9 Click the Paragraph group dialog box launcher.

10 At the Paragraph dialog box, select the number in the *Left* measurement box in the *Indentation* section and then type 0.5. Select the number in the *Right* measurement box in the *Indentation* section and then type 0.5.

11 Click OK to close the Paragraph dialog box.

12 Click anywhere in the paragraph below the *Climate* heading and then press F4.

13 Click anywhere in the paragraph below the *Holiday, Sport, and Leisure* heading and then press F4.

14 Select the text below the *Sightseeing Tours* heading except the right-aligned text and then press F4.

15 Select the three paragraphs below the *History* heading and then click the Paragraph group dialog box launcher.

16 At the Paragraph dialog box, click the *Special* option box arrow in the *Indentation* section and then click *Hanging* at the drop-down list.

17 Click OK to close the Paragraph dialog box.

18 Save **2-FCTOslo.docx**.

Figure 2.1 Ruler Indent Markers

First Line Indent   Left Indent   Hanging Indent   Right Indent

Check Your Work Compare your work to the model answer to ensure that you have completed the activity correctly.

In Addition

Indenting Text with Keyboard Shortcuts
Indent text with the following keyboard shortcuts:

Indentation	Keyboard Shortcut
Indent text from left margin	Ctrl + M
Decrease indent from left margin	Ctrl + Shift + M
Create a hanging indent	Ctrl + T
Remove hanging indent	Ctrl + Shift + T

By default, line spacing is set at 1.08. This default line spacing can be changed with the Line and Paragraph Spacing button in the Paragraph group on the Home tab, keyboard shortcuts, or with the *Line spacing* and *At* options at the Paragraph dialog box. Control spacing above and below paragraphs with options at the Line and Paragraph Spacing button drop-down list, the *Before* and *After* text boxes in the *Spacing* section in the Paragraph group on the Layout tab, or with the *Before* and *After* options in the *Spacing* section of the Paragraph dialog box with the Indents and Spacing tab selected.

What You Will Do   The Oslo document project deadline is soon. However, you have time to make a few spacing changes in the document before printing the final version.

Tutorial
Changing Line Spacing

Tutorial
Changing Spacing Before and After Paragraphs

Tutorial
Keeping Text Together

1   With **2-FCTOslo.docx** open, select the entire document by pressing Ctrl + A.

2   Click the Home tab, click the Line and Paragraph Spacing button in the Paragraph group, and then click *1.5* at the drop-down list.

3   Deselect the text and then scroll through the document.

4   After viewing the document with 1.5 line spacing, you decide to decrease the line spacing to 1.2 (which is not an option available at the Line and Paragraph Spacing button drop-down list). To begin, press Ctrl + A to select the entire document.

5   Click the Line and Paragraph Spacing button and then click *Line Spacing Options* at the drop-down list.

> You can also display the Paragraph dialog box by clicking the Paragraph group dialog box launcher.

6   Type 1.2 in the *At* measurement box in the *Spacing* section of the Paragraph dialog box.

> The Paragraph dialog box also contains a *Line spacing* option box. Click the *Line spacing* option box arrow to display a drop-down list with spacing choices.

7   Click OK to close the dialog box and then deselect the text.

8   Select the line of text beginning *Tour 1: Mini Cruise* through *Tour 4: Selected Oslo Sightseeing* and the two lines that follow.

9   Click the Line and Paragraph Spacing button and then click *1.0* at the drop-down list.

> Choosing this option changes the line spacing to single for the selected paragraphs of text. You can also change line spacing with keyboard shortcuts. Press Ctrl + 1 to change to single spacing, Ctrl + 2 to change to double spacing, and Ctrl + 5 to change to 1.5 line spacing.

10   Click anywhere in the last sentence (the sentence that begins *All tours by boat*).

11   Click the Line and Paragraph Spacing button and then click *Add Space Before Paragraph*.

> This inserts 12 points of space above the sentence.

In Brief

Change Line Spacing
1. Click Line and
   Paragraph Spacing
   button.
2. Click line spacing
   option.
OR
1. Click Line and
   Paragraph Spacing
   button.
2. Click *Line Spacing
   Options*.
3. Type line spacing in
   At text box.
4. Click OK.

12 Press Ctrl + Home to move the insertion point to the beginning of the document, click anywhere in the *History* heading, and then click the Paragraph group dialog box launcher.

13 At the Paragraph dialog box, click the *After* measurement box up arrow.

> Clicking the up arrow changes the measurement to 6 points.

14 Click OK to close the dialog box.

15 Click anywhere in the *Population* heading, click the Layout tab, and then click the *After* measurement box up arrow in the *Spacing* section of the Paragraph group.

> Clicking the up arrow changes the measurement to 6 points.

16 Click anywhere in the *Commerce and Industry* heading and then press F4.

> Pressing F4 repeats the paragraph spacing command.

17 Click anywhere in each of the remaining headings (*Climate*; *Holiday, Sport, and Leisure*; and *Sightseeing Tours*) and then press F4 after each click.

18 You decide that you want to remove the hanging indent from the paragraphs in the *History* section. To do this, select the three paragraphs of text below the *History* heading and then press Ctrl + Shift + T.

> Ctrl + Shift + T is the keyboard shortcut to remove hanging indent formatting.

19 Scroll down the page and notice that the *Climate* heading displays at the bottom of the first page while the paragraph that follows the heading displays at the top of the second page. You want to keep the heading with the paragraph of text. Begin by clicking anywhere in the *Climate* heading and then clicking the Paragraph group dialog box launcher.

20 At the Paragraph dialog box, click the Line and Page Breaks tab and then click the *Keep with next* check box to insert a check mark.

21 Click OK to close the Paragraph dialog box.

22 Save **2-FCTOslo.docx**.

Check Your Work   Compare your work to the model answer to ensure that you have completed the activity correctly.

In Addition

Changing Spacing Above or Below Paragraphs

Spacing above or below paragraphs is added in points. For example, to add 9 points of spacing below selected paragraphs, click the Layout tab or display the Paragraph dialog box with the Indents and Spacing tab selected. Select the current measurement in the *After* measurement box and then type *9*. You can also click the up or down arrows to increase or decrease the amount of spacing before or after paragraphs.

With options at the Find and Replace dialog box with the Replace tab selected, you can search for specific formatting or characters containing specific formatting and replace it with other formatting or characters. Click the More button to expand the options in the Find and Replace dialog box. Use the Format button at the expanded dialog box to specify the type of formatting to find and also the type of replacement formatting.

What You Will Do   After reviewing the Oslo document, you decide that the headings would look better set in a different font and font color. You decide to use the Find and Replace dialog box to find text with specific formatting applied and replace the text with different formatting.

Tutorial

Finding and Replacing Formatting

1. With **2-FCTOslo.docx** open, press Ctrl + Home to move the insertion point to the beginning of the document.

2. The headings in the document are set in 14-point Candara bold and dark blue color. You decide to replace that formatting with 14-point Arial bold italic and orange color. To begin, click the Replace button in the Editing group on the Home tab.

3. At the Find and Replace dialog box, press the Delete key. (This deletes any text in the *Find what* text box.)

4. Click the More button. (If a check mark displays in the *Find all word forms* check box, click the check box to remove the check mark.)

5. Click the Format button at the bottom of the dialog box and then click *Font* at the drop-down list.

6. At the Find Font dialog box, click *Candara* in the *Font* list box, click *Bold* in the *Font style* list box, click *14* in the *Size* list box, click the *Font color* option box arrow, and then click *Dark Blue* in the *Standard Colors* section.

7. Click OK to close the dialog box.

8 At the Find and Replace dialog box, select and then delete any text in the *Replace with* text box.

9 With the insertion point in the *Replace with* text box, click the Format button at the bottom of the dialog box and then click *Font* at the drop-down list.

10 At the Replace Font dialog box, click *Arial* in the *Font* list box, click *Bold Italic* in the *Font style* list box, click *14* in the *Size* list box, click the *Font color* option box arrow, and then click *Orange, Accent 2, Darker 50%* (sixth column, bottom row in the *Theme Colors* section).

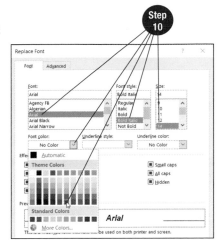

11 Click OK to close the dialog box.

12 At the Find and Replace dialog box, click the Replace All button.

13 At the message telling you that the search of the document is complete and six replacements were made, click OK.

14 With the Find and Replace dialog box open and the insertion point positioned in the *Find what* text box, click the No Formatting button at the bottom of the dialog box.

15 Click in the *Replace with* text box and then click the No Formatting button.

16 Click the Less button to reduce the size of the Find and Replace dialog box and then close the dialog box.

17 Save, print, and then close **2-FCTOslo.docx**.

> **Check Your Work** Compare your work to the model answer to ensure that you have completed the activity correctly.

In Addition

Revealing Formatting

Display formatting applied to specific text in a document at the Reveal Formatting task pane. The task pane displays font, paragraph, and section formatting applied to text where the insertion point is positioned or to selected text. Press Shift + F1 to display the Reveal Formatting task pane. Generally, a black triangle precedes *Font* and *Paragraph* in the task pane and a white triangle precedes *Section* in the *Formatting of selected text* section. Click the black triangle to hide any items below a heading and click the white triangle to reveal items. Some items in the Reveal Formatting task pane are hyperlinks. For example, click the FONT hyperlink to display the Font dialog box. Use these hyperlinks to make changes to the document formatting.

Comparing Formatting

Along with displaying formatting applied to text, you can use the Reveal Formatting task pane to compare formatting of two text selections to determine how it is different. To compare formatting, display the Reveal Formatting task pane and then select the first instance of formatting to be compared. Click the *Compare to another selection* check box to insert a check mark and then select the second instance of formatting to compare. Any differences between the two selections will display in the *Formatting differences* list box.

Activity 2.7 Creating Bulleted and Numbered Lists

If you want to draw the reader's attention to a list of items, consider inserting a bullet before each item using the Bullets button in the Paragraph group on the Home tab. If the list of items is in a sequence, consider inserting numbers before each item with the Numbering button in the Paragraph group. Create multiple-level bulleted or numbered lists with options at the Multilevel List button drop-down list in the Paragraph group.

What You Will Do First Choice Travel has created a new document on traveling in Europe by train. After reviewing the document, you decide to insert numbers and bullets before selected paragraphs to make the information easier to read.

Tutorial
Creating Numbered Lists

Tutorial
Creating Bulleted Lists

Tutorial
Creating Custom Bullets

Tutorial
Applying Multilevel List Numbering

1. Open **FCTRailTravel.docx** and then save it with the name **2-FCTRailTravel**.

2. Select text from the paragraph *Have your pass validated.* through the paragraph *Be at the right train station.* and then click the Numbering button in the Paragraph group on the Home tab.

3. Position the insertion point at the end of the second numbered paragraph (the paragraph that displays as 2. *Protect your pass.*) and then press the Enter key.

   Pressing the Enter key automatically inserts the number *3.* and renumbers the third paragraph to *4.*

4. Type Arrive 20 minutes before train departure time.

   Numbering before paragraphs changes automatically when paragraphs of text are inserted and/or deleted.

5. Select text from the paragraph that begins *Free or discount transportation* through the paragraph that begins *Reduced rental rates with* and then click the Bullets button in the Paragraph group.

   Clicking the Bullets button inserts a solid, round bullet before each paragraph. Other bullet options are available by clicking the Bullets button arrow.

6. With the text still selected, replace the round bullet with a custom bullet. To begin, click the Bullets button arrow and then click *Define New Bullet* at the drop-down list.

7. At the Define New Bullet dialog box, click the Symbol button in the *Bullet character* section.

Insert Numbers
1. Select text.
2. Click Numbering button.

Insert Bullets
1. Select text.
2. Click Bullets button.

Apply Multilevel List Numbering
1. Select text.
2. Click Multilevel List button.
3. Click option.

8 At the Symbol dialog box, click the *Font* option box arrow, type w, and then click *Webdings*.

9 Scroll to the end of the symbol list and then click the Earth symbol in the bottom row (as shown at the right; the location in the row may vary).

10 Click OK to close the Symbol dialog box.

11 Click OK to close the Define New Bullet dialog box.

12 Select the text from *Rail Passes* through *Greece-Italy*.

13 Click the Multilevel List button in the Paragraph group and then click the middle option in the top row of the *List Library* section.

> This applies multiple-level numbering to the selected text.

14 With the text still selected, change to bullets instead of numbers. To do this, click the Multilevel List button and then click the first option from the left in the middle row of the *List Library* section.

15 Deselect the text.

16 Save **2-FCTRailTravel.docx**.

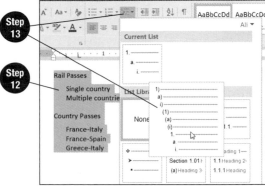

Check Your Work   Compare your work to the model answer to ensure that you have completed the activity correctly.

In Addition

Creating Numbered and/or Bulleted Text

If you type *1.* and then press the spacebar, Word indents the number approximately 0.25 inch and then hang indents the text in the paragraph approximately 0.5 inch from the left margin. When you press the Enter key after typing text, *2.* is inserted 0.25 inch from the left margin at the beginning of the next paragraph. Continue typing items and Word will continue numbering them. Press the Enter key two times to turn off numbering or click the Numbering button in the Paragraph group. Bulleted lists with hanging indents are automatically created when you begin a paragraph with the symbol *, > , or -. Type one of the symbols, press the spacebar, and the symbol bullet is inserted in the document. The type of bullet inserted depends on the type of character entered. For example, if you use the asterisk (*) symbol, a round bullet is inserted.

Turning Off Automatic Numbering and/or Bulleting

If you do not want automatic numbering or bulleting in a document, turn off the features at the AutoCorrect dialog box with the AutoFormat As You Type tab selected. To display this dialog box, click the File tab and then click *Options*. At the Word Options dialog box, click the *Proofing* option and then click the AutoCorrect Options button. At the AutoCorrect dialog box, click the AutoFormat As You Type tab. Click the *Automatic numbered lists* check box and/or *Automatic bulleted lists* check box to remove the check mark(s).

Inserting Symbols and Special Characters

Insert special symbols such as é, ö, and Å with options at the Symbol palette or the Symbol dialog box. Display the Symbol palette by clicking the Insert tab and then clicking the Symbol button in the Symbols group. Click the desired symbol to insert it in the document. To display additional symbols, display the Symbol dialog box by clicking the Symbol button and then clicking the *More Symbols* option. Click the desired symbol at the dialog box, click the Insert button, and then click the Close button. At the Symbol dialog box with the Symbols tab selected, you can change the font and display different symbols. Click the Special Characters tab to display a list of special characters and the keyboard shortcuts to insert them.

What You Will Do   You have identified a few city names in the train travel document that need special letters in their spellings, as well as a special character you need to insert in the document.

Tutorial
Inserting Symbols

Tutorial
Inserting Special
Characters

1 With **2-FCTRailTravel.docx** open, move the insertion point to the end of the document and then select and delete the multiple-level bulleted text.

2 With the insertion point positioned at the end of the document a double space below the bulleted text, type the text shown in Figure 2.2 up to the *Å* in *Århus*.

3 Display the Symbol dialog by clicking the Insert tab, clicking the Symbol button in the Symbols group, and then clicking the *More Symbols* option.

4 At the Symbol dialog box with the Symbols tab selected, click the *Font* option box arrow and then click *(normal text)* at the drop-down list. You may need to scroll up to see this option. Skip this step if *(normal text)* is already selected.

5 Scroll down the list box to somewhere between the seventh and ninth rows and then click the *Å* symbol.

6 Click the Insert button and then click the Close button.

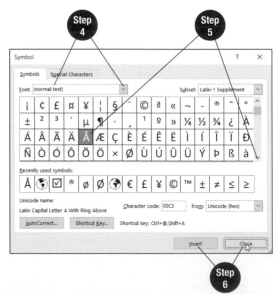

Figure 2.2 Steps 2–15

Some companies offer outstanding reductions on transportation. For example, you can travel on the ferry in Denmark between Århus and Kalundborg and between Nyborg and Korsør at a 75% discount! ScanTravel, a travel company located in Stockholm, offers the StarPass® ticket that provides you with incredible discounts on travel by train, ferry, and bus in Sweden, Norway, and Denmark.

7 Continue typing the text in Figure 2.2 up to the ø symbol. To insert the ø symbol, click the Symbol button and then click *More Symbols*.

8 At the Symbol dialog box, click the ø symbol (somewhere between the tenth and twelfth rows).

9 Click the Insert button and then click the Close button.

10 Continue typing the text up to the ® character.

11 To insert the ® character, click the Symbol button and then click *More Symbols*.

12 At the Symbol dialog box, click the Special Characters tab.

13 Click the ® character in the list box.

14 Click the Insert button.

15 Click the Close button.

16 Type the remaining text in Figure 2.2. Press the Enter key two times when you are finished.

17 Save **2-FCTRailTravel.docx**.

Step 8

Step 9

Step 12

Step 13

Step 14

Check Your Work Compare your work to the model answer to ensure that you have completed the activity correctly.

In Addition

Inserting Symbols with Keyboard Shortcuts or Character Codes

Another method for inserting symbols in a document is to use keyboard shortcuts. Click a symbol at the Symbol dialog box and the keyboard shortcut displays toward the bottom of the dialog box. For example, click the ø symbol and the keyboard shortcut Ctrl + /,O displays toward the bottom of the dialog box. To insert the ø symbol in a document using the keyboard shortcut, hold down the Ctrl key and then press the / key. Release the Ctrl key and then press the O key. Not all symbols have a corresponding a keyboard shortcut. Each symbol has an identifying character code. If you know the character code of a symbol, type the code in the *Character code* text box in the Symbol dialog box. Click a symbol at the Symbol dialog box and symbol code displays in the *Character code* text box.

Inserting Symbols Using the Palette

When you click the Symbol button in the Symbols group, a drop-down palette displays with symbol choices. The palette displays the most recently used symbols. If the palette contains the symbol you need, click the symbol to insert it in the document.

Activity 2.9 Setting Tabs on the Horizontal Ruler

Word offers a variety of default settings, including left tabs set every 0.5 inch. You can set, move, and delete your own tabs using the horizontal ruler. With a left tab, text aligns at the left edge of the tab. The other types of tabs that can be set on the horizontal ruler are center, right, decimal, and bar. The small button above the vertical ruler is called the Alignment button. Each time you click the Alignment button, a different tab or paragraph alignment symbol displays. To set a tab, display the desired tab symbol on the Alignment button and then click the horizontal ruler at the desired position.

What You Will Do You have completed some additional research on train connections in Europe. You will add airport names to the train travel document.

Tutorial
Setting and Modifying Tabs on the Horizontal Ruler

1. With **2-FCTRailTravel.docx** open, make sure the insertion point is positioned a double space below the last paragraph of text in the document.

2. Type International Airports with Train Connections and then press the Enter key two times.

3. Make sure the left tab symbol ⌊L⌋ displays in the Alignment button above the vertical ruler. (If the left tab symbol does not display in the Alignment button, click the button until it does.)

    If tabs display on the horizontal ruler, clear the tabs by clicking the Clear All Formatting button in the Font group on the Home tab.

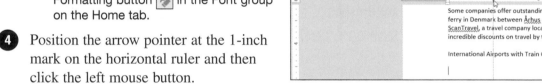

4. Position the arrow pointer at the 1-inch mark on the horizontal ruler and then click the left mouse button.

5. Click the Alignment button to display the center tab symbol ⊥.

6. Position the arrow pointer at the 3.25-inch mark on the horizontal ruler and then click the left mouse button.

7. Click the Alignment button to display the right tab symbol ⌟.

8. Position the arrow pointer at the 5.5-inch mark on the horizontal ruler and then click the left mouse button.

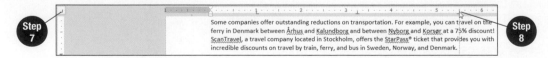

In Brief

Set Tab on Horizontal Ruler
1. Display alignment symbol in Alignment button.
2. Click position on horizontal ruler.

9 Type the text shown in Figure 2.3, pressing the Tab key before typing each tabbed entry. Make sure you press the Tab key before typing the entry in the first column and that you apply bold formatting to the text in the first row.

If your columns of text do not look similar to those in Figure 2.3, check to make sure you inserted the tab symbols at the correct locations on the horizontal ruler and that you pressed the Tab key before typing each entry in the first column.

10 After typing the last entry in the third column (*Fiumicino*), press the Enter key two times and then click the Clear All Formatting button in the Font group on the Home tab.

Clicking the Clear All Formatting button removes paragraph and character formatting. You can also remove paragraph formatting by pressing the keyboard shortcut Ctrl + Q and remove character formatting by pressing the keyboard shortcut Ctrl + spacebar.

11 Save **2-FCTRailTravel.docx**.

Figure 2.3 Step 9

Country	City	Airport
Austria	Vienna (Wein)	Schwechat
Belgium	Brussels	Nationaal
France	Paris	Orly
Germany	Berlin	Schoenefeld
Great Britain	London	Heathrow
Italy	Rome	Fiumicino

Check Your Work Compare your work to the model answer to ensure that you have completed the activity correctly.

In Addition

Moving a Tab

Move a tab on the horizontal ruler by positioning the mouse pointer on the tab symbol on the horizontal ruler, clicking and holding down the left mouse button, dragging the tab symbol to the new location on the ruler, and then releasing the mouse button.

Deleting a Tab

Delete a tab from the horizontal ruler by positioning the arrow pointer on the tab symbol, clicking and holding down the left mouse button, dragging the tab symbol down into the document screen, and then releasing the mouse button.

Setting a Decimal Tab

Set a decimal tab for column entries you want aligned at the decimal point. To set a decimal tab, click the Alignment button above the vertical ruler until the decimal tab symbol displays and then click the desired position on the horizontal ruler.

Left, right, center, and decimal tabs can be set with leaders. Leaders are useful for directing the reader's eyes across the page. Leaders can be periods, hyphens, or underlines. Set tabs with leaders by using options at the Tabs dialog box. To display the Tabs dialog box, click the Paragraph group dialog box launcher and then click the Tabs button at the Paragraph dialog box. At the Tabs dialog box, enter a tab position measurement, choose the type of tab, and then choose the type of leader.

What You Will Do   The information you found listing airports with train connections also includes schedule times. You will add this data to the train travel document.

Tutorial

Setting and Clearing
Tabs at the Tabs
Dialog Box

1 With **2-FCTRailTravel.docx** open, move the insertion point to the end of the document.

2 Click the Alignment button above the vertical ruler until the left tab symbol displays.

3 Position the arrow pointer at the 1-inch mark on the horizontal ruler and then click the left mouse button.

4 Click the Alignment button above the vertical ruler until the right tab symbol displays.

5 Position the arrow pointer at the 5.5-inch mark on the horizontal ruler and then click the left mouse button.

6 Type the headings shown in Figure 2.4 by pressing the Tab key, clicking the Bold button in the Font group, and then typing Airport.

7 Press the Tab key and then type Service.

8 Press the Enter key and then click the Clear All Formatting button to remove the bold formatting and the paragraph tab formatting.

9 Set a left tab and a right tab with leaders at the Tabs dialog box. To begin, click the Paragraph group dialog box launcher and then click the Tabs button in the lower left corner of the Paragraph dialog box.

> You can also display the Tabs dialog box by double-clicking any tab symbol on the horizontal ruler.

10 At the Tabs dialog box, select the *Left* option in the *Alignment* section of the dialog box, if necessary. With the insertion point positioned in the *Tab stop position* text box, type 1 and then click the Set button.

Set Tab with Leaders
1. Click Paragraph group dialog box launcher.
2. Click Tabs button.
3. Type tab measurement.
4. Click alignment option.
5. Click leader option.
6. Click Set.
7. Click OK.

Figure 2.4 Step 6, Step 7, and Step 14

Airport	Service
Schwechat	Train every 30 minutes
Nationaal	Train every 20 minutes
Orly..	RER train every 20 minutes
Schoenefeld	S-Bahn train every 30 minutes
Heathrow...	LT train every 10 minutes
Fiumicino....................................	Train every 10 to 20 minutes

11 Type 5.5 in the *Tab stop position* text box, click the *Right* option in the *Alignment* section of the dialog box, and then click the *2.....* option in the *Leader* section of the dialog box.

12 Click the Set button.

13 Click OK to close the dialog box.

14 Type the remaining text shown in Figure 2.4, making sure you press the Tab key before typing the text in each column.

> If your columns of text do no look similar to those in Figure 2.4, check to make sure you inserted the tab symbols at the correct measurements and that you pressed the Tab key before typing each entry in the first column.

15 Press Ctrl + Home to move the insertion point to the beginning of the document.

16 Select the four numbered paragraphs.

17 With the paragraphs selected, click the Bullets button arrow in the Paragraph group and then click the Earth bullet in the *Bullet Library* section. (The Earth bullet is the bullet you selected in Activity 2.6.) If this bullet is not available at the drop-down list, complete steps similar to those in Activity 2.7, Steps 6 through 11, to select and apply the Earth bullet.

18 Save **2-FCTRailTravel.docx**.

Check Your Work — Compare your work to the model answer to ensure that you have completed the activity correctly.

In Addition

Clearing Tabs at the Tabs Dialog Box

At the Tabs dialog box, you can clear an individual tab or all tabs. To clear all tabs, click the Clear All button. To clear an individual tab, specify the tab position and then click the Clear button.

Activity 2.11 Applying Borders and Shading

Insert a border around text and/or apply shading to text in a paragraph or selected text with the Borders button and the Shading button in the Paragraph group on the Home tab or at the Borders and Shading dialog box. At the Borders and Shading dialog box with the Borders tab selected, specify the border type, style, color, and width. Click the Shading tab and the dialog box displays options for choosing a fill color and pattern style. Click the Page Border tab and the dialog box displays options for applying a page border. You can also access the Borders and Shading dialog box with the Page Border tab selected by clicking the Design tab and then clicking the Page Borders button in the Page Background group.

What You Will Do To highlight certain information in the First Choice Travel train travel document, you will apply a border to selected text and apply border and shading formatting to the column text. You will also apply a page border to add visual appeal.

Tutorial
Applying Borders

Tutorial
Applying Shading

Tutorial
Inserting a Page Border

1 With **2-FCTRailTravel.docx** open, make sure the first four bulleted paragraphs are selected, click the Borders button arrow ⊞▾ in the Paragraph group on the Home tab, and then click *Outside Borders* at the drop-down gallery.

2 Select the second four bulleted paragraphs of text and then click the Borders button in the Paragraph group.

> This applies the outside border since that is the last border option you selected.

3 Select from the column headings *Country*, *City*, and *Airport* through the line of text containing the column entries *Italy*, *Rome*, and *Fiumicino*.

4 Click the Borders button arrow and then click *Borders and Shading* at the drop-down gallery.

5 At the Borders and Shading dialog box with the Borders tab selected, click the *Box* option in the *Setting* section.

6 Click the down arrow at the right side of the *Style* list box until the first double-line option displays and then click the double-line option.

7 Click the *Color* option box arrow and then click the *Blue, Accent 1, Darker 50%* color option (fifth column, bottom row in the *Theme Colors* section).

8 Click the *Width* option box arrow and then click ¾ pt at the drop-down list.

9 Click the Shading tab, click the *Fill* option box arrow, and then click the *Blue, Accent 1, Lighter 80%* color option (fifth column, second row in the *Theme Colors* section).

10 Click OK to close the dialog box.

11 Add the same border and shading to the other columns of text by selecting from the column headings *Airport* and *Service* through the line of text containing the column entries *Fiumicino* and *Train every 10 to 20 minutes* and then pressing F4.

12 Apply shading to the title by positioning the insertion point in the text *Traveling in Europe by Train*, clicking the Shading button arrow, and then clicking the *Blue, Accent 1, Lighter 60%* color option (fifth column, third row in the *Theme Colors* section).

Step 12

13 Insert a page border in the document. To begin, click the Borders button arrow and then click *Borders and Shading* at the drop-down list.

14 At the Borders and Shading dialog box, click the Page Border tab.

Step 14

15 Click the *Shadow* option in the *Setting* section, click the *Width* option box arrow, and then click *3 pt* at the drop-down list.

Step 15

16 Click OK to close the dialog box.

17 Change the page border to an art image. To begin, click the Design tab and then click the Page Borders button in the Page Background group.

18 At the Borders and Shading dialog box with the Page Border tab selected, click the *Box* option in the *Setting* section.

Step 18

19 Click the *Art* option box arrow, scroll down the list until the globe art images display, and then click the first set of globe images as shown at the right.

Step 19

20 Select the number in the *Width* measurement box and then type 10.

21 Click OK to close the dialog box.

22 Save **2-FCTRailTravel.docx**.

Check Your Work Compare your work to the model answer to ensure that you have completed the activity correctly.

In Addition

Applying Borders

The Borders and Shading dialog box with the Borders tab or the Page Border tab selected contains a Preview area you can use to insert borders at specfic locations. A diagram displays in the Preview area and you can click the sides, top, or bottom of the diagram to insert or remove a border line. Buttons display around the diagram that you can also use to apply borders.

A Word document is based on a template that applies default formatting such as 11-point Calibri font, line spacing of 1.08, and 8 points of spacing after each paragraph. You can change these default formats with buttons and options on the ribbon and also with styles. A style is a set of formatting instructions you can apply to text. To apply a predesigned style, click the desired style in the styles gallery in the Styles group on the Home tab. Click the More Styles button at the right side of the styles gallery to display a drop-down gallery of additional styles. Word groups styles that apply similar formatting into style sets. Style sets are available in the Document Formatting group on the Design tab. If you choose a different style set, the styles in the Styles group on the Home tab change to reflect the currently selected style set. A style set changes the formatting applied by styles. In addition to a style set, you can also apply formatting to a document with a theme. A theme is a set of formatting choices that includes a color theme (a set of colors), a font theme (a set of heading and body text fonts), and an effects theme (a set of lines and fill effects). Apply a theme with the Themes button in the Document Formatting group on the Design tab. Customize a theme (or style set) with the Colors, Fonts, and Effects buttons.

FIRST CHOICE
TRAVEL

What You Will Do   To further enhance the train travel document, you decide to apply styles, a different style set, and a theme to the document.

Tutorial
Applying Styles
and Style Sets

Tutorial
Applying and
Modifying a Theme

1   With **2-FCTRailTravel.docx** open, press Ctrl + Home to move the insertion point to the beginning of the document.

2   Click anywhere in the title *Traveling in Europe by Train* and then click the *Heading 1* style in the styles gallery on the Home tab.

> The Heading 1 style in the default style set changes the font size and font color and adds 12 points of spacing above the title. Applying the heading style also removes the shading you inserted in the previous activity.

3   Click anywhere in the heading *Rail Ticket Bonuses* and then click the *Heading 2* style in the Styles group.

4   Click anywhere in the heading *International Airports with Train Connections* and then click the *Heading 2* style.

5   Apply a different style set by clicking the Design tab, clicking the More Style Sets button at the right of the style sets gallery in the Document Formatting group, and then clicking *Lines (Stylish)*.

6   Apply a paragraph spacing option so the text fits on one page by clicking the Paragraph Spacing button in the Document Formatting group and then clicking *Compact* at the drop-down gallery.

> Display the paragraph and line formatting applied by a paragraph spacing option by hovering the mouse over the option at the drop-down gallery.

Features Summary

Feature	Ribbon Tab, Group	Button	Keyboard Shortcut
line and paragraph spacing	Home, Paragraph		
multilevel list	Home, Paragraph		
numbering	Home, Paragraph		
Paragraph dialog box	Home, Paragraph		
repeat a command			F4
remove hanging indent	Home, Paragraph		Ctrl + Shift + T
shading	Home, Paragraph		
single line spacing	Home, Paragraph		Ctrl + 1
spacing after	Layout, Paragraph		
spacing before	Layout, Paragraph		
styles	Home, Styles		
style sets	Design, Document Formatting		
subscript	Home, Font	x_2	Ctrl + =
superscript	Home, Font	x^2	Ctrl + Shift + +
Tabs dialog box	Home, Paragraph	, Tabs	
theme colors	Design, Document Formatting		
theme fonts	Design, Document Formatting	A	
themes	Design, Document Formatting	Aa	
underline	Home, Font	U	Ctrl + U

Workbook Section study tools and assessment activities are available in the *Workbook* ebook. These resources are designed to help you further develop and demonstrate mastery of the skills learned in this section.

Formatting and Enhancing a Document

Skills

- Cut, copy, and paste text
- Use the Clipboard task pane to copy and paste items
- Change page margins, orientation, and size
- Insert a watermark, page color, and page border
- Insert page numbering
- Insert a header and footer
- Format a document in MLA style
- Insert sources and citations
- Create a works cited page
- Edit a source
- Use the Click and Type feature
- Vertically align text
- Insert, size, and move images
- Prepare an envelope and mailing labels

Data Files ▷ Before beginning section work, copy the WordS3 folder to your storage medium and then make WordS3 the active folder.

Precheck ▷ Check your current skills to help focus your study of the skills taught in this section.

Projects Overview

Edit and format documents on Thailand and Juneau, Alaska; prepare an announcement about a workshop on traveling on a budget; format a report on the Middleton Valley in MLA style; prepare envelopes and labels for mailing fact sheets and announcements.

Format reports in MLA style; format a costume rental agreement.

Prepare an announcement about a workshop on employment opportunities in the movie industry; add a picture watermark.

Create an announcement for weekend work; prepare labels.

Prepare an announcement about internship positions available at Marquee Productions; prepare labels for the college.

SNAP If you are a SNAP user, launch the Precheck and Tutorials from your Assignments page.

Model Answers ▷ Preview the model answers for an overview of the projects you will complete in the section activities.

Cutting, Copying, and Pasting Text; Using Paste Options

With the Cut, Copy, and Paste buttons in the Clipboard group on the Home tab, you can move and/or copy words, sentences, or entire sections of text to other locations in a document. You can cut and paste text or copy and paste text within the same document or between documents. Specify the formatting of pasted text with the Paste Options button or options at the Paste Special dialog box.

What You Will Do   You are working on a First Choice Travel document containing information on Thailand. You decide that some of the text in the document should be reorganized, and you also decide to add additional information to the document.

Tutorial
Cutting, Copying, and Pasting Text

Tutorial
Using the Paste Options Button

Tutorial
Using Paste Special

1 Open **FCTThailand.docx** and then save it with the name **3-FCTThailand**.

2 Move the *Attractions* section below the *Traveling in Thailand* section. Begin by selecting the *Attractions* heading and the paragraph of text that follows it.

3 Click the Cut button in the Clipboard group on the Home tab.

> Clicking the Cut button places the text in a special location within Word called the *Clipboard*.

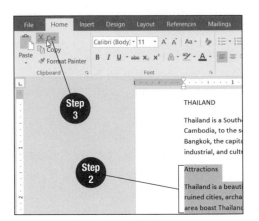

4 Move the insertion point to the beginning of the *Accommodations* heading and then click the Paste button in the Clipboard group on the Home tab.

5 Open **FCTThaiStats.docx**.

> You will copy text from this document and paste it in the Thailand information document.

6 Select the *Points of Interest* heading and the four lines of text below it and then click the Copy button in the Clipboard group.

7 Click the Word button on the taskbar and then click the **3-FCTThailand.docx** thumbnail.

8 Position the insertion point at the beginning of the heading *Passports/Visas* and then click the Paste button in the Clipboard group.

> A Paste Options button [(Ctrl)] displays below the pasted text. Click this button and a drop-down gallery of buttons displays. Use these buttons to specify the formatting of the pasted text. By default, the Keep Source Formatting button (first button from the left) is selected. With this button selected, text is pasted with the formatting from the source document. You can also click the Merge Formatting button (middle button) to merge formatting with the destination formatting or click the Keep Text Only button (third button) to paste only the text and not the formatting.

9 Click the Paste Options button and then click the Merge Formatting button (middle button) at the Paste Options button drop-down list.

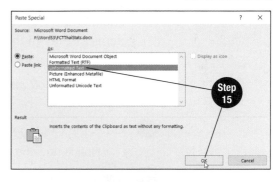

10 Click the Word button on the taskbar and then click the **FCTThaiStats.docx** thumbnail.

11 Select the text *Resources:* and the three lines below it and then click the Copy button.

12 Click the Word button on the taskbar and then click the **3-FCTThailand.docx** thumbnail.

13 Move the insertion point to the end of the document and then press the Enter key.

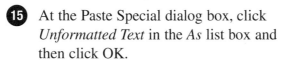

14 Paste the copied text into the document without the formatting by clicking the Paste button arrow and then clicking *Paste Special* at the drop-down list.

15 At the Paste Special dialog box, click *Unformatted Text* in the *As* list box and then click OK.

16 Select the four lines of text you just pasted in the document and then remove the spacing after the paragraphs by clicking the Layout tab and then clicking the *After* measurement box down arrow two times.

> Clicking the measurement down arrow two times will change the spacing after the selected paragraphs from 10 points to 0 points.

17 Save **3-FCTThailand.docx**.

18 Click the Word button on the taskbar, click the **FCTThaiStats.docx** thumbnail, and then close the document.

> Closing the **FCTThaiStats.docx** document displays the **3-FCTThailand.docx** document.

Check Your Work — Compare your work to the model answer to ensure that you have completed the activity correctly.

In Addition

Moving and Copying Text with the Mouse

You can move selected text using the mouse. To do this, select the text with the mouse and then move the I-beam pointer inside the selected text until the I-beam pointer turns into an arrow pointer. Click and hold down the left mouse button, drag the arrow pointer (displays with a gray box attached) to the location where you want to insert the selected text, and then release the button. Copy and move selected text by following similar steps, but hold down the Ctrl key while dragging with the mouse. When you hold down the Ctrl key, a box containing a plus symbol displays near the gray box by the arrow pointer.

Using the Clipboard task pane, you can collect up to 24 different items and then paste them in various locations in a document. Display the Clipboard task pane by clicking the Clipboard group task pane launcher. Cut or copy an item and the item displays in the Clipboard task pane. If the item is text, the first 50 characters display. Paste an item by positioning the insertion point at the desired location and then clicking the item in the Clipboard task pane. Once all desired items have been inserted, click the Clear All button in the upper right corner of the task pane.

What You Will Do You will open another document with information on Thailand, copy items in the document, and then paste the items into the Thailand document.

Tutorial

Using the Clipboard Task Pane

1. Make sure **3-FCTThailand.docx** is open and then open **FCTThaiInfo.docx**.

2. In **FCTThaiInfo.docx**, display the Clipboard task pane by clicking the Clipboard group task pane launcher. If any items display in the Clipboard task pane, click the Clear All button in the upper right corner of the task pane.

3. Select the *Food and Beverages* heading and the paragraph of text below it.

4. Click the Copy button in the Clipboard group.

   Notice how the copied item is represented in the Clipboard task pane.

5. Select the *Shopping* heading and the paragraph of text below it.

6. Click the Copy button in the Clipboard group.

7. Select the *Entertainment* heading and the paragraph of text below it.

8. Click the Copy button in the Clipboard group.

9. Click the Word button on the taskbar and then click the *3-FCTThailand.docx* thumbnail.

10. Display the Clipboard task pane by clicking the Home tab and then clicking the Clipboard group task pane launcher.

11. Move the insertion point to the beginning of the *Accommodations* heading.

12. Click the item representing *Entertainment* in the Clipboard task pane.

13. Move the insertion point to the beginning of the *Points of Interest* heading.

14. Click the item representing *Shopping* in the Clipboard task pane.

15. Click the Clear All button in the upper right corner of the Clipboard task pane.

16. Close the Clipboard task pane by clicking the Close button ☒ in the upper right corner of the task pane.

17. Click the Word button on the taskbar, click the ***FCTThaiInfo.docx*** thumbnail, and then close the document.

    The **3-FCTThailand.docx** file displays when you close **FCTThaiInfo.docx**.

18. Press Ctrl + Home to move the insertion point to the beginning of the document.

19. Click anywhere in the title *THAILAND* and then click the *Title* style in the styles gallery on the Home tab.

20. Apply the Heading 1 style to the headings in the document (*Transportation, Traveling in Thailand, Attractions, Entertainment, Accommodations, Shopping, Points of Interest,* and *Passports/Visas*).

21. Click the Design tab and then click the *Casual* style set in the Document Formatting group.

22. Press Ctrl + Home to move the insertion point to the beginning of the document.

23. Center the title *THAILAND*.

24. Save **3-FCTThailand.docx**.

Check Your Work Compare your work to the model answer to ensure that you have completed the activity correctly.

In Addition

Using Clipboard Task Pane Options

Click the Options button at the bottom of the Clipboard task pane and a pop-up menu displays with five options as shown at the right. Insert a check mark before the options you want active. For example, you can choose to display the Clipboard task pane automatically when you cut or copy text, display the Clipboard task pane by pressing Ctrl + C twice, cut and copy text without displaying the Clipboard task pane, display the Office Clipboard icon on the taskbar when the Clipboard is active, or display a status message when copying items to the Clipboard. If the last option is selected, a message such as 2 of 24 - Clipboard displays at the right side of the taskbar.

Activity 3.3 Customizing the Page Setup

In Word, a page contains default formatting such as a page size of 8.5 inches by 11 inches; top, bottom, left, and right margins of one inch; portrait page orientation; and a page break after approximately 9 inches of content on a page. You can change these defaults with buttons in the Page Setup group on the Layout tab. Change the default margins in a document with the Margins button. With the Orientation button, you can change the orientation from the default of portrait to landscape. Use the Size button in the Page Setup group to specify a paper size.

What You Will Do   To customize the Thailand document, you will change the document margins, orientation, and page size and apply a theme.

Tutorial
Changing Margins

Tutorial
Changing Page Orientation

Tutorial
Changing Paper Size

1 With **3-FCTThailand.docx** open, change the margins by clicking the Layout tab, clicking the Margins button in the Page Setup group, and then clicking the *Wide* option at the drop-down list.

> The *Wide* option changes the left and right margins to 2 inches each.

2 Change the page orientation by clicking the Orientation button in the Page Setup group on the Layout tab and then clicking *Landscape* at the drop-down list.

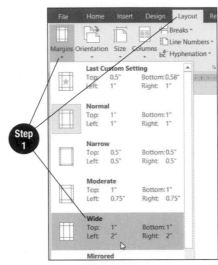

> Word considers a page in portrait orientation to be 8.5 inches wide and 11 inches tall. Word considers a page in landscape orientation to be 11 inches wide and 8.5 inches tall. You can also change page orientation at the Page Setup dialog box with the Margins tab selected.

3 Change the margins again by clicking the Margins button in the Page Setup group on the Layout tab and then clicking the *Custom Margins* option at the bottom of the drop-down list.

4 At the Page Setup dialog box with the Margins tab selected and *2"* selected in the *Top* measurement box, type 0.8.

5 Click the *Bottom* measurement box down arrow until *0.8"* displays.

6 Click OK to close the Page Setup dialog box.

7 Change the paper size by clicking the Size button in the Page Setup group and then clicking the *Legal* option at the drop-down list.

8 Scroll through the document to view the pages in legal paper size.

9 Change back to letter paper size by clicking the Size button and then clicking the *Letter* option at the drop-down list.

10 Save **3-FCTThailand.docx**. *Optional: Your instructor may want you to print the document at this point*.

11 Change the page orientation by clicking the Orientation button in the Page Setup group and then clicking *Portrait* at the drop-down list.

12 Change the margins by clicking the Margins button in the Page Setup group and then clicking *Normal* at the drop-down list.

13 Apply a theme to the document by clicking the Design tab, clicking the Themes button in the Document Formatting group, and then clicking *Integral* at the drop-down gallery.

14 Change the theme colors by clicking the Colors button in the Document Formatting group and then clicking *Red Orange* at the drop-down gallery.

15 Save **3-FCTThailand.docx**.

Check Your Work Compare your work to the model answer to ensure that you have completed the activity correctly.

In Addition

Applying Landscape Orientation

Can you imagine some instances in which you might use a landscape orientation? Suppose you are preparing a company's annual report and you need to include a couple of tables that have several columns of text. If you use the default portrait orientation, the columns will need to be quite narrow, possibly so narrow that reading becomes difficult. Changing the orientation to landscape results in three more inches of usable space. If you choose to use landscape orientation on one page, you are not committed to using it for the entire document. You can use portrait and landscape in the same document. To do this, select the text, display the Page Setup dialog box, click the desired orientation, and then change the *Apply to* option to *Selected text*.

Activity 3.4 Customizing the Page Background

The Page Background group on the Design tab contains buttons for inserting a watermark, changing the page background color, and inserting a page border. A watermark is lightened text or an image that displays behind text. Word provides a number of predesigned watermark images you can insert in a document. Apply a page background color using the Page Color button. Page background color appears on the screen but does not print. The Page Borders button in the Page Background group provides another method for displaying the Borders and Shading dialog box with the Page Border tab selected.

What You Will Do   To make sure others know that the Thailand document is still in progress, you will insert a watermark. To add visual appeal to the document, you will apply page background color and a page border.

Tutorial
Inserting and Removing a Watermark

Tutorial
Applying Page Background Color

1. With **3-FCTThailand.docx** open, press Ctrl + Home.

2. Insert a watermark by clicking the Design tab and then clicking the Watermark button in the Page Background group.

3. Scroll down the Watermark button drop-down list and then click the *DRAFT 1* option.

4. Apply a page background color to the document by clicking the Page Color button in the Page Background group.

5. Click the *Gold, Accent 5, Lighter 80%* color option (ninth column, second row).

    Page background color is designed for viewing a document on screen and does not print.

6. Click the Page Borders button in the Page Background group.

7. At the Borders and Shading dialog box with the Page Border tab selected, click the *Art* option box arrow.

8. Scroll down the list of page borders and then click the art border option shown below.

9 Click OK to close the dialog box.

10 Save **3-FCTThailand.docx**.

11 Print **3-FCTThailand.docx**.

12 Remove the page border by clicking the Design tab and then clicking the Page Borders button.

13 At the Borders and Shading dialog box, click *None* in the *Setting* section.

14 Click OK to close the dialog box.

15 Remove page background color by clicking the Page Color button in the Page Background group and then clicking *No Color*.

16 Save **3-FCTThailand.docx**.

Check Your Work Compare your work to the model answer to ensure that you have completed the activity correctly.

In Addition

Changing Page Border Options

By default, a page border displays and prints 24 points from the top, left, right, and bottom edges of the page. Some printers, particularly inkjet printers, have a non-printing area around the outside edges of the page that can interfere with the printing of a border. If part of a page border does not print, consider changing measurements at the Border and Shading Options dialog box. Display this dialog box by clicking the Design tab and then clicking the Page Borders button. At the Borders and Shading dialog box with the Page Border tab selected, click the Options button. At the dialog box, increase the margin measurements to move the page border away from the edges of the page and decrease the measurements to move the page border closer to the edges of the page.

The Pages group on the Insert tab contains buttons for adding a cover page, a blank page, and a page break. Click the Cover Page button and a drop-down list displays with predesigned cover pages. A cover page might include placeholders, which are locations where specific text is inserted. Insert a page break in a document with the keyboard shortcut Ctrl + Enter or with the Page Break button on the Insert tab. Use the Blank Page button to insert a blank page, which might be useful in a document where you want to insert a blank page for an illustration, graphic, or figure.

FIRST CHOICE TRAVEL

What You Will Do   You will insert the Motion cover page in the Thailand document and insert specific text in the cover page placeholders. You will also insert a page break and a blank page in the document.

Tutorial
Inserting and Removing a Cover Page

Tutorial
Inserting and Removing a Blank Page

Tutorial
Inserting and Removing a Page Break

1   With **3-FCTThailand.docx** open, press Ctrl + Home.

2   Click the Insert tab and then click the Cover Page button 📄 in the Pages group.

3   Insert a predesigned cover page by scrolling down the drop-down list and then clicking the *Motion* cover page option.

4   Click the *[Year]* placeholder text and then type the current year.

5   Click the *[Document title]* placeholder text and then type Discover Thailand.

6   Click the *[Company name]* placeholder text and then type First Choice Travel. If a company name already displays above the date in the bottom right corner, click the company name, click the Company tab, and then type First Choice Travel.

7   Select the name that displays above *First Choice Travel* and then type your first and last names.

8   Insert the current date below *First Choice Travel* by clicking the date, clicking the arrow at the right of the placeholder, and then clicking *Today*.

9   You need a blank page at the end of the document for information that will be added later. Press Ctrl + End to move the insertion point to the end of the document.

10 Click the Blank Page button 🗋 in the Pages group.

11 Move the insertion point to the beginning of the heading *Entertainment*.

12 Insert a page break by clicking the Page Break button 🔲 in the Pages group.

> You can also insert a hard page break with the keyboard shortcut Ctrl + Enter.

In Brief

Insert Cover Page
1. Click Insert tab.
2. Click Cover Page button.
3. Click cover page option.

Insert Blank Page
1. Click Insert tab.
2. Click Blank Page button.

Insert Page Break
1. Click Insert tab.
2. Click Page Break button.
OR
Press Ctrl + Enter.

13 Save **3-FCTThailand.docx** and then print only pages 1 and 2.

14 Delete the page break you inserted in Step 12 by positioning the insertion point at the end of the paragraph of text below the *Attractions* heading and then pressing the Delete key two times.

15 Remove the blank page. Begin by clicking the Home tab and then clicking the Show/Hide ¶ button ¶ in the Paragraph group.

> Clicking the Show/Hide ¶ button on the Home tab turns on the displays of nonprinting characters such as a paragraph symbol to indicate the press of the Enter key and a small dot to indicate the press of the spacebar.

16 Position the insertion point at the beginning of the page break that displays on the third page and then press the Delete key two times.

17 Click the Show/Hide ¶ button to turn off the display of nonprinting characters.

18 Save **3-FCTThailand.docx**.

> **Check Your Work** Compare your work to the model answer to ensure that you have completed the activity correctly.

In Addition

Inserting Page Breaks

Word assumes that you are using standard-sized paper, which is 8.5 inches wide and 11 inches long. With default top and bottom margins of 1 inch, a Word document can contain approximately 9 inches of content per page. At approximately the 10-inch mark, Word automatically inserts a page break. A page break inserted by Word is considered a *soft page break* and a page break

you insert with the Page Break button or the keyboard shortcut, Ctrl + Enter, is considered a *hard page break*. A soft page break adjusts automatically as text is added or deleted from a document. A hard page break does not adjust and therefore will remain in the place you originally inserted it.

Inserting Page Numbers, Headers, and Footers

Insert page numbers in a document with the Page Number button or in a header or footer. Click the Page Number button in the Header & Footer group on the Insert tab and a drop-down list displays with options for inserting page numbers at the top or bottom of the page or in the page margins, removing page numbers, and formatting page numbers. Text that appears at the top of every page is called a *header* and text that appears at the bottom of every page is referred to as a *footer*. Headers and footers are common in manuscripts, textbooks, reports, and other publications. Insert a predesigned header in a document with the Header button in the Header & Footer group on the Insert tab. Insert a predesigned footer in the same manner as a header. Predesigned headers and footers contain formatting that you can customize.

What You Will Do   Insert identifying information in the Thailand document using a header and footer and insert page numbers.

Tutorial
Inserting and Removing Page Numbers

Tutorial
Inserting and Removing a Predesigned Header and Footer

Tutorial
Editing a Header and Footer

1. With **3-FCTThailand.docx** open, move the insertion point to the beginning of the title *THAILAND* (located on the second page).

2. Click the Insert tab.

3. Insert page numbers at the bottom of each page by clicking the Page Number button [#] in the Header & Footer group and then pointing to *Bottom of Page*.

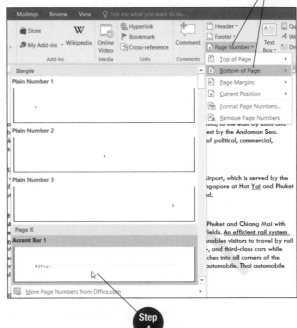

4. At the gallery of predesigned page numbers, click the *Accent Bar 1* option.

   The page number is inserted in the footer pane. With the footer pane active, the document is dimmed.

5. Click the Close Header and Footer button [x] to close the footer pane and make the document active.

6. Scroll through the document and notice how the page numbers display toward the bottom of every page except the cover page.

7. Remove page numbering by clicking the Insert tab, clicking the Page Number button in the Header & Footer group, and then clicking *Remove Page Numbers* at the drop-down list.

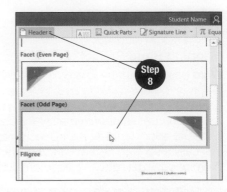

8. Insert a header in the document by clicking the Header button [ ] in the Header & Footer group, scrolling down the drop-down list, and then clicking the *Facet (Odd Page)* header.

In Brief

Insert Page Numbers
1. Click Insert tab.
2. Click Page Number button.
3. Point to location.
4. Click option at drop-down list.

Insert Header
1. Click Insert tab.
2. Click Header button.
3. Click option at drop-down list.

Insert Footer
1. Click Insert tab.
2. Click Footer button.
3. Click option.

9 Click the Close Header and Footer button to close the header pane and make the document active.

10 Click the Insert tab.

11 Insert a footer by clicking the Footer button in the Header & Footer group.

12 Scroll down the Footer button drop-down list and then click the *Ion (Dark)* footer.

> Notice how the document title you entered in the cover page is inserted in the footer, as is the author's name.

13 Click the Close Header and Footer button to close the footer pane and make the document active.

14 Scroll through the document and notice how the header and footer appear on each page except the cover page.

15 Remove the header by clicking the Insert tab, clicking the Header button in the Header & Footer group, and then clicking *Remove Header* at the drop-down list.

16 Insert a new header by clicking the Header button in the Header & Footer group, scrolling down the drop-down list, and then clicking the *Ion (Dark)* header.

17 Double-click in the body of the document.

> Close a header or footer pane by clicking the Close Header and Footer button or by double-clicking in the document.

18 Edit the footer by clicking the Insert tab, clicking the Footer button in the Header & Footer group, and then clicking *Edit Footer* at the drop-down list.

19 Press Ctrl + A to select the footer.

20 Change the font size by clicking the Home tab, clicking the *Font Size* option box arrow, and then clicking *10* at the drop-down list.

21 Click the Bold button to apply bold formatting.

22 Double-click in the document to close the footer pane and make the document active.

23 Save, print, and then close **3-FCTThailand.docx**.

> **Check Your Work** Compare your work to the model answer to ensure that you have completed the activity correctly.

In Addition

Creating Your Own Header or Footer

Create your own header or footer using the *Edit Header* or *Edit Footer* options from the corresponding button drop-down list. For example, to create a header, click the Insert tab, click the Header button, and then click *Edit Header* at the drop-down list. This opens the header pane and also displays the Header & Footer Tools Design tab with buttons and options for editing the header. Make the desired edits to the header with options on the tab and then close the header pane by clicking the Close Header and Footer button in the Close group on the Header & Footer Tools Design tab. Complete similar steps to create your own footer.

When preparing a research paper or report, consider inserting sources, citations, and a bibliography or works cited page to give credit to the sources of words, ideas, and any material summarized or quoted. Word includes some common reference styles for citing and referencing research papers and reports, including the Modern Language Association (MLA) style, which is generally used in the humanities. To create a source, display the Create Source dialog box by clicking the References tab, clicking the Insert Citation button in the Citations & Bibliography group, and then clicking *Add New Source*. At the dialog box, insert bibliography information in the required fields. Once you insert source information in the Create Source dialog box, Word will automatically save the source information. To insert a citation in a document from a source that is already saved, click the Insert Citation button in the Citations & Bibliography group and then click the desired reference at the drop-down list. If you include a direct quote from a source, you will need to include the page number. To do this, click the citation in the document to select the citation placeholder, click the Citation Options arrow, and then click *Edit Citation* at the drop-down list. At the Edit Citation dialog box, type in the page or page numbers of the quote's source.

What You Will Do   You are responsible for preparing and formatting a report on Middleton Valley for First Choice Travel. You have been asked to format the report in the MLA style.

Tutorial
Formatting a Report in MLA Style

Tutorial
Inserting Sources and Citations

1. Open **FCTMiddletonRpt.docx** and then save it with the name **3-FCTMiddletonRpt**.

2. Click the References tab, click the *Style* option box arrow in the Citations & Bibliography group, and then click *MLA* at the drop-down list.

   Refer to Table 3.1 for general guidelines on formatting a research paper or report in MLA style.

3. Press Ctrl + A to select the entire document and then change the font to 12-point Cambria.

4. With the text still selected, change the line spacing to double line spacing by clicking the Line and Paragraph Spacing button in the Paragraph group on the Home tab and then clicking *2.0* at the drop-down list.

5. With the text still selected, remove spacing after paragraphs by clicking the Layout tab, clicking in the *After* measurement box in the *Spacing* section, typing 0, and then pressing the Enter key.

Table 3.1 MLA Style General Guidelines

Use standard-sized paper (8.5 × 11 inches).
Set 1-inch top, bottom, left, and right margins.
Set text in a 12-point serif typeface (such as Cambria or Times New Roman).
Double-space text.
Indent the first line of each paragraph one-half inch.
Insert a header that prints in the upper right corner of each page the last name of the person writing the report followed by the page number.

6 Press Ctrl + Home to position the insertion point at the beginning of the document.

7 Type your name and then press the Enter key.

8 Type your instructor's name and then press the Enter key.

9 Type the title of your course and then press the Enter key.

10 Type the current date.

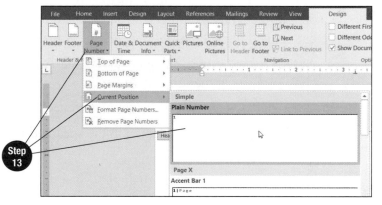

Steps 7-10

> Student Name
>
> Instructor Name
>
> Course Title
>
> Current Date
>
> Middleton
>
> The Middleton Valley is home to one of th

11 Insert a header in the document by clicking the Insert tab, clicking the Header button in the Header & Footer group, and then clicking *Edit Header* at the drop-down list.

12 Press the Tab key two times to move the insertion point to the right margin in the header pane, type your last name, and then press the spacebar.

13 Insert page numbers by clicking the Page Number button in the Header & Footer group on the Header & Footer Tools Design tab, pointing to *Current Position*, and then clicking the *Plain Number* option.

Step 13

14 Press Ctrl + A to select the header and then change the font to 12-point Cambria.

15 Click the Close Header and Footer button.

16 Insert a new source in the document. Begin by positioning the insertion point immediately right of the word *constructed* (but before the period) that ends the fifth sentence in the second paragraph.

17 Click the References tab.

18 Click the Insert Citation button in the Citations & Bibliography group and then click *Add New Source* at the drop-down list.

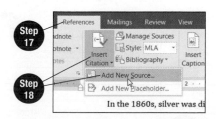

Step 17

Step 18

19 At the Create Source dialog box, click the *Type of Source* option box arrow and then click *Journal Article* at the drop-down list.

20 Click in the *Author* text box, type Joanne Henderson, and then press the Tab key three times.

21 Type Natural Resources of Middleton Valley in the *Title* text box and then press the Tab key.

22 Type Planet Earth's Resources in the *Journal Name* text box and then press the Tab key.

23 Type 2018 in the *Year* text box and then press the Tab key.

24 Type 7-9 in the *Pages* text box.

25 Click OK to close the Create Source dialog box.

26 Position the insertion point immediately right of the word *century* (but before the period) that ends the third sentence in the third paragraph, click the Insert Citation button, and then click *Add New Source* at the drop-down list.

27 At the Create Source dialog box, click the *Type of Source* option box arrow and then click *Web site* at the drop-down list.

28 Click the *Show All Bibliography Fields* check box to insert a check mark.

29 Type the following information in the specified fields:

> *Author* = Daniel Marcello
> *Name of Web Page* = Middleton Regional Planning Department
> *Year* = 2018
> *Month* = January
> *Day* = 5
> *Year Accessed* = (type current year)
> *Month Accessed* = (type current month)
> *Day Accessed* = (type current day)
> *URL* = emcp.org/middleton

30 After entering the information, click OK.

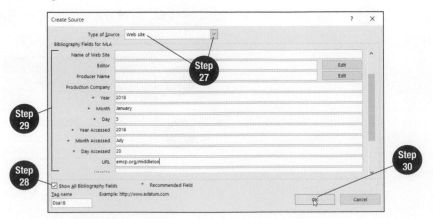

Choose Reference Style
1. Click References tab.
2. Click *Style* option box arrow.
3. Click reference style.

Insert New Source
1. Click References tab.
2. Click Insert Citation button.
3. Click *Add New Source* option.
4. At Create Source dialog box, specify type of source.
5. Enter information in appropriate text boxes.
6. Click OK.

Insert Citation
1. Position insertion point in document.
2. Click References tab.
3. Click Insert Citation button.
4. Click reference.

Edit Citation
1. Click Citation Options arrow.
2. Click *Edit Citation* option.
3. Make changes at Edit Citation dialog box.
4. Click OK.

31 Insert a citation from an existing source. Begin by positioning the insertion point between the quotation mark after the word *erosion* and the period in the second sentence in the fourth paragraph.

32 Click the Insert Citation button in the Citations & Bibliography group and then click the *Henderson, Joanne* reference at the drop-down list.

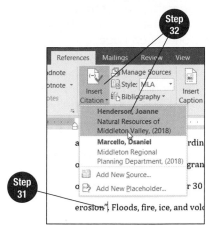

33 Because you are citing a direct quote, you need to include the page number of the journal article where you found the quote. Begin by clicking anywhere in the Henderson citation you just inserted.

This displays the citation placeholder.

34 Click the Citation Options arrow at the right side of the citation placeholder and then click *Edit Citation* at the drop-down list.

35 At the Edit Citation dialog box, type 8 in the *Pages* text box.

36 Click OK to close the Edit Citation dialog box.

37 Save **3-FCTMiddletonRpt.docx**.

Check Your Work Compare your work to the model answer to ensure that you have completed the activity correctly.

In Addition

Formatting the First Page of an MLA-Formatted Report

Your instructor may require you to omit the header on the first page of the document. To remove the header from the first page of a document, press Ctrl + Home to move the insertion point to the beginning of the document, click the Header button in the Header & Footer group on the Insert tab, and then click *Edit Header* at the drop-down list. Click the *Different First Page* check box in the Options group on the Header & Footer Tools

Design tab. This inserts a new header pane named *First Page Header*. Since you do not want a header on the first page, leave this header blank. Click the Next button in the Navigation group on the Header & Footer Tools Design tab and, if you previously created a header in the document, it displays in the header pane. If the document did not include a header, type or insert the desired header text in the header pane.

Activity 3.8 — Inserting a Works Cited Page; Editing Sources

Once you include citations in a report or research paper, you need to insert a works cited page on a separate page at the end of the document. A works cited page is an alphabetic list of the books, journal articles, web pages, and any other sources referenced in the document. To insert a works cited page, click the References tab and then click the Bibliography button in the Citations & Bibliography group. At the Bibliography drop-down list, click the desired format option. After inserting sources into a document, you may need to edit a citation to correct errors or change data. One method for editing a source is to click the desired citation in the document, click the Citation Options arrow, and then click *Edit Source* at the drop-down list. This displays the Edit Source dialog box with the information you originally typed. Make desired changes and then click OK to close the dialog box. If you edit a source, Word will not automatically update the works cited. To update the works cited, click anywhere in the works cited page and then click the Update Citations and Bibliography tab.

What You Will Do To finish the Middleton Valley report, you need to add a works cited page, edit one of the sources, and apply MLA style formatting to the works cited page.

Tutorial
Inserting a Works Cited Page

Tutorial
Editing a Citation and Source

1. With **3-FCTMiddletonRpt.docx** open, insert a works cited page at the end of the document. Begin by pressing Ctrl + End to move the insertion point to the end of the document and then pressing Ctrl + Enter to insert a hard page break.

2. Click the References tab and then click the Bibliography button in the Citations & Bibliography group.

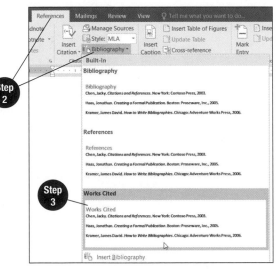

3. Click the *Works Cited* option in the *Built-In* section of the drop-down list.

4. You realize that part of the web page title is missing and you need to edit the source. Begin by clicking anywhere in the *Marcello* citation, located in the first paragraph on the second page.

   This selects the citation placeholder.

5. Click the Citation Options arrow at the right side of the citation placeholder and then click *Edit Source* at the drop-down list.

   This displays the Edit Source dialog box, which contains the same options as the Create Source dialog box.

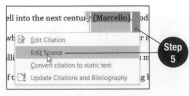

6. At the Edit Source dialog box, click in the *Name of Web Page* text box, edit the text so it displays as *Middleton Valley Regional Planning Department*, and then click OK to close the dialog box.

7. At the message telling you that the source exists in your master list and the current document and asking you if you want to update both, click Yes.

**Insert Works
Cited Page**
1. Move insertion point to
   end of document.
2. Press Ctrl + Enter.
3. Click References tab.
4. Click Bibliography
   button.
5. Click *Works Cited*
   option.

Edit Source
1. Click citation in
   document.
2. Click Citation Options
   arrow.
3. Click *Edit Source*.
4. At Edit Source dialog
   box, make desired
   changes.
5. Click OK.

**Update Works
Cited Page**
1. Click anywhere in
   works cited text.
2. Click Update Citations
   and Bibliography
   placeholder tab.

8 Update the works cited to include the edited source. Begin by pressing Ctrl + End to move the insertion point to the end of the document and then click anywhere in the works cited text.

9 Click the Update Citations and Bibliography placeholder tab.

> The placeholder tab displays above the *Works Cited* title. Notice that the updated works cited page includes the edited web page name.

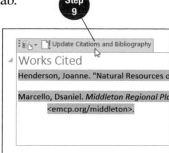

Step 9

10 Format the works cited page to MLA standards, which are listed in Table 3.2. Begin by selecting the *Works Cited* heading and the entries below it and then click the *No Spacing* style in the Styles group on the Home tab.

11 With the text still selected, change the font to Cambria, the font size to 12 points, and the line spacing to double line spacing.

12 Click anywhere in the title *Works Cited* and then click the Center button in the Paragraph group.

13 Hang-indent the works cited entries. Do this by selecting only the entries and then pressing Ctrl + T.

> You can also hang-indent the entries by clicking the Paragraph group dialog box launcher, clicking the *Special* list box arrow in the *Indentation* section, clicking *Hanging* at the drop-down list, and then clicking OK to close the Paragraph dialog box.

14 Press Ctrl + Home to move the insertion point to the beginning of the document.

15 Save, print, and then close **3-FCTMiddletonRpt.docx**.

Table 3.2 MLA Style Works Cited Page Formatting Guidelines

Begin works cited on a separate page at the end of the document.
Include the title *Works Cited* centered at the top of the page.
Double-space between and within entries.
Begin each entry at the left margin and hang-indent the second and subsequent lines in each entry.
Alphabetize the entries.

Check Your Work   Compare your work to the model answer to ensure that you have completed the activity correctly.

In Addition

Modifying Sources at the Source Manager Dialog Box

Copy, delete, edit, and create new sources at the Source Manager dialog box. Display this dialog box by clicking the References tab and then clicking the Manage Sources button in the Citations & Bibliography group. The *Master List* section of the dialog box displays all of the citations you have created in Word, and the *Current List* section displays all of the citations included in the currently open document.

You can change paragraph alignment with the Click and Type feature. To use the Click and Type feature, position the mouse pointer at the left margin, in the center of the page, or at the right margin until the pointer displays with the desired alignment symbol and then double-click the mouse button. By default, text is aligned at the top of the page. Change this vertical alignment to center, justified, or bottom with the *Vertical alignment* option at the Page Setup dialog box with the Layout tab selected. Insert an image in a document from a location on the computer with the Pictures button on the Insert tab. Use the Online Pictures button on the Insert tab to search for images on the Internet. Format an inserted image with buttons and options on the Picture Tools Format tab. This tab is active when an image is selected.

What You Will Do   First Choice Travel is planning a workshop for people interested in traveling on a budget. You will create an announcement that contains center- and right-aligned text, vertically center the text on the page, and then add visual appeal by inserting an image and the company logo.

Tutorial
Using Click and Type

Tutorial
Vertically Aligning Data

Tutorial
Inserting, Sizing, and Positioning an Image

Tutorial
Formatting an Image

1   Press Ctrl + N to display a blank document and then press the Enter key.

2   Position the I-beam pointer in the document between the left and right margins at about the 3.25-inch mark on the horizontal ruler and approximately one inch from the top of the page. When the center alignment lines display below the I-beam pointer, double-click the left mouse button.

3   Type the centered text shown in Figure 3.1, pressing the Enter key between each line of text and twice after the last line of centered text.

4   Change to right alignment by positioning the I-beam pointer near the right margin at approximately the 6.5-inch mark on the horizontal ruler and the 2-inch mark on the vertical ruler. When the right alignment lines display at the left side of the I-beam pointer, double-click the left mouse button.

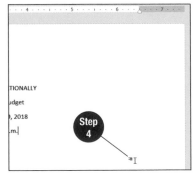

Figure 3.1 Step 3 and Step 5

TRAVELING INTERNATIONALLY

Traveling on a Budget

Thursday, April 19, 2018

7:00 to 8:30 p.m.

Sponsored by
First Choice Travel

5 Type the right-aligned text shown in Figure 3.1. After typing the first line of right-aligned text, press Shift + Enter to move the insertion point to the next line.

6 Select the centered text and then change the font to 14-point Candara bold. Select the right-aligned text, change the font to 10-point Candara bold, and then deselect the text.

7 Vertically center the text on the page. To do this, click the Layout tab and then click the Page Setup group dialog box launcher.

8 At the Page Setup dialog box, click the Layout tab, click the *Vertical alignment* option box arrow, and then click *Center* at the drop-down list.

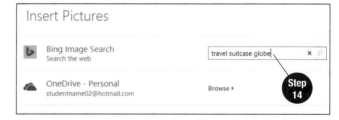

9 Click OK to close the Page Setup dialog box.

10 Save the document and name it **3-FCTTravelIntl**.

11 Print **3-FCTTravelIntl.docx**.

12 Return the vertical alignment to top alignment. To do this, click the Page Setup group dialog box launcher. At the Page Setup dialog box, click the Layout tab, click the *Vertical alignment* option box arrow, and then click *Top* at the drop-down list. Click OK to close the dialog box.

13 Click the Insert tab and then click the Online Pictures button in the Illustrations group.

This displays the Insert Pictures window with a search text box.

14 At the Insert Pictures window, click in the search box, type travel suitcase globe, and then press the Enter key.

15 Double-click the image shown at the right. If this image is not available online, click the Pictures button on the Insert tab. At the Insert Picture dialog box, navigate to the folder containing your data documents and then double-click *Suitcases.png*.

The image is inserted in the document, it is selected (sizing handles display around the image), and the Picture Tools Format tab displays as shown in Figure 3.2. A Layout Options button displays at the right side of the image. Click this button to display a list of options for positioning the image and wrapping text around the image.

Figure 3.2 Picture Tools Format Tab

16 With the image selected, click the Position button in the Arrange group and then click the *Position in Top Left with Square Text Wrapping* option (first column, first row in the *With Text Wrapping* section).

> Apply a text wrapping style to an image to specify how you want text or other items to flow around the image. Apply text wrapping with options from the Position button or with the Wrap Text button.

17 Add a shadow effect to the image by clicking the *Drop Shadow Rectangle* option in the Picture Styles group (fourth option).

18 Click the Corrections button 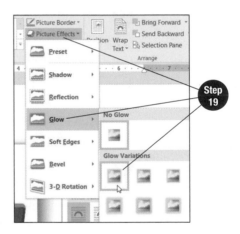 in the Adjust group and then click the *Brightness: 0% (Normal) Contrast: +40%* option (third column, bottom row in the *Brightness/Contrast* section).

19 Click the Picture Effects button in the Pictures Styles group, point to *Glow*, and then click the *Blue, 5 pt glow, Accent color 1* option (first column, first row in the *Glow Variations* section).

20 Click in the *Shape Height* measurement box in the Size group, type 1.7, and then press the Enter key.

> When you change the height measurement, the width measurement is automatically changed to maintain the proportions of the image.

21 Select and then delete the text *First Choice Travel* that displays in small font size at the right side of the document.

22 Insert the First Choice Travel logo image below *Sponsored by*. To begin, click the Insert tab and then click the Pictures button in the Illustrations group.

23 At the Insert Picture dialog box, navigate to the folder containing your data documents and then double-click *FCTLogo.jpg*.

Vertically Center Text
1. Click Layout tab.
2. Click Page Setup group dialog box launcher.
3. Click Layout tab.
4. Click *Vertical alignment* option.
5. Click *Center*.
6. Click OK.

Insert Online Image
1. Click Insert tab.
2. Click Online Pictures button.
3. Type search text in search box and then press Enter.
4. Double-click image.

Insert Image from Computer
1. Click Insert tab.
2. Click Pictures button.
3. Navigate to folder.
4. Double-click image.

24 With the logo image selected in the document, click the Layout Options button ⌷ that displays outside the upper right corner of the image and then click *Tight* (second column, first row in *With Text Wrapping* section).

25 With the logo image still selected, hold down the Shift key, click one of the corner sizing handles (white squares) and hold down the left mouse button; drag to reduce the size of the image so it displays as shown in Figure 3.3; and then release the mouse button.

Holding down the Shift key while increasing or decreasing the size of an image maintains the proportions of the image.

26 Drag the logo image so it is positioned as shown in Figure 3.3. To drag the image, position the insertion point inside the selected image until the arrow pointer displays with a four-headed arrow attached. Click and hold down the left mouse button, drag the selected image to the desired location, and then release the mouse button.

As you move an image near the top, left, right, or bottom margins of the document, green guidelines appear to help you position the image.

27 Click outside the logo to deselect it.

28 Save, print, and then close **3-FCTTravelIntl.docx**.

Figure 3.3 Activity 3.9

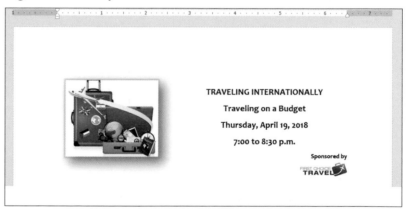

Check Your Work   Compare your work to the model answer to ensure that you have completed the activity correctly.

In Addition

Formatting an Image with Buttons on the Picture Tools Format Tab

Images inserted in a document can be formatted in a variety of ways, which might include adding fill color and border lines, increasing or decreasing the brightness or contrast, choosing a wrapping style, and cropping the image. Format an image with buttons on the Picture Tools Format tab as shown in Figure 3.2. With buttons in the Adjust group, you can correct the brightness and contrast of the image; change the image color; change to a different image; reset the image to its original size, position, and color; and compress the picture. Compress a picture to reduce resolution or discard extra information to save room on the hard drive or reduce download time. Use buttons in the Picture Styles group to apply a predesigned style, insert a picture border, or apply a picture effect. The Arrange group contains buttons for positioning the image, wrapping text around the image, and aligning and rotating the image. Use options in the Size group to crop the image and specify the height and width of the image.

Word automates the creation of envelopes with options at the Envelopes and Labels dialog box with the Envelopes tab selected. At this dialog box, type a delivery address and a return address. If you open the Envelopes and Labels dialog box in a document containing a name and address, the name and address are inserted automatically as the delivery address. If you enter a return address, Word will ask you before printing if you want to save the new return address as the default return address. Click the Yes button if you want to use the return address for future envelopes, or click the No button if you will use a different return address for future envelopes.

What You Will Do   You need to create an envelope for sending the information about Thailand to Camille Matsui at Marquee Productions.

Preparing an Envelope

1   Press Ctrl + N to display a blank document.

> You can also display a blank document by clicking the File tab, clicking the *New* option, and then clicking the *Blank document* template. Another method is to insert a New button on the Quick Access Toolbar and then click the button to display a blank document. To insert the New button on the Quick Access Toolbar, click the Customize Quick Access Toolbar button at the right side of the toolbar and then click *New* at the drop-down list.

2   Click the Mailings tab and then click the Envelopes button in the Create group.

3   At the Envelopes and Labels dialog box with the Envelopes tab selected, type the following name and address in the *Delivery address* text box. Press the Enter key at the end of each line, except the last line containing the city, state, and zip code.

> Camille Matsui
> Marquee Productions
> 955 South Alameda Street
> Los Angeles, CA 90037

In Brief

Prepare Envelope
1. Click Mailings tab.
2. Click Envelopes button.
3. Type delivery address.
4. Type return address.
5. Click either Add to Document button or Print button.

④ If any text displays in the *Return address* text box, delete it and then type the following name and address. Type your name where you see *Student Name*.

> First Choice Travel
> Student Name
> 3588 Ventura Boulevard
> Los Angeles, CA 90102

⑤ Click the Add to Document button.

Clicking the Add to Document button inserts the envelope in the document. You can also send the envelope directly to the printer by clicking the Print button.

⑥ At the message asking if you want to save the new return address as the default address, click No.

⑦ Save the document with the name **3-FCTEnvtoMP**.

⑧ Print and then close **3-FCTEnvtoMP.docx**. *Note: Manual feed of the envelope may be required. Please check with your instructor before printing the envelope.*

Check Your Work — Compare your work to the model answer to ensure that you have completed the activity correctly.

In Addition

Customizing Envelopes

With options at the Envelope Options dialog box shown at the right, you can customize an envelope. Display this dialog box by clicking the Options button at the Envelopes and Labels dialog box. At the Envelope Options dialog box, you can change the envelope size, change the font for the delivery and return addresses, and specify the positioning of the addresses in relation to the left and top edges of the envelope.

Activity 3.11   Preparing Mailing Labels

Use Word's Labels feature to print text on mailing labels, file labels, disc labels, or other types of labels. You can create labels for printing on a variety of predefined labels, which you can purchase at an office supply store. With the Labels feature, you can create a sheet of mailing labels with the same name and address or image or enter a different name and address on each label. Create a label with options at the Envelopes and Labels dialog box with the Labels tab selected.

What You Will Do   You will create a sheet of mailing labels containing the First Choice Travel name and address. You will also create mailing labels for sending the Thailand document to several First Choice Travel customers and create labels for the First Choice Travel office in Toronto.

Tutorial
Creating Mailing Labels with the Same Name and Address and an Image

Tutorial
Creating Mailing Labels with Different Names and Addresses

① Press Ctrl + N to display a blank document.

② Click the Mailings tab and then click the Labels button [icon] in the Create group.

③ Type the following information in the *Address* text box. Type your name where you see *Student Name*. (Press the Enter key at the end of each line except the last line.)

> First Choice Travel
> Student Name
> 3588 Ventura Boulevard
> Los Angeles, CA 90102

④ Click the Options button.

⑤ At the Label Options dialog box, click the *Label vendors* option box arrow and then click *Avery US Letter* at the drop-down list.

⑥ Scroll down the *Product number* list box and then click *5160 Easy Peel Address Labels*.

⑦ Click OK to close the dialog box.

⑧ Click the New Document button at the Envelopes and Labels dialog box.

⑨ Save the document and name it **3-FCTLALabels**.

⑩ Print and then close **3-FCTLALabels.docx**.

⑪ Click the Mailings tab and then click the Labels button in the Create group.

⑫ At the Envelopes and Labels dialog box, click the New Document button.

⑬ At the document, type the first name and address shown in Figure 3.4 in the first label. Press the Tab key two times to move the insertion point to the next label and then type the second name and address shown in Figure 3.4. Press the Tab key two times and then type the third name and address. Press the Tab key one time and then type the fourth name and address. Continue in this manner until you have typed all of the names and addresses in Figure 3.4.

Create Mailing Labels with Same Name and Address
1. Click Mailings tab.
2. Click Labels button.
3. Type name and address in *Address* text box.
4. Click either New Document button or Print button.

Create Mailing Labels with Different Names and Addresses
1. Click Mailings tab.
2. Click Labels button.
3. Click New Document button.
4. At document screen, type names and addresses.

Create Mailing Labels with Image
1. Click Insert tab.
2. Click Pictures button.
3. Navigate to folder.
4. Double-click image.
5. Click Mailings tab.
6. Click Labels button.
7. Click New Document button.

14 Save the document and name it **3-FCTCustLabels**.

15 Print and then close **3-FCTCustLabels.docx**.

16 At the blank document, create mailing labels for the Toronto office of First Choice Travel using an image. Begin by clicking the Insert tab and then clicking the Pictures button in the Illustrations group.

17 At the Insert Picture dialog box, navigate to the folder containing your data files and then double-click *FCTTorontoLabel.jpg*.

18 With the label image selected, click the Position button in the Arrange group on the Picture Tools Format tab and then click the *Position in Top Center with Square Text Wrapping* option (second column, first row in the *With Text Wrapping* section).

19 With the image still selected, click the Mailings tab and then click the Labels button.

20 At the Envelopes and Labels dialog box, make sure the Avery US Letter label number 5160 is selected and then click the New Document button.

> When you click the New Document button, the label image is inserted in each label in the page and inserted in a new document.

21 Save the document and name it **3-FCTTorontoLabels**.

22 Print and then close **3-FCTTorontoLabels.docx**.

23 Close the document containing the label image without saving it.

Figure 3.4 Step 13

Moreno Products 350 Mission Boulevard Pomona, CA 91767	Mr. Miguel Santos 12120 Barranca Parkway Irvine, CA 92612	Mr. and Mrs. Jack Lipinski 5534 Eagle Ridge Drive Los Angeles, CA 90092
Dr. Esther Riggins 9077 Walnut Street Los Angeles, CA 90097	Automated Services, Inc. 4394 Seventh Street Long Beach, CA 92602	Ms. Samantha Schwartz 103-B Pacific Palms Los Angeles, CA 90068

Check Your Work Compare your work to the model answer to ensure that you have completed the activity correctly.

In Addition

Customizing Labels

Click the Options button at the Envelopes and Labels dialog box with the Labels tab selected and the Label Options dialog box displays as shown at the right. At this dialog box, choose the type of printer, the desired label vendor, and the product number. This dialog box also displays information about the selected label, such as type, height, width, and paper size. When you select a label, Word automatically determines label margins. If, however, you want to customize these default settings, click the Details button at the Label Options dialog box.

Features Summary

Feature	Ribbon Tab, Group	Button, Option	Keyboard Shortcut
blank page	Insert, Pages		
Clipboard task pane	Home, Clipboard		
copy selected text	Home, Clipboard		Ctrl + C
cover page	Insert, Pages		
Create Source dialog box	References, Citations & Bibliography	, Add New Source	
cut selected text	Home, Clipboard		Ctrl + X
Envelopes and Labels dialog box with Envelopes tab selected	Mailings, Create		
Envelopes and Labels dialog box with Labels tab selected	Mailings, Create		
footer	Insert, Header & Footer		
hanging indent			Ctrl + T
header	Insert, Header & Footer		
Insert Picture dialog box	Insert, Illustrations		
Insert Pictures window	Insert, Illustrations		
page background color	Design, Page Background		
page borders	Design, Page Background		
page break	Insert, Pages		Ctrl + Enter
page margins	Layout, Page Setup		
page number	Insert, Header & Footer		
page orientation	Layout, Page Setup		
Page Setup dialog box	Layout, Page Setup		
paper size	Layout, Page Setup		
paste selected text	Home, Clipboard		Ctrl + V
Paste Special dialog box	Home, Clipboard	, Paste Special	
watermark	Design, Page Background		
works cited page	References, Citations & Bibliography		

Formatting with Special Features

Data Files ▷ Before beginning section work, copy the WordS2 folder to your storage medium and then make WordS2 the active folder.

Skills

- Create and modify WordArt text
- Create a drop cap
- Insert a text box and draw a text box
- Insert and modify shapes
- Use SmartArt to create organizational charts and diagrams
- Create, format, and modify tables
- Insert one file into another

- Insert a continuous section break
- Format text into columns and modify columns
- Insert a hyperlink
- Save a document in PDF format
- Merge letters and envelopes
- Edit a data source file

Precheck ▷ Check your current skills to help focus your study of the skills taught in this section.

Projects Overview

Format a document on special vacation activities in Hawaii; prepare an organizational chart and graphic of services; create and modify a table containing information on scenic flights on Maui; format and modify a fact sheet containing information on Petersburg, Alaska; save the fact sheet as a single file web page and insert hyperlinks to an additional document and a website; create a data source file and then merge a letter on cruise specials and an envelope document with the data source file; format a newsletter containing information on Zenith Adventures.

Create an organizational chart and graphic for the production department.

Create and format a table with information on classes offered by the Theatre Arts Division; format and modify a newsletter.

Create a data source file and then merge it with a letter asking for fabric pricing; create an organizational chart and graphic for the design department.

Create and format a table containing information on catered lunch options; create a flyer.

Create and format an announcement about an upcoming stockholders' meeting.

SNAP If you are a SNAP user, launch the Precheck and Tutorials from your Assignments page.

Model Answers ▷ Preview the model answers for an overview of the projects you will complete in the section activities.

Use the WordArt feature to distort or modify text to conform to a variety of shapes. Consider using WordArt to create a company logo, letterhead, flyer title, or heading. To insert WordArt, click the Insert tab, click the WordArt button in the Text group, and then click the desired WordArt style at the drop-down gallery. When WordArt is selected, the Drawing Tools Format tab displays. Use options and buttons on this tab to modify and customize WordArt.

FIRST CHOICE TRAVEL

What You Will Do To increase the visual appeal of a document on Hawaiian specials, you decide to insert and format WordArt.

Tutorial
Inserting, Sizing, and Positioning WordArt

Tutorial
Formatting WordArt

1. Open **FCTHawaiianSpecials.docx** and then save it with the name **4-FCTHawaiianSpecials**.

2. Complete a spelling and grammar check on the document. You determine what to correct and what to ignore. (The name *Molokini* is spelled correctly in the document.)

3. Click the Design tab, click the Fonts button in the Document Formatting group, scroll down the drop-down gallery, and then click *Calibri Light-Constantia*.

4. Click the Colors button and then click the *Green* option at the drop-down gallery.

5. With the insertion point positioned at the beginning of the document, click the Insert tab.

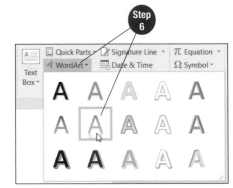

Step 6

6. Insert WordArt by clicking the WordArt button 𝐴 in the Text group and then clicking the *Gradient Fill - Aqua, Accent 1, Reflection* option (second column, second row).

7. Type HAWAIIAN SPECIALS.

   This inserts the WordArt text *HAWAIIAN SPECIALS* in the document, selects the WordArt text box, and displays the Drawing Tools Format tab.

Step 9

8. Select the border of the WordArt by positioning the arrow pointer on the dashed border that surrounds the WordArt and then clicking the left mouse button. (This changes the dashed border to a solid line border.)

9. Click the Text Fill button arrow 𝐀 in the WordArt Styles group and then click the *Blue* option (eighth option in the *Standard Colors* section).

Step 10

10. Click the Text Effects button 𝐀 in the WordArt Styles group, point to *Glow*, and then click the *Green, 5 pt glow, Accent color 1* option (first column, first row in the *Glow Variations* section).

In Brief

Insert WordArt
1. Click Insert tab.
2. Click WordArt button.
3. Click option.
4. Type text.
5. Format WordArt with options on Drawing Tools Format tab.

11 Increase the height of the WordArt text box by clicking in the *Shape Height* measurement box in the Size group, typing 1, and then pressing the Enter key.

12 Increase the width of the WordArt text box by clicking in the *Shape Width* measurement box in the Size group, typing 6.5, and then pressing the Enter key.

13 Click the Position button in the Arrange group and then click the *In Line with Text* option (first option in the drop-down gallery).

14 Click the Text Effects button in the WordArt Styles group, point to *Transform*, and then click the *Deflate* option (second column, sixth row in the *Warp* section).

15 Apply the Heading 2 style to the following headings: *White Sands Charters*, *Air Adventures*, *Deep Sea Submarines*, *Snorkeling Fantasies*, and *Bicycle Safari*.

16 Press Ctrl + A to select the entire document, click the Home tab, click the Font Color button arrow, and then click the *Turquoise, Accent 6, Darker 50%* option (last column, last row in the *Theme Colors* section).

17 Save **4-FCTHawaiianSpecials.docx**.

Check Your Work Compare your work to the model answer to ensure that you have completed the activity correctly.

In Addition

Using the Drawing Tools Format Tab

When WordArt is selected, the Drawing Tools Format tab displays as shown below. Use options in the Insert Shapes group to draw a shape or text box. With options in the Shape Styles group, you can apply a predesigned style, change the shape fill color and the shape outline color, and apply shape effects. Change the style of the WordArt text with options in the WordArt Styles group, apply text formatting to WordArt with options in the Text group, specify the layering of the WordArt text with options in the Arrange group, and identify the height and width of the WordArt text box with measurement boxes in the Size group.

Creating Drop Caps and Text Boxes; Drawing Shapes

Use a drop cap to enhance the appearance of text. A drop cap is the first letter of the first word of a paragraph that is set into a paragraph. Drop caps identify the beginning of major sections or parts of a document. Create a drop cap with the Drop Cap button in the Text group on the Insert tab. Use the Text Box button in the Text group to create a text box or insert a predesigned text box in a document. The Shapes button in the Illustrations group on the Insert tab contains a number of shape options for drawing shapes in a document including lines, rectangles, basic shapes, block arrows, flow chart shapes, stars, banners, and callouts. Click a shape and the mouse pointer displays as crosshairs. Position the crosshairs where you want the shape positioned and then click the left mouse button or click and hold down the left mouse button, drag to create the shape, and then release the mouse button. This inserts the shape in the document and also displays the Drawing Tools Format tab. Use buttons on this tab to change the shape, apply a style to the shape, arrange the shape, and change the size of the shape.

What You Will Do   You will continue to add visual appeal to the Hawaiian Specials document by creating a drop cap and a shape and inserting a predesigned text box.

Tutorial
Creating and Removing a Drop Cap

Tutorial
Inserting a Text Box

Tutorial
Formatting a Text Box

Tutorial
Inserting, Sizing, and Positioning a Shape and Line

Tutorial
Formatting a Shape and Line

1. With **4-FCTHawaiianSpecials.docx** open, position the insertion point anywhere in the heading *White Sands Charters*, click the Border button arrow in the Paragraph group on the Home tab, and then click *Borders and Shading* at the drop-down list.

2. At the Borders and Shading dialog box, make sure the single line is selected in the *Style* list box, click the *Color* option box arrow, and then click the *Turquoise, Accent 6, Darker 50%* option (last column, last row in the *Theme Colors* section).

3. Click the bottom of the diagram in the *Preview* section of the dialog box.

   This inserts a single turquoise line in the diagram.

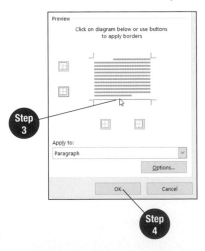

4. Click OK to close the Borders and Shading dialog box.

5. Use the Repeat command, F4, to apply the same turquoise bottom border to the remaining headings in the document (*Air Adventures*, *Deep Sea Submarines*, *Snorkeling Fantasies*, and *Bicycle Safari*).

6. Move the insertion point to the beginning of the word *Sail* that displays immediately below the heading *White Sands Charters* and then click the Insert tab.

7. Click the Drop Cap button in the Text group and then click *Dropped* at the drop-down gallery.

   If you click *Drop Cap Options*, the Drop Cap dialog box displays with options for positioning the drop cap, changing the font, identifying the number of lines for the drop cap, and setting the distance from the drop cap to the text.

8 Click anywhere in the text on the first page to deselect the *S*.

9 Insert a text box on the first page by clicking the Text Box button in the Text group on the Insert tab and then clicking the *Austin Quote* option.

Predesigned text boxes are listed in alphabetical order.

10 Type the following text in the text box: Sign up today for your Hawaiian adventure and enjoy spectacular beaches, Hawaii's natural undersea world, and beautiful bays.

11 With the Drawing Tools Format tab active, click the More Shape Styles button in the Shape Styles group and then click the *Subtle Effect - Aqua, Accent 5* option (sixth column, fourth row in the *Theme Styles* section).

12 Click the dashed line border of the text box to change the border to a solid line border.

To apply formatting to the text in the text box, the border must be changed from a dashed line to a solid line.

13 Click the Text Fill button arrow and then click the *Turquoise, Accent 6, Darker 50%* option (last column, last row in the *Theme Colors* section).

14 With the text still selected, press Ctrl + B to apply bold formatting and then press Ctrl + Shift + < to decrease the font size.

15 Click the Shape Effects button, point to *Glow*, and then click the *Turquoise, 5 pt glow, Accent color 6* option (last column, first row in the *Glow Variations* section).

16 Click the Shape Effects button, point to *Bevel*, and then click the *Circle* option (first column, first row in the *Bevel* section).

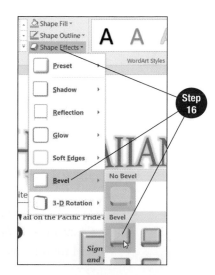

17 Click in the *Shape Width* measurement box in the Size group, type **2.9**, and then press the Enter key.

18 Click the Wrap Text button in the Arrange group and then click *Tight* at the drop-down gallery.

19 Drag the text box so it is positioned similarly to what is shown below.

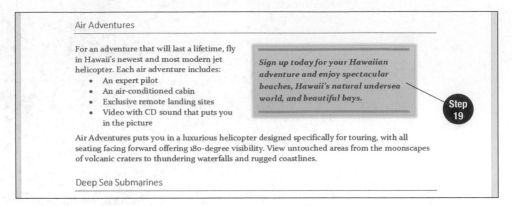

Air Adventures

For an adventure that will last a lifetime, fly in Hawaii's newest and most modern jet helicopter. Each air adventure includes:
- An expert pilot
- An air-conditioned cabin
- Exclusive remote landing sites
- Video with CD sound that puts you in the picture

Sign up today for your Hawaiian adventure and enjoy spectacular beaches, Hawaii's natural undersea world, and beautiful bays.

Step 19

Air Adventures puts you in a luxurious helicopter designed specifically for touring, with all seating facing forward offering 180-degree visibility. View untouched areas from the moonscapes of volcanic craters to thundering waterfalls and rugged coastlines.

Deep Sea Submarines

20 Press Ctrl + End to move the insertion point to the end of the document and then press the Enter key two times.

21 Click the Insert tab and then click the Shapes button in the Illustrations group.

22 Click the *Bevel* shape (first column, third row in the *Basic Shapes* section).

23 Click in the document at the location of the insertion point.

> This inserts a bevel shape in the document that is 1.14 inches in width and height.

24 Apply a shape style by clicking the More Shape Styles button in the Shape Styles group and then clicking the *Subtle Effect - Aqua, Accent 5* option (sixth column, fourth row in the *Theme Styles* section).

25 Click in the *Shape Height* measurement box, type 1.5, and then press the Enter key.

26 Click in the *Shape Width* measurement box, type 5.5, and then press the Enter key.

27 Click the Align button ▤ in the Arrange group and then click *Distribute Horizontally* at the drop-down list.

28 With the shape selected, type Sign up today for your Hawaiian adventure!

29 Select the text you just typed.

> To format text in a text box or shape, you can click the border line to change it from a dashed line border to a solid line border, or select the text in the text box or shape.

30 Click the Home tab, change the font size to 14 points, change the font color to standard dark blue, and then apply bold and italic formatting.

> Your text box should appear similar to what is shown below.

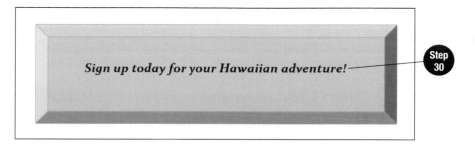

Sign up today for your Hawaiian adventure!

Step 30

31 Press Ctrl + Home to move the insertion point to the beginning of the document.

32 Save, print, and then close **4-FCTHawaiianSpecials.docx**.

> **Check Your Work** Compare your work to the model answer to ensure that you have completed the activity correctly.

In Addition

Drawing Lines

The Shapes button drop-down list contains a number of options for drawing lines in a document. Click the *Curve* option in the *Lines* section to draw curved lines by clicking at the beginning position, dragging to the location where you want the curve to appear, and then clicking the mouse button again. Continue in this manner until you have drawn all the desired curved lines. Click the *Freeform* option in the *Lines* section to draw freeform in a document. After clicking the *Freeform* option, drag in the document screen. When you want to stop drawing, double-click the left mouse button. You can also use the *Scribble* option to draw freeform in a document. The difference between the Freeform tool and the Scribble tool is that you have to double-click to stop drawing with the Freeform tool but you only need to release the mouse button to stop drawing with the Scribble tool.

Drawing and Formatting Text Boxes

Draw your own text box in a document by clicking the Insert tab, clicking the Text Box button in the Text group, and then clicking *Draw Text Box* at the drop-down list. The mouse pointer displays as crosshairs. Position the crosshairs in the document and then drag to create the text box. When you insert a text box in a document, the Drawing Tools Format tab becomes active. Use options on this tab to customize and format the text box.

Use SmartArt to create a variety of graphics to visually illustrate and present data. SmartArt includes graphics for presenting hierarchical data; making lists of data; showing data processes, cycles, and relationships; and presenting data in a matrix or pyramid. To display SmartArt graphics, click the Insert tab and then click the SmartArt button in the Illustrations group. This displays the Choose a SmartArt Graphic dialog box with *All* selected in the left panel and all available predesigned graphics displayed in the middle panel. Click the desired graphic type in the left panel and then click a graphic in the middle panel and the name of the graphic displays in the right panel along with a description of the graphic type. Double-click a graphic in the middle panel and the graphic is inserted in the document. Use buttons on the SmartArt Tools Design tab and the SmartArt Tools Format tab to customize a graphic. Some graphics are designed to include text. Type text in a graphic by selecting the object and then typing text in the object or by typing text in the *Type your text here* window at the left side of the graphic.

FIRST CHOICE
TRAVEL

What You Will Do   Terry Blessing, president of First Choice Travel, has asked you to prepare a document containing information on the organizational structure of the company and a graphic that illustrates the services provided by First Choice Travel.

Tutorial
Inserting, Sizing, and Positioning SmartArt

Tutorial
Formatting SmartArt

1 Open **FCTStructure.docx** and then save it with the name **4-FCTStructure**.

2 Move the insertion point a double space below the heading *ORGANIZATIONAL CHART* and then create the organizational chart SmartArt graphic shown in Figure 4.1. To begin, click the Insert tab and then click the SmartArt button in the Illustrations group.

3 At the Choose a SmartArt Graphic dialog box, click *Hierarchy* in the left panel and then double-click the first option in the middle panel, *Organization Chart*.

Choose a SmartArt Graphic

All
List
Process
Cycle
Hierarchy
Relationship

Step 3

> This displays the organizational chart in the document with the SmartArt Tools Design tab selected. Use buttons on this tab to add additional boxes, change the order of the boxes, choose a different layout, apply formatting with a SmartArt Style, and reset the formatting of the organizational chart SmartArt graphic.

4 If a *Type your text here* window displays at the left side of the SmartArt graphic, close it by clicking the Text Pane button in the Create Graphic group.

> You can also close the window by clicking the Close button in the upper right corner of the window.

5 Delete the bottom right box in the graphic by clicking the border of the box to select it and then pressing the Delete key.

> Make sure that the selection border that surrounds the box is a solid line and not a dashed line. If a dashed line displays, click the box border again to change it to a solid line.

6 With the bottom right box selected, click the Add Shape button arrow in the Create Graphic group and then click *Add Shape Below*.

> Your organizational chart SmartArt graphic should contain the same boxes as shown in Figure 4.1.

File   Home   Insert
Add Shape ▾   ← Promote
Add Shape After
Add Shape Before
Add Shape Above
Add Shape Below
Add Assistant

Step 6

7 Click the *[Text]* placeholder in the top box, type Terry Blessing, press the Enter key, and then type President. Click in each of the remaining boxes and type the text as shown in Figure 4.1.

8 Click inside the SmartArt graphic border but outside any objects in the graphic.

> This deselects the shape in the SmartArt graphic but keeps the graphic selected.

9 Click the More SmartArt Styles button in the SmartArt Styles group.

10 Click the *Inset* option (second column, first row in the *3-D* section).

Figure 4.1 Organizational Chart SmartArt Graphic

11 Click the Change Colors button in the SmartArt Styles group and then click the *Colorful Range - Accent Colors 5 to 6* option (last option in the *Colorful* section).

12 Click the SmartArt Tools Format tab.

> The SmartArt Tools Format tab contains buttons for changing the box shape; applying shape styles; applying WordArt styles to text; applying text fill, outline, and effects; and arranging and sizing the SmartArt graphic.

13 Click the tab (contains a left-pointing triangle) at the left side of the diagram border.

14 Click anywhere in the *Type your text here* window and then press Ctrl + A.

> This selects all of the text and shapes in the graphic.

15 Click the Change Shape button in the Shapes group and then click the *Rounded Rectangle* option (second shape in the *Rectangles* section).

16 Click the Shape Outline button arrow in the Shape Styles group and then click the *Dark Blue* color option (ninth option in the *Standard Colors* section).

17 Click the Text Fill button arrow in the WordArt Styles group and then click the *Dark Blue* color option in the *Standard Colors* section.

18 Press Ctrl + B to apply bold formatting to the text.

19 Close the Text pane by clicking the Close button in the upper right corner of the pane.

20 Deselect the shapes (but not the graphic) by clicking inside the SmartArt graphic border but outside any objects.

21 Click the Size button at the right side of the SmartArt Tools Format tab. (Your size options may display in the Size group rather than the Size button. If so, proceed to Step 22.)

22 Click in the *Shape Height* measurement box, type 4, click in the *Shape Width* measurement box, type 6.5, and then press the Enter key.

> In addition to the *Shape Height* and *Shape Width* measurement boxes, you can increase or decrease the size of a SmartArt graphic by dragging a corner of the graphic border. To maintain the proportions of the graphic, hold down the Shift key while dragging the border.

23 Press Ctrl + End to move the insertion point below the title *TRAVEL SERVICES* on the second page.

24 Click the Insert tab and then click the SmartArt button in the Illustrations group.

25 At the Choose a SmartArt Graphic dialog box, click *Cycle* in the left panel and then double-click the *Radial Cycle* graphic (second column, third row).

26 Click in each of the shapes in the graphic and then type the text as shown in Figure 4.2.

Figure 4.2 Services Diagram

27 Click inside the graphic but outside any objects.

28 Click the More SmartArt Styles button in the SmartArt Styles group and then click the *Inset* option (second column, first row in the *3-D* section).

29 Click the Change Colors button in the SmartArt Styles group and then click the *Colorful Range - Accent Colors 4 to 5* option (fourth option in the *Colorful* section).

30 Click the SmartArt Tools Format tab.

31 Hold down the Shift key, click each of the circles in the graphic, and then release the Shift key.

This selects all of the circle shapes in the graphic.

32 Click the Larger button ⊞ in the Shapes group to slightly increase the size of the circles.

33 Click the Shape Outline button arrow in the Shape Styles group and then click the *Dark Blue* color option (ninth option in the *Standard Colors* section).

34 Click the Text Fill button arrow in the WordArt Styles group and then click the *Dark Blue* color option in the *Standard Colors* section.

35 Press Ctrl + B to apply bold formatting to the text.

36 Deselect the circle shapes by clicking inside the graphic but outside any objects.

37 Click the Size button, click in the *Shape Height* measurement box, type 4, click in the *Shape Width* measurement box, type 6.5, and then press the Enter key. (Your size options may display in the Size group rather than the Size button.)

38 Click outside the graphic to deselect it.

39 Save, print, and then close **4-FCTStructure.docx**.

Check Your Work Compare your work to the model answer to ensure that you have completed the activity correctly.

In Addition

Moving or Positioning a SmartArt Graphic

Before moving a SmartArt graphic, apply text wrapping with options at the Position button drop-down gallery or the Wrap Text button drop-down gallery. With a text wrapping option applied, move a SmartArt graphic by positioning the arrow pointer on the graphic border until the pointer displays with a four-headed arrow attached, clicking and holding down the left mouse button, and then dragging the graphic to the desired location. As you move a graphic near the top, left, right, or bottom margins of the document, green guidelines appear to help you position the image.

Creating a Table and Changing the Table Layout

Word's Table feature is useful for displaying data in columns and rows. This data may be text, values, and/or formulas. Create a table using the Table button on the Insert tab or with options at the Insert Table dialog box. Once you specify the desired number of rows and columns, Word displays the table and you are ready to enter information into the cells. A cell is the box created by the intersection of a column and a row. With the insertion point positioned in a table, two tabs are available for modifying and formatting the table—the Table Tools Design tab and the Table Tools Layout tab. Use options and buttons on the Table Tools Layout tab to perform such actions as selecting a table, row, or the entire table; inserting or deleting rows and/or columns; changing the height and width of rows and columns; and specifying text alignment in cells. You can also click the Properties button to display the Table Properties dialog box with options for vertically and horizontally centering a table on the page.

What You Will Do   You are developing a new First Choice Travel information document about sightseeing flights around the island of Maui. You will create a table to display the data and then modify the table structure and apply formatting to the table and its cells.

Tutorial
Creating a Table

Tutorial
Changing the Table Layout

Tutorial
Customizing Cells in a Table

1. Open **FCTIslandFlights.docx** and then save it with the name **4-FCTIslandFlights**.

2. Press Ctrl + End to move the insertion point to the end of the document.

3. Click the Insert tab and then click the Table button ⊞ in the Tables group.

4. Drag the mouse pointer down and to the right until the number above the grid displays as *3x6* and then click the mouse button.

5. Type the text in the cells as shown in Figure 4.3. Press the Tab key to move the insertion point to the next cell or press Shift + Tab to move the insertion point to the previous cell.

    When typing text in the cells in the second column, do not press the Enter key to end a line. Type the text and let the word wrap feature wrap the text within the cell. After typing text in the last cell, do not press the Tab key. This will insert another row. If you press the Tab key accidentally, immediately click the Undo button. To move the insertion point to different cells within the table using the mouse, click in the desired cell.

Figure 4.3 Step 5

Adventure	Destination	Price
Special West Maui	Waterfalls, lush tropical valleys	$49
West Maui Tropical	West Maui mountains, Hawaii's highest waterfalls	$79
Haleakala-Keane	Haleakala crater, tropical rain forest, waterfalls	$89
Special Circle Island	Hana, Haleakala, West Maui mountains, tropical rain forest, waterfalls	$169
Molokai-West Maui	West Maui mountains, waterfalls, sea cliffs, Kalaupapa colony	$189

6 You decide to add First Choice Travel discount prices to the table. To do this, position the insertion point in the *Price* cell, make sure the Table Tools Layout tab is active, and then click the Insert Right button in the Rows & Columns group.

Figure 4.4 shows the Table Tools Layout tab.

7 Click in the top cell of the new column, type FCT, and then press the Down Arrow key. Type the money amounts in the remaining cells as shown at the right. (Press the Down Arrow key to move to the next cell down.)

8 Delete the *Special Circle Island* row. To do this, click anywhere in the text *Special Circle Island*, make sure the Table Tools Layout tab is active, click the Delete button in the Rows & Columns group, and then click *Delete Rows* at the drop-down list.

9 Insert a row above *Adventure*. To do this, click anywhere in the text *Adventure* and then click the Insert Above button in the Rows & Columns group.

10 With the new top row selected, merge the cells by clicking the Merge Cells button in the Merge group.

11 Type MAUI FLIGHTS in the top row.

12 Select all cells in the table by clicking the table move handle that displays in the upper left corner of the table (a square with a four-headed arrow inside).

13 Click the Home tab, change the font to Constantia and the font size to 12 points, and then click outside the table to deselect it.

14 Click in the top cell containing the text *MAUI FLIGHTS* and then click the Table Tools Layout tab.

15 Click in the *Table Row Height* measurement box in the Cell Size group, type 0.4, and then press the Enter key.

16 Insert a new column by clicking the Insert Left button in the Rows & Columns group.

17 With the cells in the new column selected, click the Merge Cells button in the Merge group.

Figure 4.4 Table Tools Layout Tab

18 Type Hawaiian Adventures in the new cell.

19 Click two times on the Text Direction button in the Alignment group.

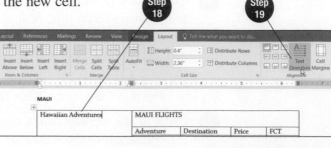

20 Click the Align Center button in the Alignment group to change the horizontal and vertical alignment of text in the cell.

21 Position the mouse pointer on the gridline between the first and second columns until the pointer turns into a double-headed arrow pointing left and right with a short double line between. Click and hold down the left mouse button, drag to the left until the table column marker displays at approximately the 0.5-inch mark on the horizontal ruler, and then release the mouse button.

22 Position the mouse pointer on the gridline between the second and third columns until the pointer turns into a double-headed arrow pointing left and right with a short double line in between, click and hold down the left mouse button, drag to the left until the table column marker displays at the 2.25-inch mark on the horizontal ruler, and then release the mouse button.

23 Following the same procedure, drag the gridline between the third and fourth columns to the left until the table column marker displays at the 4.25-inch mark on the horizontal ruler.

24 If you hold down the Alt key while dragging a gridline, column measurements display on the horizontal ruler. Use these measurements to change the width of the fourth column. To do this, position the mouse pointer on the gridline between the fourth and fifth columns, press and hold down the Alt key, click and hold down the left mouse button, drag the gridline to the left until the measurement for the fourth column on the horizontal ruler displays as *0.68"*, release the Alt key, and then release the mouse button.

25 Position the mouse pointer on the gridline at the right side of the table, press and hold down the Alt key, click and hold down the left mouse button, drag the gridline to the left until the measurement for the fifth column on the horizontal ruler displays as *0.68"*, release the Alt key, and then release the mouse button.

26 Click anywhere in the *MAUI FLIGHTS* text and then click the Align Center button in the Alignment group on the Table Tools Layout tab.

This changes the horizontal and vertical alignment for text in the cell to center.

Create Table
1. Click Insert tab.
2. Click Table button.
3. Drag in grid to select columns and rows.
OR
1. Click Insert tab.
2. Click *Insert Table* option.
3. Type number of columns.
4. Press Tab key.
5. Type number of rows.
6. Click OK.

Increase/Decrease Column/Row
1. Click Table Tools Layout tab.
2. Click in *Table Row Height* measurement box or *Table Column Width* measurement box.
3. Type measurement.
4. Press Enter.
OR
1. Position mouse pointer on gridline until it turns into a double-headed arrow.
2. Click and hold down left mouse button, drag to new position, then release mouse button.

27 Select the four cells containing the headings *Adventure*, *Destination*, *Price*, and *FCT*. To do this, position the mouse pointer in the *Adventure* cell, click and hold down the left mouse button, drag to the *FCT* cell, and then release the mouse button.

28 With the cells selected, click the Align Center button in the Alignment group and then press Ctrl + B to apply bold formatting.

29 Select all of the cells containing prices and then click the Align Top Center button in the Alignment group.

30 Horizontally center the table on the page. Begin by clicking the Properties button in the Table group.

31 At the Table Properties dialog box with the Table tab selected, click the *Center* option in the *Alignment* section.

32 Click OK to close the Table Properties dialog box.

33 Click anywhere outside the table to deselect the cells.

34 Save **4-FCTIslandFlights.docx**.

Check Your Work Compare your work to the model answer to ensure that you have completed the activity correctly.

In Addition

Creating a Table Using Other Methods

Other methods for creating a table include using options at the Insert Table dialog box or drawing a table. Display the Insert Table dialog box by clicking the Insert tab, clicking the Table button, and then clicking *Insert Table* at the drop-down list. Specify the desired number of columns and rows and then click OK to close the dialog box. Another method for creating a table is to draw a table by clicking the Table button and then clicking

Draw Table at the drop-down list. The mouse pointer changes to a pencil. Drag in the document screen to create the desired columns and rows.

Selecting Cells with the Keyboard

Besides using the mouse, you can also select cells using the following keyboard shortcuts:

To select	Press
the next cell's contents	Tab
the preceding cell's contents	Shift + Tab
the entire table	Alt + 5 (on the numeric keypad with Num Lock off)
adjacent cells	Hold Shift key and then press an arrow key repeatedly.
a column	Position insertion point in top cell of column, hold down Shift key, and then press Down Arrow key until column is selected.

The Table Tools Design tab contains a number of options for enhancing the appearance of the table. With options in the Table Styles group, apply a predesigned style that applies color and border lines to a table. Maintain further control over the predesigned style formatting applied to columns and rows with options in the Table Style Options group. Apply additional formatting to cells in a table with the Shading button in the Tables Styles group and the Borders button in the Borders group. With options in the Borders group, you can customize the borders of cells in a table. Display a list of predesigned border lines; change the line style, width, and color; add or remove borders; and apply the same border style formatting to other cells with the Border Painter button.

What You Will Do   You will add final design formatting to the Maui Flights table by applying a table style and then customizing the formatting with additional options.

Tutorial
Changing the Table Design

Tutorial
Sorting Text in a Table

1 With **4-FCTIslandFlights.docx** open, select *MAUI FLIGHTS*, change the font size to 16 points, and apply bold formatting.

2 Select the text *Hawaiian Adventures*, change the font size to 14 points, and then apply bold and italic formatting.

3 Click anywhere in the table and then click the Table Tools Design tab.

4 Click the More Table Styles button in the Table Styles group.

　　　This displays a drop-down gallery of style choices.

5 Click the *Grid Table 4 - Accent 2* option (third column, fourth row in the *Grid Tables* section; this location may vary, reference the image below to see how the option appears in the gallery).

　　　Notice the color and border style formatting applied and also notice how the style changed the cell alignment for *MAUI FLIGHTS* and *Hawaiian Adventures* from Align Center to Align Top Center.

6 Experiment with an additional style by clicking the More Table Styles button and then clicking the *Grid Table 4 - Accent 1* option (second column, fourth row in the *Grid Tables* section).

7 Change the formatting by clicking the *Banded Rows* check box in the Table Style Options group to remove the check mark. Click the *Banded Columns* check box to insert a check mark. Click the *Header Row* check box to remove the check mark and click the *First Column* check box to remove the check mark.

8 Save and then print **4-FCTIslandFlights.docx**.

9 With the insertion point positioned in a cell in the table and the Table Tools Design tab selected, click the *Header Row* check box in the Table Style Options group to insert a check mark, and click the *First Column* check box to insert a check mark. Click the *Banded Columns* check box to remove the check mark, and click the *Banded Rows* check box to insert a check mark.

10 Applying the table styles removed the horizontal alignment of the table. Horizontally align the table by clicking the Table Tools Layout tab, clicking the Properties button in the Table group, clicking the *Center* option in the *Alignment* section of the Table Properties dialog box, and then clicking OK to close the dialog box.

11 Apply the Heading 1 style to the headings *ISLAND SIGHTSEEING FLIGHTS* and *MAUI*.

12 Click the Design tab and then apply the Lines (Simple) style set, change the theme colors to Blue Green, and change the theme fonts to Calibri Light-Constantia.

13 Save, print, and then close **4-FCTIslandFlights.docx**.

Check Your Work Compare your work to the model answer to ensure that you have completed the activity correctly.

In Addition

Sorting in a Table
Sort text in a table alphabetically, numerically, or by date with options at the Sort dialog box. Display this dialog box by positioning the insertion point in a cell in the table and then clicking the Sort button in the Data group on the Table Tools Layout tab. Make sure the column you want to sort is selected in the *Sort by* option and then click OK. If the first row in the table contains data such as headings that you do not want to include in the sort, click the *Header row* option in the *My list has* section of the Sort dialog box. If you want to sort specific cells in a table, select the cells first and then click the Sort button.

Inserting a Row Using the Mouse
You can use the mouse to insert a row by moving the mouse pointer immediately left of the row where you want the new row inserted. As you move the mouse pointer to the left side of a row, a plus symbol inside a circle displays along with thin, blue, double lines across the top or bottom of the row. Move the symbol and lines to the bottom of the row and then click the plus symbol and a new row is inserted below the current row. Move the symbol and lines to the top of the row and then click the plus symbol and a row is inserted above the current row.

Inserting a File and Section Break; Creating and Modifying Newspaper Columns

Use the Object button in the Text group on the Insert tab to insert one document into another. To increase the ease with which a person can read and understand groups of words (referred to as the *readability* of a document), consider setting text in a document in newspaper columns. Newspaper columns contain text that flows up and down on the page. Create newspaper columns with the Columns button in the Page Setup group on the Layout tab or with options at the Columns dialog box. If you want to apply column formatting to only a portion of a document, insert a section break in the document with options at the Breaks button drop-down list.

What You Will Do   You are working on an informational document on Petersburg, Alaska, and realize that you need to insert additional information from another file. You also decide to improve the readability of the document by formatting the text into newspaper columns.

Tutorial
Inserting a File

Tutorial
Inserting and Deleting
a Section Break

Tutorial
Formatting Text
into Columns

1   Open **FCTPetersburgAK.docx** and then save it with the name **4-FCTPetersburgAK**.

2   Press Ctrl + End to move the insertion point to the end of the document and then click the Insert tab.

3   Insert a document into the current document by clicking the Object button arrow in the Text group and then clicking *Text from File* at the drop-down list.

4   At the Insert File dialog box, navigate to the WordS4 folder on your storage medium and then double-click *FCTPetersburgActivities.docx*.

5   Select the text you just inserted and then change the font to Constantia.

6   Apply the Heading 1 style to the title *PETERSBURG, ALASKA* and apply the Heading 2 style to the headings in the document: *Services, Visitor Attractions, Walking Tours, Accommodations, Transportation,* and *Guided Activities*.

7   Position the insertion point at the beginning of the first paragraph in the document (the paragraph that begins *Petersburg, Alaska, located on*) and then click the Layout tab.

8   Click the Breaks button in the Page Setup group. At the Breaks button drop-down list, click *Continuous* in the *Section Breaks* section.

> Click one of the other three options in the *Section Breaks* section of the Breaks button drop-down list if you want to insert a section break that begins a new page.

9   Click the View tab and then click the Draft button in the Views group.

> The section break is not visible in Print Layout view. A continuous section break separates the document into sections but does not insert a page break. In Draft view, the section break displays in the document as a double row of dots with the words *Section Break (Continuous)* in the middle.

In Brief

**Insert One File
into Another**
1. Click Insert tab.
2. Click Object button arrow.
3. Click *Text from File* option.
4. At Insert File dialog box, double-click document.

**Insert Continuous
Section Break**
1. Click Layout tab.
2. Click Breaks button.
3. Click *Continuous*.

**Format Text
into Columns**
1. Click Layout tab.
2. Click Columns button.
3. Click number of columns.

**Display Columns
Dialog Box**
1. Click Layout tab.
2. Click Columns button.
3. Click *More Columns* option.

10 With the insertion point positioned below the section break, format the text below the section break into three newspaper columns by clicking the Layout tab, clicking the Columns button 📄 in the Page Setup group, and then clicking *Three* at the drop-down list.

> Formatting text into columns automatically changes the view to Print Layout.

11 As you view the document, you decide that the three columns are too narrow. To change the columns, click the Columns button in the Page Setup group and then click *More Columns* at the drop-down list.

12 At the Columns dialog box, click *Two* in the *Presets* section.

13 Increase the spacing between the two columns by clicking the *Spacing* measurement box up arrow in the *Width and spacing* section until *0.7"* displays in the measurement box. Make sure a check mark displays in the *Equal column width* check box. (If not, click the check box to insert the check mark.)

14 Click the *Line between* check box to insert a check mark and then click OK to close the dialog box.

> Inserting a check mark in the *Line between* check box inserts a line between the two columns. The *Preview* section of the dialog box shows you what this will look like.

15 Insert page numbering by clicking the Insert tab, clicking the Page Number button in the Header & Footer group, pointing to *Bottom of Page*, and then clicking the *Plain Number 2* option.

16 Click the Close Header and Footer button.

17 Press Ctrl + End to move the insertion point to the end of the document. Looking at the columns on the last (second) page, you decide to balance the two columns. To do this, click the Layout tab, click the Breaks button in the Page Setup group, and then click *Continuous* in the *Section Breaks* section.

18 Save and then print **4-FCTPetersburgAK.docx**.

Check Your Work   Compare your work to the model answer to ensure that you have completed the activity correctly.

In Addition

Changing Column Width

One method for changing column width in a document is to drag the column marker on the horizontal ruler. To change the width (and also the spacing) of columns of text, position the arrow pointer on the left or right edge of a column marker on the horizontal ruler until the pointer turns into a double-headed arrow pointing left and right.

Click and hold down the left mouse button, drag the column marker to the left or right to make the column wider or narrower, and then release the mouse button. Press and hold down the Alt key while dragging the column marker and measurements display on the horizontal ruler.

Insert a hyperlink in a document to navigate to a specific location in the document, display a different document, open a file in a different program, or link to an email address or web site. Insert a hyperlink with the Hyperlink button on the Insert tab. If a Word document is going to be distributed to others, consider saving the document in PDF format. The abbreviation *PDF* stands for *portable document format*, which is a file format that preserves fonts, formatting, and images in a printer-friendly version that looks the same on most computers. Someone who receives a Word file saved in PDF format does not need to have the Word application on his or her computer to open, read, and print the file. Exchanging PDF files is a popular method for collaborating with others. A Word document can be saved in PDF format through the Export backstage area or with the *Save as type* option at the Save As dialog box.

FIRST CHOICE TRAVEL

What You Will Do   A document with additional information on Petersburg, Alaska, is available and you decide to link that document to the current document by inserting a hyperlink. You also decide to insert a hyperlink to an Alaska travel website. Since some of First Choice Travel's clients do not have the Word application on their computers, you decide to save the Petersburg document in PDF format.

Tutorial
Inserting and Editing a Hyperlink

Tutorial
Saving and Opening a Document in PDF Format

1️⃣ With **4-FCTPetersburgAK.docx** open, press Ctrl + End to move the insertion point to the end of the document and then type Additional Information.

2️⃣ Select the text *Additional Information*.

3️⃣ Insert a hyperlink by clicking the Insert tab and then clicking the Hyperlink button in the Links group.

Step 3

4️⃣ At the Insert Hyperlink dialog box, click the *Look in* option box arrow, navigate to the WordS4 folder on your storage medium, and then double-click *FCTPetersburgStats.docx*.

Step 4

The Insert Hyperlink dialog box closes and *Additional Information* displays as hyperlinked text.

5️⃣ Press Ctrl + End, press the Enter key, and then type Alaska Tourism.

6️⃣ Create a hyperlink to the tourism site by selecting *Alaska Tourism* and then clicking the Hyperlink button in the Links group.

7️⃣ At the Insert Hyperlink dialog box, type www.travelalaska.com in the *Address* text box and then click OK.

Step 7

Word automatically adds *http://* to the beginning of the web address. If this website is not available, try www.state.ak.us.

Insert Hyperlink
1. Select text.
2. Click Insert tab.
3. Click Hyperlink button.
4. Type file name or web address.
5. Click OK.

Save Document in PDF Format
1. Click File tab.
2. Click *Export* option.
3. Click Create PDF/XPS button.
4. Click Publish button.
5. Click Close button.

8 Display the document containing additional information on Petersburg by holding down the Ctrl key and then clicking the Additional Information hyperlink.

9 After reading the information in the document, close the document.

10 Make sure you are connected to the Internet and then connect to the Alaska tourism site by holding down the Ctrl key and then clicking the Alaska Tourism hyperlink.

> If you are not able to connect to the Alaska Tourism website, check with your instructor.

11 At the Alaska Tourism web site, click any hyperlinks that interest you. When you are finished, click the Close button in the upper right corner of the browser window.

12 Save a copy of the document as in PDF format. Begin by clicking the File tab and then clicking the *Export* option.

13 At the Export backstage area, click the Create PDF/XPS button.

14 At the Publish as PDF or XPS dialog box, make sure the WordS4 folder on your storage medium is the active folder and that the *Open file after publishing* check box contains a check mark.

15 Click the Publish button.

> This saves the document with the name **4-FCTPetersburgAK.pdf** and opens the document in Adobe Acrobat Reader.

16 After viewing the document in Adobe Acrobat Reader, click the Close button in the upper right corner of the window.

> Acrobat Acrobat Reader closes and the Word document displays on the screen.

17 Print only page 2 of the document.

18 Save and then close **4-FCTPetersburgAK.docx**.

> **Check Your Work** Compare your work to the model answer to ensure that you have completed the activity correctly.

In Addition

Downloading and Saving Web Pages and Images

You can save the image(s) and/or text that display when you open a web page as well as the web page itself. Copyright laws protect much of the information on the Internet, so check the site for restrictions before copying or downloading. If you do use information, make sure you properly cite the source. To save a web page as a file, display the desired page, right-click the page and then click *Save as* at the shortcut menu. At the Save

As dialog box, specify the folder where you want to save the web page. Select the text in the *File name* text box, type a name for the page, and then click the Save button. Save a specific web image by right-clicking the image and then clicking *Save image as*. At the Save As dialog box, type a name for the image in the *File name* text box and then press the Enter key.

If you need to mail the same basic letter to a number of clients or customers, consider using the Mail Merge feature to make the job easier and to make the letter more personalized. With Mail Merge, you can merge a data source file containing information on your clients with a main document containing the letter. You can also create an envelope document you can merge with a data source file. Click the Mailings tab to display a number of buttons for preparing a mail merge document. Generally, a merge takes two documents—the data source file and the main document. The data source file contains the variable information that will be inserted in the main document. Use buttons on the Mailings tab to create main documents and data source files for merging.

What You Will Do   First Choice Travel is offering a special cruise package, and Melissa Gehring has asked you to prepare a data source file with client information, merge it with a letter describing the cruise special, and then print envelopes for the letters.

Tutorial
Creating a Data
Source File

Tutorial
Creating a Main
Document

Tutorial
Previewing and
Merging Documents

Tutorial
Merging Envelopes

1 At a blank document, click the Mailings tab, click the Select Recipients button ⊞ in the Start Mail Merge group, and then click *Type a New List* at the drop-down list.

> This displays the New Address List dialog box with predesigned fields. You can use these predesigned fields as well as create your own custom fields.

2 Click the Customize Columns button at the bottom of the dialog box.

> The predesigned fields cover most of the fields you need for your data source file, but you decide to delete six of the predesigned fields and insert two of your own.

3 At the Customize Address List dialog box, click *Company Name* to select it and then click the Delete button.

4 At the message that displays, click Yes.

5 Complete steps similar to those in Steps 3 and 4 to delete the following fields: *Address Line 2, Country or Region, Home Phone, Work Phone,* and *E-mail Address.*

6 Click the Add button.

> If the New Address List dialog box does not provide for all variable information, create your own custom field.

7 At the Add Field dialog box, type Membership and then click OK.

8 Click the Add button, type Discount, and then click OK.

9 Click OK to close the Customize Address List dialog box.

10 At the New Address List dialog box with the insertion point positioned in the *Title* field, type Mrs. and then press the Tab key.

Step 10

> Pressing the Tab key moves the insertion point to the *First Name* field. Press the Tab key to move the insertion point to the next field and press Shift + Enter to move it to the previous field.

11 Continue typing text in the specified fields as indicated in Figure 4.5. After entering all of the information for the last client, click OK.

Step 11

> After typing *3 percent* for Jerome Ellington, do not press the Tab key. If you do, a new blank client record will be created. To remove a blank record, click the Delete Entry button and then click Yes at the message.

12 At the Save Address List dialog box, navigate to your WordS4 folder. Click in the *File name* text box, type 4-FCTDataSource, and then press the Enter key.

> Word automatically saves the data source file as an Access database.

13 Open **FCTCruiseLtr.docx** and then save it with the name **4-FCTCruiseLtrMainDoc**.

14 Click the Mailings tab, click the Select Recipients button in the Start Mail Merge group, and then click *Use an Existing List* at the drop-down list.

Figure 4.5 Step 11

Title	Mrs.	*Title*	Mr. and Mrs.
First Name	Kristina	*First Name*	Walter
Last Name	Herron	*Last Name*	Noretto
Address Line 1	4320 Jackson Street	*Address Line 1*	3420 114th Avenue
City	Long Beach	*City*	Glendale
State	CA	*State*	CA
ZIP Code	90801	*ZIP Code*	91201
Membership	Premiere Choice	*Membership*	Ultimate Choice
Discount	3 percent	*Discount*	5 percent
Title	Ms.	*Title*	Mr.
First Name	Cathy	*First Name*	Jerome
Last Name	Washington	*Last Name*	Ellington
Address Line 1	321 Wildwood Street	*Address Line 1*	12883 22nd Street
City	Torrance	*City*	Inglewood
State	CA	*State*	CA
ZIP Code	90501	*ZIP Code*	90301
Membership	Ultimate Choice	*Membership*	Premiere Choice
Discount	5 percent	*Discount*	3 percent

15 At the Select Data Source dialog box, navigate to your WordS4 folder and then double-click *4-FCTDataSource.mdb*.

16 Move the insertion point a double space above the first paragraph of text in the letter and then click the Address Block button in the Write & Insert Fields group.

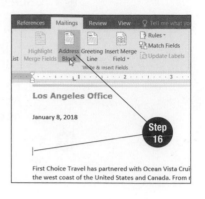

17 At the Insert Address Block dialog box, click OK.

This inserts the necessary field code to insert the client name and address in the letter.

18 Press the Enter key two times and then click the Greeting Line button in the Write & Insert Fields group.

19 At the Insert Greeting Line dialog box, click the arrow at the right side of the option box containing the comma (the box to the right of the one containing *Mr. Randall*) and then click the colon at the drop-down list.

20 Click OK to close the dialog box.

21 Move the insertion point to the end of the first paragraph, type With your, and then press the spacebar.

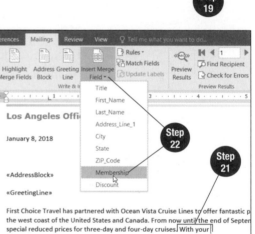

22 Insert the *Membership* field by clicking the Insert Merge Field button arrow and then clicking *Membership* at the drop-down list.

23 Press the spacebar, type membership, you will receive an additional, and then press the spacebar.

24 Insert the *Discount* field by clicking the Insert Merge Field button arrow and then clicking *Discount* at the drop-down list.

25 Press the spacebar, type discount, and then type a period.

The sentence you just typed should look like this: *With your «Membership» membership, you will receive an additional «Discount» discount.*

26 Click the Save button on the Quick Access Toolbar.

27 Merge the letter with the records in the data source file. Begin by clicking the Finish & Merge button in the Finish group on the Mailings tab and then clicking *Edit Individual Documents* at the drop-down list.

28 At the Merge to New Document dialog box, click OK.

The letters are merged with the records and displayed in a new document.

29 Save the merged letters in the normal manner and name the document **4-FCTMergedCruiseLtrs**.

In Brief

Mail Merge
1. Click Mailings tab.
2. Click Select Recipients button.
3. Click *Type a New List*.
4. Click Customize Columns button.
5. At Customize Address List dialog box, delete and/or insert fields.
6. Click OK.
7. At New Address List dialog box, type text in fields.
8. Click OK.
9. At Save Address List dialog box, navigate to folder.
10. Click in *File name* text box, type name, press Enter.
11. Open main document.
12. Click Mailings tab.
13. Click Select Recipients button.
14. Click *Use an Existing List*.
15. At Select Data Source dialog box, navigate to folder, double-click data source file.
16. Insert fields in document.
17. Click Finish & Merge button.
18. Click OK.

30 Print and then close **4-FCTMergedCruiseLtrs.docx**.

Four letters will print.

31 Save and then close **4-FCTCruiseLtrMainDoc.docx**.

32 At a blank document, prepare envelopes for the four letters. Begin by clicking the Mailings tab, clicking the Start Mail Merge button, and then clicking *Envelopes* at the drop-down list.

33 At the Envelope Options dialog box, click OK.

34 Click the Select Recipients button in the Start Mail Merge group and then click *Use an Existing List* at the drop-down list.

35 At the Select Data Source dialog box, navigate to the WordS4 folder and then double-click **4-FCTDataSource.mdb**.

36 Click in the approximate location in the envelope in the document where the client's name and address will appear.

This causes a box with a dashed gray border to display. If you do not see this box, try clicking in a different location on the envelope.

37 Click the Address Block button in the Write & Insert Fields group.

38 At the Insert Address Block dialog box, click OK.

39 Click the Finish & Merge button in the Finish group and then click *Edit Individual Documents* at the drop-down list.

40 At the Merge to New Document dialog box, click OK.

41 Save the merged envelopes document and name it **4-FCTMergedEnvs**.

42 Print **4-FCTMergedEnvs.docx**.

This document will print four envelopes. Check with your instructor about specific steps for printing envelopes. You may need to hand feed envelopes into your printer.

43 Close **4-FCTMergedEnvs.docx**.

44 Close the envelope main document without saving it.

> **Check Your Work** Compare your work to the model answer to ensure that you have completed the activity correctly.

In Addition

Using the Mail Merge Wizard

The Mail Merge feature includes a Mail Merge wizard that guides you through the merge process. To access the Wizard, click the Mailings tab, click the Start Mail Merge button, and then click *Step-by-Step Mail Merge Wizard* at the drop-down list. The first of six Mail Merge task panes displays at the right side of the screen. Complete tasks at one pane and then display the next task pane. The options in each task pane may vary depending on the type of merge you are performing.

A data source file may need editing on a periodic basis to add or delete customer names, update fields, insert new fields, or delete existing fields. To edit a data source file, select the file using the Select Recipients button on the Mailings tab. With the data source file connected to the main document, click the Edit Recipients List button in the Start Mail Merge group. At the Mail Merge Recipients dialog box, click the data source file name in the *Data Source* list box and then click the Edit button. This displays the Edit Data Source dialog box with options for editing, adding, or deleting entries.

What You Will Do   The data source file needs updating to reflect customer changes. You will edit the data source file by deleting an entry, adding a new entry, and changing the last name of an existing customer.

Tutorial

Editing a Data
Source File

1 Open **4-FCTCruiseLtrMainDoc.docx**. (If a message displays asking if you want the document to run the SQL command, click No.)

2 Click the Mailings tab, click the Select Recipients button, and then click *Use an Existing List* at the drop-down list.

3 At the Select Data Source dialog box, navigate to the WordS4 folder and then double-click **4-FCTDataSource.mdb**.

> 4-FCTDataSource.mdb is now connected to 4-FCTCruiseLtrMainDoc.docx.

4 Click the Edit Recipient List button 🖳 in the Start Mail Merge group.

5 At the Mail Merge Recipients dialog box, click *4-FCTDataSource.mdb* in the *Data Source* list box and then click the Edit button.

6 At the Edit Data Source dialog box, click the square that displays at the beginning of the row for *Mr. and Mrs. Walter Noretto* and then click the Delete Entry button.

7 At the message that displays asking if you want to delete the entry, click Yes.

Edit Data Source
1. Click Mailings tab.
2. Click Select Recipients button.
3. Click *Use an Existing List*.
4. At Select Data Source dialog box, double-click data source file.
5. Click Edit Recipient List button.
6. At Mail Merge Recipients dialog box, click data source file in *Data Source* list box.
7. Click Edit button.
8. Make changes at Edit Data Source dialog box.
9. Click OK.
10. Click Yes.
11. Click OK.

8 Click the New Entry button and then type the following text in the specified fields in the new record:

> Title: Ms.
> First Name: Jane
> Last Name: Goldberg
> Address Line 1: 530 Oak Street
> City: Torrance
> State: CA
> ZIP Code: 90501
> Membership: Premiere Choice
> Discount: 3 percent

9 Kristina Herron has changed her last name. To edit her name, click the last name *Herron* in the *Last Name* column and then type Taylor.

10 Click OK to close the Edit Data Source dialog box.

11 At the message asking if you want to update the recipient list, click Yes.

12 Click OK to close the Mail Merge Recipients dialog box.

13 Click the Merge & Finish button in the Finish group and then click *Edit Individual Documents* at the drop-down list.

14 At the Merge to New Document dialog box, make sure *All* is selected and then click OK.

> The main document is merged with the records in the data source file and a document displays with four merged letters.

15 Save the merged letters in the normal manner and name the document **4-FCTEditedDSLtrs**.

16 Print and then close **4-FCTEditedDSLtrs.docx**.

17 Save and then close **FCTCruiseLtrMainDoc.docx**.

Edit Data Source

To edit items in your data source, type your changes in the ta
recipient list fields to which they have been matched (in parer

Data source being edited: 4-FCTDataSource.mdb

Title	First Name	Last Name	Addr
Mrs.	Kristina	Taylor	432(
Ms.	Cathy	Washington	321
Mr.	Jerome	Ellington	1288
Ms.	Jane	Goldberg	530 (

Step 9

Check Your Work — Compare your work to the model answer to ensure that you have completed the activity correctly.

In Addition

Inserting a New Field in a Data Source File

A new field can be inserted in an existing data source file. To do this, display the Edit Data Source dialog box and then click the Customize Columns button. At the Customize Address List dialog box, click the Add button. At the Add Field dialog box, type the name of the new field and then click OK. Click OK to close the Customize Address List dialog box. At the Edit Data Source dialog box, type the desired information in the new field.

Selecting Specific Records

Each record in the Mail Merge Recipients dialog box contains a check mark before the first field. If you want to select specific records for merging, remove the check marks from those records you do not want to include in the merge.

Features Summary

Feature	Ribbon Tab, Group	Button	Option
columns	Layout, Page Setup		
Columns dialog box	Layout, Page Setup		*More Columns*
drop cap	Insert, Text		
Drop Cap dialog box	Insert, Text		*Drop Cap Options*
Insert Address Block dialog box	Mailings, Write & Insert Fields		
insert file	Insert, Text		*Text from File*
Insert Greeting Line dialog box	Mailings, Write & Insert Fields		
Insert Hyperlink dialog box	Insert, Links		
insert merge field	Mailings, Write & Insert Fields		
Insert Table dialog box	Insert, Tables		*Insert Table*
merge documents	Mailings, Finish		
section break (continuous)	Layout, Page Setup		*Continuous*
select recipients	Mailings, Start Mail Merge		
shapes and lines	Insert, Illustrations		
SmartArt	Insert, Illustrations		
start mail merge	Mailings, Start Mail Merge		
table	Insert, Tables		
text box	Insert, Text		
WordArt	Insert, Text		

Workbook Section study tools and assessment activities are available in the *Workbook* ebook. These resources are designed to help you further develop and demonstrate mastery of the skills learned in this section.

INDEX

A

Account option, 5
Add Field dialog box, 115
Address Block button, 112
Add Shape button, 96
Align Center button, 102
aligning
  paragraphs, 38–39, 80–81
  vertically, 80–81
Align Left button, 39
Alignment button, 50
Align Right button, 38
Align Top Center button, 102
AutoCorrect, using, 3, 14–15
automatic numbers/bulleting,
  turning off, 47

B

background, customizing page,
  68–69
backstage area, 3–4
  options, 5
backstage view, 26, 27
Bibliography button, 78
Blank document template, 2
blank page, inserting, 71
Blank Page button, 71
Bold button, 34
borders
  adding to tables, 104
  adding to text, 54–55
  applying to page, 68–69
  changing options, 69
Borders and Shading dialog box,
  54–55
Borders button, 54
boxes, enclosing text within, 92,
  93, 95
Breaks button, 106
bullets
  inserting, 46–47
  turning off automatic, 47
Bullets button, 46

C

cells
  changing size, 102–103
  changing width, 102–103
  creating, 100–102
  described, 100
  keyboard shortcuts for selecting,
    103
  moving insertion point, 100
  word wrap feature, 100
Center button, 38
center tab symbol, 50

Change Case button, 34
Change Colors button, 97
changing width, 102–103
characters, inserting special,
  48–49
citations
  creating work cited page, 78–79
  inserting, 74–77
Clear All Formatting button, 50, 51
Click and Type, aligning
  paragraphs using, 80–81
Clip Art, inserting, sizing and
  moving, 81–83
Clipboard group, 62–63
Clipboard task pane
  choosing options, 65
  using, 64–65
Close button, 7
Close option, 5, 7
closing document, 6, 7
Collapse the Ribbon button, 2,
  3, 21
color
  adding in WordArt, 90
  changing, 97, 99
  changing theme color, 57, 67
  customizing page, 68–69
  in tables, 104–105
columns
  changing size, 102–103
  changing width, 102–103, 107
  creating, 100–101
  formatting text in, 102–103
  newspaper, 106–107
Columns button, 107
Columns dialog box, 107
company logos, creating and
  modifying using WordArt,
  90–91
continuous section breaks,
  inserting, 106
Copy button, 62
copying text, 62–63
Corrections button, 82
cover page, inserting/deleting,
  70–71
Cover Page button, 70
curve, drawing, 95
Customize Address List dialog box,
  115
Customize Columns button, 115
Cut button, 62
cutting text, 62–63

D

data source file
  described, 110
  editing, 114–115
  inserting new field, 115

for mail merge, 110
decimal tab, setting, 51
default document formatting
  changing, 56–57
  elements, 5
deleting
  tabs, 51
  text, 8–9, 10–11
Design tab, 56
dictionary, downloading, 15
display percentage, changing,
  18–19
document. See also text
  changing
    default formatting, 56–57
    display percentage, 18–19
    line and paragraph spacing,
      42–43
    views, 16–17
  closing, 6, 7
  creating, 2–4
  creating using template, 28–29
  default formatting, 5
  formatting with Font group and
    Mini toolbar, 34–35
  insert one document into another,
    106–107
  main, 110
  merging with envelopes,
    110–113
  MLA style, 74–79
  naming, 7
  navigating in, 10–11
  opening, 8–9
  previewing, 27
  printing, 4–5, 26–27
  readability, 106
  resuming reading or editing, 11
  saving, 4, 6–7
    in different format, 30–31
    in PDF format, 108–109
    as web page, 109
  scrolling in, 10–11
  section break, 106–107
  spelling and grammar check,
    12–13
document icon, 30
Draft button, 16
Draft view, 16
Drawing Tools Format tab, 91
Drop Cap button, 92
drop caps, creating, 92

E

Edit Data Source dialog box,
  114–115
editing
  data source file, 114–115
  PDF file, 31

resuming, and insertion point, 11
  while checking spelling and
    grammar, 13
Edit Recipient List button, 114
envelopes
  customizing, 85
  merging documents and,
    110–113
  preparing, 84–85
Envelopes button, 84
errors, correcting
  spelling and grammar check,
    12–13
  using AutoCorrect, 3
  words not in Spelling dictionary,
    5
Export option, 5
Extend mode, 10

F

Feedback option, 5
file extension, 4, 30
files, insert one file into another,
  106–107
File tab, 2, 3, 7
Find and Replace Dialog Box
  options
    expanded options, 23
    formatting changes, 44–45
    text changes, 22–23
finding and replacing
  formatting, 44–45
  text, 22–23
Finish & Merge button, 112
folder icon, 30
folders
  creating, 30–31
  renaming, 31
Font Color button, 35
Font dialog box, 36–37
Font Group, applying formatting to
  document using, 34–35
Font group dialog box launcher, 26
fonts
  changing theme font, 57
  default, 56
  Font dialog box, 36–37
  Font Group, 34–35
  Format Painter, 36–37
  keyboard shortcuts, 37
  types of, 35
Footer button, 73
footers
  creating own, 73
  described, 72
  inserting, 73
Format Painter, applying formatting
  with, 36–37
Format Painter button, 36–37

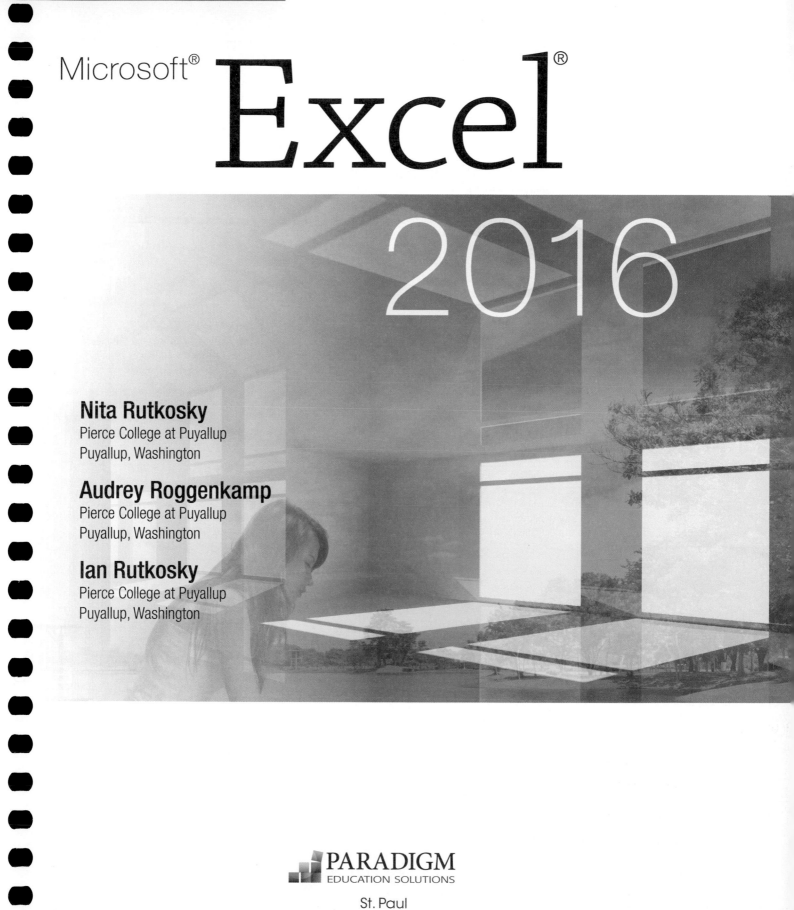

Microsoft® Excel® 2016

Nita Rutkosky
Pierce College at Puyallup
Puyallup, Washington

Audrey Roggenkamp
Pierce College at Puyallup
Puyallup, Washington

Ian Rutkosky
Pierce College at Puyallup
Puyallup, Washington

PARADIGM
EDUCATION SOLUTIONS

St. Paul

Senior Vice President	Linda Hein
Editor in Chief	Christine Hurney
Director of Production	Timothy W. Larson
Production Editors	Rachel Kats, Jen Weaverling
Cover and Text Designer	Valerie King
Copy Editor	Sarah Kearin
Senior Design and Production Specialist	Jaana Bykonich
Assistant Developmental Editors	Mamie Clark, Katie Werdick
Testers	Desiree Carvel; Ann E. Mills, Ivy Tech Community College of Indiana, Indianapolis, IN
Instructional Support Writer	Brienna McWade
Indexer	Terry Casey
Vice President Information Technology	Chuck Bratton
Digital Projects Manager	Tom Modl
Vice President Sales and Marketing	Scott Burns
Director of Marketing	Lara Weber McLellan

Care has been taken to verify the accuracy of information presented in this book. However, the authors, editors, and publisher cannot accept responsibility for Web, email, newsgroup, or chat room subject matter or content, or for consequences from application of the information in this book, and make no warranty, expressed or implied, with respect to its content.

Trademarks: Microsoft is a trademark or registered trademark of Microsoft Corporation in the United States and/or other countries. Some of the product names and company names included in this book have been used for identification purposes only and may be trademarks or registered trade names of their respective manufacturers and sellers. The authors, editors, and publisher disclaim any affiliation, association, or connection with, or sponsorship or endorsement by, such owners.

Cover Photo Credits: © whitehoune/Shutterstock.com; © manzrussali/Shutterstock.com.

We have made every effort to trace the ownership of all copyrighted material and to secure permission from copyright holders. In the event of any question arising as to the use of any material, we will be pleased to make the necessary corrections in future printings. Thanks are due to the aforementioned authors, publishers, and agents for permission to use the materials indicated.

ISBN 978-0-76386-707-2 (print)
ISBN 978-0-76386-708-9 (digital)

© 2017 by Paradigm Publishing, Inc.
875 Montreal Way
St. Paul, MN 55102
Email: educate@emcp.com
Website: ParadigmCollege.com

Printed in the United States of America

24 23 22 21 20 19 18 17 16   1 2 3 4 5 6 7 8 9 10 11 12

Contents

Excel® 2016

Microsoft Excel 2016 is a popular choice among individuals and companies to organize, analyze, and present data in columns and rows in a file called a *worksheet*. More than one worksheet can be created and saved in a file called a *workbook*. Entries are placed in a worksheet in a *cell*, which is the intersection of a column with a row. A cell is labeled with the column letter and row number, such as A1. Worksheets can be created to track, analyze, and chart any type of data that can be set up in a column and row format. Expenses, sales, assets, liabilities, grades, statistics, research study data, machine production records, weather records, and gas usage are just a few examples of the type of information that can be stored in an Excel workbook. While working in Excel, you will create and edit worksheets for the following six companies.

First Choice Travel is a travel center offering a full range of traveling services from booking flights, hotel reservations, and rental cars to offering travel seminars.

The Waterfront Bistro offers fine dining for lunch and dinner and also offers banquet facilities, a wine cellar, and catering services.

Worldwide Enterprises is a national and international distributor of products for a variety of companies and is the exclusive movie distribution agent for Marquee Productions.

Marquee Productions is involved in all aspects of creating movies from script writing and development to filming. The company produces documentaries, biographies, as well as historical and action movies.

Performance Threads maintains an inventory of rental costumes and also researches, designs, and sews special-order and custom-made costumes.

The mission of the Niagara Peninsula College Theatre Arts Division is to offer a curriculum designed to provide students with a thorough exposure to all aspects of the theatre arts.

In Section 1 you will learn how to

Create Worksheets to Analyze Data

Begin work in Excel by entering labels in columns or rows to create the worksheet layout. Next, add the values that correspond to the labels. Finally, create formulas to add, subtract, multiply, or divide to calculate the desired results. Once a worksheet has been created, the power and versatility of Excel is put to use by performing what-if analyses. What happens to net profit if sales increase by 4 percent? What happens to monthly cash flow if the wages of all employees are raised 3 percent? To answer these types of questions, edit a value and then watch Excel automatically update all other values dependent on the number changed.

Start a new worksheet by entering labels to create the worksheet layout.

	A	B	C	D	E	F	G	H	I	J	K	L
1	Payroll											
2	Week Ended: September 29, 2018											
3			Sun	Mon	Tue	Wed	Thu	Fri	Sat	Total Hours	Pay Rate	Gross Pay
4	Dayna	McGuire										
5	Heather	Kiley										
6	Pat	Soulliere										
7	Jasmine	Hill										
8	Moira	Su-Lin										
9	Carla	Modano										
10	Toni	Williams										
11	Tyler	Santini										
12	Lou	Cortez										
13	Total											

Next, add the values to record quantities, rates, or other numeric entries.

	A	B	C	D	E	F	G	H	I	J	K	L
1	Payroll											
2	Week Ended: September 22, 2018											
3			Sun	Mon	Tue	Wed	Thu	Fri	Sat	Total Hours	Pay Rate	Gross Pay
4	Dayna	McGuire	6	5	8	8	7	0	6	40	12.5	500
5	Heather	Kiley	0	8	6	8	5	5	8	40	10.25	410
6	Pat	Soulliere	8	8	0	8	7	7	0	38	10.25	389.5
7	Jasmine	Hill	8	0	8	8	0	8	6	38	11.75	446.5
8	Moira	Su-Lin	0	8	0	8	7	7	8	38	11.75	446.5
9	Carla	Cumberbatch	0	0	8	8	7	7	8	38	11.75	446.5
10	Toni	Williams	8	0	5	8	8	7	4	40	10.25	410
11	Tyler	Santini	7	0	8	8	6	7	4	40	10.25	410
12	Lou	Cortez	8	0	6	8	0	8	8	38	10.25	389.5
13	Total		45	29	49	72	47	56	52	350		3848.5

	A	B	C	D	E	F	G	H	I	J	K	L
1						Payroll						
2						Week Ended: September 22, 2018						
3			Sun	Mon	Tue	Wed	Thu	Fri	Sat	Total Hours	Pay Rate	Gross Pay
4	Dayna	McGuire	6	5	8	8	7	0	6	=SUM(C4:I4)	12.5	=J4*K4
5	Heather	Kiley	0	8	6	8	5	5	8	=SUM(C5:I5)	10.25	=J5*K5
6	Pat	Soulliere	8	8	0	8	7	7	0	=SUM(C6:I6)	10.25	=J6*K6
7	Jasmine	Hill	8	0	8	8	0	8	6	=SUM(C7:I7)	11.75	=J7*K7
8	Moira	Su-Lin	0	8	0	8	7	7	8	=SUM(C8:I8)	11.75	=J8*K8
9	Carla	Cumberbatch	0	0	8	8	7	7	8	=SUM(C9:I9)	11.75	=J9*K9
10	Toni	Williams	8	0	5	8	8	7	4	=SUM(C10:I10)	10.25	=J10*K10
11	Tyler	Santini	7	0	8	8	6	7	4	=SUM(C11:I11)	10.25	=J11*K11
12	Lou	Cortez	8	0	6	8	0	8	8	=SUM(C12:I12)	10.25	=J12*K12
13	Total		=SUM(C4:C12)	=SUM(D4:D12)	=SUM(E4:E12)	=SUM(F4:F12)	=SUM(G4:G12)	=SUM(H4:H12)	=SUM(I4:I12)	=SUM(J4:J12)		=SUM(L4:L12)

Create the formulas to add, subtract, multiply, or divide.

The desired results are shown in the finished worksheet.

	A	B	C	D	E	F	G	H	I	J	K	L
1						Payroll						
2						Week Ended: September 22, 2018						
3			Sun	Mon	Tue	Wed	Thu	Fri	Sat	Total Hours	Pay Rate	Gross Pay
4	Dayna	McGuire	6	5	8	8	7	0	6	40	$ 12.50	$ 500.00
5	Heather	Kiley	0	8	6	8	5	5	8	40	$ 10.25	$ 410.00
6	Pat	Soulliere	8	8	0	8	7	7	0	38	$ 10.25	$ 389.50
7	Jasmine	Hill	8	0	8	8	0	8	6	38	$ 11.75	$ 446.50
8	Moira	Su-Lin	0	8	0	8	7	7	8	38	$ 11.75	$ 446.50
9	Carla	Cumberbatch	0	0	8	8	7	7	8	38	$ 11.75	$ 446.50
10	Toni	Williams	8	0	5	8	8	7	4	40	$ 10.25	$ 410.00
11	Tyler	Santini	7	0	8	8	6	7	4	40	$ 10.25	$ 410.00
12	Lou	Cortez	8	0	6	8	0	8	8	38	$ 10.25	$ 389.50
13	Total		45	29	49	72	47	56	52	350		$3,848.50

In Section 2 you will learn how to

Edit and Format Worksheets

Excel provides formatting attributes and add color that enhance the appearance of a worksheet and draws a reader's attention to important titles, totals, or other results. Apply a theme which coordinates colors, fonts, and effects to create a worksheet with a professional appearance in just a few mouse clicks. A variety of formats, grouped into categories, are available for numbers, dates, and times. Insert an object such as an image or a logo to enhance a worksheet or add a corporate identity.

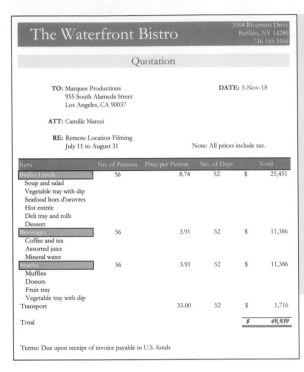

Apply formatting enhancements including:

- adding borders
- adding fill color
- adjusting row height
- adjusting column width
- applying a cell style
- applying a theme
- changing text alignment within cells
- changing font, font size, font color
- changing font attributes to bold and/or italic
- indenting text within a cell
- formatting numbers

Contact Name	Contact Phone	Event	Date	Room	Guests	Special Menu	Price Per Person
Cecily Hillmore	716 555 6598	Business Meeting	1/15/2018	Starlake	42	No	23.95
Frances Corriveau	716 555 3256	Birthday Party	1/18/2018	Westview	82	Yes	29.95
Orlando Fagan	716 555 3694	25th Wedding Anniversary	3/14/2018	Westview	95	Yes	29.95
Kim Pockovic	905 555 3698	Birthday Party	3/21/2018	Westview	65	Yes	36.95
Lane Gill	416 555 3264	Business Meeting	3/25/2018	Starlake	55	No	22.95
Percy Bresque	716 555 1248	50th Wedding Anniversary	4/12/2018	Westview	102	Yes	35.95
Max Santore	905 555 3264	Wedding	4/25/2018	Sunset	188	Yes	27.95
Omar Hamid	716 555 8796	Engagement Party	5/10/2018	Sunset	67	Yes	29.95
Jack Torrance	716 555 1469	Business Meeting	5/15/2018	Westview	34	No	24.95
Dana Russell	716 555 4965	Birthday Party	5/30/2018	Starlake	54	No	28.95
Walter Szucs	905 555 6998	Birthday Party	6/6/2018	Starlake	84	No	34.95
Nicole Griffin	905 555 4166	25th Wedding Anniversary	6/14/2018	Starlake	78	Yes	34.95
Zack Doucet	716 555 3488	Wedding	6/27/2018	Sunset	215	Yes	29.95
Jesse Golinsky	716 555 4218	Business Meeting	6/30/2018	Westview	60	No	25.95
Cora Jin Ping	716 555 7774	Baby Shower	7/11/2018	Sunset	75	Yes	22.95
Elizabeth McMaster	716 555 9442	Engagement Party	7/18/2018	Sunset	94	Yes	28.95
Reed Pavelich	716 555 2286	Wedding	7/25/2018	Starlake	145	Yes	34.95
Alfredo Juanitez	716 555 4668	Business Meeting	7/30/2018	Westview	37	No	24.95
Yanfang Guo	716 555 4856	50th Wedding Anniversary	8/2/2018	Starlake	62	No	34.95
Jelena Boskovic	716 555 3456	Business Meeting	8/7/2018	Westview	27	Yes	29.95
Priscilla Melo	716 555 3145	Business Meeting	8/21/2018	Westview	34	Yes	25.95
Tracie McIntyre	716 555 3496	Birthday Party	9/5/2018	Sunset	26	No	22.95
Krista Pressey	716 555 7469	50th Wedding Anniversary	9/13/2018	Sunset	95	No	28.95
Langford Hill	716 555 8798	Wedding	9/19/2018	Starlake	185	No	34.95
Naomi Sayers	905 555 3486	Wedding	10/10/2018	Starlake	245	Yes	24.95
Lesley Reedman	716 555 4123	Wedding	10/18/2018	Westview	110	Yes	34.95
Mitchell Langley	905 555 4637	Wedding	11/14/2018	Sunset	85	Yes	29.95
Sally Ramirez	716 555 9648	Engagement Party	12/5/2018	Starlake	34	No	25.95

Insert images, display gridlines, and apply shading to enhance the appearance of a worksheet.

In Section 3 you will learn how to

Use Function Formulas and Add Visual Elements

Excel's functions make the task of writing formulas easier. Functions are grouped into categories such as statistical, financial, date, and logical. Excel provides over 300 prebuilt formulas to perform calculations. The Insert Function dialog box is available to assist with locating and creating a function. Create charts from data to emphasize trends or compare data sets. Add emphasis to worksheets or charts by drawing arrows and adding text boxes.

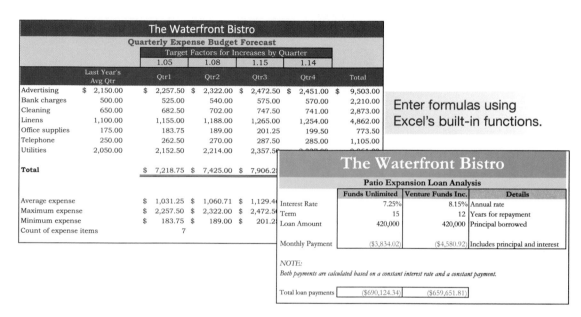

The Waterfront Bistro
Quarterly Expense Budget Forecast

	Last Year's Avg Qtr	Qtr1	Qtr2	Qtr3	Qtr4	Total
Target Factors for Increases by Quarter		1.05	1.08	1.15	1.14	
Advertising	$ 2,150.00	$ 2,257.50	$ 2,322.00	$ 2,472.50	$ 2,451.00	$ 9,503.00
Bank charges	500.00	525.00	540.00	575.00	570.00	2,210.00
Cleaning	650.00	682.50	702.00	747.50	741.00	2,873.00
Linens	1,100.00	1,155.00	1,188.00	1,265.00	1,254.00	4,862.00
Office supplies	175.00	183.75	189.00	201.25	199.50	773.50
Telephone	250.00	262.50	270.00	287.50	285.00	1,105.00
Utilities	2,050.00	2,152.50	2,214.00	2,357.50		
Total		$ 7,218.75	$ 7,425.00	$ 7,906.2		
Average expense		$ 1,031.25	$ 1,060.71	$ 1,129.4		
Maximum expense		$ 2,257.50	$ 2,322.00	$ 2,472.5		
Minimum expense		$ 183.75	$ 189.00	$ 201.2		
Count of expense items		7				

Enter formulas using Excel's built-in functions.

The Waterfront Bistro
Patio Expansion Loan Analysis

	Funds Unlimited	Venture Funds Inc.	Details
Interest Rate	7.25%	8.15%	Annual rate
Term	15	12	Years for repayment
Loan Amount	420,000	420,000	Principal borrowed
Monthly Payment	($3,834.02)	($4,580.92)	Includes principal and interest

NOTE:
Both payments are calculated based on a constant interest rate and a constant payment.

Total loan payments	($690,124.34)	($659,651.81)

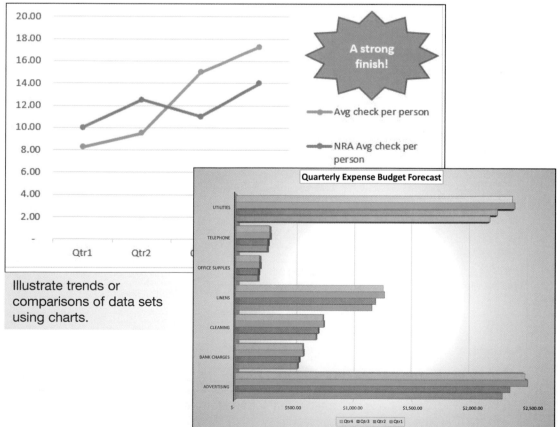

Illustrate trends or comparisons of data sets using charts.

A strong finish!

—— Avg check per person

—— NRA Avg check per person

Quarterly Expense Budget Forecast

In Section 4 you will learn how to

Work with Multiple Worksheets and Tables

Easily manage large amounts of data in Excel by separating the data into different worksheets. Worksheets can be copied or moved to rearrange the order and logically organized by renaming and applying a tab color to the sheet tabs. Formulas can be created that reference cells in other worksheets or a cell can be linked to another worksheet to ensure the data flows from one worksheet to another. A list can be formatted as a table, which can be sorted, filtered, and formatted as a separate entity within a worksheet.

Organize large amounts of data in smaller worksheets.

Create formulas and link cells to summarize worksheets.

The Waterfront Bistro
Catering Contracts

First Name	Last Name	Contact Phone	Event	Date	Room	Guests	Special Menu	Price per Person	Contract Total
Nicole	Griffin	905 555 4166	25th Wedding Anniversary	6/17/2018	Starlake	54	Yes	31.95	$ 1,725.30
Dana	Russell	716 555 4965	Birthday Party	5/30/2018	Starlake	36	No	26.95	$ 970.20
Walter	Szucs	905 555 6998	Birthday Party	6/10/2018	Starlake	42	No	28.95	$ 1,215.90
Sofia	Delgado	716 555 8465	Birthday Party	8/10/2018	Starlake	55	No	21.95	$ 1,207.25
Carlotta	Balducci	716 555 9665	Birthday Party	8/22/2018	Starlake	62	Yes	25.95	$ 1,608.90
Sonora	Yee	716 555 2668	Birthday Party	12/31/2018	Starlake	73	Yes	31.95	$ 2,332.35
Cecily	Hillmore	716 555 6598	Business Meeting	1/15/2018	Starlake	35	No	21.95	$ 768.25
Lane	Gill	416 555 3264	Business Meeting	3/29/2018	Starlake	71	No	21.95	$ 1,558.45
Mei-Yin	Zhang	716 555 2121	Business Meeting	12/1/2018	Starlake	28	Yes	31.95	$ 894.60
Cristian	Martinez	716 555 4331	Business Meeting	12/15/2018	Starlake	18	No	31.95	$ 575.10
Bianca	Vargas	716 555 3884	Engagement Party	10/15/2018	Starlake	40	Yes	31.95	$ 1,278.00
Reed	Pavelich	716 555 2286	Wedding	7/25/2018	Starlake	110	Yes	31.95	$ 3,514.50
Total						624		28.28	$ 17,648.80

Format a list as a table to filter and format the list as a separate entity.

Analyzing Data Using Excel

Data Files	Before beginning section work, copy the ExcelS1 folder to your storage medium and then make ExcelS1 the active folder.

Skills

- Start Excel and identify features in the Excel window
- Save a workbook using Save and Save As
- Close a workbook and close Excel
- Select cells
- Enter data
- Navigate a worksheet
- Scroll in a worksheet
- Use the fill handle to enter data
- Enter formulas
- Create a formula using SUM

- Copy a formula
- Editing data
- Use Undo and Redo
- Apply basic formatting to a worksheet
- Display formulas in a worksheet
- Use Tell Me feature
- Use the Help feature
- Change the page orientation to landscape
- Preview and print a worksheet

Precheck	Check your current skills to help focus your study of the skills taught in this section.

Projects Overview

 Create a payroll worksheet, create a condensed quarterly income statement.

 Create a projected distribution revenue schedule for a new movie release.

 Complete an estimated travel costs worksheet.

 Create an international student registration report and a target enrollment report.

 Create a quarterly sales report and a bookings-by-city report.

 If you are a SNAP user, launch the Precheck and Tutorials from your Assignments page.

Model Answers	Preview the model answers for an overview of the projects you will complete in the section activities.

Excel is a spreadsheet application that is used to organize numerical and financial data and to analyze and evaluate information. Information is created in Excel in a worksheet and is saved in a file called a *workbook*. A workbook can contain several worksheets. Imagine a worksheet as a page with horizontal and vertical lines drawn in a grid representing columns and rows. Data is entered into a cell, which is the intersection of a column with a row. Columns are lettered A to Z, AA to AZ, BA to BZ, and so on. The last column in the worksheet is labeled *XFD*. Rows are numbered 1, 2, 3, and so on. A column letter and a row number identify each cell. For example, A1 is the cell address for the intersection of column A with row 1. By default, an Excel workbook contains one worksheet labeled *Sheet1*. Additional sheets can be inserted as needed.

What You Will Do   You have been asked to begin creating a weekly payroll report for The Waterfront Bistro by opening a blank workbook, entering data, printing the worksheet, and then closing the workbook and Excel.

Tutorial
Opening a Blank Workbook

Tutorial
Exploring the Excel Screen

Tutorial
Saving with a New Name

Tutorial
Closing a Workbook and Closing Excel

1 At the Windows 10 desktop, click the Start button.

2 At the Start menu, click the Excel 2016 tile.

Depending on your system configuration, this step may vary.

3 At the Excel 2016 opening screen, click the *Blank workbook* template.

4 At the Excel screen, identify the various features by comparing your screen with the one shown in Figure 1.1. If necessary, maximize the Excel window. Depending on your screen resolution, your screen may vary slightly. Refer to Table 1.1 for a description of the screen features.

Figure 1.1 The Excel Screen

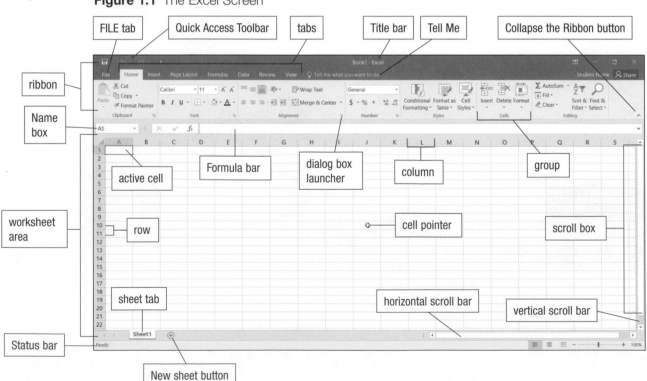

Table 1.1 Excel Screen Features

Feature	Description
active cell	location in the worksheet that will display typed data or that will be affected by a command
cell pointer	select cells when you see this icon by clicking or dragging the mouse
Collapse the Ribbon button	click to remove the ribbon; double-click a tab to redisplay the ribbon
dialog box or task pane launcher	click the downward-pointing diagonal arrow at the bottom right in a group to open a dialog box or task pane with more options for that group
File tab	displays the backstage area that contains options for working with and managing files
Formula bar	displays the contents stored in the active cell
group	area on the ribbon defined by separators that contains similar buttons or features
Name box	displays the active cell address or name assigned to active cell
New sheet button	click the button to insert a new worksheet in the workbook
Quick Access Toolbar	contains buttons for commonly used commands that can be executed with a single mouse click
ribbon	area containing the tabs with commands and buttons divided into groups
Scroll bar	used to scroll horizontally or vertically in a worksheet
sheet tab	identifies the worksheet in the workbook
Status bar	displays current mode, action messages, view buttons, and Zoom slider bar
tabs	contains commands and buttons organized into groups
Title bar	displays workbook name followed by *Excel*
vertical and horizontal scroll bars	used to view various parts of the worksheet beyond the current screen
worksheet area	contains cells used to create the worksheet

5 With cell A1 the active cell, type Payroll as the title for the new worksheet.

> When you type a new entry in a cell, the entry appears in the Formula bar as well as within the active cell in the worksheet area. To end a cell entry, press the Tab key or Enter key to move to another cell in the worksheet, or click the Enter button on the Formula bar.

6 Press the Enter key.

7 With cell A2 the active cell, type Week Ended: September 29, 2018 and then press the Enter key.

> The entry in cell A2 is overflowing into columns B, C, and D. You can allow a label to spill over into adjacent columns as long as you do not plan to enter other data in the overflow cells.

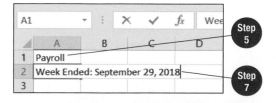

8 Click the File tab.

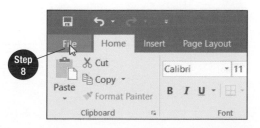

9 Click the *Print* option.

> The Print backstage area contains options, galleries, and buttons for printing the active worksheet.

10 Click the Print button.

11 Click the File tab and then click the *Save As* option.

> To save a workbook with a different name (other than *Book1.xlsx*), use the *Save As* option. Saving a workbook with a different name is useful when you want to preserve the original file.

12 At the Save As backstage area, click the *Browse* option.

13 At the Save As dialog box, click the removable disk that contains the ExcelS1 folder in the Navigation pane.

14 Double-click the *ExcelS1* folder in the Content pane.

15 Click in the *File name* text box.

16 Type the file name 1-Payroll and then click the Save button or press the Enter key.

> Press the F12 function key to display the Save As dialog box without displaying the Save As backstage area.

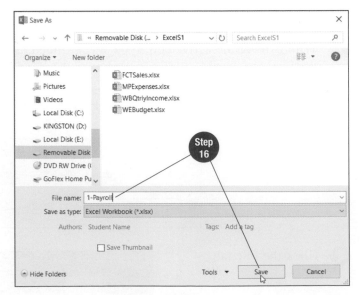

Open Excel
1. Click Start button.
2. Click Excel 2016 tile.

Enter Data
1. Make cell active.
2. Type data.

Print Workbook
1. Click File tab.
2. Click *Print* option.
3. Click Print button.

Save Workbook with New Name
1. Click File tab.
2. Click *Save As* option.
3. Click *Browse* option.
4. Navigate to folder.
5. Click in the *File name* text box.
6. Type workbook name.
7. Click Save or press Enter.

Close Workbook
1. Click File tab.
2. Click *Close* option.

Close Excel
Click Close button.

17 Click the File tab and then click the *Close* option to close the workbook.

When no workbooks are open, Excel displays a blank gray screen.

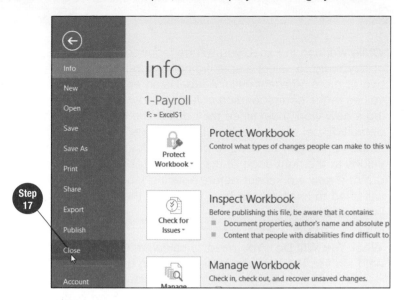

18 Click the Close button in the upper right corner of the Excel window to close Excel and return to the Windows 10 desktop.

Check Your Work Compare your work to the model answer to ensure that you have completed the activity correctly.

In Addition

Using AutoComplete

The AutoComplete feature in Excel will complete text entries for you as you start to type a new entry in a cell. If the first few letters that you type match another entry in the column, Excel automatically fills in the remaining text. Press the Tab key, the Enter key, or one of the arrow keys to accept the text Excel suggests, or continue typing the correct text. You can turn off AutoComplete by clicking the File tab and then clicking *Options*. Click *Advanced* in the left panel of the Excel Options dialog box, click the *Enable AutoComplete for cell values* check box to remove the check mark, and then click OK.

While working in Excel, you will be required to select cells in a worksheet. Use the mouse or keyboard to select a specific cell or a range of cells. A range of cells is a collection of two or more adjacent cells. A label is an entry in a cell that helps the reader relate to the values in the corresponding column or row. Labels are generally entered first when creating a new worksheet since they define the layout of the data in the columns and rows. By default, Excel aligns labels at the left edge of the column. A value is a number, formula, or function that can be used to perform calculations in the worksheet. By default, Excel aligns values at the right edge of the column. Take a few moments to plan or sketch out the layout of a new worksheet before entering labels and values. Think about the calculations you will need to execute and how to display the data so that it will be easily understood and interpreted.

Tutorial
Opening a Workbook from a Removable Disk

Tutorial
Selecting Cells

Tutorial
Entering Data

Tutorial
Saving with the Same Name

What You Will Do   You need to calculate gross pay in the payroll worksheet for the hourly paid staff at The Waterfront Bistro. Begin by entering labels and values.

1 At the Windows 10 desktop, click the Start button and then click the Excel 2016 tile.

2 Click the <u>Open Other Workbooks</u> link at the bottom of the Recent list to display the Open backstage area.

> The Open backstage area contains options, buttons, and lists for opening workbooks saved on the computer, OneDrive, and other locations.

3 Click the *Browse* option.

4 At the Open dialog box, navigate to the folder in which you saved the *1-Payroll* workbook.

5 Click *1-Payroll.xlsx* in the Content pane and then click the Open button.

6 With cell A3 the active cell, press the Down Arrow key to make cell A4 active (surrounded by a thick green border).

> The arrow keys, along with other keys, are used to make a different cell active. Refer to Table 1.2 for information on how to make a specific cell active using the keyboard.

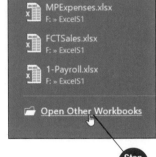

Table 1.2 Keyboard Movement Commands

Press	To move to
Alt + Page Down	one screen to the right
Alt + Page Up	one screen to the left
Arrow keys	one cell up, down, left, or right
Ctrl + Home	first cell in worksheet (cell A1)
Ctrl + End	last cell in worksheet
Home	beginning of row
Page Down	down one screen
Page Up	up one screen

Open from Removable Disk
1. Click File tab.
2. Click *Open* option.
3. Click *Browse* option.
4. Click removable disk.
5. Double-click folder.
6. Click workbook.
7. Click Open or press Enter.

Select Cell
1. Position mouse pointer over cell.
2. Click in cell.
OR
Use arrow keys.

Enter Data
1. Make cell active.
2. Type data.

Save Workbook with Same Name
Click Save button on Quick Access Toolbar.
OR
1. Click File tab.
2. Click *Save* option.

7 Type Dayna, press the Tab key, and then type McGuire.

Pressing the Tab key makes the cell to the right of the current cell active.

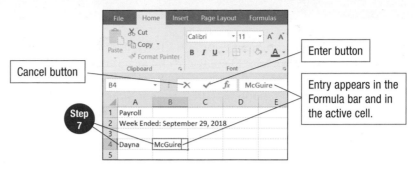

8 Click in cell J3 to make it active.

Use the mouse to select a specific cell by clicking in the desired cell when the mouse pointer displays as a white cross.

9 Type Total, press Alt + Enter, and then type Hours.

Pressing Alt + Enter inserts a line break in the cell, which places whatever is typed next on the next line. The row height will automatically adjust to accomodate the two lines of text.

10 Enter the remaining labels as shown below by making the appropriate cell active, typing the label, and then using the mouse or keyboard to make the next cell active. (Do not complete the labels for the days of the week beyond *Sun*, as this will be completed in the next activity.)

11 Click the Save button 🖫 on the Quick Access Toolbar.

Clicking the Save button on the Quick Access Toolbar saves the workbook with the same name, which overwrites the original file with the changes made in this activity.

Check Your Work ▷ Compare your work to the model answer to ensure that you have completed the activity correctly.

In Addition

Selecting Multiple Cells

A range of adjacent or nonadjacent cells is selected using the keyboard and/or mouse. Select a range of adjacent cells with the mouse by clicking in the first cell and holding down the left mouse button, dragging into the last cell, and then releasing the mouse button. Adjacent cells are selected using the keyboard by making the first cell in the range active, pressing and holding down the Shift key, pressing the arrow key in the desired direction until the last cell is selected, and then releasing the mouse button. To select nonadjacent cells, press and hold down the Ctrl key, click in the desired cells, and then release the Ctrl key.

Excel provides a variety of methods to quickly navigate a worksheet as you enter and edit data. The Name box (displays to the left of the Formula bar) and the Go To dialog box are used to navigate to a specific cell or range. A worksheet can also be navigated using keyboard shortcuts, such as Ctrl + Home. Worksheets can contain data that may not all fit in the worksheet area. Change what cells are visible by scrolling horizontally or vertically in the worksheet. To scroll, use the horizontal and vertical scroll bars, which display on the bottom right and right edge of the window. The scroll bars contain scroll buttons that are used to move the view by one column or row. The scroll bars also contain scroll boxes that can be clicked and dragged to change which cells are visible. The mouse wheel will also vertically scroll in a worksheet, making it more efficient to move up and down.

Tutorial
Navigating and
Scrolling

What You Will Do   You need to demonstrate that you can navigate the payroll worksheet using keyboard shortcuts, the Go To dialog box, and the Name box. You also need to demonstrate that you can scroll in the payroll worksheet.

1 With **1-Payroll.xlsx** open, press Ctrl + Home.

Pressing Ctrl + Home makes cell A1 the active cell.

2 Press the Page Down key.

Each time you press the Page Down key, you move the active cell down one screen.

3 Press the Page Up key.

Each time you press the Page Up key, you move the active cell up one screen.

4 Click the Find & Select button [🔍] in the Editing group on the Home tab and then click *Go To* at the drop-down list.

5 At the Go To dialog box, type L13 in the *Reference* text box and then click OK or press the Enter key.

Using Go To moved the position of the active cell to cell L13.

6 Use the Up, Down, Left, and Right Arrow keys on the keyboard to practice moving the active cell around the worksheet.

Pressing and holding down a directional arrow key causes the screen to scroll very quickly. Table 1.2 in the previous activity illustrates more keyboard movement commands.

Step 8

In Brief

Navigate to Cell with Go To
1. Click Find & Select button.
2. Type cell reference.
3. Click OK.

Navigate to Cell with Name Box
1. Click in Name box.
2. Type cell reference.
3. Press Enter key.

7 Click in the Name box, located to the left of the Formula bar, above cell A1.

Clicking in the Name box will highlight the current cell reference.

8 Type K3 and then press the Enter key.

Make sure you press the Enter key after typing a cell reference in the Name box, otherwise no action will occur.

9 Position the mouse pointer on the right scroll arrow at the right edge of the horizontal scroll bar and then click the left mouse button a few times to scroll to the right edge of the worksheet.

10 Position the mouse pointer on the horizontal scroll box, click and hold down the left mouse button, drag the scroll box to the left edge of the horizontal scroll bar, and then release the mouse button.

The width or height of the scroll box indicates the proportional number of the used cells in the worksheet that are visible in the current window. The position of the scroll box within the scroll bar indicates the relative location of the visible cells within the remainder of the worksheet.

Step 10

11 If possible, use the mouse wheel to scroll down in the worksheet area. Otherwise, click the Scroll Down button a few times to scroll down in the worksheet area.

12 Press Ctrl + Home to make cell A1 active.

13 Click the Save button on the Quick Access Toolbar.

In Addition

Entering Scroll Lock Mode

Historically, computers generally only had a keyboard as an input device. The mouse wasn't popular in the infancy of personal computing, so all commands and actions were accomplished on the keyboard. For example, scrolling in an application would require the user to turn on scroll lock and then use other keys such as the arrow keys to scroll in the application. This functionality still exists in Excel, which may be a more efficient way for some users to scroll in a worksheet. Turn on scroll lock mode by pressing the Scroll Lock key. The status bar will display the words *Scroll Lock* when the feature is turned on. Once scroll lock mode is on, use the following commands to scroll in the worksheet.

Keys	Scroll Lock Action
Arrow keys	Scrolls one column or row in the direction of the arrow keys used.
Page keys	Scrolls one screen up or down.
Home key	Makes the top left cell in the screen active.
End key	Makes the bottom right cell in the screen active.

When a cell is active, a thick, green border surrounds it and a small, green square displays in the bottom right corner of the border. This green square is called the *fill handle*. The fill handle is an AutoFill feature in Excel that enters repetitive, series, or patterned data. For example, you can type the first day of a week in a cell and then use the fill handle to populate the adjacent cells with the remaining days of the week. The entries that are automatically inserted in the adjacent cells are dependent on the contents of the active cell, which is called the source cell. Use the fill handle by making the source cell active, clicking the fill handle and holding down the left mouse button, dragging the pointer into the desired cell, and then releasing the mouse button.

Tutorial
Entering Data Using the Fill Handle

What You Will Do Finish entering the data in the payroll worksheet using the fill handle to enter repetitive and series data.

1 With **1-Payroll.xlsx** open, click in cell C3 to make it the active cell.

> You will use the fill handle in cell C3 to automatically enter the remaining days of the week in cells D3 through I3.

2 Point at the fill handle in cell C3. The cell pointer changes from the large white cross ✛ to a thin black cross ✚.

3 Click and hold down the left mouse button, drag the pointer into cell I3, and then release the mouse button.

> The entries *Mon* through *Sat* appear in cells D3 to I3. As you drag the pointer to the right, a green border surrounds the selected cells and a ScreenTip appears below the pointer indicating the label or value that will be inserted. When you release the left mouse button, the cells remain selected and the Auto Fill Options button appears.

4 Click in cell F4 to make it the active cell.

5 Type 8 and then click the Enter button ✓ on the Formula bar.

6 Click the fill handle in cell F4 and hold down the left mouse button, drag the pointer down into cell F12, and then release the mouse button.

> This time the active cell contained a value. The value *8* is copied to the adjacent cells.

In Brief

Use Fill Handle
1. Enter data in cell.
2. Drag fill handle into adjacent cell(s).

Use Fill Button
1. Select range including source cell.
2. Click Fill button.
3. Click option.

7 Enter the remaining values for employee hours as shown below. Use the fill handle where duplicate values appear in adjacent cells to enter the data as efficiently as possible.

	A	B	C	D	E	F	G	H	I	J
1	Payroll									
2	Week Ended: September 29, 2018									
3			Sun	Mon	Tue	Wed	Thu	Fri	Sat	Total Hours
4	Dayna	McGuire	6	5	8	8	7	0	6	
5	Heather	Kiley	0	8	6	8	5	5	8	
6	Pat	Soulliere	8	8	0	8	7	7	0	
7	Jasmine	Hill	8	0	8	8	0	8	6	
8	Moira	Su-Lin	0	8	0	8	7	7	8	
9	Carla	Modano	0	0	8	8	7	7	8	
10	Toni	Williams	8	0	0	8	8	7	4	
11	Tyler	Santini	8	0	8	8	6	7	0	
12	Lou	Cortez	8	0	6	8	0	8	8	
13	Total									

Step 7

8 Make cell K4 the active cell, type 10.25, and then press the Enter key.

9 Position the cell pointer over cell K4, click and hold down the left mouse button, drag down into cell K12, and then release the mouse button.

10 With the Home tab active, click the Fill button ⬇ in the Editing group and then click *Down* at the drop-down list.

11 Click the Save button on the Quick Access Toolbar.

Step 10

Check Your Work Compare your work to the model answer to ensure that you have completed the activity correctly.

In Addition

Using the Fill Handle

The fill handle is versatile and can be used to enter a series of values, dates, times, or other labels as a pattern. The pattern is established based on the cells you select before dragging the fill handle. In the worksheet shown below, the cells in columns C through J were all populated using the fill handle. In each row, the first two cells in columns A and B were selected and then the fill handle was dragged right into column J. Notice the variety of patterns used to extend a series.

Using the Fill Options Button

Use the Auto Fill Options button drop-down list to control how the series is entered. After dragging the fill handle, the Auto Fill Options button displays at the end of the series. Pointing at the button causes it to expand and display an arrow. Click the arrow and then select the desired fill action from the options in the drop-down list. By default, *Fill Series* is selected. Click the *Copy Cells* option to repeat the value in the first cell.

	A	B	C	D	E	F	G	H	I	J	K	L	M
1	Examples using the fill handle to create a series or pattern in adjacent cells												
2	In each row below, the first two cells were selected and then the fill handle dragged right.												
3	1	2	3	4	5	6	7	8	9	10			
4	10	20	30	40	50	60	70	80	90	100	○ Copy Cells		
5	9:00	10:00	11:00	12:00	13:00	14:00	15:00	16:00	17:00	18:00	◉ Fill Series		
6	2017	2019	2021	2023	2025	2027	2029	2031	2033	2035	○ Fill Formatting Only		
7	Quarter 1	Quarter 2	Quarter 3	Quarter 4	Quarter 1	Quarter 2	Quarter 3	Quarter 4	Quarter 1	Quarter 2	○ Fill Without Formatting		
8	Period 1	Period 4	Period 7	Period 10	Period 13	Period 16	Period 19	Period 22	Period 25	Period 28			
9	Year 1	Year 6	Year 11	Year 16	Year 21	Year 26	Year 31	Year 36	Year 41	Year 46			
10													

Activity 1.5 Entering Formulas

A formula is entered into a cell to perform mathematical calculations in a worksheet. All formulas in Excel begin with the equals sign (=) as the first character. After the equals sign, the cell addresses that contain the values you want to calculate are entered between mathematical operators. The mathematical operators are + (addition), - (subtraction), * (multiplication), / (division), and ^ (exponentiation). An example of a valid formula is =A3*B3. In this formula, the value in cell A3 is multiplied by the value in cell B3 and the result is placed in the formula cell. By including the cell address in the formula rather than typing the actual value, you can utilize the powerful recalculation feature in Excel. If you change a cell's content, the worksheet is automatically recalculated so that all values are current.

Tutorial
Entering Formulas
Using the Keyboard

Tutorial
Entering Formulas
Using the Mouse

Tutorial
Determining the Order
of Operations

What You Will Do   You will use two methods to enter formulas to calculate total hours and gross pay for the first two employees listed in the payroll worksheet for The Waterfront Bistro.

1 With **1-Payroll.xlsx** open, make cell J4 the active cell.

Begin a formula by making the cell active in which you want the result to appear.

2 Type =c4+d4+e4+f4+g4+h4+i4 and then press the Enter key.

The values in cells C4 through I4 are added and the result, *40*, is displayed in cell J4. You can type cell column letters in a formula in uppercase or lowercase letters. If you type lowercase column letters in a formula, Excel will convert the letters to uppercase when you press the Enter key or click the Enter button on the Formula bar.

Cell references are color-coded to the originating cell for quick reference and error checking.

3 Press the Up Arrow key to make cell J4 the active cell.

Notice that the result of the formula displays in the worksheet area and the formula used to calculate the result displays in the Formula bar.

4 Make cell J5 the active cell, type the formula =c5+d5+e5+f5+g5+h5+i5, and then press the Enter key.

Seem like too much typing? A more efficient way to add a series of cells is available. This method will be introduced in the next activity after you learn the pointing method for entering formulas.

5 Make cell L4 the active cell.

To calculate gross pay, you need to multiply the total hours by the pay rate. In Steps 6 through 10, you will enter this formula using the pointing method.

Enter a Formula Using Keyboard
1. Make formula cell active.
2. Type =.
3. Type first cell address.
4. Type operator symbol.
5. Type second cell address.
6. Continue Steps 3–5 until finished.
7. Press Enter or click Enter button.

Enter a Formula Using Pointing Method
1. Make formula cell active.
2. Type =.
3. Click first cell.
4. Type operator symbol.
5. Click second cell.
6. Repeat Steps 3–5 until finished.
7. Press Enter or click Enter button.

6 Type the equals sign (=).

7 Click in cell J4.

A moving dashed border (called a *marquee*) displays around cell J4, indicating it is the cell included in the formula, and the cell address is added to the formula cell (J4) with a blinking insertion point after the reference. The word *Point* displays at the left side of the Status bar.

8 Type an asterisk (*), which is the multiplication operator.

The marquee surrounding cell J4 disappears and cell J4 is color-coded with the cell reference *J4* within the formula cell.

9 Click in cell K4.

Marquee displays around cell K4 in Step 9.

10 Click the Enter button on the Formula bar.

The result, *410*, is displayed in cell L4. In Activity 1.9, you will learn how to display two decimal places for cells containing dollar values.

11 Click in cell K4, type 12.50, and then press the Enter key.

When the value in cell K4 was changed, the result of the formula in cell L4 changed as well.

12 Click the Save button on the Quick Access Toolbar.

Check Your Work ▷ Compare your work to the model answer to ensure that you have completed the activity correctly.

In Addition

Determining the Order of Operations

If you include several operators in a formula, Excel calculates the result using the order of operations as follows: negations (e.g., -1) first, then percents (%), then exponentiations (^), then multiplication and division (* and /), and finally addition and subtraction (+ and -). If a formula contains more than one operator at the same level of precedence—for example, both an addition and a subtraction operation—Excel calculates the equation from left to right. To change the order of operations, put parentheses around the part of the formula you want calculated first.

Formula	Calculation
=B5*C5/D5	Both operators are at the same level of precedence—Excel will multiply the value in B5 times the value in C5 and then divide the result by the value in D5.
=B5+B6+B7*C10	Multiplication takes precedence over addition, so Excel will first multiply the value in B7 by the value in C10. Excel will then take the value in B5 and add to it the value in B6 and then add the result of the multiplication operation.
=(B5+B6+B7)*C10	Because of the parentheses, Excel will first add the values in B5 through B7 and then multiply this sum by the value in C10.

The formulas to calculate the hours worked by the first two employees were lengthy. A more efficient way to calculate the total hours for Dayna McGuire in cell J4 would be to enter the formula =SUM(C4:I4). This formula includes one of Excel's built-in functions called SUM. A function is a preprogrammed formula. The structure of a formula utilizing a function begins with the equals sign (=), followed by the name of the function, and then the argument. *Argument* is the term given to the values identified within parentheses. In the example provided, the argument C4:I4 contains the starting cell and the ending cell separated by a colon (:). The colon is used to indicate the range to be summed; a range is a rectangular-shaped block of adjacent cells. Since the SUM function is used frequently, an AutoSum button is available on the Home tab.

The Waterfront BISTRO

Tutorial
Entering Formulas Using the AutoSum Button

What You Will Do   You decide to use a more efficient method of payroll calculation, so you will use the SUM function to complete the hours worked for the payroll worksheet.

1   With **1-Payroll.xlsx** open, make cell J4 the active cell and then press the Delete key.

This deletes the cell contents. There was nothing wrong with the formula already entered in cell J4. You are deleting it so that the formulas in the completed worksheet will be consistent.

2   Click the AutoSum button ∑ in the Editing group on the Home tab. (Do not click the AutoSum button arrow.)

A moving marquee surrounds cells C4 through I4 and a ScreenTip appears below the formula cell indicating the correct format for the SUM function. Excel enters the formula =SUM(C4:I4) in cell J4. The suggested range C4:I4 is selected within the formula so that you can highlight a different range with the mouse if the suggested range is not correct.

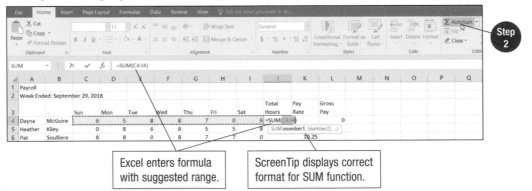

Excel enters formula with suggested range.

ScreenTip displays correct format for SUM function.

3   Press the Enter key.

Since the range Excel suggests is the correct range, you can finish the formula by pressing the Enter key or by clicking the Enter button on the Formula bar.

4   With cell J5 the active cell, press the Delete key to delete the existing formula in the cell.

5   Click the AutoSum button. When Excel displays the formula =SUM(C5:I5), click the Enter button on the Formula bar.

6   Make cell J6 the active cell and then click the AutoSum button.

This time the range of cells Excel is suggesting to add (J4:J5) is the wrong range. When you click the AutoSum button, Excel looks for multiple values in the cells immediately above the active cell. In this case, multiple values appear above cell J6, so Excel inserts J4:J5 as the range in the SUM formula.

In Brief

Enter SUM Function
1. Make result cell active.
2. Click AutoSum button.
3. Press Enter, or drag to select correct range and then press Enter.

OR
1. Drag to select range of cells to be summed including result cell.
2. Click AutoSum button.

7 Position the cell pointer over cell C6, click and hold down the left mouse button, drag the pointer into cell I6, and then release the mouse button.

8 Press the Enter key.

Now that you have seen how the AutoSum button operates, you already know that the suggested range for the next employee's total hours will be incorrect.

9 Position the cell pointer over cell C7, click and hold down the left mouse button, drag the pointer into cell J7, and then release the mouse button.

Notice you are including cell J7, the cell that will display the result, in the range of cells.

10 Click the AutoSum button.

The result, *38*, appears in cell J7.

11 Click in cell J7 and then look at the formula the SUM function created in the Formula bar: *=SUM(C7:I7)*.

Since Excel created the correct SUM formula from a range of selected cells, you decide to try calculating total hours for more than one employee in one step using the method employed in Steps 9 and 10 but with an expanded range.

12 Position the cell pointer over cell C8, click and hold down the left mouse button, drag the pointer into cell J12, and then release the mouse button.

13 Click the AutoSum button.

	A	B	C	D	E	F	G	H	I	J	
1	Payroll										
2	Week Ended: September 29, 2018										
3			Sun	Mon	Tue	Wed	Thu	Fri	Sat	Total Hours	Pay Rate
4	Dayna	McGuire	6	5	8	8	7	0	6	40	
5	Heather	Kiley	0	8	6	8	5	5	8	40	
6	Pat	Soulliere	8	8	0	8	7	7	0	38	
7	Jasmine	Hill	8	0	8	8	0	8	6	38	
8	Moira	Su-Lin	0	8	0	8	7	7	8	38	
9	Carla	Modano	0	0	8	8	7	7	8	38	
10	Toni	Williams	8	0	0	8	8	7	4	35	
11	Tyler	Santini	8	0	8	8	6	7	0	37	
12	Lou	Cortez	8	0	6	8	0	8	8	38	
13	Total										

Steps 12-13

14 Click in cells J8, J9, J10, J11, and J12 to confirm that the correct formulas appear in the Formula bar.

15 Click the Save button on the Quick Access Toolbar.

Check Your Work Compare your work to the model answer to ensure that you have completed the activity correctly.

Many times you may create a worksheet in which several formulas are basically the same. For example, in the payroll worksheet, the formula to total the hours for Dayna McGuire is =SUM(C4:I4), the formula for Heather Kiley is =SUM(C5:I5), and so on. The only difference between the two formulas is the row number. Whenever formulas are this similar, you can use the Copy and Paste feature or the fill handle to copy the formula from one cell to another. The cell containing the original formula is called the source, and the cell(s) to which the formula is copied is called the destination. When the formula is pasted, Excel automatically changes column letters or row numbers to reflect the destination location. By default, Excel assumes relative addressing, which means that cell addresses update relative to the destination.

The Waterfront
BISTRO

Tutorial ▶
Copying Formulas

What You Will Do   To simplify your completion of the payroll worksheet, you will copy formulas using two methods: Copy and Paste and the fill handle.

1 With **1-Payroll.xlsx** open, make cell L4 the active cell.

This cell contains the formula =J4*K4 to calculate the gross pay for Dayna McGuire. You will copy this formula to the remaining cells in column L to finish the *Gross Pay* column.

2 Click the Copy button in the Clipboard group on the Home tab. (Do not click the Copy button arrow.)

A moving marquee surrounds the active cell indicating that the source contents have been copied to the Clipboard, which is a temporary storage location. The source being copied is the formula =J4*K4, not the result value, *500*.

3 Select the range L5:L12. To do this, position the cell pointer over cell L5, click and hold down the left mouse button, drag the pointer to cell L12, and then release the mouse button.

marquee indicating source range

4 Click the Paste button in the Clipboard group. (Do not click the button arrow.)

Excel copies the formula to the selected cells and displays the results. The Paste Options button (Ctrl) ▼ also appears. Clicking the Paste Options button will display a drop-down list with various alternatives for pasting the data. The moving marquee remains around the source cell and the destination cells remain highlighted. The moving marquee disappears as soon as you start another activity or press the Esc key.

Paste Options button

5 Press the Esc key to remove the marquee and the Paste Options button, click in cell L5, and then look at the entry in the Formula bar: =J5*K5.

The row number in the source formula was increased by one to reflect the destination. The actions you completed in Steps 1 through 4 are called relative copying.

6 Use the Down Arrow key to check the remaining formulas in column L.

7 Make cell C13 the active cell.

In Brief

Copy Formula
1. Make source cell active.
2. Click Copy button.
3. Select destination cell(s).
4. Click Paste button.

Copy Formula with Fill Handle
1. Make source cell active.
2. Click and hold down fill handle.
3. Drag into last cell.
4. Release mouse button.

8 Click the AutoSum button and then click the Enter button on the Formula bar.

The SUM function inserts the formula *=SUM(C4:C12)*. Next, you will copy the formula using the fill handle.

9 Drag the fill handle in cell C13 into cell L13.

When the active cell contains a formula, dragging the fill handle causes Excel to copy the formula and change cell references relative to each destination location.

	A	B	C	D	E	F	G	H	I	J	K	L
1	Payroll											
2	Week Ended: September 29, 2018											
3			Sun	Mon	Tue	Wed	Thu	Fri	Sat	Total Hours	Pay Rate	Gross Pay
4	Dayna	McGuire	6	5	8	8	7	0	6	40	12.5	500
5	Heather	Kiley	0	8	6	8	5	5	8	40	10.25	410
6	Pat	Soulliere	8	8	0	8	7	7	0	38	10.25	389.5
7	Jasmine	Hill	8	0	8	8	0	8	6	38	10.25	389.5
8	Moira	Su-Lin	0	8	0	8	7	7	8	38	10.25	389.5
9	Carla	Modano	0	0	8	8	7	7	8	38	10.25	389.5
10	Toni	Williams	8	0	0	8	8	7	4	35	10.25	358.75
11	Tyler	Santini	8	0	8	8	6	7	0	37	10.25	379.25
12	Lou	Cortez	8	0	6	8	0	8	8	38	10.25	389.5
13	Total		46	29	44	72	47	56	48	342	94.5	3595.5
14												

Step 9

10 Make cell K13 the active cell and then press the Delete key.

The sum of the *Pay Rate* column is not useful information.

11 Make cell D13 the active cell and look at the entry in the Formula bar: *=SUM(D4:D12)*.

The column letter in the source formula was changed to reflect the destination.

12 Use the Right Arrow key to check the formulas in the remaining columns.

13 Click the Save button on the Quick Access Toolbar.

Check Your Work Compare your work to the model answer to ensure that you have completed the activity correctly.

In Addition

Understanding Copy and Paste versus Fill

What is the difference between copying and pasting and using the fill handle? When you use the Copy button, the contents of the source cell(s) are placed in the Clipboard. The data will remain in the Clipboard and can be pasted several times in the current worksheet, into any other worksheet that is open, or into an open file in another application. Use the Copy and Paste buttons when the formula is to be inserted more than once or into nonadjacent cells. Use the fill handle when the formula is only being copied to adjacent cells.

Data in Excel can be edited after it is entered. Once data is edited in a cell, any formulas that use the data in the edited cell will update according to the new data. This feature is useful when you want to forecast, estimate, or otherwise test how certain key variables affect the overall worksheet. Edit a cell by double-clicking in the cell and then using the keyboard to make changes. Also, you can click in a cell to make it active and then edit its contents in the Formula bar. Although it's not technically considered editing, you can replace a cell's contents by clicking in the cell to make it active and then typing the new data. After you are finished editing the contents of a cell, make sure you press the Enter key or click the Enter button on the Formula bar.

Use the Undo button on the Quick Access Toolbar to reverse the last action. Use the Redo button to restore an action that was reversed using the Undo button. Excel stores up to 100 actions that can be undone or redone, and you can repeat actions as many times as you need. Some actions (such as Save) cannot be reversed with Undo.

The Waterfront BISTRO

Tutorial
Editing Data

Tutorial
Using Undo and Redo

What You Will Do   You have been provided updated information on the employee hours and pay rates. Edit the workbook so that it contains the new information.

1   With **1-Payroll.xlsx** open, double-click in cell B6.

> Double-clicking in a cell places the insertion point in the cell in the approximate point where you double-clicked.

2   Press the Right Arrow key or Left Arrow key until the insertion point is between the two *l*s in the text *Soulliere*.

3   Press the Backspace or Delete key to remove one of the *l*s so that the text displays as *Souliere* and then press the Enter key.

4   Make cell A2 the active cell.

5   Click in the Formula bar to position the insertion point in it and then press the Right Arrow key or Left Arrow key until the insertion point is between the numbers *2* and *9* in the date.

6   Press the Delete key to remove the 9, type 2, and then click the Enter button on the Formula bar.

> The text in cell A2 should now display as *Week Ended: September 22, 2018*.

7   Click in cell B9 to make it active, type Cumberbatch, and then press the Enter key.

> The last name *Modano*, previously in cell B9, is replaced with the new last name *Cumberbatch*. Replacing data in a cell instead of editing it manually is sometimes more efficient.

Edit Data
1. Double-click in cell.
2. Make edits with keyboard.
3. Press Enter key.
OR
1. Make cell active.
2. Make edits in Formula bar.
3. Click Enter button.

8 Click in cell E10 to make it active, type 5, and then press the Enter key.

9 Make cell I11 the active cell, type 4, and then press the Enter key.

The total hours for Tyler Santini, displayed in cell J11, are one hour over 40 hours total for the week, which is a mistake in the payroll.

10 Click the Undo button ↶ on the Quick Access Toolbar.

Clicking the Undo button reverses the replacement of the 0 by 4 in the previous step.

11 Click the Redo button ↷ on the Quick Access Toolbar.

You realize that you still need to adjust some of the other data for Tyler Santini and that he in fact did work four hours on Saturday.

12 Make cell C11 the active cell, type 7, and then press the Enter key.

13 Make cell K7 the active cell, edit the cell contents in the Formula bar so that the value is *11.75*, and then click the Enter button on the Formula bar.

14 Click the fill handle in cell K7 and hold down the left mouse button, drag into cell K10, and then release the mouse button.

Using the fill handle to enter data will also replace data in cells.

J	K	L
Total Hours	Pay Rate	Gross Pay
40	12.5	500
40	10.25	410
38	10.25	389.5
38	11.75	446.5
38	11.75	446.5
38	11.75	446.5
40	11.75	470
40	10.25	410
38	10.25	389.5

Step 14

15 Click the Undo button on the Quick Access Toolbar.

You accidentally replaced the pay rate for Toni Williams.

16 Click the fill handle in cell K7 and hold down the left mouse button, drag into cell K9, and then release the mouse button.

17 Click the Save button on the Quick Access Toolbar.

Check Your Work ▸ Compare your work to the model answer to ensure that you have completed the activity correctly.

In Addition

Undoing and Redoing Multiple Actions

In addition to undoing or redoing the previous action, the Undo and Redo buttons on the Quick Access Toolbar can be used to undo or redo multiple actions. Click the button arrow to display a list of previous actions. Click an action on the Undo button drop-down list and that action, along with any preceding actions, will be undone. The same applies for redoing multiple actions. Excel will store up to 100 actions that can be undone or redone. Once a workbook is closed, the actions stored in the Undo and Redo buttons are removed.

Basic formatting should be applied to even the simplest worksheets to ensure that the information they contain is easy to understand. Some of the most basic formatting options in Excel are number, alignment, and font formatting, all of which are located on the Home tab. Apply formatting to a cell by first making it active and then using the buttons and options on the Home tab to format the cell. Formatting can also be applied to ranges of cells, which saves the time you would spend individually format each cell.

When you have finished building the worksheet, verifying the accuracy of the formulas you have entered is a good idea. The worksheet could contain formulas that are correct in structure but not mathematically correct for the situation. For example, the wrong range may be included in a SUM formula, or parentheses missing from a multioperator formula may cause an incorrect result. One method of reviewing formulas for accuracy is to display formulas in the cells of the worksheet. To display formulas in cells, click the Formulas tab and then click the Show Formulas button in the Formula Auditing group. You can also display formulas with the keyboard shortcut Ctrl + `. The displaying of formulas feature is a toggle, so clicking the Show Formulas button or pressing the keyboard shortcut again will display the results of the formulas.

Tutorial
Displaying Formulas

Tutorial
Merging and Centering Cells

What You Will Do   To improve the appearance of the payroll worksheet, you will apply basic formatting. You will also confirm the accuracy of your calculations in the payroll worksheet by displaying the formulas in the worksheet and visually checking the formulas for errors.

1 With **1-Payroll.xlsx** open, select the range K4:L13.

In columns K and L, the amount of digits displayed after the decimal point is inconsistent. Since the *Pay Rate* and *Gross Pay* columns represent money, you will format these cells to display a dollar symbol and show two digits past the decimal point.

2 Click the Accounting Number Format button $ · in the Number group on the Home tab. (Do not click the button arrow.)

The Accounting format adds a dollar symbol, a comma in the thousands place, and displays two digits after the decimal point for each value in the selection.

3 AutoFit column B so the last name in cell B9 is completely visible by double-clicking the border between the column B and column C headings.

4 Select the range A1:L1.

5 Click the Merge & Center button ⬄ in the Alignment group on the Home tab.

6 Select the range A2:L2 and then click the Merge & Center button.

7 Select the range C3:L3.

In Brief

Display Formulas
1. Click Formulas tab.
2. Click Show Formulas button.

OR
Press Ctrl + `.

8 Click the Align Right button ☰ in the Alignment group.

> The data labels are now aligned above the data below them, making identifying values in the worksheet easier.

9 Select the range A13:L13.

10 Click the Bold button in the Font group.

> The *Total* row is now bolded, making identifying the totals for each column easier.

11 If the value in cell L13 displays as pound symbols (########), AutoFit column L so the number value is completely visible by double-clicking the border between the column L and column M headings.

12 Click the Formulas tab.

13 Click the Show Formulas button 🗔 in the Formula Auditing group.

> The cells in the worksheet are automatically expanded and cells that contain formulas now display the formula in the worksheet area.

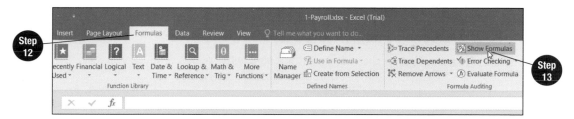

14 Click the File tab and then click the *Print* option.

15 At the Print backstage area, click the Print button.

> The worksheet will print on two pages with cell formulas visible.

16 Press Ctrl + ` to turn off the display of formulas.

> The ` symbol is the grave symbol. On the keyboard, it is usually located on the key immediately to the left of the number 1 key.

17 Click the Save button on the Quick Access Toolbar.

Check Your Work Compare your work to the model answer to ensure that you have completed the activity correctly.

In Addition

Rotating Text in Cells

The Alignment group on the Home tab contains an Orientation button, which you can use to rotate text within cells. Text can be rotated counterclockwise, clockwise, changed to a vertical alignment, rotated up vertically, or rotated down vertically. Often, text set in narrow columns is angled to improve the label appearance. In the screen shown at the right, the cells containing the days of the week in the payroll worksheet are angled counterclockwise.

A new feature in Excel 2016 is the Tell Me feature, which displays on the ribbon to the right of the tabs. The Tell Me feature provides information as well as guidance on how to perform a function. As you type a search phrase in the *Tell Me* text box, a drop-down list displays with options that are refined as you continue typing—a feature referred to as *word-wheeling*. The drop-down list will have options for performing the function you searched for along with links to articles describing the function in the Excel Help window. The Excel Help window can also be accessed by positioning the mouse pointer over the desired button or option until a ScreenTip displays and then clicking the help link in the ScreenTip. To open the Excel Help window, press the F1 function key.

Tutorial
Using the Tell Me Feature

Tutorial
Using the Help Feature

What You Will Do   After reviewing the payroll worksheet, you think the first two title rows would look better if the text was enlarged. You will use the Tell Me feature to do this.

1 With **1-Payroll.xlsx** open, make the range A1:A2 active.

> To increase the font size of the title rows above the columns in the worksheet, you decide to use the Tell Me feature.

2 Click in the *Tell Me* text box.

3 Type font in the *Tell Me* text box.

> A drop-down list appears with options such as *Font, Font Size, Theme Fonts,* and *Font Color.*

4 Position the mouse pointer on the *Font Size* option in the drop-down list.

> When you position the mouse pointer on an option with an arrow at the right side, a side menu displays.

5 At the side menu that displays, click *14*.

> The size of the text in cells A1 and A2 is increased to 14 points.

6 Make the Home tab active and then position the mouse pointer on the Font Color button ![A] in the Font group.

> A ScreenTip displays with basic information on changing the font color, along with a Tell me more hyperlink.

7 Click the Tell me more hyperlink and then read the information that displays in the Excel Help window.

> You can also access the Excel Help window by pressing the F1 function key.

In Brief

Use Tell Me
1. Click in *Tell Me* text box.
2. Type search phrase.
3. Click option.

Use Help
1. Position mouse over button.
2. Click <u>Tell me more</u> link.

OR

1. Press F1 function key.
2. Click in search text box.
3. Type search text.
4. Press Enter key.

8 Close the Excel Help window by clicking the Close button in the upper right corner of the Excel Help window.

9 Click in the *Tell Me* text box, type preview worksheet, and then click *Get Help on "preview worksheet"* toward the bottom of the *Tell Me* drop-down list.

10 At the Excel Help window, click the <u>Preview worksheet pages before you print</u> hyperlink and then read the information that displays in the window.

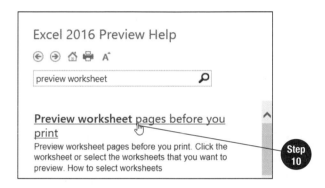

11 Close the Excel Help window.

12 Click the Save button on the Quick Access Toolbar.

Check Your Work ▷ Compare your work to the model answer to ensure that you have completed the activity correctly.

In Addition

Using Excel Help Window Buttons

The Excel Help window contains five buttons that display to the left of the search box. Use the Back and Forward buttons to navigate in the window. Click the Home button to return to the Excel Help window opening screen. If you want to print information on a topic or feature, click the Print button and then click the Print button at the Print dialog box. You can make the text in the Excel Help window larger by clicking the Use Large Text button.

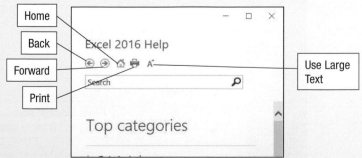

Print a worksheet so that you have a paper copy, also called a *hard copy*, to file or to attach to a report. Large, complex worksheets are often easier to proofread and check on a paper copy. Display the Print backstage area to preview the worksheet and modify print options. For example, to change the page orientation while previewing how the worksheet will print, click the File tab and then click the *Print* option. At the Print backstage area, a preview of how the worksheet will look when printed displays at the right side. The center of the Print backstage area is divided into three categories: *Print*, *Printer*, and *Settings*. Use the galleries available in each category to modify print options. Use the Print backstage area to preview the worksheet before printing to avoid wasted paper by checking in advance whether the entire worksheet will fit on one page, or to preview and/or change other print options.

Tutorial
Printing a Worksheet

What You Will Do   The payroll worksheet is finished. You want to preview the worksheet and then print a copy for the office manager.

1 With **1-Payroll.xlsx** open, make cell A15 the active cell and then type the student information your instructor has directed for printouts. For example, type your first name, press Tab, and then type your last name.

> Make sure you have checked if other identifying information such as your program or class number should be included.

2 Click the File tab and then click the *Print* option to display the worksheet in the Print backstage area as shown in Figure 1.2.

3 The right side of the backstage area displays a preview of the first page of the worksheet as it will print with the current print options. Notice the pages indicator at the bottom left of the preview shows that you are viewing page 1 of 2 pages. Click the Next Page button ▶ to the right of the current page number to display page 2.

Figure 1.2 Print Backstage Area

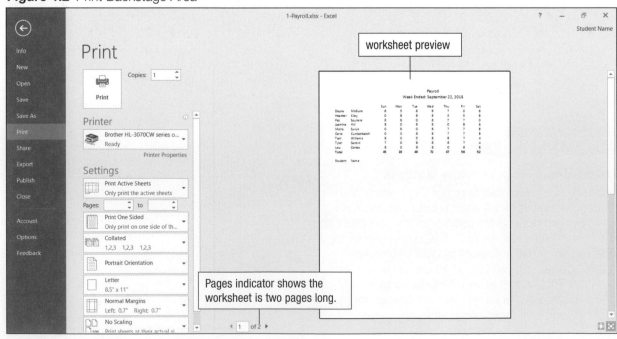

4 The second page of the printout appears showing the columns that could not fit on page 1.

5 Click the orientation gallery (currently displays *Portrait Orientation*) in the *Settings* category in the Print backstage area.

> One method to reduce the printout to one page is to change the orientation of the paper from portrait to landscape. In portrait orientation, the page is printed on paper taller than it is wide. In landscape orientation, the data is rotated to print on paper that is wider than it is tall.

6 Click *Landscape Orientation* at the drop-down list.

> The preview updates to show the worksheet in landscape orientation. Notice that all of the columns now fit on one page.

7 Click the Print button.

> The Print backstage area closes and the worksheet prints on the default printer. The default settings in the Print backstage area are to print one copy of all pages in the active worksheet. You will learn how to adjust page layout and print settings in a later section.

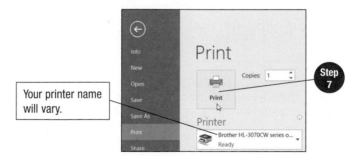

8 At the worksheet, scroll right if necessary until you see the vertical dashed line at the right of the *Gross Pay* column.

> The dashed vertical line is a page break. Page breaks appear after you have previewed or printed a worksheet. A worksheet that spans many rows will display a horizontal dashed line below the last row that can fit on the page. The dashed lines do not print.

9 Save and then close **1-Payroll.xlsx**.

Check Your Work ▸ Compare your work to the model answer to ensure that you have completed the activity correctly.

Features Summary

Feature	Ribbon Tab, Group	Button	File Tab Option	Keyboard Shortcut
Accounting format	Home, Number	$ ▾		
align right	Home, Alignment	▤		
close a workbook			*Close*	Ctrl + F4
copy	Home, Clipboard	▣		Ctrl + C
fill	Home, Editing	⬇		Ctrl + D
Go To	Home, Editing	🔍, *Go To*		Ctrl + G
Help				F1
insert line break				Alt + Enter
merge and center	Home, Alignment	▦		
new workbook			*New*	Ctrl + N
Open backstage area			*Open*	Ctrl + O
Open dialog box			*Open, Browse*	Ctrl + F12
paste	Home, Clipboard	▣		Ctrl + V
Print backstage area			*Print*	Ctrl + P or Ctrl + F2
Redo		↷		Ctrl + Y
save		💾	*Save*	Ctrl + S
save with a new name			*Save As*	F12
show formulas	Formulas, Formula Auditing	🔢		Ctrl + `
SUM function	Home, Editing	Σ		Alt + =
Undo		↶		Ctrl + Z

> **Workbook** ▶ Section study tools and assessment activities are available in the *Workbook* ebook. These resources are designed to help you further develop and demonstrate mastery of the skills learned in this section.

Excel

Editing and Formatting Worksheets

Data Files Before beginning section work, copy the ExcelS2 folder to your storage medium and then make ExcelS2 the active folder.

Skills

- Clear cells and cell formats
- Use spell check and thesaurus
- Insert and delete columns and rows
- Move and copy cells
- Use Paste Options to link cells
- Adjust column width and row height
- Change the font type, size, color, and style
- Apply numeric formats and adjust the number of digits displayed after the decimal point
- Change cell alignment
- Change indentation

- Add borders
- Add fill color
- Use Repeat
- Copy formats using Format Painter
- Apply cell styles
- Apply and modify a theme
- Find and replace cell entries and formats
- Freeze and unfreeze panes
- Change the zoom percentage
- Insert, move, and resize images

Precheck Check your current skills to help focus your study of the skills taught in this section.

Projects Overview

Edit and format a quotation and invoice for catering services. View and edit a special events booking worksheet.

Complete and format a costume cost report and an invoice for costume production.

Edit and format a revenue summary report for movie distribution.

Create a direct wages budget for a remote film shoot.

Create a room timetable.

 SNAP If you are a SNAP user, launch the Precheck and Tutorials from your Assignments page.

Model Answers Preview the model answers for an overview of the projects you will complete in the section activities.

27

The contents of a cell can be edited directly within the cell or in the Formula bar. Clearing a cell can involve removing the cell contents, format, or both. The Spelling feature is a useful tool to assist with correcting typing errors within a worksheet. After completing a spelling check, you will still need to proofread the worksheet since the spelling checker will not highlight all errors and cannot check the accuracy of the formulas or values. Other proofing tools include a Thesaurus, which will find words with similar meanings.

What You Will Do Dana Hirsch, manager of The Waterfront Bistro, has begun a catering services quotation for Marquee Productions. Dana has asked you to finish the quotation by correcting spelling, following up on costs, and improving the appearance of the document. You will be working on this quotation through most of this section.

Tutorial
Clearing Cell Contents and Formatting

Tutorial
Checking Spelling

1 Open **WBQuoteToMP.xlsx**. *Note: This worksheet contains intentional spelling errors that will be corrected in this activity.*

2 Save the workbook with the name **2-WBQuoteToMP**.

3 Make cell A7 the active cell and then press the Delete key.

> The Delete key or Backspace clears only the contents of the cell; formats applied to the cell remain in effect.

4 Make cell A1 the active cell and then press the Delete key.

> The text is deleted from the cell but the color in the background of the cell remains.

5 Select the range A1:C1. Click the Clear button in the Editing group on the Home tab and then click *Clear All* at the drop-down list.

> Clear All removes everything from a cell, including formats or comments.

6 Click in cell A1, click the Review tab, and then click the Spelling button in the Proofing group.

> Spell check begins at the active cell. Words within the worksheet that are not found in the dictionary are highlighted as potential errors. Use buttons in the Spelling dialog box to skip the word (Ignore Once or Ignore All), replace the word with the highlighted word in the *Suggestions* list box (Change or Change All), or add the word to the dictionary (Add to Dictionary) if spelled correctly.

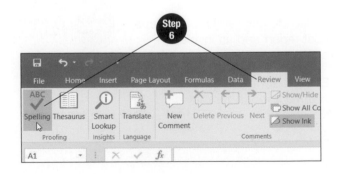

7 Click the Ignore All button in the Spelling dialog box to skip all occurrences of *Rivermist* in the worksheet since the street name is spelled correctly.

8 Click the Change button in the Spelling dialog box to replace *Remoat* with *Remote*.

9 Click the Change button in the Spelling dialog box to replace *Persns* with *Persons*.

10 Complete the spell check, changing words as required. Click OK at the message that the spelling check is complete for the entire sheet.

> Double-click the correct spelling in the *Suggestions* list box if it is not initially selected. Click in the *Not in Dictionary* text box if the correct spelling is not in the list, edit as required, and then click the Change button. You can drag the Spelling dialog box out of the way if you need to see the selected word within the worksheet.

11 Make cell A36 the active cell.

12 Click the Thesaurus button in the Proofing group on the Review tab.

> When you click the Thesaurus button, the Thesaurus task pane displays at the right side of the screen. Use the Thesaurus task pane to replace a word in the worksheet with another word with a similar meaning.

13 Point to the word *Transport* in the Thesaurus task pane word list, click the arrow that appears, and then click *Insert* at the drop-down list.

> The word *Delivery* is replaced with *Transport* in cell A36.

14 Click the Close button in the upper right corner of the Thesaurus task pane.

15 Save **2-WBQuoteToMP.xlsx**.

Check Your Work — Compare your work to the model answer to ensure that you have completed the activity correctly.

In Addition

Using the Smart Lookup Task Pane

Use the Smart Lookup task pane to search for information online without leaving the worksheet. For example, you can conduct an Internet search to look up information in online encyclopedias or business reference sites. Display the Smart Lookup task pane by making a cell active and then clicking the Smart Lookup button in the Insights group on the Review tab. The Smart Lookup task pane with the *Explore* option selected, displays information about the selected text from online sources. Click the *Define* option to display a definition of the selected text from the Oxford Dictionary.

Insert rows or columns in a worksheet using options from the Insert button in the Cells group on the Home tab or from the context-sensitive shortcut menu that displays when you right-click a selected area. Inserted rows are placed above the active cell or selected rows and existing rows are shifted down. Columns are inserted left of the active cell or selected columns and existing columns are shifted right. Delete rows or columns using options from the Delete button or from the context-sensitive shortcut menu that displays when you right-click a selected area. When rows or columns are deleted, data is automatically shifted up or left to fill in space and relative references in formulas are updated.

The Waterfront BISTRO

Tutorial
Inserting Columns and Rows

Tutorial
Deleting Columns and Rows

What You Will Do   You will add items to and delete items from the quotation by inserting and deleting rows and columns.

1 With **2-WBQuoteToMP.xlsx** open, position the cell pointer (displays as a right-pointing black arrow ➡) over row indicator *21*, click and hold down the left mouse button, drag the mouse down over row indicator *22*, and then release the mouse.

> This selects rows 21 and 22. Inserted rows are placed above the selected rows and columns are inserted to the left.

2 Click the Home tab, click the Insert button arrow in the Cells group, and then click *Insert Sheet Rows* at the drop-down list.

> Two blank rows are inserted. The amount of rows inserted into the worksheet depends on the number of rows selected. All rows below the inserted rows are shifted down.

3 Click in cell A21, type Vegetable tray with dip, and then press the Enter key.

4 Type Seafood hors d'oeuvres and then press the Enter key.

5 Make active any cell in row 29.

6 Click the Delete button arrow in the Cells group and then click *Delete Sheet Rows* at the drop-down list.

> The data in row 29 is removed from the worksheet. All rows below the deleted row shift up to fill in the space and Excel automatically adjusts the row heading numbers to remain sequential.

Insert Rows or Columns
1. Select required number of rows or columns.
2. Click Insert button arrow.
3. Click *Insert Sheet Rows* or *Insert Sheet Columns*.

Delete Rows or Columns
1. Select rows or columns to be deleted.
2. Click Delete button arrow.
3. Click *Delete Sheet Rows* or *Delete Sheet Columns*.

7 Right-click the row 19 indicator to display the shortcut menu and Mini toolbar and then click *Delete*.

8 Right-click the row 26 indicator to display the shortcut menu and Mini toolbar and then click *Delete*.

9 Delete row 30 from the worksheet.

10 Position the cell pointer over column indicator letter *F* (displays as a down-pointing black arrow ↓), right-click the mouse, and then click *Delete* at the shortcut menu.

Data in columns to the right of the deleted column are shifted left to fill in the space.

11 Click in any cell to deselect the column.

12 Make cell F8 the active cell, type November 5, 2018, and then press the Enter key.

By default, Excel displays dates in the format *d-mmm-yy* (5-Nov-18).

13 Save **2-WBQuoteToMP.xlsx**.

Check Your Work — Compare your work to the model answer to ensure that you have completed the activity correctly.

In Addition

Inserting and Deleting Cells

In this activity, you selected entire rows and columns before inserting or deleting. This practice is the more common method when you need to add to or delete data from a worksheet. Another method, used less frequently, is to insert new blank cells or delete a range of cells within the worksheet area. To insert new blank cells, select the number of cells you need to add near the location the cells will be added and then click the Insert button in the Cells group on the Home tab, or click the Insert button arrow and then click *Insert Cells* at the drop-down list to display the dialog box shown below. Using the dialog box, you can choose to shift existing cells right or down. Click the Delete button in the Cells group to delete a selected range of cells and shift up the cells below the deleted range. Click the Delete button arrow and then click *Delete Cells* to open the Delete dialog box with options similar to those for Insert.

You learned how to use copy and paste to copy formulas in the payroll worksheet for The Waterfront Bistro. You can also use cut and paste to move the contents of a cell or range of cells to another location in the worksheet. The selected cells being cut or copied are called the *source*. The cell or range of cells that is receiving the source data is called the *destination*. If data already exists in the destination cells, Excel replaces the contents. Cells cut or copied to the Clipboard can be pasted more than once in the active workbook, in another workbook, or in another Office application. Link data between cells using the Paste Options gallery or by inserting a simple formula.

What You Will Do   Continue to work on the catering quotation by moving text in the quotation, duplicating a price, linking cells containing prices, and by copying a food item description.

Tutorial
Moving Cells

Tutorial
Copying and Pasting Cells

Tutorial
Linking Data

1 With **2-WBQuoteToMP.xlsx** open, make cell A38 the active cell.

2 Click the Cut button ✂ in the Clipboard group on the Home tab.

> A moving marquee surrounds the source after you use Cut or Copy, indicating the cell contents have been placed in the Clipboard.

3 Make cell E15 the active cell and then click the Paste button 📋 in the Clipboard group. (Do not click the Paste button arrow because this displays a drop-down gallery of Paste options.)

4 Select the range of cells A14:B15.

5 Point at any one of the four borders surrounding the selected range.

> When you point at a border, the pointer changes from the thick white cross to a white arrow with the move icon attached to it (four-headed arrow).

6 Click and hold down the left mouse button, drag the top left corner of the range into cell E12, and then release the mouse button.

> A green border will appear as you drag, indicating the placement of the range when you release the mouse. The destination range displays in a ScreenTip below the green border.

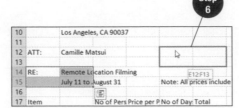

In Brief

Move or Copy Cells
1. Select source cells.
2. Click Cut button or Copy button.
3. Select starting destination cell.
4. Click Paste button.

Copy and Link Cells
1. Select source cells.
2. Click Copy button.
3. Select destination cell.
4. Click Paste button arrow.
5. Click Paste Link button.

7 Make cell D25 the active cell.

8 Click the Copy button in the Clipboard group.

9 Make cell D29 the active cell, click the Paste button arrow in the Clipboard group, and then click the Paste Link button in the *Other Paste Options* section of the Paste Options gallery.

> The existing data in cell D29 is replaced with the value copied from cell D25, and the source and destination cells are now linked. Linking the cells means that any change made to the source cell (D25) will automatically be applied to the destination cell (D29).

10 Press Esc to remove the moving marquee from cell D25 and the Paste Options button near cell D29.

11 Make cell D25 the active cell and then edit the value to *3.91*.

> The value in cell D29 is also changed automatically to 3.91.

12 Make cell A20 the active cell. Point at any one of the four borders surrounding cell A20 until the pointer displays as a white arrow with the move icon attached to it, hold down the Ctrl key, click and hold the left mouse button, and then drag into cell A33.

13 Release the mouse button first and then release the Ctrl key.

> A plus sign attached to the pointer indicates the source contents are being copied when you drag and drop using the Ctrl key.

14 If necessary, click the OK button at the message box.

15 Save **2-WBQuoteToMP.xlsx**.

Cell D29 changes automatically since the two cells are linked.

Check Your Work — Compare your work to the model answer to ensure that you have completed the activity correctly.

In Addition

Using the Paste Options Gallery

The Paste Options gallery (shown at the right) appears in three places: click the Paste button arrow in the Clipboard group, click the Paste Options button that appears after an entry has been pasted into a cell, or right-click shortcut menu. The gallery is divided into three sections: *Paste*, *Paste Values*, and *Other Paste Options*. Within each section, buttons are included for various paste options. Hover the mouse over a button in the gallery to view a ScreenTip that describes the button's purpose as well as to see a preview of the paste option applied to the cell in the worksheet. The Paste Options gallery is context sensitive, meaning the buttons that appear are dependent on the type of content that has been copied and the location in which the content is being pasted.

By default, columns are the same width and rows are the same height with columns set by default to a width of 8.11 characters and rows to a height of 14.40 points. Column width and row height can be adjusted both manually or automatically. Multiple methods are available for manually adjusting the column width or row height, such as using the Format button in the Cells group on the Home tab, or click-dragging column or row heading boundaries. As learned in Section 1, AutoFit a column or row by double-clicking a heading boundary. Excel automatically adjusts the height of rows to accommodate the size of the text within the cells. Manually increasing the row height adds more space between rows, which can be used to improve readability or as a design technique to draw attention to a series of cells.

The Waterfront BISTRO

What You Will Do   You will widen the columns in which labels are shortened to make sure each entry is entirely visible to readers and increase the height of the row containing the column headings to make them stand out from the text below.

Tutorial ▶
Adjusting Column
Width and Row Height

1 With **2-WBQuoteToMP.xlsx** open, make any cell active in column A.

2 Click the Format button in the Cells group on the Home tab and then click *Column Width* at the drop-down list.

3 At the Column Width dialog box, type 14 and then click OK or press the Enter key.

4 Position the mouse pointer on the boundary line in the column indicator row between columns D and E until the pointer changes to a vertical line with a left-and-right-pointing arrow ↔.

5 Click and hold down the left mouse button, drag the boundary line to the right until *Width: 15.00 (142 pixels)* displays in the ScreenTip, and then release the mouse button. *Note: The pixel amount in parentheses will vary depending on your monitor's settings. Use the 15.00 character measurement in this activity.*

> As you drag the boundary line to the right or left, a line appears in the column in the worksheet area, indicating the new width. If, after decreasing a column's width, cells that previously had values in them display as a series of pound symbols (######), the column is now too narrow. Widen the column to redisplay the values.

6 Position the mouse pointer on the boundary line in the column indicator row between columns C and D until the pointer changes to a vertical line with a left-and-right-pointing arrow and then double-click the left mouse button.

> Double-clicking the boundary line sets the width to fit the length of the longest entry within the column. This feature is referred to as the Autofit feature.

7 Make cell E17 the active cell, click the Format button in the Cells group, and then click *AutoFit Column Width* at the drop-down list.

In Brief

Increase or Decrease Column Width
1. Select column(s).
2. Click Format button in Cells group.
3. Click *Column Width*.
4. Type width.
5. Click OK.

Increase or Decrease Row Height
1. Select row(s).
2. Click Format button in Cells group.
3. Click *Row Height*.
4. Type height.
5. Click OK.

Adjust Width or Height Using Mouse
Drag boundary to right of column or below row, or double-click boundary to AutoFit.

AutoFit Column Width adjusts the width of the column to accommodate the amount of text in the active cell. After reviewing the worksheet, you decide all of the columns with numeric values should be the same width.

8 Position the mouse pointer on column indicator letter *C*, click and hold down the left mouse button, drag the mouse right over column F, and then release the mouse button.

This selects columns C through F.

9 Position the mouse pointer on the right boundary line for column E within the selected range of columns until the pointer changes to a vertical line with a left-and-right-pointing arrow.

Any changes made to the width of one column boundary will affect all of the selected columns.

10 Drag the boundary line right until *Width: 15.00 (142 pixels)* displays in the ScreenTip and then release the mouse button.

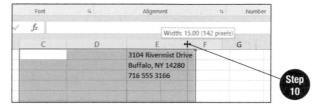

11 Click in any cell to deselect the columns.

Do not be concerned that the columns are now too wide after this step—you have many formatting tasks to complete that will improve the layout as you work through the next few activities.

12 Move E12:F13 to A14:B15 and then click in any cell to deselect the range.

Refer to Activity 2.3 if you need assistance with this step.

13 Position the mouse pointer on the boundary line below row 17 until the pointer changes to a horizontal line with an up-and-down-pointing arrow ✛ .

14 Drag the boundary line down until *Height: 21.00 (35 pixels)* displays in the ScreenTip and then release the mouse button.

15 Save **2-WBQuoteToMP.xlsx**.

Check Your Work   Compare your work to the model answer to ensure that you have completed the activity correctly.

In Addition

Using the Row Height Dialog Box

A sequence of steps similar to those used to adjust column width at the Column Width dialog box can be used to increase or decrease the height of a row with the Row Height dialog box, shown at the right. Click in any cell within the row, click the Format button in the Cells group on the Home tab, and then click *Row Height* at the drop-down list. Type the desired height and then press the Enter key or click OK.

The font is the typeface used to display and print data. The default font in Excel is Calibri, but many other fonts are available. The size of the font is measured in units called points. A point is approximately 1/72 of an inch measured vertically. The default font size in Excel is 11 points. The larger the point size, the larger the type. Each font's style can be enhanced to **bold**, *italic*, or ***bold italic***. Change the color of text to improve worksheet appearance or give emphasis to certain figures, such as changing the font color of negative numbers to red.

The Waterfront BISTRO

Tutorial
Applying Font Formatting

What You Will Do   To add to the visual appeal of the quotation, you will change the font and font size and apply attributes such as font color to the title *Quotation*.

1   With **2-WBQuoteToMP.xlsx** open, make cell A5 the active cell.

2   Click the *Font* option box arrow in the Font group on the Home tab, scroll down the drop-down gallery of fonts, and then point to *Book Antiqua* at the drop-down gallery.

> Excel applies the font you are pointing at to the active cell so that you can preview the result. This feature is called *live preview*.

3   Click *Book Antiqua* at the drop-down gallery.

Live preview shows you how the cell will look before you choose the font so you can try different font options before making your selection.

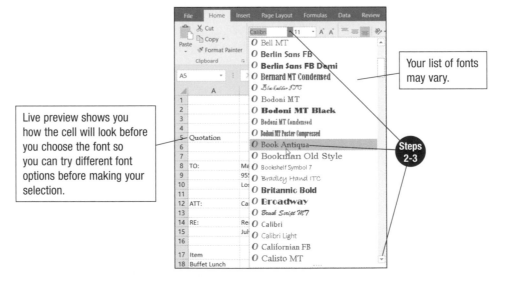

4   Click the *Font Size* option box arrow in the Font group and then click *18* at the drop-down gallery.

> The row height is automatically increased to accommodate the larger font size.

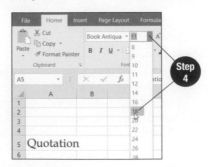

Change Font Type
1. Select cells.
2. Click *Font* option box arrow.
3. Click font.

Change Font Size
1. Select cells.
2. Click *Font Size* option box arrow.
3. Click size.

Change Font Color
1. Select cells.
2. Click Font Color button arrow.
3. Click color optoin.

Change Font Style
1. Select cells.
2. Click attribute button.

5 With cell A5 still active, click the Font Color button arrow in the Font group and then click the *Blue* color option (eighth option in the *Standard Colors* section).

6 Select the range A5:F5 and then click the Merge & Center button in the Alignment group.

7 Make cell F36 the active cell.

8 Click the Bold button **B** and then click the Italic button *I* in the Font group.

9 Save **2-WBQuoteToMP.xlsx**.

Check Your Work Compare your work to the model answer to ensure that you have completed the activity correctly.

In Addition

Using the Format Cells Dialog Box

You can use the Format Cells dialog box with the Font tab selected (shown at the right) to change the font, font size, font style, and color of text. Additional Underline style options such as *Single, Double, Single Accounting*, and *Double Accounting* are available, as well as the special effects options *Strikethrough, Superscript*, and *Subscript*. Select the cells you want to change and then click the Font group dialog box launcher to open the Format Cells dialog box with the Font tab active.

Excel provides specialized formatting options for numeric values. The Accounting format adds a dollar symbol ($), a comma in the thousands place, two digits that display after the decimal point, and displays negative values in brackets. Other numeric formats include Comma, Percentage, and Currency. By default, cells are initially set to the General format, which has no specific numeric style. The number of digits that display after the decimal point in a selected range of cells can be increased or decreased using the Increase Decimal and Decrease Decimal buttons in the Number group on the Home tab. Accountants follow a formatting standard where the top and bottom row containing monetary values display with the dollar symbol and the rest of the values do not include the dollar symbol.

Tutorial

Applying Number
Formatting

What You Will Do   To display a consistent number of characters for the numeric values, you will apply the Accounting and Comma formats to selected ranges within the quotation.

1   With **2-WBQuoteToMP.xlsx** open, make cell F18 the active cell.

2   Hold down the Ctrl key and then click in cell F36.

3   Click the Accounting Number Format button in the Number group on the Home tab.

4   Click in any cell to deselect the cells.

5   Select the range F25:F34.

6   Click the Comma Style button 🔲 in the Number group.

> The Comma Style button formats cells the same as the Accounting Number Format button with the exception of the dollar or alternative currency symbol.

7   Click in any cell to deselect the range and review the numeric values in the worksheet.

> Column D could be improved by applying a format option to the cell that is not showing the same number of digits past the decimal point as other values in the column.

In Brief

Change Numeric Format
1. Select cells.
2. Click format style button.
3. Deselect cells.

8 Make cell D34 the active cell.

9 Click the Increase Decimal button in the Number group.

> One digit past the decimal point is added to or removed from the cells in the selected range each time you click the Increase Decimal or Decrease Decimal button.

10 With cell D34 still selected, click the Increase Decimal button again.

> The value now displays as *33.00*, which is consistent with the number of digits past the decimal point for the other values in column D.

11 Select the range F18:F36 and then click the Decrease Decimal button two times.

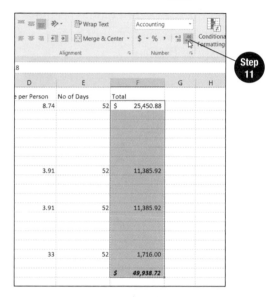

12 Save **2-WBQuoteToMP.xlsx**.

Check Your Work Compare your work to the model answer to ensure that you have completed the activity correctly.

In Addition

Accessing Additional Number Format Options

Click the Number Format button arrow in the Number group on the Home tab to display a drop-down list (shown at the right) with additional numeric format options including date, time, fraction, and scientific options. Click the *More Number Formats* option at the bottom of the list to open the Format Cells dialog box with the Number tab selected. Using this dialog box, you can access further customization options for a format, such as displaying negative values in red or creating your own custom format code.

Data in a cell can be left-aligned, right-aligned, or centered within the column. Cells that have had Merge & Center applied can be formatted to align the text in the merged cell at the left or right. Use the Increase Indent and Decrease Indent buttons to indent text from the left edge of the cell approximately one character width each time the button is clicked. Using buttons along the top row in the Alignment group on the Home tab, you can change vertical alignment, rotate text, or wrap text. Use the keyboard shortcut Ctrl + Y or F4 to repeat the last action on another cell. This is useful if you need to perform the same action several times in a row.

The Waterfront BISTRO

Tutorial
Applying Alignment Formatting

What You Will Do   To improve the appearance of the quotation, you will change the alignment of column headings and values and indent labels from the left edge of column A.

1   With **2-WBQuoteToMP.xlsx** open, edit the column headings in cells C17 and E17 to include a period (.) after the abbreviation for number. For example, the edited column heading in cell C17 will be *No. of Persons*.

2   Select the range C17:F17.

3   Click the Center button in the Alignment group on the Home tab.

4   Select the range C18:C29 and then horizontally center the data in the cells.

5   Horizontally center the entries in the range E18:E34.

6   Select the range A19:A24.

7   Click the Increase Indent button in the Alignment group.

> Each time you click the Increase Indent button, the contents of the selected cells are indented by approximately one character width. If you click Increase Indent one too many times, click the Decrease Indent button to return the text to the previous indent position.

8   Select the range A26:A28 and then click the Increase Indent button.

9   Select the range A30:A33 and then click the Increase Indent button.

10   Select the range A17:F17 and then apply bold formatting.

11   Make cell F8 the active cell and then click the Align Left button in the Alignment group.

> By default, Excel aligns date entries at the right edge of a column.

Change Horizontal or Vertical Alignment
1. Select cells.
2. Click alignment button.
3. Deselect cells.

Indent Text within Cells
1. Select cells.
2. Click Increase Indent button.
3. Deselect cells.

12 Select the range A17:F17.

In Activity 2.4, you increased the height of row 17 to 21.00 points. The Alignment group contains buttons that also allow you to control the alignment of the text between the top and bottom of the cell boundaries.

13 Click the Middle Align button ▤ in the Alignment group.

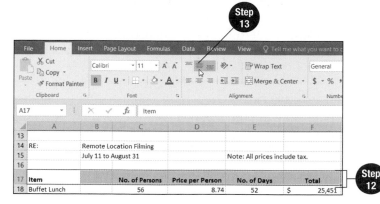

14 Deselect the range.

15 Select the range E1:F1 and then click the Merge & Center button in the Alignment group.

16 Select the range E2:F2 and then press Ctrl + Y (the Repeat command).

You can also press the F4 function key to repeat an action or you can add a Repeat button to the Quick Access Toolbar.

17 Select the range E3:F3 and then press Ctrl + Y.

You can merge and center in only one row at a time in this situation because data already exists in all three rows.

18 Select the range E1:E3 and then click the Align Right button in the Alignment group.

19 Deselect the range.

20 Save **2-WBQuoteToMP.xlsx**.

Check Your Work Compare your work to the model answer to ensure that you have completed the activity correctly.

In Addition

Wrapping Text within a Cell

A Wrap Text button ▤ is available in the Alignment group on the Home tab. Use the Wrap Text button to wrap text within a cell if you do not want to widen the column width. Text too wide for the column is displayed on multiple lines and the height of the row is automatically increased. In the example shown at the right, the original cells are shown on the left and the wrapped cells in column A are displayed on the right.

Borders in various styles and colors can be applied to display and print in selected cells within the worksheet. Borders can be added to the top, left, bottom, or right edge of a cell. Use borders to underscore headings or totals or to emphasize other cells. Fill color adds color and/or pattern to the background of a cell. Format Painter copies formatting from a selected cell to another cell. Use this feature to apply multiple format options from one cell to another cell.

Tutorial
Adding Borders to Cells

Tutorial
Adding Fill Color to Cells

Tutorial
Using Format Painter and the Repeat Command

Tutorial
Applying Formatting Using the Format Cells Dialog Box

What You Will Do   As you near completion of the quotation, you will spend time improving the presentation of the worksheet by adding borders and shading.

1   With **2-WBQuoteToMP.xlsx** open, select the range A17:F17.

2   Click the Bottom Border button arrow in the Font group on the Home tab.

> A drop-down list of border style options displays. The *More Borders* option at the bottom of the list opens the Format Cells dialog box with the Border tab selected, where you can create a custom border.

3   Click *Top and Bottom Border* at the drop-down list.

4   Click in any cell to deselect the range and view the border.

5   Select the range A18:B18, click the Top and Bottom Border button arrow, and then click *Outside Borders* at the drop-down list.

> The name of the button updates to reflect the most recently selected border style.

6   Select the range A25:B25 and then click the Outside Borders button. (Do not click the arrow.)

> Since the Borders button updates to the most recently selected border style, you can apply the *Outside Borders* option to the active cell without displaying the drop-down list.

7   Select the range A29:B29 and then click the Outside Borders button.

8   Deselect the range.

9   Make cell F36 the active cell, click the Outside Borders button arrow, and then click *Top and Double Bottom Border* at the drop-down list.

10   Make cell A8 the active cell, apply bold formatting, and right-align the cell.

11   With cell A8 still the active cell, double-click the Format Painter button in the Clipboard group.

> A moving marquee surrounds the source cell and a paintbrush displays attached to the cell pointer.

Add Borders
1. Select cells.
2. Click Borders button arrow.
3. Click border style.
4. Deselect cells.

Add Fill Color
1. Select cells.
2. Click Fill Color button arrow.
3. Click fill color option.

Copy Formats
1. Make active cell containing source formats.
2. Single-click (copy once) or double-click (copy more than once) Format Painter button.
3. Click destination cell(s).
4. If necessary, click Format Painter button to turn off feature.

12 Click in cell A12.

13 Click in cell A14.

14 Click in cell E8.

Moving marquee in cell A8 indicates cell formats are being copied from this cell.

Step 12

Step 13

Step 14

15 Click the Format Painter button to turn off the feature.

16 Click in cell A5.

17 Click the Fill Color button arrow and then click the *Blue, Accent 1, Lighter 80%* color option (fifth column, second row in the *Theme Colors* section).

18 Save **2-WBQuoteToMP.xlsx**.

Step 17

Check Your Work Compare your work to the model answer to ensure that you have completed the activity correctly.

In Addition

Creating a Custom Border

If none of the borders available in the drop-down list suit your needs, you can create a custom border. Click the *More Borders* option at the bottom of the Borders button drop-down list to open the Format Cells dialog box with the Border tab selected, as shown below. At this dialog box, you can change to a different line style by clicking another line option in the *Style* list box, and/or change the line color by clicking the *Color* option box

arrow and then choosing the desired color at the drop-down gallery. Next, specify the outside and/or inside border you want by clicking one of the buttons in the *Presets* section, clicking one or more of the Border buttons along the perimeter of the preview box, or by clicking inside the preview box at the edge of the cell along which you want the border to appear. When you are finished creating the border, click OK.

Choose the border line style here.

Change the border line color here.

Specify the border you want by clicking a button in the *Presets* section, a border button, or by clicking inside the preview box along the edge where you want the border to appear.

Cell styles contain a group of predefined formatting options stored in a name. Styles are an efficient method for consistently applying formats and creating a professional, consistent worksheet appearance. Excel includes several predefined styles that you can apply or modify; you also can choose to create your own cell style. A theme is a set of formatting choices that include a set of colors, a set of heading and body text fonts, and a set of lines and fill effects. Excel provides a variety of themes you can use to format text and cells in a worksheet.

Tutorial
Applying Cell Styles

Tutorial
Applying and Modifying Themes

What You Will Do   Your final steps in improving the presentation of the worksheet will involve applying cell styles and a theme.

1. With **2-WBQuoteToMP.xlsx** open, make cell A5 the active cell.

    You decide to change the formatting of the *Quotation* title to a predefined cell style.

2. Click the Cell Styles button 🖳 in the Styles group on the Home tab.

    A drop-down gallery appears with the predefined cell styles grouped into five sections: *Good, Bad and Neutral*; *Data and Model*; *Titles and Headings*; *Themed Cell Styles*; and *Number Format*.

3. Move the mouse pointer over several of the cell style options in the drop-down gallery and watch live preview show the style applied to the title in cell A5.

4. Click the *Title* style in the *Titles and Headings* section of the gallery.

Live preview shows how the cell will look when the Title style is applied to cell A5.

5 Select the range A17:F17, click the Cell Styles button in the Styles group, and then click the *Accent2* style in the *Themed Cell Styles* section.

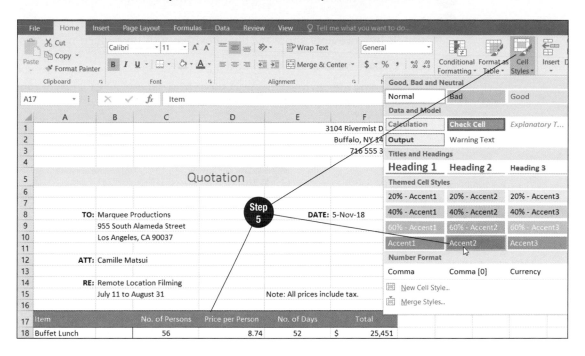

6 Select the range A18:B18, hold down the Ctrl key, select the ranges A25:B25 and A29:B29, and then release the Ctrl key.

7 Click the Cell Styles button and then click the *Accent1* style in the *Themed Cell Styles* section of the drop-down gallery.

8 Deselect the cells.

9 Click the Page Layout tab.

10 Click the Themes button in the Themes group.

11 Move the mouse pointer over several of the themes in the drop-down gallery and watch live preview show the changes that will take place in the worksheet.

12 Click *Retrospect* at the drop-down gallery.

> A theme affects the entire worksheet. You did not select a cell or range of cells before you applied a theme.

13 Click the Colors button 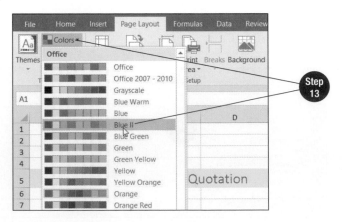 in the Themes group and then click *Blue II* at the drop-down gallery.

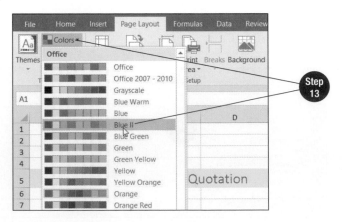

14 Click the Fonts button [A] in the Themes group, scroll down the drop-down gallery, and then click *Garamond*.

15 Make cell A1 the active cell, type The Waterfront Bistro, and then press the Enter key.

16 Select the range A1:D3 and then click the Home tab.

17 Click the Merge & Center button in the Alignment group and then click the Middle Align button.

18 With cell A1 still the active cell, click the Cell Styles button and then click *Accent2* in the *Themed Cell Styles* section of the drop-down gallery.

19 With cell A1 still the active cell, change the font size to 28 points.

20 Select the range E1:E3 and then apply the Accent2 cell style.

21 Click in any cell to deselect the range.

22 Click the File tab, click the *Print* option, and then click the Print button to print the finished quotation.

23 Save and then close **2-WBQuoteToMP.xlsx**.

Check Your Work Compare your work to the model answer to ensure that you have completed the activity correctly.

In Addition

Creating a New Style

You can create your own style using the *New Cell Style* option at the bottom of the Cell Styles drop-down gallery. First, select a cell in the current worksheet and apply all of the formatting to the cell that you want saved in the style. Second, with the cell active to which you have applied the desired formats, click the Cell Styles button and then click *New Cell Style* at the drop-down gallery. At the Style dialog box, shown at the right, type a name for the style in the *Style name* text box and then click OK. The new style will appear at the top of the Cell Styles gallery in a new section titled *Custom*. Custom styles are saved in the workbook in which they are created. You will not see the new style when you open a new workbook; however, you can copy styles from one workbook to another.

Use the Find feature to search for specific labels or values that you want to verify or edit. The Find feature will move to each cell containing the text you specify. The Replace feature will search for a label, value, or format and replace it with another label, value, or format. Use Find and Replace to ensure that all occurrences of the specified label or value are verified or edited.

What You Will Do   Dana Hirsch wants to know how many weddings are booked in 2018. You will use the Find feature to review the wedding bookings in the special events workbook. Dana has also advised you that the prices that were input at $32.95 should be $34.95. You will use the Replace feature to correct these errors.

Tutorial
Finding Data

Tutorial
Replacing Data

Tutorial
Replacing Formatting

1 Open **WBSpecEvents.xlsx** and then save it with the name **2-WBSpecEvents**.

2 Press Ctrl + Home to make cell A1 the active cell.

3 Click the Find & Select button 🔍 in the Editing group on the Home tab and then click *Find* at the drop-down list.

4 Type wedding in the *Find what* text box and then click the Find Next button.

> Excel moved to cell C6, which has the entry *25th Wedding Anniversary*. This cell contains the search text *wedding*, but you do not want to review wedding anniversary events.

5 Click the Options button in the Find and Replace dialog box, click the *Match entire cell contents* check box to insert a check mark, and then click the Find Next button.

> When you click the Options button, the dialog box expands to reveal find and replace options. When you click Find Next, Excel skips the entry *50th Wedding Anniversary* in cell C9 and moves directly to cell C10, which contains only the text *Wedding*.

6 Click the Find Next button.

7 Click the Find Next button.

8 Continue clicking the Find Next button until the active cell returns to cell C10 near the top of the worksheet.

The Options >> button changes to Options << when the dialog box has been expanded to reveal the additional find and replace settings.

> Your review has determined that seven weddings are booked in 2018. In this small worksheet, you could easily have completed this calculation by quickly scanning the contents of column C. In a large worksheet with many rows and columns, the Find feature is an efficient method of moving to a specific cell. Typing a specific value into the *Find what* text box could move to a section title or label very quickly.

9 Click the Close button to close the Find and Replace dialog box.

10 Click the Find & Select button in the Editing group and then click *Replace* at the drop-down list.

11 With *Match entire cell contents* still selected in the Find and Replace dialog box with the Replace tab selected, double-click the text *wedding* in the *Find what* text box and then type 32.95.

12 Press the Tab key to move the insertion point to the *Replace with* text box and then type 34.95.

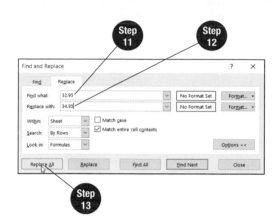

13 Click the Replace All button.

> Excel searches through the entire worksheet and automatically changes all occurrences of *32.95* to *34.95*.

14 Click OK at the message that Excel has completed the search and has made four replacements.

15 Click the *Match entire cell contents* check box to remove the check mark, click the Options button to remove the expanded find and replace options, and then click the Close button to close the Find and Replace dialog box.

16 Review the entries in column H and note that no prices exist at $32.95.

17 Save **2-WBSpecEvents.xlsx**.

> **Check Your Work** — Compare your work to the model answer to ensure that you have completed the activity correctly.

In Addition

Replacing Formats

You can use the Replace feature to find formatting and replace it with other formatting or no formatting. For example, you could use Excel to find all occurrences of bold and blue font color applied to a cell and replace them with bold and green font color. At the Find and Replace dialog box with the Replace tab selected, click the Options button to expand the dialog box and display Format buttons to the right of the *Find what* and *Replace with* text boxes (shown at the right). Use these buttons to specify the formatting options. The Preview boxes to the left (which initially display *No Format Set*) display the formatting Excel will find and replace.

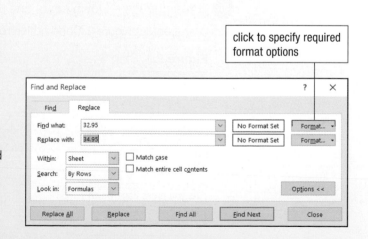

click to specify required format options

When you scroll horizontally or vertically to view parts of a worksheet that do not fit in the current window, some column or row headings may scroll off the screen, making relating to text or values difficult. Freezing panes causes rows and columns to remain fixed when scrolling. Magnify or reduce the worksheet display by dragging the Zoom slider bar button, clicking the Zoom In or Zoom Out buttons, or by specifying a percentage to zoom to at the Zoom dialog box. Changing the magnification does not affect printing since worksheets automatically print at 100% unless scaling options are changed.

The Waterfront BISTRO

What You Will Do   You will freeze column and row headings in the special events worksheet to facilitate scrolling and practice with various Zoom settings to view more cells within the current window.

Tutorial
Freezing and Unfreezing Panes

Tutorial
Changing the Zoom

1 With **2-WBSpecEvents.xlsx** open, make cell A4 the active cell.

2 Click the View tab.

3 Click the Freeze Panes button ⊞ in the Window group.

4 Click *Freeze Panes* at the drop-down list.

> The position of the active cell before you freeze panes is important since all rows above and all columns left of the active cell will be frozen. Notice you made cell A4 the active cell, so rows 1–3 are now frozen. A horizontal black line appears, indicating which rows remain fixed when scrolling.

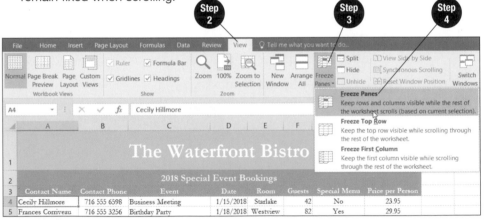

5 Press the Page Down key a few times to scroll down the worksheet.

> Look at Figure 2.1 and notice rows 1 through 3 do not scroll off the screen.

Figure 2.1 Step 5

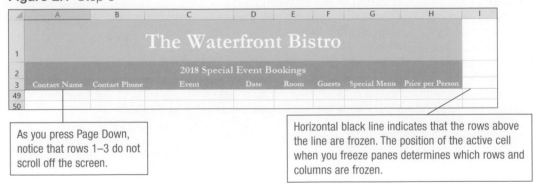

As you press Page Down, notice that rows 1–3 do not scroll off the screen.

Horizontal black line indicates that the rows above the line are frozen. The position of the active cell when you freeze panes determines which rows and columns are frozen.

Freeze Panes
1. Make cell active below and right of row or column headings to be frozen.
2. Click View tab.
3. Click Freeze Panes button.
4. Click *Freeze Panes*.

Change Zoom Setting
Drag Zoom slider bar.
OR
Click Zoom In or Zoom Out buttons.
OR
Click zoom percentage value and choose magnification option at Zoom dialog box.

6 Press Ctrl + Home. Excel returns to cell A4 instead of cell A1, since cell A1 is frozen.

7 Click the Freeze Panes button in the Window group and then click *Unfreeze Panes*.

The *Freeze Panes* option changes to *Unfreeze Panes* when rows or columns have been frozen.

8 Practice dragging the button on the Zoom slider bar (located at the right side of the Status bar above the system time) and watch the cells enlarge and shrink as you drag right and left.

9 Drag the button to the halfway mark on the slider bar to redisplay the worksheet at 100%.

10 Click *100%* at the right edge of the slider bar to open the Zoom dialog box.

11 At the Zoom dialog box, click *75%* and then click OK.

12 Click the Zoom In button at the right side of the Zoom slider bar (displays as a plus symbol).

13 Continue to click the Zoom In button until the zoom percentage returns to 100%.

When the worksheet is set to 100% magnification, clicking the Zoom In or Zoom Out buttons at either side of the slider bar magnifies or shrinks the display of the worksheet by 10% each time the button is clicked.

14 Save **2-WBSpecEvents.xlsx**.

In Addition

Using Buttons in the Zoom Group

The View tab contains a Zoom group with three buttons to change zoom settings. Click the Zoom button in the Zoom group to open the Zoom dialog box. This is the same dialog box that you displayed in Step 10. Click the 100% button to return the view to 100%. Select a range of cells and then click the Zoom to Selection button to cause Excel to scale the zoom setting so that the selected range fills the worksheet area.

Microsoft Office includes a gallery of media images you can insert in a document, such as clip art, photographs, and illustrations. Use the Online Pictures button on the Insert tab to search for and insert images from online sources. Once an image has been inserted, it can be moved, resized, or deleted. Format an image with options at the Picture Tools Format tab. A company logo or other digital image can also be inserted into a worksheet using the Pictures button in the Illustrations group on the Insert tab.

The Waterfront BISTRO

What You Will Do   Before printing the special events worksheet, you decide to add an image to the top right and the bistro's logo to the top left of the worksheet. After inserting the images, you will resize and move them.

Tutorial
Inserting an Image

Tutorial
Modifying Images

1 With **2-WBSpecEvents.xlsx** open, make cell A1 the active cell.

2 Click the Insert tab and then click the Online Pictures button in the Illustrations group.

> This displays the Insert Pictures window with a search box.

3 Click in the search box that displays to the right of the Bing Image Search option, type lobster, and then press the Enter key.

4 Double-click the image shown below. If this image is not available, choose another image related to *lobster* or *seafood*.

> The image is inserted in the worksheet starting at cell A1.

5 Position the mouse pointer on the white sizing handle in the bottom right corner of the image, click and hold down the left mouse button, drag the pointer up and left until the image fits within the first two rows and columns as shown at the right, and then release the mouse button.

Insert Online Image
1. Click Insert tab.
2. Click Online Pictures button.
3. Search for image by keyword.
4. Double-click image.
5. Move and/or resize as required.

Insert Image from File
1. Click Insert tab.
2. Click Pictures button.
3. Navigate to drive and/or folder.
4. Double-click file containing image.
5. Move and/or size as required.

6 Move the mouse pointer over the image until the four-headed arrow move icon appears attached to the pointer, click and hold down the left mouse button, and then drag the image until the right edge of the image is aligned at the right edge of the worksheet, and then release the mouse button.

7 Click in cell A1, click the Insert tab, and then click the Pictures button in the Illustrations group.

8 At the Insert Picture dialog box, navigate to the ExcelS2 folder on your storage medium and then double-click **TWBLogo.jpg**.

9 Click in the *Shape Height* measurement box in the Size group on the Picture Tools Format tab, type 1.1, and then press the Enter key.

10 Using the mouse, drag the logo image so it is positioned as shown below.

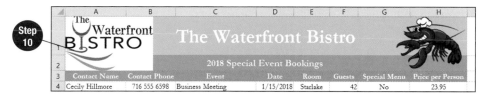

11 Click in any cell to deselect the logo image.

12 Select the range A1:A2 and add outside borders.

13 Select the range A3:H36 and add borders to all of the sides of the cells.

14 Change to landscape orientation in the Print backstage area and then print the worksheet.

15 Save and then close **2-WBSpecEvents.xlsx**.

Check Your Work — Compare your work to the model answer to ensure that you have completed the activity correctly.

In Addition

Using the Picture Tools Format Tab

When an image inserted from a file is selected, the Picture Tools Format tab becomes available. Customize the image using picture tools or picture styles. For example, use the Crop button to cut an unwanted area from the image, or set a specific height or width measurement for the image. Buttons in the Arrange group allow you to group multiple images together, as well as control the alignment, rotation, and order of the image(s) within the worksheet. Use buttons in the Adjust group to control the brightness, contrast, and color of the image(s).

Features Summary

Feature	Ribbon Tab, Group	Button	Keyboard Shortcut
align left	Home, Alignment		
borders	Home, Font		Ctrl + Shift + &
cell styles	Home, Styles		
center	Home, Alignment		
clear cell	Home, Editing		
cut	Home, Clipboard		Ctrl + X
decrease decimal places	Home, Number		
decrease indent	Home, Alignment		
delete cell, column, or row	Home, Cells		
fill color	Home, Font		
find	Home, Editing		Ctrl + F
font	Home, Font		
font color	Home, Font		
font size	Home, Font		
Format Painter	Home, Clipboard		
freeze panes	View, Window		
image from file	Insert, Illustrations		
increase decimal places	Home, Number		
increase indent	Home, Alignment		
insert cell, column, or row	Home, Cells		
middle-align	Home, Alignment		
replace	Home, Editing		Ctrl + H
Spelling	Review, Proofing		F7
theme	Page Layout, Themes		
theme colors	Page Layout, Themes		
theme fonts	Page Layout, Themes		
Thesaurus	Review, Proofing		Shift + F7

Workbook ▷ Section study tools and assessment activities are available in the *Workbook* ebook. These resources are designed to help you further develop and demonstrate mastery of the skills learned in this section.

Excel

Using Functions, Setting Print Options, and Adding Visual Elements

Data Files ▶ Before beginning the section activities, copy the ExcelS3 folder to your storage medium and then make ExcelS3 the active folder.

Skills

- Create formulas with absolute addresses
- Create AVERAGE, COUNT, MAX, and MIN formulas to perform statistical analysis
- Create NOW and TODAY formulas
- Use PMT functions to calculate loan payments
- Create and use range names
- Use an IF function to return a result based on a logical test
- Create, edit, and format a column, pie, hierarchy, and line chart
- Insert and format shapes
- Modify and format charts
- Adjust page scaling
- Change page margins
- Change horizontal and vertical centering
- Manipulate a worksheet in Page Layout view
- Insert headers and footers

Precheck ▶ Check your current skills to help focus your study of the skills taught in this section.

Projects Overview

Add functions, create charts, and change page layout options for a quarterly expense and revenue budget forecast; finish an invoice by entering dates and changing page layout options; calculate loan payment amounts for a patio expansion loan; calculate year-end bonuses; create charts for performance benchmarks.

Calculate and analyze sales commissions; create charts, apply formatting enhancements, and change page layout options in a European Destinations report.

Calculate payments for an office expansion loan for two finance companies.

Create and format charts for a grades analysis report; create a chart and apply formatting enhancements to an international student registration report.

Create two charts that depict movie attendance statistics for a staff development workshop.

 SNAP If you are a SNAP user, launch the Precheck and Tutorials from your Assignments page.

Model Answers ▶ Preview the model answers for an overview of the projects you will complete in the section activities.

In the previous two sections, when you copied and pasted formulas in worksheets, the cell addresses in the destination cells changed automatically *relative* to the destination row or column. The formulas in these worksheets used relative addressing. Sometimes you need a cell address to remain fixed when it is copied to another location in the worksheet. To do this, the formulas must include absolute addressing for those cell addresses that you do not want changed. Make a cell address absolute by typing a dollar symbol ($) in front of the column letter or row number that cannot be changed. You can also use the F4 function key to toggle through variations of the address as relative, absolute, or mixed, in which either the row is absolute and the column is relative or vice versa.

What You Will Do   Dana Hirsch has started a worksheet to forecast next year's expenses by quarter. Dana uses a model wherein next year's expenses are estimated based on last year's average quarter values multiplied by a factor that represents the expected increase for this year. For example, a factor of 1.05 means Dana is expecting the expense to increase by 5%. You will calculate each quarter's expense using the factors in the model Dana has started.

Absolute Addressing

1 Open **WBQtrExpBudg.xlsx** and then save it with the name **3-WBQtrExpBudg**.

2 Review the layout of the worksheet. The values in the range D4:G4 are factors that represent the increases by quarter for next year's expenses. For example, advertising in quarter 1 is expected to increase by a factor of 1.05 (an increase of five percent).

3 Make cell D6 active. All of the values in column D will be created by multiplying last year's average quarter amount by the factor in cell D4. The formula will include an address that should not change when the formula is copied (D4). To create a formula with an absolute address, type =b6*d4 and then press the F4 function key.

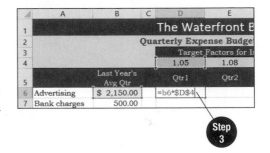

Step 3

Pressing F4 causes Excel to insert dollar symbols in front of the row number and column letter immediately left of the insertion point — *d4* becomes *$D$4*, an absolute address. You can enter column letters in formulas in either uppercase or lowercase. Excel will convert lowercase letters to uppercase automatically when you press the Enter key after typing the formula or when you press F4 to specify an absolute reference.

4 Press the Enter key.

The result $2,257.50 is entered in cell D6. In the cell D6 formula, the first cell reference (B6) is relative and the second cell reference (D4) is absolute. When the formula is copied in a later step, only cell D4 will remain the same.

5 With cell D7 active, type =b7*d4 and then press the Enter key.

You can also type the dollar symbol in front of the column letter or row number to make an address absolute.

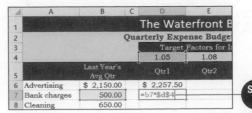

Step 5

6 Make cell D7 active and then drag the fill handle into cell D12.

In Brief

Make Cell Address
Absolute
With insertion point
positioned just after
cell address or with
cell address selected in
Formula bar, press F4.
OR
Type dollar symbol
immediately preceding
column letter and/or row
number.

7 Click in cell D8 and look at the formula in the Formula bar. The first cell address (B8) has changed relative to the current row number but the second cell address ($D$4) has remained the same as it was when the formula was copied.

8 Make cell E6 active, type =b6*e4, press F4, and then press the Enter key.

9 Make cell F6 active and then create the formula =B6*$F$4 by either typing =b6*f4 and then pressing F4 or by typing dollar symbols before *f* and *4*.

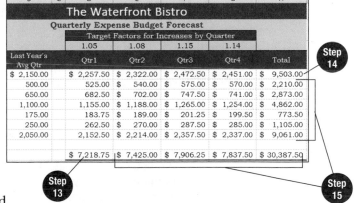

Steps 8-11

10 Make cell G6 active and then create the formula =B6*$G$4 by either typing =b6*g4 and then pressing F4 or by typing dollar symbols before *g* and *4*.

11 Select the range E6:G6 and then drag the fill handle into row 12.

12 Click a few cells in the copied range and verify that in each case, the cell reference with the dollar symbols remained the same when the formula was copied.

13 Make cell D14 active and then click the AutoSum button to calculate the total for column D. Click the AutoSum button a second time to accept the suggested formula =SUM(D6:D13).

14 Make cell H6 active, click the AutoSum button, and then press the Enter key to accept the suggested formula =SUM(D6:G6).

15 Complete the formulas in the ranges H7:H12 and E14:H14 by copying the appropriate SUM functions.

16 Select the range E7:H12 and then apply the Comma format (using the Comma Style button).

17 Save **3-WBQtrExpBudg.xlsx**.

Step 14

Step 13

Step 15

Check Your Work Compare your work to the model answer to ensure that you have completed the activity correctly.

In Addition

Learning More about Mixed Addressing

You can instruct Excel to fix only the row number or the column letter of a cell that is copied and pasted to another location. This table shows more ways that a cell address can use absolute referencing. Pressing F4 repeatedly causes Excel to scroll through each of these variations for the selected cell address.

Example	Action
=$A$12*.01	Neither the column nor the row will change.
=$A12*.01	The column will remain fixed at column A, but the row will change.
=A$12*.01	The column will change, but the row remains fixed at row 12.
=A12*.01	Both the column and row will change.

Until now, you have only used the SUM function when you click the AutoSum button in the Editing group on the Home tab. Excel includes numerous other built-in formulas that are grouped into function categories. The *Statistical* category contains several functions that can be used to perform statistical analysis on data, such as calculating medians, variances, frequencies, and so on. The structure of a function formula begins with the equals sign (=) followed by the name of the function and then the argument within parentheses. *Argument* is the term given to the values to be included in the calculation. The structure of the argument is dependent on the function being used and can include a single range of cells, multiple ranges, single cell references, or a combination thereof.

What You Will Do   Dana Hirsch has asked you to add statistics below the quarterly expenses budget forecast. Specifically, you will calculate the average, maximum, and minimum expenses, as well as the total number of expense items.

Tutorial
Using Statistical Functions

1 With **3-WBQtrExpBudg.xlsx** open, type the following labels in the cells indicated.
    A17: Average expense
    A18: Maximum expense
    A19: Minimum expense
    A20: Count of expense items

2 Make cell D17 active.

In the next steps, you will insert the AVERAGE function to determine the arithmetic mean of the expenses in column D. If an empty cell or a cell containing text is included in the argument, Excel ignores the cell when determining the result. If, however, the cell contains a zero value, it is included in the average calculation.

3 Click the AutoSum button arrow in the Editing group on the Home tab.

4 Click *Average* at the drop-down list.

Excel inserts the formula *=AVERAGE(D14:D16)* in the active cell with the suggested range highlighted. In the next step, you will drag to select the correct range and then complete the formula.

5 Position the cell pointer over cell D6, click and hold down the left mouse button, drag into cell D12, and then release the left mouse button.

Excel inserts the range *D6:D12* in the formula and the moving marquee expands to include the selected cells.

	A	B	C	D	E	
5		Last Year's Avg Qtr		Qtr1	Qtr2	
6	Advertising	$ 2,150.00		$ 2,257.50	$ 2,322.00	$ 2
7	Bank charges	500.00		525.00	540.00	
8	Cleaning	650.00		682.50	702.00	
9	Linens	1,100.00		1,155.00	1,188.00	1
10	Office supplies	175.00		183.75	189.00	
11	Telephone	250.00		262.50	270.00	
12	Utilities	2,050.00		2,152.50	2,214.00	2
13						
14	**Total**			$ 7,218.75	$ 7,425.00	$ 7
15						
16						
17	Average expense			=AVERAGE(D6:D12		
18	Maximum expense			AVERAGE(**number1**, [number2], ...)		

Step 5

In Brief

Use AVERAGE, MAX, MIN, COUNT Functions
1. Make cell active.
2. Click AutoSum button arrow.
3. Click function.
4. Type or select argument range.
5. Press Enter or click Enter button.

6 Press the Enter key or click the Enter button on the Formula bar.

7 Make cell D18 active, click the AutoSum button arrow, and then click *Max* at the drop-down list.

The MAX function returns the largest value in the argument.

8 Type d6:d12 and then press the Enter key.

Excel returns the result *$2,257.50* in cell D18. Typing the range into the formula is sometimes faster if you are sure of the starting and ending cell references.

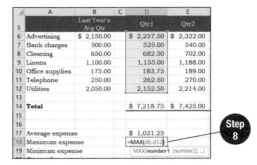

9 With cell D19 active, type the function =min(d6:d12) and then press the Enter key.

MIN returns the smallest value in the argument. As soon as you type the letter *m* after the equals sign, the Formula AutoComplete feature displays a drop-down list of functions that begin with the letter typed. Formula AutoComplete helps you to write formulas by displaying function names, descriptions, and argument syntax. You can scroll the list and point to a function name to display in a ScreenTip the function's purpose. Double-click a function name to enter the function into the cell.

10 With cell D20 active, type the function =count(d6:d12) and then press the Enter key.

COUNT returns the number of cells that contain numbers or numbers that have been formatted as text and dates. Empty cells, text labels, or error values in the range are ignored.

11 Select the range D17:D19 and then drag the fill handle into column H. (You are not including the COUNT formula in cell D20 since the count value [7] does not change.)

This copies the AVERAGE, MAX, and MIN formulas to columns E through H.

	A	B	C	D	E	F	G	H
5		Last Year's Avg Qtr		Qtr1	Qtr2	Qtr3	Qtr4	Total
6	Advertising	$ 2,150.00		$ 2,257.50	$ 2,322.00	$ 2,472.50	$ 2,451.00	$ 9,503.00
7	Bank charges	500.00		525.00	540.00	575.00	570.00	2,210.00
8	Cleaning	650.00		682.50	702.00	747.50	741.00	2,873.00
9	Linens	1,100.00		1,155.00	1,188.00	1,265.00	1,254.00	4,862.00
10	Office supplies	175.00		183.75	189.00	201.25	199.50	773.50
11	Telephone	250.00		262.50	270.00	287.50	285.00	1,105.00
12	Utilities	2,050.00		2,152.50	2,214.00	2,357.50	2,337.00	9,061.00
13								
14	**Total**			$ 7,218.75	$ 7,425.00	$ 7,906.25	$ 7,837.50	$ 30,387.50
15								
16								
17	Average expense			$ 1,031.25	$ 1,060.71	$ 1,129.46	$ 1,119.64	$ 4,341.07
18	Maximum expense			$ 2,257.50	$ 2,322.00	$ 2,472.50	$ 2,451.00	$ 9,503.00
19	Minimum expense			$ 183.75	$ 189.00	201.25	$ 199.50	$ 773.50
20	Count of expense items			7				

Step 11

12 Click in any cell to deselect the range D17:H19.

13 Save, print, and then close **3-WBQtrExpBudg.xlsx**.

Check Your Work ▸ Compare your work to the model answer to ensure that you have completed the activity correctly.

Excel provides the TODAY and NOW date and time functions that insert the current date or date and time in a worksheet. The advantage to using the functions rather than just typing the date and time is that the date and time are automatically updated when you open the worksheet. When you type a date in a cell, Excel stores the date as a serial number. Serial numbers in Excel begin with the number 1 (which represents January 1, 1900) and increase sequentially. Because dates are stored as numbers, they can be used in formulas. A date will appear in a cell based on how it is entered. Specify the appearance of dates in a worksheet with options at the Format Cells dialog box with the Number tab selected.

What You Will Do   An overdue accounts worksheet needs to be completed by entering the current date, formatting the dates, and calculating the account due dates. You will open the overdue accounts worksheet and experiment with the TODAY and NOW functions, change the formatting of the dates, and write a formula that determines the due date.

Tutorial
Using Date and Time
Functions

1 Open **WBOverdueAccts.xlsx** and then save it with the name **3-WBOverdueAccts**.

2 Make cell B4 active, type =now(), and then press the Enter key.

The current date and time are inserted in cell B4. In the next steps, you will delete the date and time and then use the TODAY function to see the difference between the two date functions. Instead of typing a function (as you did in Step 2), you can insert a date and time function with the Date & Time button on the Formulas tab.

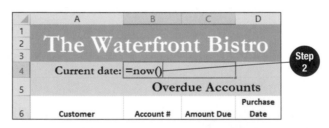

3 Make cell B4 active and then press the Delete key to delete the date and time.

4 Click the Formulas tab, click the Date & Time button 📅 in the Function Library group, and then click *TODAY* at the drop-down list.

5 At the Function Arguments dialog box, click OK.

The current date is inserted in the cell with the time displayed as *0:00*. Normally, the time does not display with the TODAY function; however, since the NOW function was used first, Excel retained the time format for the cell. In the next steps, you will change the formatting of the date.

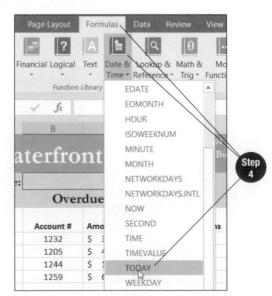

In Brief

Use a Date Function
1. Make cell active.
2. Click Formulas tab.
3. Click Date & Time button.
4. Click function.
5. If necessary, enter references in Function Arguments dialog box.
6. Click OK.

6 With cell B4 the active cell, click the Home tab, click the *Number Format* option box arrow in the Number group, and then click the *More Number Formats* option at the bottom of the drop-down list.

7 At the Format Cells dialog box, click *Date* in the *Category* list box and then double-click the fourth option in the *Type* list box (the option that displays the date as *#/##/##*).

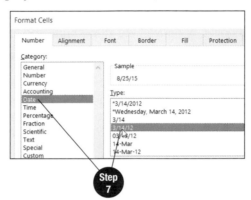

8 Select the range D7:D10 and then apply the same date formatting you applied to cell B4.

9 Turn on the display of formulas by clicking the Formulas tab and then clicking the Show Formulas button in the Formula Auditing group.

> With the display of formulas turned on, the dates in the range D7:D10 display as serial numbers.

10 Press Ctrl + ` to turn off the display of formulas.

> The grave symbol (') is located to the left of the number 1 key on most keyboards.

11 Make cell F7 active and then insert a formula that calculates the date plus the days in the *Terms* column by typing =d7+e7 and then pressing the Enter key.

> Excel used the date serial number in cell D7, added the number of days in the *Terms* column, and then inserted the due date in the date format.

12 Copy the formula in cell F7 down to the range F8:F10.

13 Save, print, and then close **3-WBOverdueAccts.xlsx**.

> **Check Your Work** — Compare your work to the model answer to ensure that you have completed the activity correctly.

In Addition

Using the TIME Function

Time values are stored as decimal numbers that represent the portion of a day starting at 0 (12:00:00 AM) and continuing up to 0.999988426 (23:59:59 PM). The format of the TIME function using the 24-hour clock is *=TIME(hour,minute,second)*. In the worksheet shown at the right, cell D2 contains the formula *=(C2-B2)*24*, which calculates how many hours an employee worked.

Use Excel's financial functions to calculate depreciation, interest rates, payments, terms, present values, future values, and so on. The PMT function is used to calculate a payment for a loan based on constant payments, a constant interest rate, and a set period of time. This function is useful if you want to borrow money and need to estimate the payment you would make given a specified interest rate and length of time to pay back the loan. To use the PMT function correctly, the time periods for the interest rate and the term have to be consistent. For example, if you want to calculate the monthly payment on a loan, make sure the interest rate and the number of periods are expressed in months, or convert the interest rate and time period to months within the formula. The PMT function requires three arguments: the interest rate for the loan (*Rate*), the number of payments to be made (*Nper*), and the amount of money that is borrowed (*Pv*).

What You Will Do   The Waterfront Bistro is planning a patio expansion next year. Dana Hirsch has received pre-approval from two finance companies and wants you to estimate monthly loan payments for each to help decide from which company to borrow funds.

Tutorial
Using Financial Functions

1 Open **WBPatioLoan.xlsx** and then save it with the name **3-WBPatioLoan**.

2 Make cell B10 active.

3 Click the Formulas tab and then click the Financial button in the Function Library group.

4 Scroll down the Financial button drop-down list and then click *PMT*.

5 If necessary, drag the Function Arguments dialog box Title bar to the right of column B.

6 With the insertion point positioned in the *Rate* text box, click in cell B6 and then type /12.

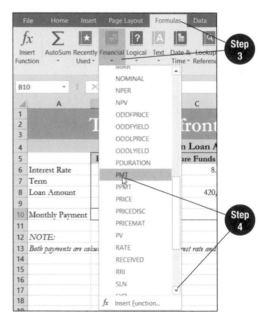

The interest rate in cell B6 is 7.25%, which is the annual interest rate. Typing */12* divides the annual interest rate by 12 to obtain a monthly interest rate. Since you want to calculate a payment per month, you need to ensure the time periods for all input values are the same.

7 Click in the *Nper* text box, click in cell B7, and then type *12.

The term in cell B7 represents the number of years that loan payments will be made. Multiplying this value by 12 represents the total number of loan payments to be made for the year. Note that you have converted both the interest rate and the number of payments within the function arguments to months.

8 Click in the *Pv* text box, click in cell B8, and then click OK.

Pv stands for *present value* and represents the principal amount that is being borrowed. Excel returns the payment amount *$3,834.02* for the Funds Unlimited loan in cell B10. Payments are displayed as negative values; in this spreadsheet file, negative values are displayed in red and within parentheses. Consider loan payments as money that is subtracted from your cash balance, which helps you relate to the negative value returned in the formula cell. If you prefer, you can enter a negative value in cell B8 (-420,000) and the calculated payment will display as a positive number.

In Brief

Use a Financial Function
1. Make cell active.
2. Click Formulas tab.
3. Click Financial button.
4. Click function.
5. Enter references in Function Arguments dialog box.
6. Click OK.

The PMT formula is entered as you complete the Function Arguments dialog box entries.

Step 6

Step 7

Step 8

9 Make cell C10 active.

10 Click the Insert Function button *fx* on the Formula bar.

> The Insert Function dialog box can be used to find an Excel function. This is useful if you do not know the category with which a function is associated. You can locate a function by typing a description of the formula and then clicking the Go button.

11 At the Insert Function dialog box, type **loan payments** in the *Search for a function* text box and then click the Go button.

12 With *PMT* already selected in the *Select a function* list box, click OK.

13 At the Function Arguments dialog box, enter the parameters below and then click OK.

> Rate   C6/12
> Nper   C7*12
> Pv   C8

Step 13

14 Make cell A15 active, type **Total loan payments**, and then press the Enter key.

15 Make cell B15 active, type **=b10*12*b7**, and then press the Enter key.

> This calculates the total amount that will have to be paid back for the loan from Funds Unlimited.

16 Use the fill handle in cell B15 to copy the formula to cell C15.

17 Use the Format Painter feature to copy the formats from cell B10 to the range B15:C15 and then apply the *All Borders* option to the range B15:C15.

> The loan from Venture Funds Inc. is a better choice for The Waterfront Bistro, provided that they can afford the higher

Steps 14-17

> monthly payments. Although the interest rate is higher than Funds Unlimited's loan rate, the shorter term means the loan is repaid faster with a lower total cost.

18 Save, print, and then close **3-WBPatioLoan.xlsx**.

Check Your Work — Compare your work to the model answer to ensure that you have completed the activity correctly.

Assigning a name to a cell or a range of cells allows you to reference the cell(s) with a descriptive label rather than the cell address or range address when creating formulas, printing, or when navigating in a large worksheet. Referencing by name makes a formula easier to understand. For example, a formula such as =*Sales-Expenses* is readily understood. A formula such as =*D3-D13* requires the reader to look at the labels next to the values in the formula cells in order to grasp the formula's purpose. A range name can be a combination of letters, numbers, underscore characters, and periods up to 255 characters. The first character in a range name must be a letter, an underscore, or a backslash (\). Spaces are not valid in a range name. To create a range name, select the desired cells and then type the name in the Name box at the left of the Formula bar.

What You Will Do The profit-sharing bonus for the employees needs to be calculated. Dana Hirsch has started the worksheet and asked you to finish it. Since the bonus amount varies depending on the employee's years of service, you decide to begin by naming cells so that you can use names in the function to help you build the correct formula.

Tutorial
Naming and Using
a Range

1. Open **WBEmpBonus.xlsx** and then save it with the name **3-WBEmpBonus**.

   To begin, you want to name the cells in column B *Years*. The first step in naming a range is to select the cell or group of cells to which the name will be associated.

2. Select the range B7:B15.

3. Point at the white box at the left side of the Formula bar (currently displays *B7*) and notice that the ScreenTip displays *Name Box*.

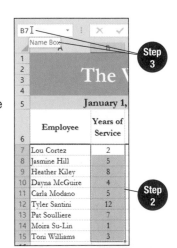

   The white box at the left side of the Formula bar is called the Name box. The Name box displays the address of the active cell. If the active cell has been named, the name appears in the Name box instead. To assign a new name to a cell or selected range, click in the Name box and then type the desired name.

4. Click in the Name box, type Years, and then press the Enter key.

   Notice that the range name now appears in the Name box. You want to assign a name to each cell that will be referenced when you create the profit-sharing formula in the next activity. In the next steps, you will assign a range name to the individual cells that will be needed to calculate the profit-sharing bonus.

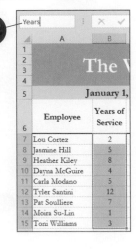

5. Make cell E7 active.

6. Click in the Name box, type Profit, and then press the Enter key.

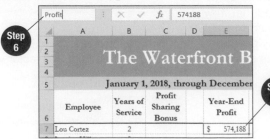

In Brief

Name a Range
1. Select cell(s).
2. Click in Name box.
3. Type range name.
4. Press Enter.

7 Make cell F7 active, click in the Name box, type FiveAndOver, and then press the Enter key.

8 Make cell G7 active, click in the Name box, type LessThanFive, and then press the Enter key.

9 Make cell A1 active and then click the arrow at the right of the Name box.

A drop-down list of range names in the current workbook appears. To move the active cell to a named cell or range, click the range name at the drop-down list.

10 Click *Years* at the drop-down list.

The range B7:B15 is selected since this is the group of cells associated with the name *Years*.

11 Make cell A19 active, type Average service, and then press the Enter key.

12 Make cell B19 active, type =average(years), and then press the Enter key.

Range names are not case sensitive when you use them in a formula. When you type the range name *years* in the formula, notice that Excel color-codes the range B7:B15 to show you the cells that are being referenced in the formula.

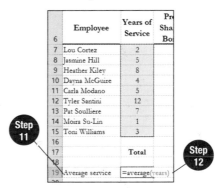

13 Format cell B19 to display only one digit past the decimal point.

14 Save **3-WBEmpBonus.xlsx**.

Check Your Work Compare your work to the model answer to ensure that you have completed the activity correctly.

In Addition

Managing Range Names

To edit or delete a range name, display the Name Manager dialog box shown at the right. To do this, click the Formulas tab and then click the Name Manager button in the Defined Names group. The Name Manager dialog box displays the range names in the active workbook and provides buttons to edit or delete them.

The IF function, also called a logical test, returns one of two values in a cell based on a true-or-false answer to a question. The format of an IF function is =IF(logical_test,value_if_true,value_if_false). For example, assume a salesperson earns a 3% commission if his or her sales are greater than or equal to $100,000, or a 2% commission for sales less than $100,000. Assume the sales value resides in cell B4. The logical test in this example would be B4>=100000. Excel can only return a true-or-false answer when this test is performed. The commission will be calculated with either B4*3% (value_if_true) or B4*2% (value_if_false). In this example, the IF function formula would be =IF(B4>=100000,B4*3%,B4*2%).

What You Will Do　The catering staff participate in a profit-sharing bonus at the end of each year. The bonus amount is based on the year-end profit and the employee's years of service—2.5% for those with 5 or more years and 1.25% for those employees with less than 5 years. Since the percentage bonus can be either one of two values, you need an IF function to calculate the bonus.

Tutorial

Using Logical IF Functions

1　With **3-WBEmpBonus.xlsx** open, make cell C7 the active cell.

2　Click the Formulas tab.

3　Click the Logical button [?] in the Function Library group.

4　Click *IF* at the drop-down list.

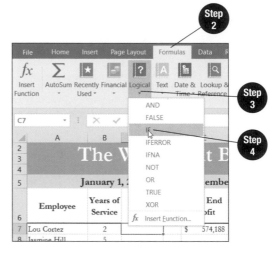

> The Function Arguments dialog box for the IF statement opens. Notice the three arguments: *Logical_test, Value_if_true,* and *Value_if_false*. To begin, you want Excel to test whether the value in the Years of Service column (column B) is less than 5.

This test determines whether Excel calculates the bonus using the lower percent paid to employees with fewer than five years of service or the higher percent paid to employees with five or more years of service. Recall that in the last project you created range names. In the next steps, you will see how using range names will make the IF statement much easier to create and understand.

5　With the insertion point positioned in the *Logical_test* text box, type years<5 and then press the Tab key.

> Watch the entries that appear at the right of each argument text box as you build the formula. Excel updates these entries to show you how the formula is working as you build each argument. Notice that next to the *Logical_test* text box you now see the TRUE and FALSE results Excel is calculating for each entry in the *Years* range.

6　With the insertion point positioned in the *Value_if_true* text box, type profit*lessthanfive and then press the Tab key.

> If the value in cell B7 is less than 5, Excel calculates the bonus as the profit (cell E7) multiplied by 1.25% (cell G7). Another advantage to using range names is that by default, range names refer to the named cell using absolute references. Since the formula will be copied to rows 8 through 15, absolute references are required for those cells that reference the profit and the percents.

Use an IF Function
1. Make cell active.
2. Click Formulas tab.
3. Click Logical button.
4. Click *IF*.
5. Type formula in *Logical_test* text box.
6. Type value or formula in *Value_if_true* text box.
7. Type value or formula in *Value_if_false* text box.
8. Click OK.

7 With the insertion point positioned in the *Value_if_false* text box, type profit*fiveandover.

If the value in cell B7 is greater than or equal to 5, the formula calculates the profit (cell E7) multiplied by 2.5% (cell F7). Notice that below the text boxes, Excel shows the result that will be placed in the active cell: = 7177.35. Looking at cell B7, you will note that Lou Cortez has 2 years of service, so Excel calculates Lou's bonus as $574,188 times 1.25%.

8 Click OK.

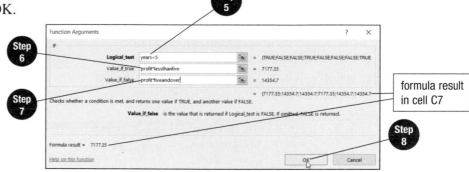

Step 5

Step 6

Step 7

Step 8

formula result in cell C7

9 Drag the fill handle in cell C7 into row 15 and then click in any cell to deselect the range.

10 Make cell C17 active, click the AutoSum button in the Function Library group, and then press the Enter key to calculate the total bonuses to be paid.

11 Apply the Comma format to the values in column C. If necessary, increase the width of column C to display the entire amounts in the column.

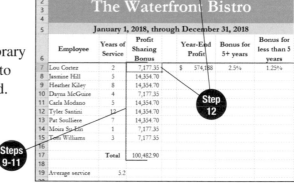

Step 12

Steps 9-11

12 Click in cell C7 and review in the Formula bar the formula that was created using the IF Function Arguments dialog box:
=IF(Years<5,Profit*LessThanFive,Profit*FiveAndOver).

The formula may be easier to comprehend if you include the range names.

13 Save and then close **3-WBEmpBonus.xlsx**.

Check Your Work — Compare your work to the model answer to ensure that you have completed the activity correctly.

In Addition

Learning More about IF Function Arguments

One advantage to creating an IF function using the Function Arguments dialog box is that the correct syntax is automatically applied to the formula. For example, in this project, you did not need to worry about typing commas between arguments or the opening and closing brackets. These elements are automatically added to the formula. Notice also that the range names in the completed formula are displayed in the case used when the range name is created. For example, you typed *profit*lessthanfive*, but the formula you reviewed in Step 12 displayed this entry as *Profit*LessThanFive*. When creating your range names, consider the readability of the formula and use upper- and lowercase letters to facilitate comprehension. Another alternative is to use underscores between words in a range name.

Numerical values are often more easily understood when presented visually in a chart. Excel includes several chart types such as column, line, pie, bar, area, scatter, and others you can use to graphically portray data. The chart can be placed in the same worksheet as the data or it can be inserted into its own sheet. To create a chart, first select the cells containing the data you want to graph and then choose the chart type. Excel graphs the data in a separate object that can be moved, resized, and formatted.

The Waterfront BISTRO

Tutorial
Creating Charts

Tutorial
Changing Chart Design

What You Will Do Dana Hirsch has asked you to create a chart to compare the quarterly expenses in the budget forecast you completed earlier in this section.

1 Open **3-WBQtrExpBudg.xlsx**, select the range A5:A12, hold down the Ctrl key, and then select the range D5:G12.

> The first step in creating a chart is to select the range of cells containing the data you want to graph. The range that you are using includes the row labels in column A. Labels are included to provide the frame of reference for each bar, column, or other chart series. If you select multiple ranges, ensure that the data in each range includes a consistent number of cells.

2 Click the Insert tab.

3 Click the Insert Column or Bar Chart button in the Charts group.

4 Click *3-D Clustered Column* at the drop-down gallery (first option in the *3-D Column* section).

> Excel graphs the data in a 3-D column chart and places the chart inside an object box in the center of the worksheet.

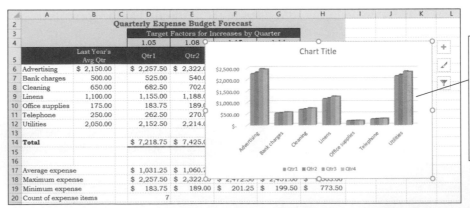

3-D column chart created in Step 4 is placed in an object box, which can be moved, resized, and formatted as needed.

5 Click the Move Chart button in the Location group on the Chart Tools Design tab.

⑥ At the Move Chart dialog box, click the *New sheet* option.

⑦ With *Chart1* selected in the *New sheet* text box, type ColumnChart and then click OK.

> The chart object is moved to a new sheet in the workbook with a tab labeled *ColumnChart*. The chart is automatically scaled to fill the entire page in landscape orientation.

⑧ Click the Quick Layout button in the Chart Layouts group and then click *Layout 3* at the drop-down gallery.

⑨ Click *Chart Title* to select the title object, click at the beginning of the text to place the insertion point inside the chart title box, delete *Chart Title*, and then type Quarterly Expense Budget Forecast.

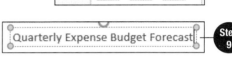

⑩ Click inside the chart area to deselect the title text.

⑪ Click the *Style 3* chart style in the Chart Styles group on the Chart Tools Design tab.

⑫ Save, print, and then close **3-WBQtrExpBudg.xlsx**.

Check Your Work — Compare your work to the model answer to ensure that you have completed the activity correctly.

In Addition

Creating a Recommended Chart

If you are not sure what type of chart will best illustrate your data, consider letting Excel recommend a chart. To do this, select the data, click the Insert tab, and then click the Recommended Charts button in the Charts group. This displays the data in a chart in the Insert Chart dialog box.

Customize the recommended chart with options in the left panel of the dialog box. Click OK to insert the recommended chart in the worksheet. You can also insert a recommended chart in the worksheet with the keyboard shortcut Alt + F1.

Hierarchy charts illustrate each data point's size in proportion to the total of all items in the parent hierarchical level and may include additional levels of hierarchy. A hierarchy chart should include at least a base hierarchical level and one sub-level. For example, a dataset could have the base hierarchical level of *Quarterly Sales* and a subcategory of *Monthly Sales*. The addition of hierarchical levels give users a further break-down of the general base level data. You can choose to display the actual values used to generate the chart using the chart buttons that display outside the top right corner of the chart and/or the Format Data Labels task pane. Other chart elements can be modified and a chart style can be applied using the chart buttons.

What You Will Do Dana Hirsch has requested a second chart from the quarterly expense budget forecast worksheet that displays each expense as a proportion of the total expenses.

1 Open **FCTSalesGraphic.xlsx** and then save it with the name **3-FCTSalesGraphic**.

Formatting with Chart Buttons

2 Select the range A3:C19.

3 Click the Insert tab.

4 Click the Insert Hierarchy Chart button in the Charts group.

5 Click the *Treemap* option at the drop-down gallery.

6 Point to the border of the chart object until the pointer displays with the four-headed-arrow move icon, click and hold down the left mouse button, and then drag the chart, positioning its top left corner in the upper left corner of cell D3.

7 Resize the chart by clicking the bottom right sizing handle and holding down the left mouse button, dragging the bottom right corner of cell J19, and then releasing the mouse button.

8 With the chart selected, click the Chart Elements button that displays at the right side of the chart.

> When a chart is selected, three buttons display outside the top right corner of the chart. With these buttons, you can insert or remove chart elements, apply chart styles, and edit what data points and names display in the chart.

9 Point to the *Data Labels* option at the drop-down list and then click the expand triangle that displays at the right side of the option.

10 Click *More Data Label Options* at the side menu.

> This displays the Format Data Labels task pane at the right side of the screen.

11 At the Format Data Labels task pane, click the Label Options icon and then click the *Label Options* heading to expand the *Label Options* section.

12 Click in the *Value* check box to insert a check mark and display the values in the chart.

In Brief

Create Pie Chart
1. Select cells.
2. Click Insert tab.
3. Click Insert Pie or Doughnut Chart button.
4. Click desired pie type.
5. Move and/or resize chart as required.
6. Apply design options.

Create Hierarchy Chart
1. Select cells.
2. Click Insert tab.
3. Click Insert Hierarchy Chart button.
4. Click desired hierarchy type.
5. Move and/or resize chart as required.
6. Apply design options.

13 Close the Format Data Labels task pane.

14 Click the Chart Styles button that displays at the right side of the chart.

15 Click the fourth style option at the side menu.

16 Click the Chart Elements button that displays at the right side of the chart and then click the *Legend* check box to remove the check mark and the legend from the chart.

17 Change the chart title to *Quarterly Sales Performance*.

Refer to Activity 3.7, Steps 9–10, if you need assistance with this step.

18 Click in the chart area to select the entire chart.

19 If necessary, click the Chart Tools Design tab and then click the Change Colors button in the Chart Styles group.

20 Click the *Color 9* option (fifth row in the *Monochromatic* section) at the drop-down gallery.

21 Click in the worksheet area to deselect the chart.

If the chart remains selected, the chart will be the only thing that is printed in the next step.

22 Change to landscape orientation.

23 Save, print, and then close **3-FCTSalesGraphic.xlsx**.

> **Check Your Work** Compare your work to the model answer to ensure that you have completed the activity correctly.

In Addition

Adding Sparklines

The Insert tab contains a Sparklines group. Sparklines are miniature charts that you can add to a cell. These miniature charts illustrate changes from a specified row or column of data. For example, in the worksheet shown below, the sparkline chart was created in cell F4 based on the values in the range B4:E4. Click the Insert tab and then click the Line, Column, or Win/Loss buttons in the Sparklines group. At the Create Sparklines dialog box, select the data range that contains the values on which you want to base the chart (B4:E4), select the cell in which to draw the chart (F4), and then click OK.

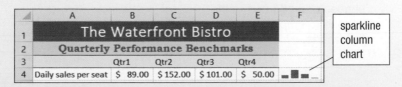

A line chart shows trends and change over time at even intervals. Line charts emphasize the rate of change over time rather than the magnitude of the change. You can easily spot trends, look for unusual points in a data series, or even predict future values based on a line chart's shape and direction. The Shapes button on the Insert tab includes buttons with which you can draw lines, rectangles, basic shapes, block arrows, equation shapes, flow-chart symbols, stars and banners, and callouts. Enclosed shapes can also contain text. Draw shapes to add emphasis or insert explanatory notes in a worksheet.

The Waterfront BISTRO

Tutorial
Inserting a Shape

Tutorial
Formatting a Shape

What You Will Do   Dana Hirsch has created a worksheet with the bistro's performance statistics by quarter, along with the National Restaurant Association's statistics. Dana would like you to create charts in order to compare the data visually.

1 Open **WBPerfStats.xlsx** and then save it with the name **3-WBPerfStats**.

2 Select the range A3:E4, hold down the Ctrl key, and then select the range A8:E8.

3 Click the Insert tab, click the Insert Line or Area Chart button [icon] in the Charts group, and then click *Line with Markers* at the drop-down gallery (fourth column, first row in the *2-D Line* section).

> The line chart clearly shows that the bistro performed below the association's average check per person for the first half of the year but finished the year well above it.

4 With the Chart Tools Design tab active, click the Quick Layout button and then click the *Layout 12* option at the drop-down gallery (third column, fourth row).

5 Point to the border of the chart object until the pointer displays with a four-headed-arrow attached, click and hold down the left mouse button, and then drag the chart below the worksheet data approximately centered below columns A through E and with the top edge in row 11.

6 Select the ranges A3:E3, A5:E5, and A9:E9 and then create a line chart similar to the one created in Steps 3 and 4.

7 Move the new line chart below the first one, leaving one blank row between the two charts.

> In the next steps, you will draw shapes and add text to the shapes to emphasize the two line charts.

line chart created in Steps 2–4

second line chart created in Steps 5–6

Create Line Chart
1. Select cells.
2. Click Insert tab.
3. Click Insert Line or Area Chart button.
4. Click desired line type.
5. Move and/or resize chart as required.
6. Apply design options.

Insert Shape
1. Click Insert tab.
2. Click Shapes button.
3. Click desired shape.
4. Click in worksheet or drag to create shape.
5. Move, resize, or format shape as required.

8 Click the Insert tab and then click the Shapes button 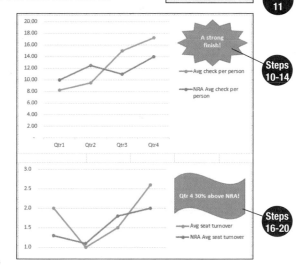 in the Illustrations group.

> The Shapes button drop-down list contains shape buttons grouped by category.

9 Click the *12-Point Star* shape in the *Stars and Banners* group (ninth column, first row).

> When a shape object tool has been selected, the pointer changes to crosshairs.

10 Click in the white space above the legend in the first line chart.

> This inserts a star shape in the worksheet with default measurements of 1 inch for the height and width. The shape contains eight white sizing handles around the perimeter as well as a white rotation handle and a yellow circle center point. The Drawing Tools Format tab becomes active with options to customize the shape.

11 With the shape selected, click in the *Shape Width* measurement box, type 1.5, and then press the Enter key.

12 With the shape still selected, type A strong finish!

> You can type text in a selected shape. You can also right-click the shape and then click *Edit Text* at the shortcut menu.

13 Select the text you just typed and then press Ctrl + E to center it horizontally in the shape. Click the Home tab, click the Middle Align button, change the font size to 10 points, and then apply bold formatting.

14 Position the shape inside the first line chart as shown at the right.

15 Click the Insert tab, click the Shapes button, and then click the *Wave* shape in the *Stars and Banners* group (seventh column, second row).

16 Click in the white space above the legend in the second line chart.

17 With the shape selected, click in the *Shape Width* measurement box, type 1.5, and then press the Enter key.

18 Type Qtr 4 30% above NRA! in the shape.

19 Select the text you just typed and then press Ctrl + E to center it horizontally. Click the Home tab, click the Middle Align button, change the font size to 10 points, and then apply bold formatting.

20 Position the shape inside the second line chart as shown above.

21 Save, print, and and then close **3-WBPerfStats.xlsx**.

Check Your Work ▶ Compare your work to the model answer to ensure that you have completed the activity correctly.

To make changes to an existing chart, click inside the chart or chart element to display a border around the chart object. Click the border to move the chart or click one of the eight sizing handles to resize it. When the chart is selected, the Chart Tools Design and Chart Tools Format tabs become available. Use these tabs to add, delete, or modify the chart or chart elements as needed.

Tutorial
Changing Chart Formatting

What You Will Do   You will modify the charts created for the quarterly expense budget forecast worksheet by formatting the legend, changing the font in the chart title, and changing the chart type.

1   Open **3-WBQtrExpBudg.xlsx** and then click anywhere inside the column chart to select the chart object.

> Once a chart is selected, two additional tabs become available—the Chart Tools Design tab and the Chart Tools Format tab.

2   Click inside the column chart legend.

> Eight sizing handles appear around the legend, indicating that the object is selected. You can drag the legend to another location or resize it using one of the handles.

3   Click the Chart Tools Format tab.

4   Click the Shape Outline button arrow in the Shape Styles group and then click the *Light Blue* color option (seventh option in the *Standard Colors* section).

> This adds a thin, light-blue border around the legend.

5   Click the chart title to select it and then click the *Colored Outline - Blue, Accent 1* option in the *Theme Styles* section in the Shape Styles gallery (second column, first row).

6   Click inside the chart area to deselect the chart title.

7   Click any one of the gray columns in the chart area.

> This selects all seven gray columns.

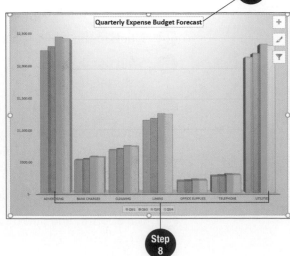

8   Click the Shape Fill button arrow in the Shape Styles group and then click the *Green* color option (sixth option in the *Standard Colors* section).

In Brief

Modify Chart
1. Click to select chart or chart element.
2. Use buttons and options on the Chart Tools Design tab or the Chart Tools Format tab to modify the chart.

9 Click in the chart area outside the columns.

10 Click the Chart Tools Design tab and then click the Change Chart Type button in the Type group.

11 At the Change Chart Type dialog box, click *Bar* in the left panel and then click the *3-D Clustered Bar* option (fourth option toward the top of the middle panel).

12 Click OK.

13 Print the chart.

14 Click the *Sheet1* worksheet tab.

15 Click the File tab and then click the *Print* option.

16 Click the scaling gallery in the *Settings* category (gallery that displays *No Scaling*) and then click *Fit Sheet on One Page* at the drop-down list.

> The worksheet is scaled so that all of the columns will print on one page.

17 Click the Print button.

18 Save and then close **3-WBQtrExpBudg.xlsx**.

Check Your Work — Compare your work to the model answer to ensure that you have completed the activity correctly.

In Addition

Editing Chart Elements

Another method to edit a chart is to right-click a chart element to display the shortcut menu. For example, right-clicking the axis labels in the bar chart displays the shortcut menu shown at the right. The bottom section of the shortcut menu changes depending on the element you click.

The Page Layout tab contains buttons to modify the page setup and scaling options for printing purposes. You can also change print options while previewing the worksheet in the Print backstage area. The margins on a worksheet are the blank spaces at the top, bottom, left, and right edges of the page and the beginning of the printed text. The default margins are 0.75-inch top and bottom and 0.7-inch left and right. Smaller worksheets can be centered horizontally and/or vertically to improve the printed appearance. For larger worksheets, you can choose to shrink the text by scaling the size of printed text to force the printout to a maximum number of pages. For example, in the previous activity you scaled the quarterly expense budget forecast to print on one page.

What You Will Do   You need to print the invoice to Performance Threads completed in Activity 3.3. Prior to printing, you will adjust the margins to improve the worksheet's appearance using the Print backstage area. Dana Hirsch would also like the worksheet printed with the loan analysis for the patio expansion. You will center the worksheet horizontally before printing.

Tutorial

Changing Page Layout Options

1   Open **3-WBOverdueAccts.xlsx**.

2   Click the File tab and then click the *Print* option to display the Print backstage area.

> The invoice is not balanced on the page. In the next steps, you will change the margins to improve the page layout.

3   Click the margins gallery in the *Settings* category (currently displays *Normal Margins*).

4   Click *Custom Margins* at the drop-down list.

The worksheet is unbalanced on the page.

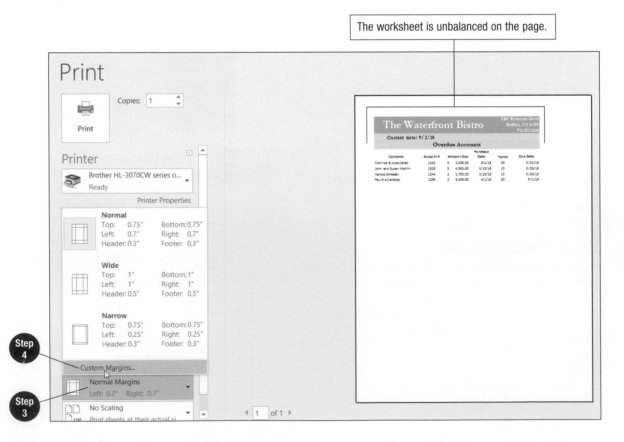

5 Select the number in the *Top* measurement box and then type 1.25. Select the number in the *Left* measurement box, type 1.25, and then click OK.

> The preview pane in the Print backstage area shows the worksheet with the new margins applied. The page layout is improved for printing.

6 Click the Print button.

7 Save and then close **3-WBOverdueAccts.xlsx**.

8 Open **3-WBPatioLoan.xlsx**.

9 Click the Page Layout tab, click the Orientation button in the Page Setup group, and then click *Landscape*.

10 Click the Margins button in the Page Setup group and then click *Custom Margins* at the drop-down list.

> The Page Setup dialog box opens with the Margins tab active. This is another way to open the same Page Setup dialog box you accessed using the margins gallery in the Print backstage area.

11 Change the top margin to 1.25 inches.

12 Click the *Horizontally* check box in the *Center on page* section and then click OK.

> Centering the worksheet horizontally is another method you can use to ensure the worksheet prints balanced between the left and right edges of the page. You can choose both the *Horizontally* and *Vertically* check boxes to print a worksheet that is centered between both the left and right edges (horizontally), and the top and bottom edges (vertically) of the page.

13 Print the worksheet.

14 Save and then close **3-WBPatioLoan.xlsx**.

Check Your Work — Compare your work to the model answer to ensure that you have completed the activity correctly.

In Addition

Printing Column or Row Headings on Multiple Pages

Use the Print Titles button in the Page Setup group on the Page Layout tab to define column or row headings that you want repeated at the top or left edge of each page. Printing column and/or row headings makes the data in rows and columns in a multipage printout easier to identify.

Page Layout view allows you to view the worksheet along with the print settings. Page Layout view also displays horizontal and vertical rulers to assist with measurements. A header is text that prints at the top of each worksheet and a footer is text that prints at the bottom of each worksheet. Excel includes pre-defined headers and footers you can select from a drop-down list or you can create your own custom header or footer text.

The Waterfront BISTRO

Tutorial

Inserting Headers and Footers

What You Will Do   Before printing the profit-sharing bonus worksheet completed earlier, you want to add identifying information in a custom header and footer and check other print options using Page Layout view.

1   Open **3-WBEmpBonus.xlsx**.

2   Click the Page Layout button 📄 at the right side of the Status bar near the Zoom slider bar.

3   If necessary, use the horizontal and vertical scroll bars to adjust the window so that the worksheet, including the white space for the top, left, and right margins, is entirely visible.

4   Hover your mouse over the text *Add header* near the top center of the page.

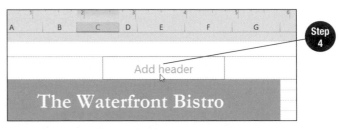

> Headers and footers are divided into three boxes. Click in the desired box and then type text or insert header and footer elements. By default, text in the left box is left-aligned, text in the center box is centered, and text in the right box is right-aligned.

5   Click in the left header box and then type your first and last names.

6   Click in the right header box, type Date Printed:, and then press the spacebar.

7   Click the Current Date button 📅 in the Header & Footer Elements group on the Header & Footer Tools Design tab.

> Excel inserts the code *&[Date]*, which causes the current date to be inserted at the location of the code when the worksheet is printed.

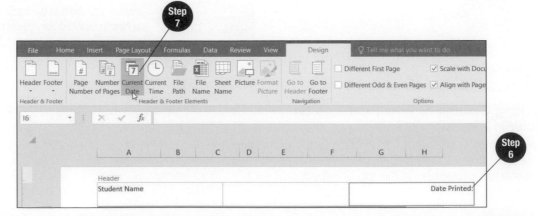

In Brief

Insert Header or Footer
1. Switch to Page Layout view.
2. Click over *Click to add header* or *Click to add footer*.
3. Insert header and footer elements and/or type text in left, center, or right box.
4. Click in the worksheet area to end header or footer editing.

8 Click the Go to Footer button in the Navigation group on the Header & Footer Tools Design tab.

> The right footer box at the bottom of the page opens for editing.

9 Click in the center footer box to open the box for editing.

10 Click the File Name button in the Header & Footer Elements group.

> Excel inserts the code *&[File]*, which causes the workbook file name to be inserted at the location of the code when the worksheet is printed.

11 Click anywhere in the worksheet area outside the footer.

12 Scroll to the top of the worksheet to view the header. Excel now displays the current date in place of the *&[Date]* code.

13 Look at the bottom of the worksheet and notice that the workbook file name now displays in place of the *&[File]* code.

14 Click the Page Layout tab.

> By default, the header and footer margin is 0.3 inch. In the next step, you will adjust the header and footer margins to provide more white space at the top and bottom of the page.

15 Click the Margins button in the Page Setup group and then click *Custom Margins* at the drop-down list. Change the margin settings as indicated below at the Page Setup dialog box with the Margins tab active:

Top:	1	*Header:*	0.5
Bottom:	1	*Footer:*	0.5
Left:	1		

16 Click OK to close the Page Setup dialog box.

17 Review the new margin settings in Page Layout view.

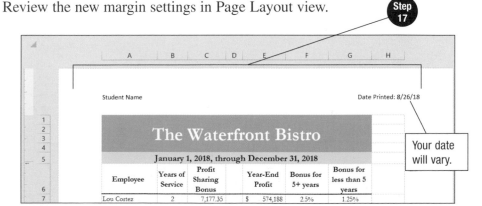

18 Print the worksheet.

19 Click the Normal button at the right side of the Status bar near the Zoom slider bar (immediately left of the Page Layout button).

20 Save and then close **3-WBEmpBonus.xlsx**.

Check Your Work Compare your work to the model answer to ensure that you have completed the activity correctly.

Features Summary

Feature	Ribbon Tab, Group	Button
change margins	Page Layout, Page Setup OR File, *Print*	
create a column chart	Insert, Charts	
create a hierarchy chart	Insert, Charts	
create a line chart	Insert, Charts	
Date & Time functions	Formulas, Function Library	
Financial functions	Formulas, Function Library	
insert a shape	Insert, Illustrations	
insert function	Formulas, Function Library	
insert header or footer	Insert, Text OR Page Layout view	
Logical functions	Formulas, Function Library	
Page Layout view	View, Workbook Views	OR
scale page width and/or height	Page Layout, Scale to Fit OR File, *Print*	
Statistical functions	Formulas, Function Library	

Workbook Section study tools and assessment activities are available in the *Workbook* ebook. These resources are designed to help you further develop and demonstrate mastery of the skills learned in this section.

Excel

Working with Multiple Worksheets, Tables, and Other File Formats

Data Files ▸ Before beginning section work, copy the ExcelS4 folder to your storage medium and then make ExcelS4 the active folder.

Skills

- Insert, delete, and rename a worksheet
- Format worksheet tabs
- Move and copy a worksheet
- Group and ungroup worksheets
- Create 3-D references in formulas
- Link cells between worksheets
- Print multiple worksheets
- Use Page Break Preview to manipulate page breaks
- Format data as a table

- Apply table design options
- Insert rows and columns into a table
- Add a total row to a table
- Sort and filter a table by single and multiple criteria
- Insert, edit, delete, and print comments
- Create a new workbook using a template
- Save a workbook in a different file format
- Create a PDF/XPS copy of a workbook

Precheck ▸ Check your current skills to help focus your study of the skills taught in this section.

Projects Overview

Complete the quarterly sales report and the payroll report; format catering contracts as a table and modify the table; format, sort, filter, and insert comments in the special events section and order workbooks; create a mortgage calculator, invoice, and billing statement using templates; save the quarterly sales report in a previous version of Excel and publish in PDF format; create a sales invoice from a template.

Produce a list of costumes with a final delivery date of August 13; insert comments in the production schedule section in preparation for the design team meeting; format the costume rentals report; and calculate the rental fees.

Import US and Canadian distributor information from text files, combine the information into one workbook, and then format and sort the report.

Create a grade summary worksheet for the Theatre Arts Co-op Internships report.

SNAP If you are a SNAP user, launch the Precheck and Tutorials from your Assignments page.

Model Answers ▸ Preview the model answers for an overview of the projects you will complete in the section activities.

A new workbook initially contains only one worksheet, named Sheet1. Additional worksheets can be added as needed. Organizing large amounts of data by grouping related topics in individual worksheets makes the task of creating, editing, and analyzing data more manageable. For example, you could keep track of your test grades in one worksheet and assignment grades in another. A summary worksheet at the beginning or end of the workbook would be used to consolidate the test and assignment grades and calculate a final grade. By breaking down the data into smaller units, you are able to view, enter, and edit cells quickly. Format worksheet tabs using different colors to visually group related sheets.

What You Will Do   Dana Hirsch has asked you to complete the quarterly sales report workbook. To begin this project, you will insert, rename, and delete a worksheet and then organize the worksheets by applying color to the worksheet tabs.

Tutorial
Inserting and
Renaming a Worksheet

1   Open **WBQtrlySales.xlsx** and then save it with the name **4-WBQtrlySales**.

　　Two additional worksheets were added to this workbook.

2   Click the Qtr2 worksheet tab and then view the worksheet.

3   Click the Sheet1 worksheet tab and then view the worksheet.

　　The quarterly sales report has been organized with each quarter's sales in a separate worksheet.

4   Click the New sheet button ⊕ at the right of the Sheet1 worksheet tab.

　　Clicking the New sheet button inserts a new worksheet to the right of the existing worksheets.

5   Right-click the Qtr1 worksheet tab.

　　Right-clicking a worksheet tab activates the worksheet and displays the shortcut menu.

6   Click *Insert* at the shortcut menu.

7   With *Worksheet* already selected at the Insert dialog box, click OK.

　　Five worksheets now exist in the workbook: Sheet3, Qtr1, Qtr2, Sheet1, and Sheet2.

8   Right-click the Sheet3 worksheet tab and then click *Rename* at the shortcut menu.

　　This selects the current worksheet name in the worksheet tab.

9   Type Summary and then press the Enter key.

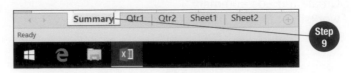

10 Double-click the Sheet1 worksheet tab.

11 Type Qtr3 and then press the Enter key.

12 Right-click the Sheet2 worksheet tab, click *Delete* at the shortcut menu, and then click the Yes button at the message box that displays.

> You can also delete the active worksheet by clicking the Delete button arrow in the Cells group on the Home tab and then clicking *Delete Sheet* at the drop-down list. If the worksheet contains data, a message box appears warning you that data may exist in the sheet and you will have to confirm the deletion. Be careful when deleting worksheets since Undo does not restore a deleted sheet.

13 Right-click the Summary worksheet tab to make the Summary worksheet active and display the shortcut menu.

14 Point to *Tab Color* and then click the *Dark Red* color option (first option in the *Standard Colors* section).

> Changing the color of worksheet tabs can help to visually identify related worksheets.

15 Right-click the Qtr1 worksheet tab, point to *Tab Color*, and then click the *Purple* color option (last option in the *Standard Colors* section).

16 Repeat Step 15 for the Qtr2 and Qtr3 worksheet tabs.

> The three worksheets containing the quarterly sales data are now formatted with the same tab color (purple). The worksheet that will later contain the summary data for the entire year is differentiated with the dark red tab color.

17 Save **4-WBQtrlySales.xlsx**.

Check Your Work ▸ Compare your work to the model answer to ensure that you have completed the activity correctly.

In Addition

Using the Worksheet Tab Scrolling Buttons

The worksheet tab scrolling buttons are located at the left edge of the horizontal scroll bar as shown below. Use these buttons if there are more tabs than currently displayed. Click the Previous button to display the previous worksheet tab and click the Next button to display the next worksheet tab. To display the first worksheet tab, press and hold down the Ctrl key and then click the Previous button. Press and hold down the Ctrl key and then click the Next button to display the last worksheet tab. Drag the tab split box to the right or left to increase or decrease the number of worksheet tabs displayed or to change the size of the horizontal scroll bar.

tab scrolling buttons

tab split box

Drag a worksheet tab to move a worksheet to a different position within the workbook. Press and hold down the Ctrl key while dragging a worksheet tab to copy it. Exercise caution when moving or copying a worksheet since calculations may become inaccurate after the worksheet has been repositioned or copied. A workbook with multiple worksheets that all have similar column and row structures can have formatting options applied to all worksheets in one step by first grouping the worksheets.

The Waterfront
BISTRO

What You Will Do   You will continue your work on the quarterly sales report by copying the Qtr3 worksheet, renaming the sheet, and then entering data for the fourth quarter's sales. Next, you will move the Summary sheet after the Qtr4 sheet. Finally, you will apply formatting options to all four quarters by grouping the worksheets.

Tutorial
Moving, Copying, and
Deleting a Worksheet

1   With **4-WBQtrlySales.xlsx** open, make sure Qtr3 is the active sheet. Position the mouse pointer over the Qtr3 worksheet tab, click and hold down the left mouse button, press and hold down the Ctrl key, drag the pointer immediately right of the Qtr3 worksheet tab, release the mouse button, and then release the Ctrl key.

A black arrow indicates the position where a worksheet will be placed.

Step 1

Pressing and holding down the Ctrl key while dragging a worksheet tab copies the worksheet. As you drag the pointer to the right, a white page with a plus sign displays with the pointer. The copied worksheet has the same label as the source worksheet with (2) added to the end of the name.

2   Double-click the Qtr3 (2) tab, type Qtr4, and then press the Enter key.

3   With Qtr4 the active worksheet, select and delete the content in the ranges B4:D6, B8:D10, and B12:D14 to remove the copied Qtr3 sales data, thereby preventing potential data entry errors when you add the Qtr4 sales data later.

4   Change cell B3 from *July* to *October*, cell C3 from *August* to *November*, and cell D3 from *September* to *December*.

The worksheet is now cleared of the third quarter's data. As new data is typed, the totals will automatically update.

5   Click the Summary worksheet tab to make it active. Position the pointer over the Summary tab, click and hold down the left mouse button, drag the pointer immediately right of the Qtr4 sheet, and then release the mouse button.

Step 5

Dragging a worksheet tab moves the worksheet. As you drag the pointer to the right, a black down-pointing arrow and a white page display with the pointer, indicating the position where the worksheet will be repositioned.

6   Click the Qtr4 worksheet tab and enter the data for the fourth quarter as shown in Figure 4.1. You do not need to type the dollar symbols, commas, or zeros after the decimal points since the cells are already formatted. Type a zero in the cells that display a dash.

In Brief

Copy Worksheet
Ctrl + drag worksheet tab.

Move Worksheet
Drag worksheet tab.

Group Worksheets
1. Click first worksheet tab.
2. Shift + click last worksheet tab, or Ctrl + click other worksheets.

Ungroup Worksheets
1. Right-click any grouped worksheet tab.
2. Click *Ungroup Sheets*.

Figure 4.1 Data for Fourth Quarter

	A	B	C	D	E
1	The Waterfront Bistro				
2	Quarterly Sales Report				
3		October	November	December	Quarter Total
4	Food - Dining Room	$ 44,875	$ 47,856	$ 55,645	$ 148,376
5	Food - Patio	1,785	-	-	1,785
6	Food - Catering	30,254	33,746	65,245	129,245
7	**Total Food**	**76,914**	**81,602**	**120,890**	**279,406**
8	Beverage - Dining Room	41,623	4,687	5,642	51,952
9	Beverage - Patio	245	-	-	245
10	Beverage - Catering	3,245	3,165	6,452	12,862
11	**Total Beverage**	**45,113**	**7,852**	**12,094**	**65,059**
12	Beer & Liquor - Dining Room	3,856	4,962	5,179	13,997
13	Beer & Liquor - Patio	215	-	-	215
14	Beer & Liquor - Catering	3,167	3,563	6,538	13,268
15	**Total Beer & Liquor**	**7,238**	**8,525**	**11,717**	**27,480**
16	**TOTAL SALES**	$ 129,265	$ 97,979	$ 144,701	$ 371,945

7 Click the Qtr1 worksheet tab, press and hold down the Shift key, and then click the Qtr4 worksheet tab.

> The four worksheets are now grouped. Notice that *[Group]* appears next to the file name in the Title bar. Any formatting options that you change apply to all four worksheets. Use the Shift key to select a group of worksheets starting with the first worksheet tab selected through to the last worksheet tab selected. Use the Ctrl key to group nonadjacent worksheets.

8 Make cell A1 active and then apply bold formatting.

9 Select the range A3:E3 and then press F4.

> This repeats the bold formatting.

10 Make cell A2 active and then apply italic formatting.

11 Right-click any of the Qtr worksheet tabs and then click *Ungroup Sheets* at the shortcut menu.

> The worksheets are no longer grouped and can be individually formatted. You can also ungroup worksheets by simply clicking one of the worksheet tabs.

12 Click the Qtr1 worksheet tab and view the formatting applied in Steps 8–10. Click each of the other quarterly sales worksheets to view the same formatting.

13 Save **4-WBQtrlySales.xlsx**.

In Addition

Using the Move or Copy Dialog Box

In Steps 1 and 5 you copied and moved a worksheet by dragging the worksheet tab with the mouse pointer. You can also use the Move or Copy dialog box (shown at the right) to move or copy worksheets within the active workbook or to another open workbook. Right-click the worksheet you want to move or copy and then click *Move or Copy* at the shortcut menu. Click the worksheet before which you want to place the moved or copied worksheet in the *Before sheet* list box and then click OK to move, or click the *Create a copy* check box to insert a check mark and then click OK to copy. To move or copy to another open workbook, select the destination file name in the *To book* drop-down list.

Activity 4.3   Using 3-D References

A formula that references the same cell in a range that extends over two or more worksheets is called a 3-D reference. A formula with 3-D references is used to consolidate data from several worksheets into one worksheet. Worksheets that will use 3-D references should have the data set up in the same manner in each worksheet. For example, if cell E4 in the Qtr1 worksheet contains the total dining room sales, then cell E4 in the remaining worksheets should contain the same value. In this project, you will create the following 3-D reference in a SUM formula: =SUM('Qtr1:Qtr4'!E4). The range Qtr1:Qtr4 within the SUM argument is the 3-D reference that instructs Excel to add the contents of cell E4 starting with the worksheet labeled *Qtr1* and ending with the worksheet labeled *Qtr4*. The 3-D range is enclosed in single quotes and an exclamation point separates the worksheet range from the cell reference.

What You Will Do   To continue the quarterly sales report, you will copy labels from the Qtr1 worksheet to the Summary worksheet and enter 3-D formulas that reference the total sales cells in the four quarterly sales worksheets.

Tutorial
Using 3-D References

1 With **4-WBQtrlySales.xlsx** open, click the Qtr1 worksheet tab.

2 Select the range A4:A19 and then click the Copy button in the Clipboard group on the Home tab.

3 Make the Summary worksheet active and then click in cell A4.

4 Click the Paste button arrow in the Clipboard group and then click *Keep Source Column Widths* (second column, second row) in the *Paste* section of the Paste Options gallery.

5 Make cell B3 active, type Total Sales, and then press the Enter key.

6 Change the width of column B to 12.00 characters.

7 Bold and center the text in cell B3.

8 Make the Qtr1 worksheet active, copy the contents of cells A1 and A2, and then paste the content into cells A1 and A2 in the Summary worksheet.

9 Select the text in cell A2 and then type Sales Summary.

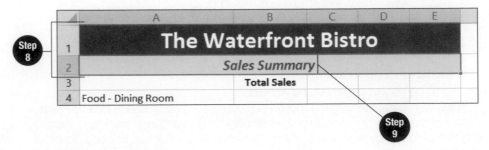

10 Save **4-WBQtrlySales.xlsx**.

Saving the workbook before consolidating data using 3-D references is a good idea in case you encounter difficulties when performing the consolidation.

In Brief

Create Formula with
3-D Reference
1. Make cell active.
2. Type =sum(.
3. Click first worksheet
   tab.
4. Shift + click last
   worksheet tab.
5. Click in cell containing
   data to be summed in
   all worksheets.
6. Press Enter.

11 With the Summary worksheet still active, click in cell B4.

12 Type =sum(.

13 Click the Qtr1 worksheet tab, press and hold down the Shift key, and then click the Qtr4 worksheet tab.

This groups the four quarterly sales worksheets and displays the Qtr1 worksheet. Watch the Formula bar each time you click the mouse to view the formula that is being built.

14 Click in cell E4 and then press the Enter key.

15 Press the Up Arrow key to make cell B4 active again and then read the completed formula in the Formula bar: *=SUM('Qtr1:Qtr4'!E4)*.

Excel inserts the closing bracket automatically. The result, *526884*, which is the total of the values in cell E4 in all four quarterly sales worksheets, appears in cell B4.

16 Drag the fill handle from cell B4 into cell B16 to copy the 3-D formula to the remaining rows.

17 Apply the Accounting format to cells B4 and B16 and then decrease the number of digits past the decimal point so that no digits display.

18 Apply the Comma format to the range B5:B15 and then decrease the number of digits past the decimal point so that no digits display.

19 Deselect the range and then save **4-WBQtrlySales.xlsx**.

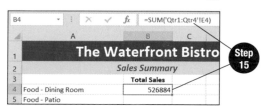

3-D formula as it is shown in Formula bar while completing Steps 12–15

Step 14

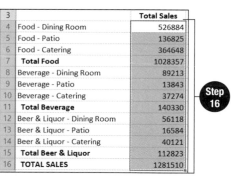

Step 15

Step 16

	Total Sales
3	
4 Food - Dining Room	526884
5 Food - Patio	136825
6 Food - Catering	364648
7 **Total Food**	1028357
8 Beverage - Dining Room	89213
9 Beverage - Patio	13843
10 Beverage - Catering	37274
11 **Total Beverage**	140330
12 Beer & Liquor - Dining Room	56118
13 Beer & Liquor - Patio	16584
14 Beer & Liquor - Catering	40121
15 **Total Beer & Liquor**	112823
16 **TOTAL SALES**	1281510

Check Your Work — Compare your work to the model answer to ensure that you have completed the activity correctly.

In Addition

Using 3-D References in Dissimilar Worksheets

You can consolidate data in multiple worksheets wherein the worksheets are not structured the same. For example, assume that you want to add two salary values from two worksheets. In the first worksheet (labeled *Marketing*), the salary value resides in cell D6, and in the second worksheet (labeled *Finance*), the salary value resides in cell H12. The following formula entered into the desired cell in the summary worksheet adds the two values: *=Marketing!D6+Finance!H12*.

In Section 2, you learned how to use the Copy and Paste buttons to link two cells. Recall that the Paste gallery includes a Paste Link button, which establishes a link between the source and destination cell(s). You can also link cells within the same workbook or between different workbooks by entering a formula that references the source cell. If the source data changes, the cell that is linked to the source will automatically update to reflect the change. To print more than one worksheet at once, group the worksheets prior to printing, or display the Print backstage area and change the selected option in the first gallery in the *Settings* category to *Print Entire Workbook*.

Tutorial
Linking Data

Tutorial
Printing Multiple Worksheets

What You Will Do   To finish the quarterly sales report, you will link to a cell in another worksheet to enter the percent of gross profit and then copy formatting to ensure consistency before setting the page layout options and printing the entire workbook.

1 With **4-WBQtrlySales.xlsx** open and with the Summary worksheet active, make cell B18 active.

2 Type =.

3 Click the Qtr1 worksheet tab, click in cell B18, and then press the Enter key.

> The value *30%* displays in cell B18 in the Summary worksheet.

4 Press the Up Arrow key to make cell B18 active again and then look at the formula that was entered in the Formula bar in Steps 2–3.

> The formula ='Qtr1'!B18 means that the contents of cell B18 in the Summary worksheet are drawn from the contents of cell B18 in the Qtr1 worksheet. Any change made to cell B18 in the Qtr1 worksheet automatically causes cell B18 in the Summary worksheet to update as well.

5 Make cell B19 active, type =b16*b18, and then press the Enter key.

6 Click the Qtr4 worksheet tab.

7 Make cell E7 active and then double-click the Format Painter button in the Clipboard group on the Home tab.

8 Click the Summary worksheet tab.

9 Click in cell B7, click in cell B11, and then click in cell B15.

10 Click the Format Painter button to turn off the feature.

11 Click the Qtr4 worksheet tab.

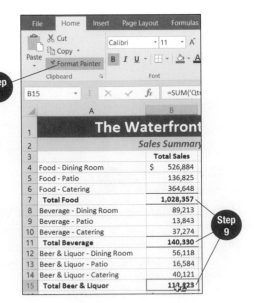

In Brief

Link Worksheet
1. Make destination cell active.
2. Type =.
3. Click worksheet tab for source cell.
4. Click source cell.
5. Press Enter.

Print Multiple Worksheets
1. Click first worksheet tab.
2. Shift + click last worksheet tab.
3. Click File tab.
4. Click *Print* option.
5. Click Print button.

12 Make cell E16 active and then click the Format Painter button.

13 Click the Summary worksheet tab and then click in cell B16.

14 Click the Qtr1 worksheet tab, press and hold down the Shift key, and then click the Summary worksheet tab.

15 Click the Insert tab and then click the Header & Footer button in the Text group.

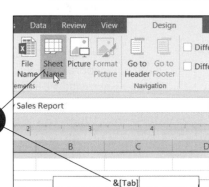

16 Click the Go to Footer button in the Navigation group on the Header & Footer Tools Design tab.

17 With the insertion point positioned in the center text box in the footer section, click the Sheet Name button in the Header & Footer Elements group on the Header & Footer Tools Design tab.

> Excel inserts the code *&[Tab]* in the footer, which will be replaced with the worksheet name when the worksheet is viewed in Page Layout view or printed.

18 Click in the worksheet area outside the footer.

19 Click the File tab and then click the *Print* option.

20 Since all of the worksheets were grouped when you opened the Print backstage area, the page navigation in the print preview area indicates that five pages will print. Click the Next Page button ▶ four times to view each preview page.

21 Click the Print button.

22 Click the View tab and then click the Normal button in the Workbook Views group.

23 Right-click any of the grouped worksheet tabs and then click *Ungroup Sheets* at the shortcut menu.

24 Save and then close **4-WBQtrlySales.xlsx**.

> **Check Your Work** ▷ Compare your work to the model answer to ensure that you have completed the activity correctly.

In Addition

Hiding a Worksheet in a Workbook

In a workbook containing multiple worksheets, you can hide a worksheet that may contain sensitive data or data you do not want to display or print with the workbook. To hide a worksheet in a workbook, click the Format button in the Cells group on the Home tab, point to *Hide & Unhide*, and then click *Hide Sheet*. You can also hide a worksheet by right-clicking a worksheet tab and then clicking the *Hide* option at the shortcut menu. To make a hidden worksheet visible, click the Format button in the Cells group, point to *Hide & Unhide*, and then click *Unhide Sheet*, or right-click a worksheet tab and then click *Unhide* at the shortcut menu. At the Unhide dialog box that displays, double-click the name of the hidden worksheet you want to display.

Activity 4.5   Using Page Break Preview

A page break displays in the worksheet as a dashed line along cell borders between columns or rows. Excel inserts the page breaks automatically based on the margin settings, page orientation, and paper size. You can adjust the page break positions if you do not like where the page break has occurred. Display the worksheet in Page Break Preview to view the worksheet with page numbers behind the cells indicating the number of pages required to print the entire worksheet and a blue dashed line indicating page break locations. Unused cells outside the printing area are grayed out but still accessible if you want to add additional data. Adjust the page breaks by dragging the blue dashed line to the preferred location. Excel automatically adjusts scaling options to accommodate the cells within the revised page break location.

What You Will Do   In the next few projects, you will be working with a catering contract summary. As your first task, you will view the worksheet in Page Break Preview to make adjustments to page layout options and page break locations.

Tutorial

Using Page Break Preview

1 Open **WBCatering.xlsx** and then save it with the name **4-WBCatering**.

2 Spend a moment reviewing the column headings and the data stored in the worksheet.

3 Click the View tab and then click the Page Break Preview button ▦ in the Workbook Views group.

In Page Break Preview, page breaks are shown as dashed or solid blue lines. A dashed line indicates an automatic page break inserted by Excel. A solid blue line indicates a manual page break.

Step 3

4 Two pages are required to print the worksheet with the current page layout settings. Click the Page Layout tab, click the Orientation button in the Page Setup group, and then click *Landscape* at the drop-down list.

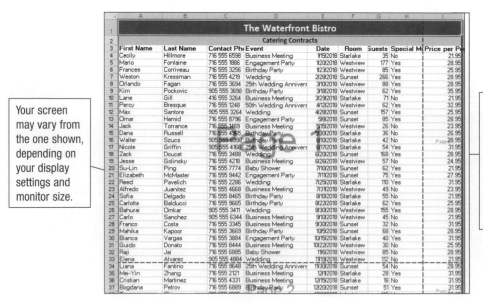

Your screen may vary from the one shown, depending on your display settings and monitor size.

The worksheet requires more pages to print when the layout is changed to landscape orientation in Step 4.

In Brief

Page Break Preview
1. Click View tab.
2. Click Page Break Preview.
OR
Click Page Break Preview button on Status bar.

5 Scroll through the worksheet to view the changes to the page breaks in landscape orientation. The worksheet now requires more pages to print.

6 Look at the number in the *Scale* measurement box in the Scale to Fit group on the Page Layout tab and notice that the current value is *100%*.

7 Position the mouse pointer on the blue dashed line between columns H and I until the pointer displays as a left-and-right-pointing arrow, click and hold down the left mouse button, drag the mouse to the right of column I, and then release the mouse button.

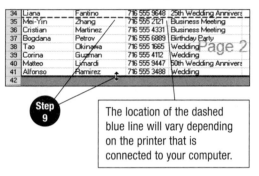

8 View the bottom of the worksheet. A few lines have been moved to page 2.

9 Position the mouse pointer on the dashed blue line between rows near the bottom of the worksheet until the pointer displays as an up-and down-pointing arrow, click and hold down the left mouse button, drag the dashed line below row 41, and then release the mouse button.

The location of the dashed blue line will vary depending on the printer that is connected to your computer.

> The entire worksheet now fits on one page. When you drag an automatic page break to a new location, the page break changes to a solid blue line indicating the break is a manual one.

10 Look at the revised value in the *Scale* measurement box in the Scale to Fit group and notice that the value has been reduced from 100%.

Your number may vary.

> Excel automatically adjusts the scaling percent downward when moving a page break causes more cells to print on a page.

11 Click the View tab and then click the Normal button in the Workbook Views group.

12 Save **4-WBCatering.xlsx**.

Check Your Work Compare your work to the model answer to ensure that you have completed the activity correctly.

In Addition

Inserting or Removing a Page Break in Normal View

Page breaks generally do not appear in Normal view until you have displayed the worksheet in the Print backstage area. Dashed lines appear between column or row borders to indicate automatic page breaks. To insert a manual page break in Normal view, position the active cell in the row below or the column to the right of which you want the page break to occur, click the

Page Layout tab, click the Breaks button in the Page Setup group, and then click *Insert Page Break* at the drop-down list (shown at the right).

Formatting Data as a Table; Applying Table Design Options

Create a table in Excel to manage data independently of other cells in a worksheet or to filter and sort a list. A worksheet can contain more than one range formatted as a table. By default, filter arrows appear in the first row of the table and a border surrounds the table range with a sizing arrow in the bottom right corner. Excel includes a variety of predefined table styles to apply professional quality formatting features to the range within a table. The Table Tools Design tab becomes available when a range of cells is defined as a table.

What You Will Do   You will format the catering contract list as a table, add a record to the list, and create a new calculated column to extend the catering contract amounts. Finally, you will add a total row to the bottom of the table to sum the catering contracts.

Tutorial
Formatting Data as a Table

Tutorial
Adding a Row to a Table

1. With **4-WBCatering.xlsx** open, select the range A3:I41.

2. Click the Home tab and then click the Format as Table button in the Styles group.

3. Click *Table Style Medium 18* (fourth column, third row in the *Medium* section) at the drop-down gallery.

   Excel includes several predefined table styles grouped into *Light*, *Medium*, and *Dark* categories with which you can add color, borders, and shading formats to cells within the table. In addition, you can create your own custom table style saved with the current workbook.

4. At the Format As Table dialog box, with *=$A$3:$I$41* selected in the *Where is the data for your table?* text box, click OK.

   Excel applies the table style formats to the range, displays filter arrows in the first row of the table, and adds a border to the table.

5. Click in any cell to deselect the range.

6. Make cell A42 active and then type text in the cells in the new row in the columns indicated. Press the Enter key after typing the price per person.

First Name	Sonora	*Room*	Starlake
Last Name	Yee	*Guests*	73
Contact Phone	716 555 2668	*Special Menu*	Yes
Event	Birthday Party	*Price per Person*	31.95
Date	12/31/2018		

Format Table
1. Select cell range.
2. Click Format as Table button.
3. Click table style.
4. Click OK.

Add Total Row
1. Click Table Tools Design tab.
2. Click *Total Row* check box.
3. If necessary, choose function in numeric columns.

Since you typed data in the row immediately below the table, Excel automatically expands the table to include the new row and applies the table style formats. You can also insert a new row by making the last cell in the table active and then pressing Tab. Pressing Tab inserts a new blank row below and the data can be typed in this new row.

| 41 | Alfonso | Ramirez | 716 555 3488 | Wedding | 12/31/2018 | Westview | 160 | Yes | 35.95 |
| 42 | Sonora | Yee | 716 555 2668 | Birthday Party | 12/31/2018 | Starlake | 73 | Yes | 31.95 |

Step 6

7 Make cell J3 active, type Contract Total, and then press the Enter key.

Typing new data in a column immediately right of the table also automatically expands the table list range.

8 With cell J4 active, type the formula =g4*i4 and then press the Enter key.

Typing a formula in a table column causes Excel to automatically categorize the column as a calculated column and duplicate the formula in the remainder of the table.

Steps 7-9

9 Select the range J4:J42, apply the Accounting format, and then change the column width to *16.00*.

10 Deselect the range by clicking a cell in the table.

11 Click the Table Tools Design tab and then click the *Total Row* check box in the Table Style Options group to insert a check mark.

Excel adds the word *Total* in the leftmost cell in the row below the table and sums the cells in column J.

Step 11

Design	♀ Tell me what you want to do...
✓ Header Row	☐ First Column
☐ Total Row	☐ Last Column
✓ Banded Rows	☐ Banded Columns
	Table Style Options

12 Make cell G43 active, click the arrow that appears, and then click *Sum* at the drop-down list.

13 Make cell I43 active, click the arrow that appears, and then click *Average* at the drop-down list.

14 Decrease the decimals in cell I43 to two digits past the decimal point.

| Westview | 160 | Yes |
| Starlake | 73 | Yes |

None
Average
Count
Count Numbers
Max
Min
Sum
StdDev

Step 12

15 Select the range A1:J1 and then click the Merge & Center button in the Alignment group on the Home tab to remove the merging of columns A through I.

160	Yes	35.95	$	5,752.00
73	Yes	31.95	$	2,332.35
3155		28.36	$	90,710.25

Step 14

16 With the range A1:J1 still selected, click the Merge & Center button a second time to merge columns A through J.

17 Correct the centering of the title in row 2 by completing steps similar to those in Steps 15–16.

18 Save **4-WBCatering.xlsx**.

Check Your Work   Compare your work to the model answer to ensure that you have completed the activity correctly.

In Section 1 you learned to sort a payroll worksheet alphabetically by last names. To sort rows in a table by single or multiple criteria involves the same process as the one used in Section 1. To sort by a single column, click in any cell in the column by which you wish to sort and then use the *Sort A to Z* or *Sort Z to A* options at the Sort & Filter button drop-down list. To group the rows first by one column and then sort the rows within each group by another column, open the Sort dialog box. You can continue to group and sort by multiple criteria as needed.

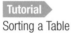
Tutorial
Sorting a Table

What You Will Do You decide to print the catering data sorted in descending order by the contract total. Next, you want a printout of the catering list grouped first by the event, then by room, and then by date.

1 With **4-WBCatering.xlsx** open, click in any cell in column J within the table range.

2 Click the Sort & Filter button in the Editing group on the Home tab.

3 Click *Sort Largest to Smallest* at the drop-down list.

The table is rearranged in descending order by contract total with the highest contract amount at the top of the list. Excel displays a black arrow in the filter arrow button to indicate that the table is ordered by the *Contract Total* column.

4 Select the range H4:I43 and then center the cells.

5 Deselect the range and then click the View tab.

6 Display the worksheet in Page Break Preview and adjust the page breaks so that the worksheet fits on one page.

7 Print the worksheet.

8 Display the worksheet in Normal view, click in any cell within the table range, and then click the Home tab.

9 Click the Sort & Filter button and then click *Custom Sort* at the drop-down list.

10 At the Sort dialog box, click the *Sort by* option box arrow in the *Column* section (currently reads *Contract Total*) and then click *Event* at the drop-down list.

11 Click the option box arrow at the right of the *Order* option box (currently reads *Z to A*) and then click *A to Z* at the drop-down list.

12 Click the Add Level button in the Sort dialog box.

13 Click the *Then by* option box arrow in the *Column* section and then click *Room* at the drop-down list.

The default entries of *Values* for *Sort On* and *A to Z* for *Order* are correct since you want the cells sorted by the room names in ascending order.

Sort Table by Single Column
1. Click in any row within column by which to sort.
2. Click the Sort & Filter button.
3. Click *Sort A to Z, or Sort Smallest to Largest,* or *Sort Z to A,* or *Sort Largest to Smallest.*

Sort Table by Multiple Columns
1. Click Sort & Filter button.
2. Click *Custom Sort.*
3. Select first column to sort by.
4. Select sort order.
5. Click Add Level.
6. Repeat Steps 3–5 for each sort column.
7. Click OK.

14 Click the Add Level button.

15 Click the second *Then by* option box arrow in the *Column* section and then click *Date* at the drop-down list.

> The default entries of *Values* for *Sort On* and *Oldest to Newest* for *Order* are correct since you want to sort the dates in ascending order.

16 Click OK to perform the sort.

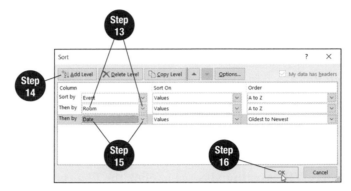

17 Examine the sorted worksheet and compare your results with the partial worksheet shown below. The rows are grouped and sorted first by event, starting with *25th Wedding Anniversary*. Within each event group, the rows are next arranged by room, and then within each room group, the rows are arranged by date.

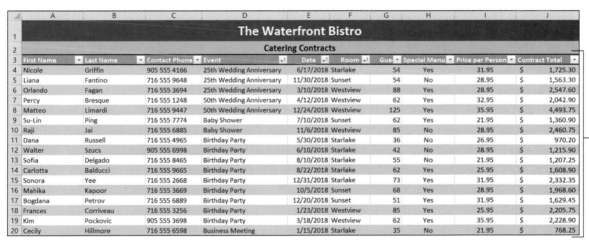

The Waterfront Bistro

Catering Contracts

First Name	Last Name	Contact Phone	Event	Date	Room	Gue	Special Menu	Price per Person	Contract Total
Nicole	Griffin	905 555 4166	25th Wedding Anniversary	6/17/2018	Starlake	54	Yes	31.95	$ 1,725.30
Liana	Fantino	716 555 9648	25th Wedding Anniversary	11/30/2018	Sunset	54	No	28.95	$ 1,563.30
Orlando	Fagan	716 555 3694	25th Wedding Anniversary	3/10/2018	Westview	88	Yes	28.95	$ 2,547.60
Percy	Bresque	716 555 1248	50th Wedding Anniversary	4/12/2018	Westview	62	Yes	32.95	$ 2,042.90
Matteo	Limardi	716 555 9447	50th Wedding Anniversary	12/24/2018	Westview	125	Yes	35.95	$ 4,493.75
Su-Lin	Ping	716 555 7774	Baby Shower	7/10/2018	Sunset	62	Yes	21.95	$ 1,360.90
Raji	Jai	716 555 6885	Baby Shower	11/6/2018	Westview	85	No	28.95	$ 2,460.75
Dana	Russell	716 555 4965	Birthday Party	5/30/2018	Starlake	36	No	26.95	$ 970.20
Walter	Szucs	905 555 6998	Birthday Party	6/10/2018	Starlake	42	No	28.95	$ 1,215.90
Sofia	Delgado	716 555 8465	Birthday Party	8/10/2018	Starlake	55	No	21.95	$ 1,207.25
Carlotta	Balducci	716 555 9665	Birthday Party	8/22/2018	Starlake	62	Yes	25.95	$ 1,608.90
Sonora	Yee	716 555 2668	Birthday Party	12/31/2018	Starlake	73	Yes	31.95	$ 2,332.35
Mahika	Kapoor	716 555 3669	Birthday Party	10/5/2018	Sunset	68	Yes	28.95	$ 1,968.60
Bogdana	Petrov	716 555 6889	Birthday Party	12/20/2018	Sunset	51	Yes	31.95	$ 1,629.45
Frances	Corriveau	716 555 3256	Birthday Party	1/23/2018	Westview	85	Yes	25.95	$ 2,205.75
Kim	Pockovic	905 555 3698	Birthday Party	3/18/2018	Westview	62	Yes	35.95	$ 2,228.90
Cecily	Hillmore	716 555 6598	Business Meeting	1/15/2018	Starlake	35	No	21.95	$ 768.25

18 Print the worksheet.

19 Save **4-WBCatering.xlsx**.

Check Your Work Compare your work to the model answer to ensure that you have completed the activity correctly.

In Addition

Understanding Sorting Order

By default, Excel sorts the data in a column alphanumerically. Alphanumeric sorting arranges rows with entries that begin with symbols first, then numbers, then letters. Notice in the catering events workbook that the events beginning with numbers, such as *25th Wedding Anniversary* and *50th Wedding Anniversary*, are the first rows in the sorted worksheet.

A filter is used to display only certain records within the table that meet specified criteria. The records that do not meet the filter criteria are temporarily hidden from view. Using a filter, you can view and/or print a subset of rows within a table. For example, you might want to print a list of catering events that have been booked into a certain room. Once you have printed the list, removing the filter redisplays all of the rows. Excel displays filter arrow buttons in the first row of the table that you can use to specify the filter criteria.

What You Will Do   To prepare for an upcoming meeting with the executive chef, Dana Hirsch has asked for a printout of the catering events that require a special menu. Another printout of the events booked into the Starlake room is needed for planning staff requirements. Finally, Dana wants a printed list of the weddings booked into the Sunset room.

Tutorial
Filtering a Table

1 With **4-WBCatering.xlsx** open, click the filter arrow button ▼ next to the label *Special Menu* in cell H3.

Filter a table by selecting the criterion from a drop-down list. For each column in the table, a filter arrow button appears. Excel looks in the active column and includes in the filter drop-down list each unique field value that exists within the column. In addition, the entries *Sort A to Z, Sort Z to A*, and *Sort by Color* appear at the top of the list.

2 Click the *No* check box to remove the check mark.

Removing a check mark from a check box instructs Excel to hide those rows within the table that match the check box entry. Since the only other entry in the column is *Yes*, the criterion for the filter is to display only those rows within the table that have the text entry *Yes* in column H.

Step 2

Step 3

3 Click OK.

Excel hides any records that have a value other than *Yes* in the column as shown below. The row numbers of the matching items that were found are displayed in blue and a filter icon appears in the filter arrow button in cell H3 to indicate H is the column that was used to filter the rows. The Status bar also shows the message that 24 of 39 records were found. A filtered worksheet can be edited, formatted, charted, or printed.

4 Print the filtered worksheet.

3	First Name	Last Name	Contact Phone	Event	Date	Room	Gue	Special Menu
4	Nicole	Griffin	905 555 4166	25th Wedding Anniversary	6/17/2018	Starlake	54	Yes
6	Orlando	Fagan	716 555 3694	25th Wedding Anniversary	3/10/2018	Westview	88	Yes
7	Percy	Bresque	716 555 1248	50th Wedding Anniversary	4/12/2018	Westview	62	Yes
8	Matteo	Limardi	716 555 9447	50th Wedding Anniversary	12/24/2018	Westview	125	Yes
9	Su-Lin	Ping	716 555 7774	Baby Shower	7/10/2018	Sunset	62	Yes
14	Carlotta	Balducci	716 555 9665	Birthday Party	8/22/2018	Starlake	62	Yes
15	Sonora	Yee	716 555 2668	Birthday Party	12/31/2018	Starlake	73	Yes
16	Mahika	Kapoor	716 555 3669	Birthday Party	10/5/2018	Sunset	68	Yes
17	Bogdana	Petrov	716 555 6889	Birthday Party	12/20/2018	Sunset	51	Yes
18	Frances	Corriveau	716 555 3256	Birthday Party	1/23/2018	Westview	85	Yes
19	Kim	Pockovic	905 555 3698	Birthday Party	3/18/2018	Westview	62	Yes
22	Mei-Yin	Zhang	716 555 2121	Business Meeting	12/1/2018	Starlake	28	Yes
30	Bianca	Vargas	716 555 3884	Engagement Party	10/15/2018	Starlake	40	Yes
31	Omar	Hamid	716 555 8796	Engagement Party	5/8/2018	Sunset	85	Yes
32	Elizabeth	McMaster	716 555 9442	Engagement Party	7/11/2018	Sunset	75	Yes
33	Mario	Fontaine	716 555 1886	Engagement Party	1/20/2018	Westview	177	Yes
34	Reed	Pavelich	716 555 2286	Wedding	7/25/2018	Starlake	110	Yes
35	Weston	Kressman	716 555 4219	Wedding	2/28/2018	Sunset	266	Yes
36	Max	Santore	905 555 3264	Wedding	4/28/2018	Sunset	157	Yes
37	Zack	Doucet	716 555 3488	Wedding	6/20/2018	Sunset	168	Yes
38	Bahurai	Omkar	905 555 3411	Wedding	8/30/2018	Westview	155	Yes
40	Tao	Okinawa	716 555 1665	Wedding	12/21/2018	Westview	110	Yes
41	Corina	Guzman	716 555 4112	Wedding	12/22/2018	Westview	85	Yes
42	Alfonso	Ramirez	716 555 3488	Wedding	12/31/2018	Westview	160	Yes

Filter icon indicates the column used to filter the table.

Excel hides rows that do not meet the criterion. Matching row numbers are displayed in blue.

In Brief

Filter Table
1. Click filter arrow button.
2. Remove check marks from check boxes for items you do not want to view.
3. Click OK.

Remove Filter
1. Click filter arrow button.
2. Click *Clear Filter From (column title)*.

5 Point to the filter icon in the filter arrow button in cell H3 and notice the filter criterion that displays in the ScreenTip.

6 Click the filter arrow button in cell H3.

7 Click *Clear Filter From "Special Menu"* at the drop-down list.

> All rows within the table are restored to view.

8 Click the filter arrow button in cell F3.

9 Click the *Sunset* and *Westview* check boxes at the drop-down list to remove the check marks and then click OK.

> Only the catering events for which Starlake is the specified room are displayed.

3	First Name	Last Name	Contact Phone	Event	Date	Room
4	Nicole	Griffin	905 555 4166	25th Wedding Anniversary	6/17/2018	Starlake
11	Dana	Russell	716 555 4965	Birthday Party	5/30/2018	Starlake
12	Walter	Szucs	905 555 6998	Birthday Party	6/10/2018	Starlake
13	Sofia	Delgado	716 555 8465	Birthday Party	8/10/2018	Starlake
14	Carlotta	Balducci	716 555 9665	Birthday Party	8/22/2018	Starlake
15	Sonora	Yee	716 555 2668	Birthday Party	12/31/2018	Starlake
20	Cecily	Hillmore	716 555 6598	Business Meeting	1/15/2018	Starlake
21	Lane	Gill	416 555 3264	Business Meeting	3/29/2018	Starlake
22	Mei-Yin	Zhang	716 555 2121	Business Meeting	12/1/2018	Starlake
23	Cristian	Martinez	716 555 4331	Business Meeting	12/15/2018	Starlake
30	Bianca	Vargas	716 555 3884	Engagement Party	10/15/2018	Starlake
34	Reed	Pavelich	716 555 2286	Wedding	7/25/2018	Starlake

table filtered by *Starlake* in Step 9

10 Print the filtered worksheet.

11 Click the filter arrow button in cell F3.

12 Click the *(Select All)* check box to insert a check mark and then click OK.

> Choosing the *(Select All)* check box is another way to redisplay the entire table.

13 Click the filter arrow button in cell D3.

14 Click the *(Select All)* check box to remove the check marks from all check boxes in the drop-down list, click the *Wedding* check box to insert a check mark, and then click OK.

15 Click the filter arrow button in cell F3.

16 Click the *Starlake* and *Westview* check boxes to remove the check marks and then click OK.

3	First Name	Last Name	Contact Phone	Event	Date	Room
35	Weston	Kressman	716 555 4219	Wedding	2/28/2018	Sunset
36	Max	Santore	905 555 3264	Wedding	4/28/2018	Sunset
37	Zack	Doucet	716 555 3488	Wedding	6/20/2018	Sunset
43	Total					

table filtered first by *Wedding* event and then by *Sunset* room in Steps 13–16

17 Print the filtered worksheet.

18 Redisplay all records for both filtered columns.

19 Save **4-WBCatering.xlsx**.

Check Your Work   Compare your work to the model answer to ensure that you have completed the activity correctly.

In Addition

Filtering Data Not Formatted as a Table

Data in a worksheet that has not been formatted as a table can also be filtered using techniques similar to those you learned in this activity. Select the range of cells that you wish to filter, click the Sort & Filter button in the Editing group on the Home tab, and then click *Filter* at the drop-down list. Excel adds filter arrow buttons in each column of the first row of the selected range.

Inserting, Editing, Deleting, and Printing Comments

A comment is a pop-up box containing text that can be attached to a cell and that displays when the cell pointer is positioned over a cell with an attached comment. A diagonal red triangle in the upper right corner of a cell alerts the reader that a comment exists. The Review tab contains buttons to insert and delete comments, show or hide all comment boxes, and scroll through comments within a worksheet. Use comments to provide instructions, ask questions, or add other explanatory text to a cell.

Tutorial

Inserting, Editing, and Printing Comments

What You Will Do   Dana Hirsch has given you two notes and a reminder that should be inserted into the appropriate event information in the catering contracts workbook.

1 With **4-WBCatering.xlsx** open, make cell G10 active.

2 Click the Review tab.

3 Click the New Comment button in the Comments group.

> A comment box displays anchored to the active cell with the user's name inserted in bold text at the top of the box. In worksheets accessed by multiple people, the name helps the reader identify the person who made the comment.

4 Type Waiting for Frances to confirm the final number of guests.

> If the Show All Comments button is active, click it once to turn off the Show All Comments feature.

5 Click in the worksheet outside the comment box.

> A diagonal red triangle appears in the upper right corner of cell G10, indicating that a comment exists for the cell.

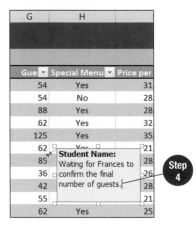

6 Right-click in cell H19 and then click *Insert Comment* at the shortcut menu.

7 Type Remind Pierre that five guests require a diabetic menu.

8 Click in the worksheet outside the comment box.

9 Hover the cell pointer over cell G10.

> Hovering the cell pointer over a cell that contains a comment causes the comment box to pop up.

10 Click in cell I24, click the New Comment button in the Comments group, type Signed contract not yet received. Follow up in two weeks., and then click in the worksheet outside the comment box.

11 Right-click in cell H19 and then click *Edit Comment* at the shortcut menu.

Steps 11

12 Move the insertion point and insert and delete text as needed to change the comment text from *five* to *six* guests that require a diabetic menu.

13 Click in the worksheet outside the comment box and then press Ctrl + Home to make cell A1 active.

14 Click the Next button in the Comments group.

Excel opens the comment box in cell G10.

Steps 14-15

15 Click the Next button to move to the next comment box.

16 Click the Next button to move to the third comment box and then click the Delete button in the Comments group.

Step 16

17 Click the Show All Comments button in the Comments group.

By default, comments do not print with the worksheet.

18 Click the Page Layout tab.

Step 18

19 Click the Page Setup group dialog box launcher in the bottom right corner of the Page Setup group.

Step 19

20 Click the Sheet tab at the Page Setup dialog box, click the *Comments* option box arrow in the *Print* section, click *As displayed on sheet* at the drop-down list, and then click OK.

21 Print the worksheet.

22 Click the Review tab and then click the Show All Comments button to remove the display of the comment boxes.

23 Save and then close **4-WBCatering.xlsx**.

Step 20

Check Your Work Compare your work to the model answer to ensure that you have completed the activity correctly.

Activity 4.10   Creating a Workbook from a Template

Excel includes worksheets that are formatted and have text and formulas for specific uses such as creating budgets, inventories, mortgage loan calculators, sales reports, and financial statements. These preformatted worksheets are called *templates*. Templates can be customized and saved with a new name to reflect individual company data. Templates are available at the New backstage area and can be downloaded from Office.com.

What You Will Do   Dana Hirsch is considering expanding the catering services offered by The Waterfront Bistro and is interested in purchasing a new property. She has asked you to find a mortgage loan calculator template and determine the payments for various loan and interest amounts.

Tutorial
Using Templates

1 Click the File tab and then click the *New* option.

2 At the New backstage area, search for mortgage loan calculator templates by clicking in the search text box (displays with *Search for online templates*), typing mortgage loan calculator, and then pressing the Enter key.

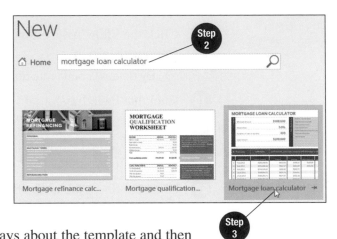

3 Click the mortgage loan calculator template shown at the right.

4 Read the information that displays about the template and then click the Create button.

5 Look at the template and notice the type of information required and the way the data is arranged on the page. Save the workbook with the name **4-WBMortgageLoan**.

6 The first property Dana Hirsch is interested in is priced at $375,000. She wants you to calculate the loan with a $50,000 down payment and an interest rate of 5.5%. Click the amount *$300,000* in the template, type 375000 as the mortgage amount, and then press the Enter key.

7 Type 5.5 as the interest rate and then press the Enter key two times.

8 Type 325000 as the loan amount and then press the Enter key.

The information that displays about the loan, such as the monthly payments, total amount of loan payments, and the interest paid automatically updates as variables are changed.

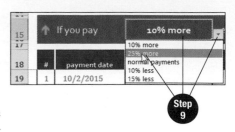

In Brief

Create Workbook from Template
1. Click File tab.
2. Click *New* option.
3. Click in search text box.
4. Type search text.
5. Press Enter.
6. Click template.
7. Click Create button.

9 The template contains a formula for determining the change in total months and payment duration if loan payments increase by 10%. Notice the information that displays with a darker gray background in the template. Click in the cell containing *10% more*, click the arrow at the right side of the cell, and then click *25% more* at the drop-down list.

> The information that displays to the right of *25% more* indicates the decrease in months and duration of the loan if payments are increased by 25%.

10 Print the first page of the worksheet. To do this, click the File tab and then click the *Print* option. At the Print backstage area, click in the *Pages* measurement box in the *Settings* category, type 1, and then press the Tab key. Type 1 in the second measurement box (after the word *to*) and then click the Print button.

11 Dana has located another property that is priced at $529,000. She wants you to calculate the loan with a $65,000 down payment and an interest rate of 4.8%. Click in the cell containing $375,000, type 529000, and then press the Enter key. Type 4.8 as the interest rate and then press the Enter key two times. Type 464000 as the loan amount and then press the Enter key.

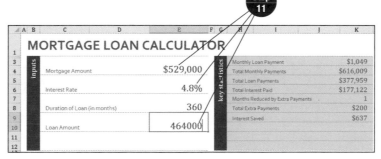

12 Print only the first page of the worksheet.

13 Save and then close **4-WBMortgageLoan.xlsx**.

> **Check Your Work** — Compare your work to the model answer to ensure that you have completed the activity correctly.

In Addition

Pinning a Template

If you use a template on a regular basis, consider pinning the template to the New backstage area. To do this, hover your mouse over the template and then click the gray left-pointing stick pin (*Pin to list*) that displays to the right of the template name. To unpin a template, click the down-pointing stick pin (*Unpin from list*).

You can save an Excel file in a different file format. This might be useful for saving a file in an earlier version of Excel, as a template, or in the OpenDocument format. Save files in a different format with options at the Export backstage area. In this backstage area, you can also save an Excel file in the PDF or XPS format. Portable Document Format (PDF) is a file format that preserves fonts, formatting, and images in a printer-friendly version that looks the same on most computers. The recipient of a PDF file does not have to have the Excel application on his or her computer to open, read, or print the file. A PDF file can be opened in various applications including Word and Adobe Acrobat Reader if Adobe Acrobat Reader is installed on the computer. Adobe Acrobat Reader is available free of charge for download from Adobe's website. Exchanging PDF files has become a popular method for collaborating with others since compatibility does not become an issue and each person keeps his or her original Excel file intact. The XML Paper Specification (XPS) format, developed by Microsoft, is a fixed-layout format with all formatting preserved (similar to PDF).

The Waterfront BISTRO

What You Will Do   Dana needs to send the quarterly sales report workbook to a colleague who uses Excel 2003 and has asked you to save the workbook in the Excel 97-2003 Workbook (*.xls) format. She has also asked you to send an investment workbook to the bistro's financial advisor. You decide to send her a PDF version of the investment workbook since you want to keep the original workbook with the formulas intact.

Tutorial
Saving a Workbook in a Different File Format

1 Open **4-WBQtrlySales.xlsx**.

2 Click the File tab and then click the *Export* option.

3 At the Export backstage area, click the *Change File Type* option.

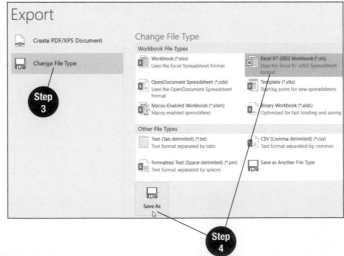

4 Click the *Excel 97-2003 Workbook (*.xls)* option in the *Change File Type* section and then click the Save As button.

5 At the Save As dialog box with **4-WBQtrlySales.xls** in the *File name* text box and *Excel 97-2003 Workbook (*.xls)* selected in the *Save as type* option box, click the Save button.

6 At the Microsoft Excel - Compatibility Checker dialog box, click the Continue button.

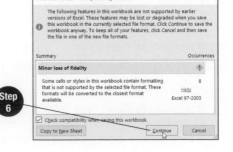

7 Close **4-WBQtrlySales.xls**.

8 Open **WBInvestment.xlsx**.

9 Click the File tab and then click the *Export* option.

10 At the Export backstage area, click the Create PDF/XPS button in the *Create a PDF/XPS Document* section.

11 At the Publish as PDF or XPS dialog box, with *WBInvestment.pdf* in the *File name* text box and with the *Save as type* already set to *PDF (*.pdf)*, make sure the *Open file after publishing* check box contains a check mark (if not, click the option), and then click the Publish button.

> The worksheet is converted to a PDF file and the published file opens in an Adobe Acrobat Reader window.

12 Print the document from the Adobe Acrobat Reader window by pressing Ctrl + P to display the Print dialog box and then clicking the Print button.

13 Close the Adobe Acrobat Reader window.

14 At the Excel window, close **WBInvestment.xlsx**.

Check Your Work Compare your work to the model answer to ensure that you have completed the activity correctly.

In Addition

Saving and Opening a File in XPS Format

Save a file in XPS format in the same manner as saving a file in PDF format. Click the File tab and then click the *Export* option. At the Export backstage area, click the Create PDF/XPS button. At the Publish as PDF or XPS dialog box, click the *Save as type* option, click *XPS Document (*.xps)* at the drop-down list, and then click the Publish button. To open an XPS file, open the File Explorer in Windows 10, navigate to the folder containing the file, and then double-click the file. This opens the file in XPS Viewer. To close the file, click the Close button in the upper right corner of the XPS Viewer window.

Features Summary

Feature	Ribbon Tab, Group	Button	File Tab Option	Keyboard Shortcut
delete comment	Review, Comments			
delete worksheet	Home, Cells			
edit comment	Review, Comments			
filter table	Home, Editing			
format sheet tab	Home, Cells			
format table	Home, Styles			
insert comment	Review, Comments			Shift + F2
insert worksheet	Home, Cells			Shift + F11
move or copy worksheet	Home, Cells			
page break preview	View, Workbook Views			
print comments	Page Layout, Page Setup			
rename worksheet	Home, Cells			
save in different file format			*Export* OR *Save As*	F12
show all comments	Review, Comments			
sort	Home, Editing			
templates			*New*	

Workbook Section study tools and assessment activities are available in the *Workbook* ebook. These resources are designed to help you further develop and demonstrate mastery of the skills learned in this section.

Word and Excel

Data Files Before beginning the section activities, copy the Integrating1 folder to your storage medium and then make Integrating1 the active folder.

Skills

- Copy and paste Word data into an Excel worksheet
- Link an Excel worksheet with a Word document
- Update linked data
- View linked data as an icon

- Link an Excel chart with a Word document
- Embed an Excel worksheet into a Word document
- Edit an embedded worksheet

Precheck Check your current skills to help focus your study of the skills taught in this section.

Projects Overview

 Copy data on costume research, design, and sewing hours for employees from a Word document into an Excel worksheet. Copy data in an Excel worksheet on employee payroll and then link the data to a Word document. Update the payroll hours for the employees for the next week. Copy employee payroll data in an Excel worksheet to a Word document and then update the data in Word.

 Link a chart containing sales commissions for agents with a Word document and then update the sales commissions to reflect a higher percentage.

 NIAGARA PENINSULA COLLEGE Copy Word data on student scores into an Excel worksheet. Copy an Excel chart containing data on student areas of emphasis in the Theatre Arts Division into a Word document and then update the chart in Excel.

 Worldwide Enterprises Copy data in an Excel worksheet on theatre company revenues into a Word document and then update the data in Word.

 SNAP If you are a SNAP user, launch the Precheck and Tutorials from your Assignments page.

Model Answers Preview the model answers for an overview of the projects you will complete in the section activities.

Microsoft Office is a suite that allows integration, which is the combining of data from two or more programs into one file. Integration can occur by copying and pasting data between programs. The program containing the data to be copied is called the source program and the program where the data is pasted is called the destination program. For example, you can copy data from a Word document into an Excel worksheet. Copy and paste data between programs in the same manner as you would copy and paste data within a program.

What You Will Do You have been handed a Word document containing data on costume research, design, and sewing hours, and you need to copy the data to an Excel worksheet.

1 Open Word and then open **PTWordJuneHrs.docx**.

2 Open Excel and then open **PTExcelJuneHrs.xlsx**.

3 Save the workbook with the name **1-PTExcelJuneHrs**.

4 Click the Word button on the taskbar.

5 Select the five lines of text in columns.

6 Click the Copy button 📋 in the Clipboard group on the Home tab.

7 Click the Excel button on the taskbar.

8 Make sure cell A2 is active and then click the Paste button 📋 in the Clipboard group.

9 Click in cell E2 to deselect the text and then double-click the gray column boundary line between columns A and B.

> This increases the width of column A so the names display.

10 With cell E2 active, click the Bold button **B** in the Font group and then type Total.

In Brief

Copy Data from One Program to Another
1. Open programs and files.
2. Select data in source program.
3. Click Copy button.
4. Click button on taskbar representing destination program.
5. Click Paste button.

11 Make cell E3 active, click the AutoSum button Σ in the Editing group on the Home tab, and then press the Enter key.

> This inserts a formula that calculates the total number of hours for Scott Bercini.

12 Using the fill handle, copy the formula in cell E3 to the range E4:E6.

13 Make cell A7 active, click the Bold button, and then type Total.

14 Make cell B7 active, click the AutoSum button in the Editing group, and then press the Enter key.

> This inserts a formula that calculates the total number of research hours.

15 Using the fill handle, copy the formula in cell B7 to the range C7:E7.

	A	B	C	D	E	F
1						
2	Employee	Research	Design	Sewing	Total	
3	Scott Bercini	3	8	14	25	
4	Terri Cantrell	5	10	18	33	
5	Paul Gottlieb	2	7	10	19	
6	Tae Jeong	6	12	20	38	
7	Total	16	37	62	115	
8						
9						

Steps 11-12

Step 13

Steps 14-15

16 Select the range A2:E7.

17 Click the Format as Table button in the Styles group on the Home tab and then click *Table Style Light 11* (fourth column, second row in the *Light* section).

Step 17

18 At the Format As Table dialog box, click OK.

19 Remove the filtering arrows that display in the range A2:E2. To do this, click the Sort & Filter button in the Editing group on the Home tab and then click *Filter* at the drop-down list.

Step 19

20 Make any other changes needed to improve the visual display of the data in cells A2 through E7.

21 Save, print, and then close **1-PTExcelJuneHrs.xlsx**.

22 Click the Word button on the taskbar.

23 Close **PTWordJuneHrs.docx**.

Check Your Work Compare your work to the model answer to ensure that you have completed the activity correctly.

In Addition

Cycling through Open Programs

Switch between open programs by clicking the button on the taskbar representing the desired program. You can also cycle through open programs by pressing Alt + Tab. Pressing Alt + Tab causes a window to display. Continue holding down the Alt key and pressing the Tab key until the desired program icon is selected in the window and then release the Tab key and the Alt key.

Linking an Excel Worksheet with a Word Document

In the previous activity, you copied data from a Word document and pasted it into an Excel worksheet. If you continuously update the data in the Word document, you would need to copy and paste the data into the Excel worksheet to keep it updated as well. To keep data updated in all programs, consider copying and linking the data. When data is linked, it exists in the source program but not as separate data in the destination program. The destination program contains only a code that identifies the name and location of the source program and the location in the source file. Since the data is located only in the source program, changes made to the data in the source program are reflected in the destination program. Office updates a link automatically whenever you open the destination program or edit the linked data in the destination program.

What You Will Do   Copy data in an Excel worksheet on employee payroll for Performance Threads and then link the data to a Word document.

1. With Word active, open **PTWordOctPay.docx**.

2. Save the document with the name **1-PTWordOctPay**.

3. Make Excel active and then open **PTExcelOctPay.xlsx**.

4. Save the workbook with the name **1-PTExcelOctPay**.

5. Link the data in the worksheet to the Word document by selecting the range A3:D8.

6. Click the Copy button in the Clipboard group on the Home tab.

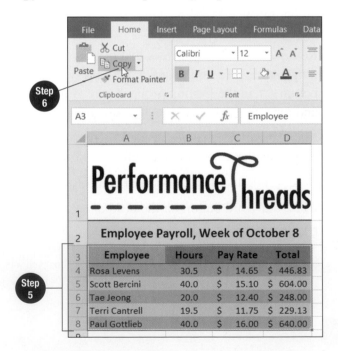

7. Click the Word button on the taskbar.

8. Press Ctrl + End to move the insertion point to the end of the document. (The insertion point is positioned a double space below *Week of October 8, 2018*.)

In Brief

Link Data between Programs
1. Open programs and documents.
2. Select data in source program.
3. Click Copy button.
4. Click button on taskbar representing destination program.
5. Click Paste button arrow.
6. Click *Paste Special*.
7. Click object in *As* list box.
8. Click *Paste link*.
9. Click OK.

9 Click the Paste button arrow and then click *Paste Special* at the drop-down gallery.

10 At the Paste Special dialog box, click *Microsoft Excel Worksheet Object* in the *As* list box.

11 Click the *Paste link* option at the left side of the dialog box.

12 Click OK to close the dialog box.

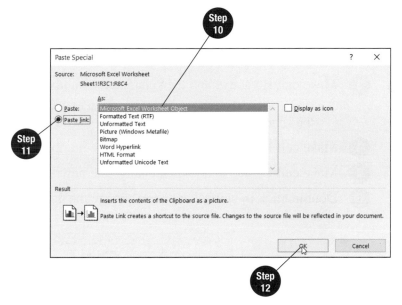

13 Save, print, and then close **1-PTWordOctPay.docx**.

The table gridlines do not print.

14 Click the Excel button on the taskbar.

15 Press the Esc key on the keyboard to remove the moving marquee around the range A3:D8 and then click in cell A3 to make it active.

16 Close **1-PTExcelOctPay.xlsx**.

Check Your Work Compare your work to the model answer to ensure that you have completed the activity correctly.

In Addition

Linking Data within a Program

Linking does not have to be between two different programs—you can link data between files in the same program. For example, you can create an object in a Word document such as a table or chart and then link the object with another Word document (or several Word documents). If you make a change to the object in the original document, the linked object in the other document (or documents) is automatically updated.

The advantage of linking data over copying data is that editing the data in the source program will automatically update the data in the destination program. To edit linked data, open the file in the source program, make the desired edits, and then save the document. The next time you open the file in the destination program, the data will be updated. The display of the linked data in the destination program can be changed to an icon. The icon represents the file and program to which the object is linked.

What You Will Do   Update the payroll hours for the employees of Performance Threads in the Excel worksheet for the week of October 15, 2018.

1 With Excel active, open **1-PTExcelOctPay.xlsx**.

2 Make cell B4 active and then change the number to *20.0*.

> The cells in the range D4:D8 contain a formula that multiplies the number in the cell in column B by the number in the cell in column C.

3 Make cell B6 active and then change the number to *25.5*.

> When you make cell B6 active, the result of the formula in cell D6 is updated to reflect the change you made to the number in cell B6.

4 Make cell B7 active and then change the number to *15.0*.

5 Make cell C7 active and then change the pay rate to *12.00*.

6 Double-click in cell A2 and then change the date from *October 8* to *October 15*.

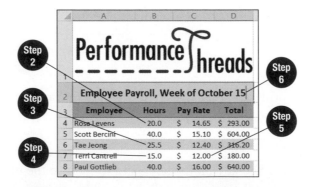

7 Save, print, and then close **1-PTExcelOctPay.xlsx**.

8 Make Word active and then open **1-PTWordOctPay.docx**.

9 At the message asking if you want to update the document, click Yes.

> The document opens and is automatically updated to reflect the changes you made in **1-PTExcelOctPay.xlsx**.

10 Change the date above the table from *October 8* to *October 15*.

11 Save and then print **1-PTWordOctPay.docx**.

Update Linked Data
1. Open file in source program.
2. Make edits.
3. Save and close file.
4. Open document in destination program.
5. Click Yes to update links.
6. Save and close file.

Display Linked Object as an Icon
1. Select object.
2. Right-click object icon.
3. Point to *Linked Worksheet Object* and then click *Convert*.
4. At Convert dialog box, click *Display as icon* check box.
5. Click OK.

12 Display the linked table as an icon. Begin by right-clicking in the table, pointing to *Linked Worksheet Object*, and then clicking *Convert*.

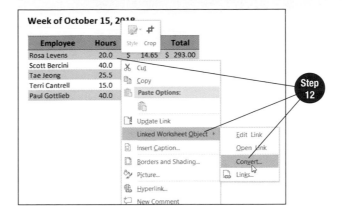

13 At the Convert dialog box, click the *Display as icon* check box to insert a check mark and then click OK.

Notice how the table changes to an icon representing the linked file.

14 Print **1-PTWordOctPay.docx**.

15 Make sure the linked object icon is still selected and then redisplay the table. To begin, right-click the object icon, point to *Linked Worksheet Object*, and then click *Convert*.

16 At the Convert dialog box, click the *Display as icon* check box to remove the check mark and then click OK.

17 Save and then close **1-PTWordOctPay.docx**.

Check Your Work Compare your work to the model answer to ensure that you have completed the activity correctly.

In Addition

Breaking a Link

The link between an object in the destination and source programs can be broken. To break a link, right-click the object icon, point to *Linked Worksheet Object*, and then click *Links*. At the Links dialog box, click the Break Link button. At the question asking if you are sure you want to break the link, click Yes.

While a worksheet does an adequate job of representing data, you can present some data more effectively in a chart. A chart is a visual representation of numeric data and, like a worksheet, can be linked to a document in another program. Link a chart in the same manner as you would link a worksheet.

What You Will Do Link a chart containing sales commissions for agents of First Choice Travel with a Word document. Change the sales commission in the worksheet chart from 3% to 4%.

1. Make Word active and then open **FCTWordSalesCom.docx**.

2. Save the document with the name **1-FCTWordSalesCom**.

3. Make Excel active and then open **FCTExcelSalesCom.xlsx**.

4. Save the workbook with the name **1-FCTExcelSalesCom**.

5. Click in the chart area to select it. (A border displays around the chart.)

   Make sure you do not select a specific chart element.

6. Click the Copy button in the Clipboard group on the Home tab.

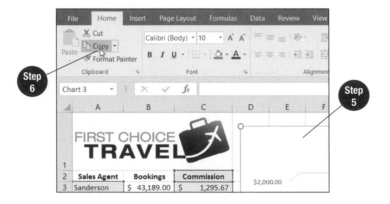

7. Click the Word button on the taskbar.

8. Press Ctrl + End to move the insertion point to the end of the document.

9. Link the chart by clicking the Paste button arrow and then clicking *Paste Special* at the drop-down list.

10. At the Paste Special dialog box, click *Microsoft Excel Chart Object* in the *As* list box, click the *Paste link* option, and then click OK.

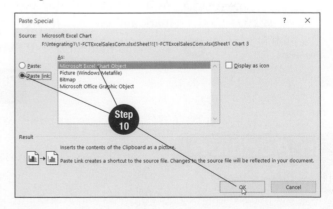

11. Save, print, and then close **1-FCTWordSalesCom.docx**.

12 Click the Excel button on the taskbar.

13 The chart is based on a sales commission of 3%. Change the formula so it calculates a sales commission of 4%. Double-click in cell C3 and then change *0.03* in the formula to *0.04*.

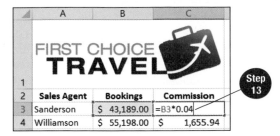

14 Press the Enter key.

> Pressing the Enter key displays the result of the formula calculating commissions at 4%.

15 Using the fill handle, copy the formula in cell C3 to the range C4:C8.

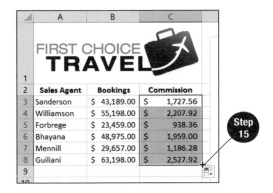

16 Save and then close **1-FCTExcelSalesCom.xlsx**.

17 Click the Word button on the taskbar and then open **1-FCTWordSalesCom.docx**.

18 At the message asking if you want to update the document, click Yes.

> Notice the change in the amounts in the chart. If your chart does not update, click the chart to select it and then press the F9 function key.

19 Save, print, and then close **1-FCTWordSalesCom.docx**.

Check Your Work Compare your work to the model answer to ensure that you have completed the activity correctly.

In Addition

Customizing a Link

By default, a linked object is updated automatically and can be edited. You can change these defaults with options at the Links dialog box. Display this dialog box by right-clicking the linked object, pointing to *Linked Worksheet Object*, and then clicking *Links*. At the Links dialog box, click the *Manual update* option if you want to control when to update linked data. With the *Manual update* option selected, update linked objects by clicking the Update Now button at the right side of the Links dialog box. If you do not want a linked object updated, click the *Locked* check box in the Links dialog box to insert a check mark.

Embedding an Excel Worksheet into a Word Document

You can copy an object between files in a program, link an object, or embed an object. A linked object resides in the source program but not as a separate object in the destination program. An embedded object resides in the file in the source program as well as in the destination program. If a change is made to an embedded object in the source program, the change is not made to the object in the destination program. Since an embedded object is not automatically updated like a linked object, the only advantage to embedding rather than simply copying and pasting is that you can edit an embedded object in the destination program using the tools of the source program.

What You Will Do   Copy data in an Excel worksheet on employee payroll for Performance Threads and then embed the data in a Word document. Update the payroll hours for the week of November 12 in the embedded Excel worksheet.

1. With Word active, open **PTWordNovPay.docx**.

2. Save the document with the name **1-PTWordNovPay**.

3. Make Excel active and then open **PTExcelNovPay.xlsx**.

4. Save the workbook with the name **1-PTExcelNovPay**.

5. Embed cells into the Word document. Start by selecting the range A3:D8.

6. Click the Copy button in the Clipboard group on the Home tab.

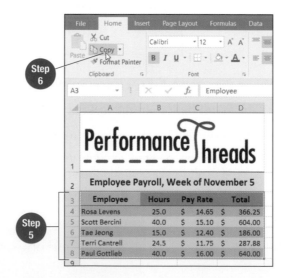

7. Click the Word button on the taskbar.

8. Press Ctrl + End to move the insertion point to the end of the document. (The insertion point is positioned a double space below *Week of November 5, 2018*.)

9. Click the Paste button arrow and then click *Paste Special* at the drop-down list.

Embed Data
1. Open programs and files.
2. Select data in source program.
3. Click Copy button.
4. Click button on taskbar representing destination program.
5. Click Paste button arrow.
6. Click *Paste Special*.
7. Click object in *As* list box.
8. Click OK.

Edit Embedded Object
1. In source program, double-click embedded object.
2. Make edits.
3. Click outside object.

10 At the Paste Special dialog box, click *Microsoft Excel Worksheet Object* in the *As* list box.

11 Click OK.

12 Save and print **1-PTWordNovPay.docx**.

13 Click the Excel button on the taskbar.

14 Press the Esc key to remove the moving marquee around the range A3:D8.

15 Click in cell A2 to make it active and then close **1-PTExcelNovPay.xlsx**.

16 Click the Word button on the taskbar.

17 Change the date above the table from *November 5* to *November 12*.

18 Position the arrow pointer anywhere in the worksheet and then double-click the left mouse button.

> In a few moments, the worksheet displays surrounded by column and row designations and the Excel tabs.

19 To produce the ordered costumes on time, the part-time employees worked a full 40 hours for the week of November 12. Make cell B4 active and then change the number to *40.0*.

20 Make cell B6 active and then change the number to *40.0*.

21 Make cell B7 active and then change the number to *40.0*.

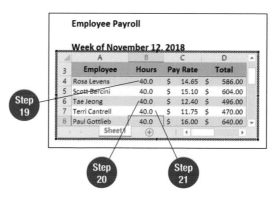

22 Bobbie Sinclair, the business manager, wants to know the payroll total for the week of November 12 to determine the impact it has on the monthly budget. Add a new row to the table by making cell A8 active and then pressing the Down Arrow key.

23 With cell A9 active, type Total.

24 Make cell D9 active and then click the AutoSum button in the Editing group.

25 Make sure the sum of the range D4:D8 displays in cell D9 and then press the Enter key.

26 Increase the height of the worksheet by one row by positioning the arrow pointer on the bottom middle black sizing square until the pointer turns into an up-and-down-pointing arrow. Click and hold down the left mouse button, drag down one row, and then release the mouse button.

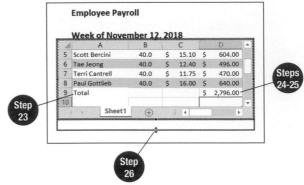

27 Using the arrow keys on the keyboard, make cell A3 active and position cell A3 in the upper left corner of the worksheet. (This will display all cells in the worksheet containing data.)

28 Click outside the worksheet to deselect it.

29 Save, print, and then close **1-PTWordNovPay.docx**.

The gridlines do not print.

Check Your Work Compare your work to the model answer to ensure that you have completed the activity correctly.

In Addition

Inserting an Embedded Object from an Existing File

You embedded an Excel worksheet in a Word document using the Copy button and options at the Paste Special dialog box. Another method is available for embedding an object from an existing file. In the destination program document, position the insertion point where you want the object embedded and then click the Object button in the Text group on the Insert tab. At the Object dialog box, click the Create from File tab. At the Object dialog box with the Create from File tab selected, type the desired file name in the *File name* text box or click the Browse button and then select the desired file from the appropriate folder. At the Object dialog box, make sure the *Link to file* check box does not contain a check mark and then click OK.

Troubleshooting Linking and Embedding Problems

If you double-click a linked or embedded object and a message appears telling you that the source file or source program cannot be opened, consider the following troubleshooting options. Check to make sure that the source program is installed on your computer. If the source program is not installed, convert the object to the file format of a program that is installed. Check to make sure the source program does not have any dialog boxes open and, if it is a linked object, check to make sure someone else is not working in the source file.

Workbook Section assessment activities are available in the *Workbook* ebook. These activities are designed to help you demonstrate mastery of the skills learned in this section.

INDEX

MARQUEE SERIES

Microsoft® Access® 2016

Nita Rutkosky
Pierce College at Puyallup
Puyallup, Washington

Audrey Roggenkamp
Pierce College at Puyallup
Puyallup, Washington

Ian Rutkosky
Pierce College at Puyallup
Puyallup, Washington

PARADIGM
EDUCATION SOLUTIONS

St. Paul

Senior Vice President	Linda Hein
Editor in Chief	Christine Hurney
Director of Production	Timothy W. Larson
Production Editors	Rachel Kats, Jen Weaverling
Cover and Text Designer	Valerie King
Copy Editor	Sarah Kearin
Senior Design and Production Specialist	Jaana Bykonich
Assistant Developmental Editors	Mamie Clark, Katie Werdick
Testers	Desiree Carvel; Ann E. Mills, Ivy Tech Community College of Indiana, Indianapolis, IN
Instructional Support Writer	Brienna McWade
Indexer	Terry Casey
Vice President Information Technology	Chuck Bratton
Digital Projects Manager	Tom Modl
Vice President Sales and Marketing	Scott Burns
Director of Marketing	Lara Weber McLellan

Care has been taken to verify the accuracy of information presented in this book. However, the authors, editors, and publisher cannot accept responsibility for Web, email, newsgroup, or chat room subject matter or content, or for consequences from application of the information in this book, and make no warranty, expressed or implied, with respect to its content.

Trademarks: Some of the product names and company names included in this book have been used for identification purposes only and may be trademarks or registered trade names of their respective manufacturers and sellers. Access, Excel, Internet Explorer, Microsoft, PowerPoint, and Windows are trademarks of Microsoft Corporation in the United States and/or other countries. The authors, editors, and publisher disclaim any affiliation, association, or connection with, or sponsorship or endorsement by, such owners.

Cover Photo Credits: © whitehoune/Shutterstock.com; © Fuatkose/iStock.com

We have made every effort to trace the ownership of all copyrighted material and to secure permission from copyright holders. In the event of any question arising as to the use of any material, we will be pleased to make the necessary corrections in future printings. Thanks are due to the aforementioned authors, publishers, and agents for permission to use the materials indicated.

ISBN 978-0-76386-715-7 (print)
ISBN 978-0-76386-716-4 (digital)

© 2017 by Paradigm Publishing, Inc.
875 Montreal Way
St. Paul, MN 55102
Email: educate@emcp.com
Website: ParadigmCollege.com

Printed in the United States of America

24 23 22 21 20 19 18 17 16   1 2 3 4 5 6 7 8 9 10 11 12

Contents

Access® 2016

Microsoft Access 2016 is a *database management system (DBMS)* included with the Microsoft Office suite. Interacting with a DBMS occurs often as one performs daily routines such as withdrawing cash from the ATM, purchasing gas using a credit card, or looking up a telephone number in an online directory. In each of these activities a DBMS is accessed to retrieve information, and data is viewed, updated, and/or printed. Any application that involves storing and maintaining a large amount of data in an organized manner can be set up as an Access database. Examples include customers and invoices, suppliers and purchases, inventory and orders. While working in Access, you will create and maintain databases for the following six companies.

First Choice Travel is a travel center offering a full range of traveling services from booking flights, hotel reservations, and rental cars to offering travel seminars.

The Waterfront Bistro offers fine dining for lunch and dinner and also offers banquet facilities, a wine cellar, and catering services.

Worldwide Enterprises is a national and international distributor of products for a variety of companies and is the exclusive movie distribution agent for Marquee Productions.

Marquee Productions is involved in all aspects of creating movies from script writing and development to filming. The company produces documentaries, biographies, as well as historical and action movies.

Performance Threads maintains an inventory of rental costumes and also researches, designs, and sews special-order and custom-made costumes.

The mission of the Niagara Peninsula College Theatre Arts Division is to offer a curriculum designed to provide students with a thorough exposure to all aspects of the theatre arts.

In Section 1 you will learn how to
Maintain Data in Tables

Access databases are comprised of a series of objects. A table is the first object that is created in a new Access database. Information in the database is organized by topic, and a table stores data for one topic. For example, one table in a customer database might store customer names and addresses while another table stores the customer invoices and yet another table stores the customer payments. Table datasheets are organized like a spreadsheet, with columns and rows. Each column in the table represents one *field*, which is a single unit of information about a person, place, item, or object. Each row in the table represents one *record*, which includes all of the related fields for one person, place, item, or object. Working in tables involves adding or deleting records; editing fields; and sorting, filtering, or formatting datasheets. Access provides the Navigation pane for managing database objects.

Group objects in the database by various categories and display them in the Navigation pane.

Data in tables display in a datasheet comprised of columns and rows similar to an Excel worksheet. Each column in a table datasheet represents one field. Each row in a table datasheet represents one record.

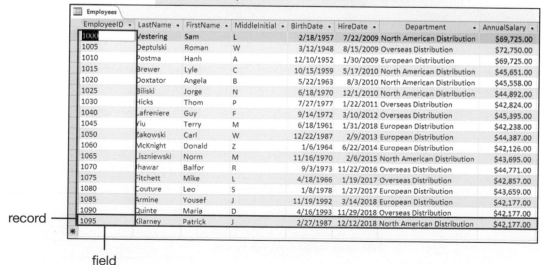

record

field

In Section 2 you will learn how to
Create New Tables and Establish Relationships

New tables can be created starting with a blank datasheet or by creating the table structure by defining fields in a view called *Design view*. Each field in a table has a set of *field properties*, which are characteristics that control how the field interacts with data in objects such as tables, forms, queries, or reports. The ability to create a relationship between two tables allows one to maintain or extract data in multiple tables as if they were one large table.

Create a new table in Table Design view by assigning each field a field name, a data type, and field properties.

Designate one field in a table as a primary key—a field that will contain unique data for each record.

field properties

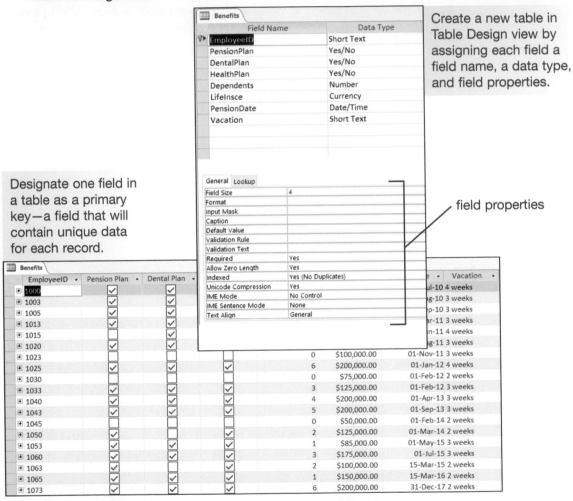

Create relationships between tables by joining one table to another on a common field. These relationships are displayed in the Relationships window using black join lines between table field list boxes.

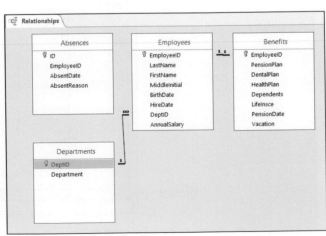

In Section 3 you will learn how to

Create Queries, Forms, and Reports

Queries and forms are objects based on tables and are created to extract, view, and maintain data. Queries can be used to view specific fields from tables that meet a particular criterion. For example, create a query to view customers from a specific state or zip code. Forms provide a more user-friendly interface for entering, editing, deleting, and viewing records in tables. Create a report to generate professionally designed printouts of information from tables or queries.

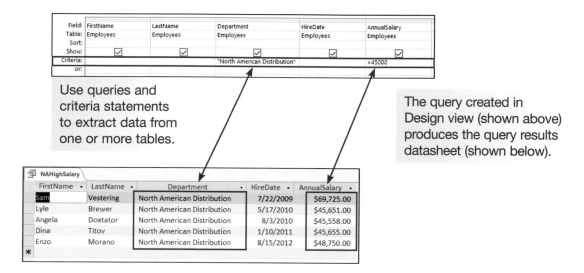

Use queries and criteria statements to extract data from one or more tables.

The query created in Design view (shown above) produces the query results datasheet (shown below).

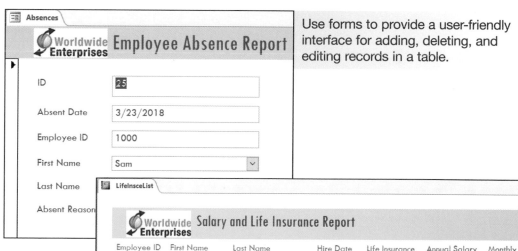

Use forms to provide a user-friendly interface for adding, deleting, and editing records in a table.

Create professional-quality printed reports using the Report tool. Report columns can be easily moved, resized, and formatted in Layout view.

Salary and Life Insurance Report

Employee ID	First Name	Last Name	Hire Date	Life Insurance	Annual Salary	Monthly Salary
1085	Yousef	Armine	3/12/2018	$125,000.00	$42,177.00	$506,124.00
1083	Drew	Arnold	6/28/2018	$75,000.00	$43,659.00	$523,908.00
1025	Jorge	Biliski	12/1/2012	$200,000.00	$44,892.00	$538,704.00
1015	Lyle	Brewer	5/19/2012	$185,000.00	$45,651.00	$547,812.00
1023	Aleksy	Bulinkski	10/13/2012	$100,000.00	$51,450.00	$617,400.00
1013	Gregg	Chippewa	2/11/2012	$200,000.00	$48,650.00	$583,800.00
1080	Leo	Couture	1/29/2018	$150,000.00	$43,659.00	$523,908.00
1005	Roman	Deptulski	8/15/2011	$150,000.00	$72,750.00	$873,000.00
1020	Angela	Doxtator	8/4/2012	$200,000.00	$45,558.00	$546,696.00
1030	Thom	Hicks	1/5/2013	$75,000.00	$42,824.00	$513,888.00
1073	Marsha	Judd	11/29/2017	$200,000.00	$44,771.00	$537,252.00
1095	Patrick	Kilarney	12/10/2018	$200,000.00	$42,177.00	$506,124.00
1040	Guy	Lafreniere	3/8/2014	$200,000.00	$45,395.00	$544,740.00

Summarize Data and Create Calculations

Large amounts of data in tables can be summarized using various tools available within Access. Aggregate functions calculate statistics such as the sum, average, maximum, and minimum values on a numeric field. Crosstab queries use functions on a numeric field to group data by two fields. Forms and reports can have data conditionally formatted, and you can add a calculated field to a form and/or report to calculate a result from a numeric field. Reports can be more meaningful when like data is grouped and sorted. Mailing labels are produced easily with the assistance of the Labels Wizard.

SalaryStatsByDept

SumOfAnnualSalary ▾	AvgOfAnnualSalary ▾	MaxOfAnnualSalary ▾	MinOfAnnualSalary ▾	Department ▾
$314,687.00	$44,955.29	$51,450.00	$42,126.00	European Distribution
$645,975.00	$46,141.07	$69,725.00	$41,875.00	North American Distribution
$203,146.00	$50,786.50	$72,750.00	$42,177.00	Overseas Distribution

Summarize data by calculating statistics such as sum, average, maximum, and minimum. Show statistics for the entire table or group them by a field.

Use a crosstab query to group data by two fields. In this example, tuition payments are grouped by employee (rows) and by quarter (columns).

PayrollByDeptByYear

Department ▾	Total Of AnnualSalary ▾	2011 ▾	2012 ▾	2013 ▾	2014 ▾	2015 ▾	2016 ▾	2017 ▾	2018 ▾
European Distribution	$314,687.00		$100,100.00			$86,625.00	$42,126.00		$85,836.00
North American Distribution	$645,975.00	$111,600.00	$136,101.00	$45,655.00	$48,750.00		$43,695.00	$132,161.00	$128,013.00
Overseas Distribution	$203,146.00	$72,750.00		$42,824.00	$45,395.00				$42,177.00

PDCourses

Worldwide Enterprises

Professional Development Course Reimbursement

Add labels, calculations, and images to forms (as shown at left) and group and sort reports (as shown below).

EmployeeID	1020
Course Description	Introduction to Accounting
Registration Date	05-Sep-17
End Date	15-Dec-17
Grade	B-
Tuition	$485.00
Accredited School	☑
Transcript Received	☑
Date Reimbursed	23-Jan-18

MINIMUM GRADE OF C- IS REQUIRED.

EmployeesByDept

Employee Salaries by Department

12:13:21 PM

Department	Employee ID	First Name	Last Name	Hire Date	Annual Salary
European Distribution					
	1085	Yousef	Armine	3/12/2018	$42,177.00
	1023	Aleksy	Bulinkski	10/13/2012	$51,450.00
	1013	Gregg	Chippewa	2/11/2012	$48,650.00
	1080	Leo	Couture	1/29/2018	$43,659.00
	1060	Donald	McKnight	6/22/2016	$42,126.00
	1045	Terry	Yiu	1/31/2015	$42,238.00
	1050	Carl	Zakowski	2/9/2015	$44,387.00
North American Distribution					
	1083	Drew	Arnold	6/28/2018	$43,659.00
	1025	Jorge	Biliski	12/1/2012	$44,892.00

Access

Maintaining Data in Access Tables

Data Files ▶ Before beginning section work, copy the AccessS1 folder to your storage medium and then make AccessS1 the active folder.

Skills

- Open and close Access
- Open and close an existing database
- Open and close tables, queries, forms, and reports
- Explore and navigate in tables
- Adjust field column widths
- Find and replace data
- Add and delete records in a table and form

- Sort and filter records
- Preview and print a table
- Change margins
- Change the page orientation
- Use the Help and Tell Me features
- Change the font size for records in a table
- Hide columns in a table

Precheck ▶ Check your current skills to help focus your study of the skills taught in this section.

Projects Overview

Add, delete, find, sort, and filter records; change page orientation and margins; format and hide columns in a table in two databases.

Find student records and enter grades into the Grades database.

Maintain the Inventory database by adding and deleting records. Add, delete, and modify records; sort, filter, and set print options for a Catering Event database.

Delete records and sort and print a report from the Costume Inventory database. Create field names and table names for a new Custom Costume database.

 If you are a SNAP user, launch the Precheck and Tutorials from your Assignments page.

Note: On some computer systems, a file downloaded from the Internet, or copied from a storage medium retains the source file's read-only attribute. If this occurs, you will not be able to make changes to the database file. Complete the following steps to check and then remove a file's read-only status:

1. Open a File Explorer window.
2. Navigate to the drive representing your storage medium.
3. Navigate to the AccessS1 folder.
4. Right-click a database file and then click *Properties* at the shortcut menu.
5. At the Properties dialog box with the General tab selected, look at the *Read-only* check box in the *Attributes* section. If it contains a check mark, click the check box to remove it; if the check box is empty, the read-only attribute is not turned on (no action is required).
6. Click OK.

If the read-only attribute is not active for one file in the copied folder, then you can assume all files copied without an active read-only attribute. If you cleared the *Read-only* check box for one file, you will need to clear the attribute for all files after downloading from the ebook. You can select multiple files and remove the read-only attribute in one operation.

Model Answers ▶ Preview the model answers for an overview of the projects you will complete in the section activities.

Opening and Closing a Database and Database Objects

Organizations use databases to keep track of customers, suppliers, employees, inventory, sales, orders, purchases, and much more. A database can be defined as a collection of data that has been organized so that the data can be easily stored, sorted, extracted, and reported. A key concept for understanding databases is that the data has to be organized. Data is organized first into a series of tables within the database, where one table contains all of the data that describe a person, place, object, event, or other subject. Within a database, a series of objects exist for entering, managing, and viewing data. The first objects created are tables. Once a table exists, other objects can be created that use the table structure as a means to enter and view the data. Some other database objects include queries, forms, and reports.

Worldwide Enterprises

What You Will Do You will open a database used by Worldwide Enterprises to keep track of distributors, orders, and movies and open and close the objects in the database to gain an understanding of important Access concepts and terminology.

Note: Make sure you have downloaded the files from the ebook to your storage medium. Open all database files from your removable storage device and NOT directly from the Student Resource Center since Access database files at the Student Resource Center are read-only. Please refer to the note on page 1 regarding checking and removing read-only attributes before proceeding with the activities in this section.

Tutorial
Opening an Existing Database

Tutorial
Opening and Closing an Object

Tutorial
Closing a Database and Closing Access

1. At the Windows 10 desktop, click the Start button and then click the Access 2016 tile.

2. At the Access opening screen, click the Open Other Files hyperlink at the bottom of the Recent list.

3. At the Open backstage area, click the *Browse* option.

4. At the Open dialog box, click *Removable Disk (F:)* in the Navigation pane.

   If you are opening and saving files in a location other than a USB flash drive, please check with your instructor. You can bypass the Open backstage area and go directly to the Open dialog box by pressing Ctrl + F12.

5. Double-click the *AccessS1* folder in the Content pane of the Open dialog box.

6. Double-click *1-WEDistributors.accdb* in the Content pane.

   A security warning message bar displays if Access determines the file you are opening did not originate from a trusted location on your computer. This often occurs when you copy a file from another medium (such as a flash drive or the Web).

7. If a security warning message bar displays, click the Enable Content button.

   Identify the various features of the Access screen by comparing your screen with the one shown in Figure 1.1.

Figure 1.1 The Access Screen

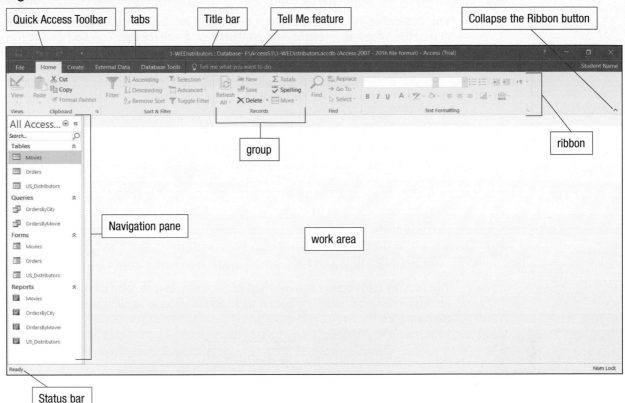

Quick Access Toolbar | tabs | Title bar | Tell Me feature | Collapse the Ribbon button

group | ribbon

Navigation pane | work area

Status bar

8 Double-click the *Orders* table in the Tables group in the Navigation pane.

The Orders table opens in Datasheet view in the work area with a tab in the upper left corner identifying the table name. Each column in the table contains only one unit of information and each row represents one record. A table is an object in a database and other objects are created using data from a table or multiple tables. Refer to Table 1.1 for a description of database objects.

Step 8

Table 1.1 Database Objects

Object	Description
table	organizes data in fields (columns) and records (rows); a database must contain at least one table. The table is the base upon which other objects are created
query	displays data from one or more tables that meets a conditional statement (for example, records in which the city is Toronto); performs calculations
form	allows fields and records to be presented in a different layout than the datasheet; used to facilitate data entry and maintenance
report	prints data from tables or queries
macro	automates repetitive tasks
module	advances automation through programming using Visual Basic for Applications

9 Double-click the *OrdersByCity* query in the Queries group in the Navigation pane.

> The OrdersByCity query opens in a new tab in the work area. A query resembles a table in that the information displays in a column-and-row format. The purpose of a query is to display data from one or more related tables that meets a conditional statement.

10 Double-click the *Movies* form in the Forms group in the Navigation pane. (Make sure you double-click *Movies* in the Forms group and not one of the other groups.)

> The Movies form opens in a new tab in the work area. A form presents fields and records in a layout different from a table and is used to facilitate data entry and maintenance.

11 Right-click the *US_Distributors* report in the Reports group in the Navigation pane. (Make sure you right-click *US_Distributors* in the Reports group and not one of the other groups.)

> Right-clicking the report displays the shortcut menu. The shortcut menu provides another method for opening an object.

12 Click *Open* at the shortcut menu.

> The US_Distributors report opens in a new tab in the work area. Reports are used to display or print data from one or more tables in a specific layout. In a report, data can be arranged, formatted, grouped, and sorted. Descriptive labels, a logo, or other items can be included.

13 Click the Orders tab in the work area.

> Clicking a tab in the work area moves that object to the foreground.

14 Close the Orders table by clicking the Close button in the upper right corner of the work area.

In Brief

Open Database
1. Click Open Other Files hyperlink.
2. Click *Browse* option.
3. Click *Removable Disk (F:)*.
4. Navigate to folder.
5. Double-click database file.
OR
1. Click File tab and then click *Open*.
2. Click *Browse* option.
3. Click *Removable Disk (F:)*.
4. Navigate to folder.
5. Double-click database file.

Open Object
Double-click object in Navigation pane.
OR
1. Right-click object.
2. Click *Open*.

Close Object
Click Close button.
OR
1. Right-click object tab.
2. Click *Close*.

15 Close the US_Distributors report by right-clicking the tab and then clicking *Close* at the shortcut menu.

The shortcut menu provides another method for closing an object.

Step 15

16 Close both of the two open objects by right-clicking the Movies tab and then clicking *Close All* at the shortcut menu.

17 Close the **1-WEDistributors.accdb** database by clicking the File tab and then clicking the *Close* option.

Clicking the File tab displays the backstage area with options for working with and managing databases.

Step 17

18 Close Access by clicking the Close button in the upper right corner of the screen.

In Addition

Learning More about the Access User Interface

While you can have several files of the same type open in the other Microsoft Office applications, only one Access database can be open at a time. If a database is open and you open another one, the first database closes. In other Microsoft Office applications, you have to save your revisions after editing text or values. In a database, changes to the data are saved automatically when you move to the next record. For this reason, the Undo command is often unavailable. If you are prompted to save changes when you close an object in Access, the prompt is referring to changes made to the layout and/or formatting of the object.

In a database, tables are the first objects created, since all other objects rely on tables as the source for their data. Each table in a database contains data for one subject such as customers, orders, suppliers, and so on. Within a table, the data is broken down into units of information about the subject, called *fields*. All of the data about one subject in the table is called a *record*. For example, in a table containing data on suppliers, one record contains the data for one supplier. Navigate in an open table using the mouse, keys on the keyboard, and/or the Record Navigation bar at the bottom of the work area.

Worldwide Enterprises

What You Will Do   You will open the database used by Worldwide Enterprises and examine the tables to determine how information is organized. You will also navigate to various fields and records in the tables.

Tutorial
Navigating in Objects

1. Open Access and then open the **1-WEDistributors.accdb** database from the AccessS1 folder on your storage medium and enable the contents, if necessary.

2. Double-click the *US_Distributors* table in the Navigation pane.

   Each column in the table in Datasheet view contains only one unit of information. Each column represents one field. Identify the fields and field names at the top of each column by comparing your screen with the one shown in Figure 1.2. The field names *DistID*, *CompanyName*, *StreetAdd1*, and so on display in the header row at the top of the table.

3. Double-click the *Movies* table in the Navigation pane.

   The Movies table opens in the work area on top of the US_Distributors table. Examine the fields and records in the table to determine how the information is organized.

4. Double-click the *Orders* table in the Navigation pane.

   The Orders table opens in the work area on top of the other two tables. Database designers often create a visual representation of the database's structure in a diagram similar to the one in Figure 1.3. Each table is represented in a box with the table name at the top of the box. Within each box, the fields that will be stored in the table are listed. The field with the asterisk is called the *primary key field*, which holds the data that uniquely identifies each record in the table (usually an identification number).

Figure 1.2 US_Distributors Table in Datasheet View

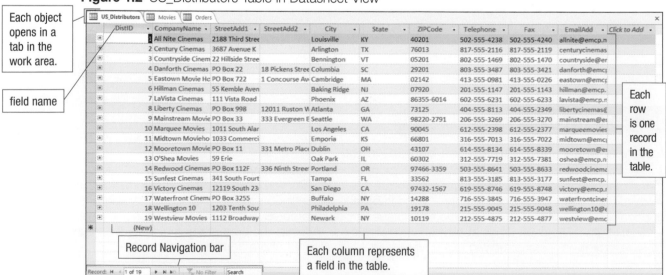

Figure 1.3 Database Diagram for 1-WEDistributors Database

⑤ Change how objects display in the Navigation pane by clicking the menu bar at the top of the Navigation pane and then clicking *Tables and Related Views* at the drop-down list.

> Originally, the Navigation pane displayed the objects grouped by type (table, query, form, and report). Clicking *Tables and Related Views* displays each table in the Navigation pane followed by the objects related to the table.

⑥ Show only the Orders table and related objects by clicking the Navigation pane menu bar and then clicking *Orders* in the *Filter By Group* section of the drop-down list.

⑦ Redisplay by object type by clicking the button on the menu bar containing a down-pointing triangle in a circle and then clicking *Object Type* at the drop-down list.

> Clicking *Object Type* displays *All Access Objects* in the *Filter By Group* section of the drop-down list. Display the Navigation pane drop-down list by clicking the menu bar or by clicking the button on the menu bar. The name of the button changes depending on what is selected.

⑧ To view more of the open objects in the work area, click the Shutter Bar Open/Close Button in the upper right corner of the Navigation pane.

> The Navigation pane collapses to a bar at the left side of the screen with the text *Navigation Pane* displayed vertically.

⑨ Redisplay the Navigation pane by clicking the Shutter Bar Open/Close Button.

> You can also collapse or redisplay the Navigation pane by pressing the F11 function key.

10 Close the Orders table by right-clicking the Orders tab and then clicking *Close* at the shortcut menu.

11 Close the Movies table by right-clicking the Movies tab and then clicking *Close* at the shortcut menu.

The US_Distributors table should be the only open table.

12 Press the Tab key to make the next field in the current record active.

Navigate in a table using keys on the keyboard, the mouse, or the Record Navigation bar. Pressing the Tab key makes the next field in the current record active. Refer to Table 1.2 for information on keyboard commands for navigating in a table.

13 Press Shift + Tab to make the previous field in the current record active.

14 Press Ctrl + End to make the last field in the last record active.

15 Press Ctrl + Home to make the first field in the first record active.

16 Move the insertion point to a field in the *CompanyName* field column by clicking anywhere in the company name *Century Cinemas* in record 2.

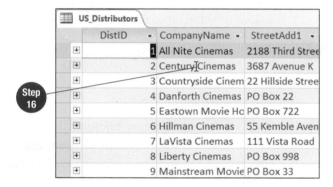

17 Make record 3 active by clicking the Next record button on the Record Navigation bar.

18 Make the last record active by clicking the Last record button on the Record Navigation bar.

Table 1.2 Navigating in an Access Table Using the Keyboard

Press	To move to
Home	first field in the current record
End	last field in the current record
Tab	next field in the current record
Shift + Tab	previous field in the current record
Ctrl + Home	first field in the first record
Ctrl + End	last field in the last record

In Brief

Change Navigation Pane View
1. Click All Access Objects button at top of Navigation pane.
2. Click view.

19 Make the first record active by clicking the First record button on the Record Navigation bar.

Step
19

20 Navigate to record 14 by triple-clicking the text *1 of 19* that displays in the *Current Record* text box on the Record Navigation bar, typing 14, and then pressing the Enter key.

Step
20

21 Close the US_Distributors table by clicking the Close button in the upper right corner of the work area.

In Addition

Planning and Designing a Table

The table below describes the steps involved in planning and designing a new database. The design process may seem time-consuming; however, the time expended to produce a well-designed database saves time later. A database that is poorly designed will likely have logical or structural errors that require redefining of data or objects after live data has been entered.

Step	Description
1. Determine the purpose of the database.	Describe who will use the database and for what purpose. This helps to focus the efforts for the remaining steps on the mission the database is to fulfill.
2. Determine all of the data that will need to be tracked in the database.	Gather all of the data elements that you will need to store in the database. You can find this information by looking at records of invoices, inventory lists, purchase orders, and so on. You can also ask individuals what information they want to get out of the database to help you determine the required data.
3. Group the data elements into tables.	Divide the information into subjects (also referred to as entities) so that one table will be about one subject only.
4. Decide the fields and field names for each table.	Break down each data element into its smallest unit. For example, a person's name could be broken down into first name, middle name, and last name.
5. Make sure each table includes a field that will be used to uniquely identify each record in the table.	Access can create an *ID* field for you if you do not have an existing unique identification number such as a product number, student number, social security number, or similar field.
6. Decide which tables need to be linked by a relationship and include in the table the common field upon which to join the tables if necessary.	Identifying relationships at this stage helps you determine if you need to add a field to a related table to allow you to join the table. You will learn more about relationships in Section 2.

Access creates columns in a table with a default width of 13.1111 characters, which is the approximate number of characters that will display in a column. Column width can be increased or decreased to accommodate the data with options at the Column Width dialog box, by double-clicking the column boundary line to adjust the width to the longest entry (referred to as best fit), or by dragging a column boundary line to the desired position. The width of multiple adjacent columns can be best fit by selecting the columns and then clicking one of the column boundary line.

Worldwide Enterprises

What You Will Do   You will reopen the US_Distributors table and adjust column widths to accommodate the longest entries in each column.

Tutorial
Adjusting Field
Column Width

1   With the **1-WEDistributors.accdb** database open, double-click the US_Distributors table in the Navigation pane.

2   With the first field selected in the *DistID* field column, click the More button in the Records group on the Home tab.

3   Click *Field Width* at the drop-down list.

4   At the Column Width dialog box with the current width selected in the *Column Width* measurement box, type 8 and then click OK.

> If the data entered in field in a column does not fill the entire field, consider decreasing the column width to save space in the work area and when the table is printed.

5   Click anywhere in the first field in the *CompanyName* field column (the field containing the text *All Nite Cinemas*).

> Clicking in a field in the *CompanyName* field column makes the column active and *CompanyName* in the header row displays with an orange background.

6   Click the More button in the Records group and then click *Field Width* at the drop-down list.

7   At the Column Width dialog box with the current width selected in the *Column Width* measurement box, type 20 and then click OK.

8   Click anywhere in the first field in the *StreetAdd1* field column (the field containing the text *2188 Third Street*).

Adjust Column Width
1. Position insertion point in column.
2. Click More button.
3. Click *Field Width*.
4. Type column width number or click Best Fit button.
OR
Drag or double-click right column boundary line in header row.

9 Click the More button and then click *Field Width* at the drop-down list.

10 At the Column Width dialog box, click the Best Fit button.

Clicking the Best Fit button causes the width of the *StreetAdd1* column to adjust to accommodate the longest entry.

11 Use the mouse to adjust the *StreetAdd2* field column. To do this, position the mouse pointer on the column boundary line between the *StreetAdd2* and *City* field column headings until the pointer displays as a left-and-right pointing arrow with a vertical line between, click and hold down the left mouse button, drag to the right approximately one-half inch, and then release the mouse button. Make sure all of the entries in the column are visible. If not, continue to increase the width of the column.

12 Select the remaining columns by positioning the mouse pointer in the *City* field column heading, clicking and holding down the left mouse button, dragging to the right to the *EmailAdd* field column heading, and then releasing the mouse button.

13 With the columns selected, double-click the column boundary line between the *City* and *State* field column headings.

Double-clicking the column boundary line best fits all of the selected columns. Double-check that the *EmailAdd* field column has fully expanded to display all entries. If not, double-click the column boundary line between the Fax and EmailAdd field column headings. You may need to scroll to the right to display the entire field.

14 Click the First record button on the Record Navigation bar.

15 Click the Save button on the Quick Access Toolbar.

Clicking the Save button saves the changes made to the column widths.

16 Close the US_Distributors table.

Check Your Work Compare your work to the model answer to ensure that you have completed the activity correctly.

In Addition

Using the Record Navigation Bar Search Text Box

Use the Record Navigation bar search text box to search for a specific entry in a field in a table. To use the search text box, click in the text box and then begin typing the search data. As you begin typing, text that matches what you type is selected in the table, which is referred to as "word-wheeling." For example, to search for Mooretown Movies in the US_Distributors table, you would start by clicking at the beginning of the first field below the *CompanyName* field column heading, clicking in the search text box, and then typing *m*. This causes Access to select the letter *m* in *Cinemas* in the first entry in the *CompanyName* field column. Type the letter *o* and Access selects *Mo* in the *Eastown Movie House* entry. Type the letter *o* again and Access selects *Moo* in *Mooretown Movies*.

In a table, you can search for specific data using the Find and Replace dialog box with the Find tab selected. Display this dialog box with the Find button on the Home tab. Using the Find and Replace dialog box saves time when searching for data when the table contains many records that are not all visible on the screen. Use the Find and Replace dialog box with the Replace tab selected to find specific data in a table and replace it with other data. Display this dialog box with the Replace button on the Home tab. Use options at the Find and Replace dialog box with either tab selected to specify where to search, such as the current field or the entire table, and what to search, such as any part of a field, the whole field, or the start of a field.

Worldwide Enterprises

What You Will Do   You have received a note from Sam Vestering that the city for Westview Movies was entered incorrectly and should be *New York* instead of *Newark*. He also indicated that the post office reference in the addresses should appear as *P.O.* and not *PO*. You will use the Find and Replace dialog box to locate and make the changes.

Tutorial
Finding Data

Tutorial
Finding and Replacing Data

1 Open the US_Distributors table and then click the first field in the *City* field column (contains the text *Louisville*).

2 Click the Find button 🔍 in the Find group on the Home tab.

Clicking the Find button opens the Find and Replace dialog box with the Find tab selected.

3 Type Newark in the *Find What* text box.

4 Click the Find Next button.

The city *Newark* is selected in record 19.

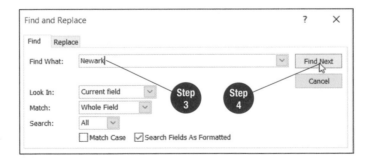

5 Click the Cancel button to close the Find and Replace dialog box.

6 Type New York.

As you type *New York* a pencil icon displays in the record selector bar at the left side of the table, indicating that the current record is being edited and the change has not been saved. When you complete Step 7, the change is saved and the pencil icon disappears.

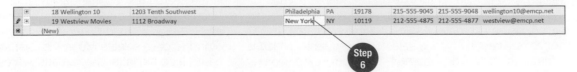

7 Click in the first field in the *DistID* field column (contains the number *1*).

In Brief

Find Data
1. Click in field in column to be searched.
2. Click Find button.
3. Type search text in *Find What* text box.
4. Click Find Next button.

Find and Replace Data
1. Click in field in column to be searched.
2. Click Replace button.
3. Type search text in *Find What* text box.
4. Press Tab.
5. Type replace text in *Replace With* text box.
6. Click Replace All button.

8 Click the Replace button in the Find group on the Home tab.

Step 8

9 At the Find and Replace dialog box with the Replace tab selected, type PO in the *Find What* text box.

10 Press the Tab key to move the insertion point to the *Replace With* text box and then type P.O.

11 Click the *Look In* option box arrow and then click *Current document* at the drop-down list.

> Changing the *Look In* option to *Current document* tells Access to search all fields in the table.

12 Click the *Match* option box arrow and then click *Any Part of Field* at the drop-down list.

> Changing the *Match* option to *Any Part of Field* tells Access to search for data that matches any part of a field—not only the entire field.

13 Click the *Match Case* check box to insert a check mark.

> Inserting a check mark in the *Match Case* check box tells Access to search only for the uppercase letters *PO*.

14 Click the Replace All button.

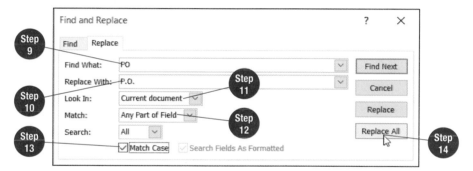

15 At the message indicating that you cannot undo the action and asking if you want to continue, click the Yes button.

> Clicking the Yes button closes the message and replaces all occurrences of *PO* with *P.O.*

16 Click the Cancel button to close the Find and Replace dialog box.

Check Your Work Compare your work to the model answer to ensure that you have completed the activity correctly.

In Addition

Exploring the Find and Replace Dialog Box Options

By default, the *Look In* option at the Find and Replace dialog box is set to *Current field*. At this setting, Access will only search in the field where the insertion point is positioned. Change this option to *Current document* and Access will search all fields in the table. The *Match* option has a default setting of *Whole Field*, which means Access will search for data that matches the entire entry in a field. If you want to search for data that matches only partial field entries, change the *Match* option to *Any Part of Field*, or *Start of Field* if you want Access to search

entries in fields that begin with the data entered in the *Find What* text box. The *Search* option has a default setting of *All*, which means Access will search all of the data in the specific field or table. This can be changed to *Up* to search from the insertion point to the beginning of the table or *Down* to search from the insertion point to the end of the table. To find data that contains specific uppercase or lowercase letters, insert a check mark in the *Match Case* check box.

Tables are the first objects created in a database and all other objects rely on a table as the source for their data. Managing the tables in a database is important for keeping the database up to date and may include adding and deleting records. Add a new record to a table in Datasheet view by clicking the New (blank) record button on the Record Navigation bar, or clicking the New button in the Records group on the Home tab. Delete a record in a table by clicking in any field in the record, clicking the Delete button arrow in the Records group on the Home tab and then clicking *Delete Record* at the drop-down list. Another method for deleting a record is to select the record by clicking the record selector bar at the left side of the record and then clicking the Delete button on the Home tab.

Worldwide Enterprises

What You Will Do   Worldwide Enterprises has signed two new distributors in the United States and one company has signed with another movie distributing company. You will add the new information in two records in the US_Distributors table and delete the old company.

Tutorial
Adding and Deleting
Records in a Table

1 With the US_Distributors table open, click the New (blank) record button ▶⃰ in the Record Navigation bar.

> The insertion point moves to the first field in the blank row at the bottom of the table in the *DistID* field column. The *Current Record* text box in the Record Navigation bar indicates you are editing record 20 of 20 records.

2 Press the Tab key to move past the *DistID* field (currently displays *(New)*) since Access automatically assigns the next sequential number to this field.

> You will learn more about the AutoNumber data type field in Section 2. The number will not appear in the field until you type an entry in the next field.

3 Type Dockside Movies in the *CompanyName* field and then press the Tab key.

⊞		18	Wellington 10	1203 Tenth Southwest
⊞		19	Westview Movies	1112 Broadway
✎ ⊞		20	Dockside Movies	
✳			(New)	

Step 3

Record: ◄ ◄ 20 of 20 ► ►I ►⃰   No Filter   Search ◄

4 Type P.O. Box 224 and then press the Tab key.

5 Type 155 Central Avenue and then press the Tab key.

6 Type Baltimore and then press the Tab key.

7 Type MD and then press the Tab key.

8 Type 21203 and then press the Tab key.

⊞	19	Westview Movies	1112 Broadway		New York	NY	10119
⊞	20	Dockside Movies	P.O. Box 224	155 Central Avenue	Baltimore	MD	21203
✳		(New)					

Steps 4-8

9 Type 301-555-7732 and then press the Tab key.

10 Type 301-555-9836 and then press the Tab key.

Add Records to Datasheet
1. Open table.
2. Click New (blank) record button in Navigation bar or click New button in Records group.
3. Type data in fields.

11 Type dockside@emcp.net and then press the Tab key.

The insertion point moves to a new row when you press the Tab key or the Enter key after the last field in a new record to allow you to continue typing the next new record in the table. The record just entered is saved automatically.

12 Type the following information in the appropriate fields in the next row:

Renaissance Cinemas
3599 Woodward Avenue
Detroit, MI 48211
313-555-1693
313-555-1699
rencinemas@emcp.net

⊞ Redwood Cinemas	P.O. Box 112F	336 Ninth Street	Portland	OR	97466-3359	503-555-8641	503-555-8633	redwoodcinemas@emcp.net
⊞ Sunfest Cinemas	341 South Fourth Avenue		Tampa	FL	33562	813-555-3185	813-555-3177	sunfest@emcp.net
⊞ Victory Cinemas	12119 South 23rd		San Diego	CA	97432-1567	619-555-8746	619-555-8748	victory@emcp.net
⊞ Waterfront Cinemas	P.O. Box 3255		Buffalo	NY	14288	716-555-3845	716-555-3947	waterfrontcinemas@emcp.net
⊞ Wellington 10	1203 Tenth Southwest		Philadelphia	PA	19178	215-555-9045	215-555-9048	wellington10@emcp.net
⊞ Westview Movies	1112 Broadway		New York	NY	10119	212-555-4875	212-555-4877	westview@emcp.net
⊞ Dockside Movies	P.O. Box 224	155 Central Avenue	Baltimore	MD	21203	301-555-7732	301-555-9836	dockside@emcp.net
⊞ Renaissance Cinemas	3599 Woodward Avenue		Detroit	MI	48211	313-555-1693	313-555-1699	rencinemas@emcp.net

Step 12

13 Position the mouse pointer in the record selector bar (empty column to the left of the *DistID* field) for record 3 (*Countryside Cinemas*) until the pointer changes to a right-pointing black arrow and then click the left mouse button.

This action selects the entire record.

14 Click the Delete button in the Records group on the Home tab.

Step 14

15 Access displays a message box indicating you are about to delete 1 record and that the undo operation is not available after this action. Click the Yes button to confirm the deletion.

Access does not renumber the remaining records in the *DistID* field once record 3 has been deleted from the table. The *DistID* field is defined as an AutoNumber data type field. For this field data type, once a number has been used, Access does not make the number available again for another record even after the record is deleted.

16 Close the US_Distributors table.

Check Your Work ▸ Compare your work to the model answer to ensure that you have completed the activity correctly.

In Addition

Understanding the Primary Key Field

In each table, one field is designated as the primary key field. A primary key field is the field by which the table is sorted whenever the table is opened. The primary key field must contain unique data for each record. When a new record is added to a table, Access checks to ensure that no record exists with the same data in the primary key field. If a record does exist with the same data in the primary key field, Access displays an error message indicating there are duplicate values and will not allow the record to be saved. The primary key field cannot be left blank when a new record is added, since it is the field that is used to sort and check for duplicates. Access includes a feature where a field named *ID* defined as the primary key field is included automatically in a new table that is created in a blank datasheet. The *ID* field uses the AutoNumber data type, which assigns the first record a field value of *1* and each new record the next sequential number.

Forms are used to enter, edit, view, and print data. Adding records in a form is easier than using a table since all of the fields in the table are presented in a different layout, which usually allows all fields to be visible at the same time. Other records in the table do not distract the user since only one record displays at a time. Add records to a form using the New (blank) record button on the Record Navigation bar or with the New button in the Records group on the Home tab. Delete a record in a form by making the record active and then clicking the Delete button in the Records group on the Home tab.

Worldwide Enterprises

What You Will Do   Worldwide Enterprises has just signed two new distributors in New York and one company has signed with another movie distributing company. You will add two new records and delete one record from the US_Distributors table using a form.

Tutorial
Adding and Deleting
Records in a Form

1. With **1-WEDistributors.accdb** open, double-click the *US_Distributors* form in the Forms group in the Navigation pane.

   The US_Distributors form opens with the first record in the US_Distributors table displayed in the form.

2. Click the New button in the Records group on the Home tab.

   A blank form displays and the Record Navigation bar indicates you are editing record number 21. The New (blank) record and Next record buttons on the Record Navigation bar are dimmed.

3. Press the Tab key to move to the *CompanyName* field, since Access automatically assigns the next sequential number to the *DistID* field.

   The *DistID* field does not display a field value until you begin to type data in another field in the record.

4. Type Movie Emporium and then press the Tab key or the Enter key.

5. Type 203 West Houston Street and then press the Tab key or the Enter key.

   Use the same navigation methods you learned in Activity 1.5 to add the record to the table.

6. Type the remaining field values as shown at the right. Press the Tab key or the Enter key after typing the last field.

   When you press the Tab key or the Enter key after the *EmailAdd* field, a new form will appear in the work area.

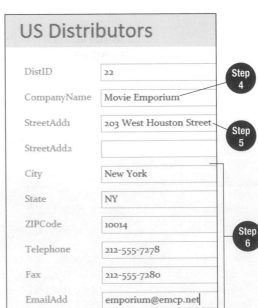

Step 1 (Navigation pane showing All Access... with Tables: Movies, Orders, US_Distributors; Queries: OrdersByCity, OrdersByMovie; Forms: Movies, Orders, US_Distributors; Reports: Movies, OrdersByCity)

US Distributors

Field	Value
DistID	22
CompanyName	Movie Emporium
StreetAdd1	203 West Houston Street
StreetAdd2	
City	New York
State	NY
ZIPCode	10014
Telephone	212-555-7278
Fax	212-555-7280
EmailAdd	emporium@emcp.net

Step 4 — CompanyName / Movie Emporium
Step 5 — StreetAdd1 / 203 West Houston Street
Step 6 — remaining fields

7 Type the following information in the appropriate fields in a new form for record 22:

Cinema Festival 212-555-9715
318 East 11th Street 212-555-9717
New York, NY 10003 cinemafest@emcp.net

8 Click the First record button in the Record Navigation bar.

This displays the record for All Nite Cinemas.

9 Click in the first field in the *CompanyName* field column, click the Home tab, and then click the Find button.

10 At the Find and Replace dialog box with the Find tab selected, type Victory Cinemas and then click the Find Next button.

11 When the record for Victory Cinemas displays, click the Cancel button to close the Find and Replace dialog box.

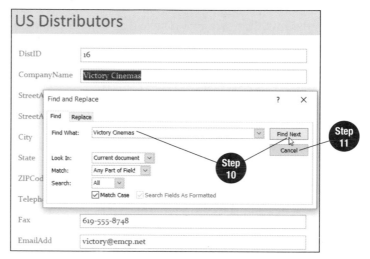

12 Click the Delete button arrow in the Records group on the Home tab and then click *Delete Record* at the drop-down list.

13 Click Yes to confirm the deletion.

14 Close the US_Distributors form.

15 Open the US_Distributors table and then view the two records added to and the one record deleted from the table using the form.

16 Close the US_Distributors table.

Check Your Work Compare your work to the model answer to ensure that you have completed the activity correctly.

In Addition

Navigating in Form View Using the Keyboard

Navigate records in a form using the following keyboard commands:
- Press Page Down to display the next record.
- Press Page Up to display the previous record.
- Press Ctrl + End to move to the last field in the last record.
- Press Ctrl + Home to move to the first field in the first record.

Records in a table are displayed alphanumerically and sorted in ascending order by the primary key field values. To rearrange the order of records in a table, click in any entry in the field you want to sort by and then click the Ascending button or Descending button in the Sort & Filter group on the Home tab. Text is sorted from A to Z (ascending) or Z to A (descending), numbers (values) are sorted from lowest to highest (ascending) or highest to lowest (descending), and dates are sorted from earliest to latest (ascending) or latest to earliest (descending). To sort by more than one field column, select the field columns first and then click the Ascending button or Descending button. Access sorts first by the leftmost field column in the selection and then by the next field column. Select adjacent field columns by positioning the mouse pointer on the header row of the first field column to be selected, click and hold down the left mouse button, drag to the header row of the last field column, and then release the mouse button. When a field is sorted, a sort icon displays in the field's header row. The sort icon displays as an up-pointing arrow if the sort is in ascending order and a down-pointing arrow if the sort is in descending order. Remove a sort by clicking the Remove Sort button on the Home tab. When a sort is removed, the records are sorted by the primary key field.

Worldwide Enterprises

What You Will Do   You will sort records in the *CompanyName* field, sort the records in the *ZIPCode* field, remove the sort, and then perform a multiple-field sort.

Tutorial
Sorting Records
in a Table

1 With **1-WEDistributors.accdb** open, open the US_Distributors table.

2 Click in any record in the *CompanyName* field column.

3 Click the Ascending button ⬛ in the Sort & Filter group on the Home tab.

The records are rearranged to display the company names in ascending alphabetic order (A to Z) and a sort icon displays to the right of *CompanyName* in the header row.

4 Click the Descending button ⬛ in the Sort & Filter group.

The records are rearranged to display the companies in descending alphabetic order (Z to A). The sort icon changes from an up-pointing arrow to a down-pointing arrow.

5 Click in any record in the *ZIPCode* field column.

6 Click the Descending button in the Sort & Filter group.

7 Click the Remove Sort button in the Sort & Filter group.

Removing the sort from the *ZIPCode* field sorts the records by the primary key field (the *DistID* field).

Sort Datasheet by Single Field
1. Open table.
2. Click in field in column by which to sort.
3. Click Ascending or Descending button.

Sort Datasheet by Multiple Fields
1. Open table.
2. Select columns from left to right in order of the sort.
3. Click Ascending or Descending button.

8 Position the mouse pointer in the *State* header row until the pointer changes to a down-pointing black arrow, click and hold down the left mouse button, drag to the right to select the *ZIPCode* field column, and then release the mouse button.

> The *State* and *ZIPCode* field columns are both selected.

Step 8

City	State	ZIPCode	Telephone
Louisville	KY	40201	502-555-4238
Arlington	TX	76013	817-555-2116
Columbia	SC	29201	803-555-3487
Cambridge	MA	02142	413-555-0981

9 Click the Ascending button.

10 Click in any field to deselect the two field columns.

> The records are sorted first by state and then by ZIP code within each state, as shown in Figure 1.4.

11 Close the US_Distributors table. Click Yes when prompted to save the design changes.

Figure 1.4 Records Sorted by State and Then by ZIP Code Within Each State

	DistID	CompanyName	StreetAdd1	StreetAdd2	City	State	ZIPCode
+	7	LaVista Cinemas	111 Vista Road		Phoenix	AZ	86355-6014
+	10	Marquee Movies	1011 South Alameda Street		Los Angeles	CA	90045
+	15	Sunfest Cinemas	341 South Fourth Avenue		Tampa	FL	33562
+	8	Liberty Cinemas	P.O. Box 998	12011 Ruston Way	Atlanta	GA	73125
+	13	O'Shea Movies	59 Erie		Oak Park	IL	60302
+	11	Midtown Moviehouse	1033 Commercial Street		Emporia	KS	66801
+	1	All Nite Cinemas	2188 Third Street		Louisville	KY	40201
+	5	Eastown Movie House	P.O. Box 722	1 Concourse Avenue	Cambridge	MA	02142
+	20	Dockside Movies	P.O. Box 224	155 Central Avenue	Baltimore	MD	21203
+	21	Renaissance Cinemas	3599 Woodward Avenue		Detroit	MI	48211
+	6	Hillman Cinemas	55 Kemble Avenue		Baking Ridge	NJ	07920
+	23	Cinema Festival	318 East 11th Street		New York	NY	10003
+	22	Movie Emporium	203 West Houston Street		New York	NY	10014
+	19	Westview Movies	1112 Broadway		New York	NY	10119
+	17	Waterfront Cinemas	P.O. Box 3255		Buffalo	NY	14288
+	12	Mooretown Movies	P.O. Box 11	331 Metro Place	Dublin	OH	43107
+	14	Redwood Cinemas	P.O. Box 112F	336 Ninth Street	Portland	OR	97466-3359
+	18	Wellington 10	1203 Tenth Southwest		Philadelphia	PA	19178
+	4	Danforth Cinemas	P.O. Box 22	18 Pickens Street	Columbia	SC	29201
+	2	Century Cinemas	3687 Avenue K		Arlington	TX	76013
+	9	Mainstream Movies	P.O. Box 33	333 Evergreen Building	Seattle	WA	98220-2791

The ZIP codes are sorted in ascending order within each state.

Check Your Work Compare your work to the model answer to ensure that you have completed the activity correctly.

In Addition

Learning More about Sorting

When sorting records, consider the following alphanumeric rules:
- Numbers stored in fields that are not defined as numeric, such as social security numbers or telephone numbers, are sorted as characters (not numeric values). To sort them as numbers, all field values must be the same length.
- Records in which the selected field is empty are listed first.
- Numbers are sorted before letters.

Moving a Column

When sorting on more than one column, the columns must be adjacent. If necessary, columns can be moved to accommodate a multiple-field sort. To move a column, click the field name in the header row to select the column. Position the mouse pointer on the field name of the selected column, click and hold down the left mouse button, drag the thick black line that displays to the desired location, and then release the mouse button.

A filter is used to view only those records that meet specified criteria. The records that do not meet the filter criteria are hidden from view temporarily. Using a filter, you can view, edit, and/or print a subset of rows within the table. For example, you might want to view only those records of distributors in one state. Apply a filter using the filter arrow that displays to the right of the column heading or click the Filter button on the Home tab. Insert or remove check marks from the field entries to be filtered. Toggle between the data in the table and the filtered data using the Toggle Filter button on the Home tab and use the *Clear All Filters* option from the Advanced button drop-down list to clear all filters from the table. Records can be sorted by specific values using the *Text Filters* option at the filter drop-down list for fields containing text, the *Number Filters* option for fields that contain number values, or the *Date Filters* option for fields containing dates.

Worldwide Enterprises

What You Will Do   You want to view a list of distributors in New York state and then further filter the list to display only those in the city of New York. In a second filter operation, you will view the distributors located in California and Georgia.

Tutorial
Filtering Records

1   With **1-WEDistributors.accdb** open, open the US_Distributors table.

2   Click in any field in the *State* field column.

3   Click the Filter button 🔽 in the Sort & Filter group on the Home tab.

4   Click the (*Select All*) check box to remove the check marks from all of the check boxes.

> At the drop-down list, click the check boxes for those states that you do not wish to view to remove the check marks.

5   Scroll down the filter list box, click the check box next to *NY*, and then click OK.

> The filter list box closes and only four records remain, as shown below. Two icons display next to *State* indicating the field is both filtered and sorted and the message *Filtered* displays in the Record Navigation bar.

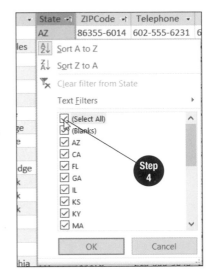

Only those records that meet the filter criterion, the *State* field, are displayed in Step 5.

City	State	ZIPCode	Telephone	Fax
New York	NY	10003	212-555-9715	212-555-9717
New York	NY	10014	212-555-7278	212-555-7280
New York	NY	10119	212-555-4875	212-555-4877
Buffalo	NY	14288	716-555-3845	716-555-3947

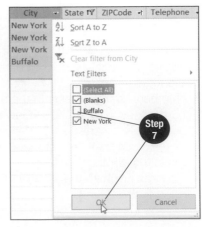

6   Click the filter arrow to the right of *City* in the header row to display the filter drop-down list.

7   Click the check box next to *Buffalo* to remove the check mark and then click OK.

> The record for the company located in Buffalo is removed and only three records remain.

In Brief

Filter Records
1. Open table.
2. Click in field by which to filter.
3. Click Filter button or click down-pointing arrow next to field name.
4. Remove check marks from check boxes for items you do not want to view.
5. Click OK.

Remove Filter
Click Toggle Filter button.

Clear All Filters
1. Click Advanced button.
2. Click *Clear All Filters*.

8 Click the Toggle Filter button 🔽 in the Sort & Filter group.

> Click the Toggle Filter button to toggle between the data in the table and the filtered data. The message in the Record Navigation bar changes to *Unfiltered*.

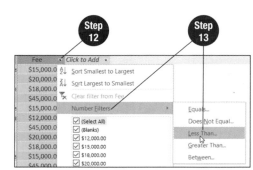

9 Remove both filters from the table by clicking the Advanced button 🔲 in the Sort & Filter group on the Home tab and then clicking *Clear All Filters*.

10 Save and then close the US_Distributors table.

11 Open the Orders table and then click in any field in the *Fee* field column.

12 Click the filter arrow to the right of *Fee* in the header row.

13 Point to *Number Filters* and then click *Less Than* at the side menu.

14 At the Custom Filter dialog box, type 15000.

> Typing 15000 in the Custom Filter dialog box specifies that you want to filter and display only those records with a fee amount less than or equal to $15,000.

15 Click OK.

> Six records display with a fee amount less than or equal to $15,000.

16 Close the Orders table and at the message that displays asking if you want to save the changes, click the No button.

In Addition

Filtering by Selection

Another method for filtering is to select specific text in a field and then click the Selection button in the Sort & Filter group on the Home tab. A drop-down list displays with filtering options such as *Equals* and *Does Not Equal*. The options vary depending on the data selected. For example, select *NY* in the *State* field in the US_Distributors table and the drop-down list displays the options *Equals "NY"*, *Does Not Equal "NY"*, *Contains "NY"*, and *Does Not Contain "NY"*. Click one of the options to filter the data.

Previewing and Printing; Changing Margins and Page Orientation

To print a table in Datasheet view, click the File tab, click the *Print* option in the backstage area and then click the *Quick Print* or *Print* option. To avoid wasting paper, use the *Print Preview* option at the Print backstage area to see how the table will appear on the page before you print. By default, Access prints a table on letter-size paper in portrait orientation. Change the paper size, orientation, or margins using buttons in the Page Size and Page Layout groups on the Print Preview tab.

Worldwide Enterprises

What You Will Do   Sam Vestering has requested a list of the US distributors. You will open the US_Distributors table, preview the printout, change the page orientation, change the left and right margins, and then print the table.

Tutorial
Previewing and Printing a Table

1   With **1-WEDistributors.accdb** open, open the US_Distributors table.

2   Click the File tab, click the *Print* option, and then click the *Print Preview* option.

   The table displays in the Print Preview window as shown in Figure 1.5.

3   Move the mouse pointer (displays as a magnifying glass) over the top center of the table and then click the left mouse button.

   Clicking the left mouse button changes the display percentage to 100%. Access prints the table name at the top center and the current date at the top right of the page. At the bottom center, Access prints the word *Page* followed by the current page number.

4   Click the left mouse button again to display the current page in the Print Preview window.

5   Click the Next Page button on the Navigation bar at the bottom left of the Print Preview window.

   The US_Distributors table requires two pages to print with the default margins and orientation. In the next step, you will change to landscape orientation to see if all of the columns will fit on one page.

Figure 1.5 Print Preview Window

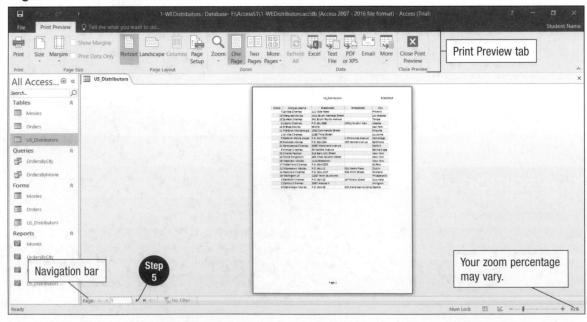

In Brief

Display Table in Print Preview
1. Click File tab.
2. Click *Print* option.
3. Click *Print Preview* option.

Change to Landscape Orientation
1. Display table in Print Preview window.
2. Click Landscape button.
3. Click Close Print Preview button.

Change Margins
1. Display table in Print Preview window.
2. Click Margins button.
3. Click predefined margins option.
OR
1. Display table in Print Preview window.
2. Click Page Setup button.
3. Change margins settings.
4. Click OK.

6 Click the Landscape button ▤ in the Page Layout group on the Print Preview tab.

> Landscape orientation rotates the printout to print wider than it is tall. Changing to landscape orientation allows more columns to fit on a page, but the US_Distributors table still needs two pages to print.

7 Click the Margins button ▦ in the Page Size group and then click the *Narrow* at the drop-down list.

> The *Narrow* option changes all margins to 0.25 inches.

8 Click the Page Setup button ▤ in the Page Layout group.

9 At the Page Setup dialog box with the Print Options tab active, select *0.25* in the *Top* measurement box and then type 2.

10 Select *0.25* in the *Left* measurement box and then type .75.

11 Click OK.

12 Click the Print button ▤ in the Print group and then click OK at the Print dialog box.

> In a few seconds, the table will print on the default printer installed on your computer. Even in landscape orientation with narrow margins, the table does not fit on one page. In Section 3, you will learn how to create a report for a table. Using a report, you can control the data layout on the page and which columns are printed.

13 Click the Close Print Preview button ✕ in the Close Preview group.

14 Close the US_Distributors table.

Step 6

Step 9   Step 10

Step 11

Check Your Work ➤ Compare your work to the model answer to ensure that you have completed the activity correctly.

In Addition

Previewing Multiple Pages

Use buttons in the Zoom group on the Print Preview tab to view a specific number of pages in a multiple-page table. Click the Two Pages button to view the table with two pages side-by-side. Click the More Pages button and then choose *Four Pages*, *Eight Pages*, or *Twelve Pages* at the drop-down list. The US_Distributors table is shown at the right in the Two Pages view.

Using the Help and Tell Me Features; Hiding Columns in a Table

An online Help resource is available that contains information on Access features and commands. Click the Microsoft Access Help button in the upper right corner of the screen to open the Access Help window. You can also get help within a dialog box, at the backstage area, or from a button's ScreenTip. Access also includes the Tell Me feature, which provides information and guidance on how to complete a function. To use Tell Me, click in the *Tell Me* text box on the ribbon and then type the function for which you want help. As you type, a drop-down list displays with options for completing the function or displaying information on the function in the Access Help window. When you click in the *Tell Me* text box, a drop-down list displays containing the last five functions entered. Hide a column in a table in Datasheet view if a field exists in the table that you do not need for data entry or editing purposes. Hiding the column provides more space in the work area, and hidden columns do not print. To hide a column, right-click the field name in the header row and then click *Hide Fields* at the shortcut menu.

Worldwide Enterprises

What You Will Do   You will explore topics in the Help feature and use the Tell Me feature to change the font size of the text in the datasheet. Finally, you will reprint the formatted datasheet with two columns hidden that you decide you do not need on the printout.

Note: The following steps assume you are connected to the Internet to access online resources.

Tutorial
Using the Help and Tell Me Features

1 With **1-WEDistributors.accdb** open, open the US_Distributors table.

2 Click the Microsoft Access Help button [?] in the upper right corner of the screen.

Find information in Help resources by typing a search word or phrase and then pressing the Enter key or clicking the Search help button.

3 Click in the search text box in the Access Help window, type keyboard shortcuts, and then press the Enter key.

Keyboard shortcuts are helpful to know since they help you perform frequently used commands more quickly.

4 Click the Keyboard shortcuts for Access hyperlink.

5 Scroll down the article in the Access Help window and then click the Shortcut keys for working with text and data in Access hyperlink.

6 Scroll down the article to the *Selecting a field or record* section.

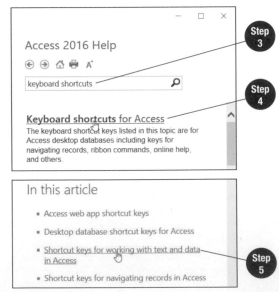

In Brief

Use Help Feature
1. Click Microsoft Access Help button.
2. Type term, phrase, or question.
3. Press Enter.
4. Click article hyperlink.
5. Close Access Help window.

Use Tell Me Feature
1. Click in *Tell Me* text box.
2. Type function.
3. Click option at drop-down list.

7 Read the descriptions and keyboard shortcuts.

8 Close the Access Help window.

9 At the US_Distributors table, click in the *Tell Me* text box and then type font size.

A drop-down list displays with options such as *Font Size*, *Font*, and *Font Color*.

10 Position the mouse pointer on the *Font Size* option at the drop-down list and then click *10* at the side menu.

The Tell Me feature guided you through the steps for changing font size.

11 Right-click the *DistID* field name in the header row and then click *Hide Fields* at the shortcut menu.

12 Right-click the *EmailAdd* field name and then click *Hide Fields* at the shortcut menu.

13 Click the File tab, click the *Print* option, and then click the *Print Preview* option.

14 Change to landscape orientation.

15 Print the table by clicking the Print button on the Print Preview tab and then clicking OK at the Print dialog box.

16 Close the Print Preview window and then close the US_Distributors table. Click Yes when prompted to save the layout changes.

17 Click the File tab and then click the *Close* option.

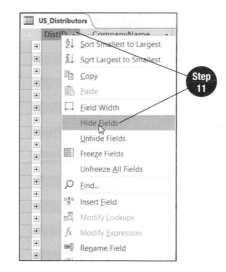

Check Your Work Compare your work to the model answer to ensure that you have completed the activity correctly.

In Addition

Accessing the Help Feature

In addition to the Microsoft Access Help button, the following options are available for displaying the Access Help window:
- Press the F1 function key.
- Hover the mouse over a button and if the ScreenTip displays a Tell me more hyperlink, click the hyperlink.

- Type a function in the *Tell Me* text box and then click the last option.
- Display the backstage area and then click the Microsoft Access Help button that displays in the upper right corner of the backstage area.

Features Summary

Feature	Ribbon Tab, Group	Button	Keyboard Shortcut
add records	Home, Records	[icon] OR [icon]	Ctrl + +
change font size	Home, Text Formatting		
change margins	Print Preview, Page Size OR Page Layout	[icon] OR [icon] to open Page Setup	
column width	Home, Records	[icon]	
delete records	Home, Records	[icon]	Delete
filter	Home, Sort & Filter	[icon]	
Find	Home, Find	[icon]	Ctrl + F
Help		[?]	F1
landscape orientation	Print Preview, Page Layout	[icon]	
Print backstage area	File, *Print*		
Print dialog box	File, *Print, Print*		Ctrl + P
Print Preview	File, *Print, Print Preview*		
save		[icon]	Ctrl + S
sort ascending order	Home, Sort & Filter	[icon]	
sort descending order	Home, Sort & Filter	[icon]	
Tell Me feature	*Tell Me* text box		Alt + Q

Workbook ▶ Section study tools and assessment activities are available in the *Workbook* ebook. These resources are designed to help you further develop and demonstrate mastery of the skills learned in this section.

Access

Creating Tables and Relationships

Data Files Before beginning section work, copy the AccessS2 folder to your storage medium and then make AccessS2 the active folder.

Skills

- Create a new database
- Create a table in Datasheet view
- Assign data types to fields
- Create captions for fields
- Limit the number of characters allowed in a field
- Create a default value for a field
- Create and modify a table in Design view
- Set the primary key field for a table
- Verify data entry using a validation rule
- Restrict data entry using an input mask

- Set the format for displaying data
- Create a lookup list in a field
- Insert, move, and delete fields
- Apply formatting to data in a table
- Add a total row to a table
- Create, edit, and delete a one-to-many relationship
- Create and print a relationship report
- Create and edit a one-to-one relationship

Precheck Check your current skills to help focus your study of the skills taught in this section.

Projects Overview

Create and modify tables to store distributor contract information and employee benefit and review information; create relationships between tables. Review tables in an existing database and improve the table design.

Create a table to store student grades for a course in the Theatre Arts Division.

Create a new database to store local event information.

Create a new database to store employee expense claims. Modify a database on tour bookings.

Modify and correct field properties in a costume inventory table to improve the design.

 SNAP If you are a SNAP user, launch the Precheck and Tutorials from your Assignments page.

Model Answers Preview the model answers for an overview of the projects you will complete in the section activities.

27

Creating a New Database; Creating a Table in Datasheet View

Tables form the basis for all other objects in a database and each table must be planned to adhere to database design principles. Creating a new table generally involves determining fields, assigning a data type to each field, designating the primary key field, and naming the table. This process is referred to as *defining the table structure*. As you learned in Section 1, Access saves data automatically as you enter records into a datasheet. For this reason, to begin a new database, you choose the Blank desktop database template at the Access opening screen, assign the database a file name, and navigate to the desired storage location. Once the database has been created, a new blank table is presented in Datasheet view. Create the table and then enter records in the table.

Worldwide Enterprises

What You Will Do   Riya Singh, a paralegal at Worldwide Enterprises, has asked you to create a new database in which distributor contracts can be maintained. You will create a new database file in which to store the contracts and then create the Contracts table. After the table is created, you will look at the table in a view that allows you to make changes to the table's structure.

Tutorial
Opening a Blank
Database

Tutorial
Creating a Table in
Datasheet View

1 Open Access and then click the *Blank desktop database* template at the Access opening screen.

2 At the Blank desktop database window, click in the *File Name* text box and then type 2-WEContracts.

> One of the differences between Access and other programs is that the file name is assigned before any data is entered. Do not remove your storage medium while working in Access since the file will frequently have data written to it.

3 Click the Browse button 📁 at the right of the *File Name* text box.

4 At the File New Database dialog box, navigate to the AccessS2 folder on your storage medium and then click OK.

5 Click the Create button.

> A blank table appears in the work area with a tab labeled *Table1*. A column with the field name *ID* has been created automatically. The heading *Click to Add* appears at the top of the first blank column.

6 Review the table design shown in Figure 2.1. This is the table you will create in Steps 7–23. Refer to Table 2.1 for guidelines for naming fields. Note that in the Contracts table design the *ID* field that Access automatically creates will be used for the primary key field.

> Before you begin creating a table, refer to Table 2.2 on page 30 for information on field data types.

Figure 2.1 Fields for Contracts Table

Contracts		
Field Name	**Data Type**	**Sample Data**
*ID	AutoNumber	
ContractNo	Short Text	2018-034
Company	Short Text	West Coast Movies
ContactFN	Short Text	Jordan
ContactLN	Short Text	Daniels
Phone	Short Text	604-555-2886
Renewal	Yes/No	Yes
StartDate	Date & Time	July 1, 2018
EndDate	Date & Time	June 30, 2020
ShipFee	Currency	$500
Percentage	Number	10
Notes	Long Text	Jordan is an active member of the Western Film Association.

Table 2.1 Field Name Guidelines

A field name can be up to 64 characters and can include both letters and numbers. Some symbols are permitted, but others are excluded, so avoiding symbols is best. An exception is the underscore, which is often used as a word separator.
Do not use a space in a field name. Although a space is an accepted character, most database designers avoid using spaces in field names and object names. This practice facilitates easier management of the data with scripting or other database programming tools. Use compound words for field names or the underscore character as a word separator. For example, a field to hold a person's last name could be named *LastName*, *Last_Name*, or *LName*.
Abbreviate field names so that the names are as short as possible while still able to be readily understood. For example, a field such as *ContactLastName* could be abbreviated to *ContactLN* or a field such as *Telephone* to *Phone*. Shorter names are easier to manage and type into expressions.

7 Click the Short Text button [AB] in the Add & Delete group on the Table Tools Fields tab.

> Access adds a new column to the datasheet with the Short Text data type assigned and selects the field name in the table header row for you to type the correct field name.

8 Type ContractNo and then press the Enter key.

> Access moves to the *Click to Add* column and opens the data type drop-down list for the next new column.

9 Click *Short Text* at the drop-down list.

10 Type Company and then press the Enter key.

11 Click *Short Text* at the drop-down list, type ContactFN, and then press the Enter key.

12 Click *Short Text* at the drop-down list, type ContactLN, and then press the Enter key.

13 Click *Short Text* at the drop-down list, type Phone, and then press the Enter key.

14 Click *Yes/No* at the drop-down list.

> The *Renewal* column will contain only one of two entries: *Yes* for those records that represent renewals of existing contracts or *No* if the record is a contract for a new distributor. When you change the data type to *Yes/No*, a check box is inserted in the column.

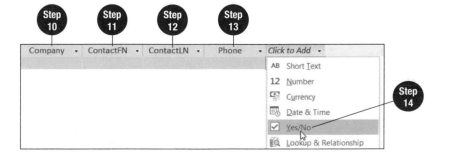

Table 2.2 Common Data Types in Datasheet View

Option	Description
Short Text	Alphanumeric data up to 255 characters in length, such as a name, address, or value such as a telephone number or social security number that is used as an identifier and not for calculating.
Number	Positive or negative values that can be used in calculations; do not use for values that will calculate monetary amounts (see *Currency*).
Currency	Values that involve money; Access will not round off during calculations.
Date & Time	Use this type to ensure dates and times are entered and sorted properly.
Yes/No	Data in the field will be either Yes or No, True or False, On or Off.
Lookup & Relationship	Can be used to enter data in the field from another existing table or display a list of values in a drop-down list for the user to choose from.
Long Text	Alphanumeric data up to 64,000 characters in length.
AutoNumber	Access automatically numbers each record sequentially (incrementing by 1) when you begin typing a new record.
Calculated Field	The contents of a calculated field are generated by Access from an expression you create; for example, a total cost could be calculated by adding a price plus a sales tax column.

15 Type Renewal and then press the Enter key.

16 Continue changing the data types and typing the field names for the remainder of the fields as shown in Figure 2.1 on page 28.

17 Press the Enter key after typing *Notes*. Click in any empty field below a column heading to remove the drop-down list and end the table.

18 If necessary, scroll to the left edge of the table. Click in the empty field below *ContractNo*, type 2018-034, and then press the Enter key or the Tab key to move to the next field.

19 Continue typing the sample data for the remainder of the fields as shown in Figure 2.1. At the first field in the *Renewal* column, click the check box or press the spacebar to insert a check mark in the box, indicating that the field entry is *Yes*.

> Access converts dates you enter into the format *m/d/yyyy*. When entering dates, be careful to use the proper punctuation and spacing between the month, day, and year so that Access recognizes the entry as a valid date.

20 Click the Save button 🖫 on the Quick Access Toolbar.

21 At the Save As dialog box with *Table1* selected in the *Table Name* text box, type Contracts and then press the Enter key or click OK.

22 Click the View button in the Views group on the Home tab. (Do not click the button arrow.)

> The View button toggles between Design view and Datasheet view. In Design view, each row represents one field in the table and is used to define the field name, the field's data type, and an optional description. The *Field Properties* section in the lower half of the work area displays the properties for the active field. The properties will vary depending on the active field. A key icon displays in the field selector bar (blank column to the left of the field names) for the *ID* field, identifying it as the primary key field.

23 Compare the entries in the *Field Name* and *Data Type* columns for each field with those shown in Figure 2.1. If necessary, correct a typing error in a field name by positioning the insertion point over the existing field name, clicking to open the field, and then inserting or deleting text as necessary. To change a data type, click in the *Data Type* column for the field, click the down-pointing arrow that displays, and then click the correct data type at the drop-down list.

24 Click the View button in the Views group on the Table Tools Design tab. If you made changes while in Design view, you will be prompted to save the table when you switch views. If necessary, click Yes at any prompts that appear.

> Since you were in Design view, the View button changed to the Datasheet view button. Click the button to change back to Datasheet view.

25 Adjust the width of the columns to best fit the longest entries.

26 Print the table in landscape orientation and then close the table, saving the changes to the table layout.

Check Your Work Compare your work to the model answer to ensure that you have completed the activity correctly.

In Addition

Pinning/Unpinning a Database File

At the Access opening screen and the Open backstage area, Access displays the most recently opened databases. If you open a database on a regular basis, consider pinning the database to the Recent list at the Access opening screen or to the *Recent* option list in the Open backstage area. To pin a database, hover the mouse over the database file name and then click the push pin that displays to the right of the file name. Whether a database file is pinned at the Access opening screen or the Open backstage area, it displays in both. Unpin a database file by hovering the mouse over the database file name and then clicking the push pin that displays to the right of the file.

Each field has characteristics associated with it, called *field properties*. Field properties are used to control the behavior or interactivity of the field in database objects. Use buttons and options in the Properties group on the Table Tools Fields tab to modify field properties. Click the Name & Caption button and the Enter Field Properties dialog box displays with options for creating a descriptive title for fields. This is useful if you abbreviate a field name but want a more descriptive name to display in the table or if you want to show spaces between words in a compound field name. Type a description in the *Description* text box and the description displays above the Status bar when entering records in the table. Use the *Field Size* option box to limit the number of characters that are allowed in a field entry. A field size of *4* for an *ID* field would prevent ID numbers longer than four characters from being stored in a record. If most records are likely to contain the same data, create a default entry to save typing and reduce errors. Click the Default Value button in the Properties group to display the Expression Builder dialog box with options for entering a default value.

Worldwide Enterprises

What You Will Do   You will modify the field properties of some of the fields in the Contracts table by providing a caption and description, specifying a field size, and/or providing a default value.

Tutorial
Modifying Field
Properties in
Datasheet View

① With **2-WEContracts.accdb** open, open the Contracts table.

② Click the *ContactFN* field name in the header row.

③ Click the Table Tools Fields tab.

④ Click the Name & Caption button 📋 in the Properties group.

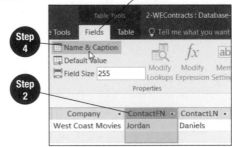

⑤ At the Enter Field Properties dialog box, click in the *Caption* text box and then type First Name.

⑥ Click in the *Description* text box and then type Enter contact's first name.

⑦ Click OK to close the dialog box.

> The caption *First Name* now displays in the header row instead of *ContactFN*. The field name is still *ContactFN*, but the user-friendly caption displays in the header row.

⑧ Limit the field size for the contact's first name by clicking the number *255* in the *Field Size* option box in the Properties group, typing 20, and then pressing Enter.

⑨ At the message that displays indicating that the size of the field has been changed to a shorter size and asking if you want to continue, click the Yes button.

10 Click the *ContactLN* field name in the header row.

11 Click the Name & Caption button in the Properties group.

12 At the Enter Field Properties dialog box, click in the *Caption* text box and then type Last Name.

13 Click in the *Description* text box, type Enter contact's last name, and then click OK.

14 Click the number *255* in the *Field Size* option box, type 25, and then press the Enter key.

15 At the message that displays indicating that the size of the field has been changed to a shorter size and that some of the data may be lost, click the Yes button.

16 Click the *Renewal* field name in the header row.

17 Click the Default Value button in the Properties group.

18 At the Expression Builder dialog box, select the current default value *No* in the dialog box text box and then type Yes.

19 Click OK.

With a default value of *Yes*, a check mark will automatically appear in the *Renewal* check box for new records entered in the table.

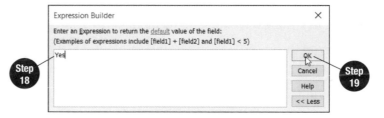

20 Print the table in landscape orientation and then close the table, saving the changes to the table layout.

21 Close **2-WEContracts.accdb**.

Check Your Work Compare your work to the model answer to ensure that you have completed the activity correctly.

In Addition

Changing an AutoNumber Data Type Field

Access automatically applies the AutoNumber data type to the first field in a table created in Datasheet view and assigns a unique number to each record. In many cases, letting Access automatically assign a number to a record is a good idea. Some situations may arise, however, when you want the unique value in the first field to be something other than a number. If you try to change the AutoNumber data type in the first column by clicking one of the data type buttons in the Add & Delete group on the Table Tools Fields tab, Access creates another field. To change the AutoNumber data type for the first field, click the *Data Type* option box arrow in the Formatting group on the Table Tools Fields tab and then click the desired data type at the drop-down list.

As an alternative to creating a table in Datasheet view, you can create a table in Design view. In Design view, you can set the field's properties the way you need them right away. When you use Design view, Access does not add the *ID* field to the new table automatically. As mentioned previously, a table should have a primary key field, or a field used to store a unique value for each record. Examples of fields suitable for a primary key field are those that store an identification value such as an employee number, a part number, a vendor number, or a customer number. If, when you are working on a table's design, you do not have any data suited to a primary key field, create a field labeled *ID* and set the data type to *AutoNumber*. When creating a table in Datasheet view, the Properties group on the Table Tools Fields tab contains buttons and an option for modifying or adding field properties. In Design view, the *Field Properties* section contains property boxes with options for adding or modifying field properties.

Worldwide Enterprises

What You Will Do Rhonda Trask, human resources manager, has asked you to work in the employees database. Rhonda would like you to create a new table in the file in which to store the employee benefit plan information. You decide to create this table in Design view and add and modify field properties.

Tutorial
Creating a Table in Design View

Tutorial
Setting the Primary Key Field

Tutorial
Modifying Field Properties in Design View

1. Open **2-WEEmployees.accdb** and enable the contents, if necessary.

   This database is similar to the database you worked with in the Skills Review for Section 1. This version of the database has additional records added.

2. Click the Create tab and then click the Table Design button in the Tables group.

3. With the insertion point positioned in the *Field Name* column in the first row, type EmployeeID and then press the Enter key or the Tab key to move to the next column.

4. With *Short Text* already entered in the *Data Type* column, change the default field size from *255* to *4* by double-clicking the number 255 in the *Field Size* property box in the *Field Properties* section and then typing 4.

   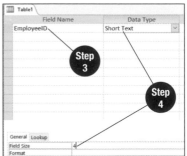

   The *EmployeeID* field will contain numbers; however, leave the data type defined as *Short Text* since no calculations will be performed with employee numbers. Notice the information that displays in the bottom right corner of the Design window. Access displays information about the field in which the insertion point is positioned.

5. Click in the *Description* column to the right of *Short Text*, type Type the four-digit employee number, and then press the Enter key to move to the second row.

6. Type PensionPlan in the *Field Name* column in the second row and then press the Enter key.

7. Click the arrow at the right of the *Data Type* column and then click *Yes/No* at the drop-down list.

   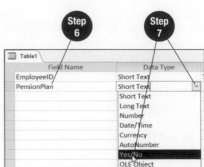

   In this field, the data is only one of two entries: *Yes* if the employee is enrolled in the pension plan or *No* if the employee is not.

8 Change the default value from *No* to *Yes* by double-clicking *No* in the *Default Value* property box in the *Field Properties* section and then typing Yes.

Step 8

9 Click in the *Description* column to the right of *Yes/No*, type Click or press spacebar for Yes; leave empty for No, and then press the Enter key.

10 Enter the remaining field names, data types, and descriptions as shown in Figure 2.2 by completing steps similar to those in Steps 3–9. Change the default value for the *HealthPlan* field to *Yes*.

11 Click anywhere in the *EmployeeID* field name.

12 Click the Primary Key button in the Tools group on the Table Tools Design tab.

Step 12

Step 11

> A key icon appears in the field selector bar to the left of *EmployeeID*, indicating the field is the primary key field.

13 Click the Save button on the Quick Access Toolbar.

14 At the Save As dialog box, type Benefits in the *Table Name* text box and then press the Enter key or click OK.

Step 14

15 Close the Benefits table.

Figure 2.2 Design View Table Entries

Field Name	Data Type	Description (Optional)
EmployeeID	Short Text	Type the four-digit employee number
PensionPlan	Yes/No	Click or press spacebar for Yes; leave empty for No
DentalPlan	Yes/No	Click or press spacebar for Yes; leave empty for No
HealthPlan	Yes/No	Click or press spacebar for Yes; leave empty for No
Dependents	Number	Type the number of dependents related to this employee
LifeInsce	Currency	Type the amount of life insurance subscribed by this employee

Check Your Work Compare your work to the model answer to ensure that you have completed the activity correctly.

In Addition

Using the More Button on the Table Tools Fields tab in Datasheet View

Click the More Fields button to choose from a list of other field data types and fields that have predefined field properties. Scroll down the More Fields drop-down list to the *QuickStart* category. Options in this category allow you to add a group of related fields in one step. For example, click *Address* to add five new fields: *Address*, *City*, *StateProvince*, *ZIPPostal*, and *CountryRegion*.

Activity 2.4 Applying Validation Rules

The accuracy of data in a table is extremely important. To control the data entered in a field and improve the accuracy of the data, apply a validation rule. For example, a validation rule can be applied that specifies amounts entered in a field must be less than a certain number. Apply a validation rule to a field in Datasheet view with the Validation button in the Field Validation group on the Table Tools Fields tab or with the *Validation Rule* property box in Design view. A validation message can be included that displays if the data entered in a field violates the validation rule. Use the Validation button in Datasheet view or the *Validation Text* property box in Design view to create a validation message.

Worldwide Enterprises

What You Will Do   Worldwide Enterprises offers health benefits to a maximum of five dependents. You will use the Validation button on the Table Tools Fields tab to add a validation rule and message indicating that the number in the *Dependents* field must be less than six. The company offers life insurance in amounts up to a maximum of $200,000 per employee. You will use field properties in Design view to ensure that no amounts greater than $200,000 are entered in the *LifeIns* field.

Tutorial
Applying a Validation
Rule in Datasheet View

Tutorial
Applying a Validation
Rule in Design View

1. With **2-WEmployees.accdb** open, open the Benefits table in Datasheet view.

2. Click *Dependents* in the header row.

3. Click the Table Tools Fields tab.

4. Click the Validation button 🗐 in the Field Validation group and then click the *Field Validation Rule* option.

5. Type <6 in the *Expression Builder* text box and then click OK.

6. Click the Validation button and then click the *Field Validation Message* option.

7. Type Enter a number less than 6 in the text box in the Enter Validation Message dialog box and then click OK.

8. Click the View button in the Views group to switch to Design view.

9. Click *LifeInsce* in the *Field Name* column to display the associated field properties.

10. Click in the *Validation Rule* property box, type <=200000, and then press the Enter key.

> Pressing the Enter key after typing the validation rule moves the insertion point to the *Validation Text* property box. If an invalid syntax error displays, check your typing. Do not type a dollar sign or comma in the validation rule statement. Also, make sure you have the correct less-than symbol (<) and equals symbol (=) and that the order is <=.

11. Type Enter a value that is less than or equal to $200,000 and then press the Enter key.

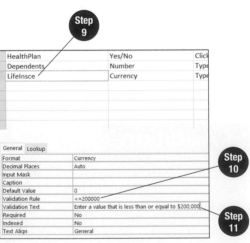

12 Click the Save button.

13 Click the View button in the Views group to switch to Datasheet view.

14 Add the following record to the table:

EmployeeID	1003
PensionPlan	Yes
DentalPlan	Yes
HealthPlan	Yes
Dependents	2
LifeInsce	210000

When you enter *210000* into the *LifeInsce* field and then press the Enter key or the Tab key, Access displays an error message. The text in the error message is the text you entered in the *Validation Text* property box.

15 Click OK at the Microsoft Access error message.

Step 15

16 Delete *210000*, type 200000, and then press the Enter key.

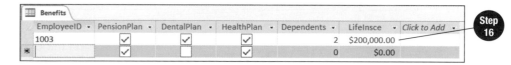

Step 16

17 Close the Benefits table.

Check Your Work   Compare your work to the model answer to ensure that you have completed the activity correctly.

In Addition

Understanding Other Types of Validation Rules

Validation rules should be created whenever possible to avoid data entry errors. The examples at the right illustrate various ways to use a validation rule to verify data.

Field Name	Validation Rule	Data Check
CustomerNo	>1000 And <1100	Limits customer numbers to 1001 through 1099.
CreditLimit	<=5000	Restricts credit limits to values of 5000 or less.
State	"CA"	Only the state of California is accepted.
Country	"CA" Or "US"	Only the United States or Canada is accepted.
OrderQty	>=25	Quantity ordered must be a minimum of 25.

An input mask displays a pattern in a table or form indicating how data is to be entered into a field. For example, an input mask in a telephone number field that displays (___)___-____ indicates to the user that a three-digit area code is to be entered in front of all telephone numbers. Input masks ensure that data is entered consistently in tables. In addition to specifying the position and number of characters in a field, you can create masks that restrict the data entered to digits, letters, or characters, and specify whether or not each digit, letter, or character is required or optional. Create an input mask in Design view with the *Input Mask* property box. Use the *Format* property box to control how the data is displayed in the field after it has been entered.

What You Will Do   You will create a new field in the Benefits table for pension plan eligibility dates and include an input mask and format property in the field.

Creating an Input Mask

1   With **2-WEEmployees.accdb** open, open the Benefits table in Design view.

2   Click in the *Field Name* column in the blank row below *LifeInsce*, type PensionDate, and then press the Enter key.

3   Change the data type to *Date/Time* and then press the Enter key.

4   Type Type date employee is eligible for pension plan in the format dd-mmm-yy (example: 31-Dec-18).

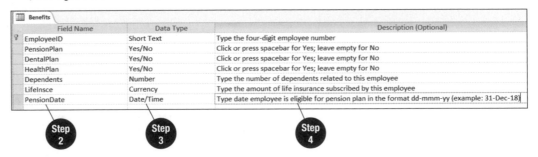

Field Name	Data Type	Description (Optional)
EmployeeID	Short Text	Type the four-digit employee number
PensionPlan	Yes/No	Click or press spacebar for Yes; leave empty for No
DentalPlan	Yes/No	Click or press spacebar for Yes; leave empty for No
HealthPlan	Yes/No	Click or press spacebar for Yes; leave empty for No
Dependents	Number	Type the number of dependents related to this employee
LifeInsce	Currency	Type the amount of life insurance subscribed by this employee
PensionDate	Date/Time	Type date employee is eligible for pension plan in the format dd-mmm-yy (example: 31-Dec-18)

Step 2   Step 3   Step 4

5   Click the Save button.

6   With the *PensionDate* field active, click in the *Input Mask* property box in the *Field Properties* section and then click the Build button [...] at the right side of the box.

7   Click *Medium Date* at the first Input Mask Wizard dialog box and then click the Next button.

The input masks that display in the list in the first dialog box are dependent on the data type for the field for which you are creating an input mask.

8   Click the Next button at the second Input Mask Wizard dialog box.

This dialog box displays the input mask code in the *Input Mask* text box and sets the placeholder character that displays in the field. The default placeholder is the underscore character.

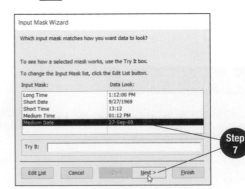

Step 7

In Brief

Use Input Mask Wizard
1. Open table in Design view.
2. Click in field row.
3. Click in *Input Mask* property box.
4. Click Build button.
5. Click input mask you want to create.
6. Click Next.
7. Select placeholder character.
8. Click Next.
9. Click Finish at the last wizard dialog box.
10. Click Save button.

9 Click the Finish button at the last Input Mask Wizard dialog box to complete the entry in the *Input Mask* property box and then press the Enter key.

10 Click in the *Format* property box.

The input mask controls how a date is entered into the field; however, by default, Access displays dates in the format *m/d/yyyy*. To avoid confusion, you will format the field to display the date in the same format that the input mask accepts the data.

11 Click the arrow at the right side of the property box and then click *Medium Date* at the drop-down list.

12 Click in the *Caption* property box and then type Pension Date.

13 Click the Save button and then switch to Datasheet view.

14 Click in the first field in the *Pension Date* column in the datasheet.

The input mask __-__-__ appears in the field.

15 Type 080718.

A beep sounds as you type every character after *08*. The only characters allowed after the first hyphen are letters. Notice the insertion point remains in the month section of the field.

16 Type 08jul18 and then press the Enter key.

Notice that you did not have to type the hyphens or capitalize the first letter of the month. The greater than symbol (>) preceding *L* in the mask causes Access to convert the first character to uppercase.

17 Adjust the width of the *Pension Date* column to best fit the longest entry.

18 Close the Benefits table. Click Yes when prompted to save changes to the layout.

> **Check Your Work** Compare your work to the model answer to ensure that you have completed the activity correctly.

In Addition

Input Mask Codes

The Input Mask Wizard is only available for fields with the Short Text or Date/Time data types. For fields with data types such as Number or Currency or for an input mask for which the wizard does not provide an option, you can create your own by entering the codes directly into the property box. At the right is a list of commonly used input mask codes.

Use	To restrict data entry to
0	digit, zero through nine, entry is required
9	digit or space, entry is not required
L	letter, A through Z, entry is required
?	letter, A through Z, entry is not required
>	all characters following are converted to uppercase
<	all characters following are converted to lowercase

Create a lookup field when you want to restrict the data entered into the field to a list of values from an existing table or a list of values that you create. The Lookup tab in the *Field Properties* section in Design view contains the options used to create a lookup field. Access includes the Lookup Wizard to facilitate entering the lookup settings.

Worldwide Enterprises

What You Will Do   You will create a new field in the Benefits table to store vacation entitlement for each employee. You want the field to display a drop-down list of vacation periods and restrict the field to accept only those entries that match items in the list.

Tutorial
Creating a Lookup Field

1 With **2-WEEmployees.accdb** open, open the Benefits table in Design view.

2 Click in the *Field Name* column in the blank row below *PensionDate*, type Vacation, and then press the Enter key.

3 Click the arrow at the right of the *Data Type* column and then click *Lookup Wizard* at the drop-down list.

4 At the first Lookup Wizard dialog box, click the *I will type in the values that I want* option and then click the Next button.

> If you press the Enter key by mistake and find yourself at the next step in the Lookup Wizard, click the Back button to return to the previous dialog box.

5 Click in the blank row below *Col1*, type 1 week, and then press the Tab key.

6 Type 2 weeks and then press the Tab key.

7 Type 3 weeks and then press the Tab key.

8 Type 4 weeks and then click the Next button.

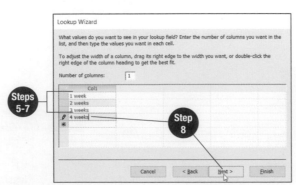

9 Click the Finish button in the last Lookup Wizard dialog box to accept the default label *Vacation*. No entry is required in the *Description* column.

In Brief

Create List of Values Using Lookup Wizard
1. Open table in Design view.
2. Type field name and press Enter.
3. Change data type to *Lookup Wizard.*
4. Click *I will type in the values that I want.*
5. Click Next.
6. Type field values in *Col1* column.
7. Click Next.
8. Click Finish.
9. Click Save.

10 Click the Lookup tab in the *Field Properties* section and then view the entries made to each property by the Lookup Wizard.

11 Click in the *Limit To List* property box, click the arrow that appears, and then click *Yes.*

> By changing the *Limit To List* property to *Yes*, you are further restricting the field to only those items in the drop-down list. If someone attempts to type an entry other than *1 week*, *2 weeks*, *3 weeks*, or *4 weeks*, Access will display an error message and will not store the data.

12 Click in the *Allow Value List Edits* property box, click the arrow that appears, and then click *No.*

> You want to make sure that changes to the list that you created are not allowed by someone using the table or a form.

13 Click the Save button and then click the View button to switch to Datasheet view.

14 If necessary, scroll right in the table, click in the first field in the *Vacation* column, type 6 weeks, and then press the Enter key.

15 Click OK at the message that displays informing you that the text entered isn't an item in the list.

16 Click *3 weeks* at the drop-down list and then press the Enter key.

17 Display the table in Print Preview. Change to landscape orientation and then print the table.

18 Close the Benefits table.

Check Your Work ▸ Compare your work to the model answer to ensure that you have completed the activity correctly.

In Addition

Looking Up Data from Another Table

Items in a drop-down list can also be generated by specifying an existing field in another table or query. To do this, click the Next button at the first Lookup Wizard dialog box to accept the default setting *I want the lookup field to get the values from another table or query*. In the remaining wizard dialog boxes, you choose the table or query and the field you want to use, choose the sort order for displaying the field values, adjust the column width for the lookup list, select the value to store, and assign a label to the column. Creating field entries using this method ensures that data is consistent between tables and eliminates duplicate typing of information that can lead to data errors. For example, in a database used to store employee information, one table could be used to enter employee numbers and then the remaining tables look up the employee number by scrolling a list of employee names.

Managing Fields; Formatting Data; Inserting a Total Row

Fields in Datasheet view can be inserted, moved, deleted, hidden, or frozen. Perform most field management tasks with buttons in the Records group on the Home tab. In Design view, fields can be inserted, moved, and deleted. Apply formatting to data in a table in Datasheet view with buttons and options in the Text Formatting group on the Home tab. Use the Totals button in the Records group on the Home tab to add a total row to a datasheet and then choose from a list of functions to find the sum, average, maximum, minimum, count, standard deviation, or variance result in a numeric column.

Worldwide Enterprises

What You Will Do   You will make changes to the structure of the Employees table in Datasheet view and Design view, apply formatting to the data in the table, and then add a total row and sum the amounts in the *AnnualSalary* column.

Tutorial
Managing Fields in Datasheet View

Tutorial
Managing Fields in Design View

Tutorial
Formatting Table Data

Tutorial
Inserting a Total Row

1 With **2-WEEmployees.accdb** open, open the Employees table in Datasheet view.

2 Click the *MiddleInitial* field column heading.

3 Click the Delete button ⊠ in the Records group on the Home tab.

4 At the message asking you to confirm the deletion, click Yes.

5 Select the *Department* field column by clicking the *Department* column heading.

6 Position the mouse pointer in the *Department* column heading (make sure the mouse displays as a white arrow); click and hold down the left mouse button, drag the thick, black, vertical line to the left so it is positioned between the *EmployeeID* and *LastName* field columns; and then release the mouse button.

When you release the mouse button, the *Department* field column is moved between the *EmployeeID* and *LastName* field columns.

7 Click the View button to switch to Design view.

Even though the *Department* field column was moved in Datasheet view, the field remains in its original location in Design view.

8 Select the *AnnualSalary* field row by positioning the mouse pointer on the field selector bar to the left of *AnnualSalary* field row and then clicking the left mouse button.

9 Position the mouse pointer (white arrow) in the field selector bar for *AnnualSalary* field row; drag the black, horizontal line up so it displays between the *BirthDate* and *HireDate* field row; and then release the left mouse button.

The field moved in Design view remains in the original location in Datasheet view.

10 Click in a field in the *Department* row.

11 Click the Insert Rows button in the Tools group on the Table Tools Design tab.

A new blank row is inserted above the *Department* field row.

Delete Field in Datasheet View
1. Click field name in header row.
2. Click Delete button.
3. Click Yes.

Delete Field in Design View
1. Select field row.
2. Click Delete button.
3. Click Yes.

Insert Field in Design View
1. Make field active that will display after new field.
2. Click Insert Rows button.

Move Field in Datasheet View
1. Click field name in header row.
2. Drag vertical line to new position and then release button.

Move Field in Design View
1. Select field using field selector bar.
2. Drag horizontal line to new position and then release mouse button.

Insert Total Row
1. Display table in Datasheet view.
2. Click Totals button.

12 With the insertion point positioned in the *Field Name* column for the new row, type Supervisor and then press the Enter key. (Access will automatically assign the *Short Text* data type.)

13 Click the Save button and then click the View button to switch to Datasheet view.

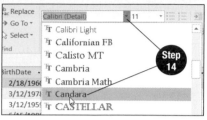

14 Click the *Font* option box arrow in the Text Formatting group on the Home tab, scroll down the drop-down list, and then click *Candara*.

15 Click the *Font Size* option box arrow in the Text Formatting group and then click *12* at the drop-down list.

16 Click the Alternate Row Color button arrow in the Text Formatting group and then click the *Tan, Background 2* color option (third column, first row in the *Theme Colors* section).

17 Click the Gridlines button in the Text Formatting group and then click *Gridlines: None* at the drop-down list.

18 Select the *EmployeeID* field by clicking the *EmpoyeeID* column heading.

19 Click the Center button in the Text Formatting group.

20 Click the Totals button ∑ in the Records group on the Home tab.

Access adds a row to the bottom of the table with the label *Total* at the left.

21 Click in the field in the *Total* row in the *AnnualSalary* column.

22 Click the arrow that appears at the left, click *Sum* at the drop-down list, and then click in any field in the table to deselect the total amount.

The sum *$1,163,808.00* appears at the bottom of the *AnnualSalary* field column.

23 Automatically adjust the width of the *Department* column to best fit the longest entry.

24 Display the table in Print Preview, change to landscape orientation, and then print the table.

25 Close the Print Preview window and then close the Employees table. Click Yes when prompted to save changes.

26 Click the File tab and then click the *Close* option.

Check Your Work Compare your work to the model answer to ensure that you have completed the activity correctly.

In Addition

Working with Wide Tables

When working in a table with many columns, scrolling right can make relating to the record in which you need to make a change difficult, since descriptor field columns such as *EmployeeID* or *LastName* may have scrolled off the screen. To alleviate this problem, you can freeze columns so they do not disappear when the datasheet is scrolled right. To do this, select the columns you want to freeze, click the More button in the Records group on the Home tab, and then click *Freeze Fields*.

Access is referred to as a *relational database management system*. A *relational database* is one in which tables have been joined. When two or more tables are joined to create a relationship, you can look up or create reports from multiple tables as if they were one table. Relationships help avoid data duplication. For example, in an employee database, the employee's first and last names would only need to appear in one table. In the remaining tables, only the employee identification number is needed. In most cases, tables are joined by a common field that exists in both tables. When two tables are joined in a relationship, one table is called the *primary table* and the other table is called the *related table*. One type of relationship is a one-to-many relationship, where one table in the relationship contains one unique record in the field used to join the tables while the other table can have several records with a matching field value in the joined field. In this type of relationship, the common field is the primary key field in the primary table and the field in the related table is the foreign key field. The referential integrity in a relationship can be enforced, which means that a value for the primary key field must first be entered in the primary table before it can be entered in the related table. Once referential integrity is enforced, other options become available for specifying that any change to the primary key field in the primary table is automatically updated in the related table and any record deleted in the primary table is automatically deleted in the related table. Establish a relationship between tables at the Relationships window. Display this window by clicking the Relationships button on the Database Tools tab.

Worldwide Enterprises

What You Will Do   You have been given a new employee database file that has additional records in the Benefits table and a new table that is used to store absence reports. You will create a one-to-many relationship between the Employees table and the Absences table using the common *EmployeeID* field. You will enforce referential integrity and cascade updated and deleted fields.

Tutorial
Creating a One-to-Many Relationship

1   Open **2-WEEmpRelationships.accdb** and enable the contents, if necessary.

2   Open the Absences table and review the entries.

   This table is used to record employee absence reports. Notice that some employees have more than one record in the table.

3   Open the Benefits table and review the entries.

4   Open the Employees table and review the entries.

   Notice that the Employees table includes fields for the employees' names.

5   Click the Absences table tab at the top of the work area and notice that the names are not duplicated in the table. However, all three tables contain an *EmployeeID* field.

Step 5

6   Close all three tables.

7   Click the Database Tools tab.

8   Click the Relationships button in the Relationships group.

   The Relationships window opens in the work area.

Step 8   Step 7

In Brief

Arrange Tables in Relationships Window
1. Click Database Tools tab.
2. Click Relationships button.
3. Add tables to window at Show Table dialog box.
4. Close Show Table dialog box.
5. Resize table field list boxes as necessary.
6. Move table field list boxes as necessary.
7. Save layout.

9 If necessary, click the Show Table button 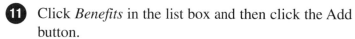 in the Relationships group. (Skip this step if the Show Table dialog box displays in the Relationships window.)

10 At the Show Table dialog box with the Tables tab selected and *Absences* selected in the list box, click the Add button.

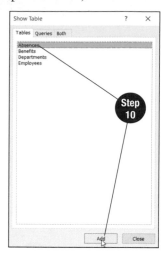

> A table field list box for the Absences table is added to the Relationships window. The Show Table dialog box remains open for you to add the next table.

11 Click *Benefits* in the list box and then click the Add button.

> Depending on the position of the Show Table dialog box in the Relationships window, the Benefits table field list box may be hidden behind the dialog box. If necessary, drag the Show Table dialog box title bar to move the dialog box out of the way.

12 Double-click *Employees* in the list box.

> Double-clicking a table name is another way to add a table field list box to the Relationships window.

13 Click the Close button in the Show Table dialog box.

> The three table field list boxes are side by side in the window. The *EmployeeID* field is the primary key field in the Employees table, but it is not the primary key field in the Absences table. This is because an employee can be absent many times; therefore, the *EmployeeID* field could not be a primary key field in the Absences table.

14 Position the mouse pointer on the bottom border of the Benefits table field list box until the pointer changes to an up-and-down-pointing arrow and then drag the bottom border down until the vertical scroll bar disappears.

> This action expands the height of the table field list box so you can see all of the field names in the box.

15 Expand the height of the Employees table field list box to see all of the field names by completing a step similar to Step 14.

16 Position the mouse pointer on the Employees table field list box title bar and then drag the table field list box below the Benefits table field list box.

17 Move the Benefits table field list box to the right and then move the Employees table field list box up to fill in the space as shown below by dragging the table field list box title bars.

> You have been arranging the table field list boxes in the Relationships window to position the Employees table in the middle of the other two tables that will be joined. This layout will make it easier to create the relationship and understand the join lines that will appear.

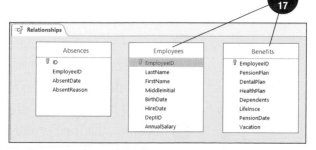

18 Position the mouse pointer on the *EmployeeID* field in the Employees table field list box, click and hold down the left mouse button, drag the pointer left to the *EmployeeID* field in the Absences table field list box, and then release the mouse button.

> A relationship is created by dragging the common field name from the primary table field list box to the related table field list box.

19 At the Edit Relationships dialog box, notice that *One-To-Many* displays in the *Relationship Type* section of the dialog box.

> Access determined the relationship type based on the common field that was used to join the tables. In the primary table (Employees), *EmployeeID* is the primary key field while in the related table (Absences), the *EmployeeID* field is not the primary key field. In the Absences table, the *EmployeeID* field is referred to as the *foreign key*.

20 Click the *Enforce Referential Integrity* check box to insert a check mark.

> *Referential integrity* means that Access will ensure that a record with the same employee number already exists in the primary table when a new record is added to the related table. This prevents what are known as *orphan records*—records in a related table for which no matching records are found in the primary table.

21 Click the *Cascade Update Related Fields* check box to insert a check mark.

> With a check mark in the *Cascade Update Related Fields* check box, make a change to a primary key field value and Access will automatically update the matching value in the related table.

22 Click the *Cascade Delete Related Records* check box to insert a check mark.

> With a check mark in the *Cascade Delete Related Records* check box, delete a record in the primary table and Access will delete any related records in the related table.

23 Click the Create button.

> A black line, called the *join line*, displays connecting the *EmployeeID* field in the Employees table field list box to the *EmployeeID* field in the Absences table field list box. Because you enforced referential integrity in the relationship, the join line displays with a *1* at the Employees table field list box and an infinity symbol at the Absences table field list box.

24 Click the Show Table button in the Relationships group.

25 At the Show Table dialog box, double-click *Departments* in the list box.

26 Click the Close button to close the Show Table dialog box.

> Join line illustrating the relationship that links the tables at the common field in each table.

27 Position the mouse pointer on the *DeptID* field in the Departments table field list box, click and hold down the left mouse button, drag the pointer to the *DeptID* field in the Employees table field list box, and then release the mouse button.

28 Click the Create button.

Since referential integrity was not enforced in this relationship, the black join line does not display with a 1 at one end and the infinity symbol at the other.

29 Click the Save button.

30 Click the Close button ⊠ on the Relationship Tools Design tab to close the Relationships window.

31 Open the Absences table.

32 Click in the blank row at the bottom of the datasheet in the *EmployeeID* field column, type 1099, and then press the Enter key.

33 Type March 3, 2018 in the *Absent Date* field column and then press the Enter key.

34 With *Sick Day* the default value in the *Absent Reason* field column, press the Enter key to accept the entry.

Access displays an error message indicating you cannot add or change a record because a related record is required in the Employees table.

35 Click OK at the Microsoft Access message box.

36 Close the Absences table. Click OK at the Microsoft Access error message that appears for the second time.

37 Click Yes at the second error message box to close the table and confirm that the data changes will be lost.

> **Check Your Work** — Compare your work to the model answer to ensure that you have completed the activity correctly.

In Addition

Clearing the Relationships Window Layout

If you are not satisfied with the layout of the table field list boxes in the Relationships window and want to remove relationships created between tables, click the Clear Layout button in the Tools group on the Relationship Tools Design tab. At the message that displays indicating the the layout will be cleared and asking if you want to continue, click the Yes button.

Editing and Deleting a Relationship; Creating a Relationship Report

A relationship between tables can be edited with options at the Edit Relationships dialog box. Display this dialog box at the Relationships window by clicking the Edit Relationships button on the Relationship Tools tab. Relationships can be deleted if you redesign the database and the existing relationship no longer applies. You may also need to delete a relationship in order to make a structural change to a table. In this case, the relationship can be deleted, the change made, and then the relationship re-created. Once all relationships have been created in a database, printing a hard copy of the relationship report to file away for future reference is a good idea. This documentation is a quick reference that displays at a glance all of the table names, fields within each table, and relationships between the tables. Should you ever have to re-create a relationship, this documentation will be of assistance to you.

Worldwide Enterprises

What You Will Do You will edit the relationship between the Departments table and Employees table, delete a relationship, and then create and then print a relationship report.

Tutorial
Editing and Deleting a Relationship

Tutorial
Creating a Relationship Report

1 With **2-WEEmpRelationships.accdb** open, open the Relationships window by clicking the Database Tools tab and then clicking the Relationships button in the Relationships group.

2 Click the Edit Relationships button in the Tools group.

Step 2

3 At the Edit Relationships dialog box, click the *Table/Query* option box arrow and then click *Departments* at the drop-down list.

> Since the Departments table contains only one relationship, *Employees* automatically displays in the *Related Table/Query* option box and *DeptID* displays below each table name.

Step 3   Step 5

Step 4

4 Click the *Enforce Referential Integrity* check box, the *Cascade Update Related Fields* check box, and the *Cascade Delete Related Records* check box to insert check marks.

5 Click OK.

6 Right-click the black join line between the Absences table field list box and the Employees table field list box.

7 Click *Delete* at the shortcut menu.

Right-click the join line to display the shortcut menu.

Step 7

Delete a Relationship
1. Open Relationships window.
2. Right-click join line between tables.
3. Click *Delete*.
4. Click Yes.

Print a Relationship Report
1. Open Relationships window.
2. Click Relationship Report button.
3. Click Print.
4. Click OK.
5. Click Close Print Preview.
6. Close report in work area.
7. Click Yes to save report, or No to close without saving.
8. Type report name.
9. Click OK.
10. Close Relationships window.

8 Click Yes at the Microsoft Access message box asking if you are sure you want to permanently delete the relationship.

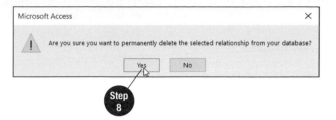

Step 8

9 Click the Relationship Report button 🖼 in the Tools group on the Relationship Tools Design tab.

Access generates the report and displays it in Print Preview in a new tab in the work area.

10 Click the Print button 🖨 in the Print group.

11 At the Print dialog box, click OK.

12 Click the Close button at the top right of the work area to close the report.

Step 10

13 Click Yes at the Microsoft Access message box asking if you want to save the report.

14 At the Save As dialog box with the existing report name already selected in the *Report Name* text box, type Relationships and then click OK or press the Enter key.

Step 14

15 Close the Relationships window.

Check Your Work Compare your work to the model answer to ensure that you have completed the activity correctly.

In Addition

Displaying Records in a Subdatasheet

When two tables are joined, you can view related records within a subdatasheet. A subdatasheet is a datasheet within a datasheet. When you open the primary table in Datasheet view, a column of plus symbols (referred to as *expand indicators*) displays between the record selector bar and the first column. Click the expand indicator next to the record for which you want to view related records. A subdatasheet opens, similar to the one shown below. The plus symbol changes to a minus symbol when a record has been expanded. Click the minus symbol (referred to as a *collapse indicator*) to close the subdatasheet.

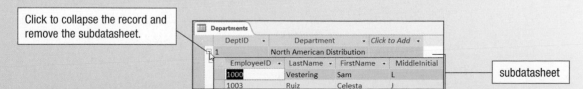

Click to collapse the record and remove the subdatasheet.

subdatasheet

A one-to-one relationship exists when both the primary table and the related table contain only one record with a matching field value in the common field. In this relationship, the common field used to join the tables is the primary key field in each table. For example, the Employees table would contain only one record for each employee. The Benefits table would also contain only one record for each employee. If these tables are joined on the common *EmployeeID* field, a one-to-one relationship would be created. In this type of relationship, consider the primary table to be the table with the fields (such as the employee names) that describe the identity of each employee number (the person for whom the employee number was created).

Worldwide Enterprises

What You Will Do   You will create a one-to-one relationship between the Employees and the Benefits tables and then edit the relationship after it has been created.

Tutorial

Creating a One-to-One Relationship

1 With **2-WEEmpRelationships.accdb** open, open the Relationships window.

2 Notice the *EmployeeID* field is the primary key field in both the Employees table field list box and the Benefits table field list box.

3 Position the mouse pointer on the *EmployeeID* field in the Employees table field list box, click and hold down the left mouse button, drag the pointer to the *EmployeeID* field in the Benefits table field list box, and then release the mouse button.

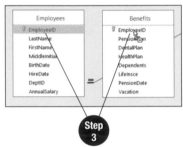

Access determined the relationship type as one-to-one since the common field that was used to join the two table field list boxes is the primary key field in each table. In both tables, only one record can exist for each unique employee number.

4 Click the Create button.

The black join line connecting the two *EmployeeID* fields appears between the two table field list boxes in the Relationships window. The join line does not show a *1* at each end because referential integrity was not enforced.

5 Click the Save button.

6 Click the Close button on the Relationship Tools Design tab to close the Relationships window.

In the next steps, you will add a record to the Benefits table to illustrate why referential integrity is a good idea to ensure primary tables are updated first.

7 Open the Benefits table and then add the following record to the table:

EmployeeID	1100
Pension Plan	Yes
Dental Plan	Yes
Health Plan	Yes
Dependents	5
Life Insurance	200000
Pension Date	31-Dec-18
Vacation	1 week

⊞ 1095				1	$200,000.00	31-Dec-18	1 week
⧊ ⊞ 1100	✓	✓	✓	5	$200,000.00	31-Dec-18	1 week

Step 7

Create a One-to-One
Relationship
1. Open Relationships
   window.
2. If necessary, add
   tables to window.
3. Close Show Table
   dialog box.
4. Drag common field
   name from primary
   table field list box to
   related table field list
   box.
5. Specify relationship
   options.
6. Click Create.
7. Click Save.

8 Open the Employees table. If necessary, scroll down to view the last record in the table. No employee record exists in the table with an employee ID of 1100.

> Since referential integrity was not turned on when the relationship was created between the Employees and the Benefits tables, you were able to add a record to the related table for which no matching record is found in the primary table. Although you could easily add the matching record to the Employees table afterwards, establishing the employee's record in the first primary table is considered good practice.

9 Close the Employees table.

10 Delete the record you added at Step 7, the record with *1100* in the *EmployeeID* field in the Benefits table, and then close the table.

11 Open the Relationships window.

12 Right-click the black join line between the Employees table field list box and the Benefits table field list box and then click *Edit Relationship* at the shortcut menu.

13 Click the *Enforce Referential Integrity* check box at the Edit Relationships dialog box and then click OK.

> Join line displays 1 at each end now that referential integrity is turned on.

With referential integrity turned on, the join line displays a *1* at each end.

14 Close the Relationships window.

15 Close **2-WEEmpRelationships.accdb**.

Check Your Work — Compare your work to the model answer to ensure that you have completed the activity correctly.

Features Summary

Feature	Ribbon Tab, Group	Button
alternate row color	Home, Text Formatting	
create table	Create, Tables	
create table in Design view	Create, Tables	
Datasheet view	Home, Views	
delete fields	Table Tools Design, Tools	
edit relationship	Relationship Tools Design, Tools	
font	Home, Text Formatting	
font size	Home, Text Formatting	
gridlines	Home, Text Formatting	
insert fields	Table Tools Design, Tools	
insert totals	Home, Records	
primary key field	Table Tools Design, Tools	
relationship report	Relationship Tools Design, Tools	
relationships	Database Tools, Relationships	

Workbook Section study tools and assessment activities are available in the *Workbook* ebook. These resources are designed to help you further develop and demonstrate mastery of the skills learned in this section.

Access

Creating Queries, Forms, and Reports

Data Files ▶ Before beginning section work, copy the AccessS3 folder to your storage medium and then make AccessS3 the active folder.

Skills

- Create a query using the Simple Query Wizard
- Create a query in Design view using one table
- Create a query in Design view using multiple tables
- Add criteria statements to a query
- Sort and hide columns in a query results datasheet
- Design a query with an *And* criteria statement and design a query with an *Or* criteria statement

- Perform calculations in a query
- Create and format a form
- Add an existing field to a form
- Manage control objects in a form
- Create and format a report
- Manage control objects in a report

Precheck ▶ Check your current skills to help focus your study of the skills taught in this section.

Projects Overview

Worldwide Enterprises
Create queries to produce custom employee lists, add criteria, and calculate pension contributions and monthly salaries; create and modify forms to facilitate data entry and viewing of records; create and modify reports to produce custom printouts of data.

Performance Threads
Create a query, and create and print a report that lists all costumes rented in a particular month; create and modify a form for browsing the costume inventory and entering new records; continue design work on a new database for custom costume activities by creating a form and a report.

Niagara Peninsula College
Create and print a query to extract records of students who achieved A+ in all of their courses.

The Waterfront Bistro
Create queries and design a report for the catering events database to extract event information for a banquet room, extract all events booked in a particular month, and calculate the estimated revenue from the catering events.

SNAP If you are a SNAP user, go to your SNAP Assignments page to complete the Precheck, Tutorials, and Recheck.

Model Answers ▶ Preview the model answers for an overview of the projects you will complete in the section activities.

Activity 3.1

Creating a Query Using the Simple Query Wizard

A query is an Access object designed to extract data from one or more tables. Usually a query is created to select records that answer a question. For example, a question such as *Which employees are enrolled in the Pension Plan?* could be answered with a query. The query would be designed to select records for those employees with a *Yes* in the *PensionPlan* field. Query results display in a datasheet that pulls the data from existing tables. A query can be created to serve a variety of purposes, from very simple field selections to complex conditional statements or calculations. In its simplest form, a query may be used to display or print selected fields from two tables. Access includes the Simple Query Wizard to facilitate creating a query.

Worldwide Enterprises

What You Will Do Using the Simple Query Wizard, you will generate a list of each employee's first and last names and benefit selections. This will allow you to print a list by selecting fields from two tables.

Tutorial
Creating a Query Using the Simple Query Wizard

1 Open **3-WEEmployees.accdb** and enable the contents, if necessary.

2 Click *Employees* in the Tables group in the Navigation pane and then click the Create tab.

3 Click the Query Wizard button 📊 in the Queries group.

4 At the New Query dialog box, with *Simple Query Wizard* already selected in the list box, click OK.

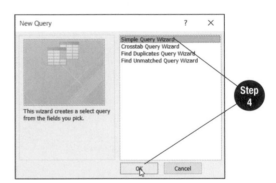

5 At the first Simple Query Wizard dialog box, with *Table: Employees* selected in the *Tables/Queries* option box and *EmployeeID* selected in the *Available Fields* list box, click the One Field button > to move *EmployeeID* to the *Selected Fields* list box.

6 With *LastName* now selected in the *Available Fields* list box, click the One Field button to move *LastName* to the *Selected Fields* list box.

7 Click the One Field button to move *FirstName* to the *Selected Fields* list box.

8 Click the the *Tables/Queries* option box arrow and then click *Table: Benefits* at the drop-down list.

> The list of fields in the *Available Fields* list box changes to display the field names from the Benefits table.

9 Double-click *PensionPlan* in the *Available Fields* list box.

> Double-clicking a field name is another way to move a field to the *Selected Fields* list box.

In Brief

Create Query Using
Simple Query Wizard
1. Click Create tab.
2. Click Query Wizard
   button.
3. Click OK.
4. Choose table(s) and
   field(s) to include in
   query.
5. Click Next.
6. Choose *Detail* or
   Summary query.
7. Click Next.
8. Type title for query.
9. Click Finish.

10 Double-click the following fields in the *Available Fields* list box to move them to the *Selected Fields* list box:

  DentalPlan
  HealthPlan
  Vacation

11 Click the Next button.

12 Click the Next button at the second Simple Query Wizard dialog box to accept *Detail (shows every field of every record)* in the *Would you like a detail or summary query?* section.

13 At the third Simple Query Wizard dialog box, select the current text in the *What title do you want for your query?* text box, type BenefitPlans, and then click the Finish button.

> View the query results datasheet shown in Figure 3.1. A query results datasheet can be sorted, edited, or formatted in a manner similar to a table. Data displayed in query results is not stored as a separate entity—the query is simply another interface for viewing and editing data in the associated table(s). Each time a saved query is opened, Access dynamically updates the query results by running the query.

14 Display the query in Print Preview, change to landscape orientation, and then print the query.

15 Close the Print Preview window and then close the BenefitPlans query.

Figure 3.1 BenefitPlans Query Results Datasheet

EmployeeID	LastName	FirstName	Pension Plan	Dental Plan	Health Plan	Vacation
1000	Vestering	Sam	✓	✓	✓	4 weeks
1003	Ruiz	Celesta	✓	✓	✓	3 weeks
1005	Deptulski	Roman	✓	✓		3 weeks
1013	Chippewa	Gregg	✓	✓	✓	3 weeks
1015	Brewer	Lyle		✓	✓	4 weeks
1020	Doxtator	Angela	✓	✓		3 weeks
1023	Bulinkski	Aleksy				3 weeks
1025	Biliski	Jorge	✓	✓	✓	4 weeks
1030	Hicks	Thom				2 weeks
1033	Titov	Dina	✓	✓	✓	3 weeks
1040	Lafreniere	Guy	✓	✓	✓	3 weeks
1043	Morano	Enzo	✓	✓	✓	3 weeks
1045	Yiu	Terry				2 weeks
1050	Zakowski	Carl	✓		✓	2 weeks
1053	O'Connor	Shauna	✓	✓	✓	3 weeks
1060	McKnight	Donald	✓	✓	✓	3 weeks
1063	McPhee	Charlotte	✓		✓	2 weeks
1065	Liszniewski	Norm	✓	✓	✓	2 weeks
1073	Judd	Marsha	✓	✓	✓	2 weeks
1080	Couture	Leo	✓	✓		1 week
1083	Arnold	Drew	✓		✓	1 week
1085	Armine	Yousef		✓	✓	1 week
1090	Quinte	Maria	✓		✓	1 week
1093	Vaquez	Luis	✓	✓		1 week
1095	Kilarney	Patrick				1 week

Check Your Work Compare your work to the model answer to ensure that you have completed the activity correctly.

Creating a Query in Design View Using a Single Table

In Section 2, you learned to work with tables in Design view to define or modify the table structure. Similarly, you can use Design view to create a query for which you define the structure. In Design view, you begin by choosing the table from which you wish to select records. You use the table field list box to select the fields to display in the query results datasheet. When you have finished selecting fields, you instruct Access to display the records by switching to Datasheet view or by clicking the Run button.

Worldwide Enterprises

What You Will Do   Rhonda Trask, human resources manager, has asked for a list of employees with their annual salaries and hire dates. You will produce the list by creating a query to obtain the required fields from the Employees table.

Tutorial

Creating a Query in Design View

1   With **3-WEEmployees.accdb** open and the Create tab active, click the Query Design button in the Queries group.

2   At the Show Table dialog box with the Tables tab selected, double-click *Employees*.

> A table field list box for the Employees table is added to the query. The first step in building a query in Design view is to add a table field list box for each table from which records will be selected.

3   Click the Close button to close the Show Table dialog box.

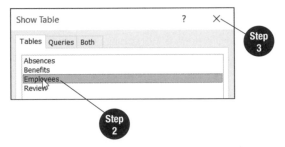

4   Double-click the *EmployeeID* field in the Employees table field list box.

> The blank columns at the bottom represent the columns in the query results datasheet and are referred to as the *query design grid*. You place the field names in the columns in the order in which you want the fields displayed in the query results datasheet. Double-clicking a field name adds the field to the next available column. In Steps 5 and 6, you will practice two other methods of adding fields to the query design grid.

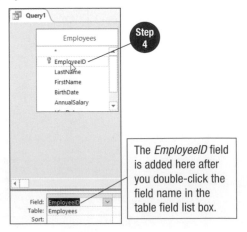

The *EmployeeID* field is added here after you double-click the field name in the table field list box.

5 Position the mouse pointer on the *FirstName* field in the Employees table field list box, click and hold down the left mouse button, drag to the second field in the *Field* row of the query design grid, and then release the mouse button.

6 Click in the third field in the *Field* row of the query design grid, click the arrow that appears, and then click *LastName* at the drop-down list.

7 Using any of the three methods in Steps 4–6, add the *AnnualSalary* and *HireDate* fields from the Employees table field list box to the query design grid.

8 Click the Save button 🖫 on the Quick Access Toolbar.

9 At the Save As dialog box, type SalaryList in the *Query Name* text box and then press the Enter key or click OK.

10 Click the Run button ❗ in the Results group on the Query Tools Design tab.

> A query stores instructions on how to select data. The Run command instructs Access to carry out the instructions and display the results.

11 Print the query.

12 Close the SalaryList query.

Check Your Work — Compare your work to the model answer to ensure that you have completed the activity correctly.

In Addition

Understanding Action Queries

In the last activity and in this activity, you created select queries that displayed selected fields from tables. Another type of query, called an *action query*, makes changes to a group of records. Four types of action queries are available in Access: delete, update, append, and make-table. A delete query deletes records. An update query makes global changes to a field. An append query adds a group of records from one table to the end of another table. A make-table query creates a new table from all or part of the data in existing tables.

Activity 3.3 — Creating a Query in Design View Using Multiple Tables

Often a query is used to select records from more than one table. In Activity 3.1, you were able to view records from the Employees table and the Benefits table in a query results datasheet. In Design view, multiple tables are added to the query at the Show Table dialog box. Once you have added a table field list box for each table, you can then add the fields to the query design grid in the desired order using any one of the three methods learned in the last activity.

Worldwide Enterprises

What You Will Do   Rhonda Trask has asked for a list of employees, along with their hire and review dates. This data is stored in two different tables. You will produce the list by creating a query to obtain the required fields from each table to generate the list.

Tutorial
Creating a Query in Design View Using Multiple Tables

1 With **3-WEEmployees.accdb** open and the Create tab active, click the Query Design button.

2 At the Show Table dialog box with the Tables tab selected, double-click *Employees*.

3 Double-click *Review* and then click the Close button to close the Show Table dialog box.

A black join line with *1* at each end of the line between the Employees table field list box and the Review table field list box illustrates the one-to-one relationship that has been defined between the two tables.

4 Double-click the *EmployeeID* field in the Employees table field list box.

5 Double-click the *FirstName* field in the Employees table field list box.

6 Double-click the *LastName* field in the Employees table field list box.

7 Double-click the *SupervisorFName* field and then double-click the *SupervisorLName* field in the Review table field list box to add the fields from the second table to the query design grid.

8 Double-click the *HireDate* field in the Employees table field list box.

You can add fields in any order from either table to the query design grid.

In Brief

Create Query in Design View with Multiple Tables
1. Click Create tab.
2. Click Query Design button.
3. Double-click tables in Show Table dialog box.
4. Close Show Table dialog box.
5. Add field names from table field list boxes to columns in query design grid.
6. Click Save button.
7. Type query name and click OK.
8. Click Run button.

9 Double-click the *AnnualRevDate* field in the Review table field list box.

10 Look at the table names in the *Table* row in the query design grid. The table with which each field is associated is displayed.

Field:	EmployeeID	FirstName	LastName	SupervisorFName	SupervisorLName	HireDate	AnnualRevDate
Table:	Employees	Employees	Employees	Review	Review	Employees	Review
Sort:							
Show:	☑	☑	☑	☑	☑	☑	☑

Step 10

11 Click the Save button on the Quick Access Toolbar.

12 At the Save As dialog box, type ReviewList in the *Query Name* text box and then press the Enter key or click OK.

Save As   ? ×

Query Name:

ReviewList

OK   Cancel

Step 12

13 Click the Run button in the Results group on the Query Tools Design tab.

View the query results in Figure 3.2.

14 Display the datasheet in Print Preview, change to landscape orientation, and then print the datasheet.

15 Close the Print Preview window and then close the ReviewList query.

Figure 3.2 ReviewList Query Results Datasheet

EmployeeID	FirstName	LastName	Supervisor First Name	Supervisor Last Name	HireDate	Annual Review Date
1013	Gregg	Chippewa	Sam	Vestering	2/10/2010	10-Feb-17
1015	Lyle	Brewer	Sam	Vestering	5/17/2010	17-May-17
1020	Angela	Doxtator	Celesta	Ruiz	8/3/2010	03-Aug-18
1023	Aleksy	Bulinkski	Sam	Vestering	10/10/2010	15-Oct-18
1025	Jorge	Biliski	Roman	Deptulski	12/1/2010	01-Dec-18
1030	Thom	Hicks	Roman	Deptulski	1/22/2011	22-Jan-18
1033	Dina	Titov	Roman	Deptulski	1/10/2011	01-Jan-18
1040	Guy	Lafreniere	Celesta	Ruiz	3/10/2012	10-Mar-18
1043	Enzo	Morano	Roman	Deptulski	8/15/2012	15-Aug-18
1045	Terry	Yiu	Celesta	Ruiz	1/31/2013	01-Jan-18
1050	Carl	Zakowski	Sam	Vestering	2/9/2013	09-Feb-18
1053	Shauna	O'Connor	Sam	Vestering	4/15/2014	15-Apr-17
1060	Donald	McKnight	Roman	Deptulski	6/22/2014	25-Jun-18
1063	Charlotte	McPhee	Celesta	Ruiz	2/6/2015	10-Feb-17
1065	Norm	Liszniewski	Sam	Vestering	2/6/2015	10-Feb-17
1073	Marsha	Judd	Roman	Deptulski	11/30/2016	30-Nov-17
1080	Leo	Couture	Roman	Deptulski	1/27/2017	27-Jan-17
1083	Drew	Arnold	Celesta	Ruiz	6/22/2017	22-Jun-17
1085	Yousef	Armine	Celesta	Ruiz	3/14/2017	14-Mar-17
1090	Maria	Quinte	Sam	Vestering	11/29/2017	30-Nov-17
1093	Luis	Vaquez	Sam	Vestering	12/5/2017	10-Dec-17
1095	Patrick	Kilarney	Celesta	Ruiz	12/12/2017	15-Dec-17

Check Your Work Compare your work to the model answer to ensure that you have completed the activity correctly.

In Addition

Learning More about Adding Tables to the Query Design Grid

If you have closed the Show Table dialog box and then realize you need to add another table field list box to the query design grid, you do not need to start over again. The Show Table button in the Query Setup group on the Query Tools Design tab will redisplay the Show Table dialog box, from which you can add more tables to the query design grid.

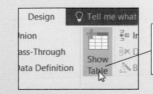

Click the Show Table button to add a table field list box to the query design grid.

Adding a Criteria Statement to a Query; Sorting and Hiding Columns

In the previous queries, all records from the tables were displayed. Adding a criterion statement to the query design grid will cause Access to display only those records that meet the criterion. For example, you could generate a list of employees who are entitled to four weeks of vacation. Extracting specific records from tables is where the true power in creating queries is found, since you are able to separate out only those records that serve your purpose. Use the *Sort* row in the design grid to specify the field by which records should be sorted. By default, each check box in the *Show* row in the query design grid contains a check mark, meaning the column will be displayed in the query results datasheet. Clear the check mark from a field's *Show* row to hide the column in the query results datasheet.

What You Will Do   Rhonda Trask has requested a list of employees who receive four weeks of vacation. Since you already have the employee names and vacation fields set up in an existing query, you decide to modify the query by adding the vacation criteria and then save the query using a new name.

Tutorial
Adding a Criteria
Statement to a Query

Tutorial
Sorting Data and
Showing/Hiding Fields
in Query Results

1 With **3-WEEmployees.accdb** open, right-click *BenefitPlans* in the Queries group in the Navigation pane and then click *Design View* at the shortcut menu.

2 Click the File tab, click the *Save As* option, and then click the *Save Object As* option in the *File Types* section of the Save As backstage area.

3 Click the Save As button 🖫.

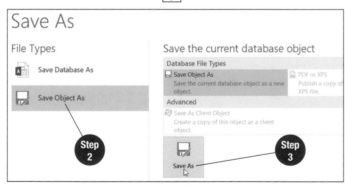

4 Type 4WksVac in the *Save 'BenefitPlans' to* text box at the Save As dialog box and then click OK.

5 With the Query Tools Design tab active, click in the field in the *Criteria* row in the *Vacation* column in the query design grid (the blank field below the check box).

> Before you type a criteria statement, make sure you have placed the insertion point in the *Criteria* row for the field by which you will be selecting records.

6 Type 4 weeks and then press the Enter key.

> The insertion point moves to the field in the *Criteria* row in the next column and Access inserts quotation marks around *4 weeks* in the field in the *Vacation* column. Since quotation marks are required in criteria statements for text fields, Access automatically inserts them if they are not typed into the field in the *Criteria* row.

7 Click in the field in the *Sort* row in the *LastName* column, click the down arrow, and then click *Ascending* at the drop-down list.

8 Click the Run button in the Results group on the Query Tools Design tab.

9 View the query results in the datasheet (the results are sorted in alphabetic order by last name) and then click the View button in the Views group on the Home tab to switch to Design view. (Do *not* click the View button arrow.)

> Since Rhonda Trask is interested only in the employee names and vacation, you will instruct Access not to display the other fields in the query results datasheet.

10 Click the check box in the *Show* row in the *PensionPlan* column to remove the check mark.

> Removing the check mark instructs Access to hide the column in the query results datasheet.

Step 10   Step 11

11 Remove the check marks from the *Show* check box in the *DentalPlan* and *HealthPlan* columns in the query design grid.

12 Click the View button to switch to Datasheet view.

> The columns for which you removed the check mark from the *Show* check box do not display in the query results. Notice that you displayed the query results datasheet by switching views. Clicking the Run button or switching views achieves the same result.

13 Print the query results datasheet.

14 Close the 4WksVac query. Click Yes to save changes to the design of the query.

Check Your Work — Compare your work to the model answer to ensure that you have completed the activity correctly.

In Addition

Learning More about Criteria Statement

The following are examples of criteria statements for text, number, and date fields showing the proper syntax required by Access. Access inserts the quotation marks (") automatically for text fields and the pound symbols (#) automatically for date fields when you type a valid entry in a field in the *Criteria* row.

Criterion Statement	Records That Would Be Extracted
"Finance Department"	those with Finance Department in the field
Not "Finance Department"	all except those with Finance Department in the field
"Fan*"	those that begin with Fan and end with any other characters in the field
>15000	those with a value greater than 15,000 in the field
#5/1/18#	those that contain the date May 1, 2018 in the field
>#5/1/18#	those that contain dates after May 1, 2018 in the field

You may need to select records by using more than one criterion. For example, you may wish to view records of those employees who have enrolled in more than one benefit plan. More than one column in the query design grid can have an entry in the *Criteria* row. Multiple criteria all entered in the same *Criteria* row becomes an *And* statement wherein each criterion must be met for the record to be selected. For example, the word *Yes* in the *PensionPlan* column and the *DentalPlan* column in the *Criteria* row would mean a record would need to have a check mark in both check boxes in order for Access to display the record in the query results datasheet.

Worldwide Enterprises

What You Will Do   Rhonda Trask is reviewing salaries and has requested a list of employees who work in the North American Distribution Department and earn over $45,000. You will create a new query in Design view to produce the list.

Tutorial
Designing a Query with an *And* Criteria Statement

1 With **3-WEEmployees.accdb** open, click the Create tab and then click the Query Design button.

2 At the Show Table dialog box, double-click *Employees* and then click the Close button.

3 Double-click the following fields to add them to the query design grid. *Note: You may have to scroll down the table field list box to see all of the fields*.
> *FirstName*
> *LastName*
> *Department*
> *HireDate*
> *AnnualSalary*

4 Click in the field in the *Criteria* row in the *Department* column in the query design grid, type North American Distribution, and then press the Enter key.

5 Position the mouse pointer on the right column boundary line for the *Department* field in the gray header row at the top of the query design grid until the pointer changes to a left-and-right-pointing arrow with a vertical line in the middle and then double-click to best fit the column width.

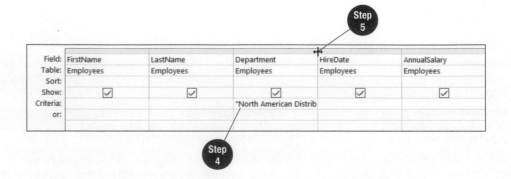

Step 5

Field:	FirstName	LastName	Department	HireDate	AnnualSalary
Table:	Employees	Employees	Employees	Employees	Employees
Sort:					
Show:	☑	☑	☑	☑	☑
Criteria:			"North American Distrib		
or:					

Step 4

In Brief

Designing a Query with an *And* Statement
1. Start new query in Design view.
2. Add table(s) and field(s) to query design grid.
3. Click in *Criteria* row in column in which you want to write criterion statement.
4. Type criterion statement.
5. Repeat Steps 3–4 for the remaining criterion fields.
6. Save query.
7. Run query.

6 Click in the field in the *Criteria* row in the *AnnualSalary* column, type >45000, and then press the Enter key.

Placing multiple criterion statements on the same row in the query design grid means that each criterion must be satisfied in order for Access to select the record.

Step 6

7 Click the Run button.

8 Review the records selected in the query results datasheet.

The field value for each record in the *Department* column is *North American Distribution* and the field values in the *AnnualSalary* column are all greater than $45,000.

FirstName	LastName	Department	HireDate	AnnualSalary
Sam	Vestering	North American Distribution	7/22/2009	$69,725.00
Lyle	Brewer	North American Distribution	5/17/2010	$45,651.00
Angela	Doxtator	North American Distribution	8/3/2010	$45,558.00
Dina	Titov	North American Distribution	1/10/2011	$45,655.00
Enzo	Morano	North American Distribution	8/15/2012	$48,750.00

Step 8

9 Click the Save button, type NAHighSalary in the *Query Name* text box, and then press the Enter key or click OK.

10 Print the query results datasheet.

11 Close the NAHighSalary query.

Check Your Work Compare your work to the model answer to ensure that you have completed the activity correctly.

In Addition

Learning More about *And* Criteria Statements

The following are additional examples of *And* criteria statements.

Criterion Statement in *PensionPlan* Column	Criterion Statement in *HireDate* Column	Criterion Statement in *AnnualSalary* Column	Records That Would Be Extracted
	>#1/1/2018#	>40000 And <50000	employees hired after January 1, 2018 who earn between $40,000 and $50,000
Yes	>#1/1/2018#	>45000	employees hired after January 1, 2018 who are enrolled in the pension plan and earn over $45,000
No	Between #1/1/2018# And #12/31/2018#	<50000	employees hired between January 1, 2018 and December 31, 2018 who are not enrolled in the pension plan and earn less than $50,000

Multiple criterion statements on different rows in the query design grid become an *Or* statement in which any of the criteria can be met in order for Access to select the record. For example, in this activity, you will generate a list of employees who are entitled to either three or four weeks of vacation. Creating select queries with *Or* statements is often done to generate mailing lists. For example, if a business wants to create mailing labels for customers who live in either Texas or Nevada, the query to select the records needs to be an *Or* statement since the *State* field in a customer table would have a value of *Texas* or *Nevada*. (It would not be possible to have both state names in the same record.)

Worldwide Enterprises

What You Will Do   Rhonda Trask has requested a list of employees who receive either three or four weeks of vacation. Since you already have a query created that selected the records of employees with four weeks of vacation, you decide to modify the existing query by adding the second vacation criteria.

Tutorial

Designing a Query with an *Or* Criteria Statement

1 With **3-WEEmployees.accdb** open, right-click *4WksVac* in the Queries group in the Navigation pane and then click *Design View* at the shortcut menu.

2 Click the File tab, click the *Save As* option, and then click the *Save Object As* option in the *File Types* section of the Save As backstage area.

3 Click the Save As button.

4 Type 3or4WksVac in the *Save '4WksVac' to* text box at the Save As dialog box and then click OK.

5 With the Query Tools Design tab active, click in the field in the *or* row in the *Vacation* column in the query design grid (the blank row below *"4 weeks"*), type 3 weeks, and then press the Enter key.

Including a second criterion below the first one instructs Access to display records that meet either of the two criteria.

Field:	EmployeeID	LastName	FirstName	Vacation
Table:	Employees	Employees	Employees	Benefits
Sort:		Ascending		
Show:	☑	☑	☑	☑
Criteria:				"4 weeks"
or:				"3 weeks"

6 Click the Run button.

Extract Records Using
***Or* Criteria**
1. Start new query in Design view.
2. Add table(s) and field(s) to query design grid.
3. Click in *Criteria* row in column in which you want to write criterion statement.
4. Type criterion statement.
5. Click in *or* row in column below the *Criteria* row in the column containing the first criterion statement.
6. Type criterion statement.
7. Repeat Steps 5–6 as necessary, moving down one field in *Criteria* row for each new criterion.
8. Save query.
9. Run query.

7 View the query results datasheet.

The records that have been selected contain either *4 weeks* or *3 weeks* in the *Vacation* field column.

3or4WksVac			
EmployeeID ▾	LastName ▾	FirstName ▾	Vacation ▾
1025	Biliski	Jorge	4 weeks
1015	Brewer	Lyle	4 weeks
1023	Bulinkski	Aleksy	3 weeks
1013	Chippewa	Gregg	3 weeks
1005	Deptulski	Roman	3 weeks
1020	Doxtator	Angela	3 weeks
1040	Lafreniere	Guy	3 weeks
1060	McKnight	Donald	3 weeks
1043	Morano	Enzo	3 weeks
1053	O'Connor	Shauna	3 weeks
1003	Ruiz	Celesta	3 weeks
1033	Titov	Dina	3 weeks
1000	Vestering	Sam	4 weeks
*			

Step 7

8 Print the query results datasheet.

9 Click the Save button to save the revised query.

10 Close the 3or4WksVac query.

Check Your Work Compare your work to the model answer to ensure that you have completed the activity correctly.

In Addition

Combining *And* and *Or* Criteria Statements

Assume that Rhonda Trask wants to further explore the vacation entitlements for the North American Distribution employees only. Rhonda wants a list of employees who work in the North American Distribution Department *and* have four weeks of vacation *or* who work in the North American Distribution Department *and* have three weeks of vacation. To perform this query, you would use two rows in the query design grid to enter the criteria as shown below. Note that the *Department* column has been added to the query design grid.

Field:	EmployeeID	LastName	FirstName	Vacation	Department
Table:	Employees	Employees	Employees	Benefits	Employees
Sort:		Ascending			
Show:	☑	☑	☑	☑	☑
Criteria:				"4 weeks"	"North American Distribution"
or:				"3 weeks"	"North American Distribution"

multiple *And/Or* criteria

3or4WksVac				
EmployeeID ▾	LastName ▾	FirstName ▾	Vacation ▾	Department ▾
1025	Biliski	Jorge	4 weeks	North American Distribution
1015	Brewer	Lyle	4 weeks	North American Distribution
1020	Doxtator	Angela	3 weeks	North American Distribution
1043	Morano	Enzo	3 weeks	North American Distribution
1053	O'Connor	Shauna	3 weeks	North American Distribution
1003	Ruiz	Celesta	3 weeks	North American Distribution
1033	Titov	Dina	3 weeks	North American Distribution
1000	Vestering	Sam	4 weeks	North American Distribution
*				

query results datasheet

Activity 3.7   Performing Calculations in a Query

Calculations involving mathematical operations such as adding or multiplying a field value can be included in a query. In a blank field in the *Field* row in Query Design view, type the text you want to appear as the column heading, followed by a colon (:) and then the mathematical expression for the calculated values. Field names in the mathematical expression are encased in square brackets. For example, the entry *TotalSalary:[BaseSalary]+[Commission]* would add the value in the field named *BaseSalary* to the value in the field named *Commission*. The result would be placed in a new column in the query datasheet with the column heading *TotalSalary*. Calculated columns do not exist in the associated table; the values are calculated dynamically each time the query is run. Numeric format and the number of digits after the decimal point for calculated columns are set using the Format property box in the Property Sheet task pane in Design view.

Worldwide Enterprises

What You Will Do   Worldwide Enterprises contributes 3% of each employee's annual salary to a registered pension plan. You will create a new query to calculate the employer's annual pension contributions.

Tutorial
Performing Calculations in a Query

1. With **3-WEEmployees.accdb** open, click the Create tab and then click the Query Design button.

2. At the Show Table dialog box, double-click *Employees* and then click the Close button.

3. Double-click the following fields in the order shown to add them to the query design grid:
   EmployeeID
   FirstName
   LastName
   AnnualSalary

4. Click in the field in the *Field* row to the right of the *AnnualSalary* column in the query design grid.

5. Type PensionContribution:[AnnualSalary]*.03 and then press the Enter key.

6. Position the mouse pointer on the right vertical boundary line for the *PensionContribution* column in the gray field selector bar at the top of the query design grid until the pointer changes to a left-and-right-pointing arrow with a vertical line in the middle and then double-click the left mouse button.

Create Calculated Field in Query
1. Open query in Design view.
2. Click in first available blank field row in query design grid.
3. Type column heading for calculated field.
4. Type colon.
5. Type the mathematical expression.
6. Press Enter or click in another field.
7. Click Save button.
8. Click Run button.

Format Calculated Field
1. Open query in Design view.
2. Click in field containing calculated expression.
3. Click Query Tools Design tab.
4. Click Property Sheet button.
5. Click in Format property box.
6. Click arrow.
7. Click format at drop-down list.
8. Close Property Sheet task pane.
9. Save query.
10. Run query.

7 Click the Save button. At the Save As dialog box, type PensionCont in the *Query Name* text box and then press the Enter key or click OK.

8 Click the Run button.

9 In the query results datasheet, adjust the column width to best fit the entries in the *PensionContribution* column.

> The values in the calculated column need to be formatted to display a consistent number of decimal places.

10 Switch to Design view.

11 Click anywhere within the first field in the *PensionContribution* column in the query design grid.

12 Click the Property Sheet button 🗐 in the Show/Hide group on the Query Tools Design tab.

> Available properties for the active field display in the Property Sheet task pane at the right side of the work area.

13 Click in the *Format* property box in the Property Sheet task pane, click the down arrow that appears, and then click *Currency* at the drop-down list.

14 Click the Close button in the top right corner of the Property Sheet task pane.

Step 14

Property Sheet ✕

Selection type: Field Properties

General Lookup

Description	
Format	∨
Decimal Places	General Num
Input Mask	Currency
Caption	Euro
	Fixed
	Standard

Step 13

15 Click the Save button and then click the Run button.

16 Click the Totals button Σ in the Records group to add a total row to the bottom of the datasheet and then add a Sum function to the bottom of the *AnnualSalary* and *PensionContribution* field columns. *Note: Refer to Activity 2.7 if you need assistance with this step.*

17 Print the query results datasheet.

18 Close the PensionCont query. Click Yes when prompted to save changes to the query.

PensionCont

EmployeeID	FirstName	LastName	AnnualSalary	PensionContribution
1000	Sam	Vestering	$69,725.00	$2,091.75
1003	Celesta	Ruiz	$41,875.00	$1,256.25
1005	Roman	Deptulski	$72,750.00	$2,182.50
1013	Gregg	Chippewa	$48,650.00	$1,459.50
1015	Lyle	Brewer	$45,651.00	$1,369.53
1020	Angela	Doxtator	$45,558.00	$1,366.74
1023	Aleksy	Bulinkski	$51,450.00	$1,543.50
1025	Jorge	Biliski	$44,892.00	$1,346.76
1030	Thom	Hicks	$42,824.00	$1,284.72
1033	Dina	Titov	$45,655.00	$1,369.65
1040	Guy	Lafreniere	$45,395.00	$1,361.85
1043	Enzo	Morano	$48,750.00	$1,462.50
1045	Terry	Yiu	$42,238.00	$1,267.14
1050	Carl	Zakowski	$44,387.00	$1,331.61
1053	Shauna	O'Connor	$43,695.00	$1,310.85
1060	Donald	McKnight	$42,126.00	$1,263.78
1063	Charlotte	McPhee	$43,695.00	$1,310.85
1065	Norm	Liszniewski	$43,695.00	$1,310.85
1073	Marsha	Judd	$44,771.00	$1,343.13
1080	Leo	Couture	$43,659.00	$1,309.77
1083	Drew	Arnold	$43,650.00	$1,309.77
Total			**$1,163,808.00**	**$34,914.24**

Step 16

Check Your Work ▷ Compare your work to the model answer to ensure that you have completed the activity correctly.

Recall from Section 1 that forms provide a user-friendly interface for viewing, adding, editing, and deleting records. The Form button creates a new form with one mouse click. All fields in the selected table are added to the form in a columnar layout. The form is comprised of a series of objects referred to as *controls*. Each field from the table has a label control and a text box control object. The label control object contains the field name or caption and the text box control object is the field placeholder where data is entered or edited. A form may also contain other controls such as a title, logo, and date and time control object. The form appears in the work area in Layout view, which is used to make changes to the form. Three tabs become active when a form has been created. Use buttons on the Form Layout Tools Design tab to change the theme or add new control objects to the form. The Form Layout Tools Arrange tab contains buttons to rearrange the fields from columnar to tabular or stacked or to otherwise modify the position of the control objects on the form. To make changes to the form's font, font attributes, or other format characteristics, use the Form Layout Tools Format tab. In the Form Wizard, the user is guided through a series of dialog boxes to generate the form, including selecting the fields to be included and the form layout.

Worldwide Enterprises

What You Will Do   You decide to create two forms for the assistant who works with you since she prefers to see only one record at a time while entering data. One form will be used to record employee absences and the other will be used to enter new employee records.

Tutorial
Creating a Form Using the Form Button

Tutorial
Formatting a Form

Tutorial
Creating a Form Using the Form Wizard

1 With **3-WEEmployees.accdb** open, click *Absences* in the Tables group in the Navigation pane to select but not open the table.

> In order to create a form using the Form tool, you first select the table or query object upon which to base the new form.

2 Click the Create tab and then click the Form button in the Forms group.

> Access creates the form using all fields in the table in a vertical layout and displays the form in Layout view with the Form Layout Tools Design tab active.

3 Click the View button in the Views group on the Form Layout Tools Design tab to switch to Form view.

> When working in a form, you can use the View button to switch back and forth between Form view, where you view the data, and Layout view, where you make changes to the form's appearance and structure.

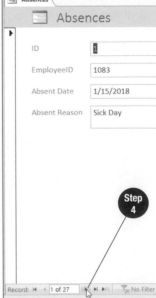

4 Click the Next record button on the Record Navigation bar a few times to scroll through a few records in Form view.

5 Click the View button in the Views group on the Home tab to return to Layout view.

In Brief

Create Form Using Form Button
1. Click table name in Navigation pane.
2. Click Create tab.
3. Click Form button.

Create Form Using Form Wizard
1. Click Create tab.
2. Click Form Wizard button.
3. Choose table or query from which to create form.
4. Select fields to include in form.
5. Click Next.
6. Choose form layout.
7. Click Next.
8. Type form title.
9. Click Finish.

6 Click the Themes button in the Themes group on the Form Layout Tools Design tab and then click *Retrospect* at the drop-down gallery.

> Themes in the Microsoft Office suite are standardized across the applications. A business can apply a consistent look to documents, workbooks, presentations, and databases by using the same theme in each application.

7 Click the Colors button in the Themes group and then click *Green* at the drop-down list.

8 Click the Fonts button and then click *Candara* at the drop-down list.

9 Click the Title button ⬜ in the Header/Footer group.

Clicking the Title button selects the text *Absences* that displays in the title control object.

10 Type Employee Absences and then press the Enter key.

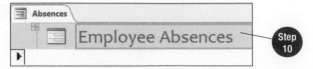

11 Click the Form Layout Tools Format tab.

12 Click the *Font Size* option box arrow in the Font group on the Form Layout Tools Format tab and then click *24* at the drop-down list.

13 Press Ctrl + A to select all of the control objects in the form.

14 Click the Font Color button arrow and then click the *Dark Blue* color option (ninth column, bottom row in the *Standard Colors* section).

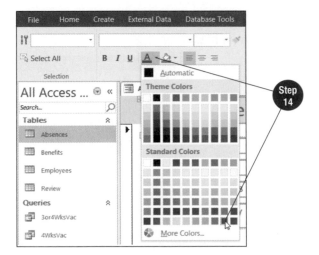

15 Close the Absences form. Click Yes to save the changes to the form's design and then click OK at the Save As dialog box to accept the default form name *Absences*.

16 Click the Create tab and then click the Form Wizard button 🖳 in the Forms group.

17 At the first Form Wizard dialog box, click the *Tables/Queries* option box arrow and then click *Table: Employees* at the drop-down list.

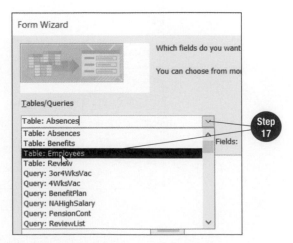

18 Click the All Fields button `>>` to move all of the fields in the *Available Fields* list box to the *Selected Fields* list box and then click the Next button.

19 At the second Form Wizard dialog box with *Columnar* already selected as the form layout, click the Next button.

20 Click the Finish button at the last Form Wizard dialog box to accept the default title of *Employees* and the option *Open the form to view or enter information.*

21 Click the Next record button on the Record Navigation bar a few times to scroll through a few records in Form view and then close the Employees form.

Check Your Work Compare your work to the model answer to ensure that you have completed the activity correctly.

In Addition

Applying Conditional Formatting

Use the Conditional Formatting button to apply formatting to data that meets a specific criterion. For example, conditional formatting can be applied to sales amounts that displays amounts greater than a specified number in a different color. To apply conditional formatting, click the Conditional Formatting button in the Control Formatting group on the Form Layout Tools Format tab and the Conditional Formatting Rules Manager dialog box displays. At this dialog box, click the New Rule button and the New Formatting Rule dialog box displays. Use options in this dialog box to specify the conditional formatting that is to be applied to data in a field that matches a specific condition.

Activity 3.9   Adding an Existing Field to a Form

When two tables have been joined by a relationship, you can add fields from a related table to a form. For example, in the Absences form created in the previous activity, the names of the employees are not on the form because the first and last name fields are not in the Absences table. It would be helpful to be able to see the employee's name while entering an absence report so that the correct employee ID can be verified as a new record is being added. You can add fields from another table to a form using the Field List task pane in Layout view.

Worldwide Enterprises

What You Will Do   You will edit the Absences form to add the employee's first and last names from the Employees table.

Tutorial

Adding an Existing Field to a Form

1 With **3-WEEmployees.accdb** open, double-click *Absences* in the Forms group in the Navigation pane to open the form.

2 Click the View button in the Views group on the Home tab to switch to Layout view.

3 With the Form Layout Tools Design tab active, click the Add Existing Fields button [icon] in the Tools group.

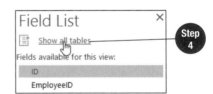

> The Field List task pane opens at the right side of the work area in one of two states: with one section titled *Fields available for this view* and with a Show all tables hyperlink at the top of the Field List task pane; or, with three sections titled *Fields available for this view*, *Fields available in related tables*, and *Fields available in other tables*. A Show only fields in the current record source hyperlink is at the top of the Field List task pane when it displays three sections.

4 Click Show all tables at the top of the Field List task pane. *Note: Skip this step if the hyperlink at the top of the Field List task pane on your computer reads* **Show only fields in the current record source.**

> Clicking Show all tables in the Field List task pane displays two new sections: *Fields available in related tables* and *Fields available in other tables*. Within each section box, each table name displays with an expand button (plus symbol) you can use to display the fields in the related table.

5 Click the expand button next to the *Employees* table name in the *Fields available in related tables* list box to expand the list.

6 Click to select *FirstName* in the expanded Employees table field list.

7 Position the mouse pointer on the selected *FirstName* field in the Field List task pane, click and hold down the left mouse button, drag the field name to the form between the *EmployeeID* and *Absent Date* fields, and then release the mouse button.

> As you drag the field over the form, a pink indicator bar identifies where the field will be positioned between existing fields. When you release the mouse, the field is added to the form. The Field List task pane updates to move the Employees table to the *Fields available for this view* section. By adding a field from the related table, the Employees table is now associated with the Absences table.

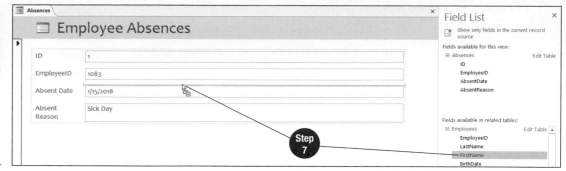

8 Position the mouse pointer on the *LastName* field in the *Fields available for this view* section of the Field List task pane, click and hold down the left mouse button, drag the field name to the form between the *FirstName* and *Absent Date* fields, and then release the mouse button.

9 Click the Close button in the upper right corner of the Field List task pane.

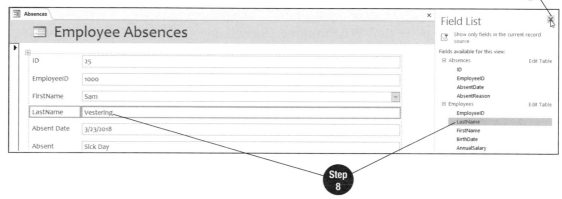

10 Click the Save button to save the revised form design.

11 Switch to Form view and scroll through a few records.

12 Click the New button 🔲 in the Records group on the Home tab, press the Tab key to move past the *ID* AutoNumber data type field, type 1063 in the *EmployeeID* field, and then press the Tab key or Enter key.

> Access automatically displays *Charlotte* in the *FirstName* field, *McPhee* in the *LastName* field, and *Sick Day* in the *Absent Reason* field. Since the Employees and Absences tables are related, Access matches the *EmployeeID* field values and displays the three field entries from the primary table.

13 Press the Tab key two times to move to the *Absent Date* field, type 3/30/2018, press the Tab key (this selects the current text), type Personal leave day in the *Absent Reason* field, and then press the Enter key.

14 Close the Absences form.

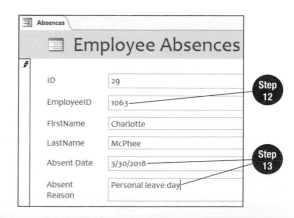

Check Your Work — Compare your work to the model answer to ensure that you have completed the activity correctly.

As you learned in Activity 3.8, a form is comprised of a series of objects referred to as *controls*. Each field from the table has a label control and a text box control object placed side by side, with the label control object placed first. The label control object contains the field name or the caption property text if a caption has been added to the field's properties. The text box control object is the field placeholder where data is entered or edited. The controls can be moved, resized, formatted, or deleted from the form. Use buttons on the Form Layout Tools Design tab and Form Layout Tools Arrange tab to manage control objects. The Property Sheet task pane contains options for changing the width and height of control objects in the form.

Worldwide Enterprises

What You Will Do   You decide to further customize the Absences form by inserting the Worldwide Enterprises logo, resizing control objects, changing the width and height of control objects, and moving control objects.

Tutorial
Managing Control Objects in a Form

1 With **3-WEEmployees.accdb** open, right-click *Absences* in the Forms group in the Navigation pane and then click *Layout View* at the shortcut menu.

2 Click the Logo button 🖼 in the Header/Footer group on the Form Layout Tools Design tab.

3 At the Insert Picture dialog box, navigate to the AccessS3 folder on your storage medium (if AccessS3 is not the current folder) and then double-click *WELogo-Small.jpg*.

4 Position the mouse pointer on the right edge of the selected logo control object until the pointer changes to a left-and-right-pointing arrow, click and hold down the left mouse button, drag the control to the approximate width shown at the right, and then release the mouse button. Resize the object as necessary until you can see the entire logo within the control object.

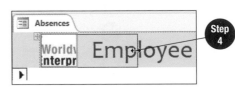

5 Click in the text box control object containing the number *25* (to the right of the ID label control object).

6 Click the Property Sheet button in the Tools group.

7 In the Property Sheet task pane with the Format tab active, select the current measurement in the *Width* property box, type 2.2, and then press the Enter key.

8 With the current measurement in the *Height* property box selected, type 0.3 and then press the Enter key.

9 Click in the label control object containing the text *ID*.

10 In the Property Sheet task pane, select the current measurement in the *Width* property box, type 1.1, and then click the Close button to close the Property Sheet task pane.

11 Click the *Absent Date* label control object, hold down the Shift key, click the text box control object containing the date *3/23/2018*, and then release the Shift key.

12 Click the Form Layout Tools Arrange tab.

13 Click the Move Up button ⬆ in the Move group three times to move the *Absent Date* label control and text box control objects above *EmployeeID*.

14 Click to select the *EmployeeID* label control object and then click the object again. Move the insertion point between the *e* and the *I* in *EmployeeID*, press the spacebar to insert a space, and then press the Enter key.

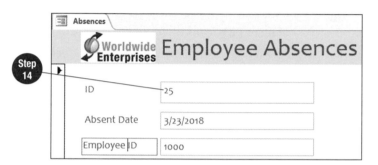

15 Edit the *FirstName* label control to *First Name* and the *LastName* label control to *Last Name* by completing steps similar to those in step 14.

16 Scroll through the records in the form until you reach the absence report for employee ID 1063 (Charlotte McPhee).

17 Display the form in Print Preview.

18 Click the Columns button 📄 in the Page Layout group on the Print Preview tab.

19 Select the current measurement in the *Width* measurement box, type 8, and then click OK.

20 Close Print Preview and then press Ctrl + P to display the Print dialog box.

21 Click *Selected Records(s)* in the *Print Range* section and then click OK.

22 Close the Absences form. Click Yes when prompted to save changes to the form's design.

> **Check Your Work** Compare your work to the model answer to ensure that you have completed the activity correctly.

Information from a database can be printed while viewing tables in Datasheet view, while viewing a query results datasheet, or while browsing through forms. In these printouts, all of the fields are printed in a tabular layout for datasheets or in the designated layout for forms. Create a report when you want to specify which fields to print and to have more control over the report layout and format. Access includes a Report button (similar to the Form button) that can be used to generate a report with one mouse click. Reports are generally created for viewing and printing purposes only.

Worldwide Enterprises

What You Will Do   Rhonda Trask has requested a hard copy of the NAHighSalary query. You decide to experiment with the Report feature to print the data.

Tutorial
Creating a Report

Tutorial
Formatting a Report

1   With **3-WEEmployees.accdb** open, click *NAHighSalary* in the Queries group in the Navigation pane and then click the Create tab.

Select a table or query before clicking the Report button.

2   Click the Report button [image] in the Reports group.

Access generates the report using a tabular layout with records displayed in rows. A title, along with the current day, date, and time are placed automatically at the top of the report, as is a container for an image such as a logo at the left of the title text.

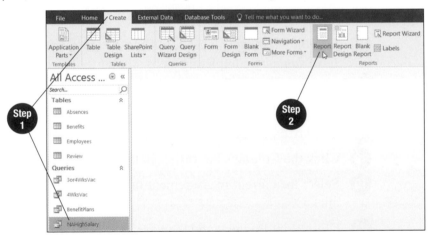

3   Click the Themes button in the Themes group on the Report Layout Tools Design tab and then click the *Integral* theme.

4   Click the Colors button in the Themes group and then click the *Yellow Orange* color option.

5   Click the Title button in the Header/Footer group.

6   Type Employees in North American Distribution, press Shift + Enter to insert a line break, type Earning over $45,000, and then press the Enter key.

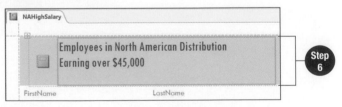

7   With the title control object still selected, click the Report Layout Tools Format tab, click the *Font Size* option box arrow in the Font group, and then click *14* at the drop-down list.

In Brief

Create Report Using Report Tool
1. Click object name in Navigation pane.
2. Click Create tab.
3. Click Report button.

8 Click the Report Layout Tools Design tab and then click the Logo button in the Header/Footer group.

9 At the Insert Picture dialog box, navigate to the AccessS3 folder on your storage medium (if AccessS3 is not the current folder) and then double-click *WELogo-Small.jpg*. Resize the logo object to the approximate width shown below.

10 Click the Report Layout Tools Format tab and then click the Select All button in the Selection group.

11 Click the Font Color button arrow and then click the *Dark Blue* color option (ninth column, bottom row in the *Standard Colors* section).

12 Click the total amount at the bottom of the *AnnualSalary* field column and then double-click the bottom border to display the entire amount.

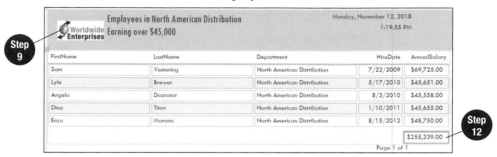

13 Minimize the Navigation pane by clicking the Shutter Bar Open/Close Button at the top of the Navigation pane.

> A dashed line in the middle of the *HireDate* field column indicates a page break. Changing to landscape orientation will allow all of the columns to print on the same page.

14 Click the Report Layout Tools Page Setup tab.

15 Click the Landscape button in the Page Layout group.

> The page break disappears, indicating all columns now fit on one page.

16 Click the Save button. At the Save As dialog box, click OK to accept the default report name *NAHighSalary*.

17 Print and then close the report.

18 Redisplay the Navigation pane by clicking the Shutter Bar Open/Close Button.

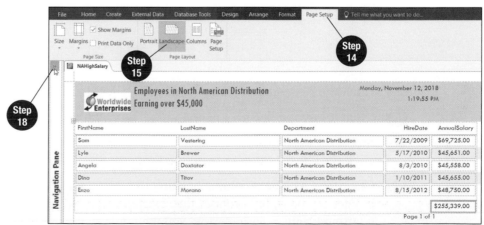

Check Your Work — Compare your work to the model answer to ensure that you have completed the activity correctly.

Once a report has been created, it can be modified by opening it in Layout view. A report is similar to a form in that it is comprised of a series of controls. Control objects in a report can be resized, moved, and deleted.

What You Will Do Rhonda Trask would like a hard copy of the ReviewList query. You decide to create a new report and move and resize columns to provide a better layout for the report.

Tutorial

Managing Control
Objects in a Report

1 With **3-WEEmployees.accdb** open, click *ReviewList* in the Queries group in the Navigation pane, click the Create tab, and then click the Report button.

2 Minimize the Navigation pane.

3 With the report displayed in Layout view, click to select the control object containing the *HireDate* column heading. (You may need to scroll to the right to see the column.)

4 Press and hold down the Shift key and then click in any field below the *HireDate* column heading.

This selects the entire column, as indicated by the gold borders around all of the cells in the column.

HireDate
2/10/2010
5/17/2010
8/3/2010
10/10/2010
12/1/2010

Steps 3-5

5 Position the mouse pointer inside the selected control object containing the *HireDate* column heading until the pointer displays with the four-headed arrow attached.

6 Drag the column to the left, between the *LastName* column and the *Supervisor First Name* column.

A vertical pink indicator bar identifies the location where the column will be placed when you release the mouse.

1:08:18 PM			
Supervisor First Name		Supervisor Last Name	HireDate
Sam		Vestering	2/10/2010
Sam		Vestering	5/17/2010
Celesta		Ruiz	8/3/2010
Sam		Vestering	10/10/2010
Roman		Deptulski	12/1/2010

Step 6

7 Click the *FirstName* column heading to select the control object.

8 Click the Property Sheet button in the Tools Group.

9 Select the current measurement in the *Width* measurement box, type 0.8, and then click the Close button to close the Property Sheet task pane.

10 Click the LastName column heading to select the control object, position the mouse pointer on the right border of the selected control object until the pointer displays as a left-and-right-pointing arrow and then drag to the left until *Lines: 1 Characters: 14* displays at the left side of the Status bar.

In Brief

Move Report Columns
1. Open report in Layout view.
2. Click column heading.
3. Press and hold down Shift key and click over data below column heading.
4. Position mouse pointer inside selected column.
5. Drag column to new location.
6. Save report.

Resize Report Columns
1. Open report in Layout view.
2. Click column heading.
3. Drag right or left border of selected column heading to change width.
4. Save report.

In addition to the Column property box at the Property Sheet task pane, a column width can be changed to a specific width using the line and character numbers that display at the left side of the Status bar.

11 Decrease the width of the *Supervisor First Name* column and the *Supervisor Last Name* column to *Lines 1: Characters 24*.

12 Click the Report Layout Tools Page Setup tab and then change to landscape orientation.

13 Edit the title text to *Employee Review List*.

14 Click to select the logo control object and then press the Delete key.

15 Click to select the control object that contains the current day and date. Position the mouse pointer on the right edge of the selected control until the pointer changes to a left-and-right-pointing arrow. Click and hold down the left mouse button, drag right until the right edge of the date aligns with the right edge of the last column, and then release the mouse button.

Access prints the current day, date, and time on all reports. In businesses with time-sensitive report needs, the inclusion of these controls is important.

16 Click the total amount at the bottom of the *EmployeeID* column, press the Delete key, click the remaining bar, and then press the Delete key again.

17 Save the report, accepting the default report name of *ReviewList*.

18 Print and then close the ReviewList report.

19 Redisplay the Navigation pane and then close **3-WEEmployees.accdb**.

Check Your Work ▷ Compare your work to the model answer to ensure that you have completed the activity correctly.

In Addition

Understanding Report Sections

A report is divided into five sections, described below.

Report Section	Description
Report Header	Controls in this section are printed once at the beginning of the report, such as the report title.
Page Header	Controls in this section are printed at the top of each page, such as column headings.
Detail	Controls in this section make up the body of the report by printing the data from the associated table or query.
Page Footer	Controls in this section are printed at the bottom of each page, such as the report date and page numbers.
Report Footer	Controls in this section are printed once at the end of the report, such as column totals.

Features Summary

Feature	Ribbon Tab, Group	Button	Keyboard Shortcut
add fields to a form	Form Layout Tools Design, Tools		
create query in Design view	Create, Queries		
Design view	Home, Views		
Form tool	Create, Forms		
Form view	Home, Views		
Form Wizard	Create, Forms		
insert logo in form or report	Form Layout Tools Design, Header/Footer OR Report Layout Tools Design, Header/Footer		
Layout view	Home, Views		
minimize Navigation pane			
Property Sheet task pane	Query Tools Design, Show/Hide OR Form Layout Tools Design, Tools OR Report Layout Tools Design, Tools		Alt + Enter
redisplay Navigation pane			
Report tool	Create, Reports		
run a query	Query Tools Design, Results		
Simple Query Wizard	Create, Queries		

Workbook Section study tools and assessment activities are available in the *Workbook* ebook. These resources are designed to help you further develop and demonstrate mastery of the skills learned in this section.

Access

SECTION 4

Summarizing Data and Calculating in Forms and Reports

Data Files Before beginning section work, copy the AccessS4 folder to your storage medium and then make AccessS4 the active folder.

Skills

- Use aggregate functions to calculate statistics in a query
- Summarize data in a crosstab query
- Create a find duplicates query
- Create a find unmatched query
- Insert control objects in a form and report
- Insert a calculation in a form and report
- Sort records in a form
- Group and sort in a report
- Apply conditional formatting to a report
- Create mailing labels
- Compact and repair a database
- Back up a database

Precheck Check your current skills to help focus your study of the skills taught in this section.

Projects Overview

 Worldwide Enterprises
Create a query to summarize and group salaries; use a query to find duplicate records and display records from a table that have no matching record in a related table; modify forms and reports to include descriptive text and calculations; and create and modify a report and mailing labels to print names and addresses of distributors.

 Performance Threads
Modify a form to include a calculation that displays the rental fee including tax and create a report that prints costume rental revenue grouped by month.

 The Waterfront BISTRO
Create a query to summarize and calculate statistics from inventory items and purchases and create a report to summarize catering event revenue.

 SNAP If you are a SNAP user, launch the Precheck and Tutorials from your Assignments page.

Model Answers Preview the model answers for an overview of the projects you will complete in the section activities.

81

Aggregate functions such as Sum, Avg, Min, Max, and Count can be used in a query to calculate statistics. When an aggregate function is used, Access displays one row in the query results datasheet with the result for each statistic in the query. To display the aggregate function list, click the Totals button in the Show/Hide group on the Query Tools Design tab. Access adds a *Total* row to the query design grid with a drop-down list from which you can select a function. Using the *Group By* option in the *Total* drop-down list, you can add a field to the query upon which Access will group records for statistical calculations.

Worldwide Enterprises

What You Will Do Rhonda Trask, human resources manager, has asked for statistics on the salaries currently paid to employees. You will create a new query and use aggregate functions to find the total of all salaries, the average salary, and the maximum and minimum salary. In a second query, you will calculate the same statistics by department.

Tutorial
Using Aggregate Functions

1 Open **4-WEEmployees.accdb** and enable the contents, if necessary.

2 Click the Create tab and then click the Query Design button.

3 At the Show Table dialog box with the Tables tab selected, double-click *Employees* and then click the Close button.

4 Double-click *AnnualSalary* in the Employees table field list box to add the field name to the first field in the *Field* row in the query design grid. Double-click *AnnualSalary* again to add the field name to the second field in the *Field* row. Repeat two more times so that *AnnualSalary* appears in the first four fields in the *Field* row.

> The field upon which the statistics are to be calculated is added to the query design grid once for each aggregate function you want to use.

Step 4

5 Click the Totals button Σ in the Show/Hide group on the Query Tools Design tab.

> A *Total* row is added to the query design grid between the *Table* and *Sort* rows with the default option *Group By*.

6 Click in the first *AnnualSalary* field in the *Total* row in the query design grid, click the down arrow that displays, and then click *Sum* at the drop-down list.

Step 6

7 Click in the second *AnnualSalary* field in the *Total* row, click the down arrow that displays, and then click *Avg* at the drop-down list.

8 Change the Group By option to *Max* for the third *AnnualSalary* field in the *Total* row.

9 Change the Group By option to *Min* for the fourth *AnnualSalary* field in the *Total* row.

10 Click the Save button, type SalaryStats in the *Query Name* text box at the Save As dialog box, and then press the Enter key or click OK.

11 Click the Run button.

Access calculates the Sum, Avg, Max, and Min functions for all salary values and displays one row with the results. Access assigns column headings in the query results datasheet using the function name, the word *Of*, and the field name from which the function has been derived; for example, *SumOfAnnualSalary*.

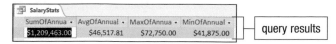

query results

12 Adjust all column widths to best fit the entries in the query results datasheet and then print the datasheet.

13 Switch to Design View.

14 Click the File tab and then click the *Save As* option.

15 Click the *Save Object As* option in the *File Types* section and then click the Save As button.

16 Type SalaryStatsByDept in the *Save 'SalaryStats' to* text box and then press the Enter key or click OK.

17 Click the Query Tools Design tab and then double-click *Department* in the Employees table field list box. ***Note: You may have to scroll down the table field list box to find the* Department *field*.

The *Department* field is added to the query design grid with *Total* automatically set to *Group By*. Adding this field produces a row in the query results datasheet in which Access calculates the aggregate functions for each department.

18 Run the query and then print the query results datasheet.

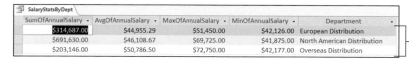

Steps 17-18

19 Close the SalaryStatsByDept query. Click Yes when prompted to save changes to the query design.

Check Your Work Compare your work to the model answer to ensure that you have completed the activity correctly.

In Addition

Using the Caption Property Box

Access assigned column headings in the query results datasheet using the function name, the word *Of*, and the field name from which the function was derived. These default column headings can be changed using the *Caption* property box in the Property Sheet task pane. Display the task pane by clicking the Property Sheet button in the Show/Hide group on the Query Tools Design tab. Click in a row in a column in the query design grid, click in the *Caption* property box, and then type a new name for the column heading. After renaming each column heading, close the Property Sheet task pane by clicking the Close button in the upper right corner of the task pane.

Summarizing Data Using a Crosstab Query

A crosstab query calculates aggregate functions such as Sum and Avg in which field values are grouped by two fields. Access includes a wizard to guide you through the steps to create the query. The first field selected causes one row to display in the query results datasheet for each group. The second field selected displays one column in the query results datasheet for each group. The third field specified is the numeric field to be summarized. The cell at the intersection of each row and column holds a value that is the result of the specified function for the designated row and column group. For example, suppose you want to find the total sales achieved by each salesperson by state. Each row in the query results could be used to display a salesperson's name with the state names in columns. Access summarizes the total sales for each person for each state and shows the results in a spreadsheet-type format.

Worldwide Enterprises

What You Will Do   Rhonda Trask wants to find out the salary cost that has been added to the payroll each year by department. You will use a crosstab query to calculate the total value of annual salaries for new hires in each year by each department.

Tutorial
Creating a Crosstab
Query

1 With **4-WEEmployees.accdb** open, click the Create tab and then click the Query Wizard button.

2 Click *Crosstab Query Wizard* in the New Query dialog box and then click OK.

> The fields that you want to use for grouping must all exist in one table or query. In situations in which the fields that you want to group by are in separate tables, you would first create a new query that contains the fields you need and then start the Crosstab Query Wizard. In this activity, all three fields you need are in one table.

3 At the first Crosstab Query Wizard dialog box with *Tables* selected in the *View* section, click *Table: Employees* in the list box and then click the Next button.

4 At the second Crosstab Query Wizard dialog box, double-click *Department* in the *Available Fields* list box to move the field to the *Selected Fields* list box and then click the Next button.

> At the second Crosstab Query Wizard dialog box, you choose the field in which the field's values become the row headings in the query results datasheet.

In Brief

Create Crosstab Query
1. Click Create tab.
2. Click Query Wizard button.
3. Click *Crosstab Query Wizard* and click OK.
4. Choose table or query name and click Next.
5. Choose field for row headings and click Next.
6. Choose field for column headings and click Next.
7. Choose numeric field to summarize and function to calculate and click Next.
8. Type query name and click Finish.

5 At the third Crosstab Query Wizard dialog box, click *HireDate* in the field list box and then click the Next button.

Whenever a date/time field is chosen for the column headings, Access displays a dialog box asking you to choose the time interval to summarize by, with the default option set to *quarter*.

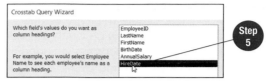

6 At the fourth Crosstab Query Wizard dialog box, click *Year* in the list box and then click the Next button.

At the fourth dialog box, you choose the field in which the field's values become the column headings in the query results datasheet.

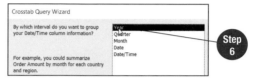

7 At the fifth Crosstab Query Wizard dialog box, click *AnnualSalary* in the *Fields* list box and then click *Sum* in the *Functions* list box.

At the fifth Crosstab Query Wizard dialog box, you select the numeric field to be summarized and the function to be used to calculate the values.

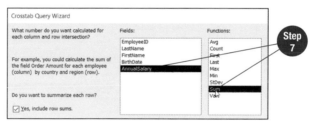

8 Notice how the datasheet layout displays in the *Sample* section and then click the Next button.

9 Select the existing text in the *What do you want to name your query?* text box, type PayrollByDeptByYear, and then click the Finish button.

10 Minimize the Navigation pane and adjust each column's width to best fit the entries.

The query results datasheet displays as shown below. Notice the total column next to each department name and the columns that break down the totals to show the payroll cost for each year.

Department	Total Of AnnualSalary	2011	2012	2013	2014	2015	2016	2017	2018
European Distribution	$314,687.00		$100,100.00			$86,625.00	$42,126.00		$85,836.00
North American Distribution	$691,630.00	$111,600.00	$136,101.00	$91,310.00	$48,750.00		$43,695.00	$132,161.00	$128,013.00
Overseas Distribution	$203,146.00	$72,750.00		$42,824.00	$45,395.00				$42,177.00

11 Print the query results datasheet in landscape orientation.

12 Close the PayrollByDeptByYear query. Click Yes to save changes to the layout.

13 Redisplay the Navigation pane.

Check Your Work Compare your work to the model answer to ensure that you have completed the activity correctly.

A find duplicates query searches a table or query for duplicate values within a designated field or group of fields. Create this type of query if you suspect a record, such as a product record, has been entered twice, such as under two different product numbers. Other applications for this type of query are included in the In Addition section at the end of this activity. Access provides the Find Duplicates Query Wizard to help you build the query by making selections in a series of dialog boxes.

Worldwide Enterprises

Tutorial
Creating a Find Duplicates Query

What You Will Do   You printed new ID cards for employees and received one more card than the number of employees. You suspect that a duplicate ID card was printed. You will use a find duplicates query to check for a duplicated record in the Employees table.

1 With **4-WEEmployees.accdb** open, click the Create tab and then click the Query Wizard button.

2 Click *Find Duplicates Query Wizard* in the New Query dialog box and then click OK.

3 With *Tables* selected in the *View* section of the first Find Duplicates Query Wizard dialog box, click *Table: Employees* in the list box and then click the Next button.

> At the first Find Duplicates Query Wizard dialog box, you choose the table or query in which you want Access to look for duplicate field values.

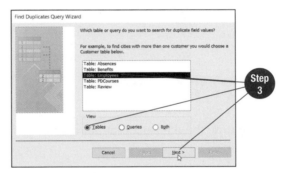

4 Double-click *LastName* and *FirstName* in the *Available fields* list box to move them to the *Duplicate-value fields* list box and then click the Next button.

> In the second Find Duplicates Query Wizard dialog box, you choose the fields that may contain duplicate field values. Since *EmployeeID* is the primary key field in the Employees table, you know that it is not possible for an employee record to be duplicated using the same employee number; therefore, you will use the name fields to check for duplicates.

Create Find Duplicates Query
1. Click Create tab.
2. Click Query Wizard button.
3. Click *Find Duplicates Query Wizard* and click OK.
4. Choose table or query to search for duplicates and click Next.
5. Choose field(s) that might contain duplicate field values and click Next.
6. Choose additional fields to display in query results and click Next.
7. Type query name and click Finish.

5 Move all of the fields from the *Available fields* list box to the *Additional query fields* list box and then click the Next button.

If an employee record has been duplicated, you want to see all of the fields to ensure that the information in both records is exactly the same. If not, you need to figure out which record contains the accurate information before deleting the duplicate.

6 With the text already selected in the *What do you want to name your query?* text box, type DupRecordCheck and then click the Finish button.

The query results datasheet displays, showing that Dina Titov has two records in the Employees table under two different employee numbers.

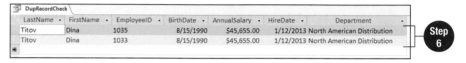

7 Print the query results datasheet in landscape orientation.

8 Move the mouse pointer in the record selector bar next to the record with the employee ID 1035 until the pointer changes to a right-pointing black arrow. Right-click the record selector bar and then click *Delete Record* at the shortcut menu.

9 Click Yes to confirm the record deletion.

10 Close the DupRecordCheck query.

11 Double-click *DupRecordCheck* in the Queries group in the Navigation pane to reopen the query. The query results datasheet is now blank. Since you deleted the duplicate record for Dina Titov in Step 8, duplicate records no longer exist in the Employees table.

12 Close the DupRecordCheck query.

Check Your Work Compare your work to the model answer to ensure that you have completed the activity correctly.

In Addition

Understanding When to Use a Find Duplicates Query

In this activity, you used a find duplicates query to locate and then delete an employee record that was entered twice. A find duplicates query has several other applications. Consider the following examples:
- Find the records in an Orders table with the same customer number so that you can identify your most loyal customers.

- Find the records in a Customer table with the same last name and mailing address so that you send only one mailing to a household, saving on printing and postage costs.
- Find the records in an Expenses table with the same employee number so that you can see which employee is submitting the most claims.

Use a find unmatched query when you want Access to compare two tables and produce a list of the records in one table that have no matching record in the other related table. This type of query is useful to produce lists such as customers who have never placed an order, invoices with no payment, or employees with no absences. Access provides the Find Unmatched Query Wizard to help you build the query by guiding you through a series of dialog boxes.

Worldwide Enterprises

What You Will Do   You are not sure that benefits have been entered for all employees. You decide to create a find unmatched query to make sure that a record exists in the Benefits table for all employees.

Tutorial
Creating a Find
Unmatched Query

1 With **4-WEEmployees.accdb** open, click the Create tab and then click the Query Wizard button.

2 Double-click the *Find Unmatched Query Wizard* option in the New Query dialog box.

3 With *Tables* selected in the *View* section of the first Find Unmatched Query Wizard dialog box, click *Table: Employees* in the list box and then click the Next button.

At the first Find Unmatched Query Wizard dialog box, you choose the table or query in which you want to view records in the query results datasheet. If an employee is missing a record in the Benefits table, you will need the employee's name and employee number, which are in the Employees table.

4 At the second Find Unmatched Query Wizard dialog box, click *Table: Benefits* and then click the Next button.

At the second dialog box, you choose the table or query that you want Access to compare with the first table selected. For Access to compare records, you need to specify the field in each table that would have matching field values.

5 With *EmployeeID* already selected in the *Fields in 'Employees'* and *Fields in 'Benefits'* list boxes at the third Find Unmatched Query Wizard dialog box, click the Next button.

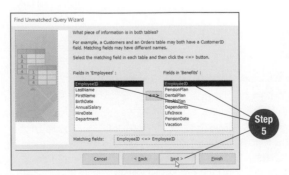

In Brief

Create Find Unmatched Query
1. Click Create tab.
2. Click Query Wizard button.
3. Click *Find Unmatched Query Wizard* and click OK.
4. Choose table or query to display in query results and click Next.
5. Choose related table or query and click Next.
6. Choose matching field in each table field list and click Next.
7. Choose fields you want to view in query results and click Next.
8. Type query name and click Finish.

6 At the fourth Find Unmatched Query Wizard dialog box, double-click *EmployeeID*, *LastName*, and *FirstName* to move the fields from the *Available fields* list box to the *Selected fields* list box and then click the Next button.

7 With the text already selected in the *What would you like to name your query?* text box, type UnmatchedBenefits and then click the Finish button.

8 Look at the three records displayed in the query results datasheet. These are the employee records for which no record with a matching employee number exists in the Benefits table.

9 Print the query results datasheet and then close the UnmatchedBenefits query.

10 Open the Benefits table and then add the records shown in Figure 4.1 to the table.

11 Close the Benefits table.

12 Double-click *UnmatchedBenefits* in the Queries group in the Navigation pane. The query results datasheet is now blank since all employees now have a matching record in the Benefits table.

13 Close the UnmatchedBenefits query.

Figure 4.1 Step 10

Employee ID	Pension Plan	Dental Plan	Health Plan	Dependents	Life Insurance	Pension Date	Vacation
1045	Yes	No	Yes	3	$150,000	01-May-12	3 weeks
1080	Yes	No	No	0	$100,000	01-Feb-17	2 weeks
1085	Yes	Yes	Yes	4	$185,000	01-Jan-18	1 week

Check Your Work Compare your work to the model answer to ensure that you have completed the activity correctly.

The gallery in the Controls group on the Form Layout Tools Design tab contains buttons with which you can insert control objects in a form, such as a title, the date and time, and a picture or other image, to name a few. A label control object contains text that is not associated with an existing field in a table or query. Think of a label control object like a text box that can be used to add instructions or other explanatory text for the users of a form. To sort data in a form, click in the field by which you wish to arrange records and then click the Ascending button or the Descending button in the Sort & Filter group on the Home tab.

Worldwide Enterprises

What You Will Do   Worldwide Enterprises reimburses employees for tuition paid for work-related courses, provided the employee achieves a grade of C- or higher. A form has already been created to enter the records into the PDCourses table. You decide to add objects to the form to enhance its appearance and functionality.

Tutorial

Inserting Control Objects

1   With **4-WEEmployees.accdb** open, double-click *PDCourses* in the Forms group in the Navigation pane to open the form.

2   Scroll through a few records in the form to become familiar with the form's data and purpose. Display the first record in the form and then click the View button in the Views group on the Home tab to switch to Layout view.

> In the next steps, you will insert a label control object in the form to add an explanation about the minimum grade requirement.

3   Click the Label button 🅰 in the gallery in the Controls group on the Form Layout Tools Design tab.

Step 3

> When a control button has been selected, the pointer changes to crosshairs with an icon attached that indicates the type of control object to be created. A label control object displays an uppercase *A* as the icon.

4   Position the crosshairs with the label icon attached at the left edge of the form, just below the *Date Reimbursed* field.

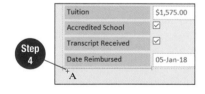
Step 4

> A vertical pink indicator bar appears just below the *Date Reimbursed* label to show you where the new control object will be placed.

5   Click to insert a label control object. The insertion point is positioned in the label control object. Type Minimum grade of C- is required. and then press the Enter key.

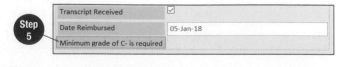
Step 5

> The column width automatically expands to accommodate the length of the text entry. Press Shift + Enter to insert a line break when you want to move down one line in the label control object. A line break can help readability of long entries. In the next steps, you will add a picture to the form to create visual interest.

6   Click the Image button 🖼 in the gallery in the Controls group.

Step 6

7 Position the crosshairs with the image icon attached below the date entry in the *Date Reimbursed* field until a pink indicator bar appears inside a rectangle next to the label control object and then click the left mouse button.

Step 7

8 At the Insert Picture dialog box, navigate to the AccessS4 folder on your storage medium and then double-click *Classroom.jpg*.

9 Position the mouse pointer on the bottom of the image control object until the pointer displays as an up-and-down-pointing arrow and then drag the mouse down approximately 2 inches to resize the image as shown at the right.

Step 9

10 Click to select the label control object to the left of the picture and then click the Form Layout Tools Format tab.

11 Change the font to Copperplate Gothic Light and the font size to 14 points.

12 Click outside the label control object to deselect the object.

13 Save the form and then switch to Form view.

14 At the first record displayed in Form view, click anywhere within the *Tuition* field and then click the Ascending button in the Sort & Filter group on the Home tab.

first record displayed when form is sorted in ascending order on the *Tuition* field in Step 14

> The records are rearranged to display from the lowest to highest tuition reimbursed.

15 Print the first record only.

16 Close the PDCourses form, saving changes if prompted.

Check Your Work Compare your work to the model answer to ensure that you have completed the activity correctly.

Create a calculated control object containing a formula by using the Text Box button. Like a calculated field in a query, a calculated control object in a form is not stored as a field—each time the form is opened, the results are calculated dynamically. Display a form in Layout view to add a text box control object.

What You Will Do   Worldwide Enterprises pays its employees 4% of their annual salary each year as vacation pay. You decide to show the vacation pay calculation within the Employees form.

Tutorial
Inserting a Calculation in a Form

1 With **4-WEEmployees.accdb** open, right-click *Employees* in the Forms group in the Navigation pane and then click *Layout View* at the shortcut menu.

2 Click the Text Box button abl in the Controls group on the Form Layout Tools Design tab.

3 Position the crosshairs with the text box icon attached between the *Annual Salary* and *Hire Date* fields until a horizontal pink indicator bar displays between the field boxes and then click the left mouse button.

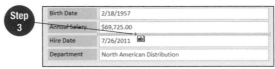

> With the Text Box button selected, clicking in the form inserts two control objects: a label control object and a text box control object.

4 Click to select the empty text box control object (white box below *$69,725.00*) and then click the Property Sheet button in the Tools group on the Form Layout Tools Design tab.

5 Click the Data tab in the Property Sheet task pane.

6 Click in the *Control Source* property box, type =[AnnualSalary]*.04, and then press the Enter key.

> Similar to a query, a formula is typed by placing field names in square brackets. The field name for the salary field is *AnnualSalary* (with no spaces between the words). In the form, recall that the label controls next to the fields can contain spaces to improve readability and appearance; however, in a formula, you must refer to the proper field name in which the data resides in the table. The Property Sheet task pane can be widened to display the entire formula.

7 Click the Close button in the upper right corner of the Property Sheet task pane to close the task pane.

In Brief

Add Calculated Control Object to Form
1. Open form in Layout view.
2. Click Text Box button.
3. Click crosshairs at specific location to insert control object.
4. Click to select empty text box control object.
5. Open Property Sheet task pane.
6. Click Data tab.
7. Click in *Control Source* property box.
8. Type formula beginning with equals symbol.
9. Close Property Sheet task pane.

8 With the text box control object still selected (contains *2789*), click the Form Layout Tools Format tab.

9 Click the Apply Currency Format button $ in the Number group.

Applying currency formatting changes the amount in the text box control object to *$2,789.00*.

10 Click the label control object adjacent to the calculated text box control (currently displays *Text##* [where ## is the number of the label object]).

11 Double-click the text in the label control object to select it, type Vacation Pay, and then press the Enter key.

12 Position the mouse pointer on the right edge of the selected *Vacation Pay* label control object until the pointer displays as a left-and-right-pointing arrow and then drag right approximately 0.25 inch to widen the label column. (This changes the width of the entire column.)

Employee ID	1000
Last Name	Vestering
First Name	Sam
Birth Date	2/18/1957
Annual Salary	$69,725.00
Vacation Pay	$2,789.00
Hire Date	7/26/2011
Department	North Americ

Step 12

13 Click in a blank area outside the label control object to deselect the object.

14 Switch to Form view and then scroll through the records, viewing the calculated control object for each record.

15 Display the first record in the form and then print the selected record.

16 Save and then close the Employees form.

Check Your Work ▶ Compare your work to the model answer to ensure that you have completed the activity correctly.

In Addition

Using the Expression Builder Dialog Box

In addition to typing a calculation into the *Control Source* property box, you can create a calculation using the Expression Builder dialog box. Display the dialog box by clicking in the *Control Source* property box in the Property Sheet task pane and then clicking the Build button that displays at the right side of the property box. To insert the formula for the vacation pay, you would scroll down the *Expression Categories* list box and then double-click *AnnualSalary*. The Expression Builder adds the field name in square brackets to the text box in the top portion of the dialog box. To complete the calculation, you would type *.04 and then press the Enter key. Close the Expression Builder dialog box by clicking the Close button in the upper right corner.

Labels, images, and calculated control objects can be added to a report using similar techniques as those learned in the previous activities with forms. A calculation can be inserted in a report using the Text Box button in the gallery in the Controls group on the Report Layout Tools Design tab. Insert a calculation in a text box in the same manner as inserting a calculation in a form. Display the Property Sheet task pane and then type the calculation in the *Control Source* property box.

What You Will Do   Rhonda Trask estimates that Worldwide Enterprises incurs an additional 22% of an employee's annual salary to pay for the employee's benefit plan. You will create a query and then a report and insert a calculation to show the estimated benefit cost by employee.

Inserting a Calculation in a Report

1. With **4-WEEmployees.accdb** open, click the Create tab, click the Query Design button, and then create a new query as follows:
   - Add the Employees table to the query design grid.
   - Add the following fields in this order: *EmployeeID*, *FirstName*, *LastName*, *HireDate*, *Department*, and *AnnualSalary*.
   - Save the query and name it *EmployeeList*.

2. Run the query, view the query results datasheet, and then close the query.

3. Click *EmployeeList* in the Queries group in the Navigation pane, click the Create tab, and then click the Report button in the Reports group.

4. Minimize the Navigation pane.

5. Click the Report Layout Tools Page Setup tab and then click the Landscape button in the Page Layout group.

6. Click to select the control object containing the *FirstName* column heading and then drag the right edge of the *FirstName* control object left until *Lines: 1 Characters: 15* displays at the left side of the Status bar.

7. Click to select the control object containing the *LastName* column heading and then drag the right edge of the *LastName* control object left until *Lines 1: Characters: 15* displays at the left side of the Status bar.

8. Click the Report Layout Tools Design tab.

9. Click the Text Box button in the Controls group and then position the crosshairs with the text box icon attached at the right of the *AnnualSalary* column heading until a vertical pink indicator bar appears.

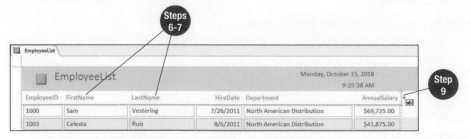

10. Click the left mouse button to insert a new column.

Add Calculated Control Object to Report
1. Open report in Layout view.
2. Click Text Box button.
3. Click crosshairs in report to insert control object.
4. Click to select empty cells in new column.
5. Open Property Sheet task pane.
6. Click Data tab.
7. Click in *Control Source* property box.
8. Type formula or click Build button to enter formula in Expression Builder.
9. Change format property for calculated control as required.
10. Close Property Sheet task pane.
11. Type label in label control.
12. Save report.

11 Click in the empty cells below the *Text##* field column heading (where ## is the number Access has assigned to the text box control object) to select the cells below the heading.

12 Click the Property Sheet button in the Tools group on the Report Layout Tools Design tab.

13 Click the Data tab, click in the *Control Source* property box, type =[AnnualSalary]*.22, and then close the Property Sheet task pane.

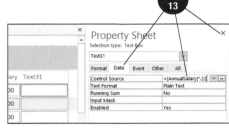

14 Click the Report Layout Tools Format tab and then click the Apply Currency Format button in the Number group.

15 Double-click the label control object at the top of the calculated column, delete the current text, type Benefit Cost, and then press the Enter key.

16 Drag the right edge of the *Benefit Cost* label control object to the right until *Lines: 1 Characters: 14* displays at the left side of the Status bar.

17 Click to select the logo control at the top left of the report and then press the Delete key to delete the control object.

18 Double-click the report title *EmployeeList*, delete the current text, type Employee Benefit Costs, and then press the Enter key.

19 Add a space between the words in the field names for those column headings that do not currently have a space.

20 Scroll to the bottom of the report and then select and delete the total and the line at the bottom of the *Annual Salary* field column. (Select the cell and then press the Delete key. Click the remaining line and then press the Delete key.)

21 Display the report in Print Preview and then return to Layout view. Widen any columns that displayed pound symbols (#) in Print Preview.

22 Click the table select handle located above and to the left of the *Employee ID* column heading to select all records in the report.

23 Click the Report Layout Tools Arrange tab, click the Control Padding button in the Position group, and then click *None* at the drop-down list.

> Control padding adds extra space between rows in a report. Removing the padding allows the report to better fit on one page.

24 Click to select the current day, date, and time control object and then drag the right edge of the selected controls to the right until the control aligns with the right edge of the *Benefit Cost* calculated column.

25 Save the report, accepting the default name *EmployeeList*, and then print and close the report.

26 Redisplay the Navigation pane.

Check Your Work Compare your work to the model answer to ensure that you have completed the activity correctly.

Use the Group, Sort, and Total pane in Layout view to group together records with a similar characteristic. For example, you could arrange the records in the report by department so that all of the employees in the North American Distribution Department are shown together. By default, when a report is grouped, the records are sorted by the grouped field. You can change the sort order or specify multiple-level sorting to sort by another field within a group (such as last name). Display the Group, Sort, and Total pane by clicking the Group & Sort button in the Grouping & Totals group on the Report Layout Tools Design tab.

What You Will Do   Rhonda Trask has asked for a new report that groups the salaries by department. You decide to create a report based on the EmployeeList query and add grouping to the report.

Grouping and Sorting
Records in a Report

1 With **4-WEEmployees.accdb** open, click *EmployeeList* in the Queries group in the Navigation pane, click the Create tab, and then click the Report button.

2 Minimize the Navigation pane.

3 Click the Report Layout Tools Page Setup tab and then click the Landscape button.

4 Click the Report Layout Tools Design tab and then click the Group & Sort button in the Grouping & Totals group. *Note: Skip this step if the Group, Sort, and Total pane is already open at the bottom of the work area.*

The Group, Sort, and Total pane opens at the bottom of the work area. The Group & Sort button is a toggle button that opens or closes the pane.

5 Click the Add a group button in the Group, Sort, and Total pane.

Access adds a grouping level row in the Group, Sort, and Total pane and a list box of available fields displays next to *select field* in which you choose the field by which the records should be grouped.

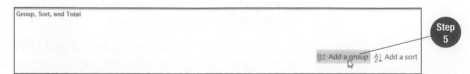

6 Click *Department* in the list box of available fields in the Group, Sort, and Total pane.

Access reorganizes the records in the report and displays a group for each department name with the associated employee records for each group.

In Brief

Group Data in Report
1. Open report in Layout view.
2. If necessary, click Report Layout Tools Design tab.
3. Click Group & Sort button.
4. Click Add a group button.
5. Click field name by which to group.
6. Close Group, Sort, and Total pane.
7. Save report.

Sort Data in Report
1. Open report in Layout view.
2. If necessary, click Report Layout Tools Design tab.
3. Click Group & Sort button.
4. Click Add a sort button.
5. Click field name by which to sort.
6. Close Group, Sort, and Total pane.
7. Save report.

7 Observe that the department names are automatically sorted in ascending order.

Department		EmployeeID	FirstName	LastName	HireDate	AnnualSalary
European Distribution						
		1050	Carl	Zakowski	2/9/2015	$44,387.00
		1013	Gregg	Chippewa	2/11/2012	$48,650.00
		1023	Aleksy	Bulinkski	10/13/2012	$51,450.00
		1045	Terry	Yiu	1/31/2015	$42,238.00
		1060	Donald	McKnight	6/22/2016	$42,126.00
		1085	Yousef	Armine	3/12/2018	$42,177.00
		1080	Leo	Couture	1/29/2018	$43,659.00
North American Distribution						
		1065	Norm	Liszniewski	2/6/2017	$43,695.00
		1063	Charlotte	McPhee	2/6/2017	$43,695.00

Step 7

8 Click the Add a sort button [A↓] in the Group, Sort, and Total pane.

Access inserts a sorting row below the grouping level row and a list box of available fields displays from which you choose the field by which to sort the records within each group.

9 Click *LastName* in the list box of available fields.

The records are now arranged in ascending order by last name within each group.

Step 9

10 Click the Group & Sort button in the Grouping & Totals group on the Report Layout Tools Design tab to close the Group, Sort, and Total pane.

11 Make the following changes to the report:
- Apply the Integral theme.
- Delete the logo control object.
- Delete the total and line at the bottom of the *AnnualSalary* field column.
- Change the report title to *Employee Salaries by Department*.
- Add spaces between words in the column headings.
- Adjust column widths to better fit data on the page.
- Change the Control Padding to *None*.
- Move the date and time controls to align at the right edge of the report.

Step 11

12 Save the report and name it *EmployeesByDept*.

13 Print and close the report and then redisplay the Navigation pane.

> **Check Your Work** — Compare your work to the model answer to ensure that you have completed the activity correctly.

Applying Conditional Formatting to a Report

Conditional formatting allows you to apply font formatting options to field values in a report that meet a specific criterion. For example, you could instruct Access to apply a different font color to all salaries that are greater than a certain value. Click the Conditional Formatting button on the Report Layout Tools Format tab to open the Conditional Formatting dialog box, click the New Rule button, and then specify the criterion and the formatting to apply at the New Formatting Rule dialog box.

What You Will Do   Rhonda Trask has requested a report that shows the employees who have participated in the tuition reimbursement program. She is specifically interested in the courses that were reimbursed that cost over $1,000.00.

Tutorial

Applying Conditional Formatting to a Report

1. With **4-WEEmployees4.accdb** open, click the Create tab, click the Query Design button, and then create a new query as follows:
   - Add the Employees and the PDCourses tables to the query window.
   - Add the following fields in order: *EmployeeID*, *FirstName*, *LastName*, *CourseDescr*, *Grade*, *Tuition*, and *Reimbursed*.
   - Save the query and name it *TuitionReimbursed*.

2. Run the query, view the query results datasheet, and then close the query.

3. Create a new report with the TuitionReimbursed query.

4. Minimize the Navigation pane.

5. Change the report to landscape orientation and adjust the column widths so that all of the fields fit on one page.

6. Position the mouse pointer over the values in the *Tuition* field column and then click to select the column.

7. Click the Report Layout Tools Format tab and then click the Conditional Formatting button ![icon] in the Control Formatting group.

   The Conditional Formatting Rules Manager dialog box opens, in which you can create a new criterion, referred to as a *rule*, or edit or delete an existing rule.

8. Click the New Rule button in the Conditional Formatting Rules Manager dialog box.

   The New Formatting Rule dialog box opens. By default, the new rule type is *Check values in the current record or use an expression*.

9. Click the second option box arrow (currently displays *between*) in the *Edit the rule description* section and then click *greater than or equal to* at the drop-down list.

Apply Conditional Formatting to a Report
1. Open report in Layout view.
2. Select field values to format.
3. Click Report Layout Tools Format tab.
4. Click Conditional Formatting button.
5. Click New Rule button.
6. Change *between* list option as required.
7. Type criterion text or value.
8. Change formatting options as required.
9. Click OK.
10. Click OK.

10 Click in the blank text box next to *greater than or equal to* and then type 1000.

11 Click the Font color button arrow below the text box and then click the *Dark Red* color option (first column, last row in the *Standard Colors* section).

12 Click the Bold button.

13 Click OK to close the New Formatting Rule dialog box.

The new rule is shown in the *Rule* list in the Conditional Formatting Rules Manager dialog box.

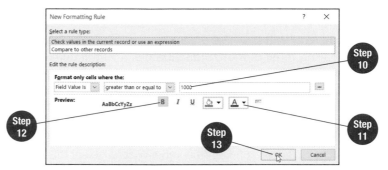

14 Click OK to close the Conditional Formatting Rules Manager dialog box.

The rule is applied to the selected column when you close the dialog box.

15 Notice that the values in the *Tuition* field column that are over $1,000.00 appear in bold, dark red font.

16 Make the following changes to the report:
- Delete the logo control object.
- Change the report title to *Employee Tuition Reimbursement Report*.
- Add spaces between words in the column headings whose field names are compound words.
- Move the date and time controls to align at the right edge of the report.
- Delete the total amount and line at the bottom of the *Tuition* field column.

Employee Tuition Reimbursement Report						Monday, October 15, 2018 10:49:04 AM
Employee ID	First Name	Last Name	Course Description	Grade	Tuition	Date Reimbursed
1000	Sam	Vestering	Global Finance	B+	$1,575.00	05-Jan-18
1005	Roman	Deptulski	Operations Management	A-	$1,145.00	05-Jan-18
1020	Angela	Doxtator	Introduction to Accounting	B-	$485.00	23-Jan-18
1030	Thom	Hicks	Marketing Research Methods	B+	$674.00	30-Jan-18
1045	Terry	Yiu	Marketing E-Commerce Strategies	A	$985.00	16-Feb-18
1000	Sam	Vestering	Information Systems	B	$543.00	01-May-18
1005	Roman	Deptulski	Database Management	A-	$750.00	15-Jun-18
1020	Angela	Doxtator	Intermediate Accounting	B+	$510.00	15-May-18
1045	Terry	Yiu	Operations Management	A	$1,145.00	15-May-18

Step 16

17 Save the report with the default name *TuitionReimbursed*.

18 Print and then close the report.

19 Redisplay the Navigation pane and then close **4-WEEmployees.accdb**.

Check Your Work ▷ Compare your work to the model answer to ensure that you have completed the activity correctly.

Often, an Access database contains the names and addresses of customers, employees, vendors, or other individuals or companies to whom you want to send a mailing. Access includes a wizard to assist you with creating a report that can be used to print names and addresses on a sheet of labels. The Label Wizard includes predefined formatting for all of the common label products available in office supply stores.

Worldwide Enterprises

What You Will Do   Sam Vestering, manager of North American Distributors, wants to send a mailing to all of the US distributors. You will generate a sheet of mailing labels to be used to address the envelopes.

Tutorial
Creating Mailing Labels

1   Open **4-WEDistributors.accdb** and enable the contents, if necessary.

2   Click *US_Distributors* in the Tables group in the Navigation pane.

> Before you start the Label Wizard, select the table or query in the Navigation pane that contains the name and address fields.

3   Click the Create tab and then click the Labels button ⊞ in the Reports group.

4   At the first Label Wizard dialog box, make sure *Avery* is selected next to *Filter by manufacturer*. Scroll up or down the list box below *What label size would you like?* and then click *5163* in the *Product number* column. **Note: Many labels are manufactured by Avery and you may need to scroll for a while to find the 5163 product number**.

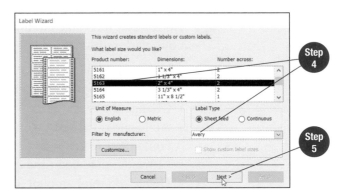

5   Click the Next button.

6   At the second Label Wizard dialog box, change the font size to *10* (if *10* is not currently selected) and then click the Next button.

7   At the third Label Wizard dialog box, double-click *CompanyName* in the *Available fields* list box to move the field name to the first line in the *Prototype label* box.

> Access adds *CompanyName* in brace brackets on the first line of the prototype label. The prototype label represents a sample of the label that will be generated when you complete the wizard.

8   Press the Enter key to move the insertion point to the next line.

9   Double-click *StreetAdd1* in the *Available fields* list box and then press the Enter key.

10   Double-click *StreetAdd2* in the *Available fields* list box and then press the Enter key.

In Brief

Create Mailing Labels
1. Click table or query name in Navigation pane.
2. Click Create tab.
3. Click Labels button.
4. Select label product and click Next.
5. Select font characteristics and click Next.
6. Add fields including spacing and punctuation to prototype label and click Next.
7. Specify sort field and click Next.
8. Click Finish.

11 Double-click *City*, type a comma (,), press the spacebar, double-click *State*, press the spacebar, and then double-click *ZIPCode*.

12 Click the Next button.

13 At the fourth Label Wizard dialog box, double-click the *State* field name in the *Available fields* list box to move the field to the *Sort by* list box and then click the Next button.

> The labels will be sorted alphabetically by the *State* field.

14 Click the Finish button at the last Label Wizard dialog box to accept the default report name *Labels US_Distributors*.

15 Click OK if a message box displays indicating some data may be lost because there is not enough horizontal space on the page.

> The labels report opens in Print Preview.

16 Scroll through the labels report and note that the labels are arranged in alphabetical order by the *State* field.

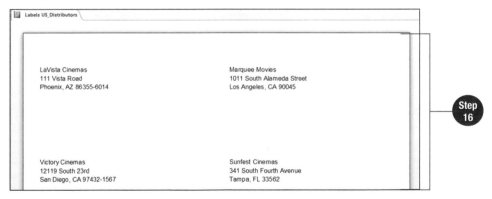

17 Print the labels report. Click OK if the message box reappears warning that some data may be lost.

18 Close the Labels US_Distributors report. ***Note: If the report displays in a Design view window after closing Print Preview, click the Close button in the top right of the work area.***

Check Your Work Compare your work to the model answer to ensure that you have completed the activity correctly.

Compacting and Repairing a Database; Backing Up a Database

Once you have been working with a database file for a period of time, the data can become fragmented because of records and objects that have been deleted. The disk space the database uses may be larger than is necessary. Compacting the database defragments the file and reduces the required disk space. Compacting and repairing a database also ensures optimal performance while using the file. The database can be set to compact automatically each time the file is closed. Databases should be regularly backed up to protect a business from data loss and to provide a historical record of tables before records are added, deleted, or modified. Access includes a backup utility to facilitate this process.

Worldwide Enterprises

What You Will Do   You decide to compact the Worldwide Enterprises Distributors database file and then turn on the *Compact on Close* option so that the database is compacted automatically each time the file is closed. You will also create a backup copy of the database.

Tutorial
Compacting and Repairing a Database

Tutorial
Backing Up a Database

1 With **4-WEDistributors.accdb** open, click the Minimize button on the Title bar to reduce Access to a button on the taskbar.

> In the next steps, you will view the current file size of the database to determine the impact of compacting the database by comparing the before and after file sizes once you have compacted it.

2 Open File Explorer and then navigate to your AccessS4 folder.

3 If necessary, change to the Tiles view. To do this, click the View tab and then click the *Tiles* option in the Layout group.

> If the *Tiles* option is not visible, click the More button in the Layout group.

4 Locate the file named **4-WEDistributors.accdb** and then write down the file size of the database.

> File size = _____

> Two files will appear in the file list: **4-WEDistributors.accdb** and **4-WEDistributors.laccdb**. Notice the .laccdb file displays with a a lock icon. This file is used to lock records so that two users cannot request the same record at the same time.

5 Click the Access button on the taskbar.

6 Click the File tab and then click the Compact & Repair Database button at the Info backstage area.

> Compacting may take a few seconds.

7 Click the File Explorer button on the taskbar.

8 Write down the new file size of **4-WEDistributors.accdb**. Notice that the amount of disk space used for the database is now lower.

> File size = _____

9 Close File Explorer.

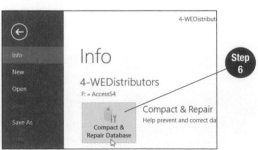

In Brief

Compact and Repair Database
1. Open database.
2. Click File tab.
3. If necessary, click Info tab.
4. Click Compact and Repair Database button.

Turn on Compact on Close Option
1. Open database.
2. Click File tab.
3. Click *Options*.
4. Click *Current Database*.
5. Click *Compact on Close*.
6. Click OK.

Back Up Database
1. Open database.
2. Click File tab.
3. Click *Save As*.
4. Double-click *Back Up Database*.
5. Click Save.

10 With **4-WEDistributors.accdb** open, click the File tab and then click *Options*.

11 At the Access Options dialog box, click the *Current Database* option in the left panel.

12 Click the *Compact on Close* check box in the *Application Options* section to insert a check mark.

13 Click OK to close the Access Options dialog box and then click OK at the message box that informs you that you must close and reopen the current database for the option to take effect.

14 Click the File tab and then click the *Save As* option.

15 At the Save As backstage area, double-click *Back Up Database* in the *Advanced* section.

16 At the Save As dialog box, click the Save button to accept the default settings.

By default, Access saves the backup copy of the database using the original file name with the current date appended to the end of the name. The backup copy is stored in the same location as the original database unless you change the drive and/or folder before saving.

17 Close **4-WEDistributors.accdb**.

In Addition

Editing Database Properties

Use the Database Properties dialog box (shown at the right) to store additional information about a database. For example, you can add information in the *Comments* text box about the data history in the backup copy of a database. To do this, open the backup copy of the database, click the File tab, and then click the <u>View and edit database properties</u> hyperlink in the right panel.

Features Summary

Feature	Ribbon Tab, Group	Button
aggregate functions	Query Tools Design, Show/Hide	Σ
backup database	File, *Save As*	
compact and repair database	File, *Info*	
conditional formatting in form or report	Form Layout Tools Format, Control Formatting OR Report Layout Tools Format, Control Formatting	
Crosstab Query Wizard	Create, Queries	
Find Duplicates Query Wizard	Create, Queries	
Find Unmatched Query Wizard	Create, Queries	
Group, Sort, and Total pane	Report Layout Tools Design, Grouping & Totals	
Label Wizard	Create, Reports	
Property Sheet task pane	Form Layout Tools Design, Tools OR Report Layout Tools Design, Tools	
sort a record in a form in ascending order	Home, Sort & Filter	

Workbook Section study tools and assessment activities are available in the *Workbook* ebook. These resources are designed to help you further develop and demonstrate mastery of the skills learned in this section.

Word, Excel, and Access

Data Files ⟩ Before beginning the section activities, copy the Integrating2 folder to your storage medium and then make Integrating2 the active folder.

Skills

- Export Access data in a table to Excel
- Export Access data in a table to Word
- Export Access data in a report to Word
- Import Excel data to a new Access table

- Link data between an Excel worksheet and an Access table
- Edit linked data

Precheck ⟩ Check your current skills to help focus your study of the skills taught in this section.

Projects Overview

 NIAGARA PENINSULA COLLEGE
Export grades from an Access table to an Excel worksheet. Import grades from an Excel worksheet into an Access database table. Link grades between an Excel worksheet and an Access database table.

 Worldwide Enterprises
Export data on US Distributors from an Access table to a Word document. Export data on Canadian Distributors from an Access report to a Word document.

 The Waterfront BISTRO
Export data on inventory from an Access table to a Word document.

 Performance Threads
Export data on costume inventory from an Access table to an Excel worksheet. Export data on costume inventory from an Access report to a Word document. Import data on costume design hours from an Excel worksheet into an Access table.

 FIRST CHOICE TRAVEL
Link data on booking commissions between an Excel worksheet and an Access table and then update the data in the Excel worksheet.

 SNAP If you are a SNAP user, launch the Precheck and Tutorials from your Assignments page.

Model Answers ⟩ Preview the model answers for an overview of the projects you will complete in the section activities.

Activity 2.1 Exporting Access Data to Excel

One of the advantages of a suite like Microsoft Office is the ability to exchange data between programs. Access, like the other programs in the suite, offers a feature to export data into other programs—in this case, Excel and Word. Export data to Excel using the Excel button in the Export group on the External Data tab. You can export an Access object such as a table, form, or query.

NIAGARA PENINSULA COLLEGE

What You Will Do   You are Katherine Lamont, Theatre Arts Division instructor at Niagara Peninsula College. You want to work on your grades for your AC-215 class over the weekend and you do not have Access installed on your personal laptop. You decide to export your Access grading table to Excel.

1. Open **2-NPCStudentGrades.accdb** from the Integrating2 folder and then enable the contents.

2. Click the down-pointing arrow in the upper right corner of the Navigation pane and then click *Object Type* at the drop-down list.

3. Click the *StudentGradesAC215-03* query.

4. Click the External Data tab.

5. Click the Excel button in the Export group.

6. At the Export - Excel Spreadsheet dialog box, click the Browse button.

7. At the File Save dialog box, navigate to the Integrating2 folder on your storage medium.

8. Click in the *File name* text box, press the Home key to move the insertion point to the beginning of the file name, type 2- (the file name should appear as **2-StudentGradesAC215-03.xlsx**), and then click the Save button.

   The name of the query was automatically inserted in the *File name* text box.

In Brief

Export Access Table, Form, or Query to Excel
1. Open database.
2. Click object in Navigation pane.
3. Click External Data tab.
4. Click Excel button in Export group.
5. At Export - Excel Spreadsheet dialog box, click Browse button.
6. At File Save dialog box, navigate to folder.
7. Click Save button.
8. Click options at Export - Excel Spreadsheet dialog box.
9. Click OK.

9 At the Export - Excel Spreadsheet dialog box, click the *Export data with formatting and layout* check box to insert a check mark.

10 Click the *Open the destination file after the export operation is complete* check box to insert a check mark and then click OK.

Excel opens with the grades from the query in cells in the workbook.

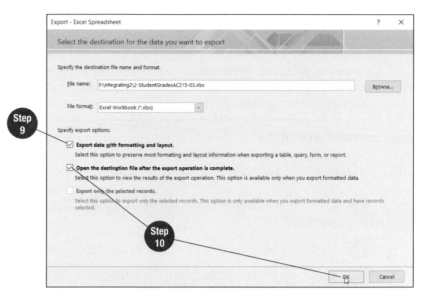

11 If Access is not active, click the Access button on the taskbar.

12 Click the Close button at the Export - Excel Spreadsheet dialog box.

13 Close **2-NPCStudentGrades.accdb**.

14 Click the Excel button on the taskbar.

15 In **2-StudentGradesAC215-03.xlsx**, insert the following grades in the specified cells in the worksheet:

D4:	C
D8:	B
D10:	F
D14:	A
D16:	C
D18:	B

	A	B	C	D
1	Student_No	Last_Name	First_Name	Grade
2	111-785-156	Bastow	Maren	B
3	118-487-578	Andre	Ian	A
4	137-845-746	Knowlton	Sherri	C
5	138-456-749	Yiu	Terry	A
6	146-984-137	Rhodes	Tari	A+
7	157-457-856	Dwyer	Barbara	C
8	184-457-156	Van Este	Doranda	B
9	197-486-745	Koning	Jeffrey	D
10	198-744-149	Lysenko	Earl	F
11	211-745-856	Uhrig	Andrew	A
12	217-458-687	Husson	Ahmad	A+
13	221-689-478	Bhullar	Ash	D
14	229-658-412	Mysior	Melanie	A
15	255-158-498	Gibson	Kevin	A+
16	274-658-986	Woollatt	Bentley	C
17	314-745-856	Morgan	Bruce	C
18	321-487-659	Loewen	Richard	B
19	325-841-469	Clements	Russell	A

16 Save, print, and then close **2-StudentGradesAC215-03.xlsx**.

Check Your Work Compare your work to the model answer to ensure that you have completed the activity correctly.

In Addition

Exporting Limitations

You can export to Excel a table, form, or query but you cannot export a macro, module, or report. If a table contains subdatasheets or a form contains subforms, you must export each subdatasheet or subform to view them in Excel.

Export data from Access to Word in a manner similar to exporting data to Excel. To export data to Word, open the database, select the object, click the External Data tab, click the More button in the Export group, and then click *Word* at the drop-down list. At the Export - RTF File dialog box, make changes and then click OK. Word automatically opens and the data displays in a Word document that is automatically saved with the same name as the database object. The difference is that the file extension *.rtf* is added to the name rather than the Word file extension, *.docx*. An RTF file is saved in "rich-text format," which preserves formatting such as fonts and styles.

Worldwide Enterprises

What You Will Do Sam Vestering, the manager of North American Distribution for Worldwide Enterprises, needs information on US Distributors for an upcoming meeting. He has asked you to export the information from an Access database to a Word document.

1 Open **2-WEDistributors.accdb** from the Integrating2 folder and then enable the contents.

2 Click the *US_Distributors* table in the Tables group in the Navigation pane.

3 Click the External Data tab, click the More button ⊞ in the Export group, and then click *Word* at the drop-down list.

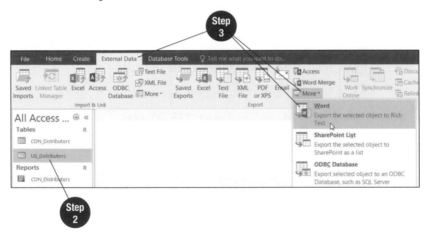

4 At the Export - RTF File dialog box, click the Browse button.

5 At the File Save dialog box, navigate to the Integrating2 folder on your storage medium.

6 Click in the *File name* text box, press Home to move the insertion point to the beginning of the file name, type 2- (the file name should appear as *2-US_Distributors.rtf*), and then click the Save button.

7 At the Export - RTF File dialog box, click the *Open the destination file after the export operation is complete* check box and then click OK.

Microsoft Word opens and the information for US Distributors displays in a document.

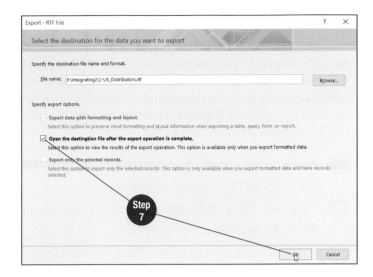

8 If Access is not the active program, click the Access button on the taskbar.

9 Click the Close button at the Export - RTF File dialog box.

10 Close **2-WEDistributors.accdb**.

11 Click the Word button on the taskbar.

12 Change to landscape orientation by clicking the Layout tab, clicking the Orientation button in the Page Setup group, and then clicking *Landscape* at the drop-down list.

13 Click in any cell in the table.

14 Autofit the contents by clicking the Table Tools Layout tab, clicking the AutoFit button in the Cell Size group, and then clicking *AutoFit Contents* at the drop-down list.

15 Save, print, and then close **2-US_Distributors.rtf**.

> **Check Your Work**   Compare your work to the model answer to ensure that you have completed the activity correctly.

In Addition

Adjusting a Table

In this activity, you adjusted the Word table to the cell contents. The table AutoFit feature contains three options for adjusting table contents as described at the right.

Option	Action
AutoFit Contents	adjusts table to accommodate table text
AutoFit Window	resizes table to fit within window or browser; if browser changes size, table size automatically adjusts to fit within window
Fixed Column Width	adjusts each column to fixed width using current widths of the columns

You can also export an Access report to a Word document. Export a report to Word by using the *Word* option at the More button drop-down list in the Export group on the External Data tab. One of the advantages to exporting a report to Word is that you can apply formatting to the report using Word formatting features.

Worldwide Enterprises

What You Will Do   Sam Vestering needs a list of Canadian Distributors. He has asked you to export a report to Word and then apply specific formatting to the report. He needs some of the information for a contact list.

1   Make Access active and then open **2-WEDistributors.accdb**. If necessary, enable the contents.

2   Click the *CDN_Distributors* report in the Reports group in the Navigation pane.

3   Click the External Data tab, click the More button in the Export group, and then click *Word* at the drop-down list.

Step 2

4   At the Export - RTF File dialog box, click the Browse button.

5   At the File Save dialog box, navigate to the Integrating2 folder on your storage medium.

6   Click in the *File name* text box, press Home to move the insertion point to the beginning of the file name, type 2- (the file name should appear as *2-CDN_Distributors.rtf*), and then click the Save button.

7   At the Export - RTF File dialog box, click the *Open the destination file after the export operation is complete* check box and then click OK.

> Microsoft Word opens and the Canadian Distributors report displays in a document.

8   If Access is not the active program, click the Access button on the taskbar.

9   Click the Close button at the Export - RTF File dialog box.

10   Close **2-WEDistributors.accdb**.

11   Click the Word button on the taskbar.

12   Convert the text to a table. To begin, click the Show/Hide ¶ button ¶ in the Paragraph group on the Home tab.

Step 14

13   Move the insertion point to the left of the tab symbol that displays immediately left of the text *CompanyName*, press F8, and then press Ctrl + End.

> The keyboard shortcut F8 turns on the select mode.

14   Click the Insert tab, click the Table button, and then click *Convert Text to Table* at the drop-down list.

In Brief

Export Access Report to Word
1. Open database.
2. Click report in Navigation pane.
3. Click External Data tab.
4. Click More button in Export group.
5. Click *Word*.
6. At Export - RTF File dialog box, click Browse button.
7. At File Save dialog box, navigate to folder.
8. Click Save button.
9. Click options at Export - RTF File dialog box.
10. Click OK.

15 At the Convert Text to Table dialog box, make sure *7* displays in the *Number of columns* text box, make sure *Tabs* is selected in the *Separate text at* section, and then click OK.

16 Turn off the display of nonprinting characters by clicking the Show/Hide ¶ button in the Paragraph group on the Home tab.

17 Click in any cell in the first column (this column does not contain data) and then click the Table Tools Layout tab. Click the Delete button in the Rows & Columns group and then click *Delete Columns* at the drop-down list.

18 Change the left and right margins by clicking the Layout tab, clicking the Margins button in the Page Setup group, and then clicking *Normal* at the drop-down list.

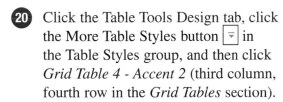

19 Click the Table Tools Layout tab, click the AutoFit button in the Cell Size group, and then click *AutoFit Contents* at the drop-down list.

20 Click the Table Tools Design tab, click the More Table Styles button in the Table Styles group, and then click *Grid Table 4 - Accent 2* (third column, fourth row in the *Grid Tables* section).

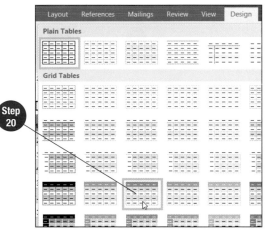

21 Click in the title *Canadian Distributors* and then click the Center button in the Paragraph group on the Home tab.

22 Save, print, and then close **2-CDN_Distributors.rtf**. Close Word.

Check Your Work Compare your work to the model answer to ensure that you have completed the activity correctly.

In Addition

Merging Access Data with a Word Document

Word includes a Mail Merge feature you can use to create letters and envelopes, and much more, with personalized information. Generally, a merge requires two documents—the *data source file* and the *main document*. The data source contains the variable information that will be inserted in the main document. Create a data source file in Word or use data from an Access table. When merging Access data, you can either type the text in the main document or merge Access data with an existing Word document. To merge data in an Access table, open the database and then click the table in the Navigation pane. Click the External Data tab and then click the Word Merge button in the Export group. Follow the steps presented by the Mail Merge wizard.

Activity 2.4 Importing Data into an Access Table

In the previous three activities, you exported Access data to Excel and Word. You can also import data from other programs into an Access table. For example, you can import data from an Excel worksheet and create a new table in a database file. Data in the original program is not connected to the data imported into an Access table. If you make changes to the data in the original program, those changes are not reflected in the Access table.

NIAGARA
PENINSULA
COLLEGE

What You Will Do   You are Gina Simmons, theatre arts instructor. You have recorded grades in an Excel worksheet for students in the Beginning Theatre class. You want to import those grades into a database.

1 Make Access active and then open **2-NPCStudentGrades.accdb**. If necessary, enable the contents.

2 Click the External Data tab.

3 Click the Excel button [icon] in the Import & Link group.

4 At the Get External Data - Excel Spreadsheet dialog box, click the Browse button.

5 At the File Open dialog box, navigate to the Integrating2 folder on your storage medium and then double-click *NPCBegThGrades.xlsx*.

6 At the Get External Data - Excel Spreadsheet dialog box, click OK.

7 At the first Import Spreadsheet Wizard dialog box, insert a check mark in the *First Row Contains Column Headings* check box and then click the Next button.

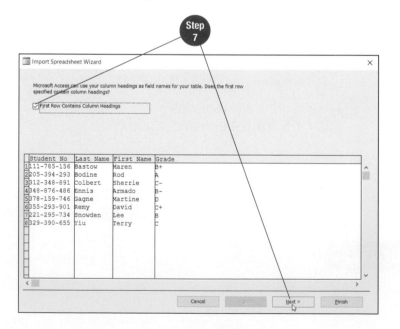

8 At the second Import Spreadsheet Wizard dialog box, click the Next button.

Import Data to New Table
1. Open database.
2. Click External Data tab.
3. Click Excel button in Import & Link group.
4. Click OK at Get External Data - Excel Spreadsheet dialog box.
5. Follow Import Spreadsheet Wizard steps.

9 At the third Import Spreadsheet Wizard dialog box, click the *Choose my own primary key* option (this inserts *Student No* in the text box located to the right of the option) and then click the Next button.

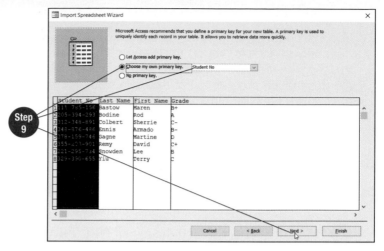

10 At the fourth Import Spreadsheet Wizard dialog box, type BegThGrades in the *Import to Table* text box and then click the Finish button.

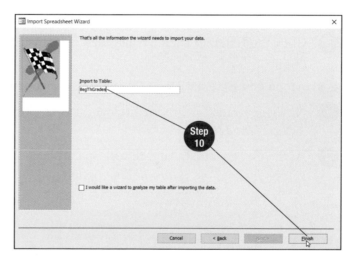

11 At the Get External Data - Excel Spreadsheet dialog box, click the Close button.

12 Open the new table by double-clicking *BegThGrades* in the Navigation pane.

13 Print and then close the BegThGrades table.

14 Close **2-NPCStudentGrades.accdb**.

> **Check Your Work** Compare your work to the model answer to ensure that you have completed the activity correctly.

In Addition

Importing or Linking a Table

You can import data from another program into an Access table or you can link the data. Choose the method depending on how you are going to use the data. Consider linking an Excel file instead of importing if you want to keep data in an Excel worksheet but use Access to perform queries and create reports. In Access, you can only update linked data in one direction. Once an Excel table is linked to Access, you cannot edit data in the Access table. You can update the data in the Excel file and see the changes reflected in Access, but you cannot update data within Access.

Activity 2.5   Linking Excel Data to an Access Table

Imported data is not connected to the source program. If you know that you will use your data only in Access, import it. However, if you want to update data in a program other than Access, link the data. Changes made to linked data are reflected in both the source and the destination programs. For example, you can link an Excel worksheet with an Access table and when you make changes in the Excel worksheet, the changes will be reflected in the Access table.

NIAGARA
PENINSULA
COLLEGE

What You Will Do   You are Cal Rubine, theatre arts instructor at Niagara Peninsula College. You record students' grades in an Excel worksheet and link the grades to an Access database table. With the data linked, changes you make to the Excel worksheet are reflected in the Access table.

1 Make Excel active and then open **NPCTRA220.xlsx**.

2 Save the workbook with the name **2-NPCTRA220**.

3 Print and then close **2-NPCTRA220.xlsx**.

4 Make Access active and then open **2-NPCStudentGrades.accdb**.

5 Click the External Data tab and then click the Excel button in the Import & Link group.

6 At the Get External Data - Excel Spreadsheet dialog box, click the Browse button.

7 Navigate to the Integrating2 folder on your storage medium and then double-click *2-NPCTRA220.xlsx*.

8 At the Get External Data - Excel Spreadsheet dialog box, click the *Link to the data source by creating a linked table* option and then click OK.

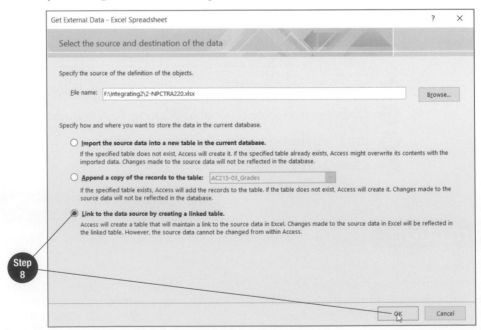

Link Data to New Table
1. Open database.
2. Click External Data tab.
3. Click Excel button in Import & Link group.
4. At Get External Data - Excel Spreadsheet dialog box, click Browse button.
5. Navigate to folder, then double-click file.
6. Click *Link to the data source by creating a linked table* option at Get External Data - Excel Spreadsheet dialog box, then click OK.
7. Follow Link Spreadsheet Wizard steps.

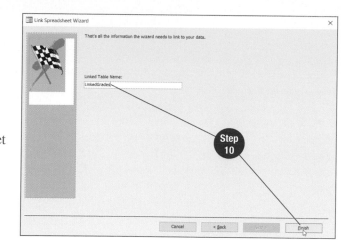

9 At the first Link Spreadsheet Wizard dialog box, make sure the *First Row Contains Column Headings* check box contains a check mark and then click the Next button.

10 At the second Link Spreadsheet Wizard dialog box, type LinkedGrades in the *Linked Table Name* text box and then click the Finish button.

11 At the message stating that the link is finished, click OK.

> Access uses different icons to represent linked tables and tables that are stored in the current database. Notice the icon that displays before the LinkedGrades table.

12 Open the new LinkedGrades table in Datasheet view.

13 Close the LinkedGrades table.

14 Make Excel the active program and then open **2-NPCTRA220.xlsx**.

15 Make cell E2 active, click the AutoSum button arrow in the Editing group, click *Average* at the drop-down list, and then press the Enter key.

> This inserts *3.00* in cell E2.

16 Copy the formula in cell E2 down to the range E3:E9.

17 Save, print, and then close **2-NPCTRA220.xlsx**.

18 Close Excel.

19 With **2-NPCStudentGrades.accdb** open, open the LinkedGrades table and notice that the worksheet contains the average amounts.

20 Print and then close the table.

21 Close **2-NPCStudentGrades.accdb** and then close Access.

Check Your Work ▶ Compare your work to the model answer to ensure that you have completed the activity correctly.

In Addition

Deleting the Link to a Linked Table

If you want to delete the link to a table, open the database and then click the table in the Navigation pane. Click the Home tab and then click the Delete button in the Records group. At the question asking if you want to remove the link to the table, click Yes. Access deletes the link and removes the table's name from the Navigation pane. When you delete a linked table, you are deleting the information Access uses to open the table, not the table itself. You can link to the same table again if necessary.

Workbook ▶ Section assessment activities are available in the Workbook pages of the ebook. These activities are designed to help you demonstrate mastery of the skills learned in this section.

MARQUEE SERIES

Microsoft®

PowerPoint®

2016

Nita Rutkosky
Pierce College Puyallup
Puyallup, Washington

Audrey Roggenkamp
Pierce College Puyallup
Puyallup, Washington

Ian Rutkosky
Pierce College Puyallup
Puyallup, Washington

PARADIGM
EDUCATION SOLUTIONS

St. Paul

Senior Vice President	Linda Hein
Editor in Chief	Christine Hurney
Director of Production	Timothy W. Larson
Production Editors	Rachel Kats, Jen Weaverling
Cover and Text Designer	Valerie King
Copy Editor	Sarah Kearin
Senior Design and Production Specialist	Jaana Bykonich
Assistant Developmental Editors	Mamie Clark, Katie Werdick
Testers	Desiree Carvel; Ann E. Mills, Ivy Tech Community College of Indiana, Indianapolis, IN
Instructional Support Writer	Brienna McWade
Indexer	Terry Casey
Vice President Information Technology	Chuck Bratton
Digital Projects Manager	Tom Modl
Vice President Sales and Marketing	Scott Burns
Director of Marketing	Lara Weber McLellan

Care has been taken to verify the accuracy of information presented in this book. However, the authors, editors, and publisher cannot accept responsibility for Web, email, newsgroup, or chat room subject matter or content, or for consequences from application of the information in this book, and make no warranty, expressed or implied, with respect to its content.

Trademarks: Microsoft is a trademark or registered trademark of Microsoft Corporation in the United States and/or other countries. Some of the product names and company names included in this book have been used for identification purposes only and may be trademarks or registered trade names of their respective manufacturers and sellers. The authors, editors, and publisher disclaim any affiliation, association, or connection with, or sponsorship or endorsement by, such owners.

Cover Photo Credits: © whitehoune/Shutterstock.com; © Bohbeh/Shutterstock.com.

We have made every effort to trace the ownership of all copyrighted material and to secure permission from copyright holders. In the event of any question arising as to the use of any material, we will be pleased to make the necessary corrections in future printings. Thanks are due to the aforementioned authors, publishers, and agents for permission to use the materials indicated.

ISBN 978-0-76386-723-2 (print)
ISBN 978-0-76386-724-9 (digital)

© 2017 by Paradigm Publishing, Inc.
875 Montreal Way
St. Paul, MN 55102
Email: educate@emcp.com
Website: ParadigmCollege.com

Printed in the United States of America

24 23 22 21 20 19 18 17 16   1 2 3 4 5 6 7 8 9 10 11 12

Contents

PowerPoint® 2016

Create colorful and powerful presentations using PowerPoint, Microsoft's presentation program that is included in the Office 2016 suite. Use PowerPoint to organize and present information and create visual aids for a presentation. PowerPoint is a full-featured presentation program that provides a wide variety of editing and formatting features as well as sophisticated visual elements such as images, pictures, SmartArt, WordArt, and drawn objects. While working in PowerPoint, you will produce presentations for the following six companies.

First Choice Travel is a travel center offering a full range of traveling services from booking flights, hotel reservations, and rental cars to offering travel seminars.

The Waterfront Bistro offers fine dining for lunch and dinner and also offers banquet facilities, a wine cellar, and catering services.

Worldwide Enterprises is a national and international distributor of products for a variety of companies and is the exclusive movie distribution agent for Marquee Productions.

Marquee Productions is involved in all aspects of creating movies from script writing and development to filming. The company produces documentaries, biographies, as well as historical and action movies.

Performance Threads maintains an inventory of rental costumes and also researches, designs, and sews special-order and custom-made costumes.

The mission of the Niagara Peninsula College Theatre Arts Division is to offer a curriculum designed to provide students with a thorough exposure to all aspects of the theatre arts.

In Section 1 you will learn how to

Prepare a Presentation

Prepare a presentation using a template provided by PowerPoint or create a presentation and apply formatting with a design theme. Preparing a presentation consists of general steps such as creating and editing slides; adding enhancements to slides; and saving, previewing, printing, and closing a presentation and running a slide show. When running a slide show, the way in which one slide is removed from the screen and the next slide is displayed is referred to as a *transition*. Interesting transitions can be added to slides as well as transition sounds to a presentation.

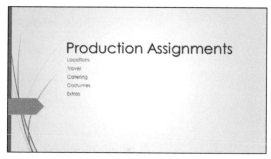

Create presentations using PowerPoint design themes and apply various slide layouts to change the appearance of slides.

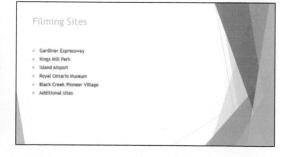

In Section 2 you will learn how to

Edit and Enhance Slides

Edit slides and slide elements in a presentation to customize and personalize the presentation. Editing can include such functions as rearranging and deleting slides; cutting, copying, and pasting text; changing the font, paragraph alignment, and paragraph spacing; and changing the design theme, theme color, and theme font. Add visual appeal to a presentation by inserting images, pictures, and SmartArt organizational charts and graphics.

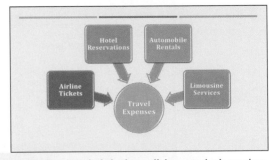

Edit slides by performing such actions as rearranging and deleting slides and changing slide size. Perform editing tasks on text in slides such as changing the font, paragraph alignment, and spacing. Enhance the visual appeal of a presentation by inserting such elements as a company logo, image, an organizational chart, and a graphic.

In Section 3 you will learn how to

Customize Presentations

Customize a presentation with the WordArt feature and by drawing and formatting objects and text boxes. Additional features for customizing a presentation include using the Clipboard; inserting and formatting a table; inserting actions buttons, hyperlinks, and headers and footers; and inserting audio and video files.

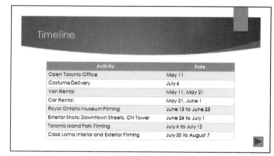

Further customize presentations with features such as headers and footers, audio and video files, WordArt, shapes, text boxes, and tables.

PowerPoint

Preparing a Presentation

Data Files — Before beginning section work, copy the PowerPointS1 folder to your storage medium and then make PowerPointS1 the active folder.

Skills

- Open, save, and close a presentation
- Run a slide show
- Choose a design theme
- Add a new slide to a presentation
- Navigate in a presentation
- Insert a slide in a presentation
- Change the slide layout
- Change the presentation view
- Rearrange, delete, and hide slides
- Use the Tell Me and Help features

- Check spelling in a presentation
- Use Thesaurus to display synonyms for words
- Run a slide show and use the pen during a slide show
- Use ink tools
- Add transitions and transition sounds to a presentation
- Print and preview a presentation

Precheck — Check your current skills to help focus your study of the skills taught in this section.

Projects Overview

 Use an installed template to prepare a presentation about the new features in PowerPoint 2016; prepare a movie production meeting presentation and a location team meeting presentation.

 Prepare a presentation on Toronto, Ontario, Canada.

 Prepare a presentation for a costume meeting.

 Prepare an executive meeting presentation for Worldwide Enterprises.

 Prepare a presentation containing information on the accommodations and services offered by The Waterfront Bistro.

 SNAP If you are a SNAP user, launch the Precheck and Tutorials from your Assignments page.

Model Answers — Preview the model answers for an overview of the projects you will complete in the section activities.

PowerPoint is a presentation graphics program you can use to organize and present information. With PowerPoint, you can create visual aids for a presentation and then print copies of the aids as well as run the slide show. To open a predesigned PowerPoint template, open the PowerPoint program, click the desired template, and then click the Create button. The presentation screen contains a variety of features for working with a presentation, such as the Title bar, Quick Access Toolbar, ribbon, and Status bar. After creating a presentation, save the presentation so it is available for future use. Save a presentation at the Save As backstage area.

What You Will Do   You are an employee of Marquee Productions and Office 2016 has just been installed on your computer. You need to prepare a presentation in the near future so you decide to open a PowerPoint file and experiment with running the slide show.

Tutorial
Opening a
Presentation Based
on a Template

Tutorial
Exploring the
PowerPoint Screen

Tutorial
Running a Slide Show

Tutorial
Saving to a Removable
Disk

Tutorial
Closing a Presentation
and Closing
PowerPoint

1   At the Windows 10 desktop, click the Start button and then click the PowerPoint 2016 tile at the Start menu.

> Depending on your system configuration, these steps may vary.

2   At the PowerPoint 2016 opening screen, click the *Welcome to PowerPoint* template.

> If this template is not visible, you will need to search for it. To do this, click in the search text box, type Welcome to PowerPoint, and then press the Enter key.

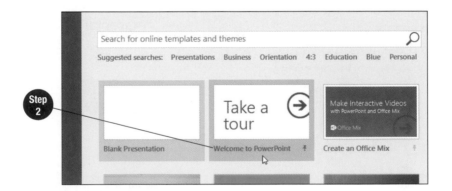

3   Click the Create button.

> The Welcome to PowerPoint template opens in the PowerPoint window. What displays in the PowerPoint window will vary depending on what type of presentation you are creating. However, the PowerPoint window contains some consistent elements, as those identified in Figure 1.1. Refer to Table 1.1 for a description of the window elements.

4   Run the slide show by clicking the Start From Beginning button 🖳 on the Quick Access Toolbar.

5 When the first slide fills the screen, read the information and then click the left mouse button. Continue reading the information in each slide and clicking the left mouse button to advance to the next slide. When a black screen displays, click the left mouse button to end the slide show.

FIGURE 1.1 PowerPoint Window

Table 1.1 PowerPoint Window Elements

Feature	Description
Collapse the Ribbon button	when clicked, removes ribbon from screen
File tab	when clicked, displays backstage area that contains options for working with and managing presentations
I-beam pointer	used to move insertion point or to select text
insertion point	indicates location of next character entered at keyboard
Tell Me feature	used to look up features and provide options for using them
placeholder	location on slide with dotted border; holds text or objects
Quick Access Toolbar	contains buttons for commonly used commands
ribbon	area containing tabs with options and buttons divided into groups
scroll box	used to scroll through slides in presentation; click and hold mouse button on scroll box to indicate slide number and title
slide pane	displays slide and slide contents
slide thumbnails pane	left side of screen; displays slide thumbnails
Status bar	displays slide number, view buttons, and Zoom slider bar
tabs	contain commands and buttons organized into groups
Title bar	displays presentation name followed by program name
vertical scroll bar	used to display specific slides
view area	contains buttons for changing presentation view

6 Save the presentation by clicking the Save button 🖫 on the Quick Access Toolbar.

7 At the Save As backstage area, click the *Browse* option.

8 At the Save As dialog box, click the drive in the Navigation pane that contains your storage medium.

Press the F12 function key to display the Save As dialog box without displaying the Save As backstage area.

9 Double-click the *PowerPointS1* folder in the Content pane.

10 Click in the *File name* text box, type 1-MPPowerPoint2016, and then press the Enter key (or click the Save button).

PowerPoint automatically adds the file extension *.pptx* to the end of a presentation name.

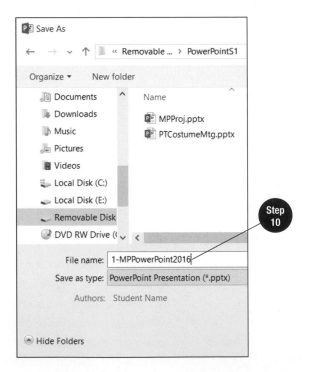

11 At the PowerPoint window, print the presentation information in outline layout by clicking the File tab and then clicking the *Print* option.

> The File tab is in the upper left corner of the screen at the left side of the Home tab. When you click the File tab, the backstage area displays with options for working with and managing presentations.

12 At the Print backstage area, click the second gallery in the *Settings* category (the gallery containing the text *Full Page Slides*) and then click *Outline* in the *Print Layout* section of the drop-down list.

13 Click the Print button. ***Note: If working in a lab, check with your instructor before printing.***

14 Close the presentation by clicking the File tab and then clicking the *Close* option.

> If a message displays asking if you want to save the presentation, click Yes.

15 Close PowerPoint by clicking the Close button that displays in the upper right corner of the screen.

Check Your Work — Compare your work to the model answer to ensure that you have completed the activity correctly.

In Addition

Using Tabs

The ribbon area displays below the Quick Access Toolbar. The buttons and options in the ribbon area vary depending on the tab selected and the width of the window displayed on the screen. PowerPoint features are organized into tabs that display in the ribbon area. Commands and buttons are organized into groups within a tab. For example, the Home tab, which is the default tab, contains the Clipboard, Slides, Font, Paragraph, Drawing, and Editing groups. When you hover the mouse pointer over a button, a ScreenTip displays with the name of the button, a keyboard shortcut (if any), and a description of the purpose of the button.

Create a PowerPoint presentation using an installed template as you did in the previous activity or begin with a blank presentation and apply your own formatting or a slide design theme. To display a blank PowerPoint presentation, use the keyboard shortcut Ctrl + N, or click the File tab, click the *New* option, and then click the *Blank Presentation* template in the New backstage area. A PowerPoint presentation screen displays in Normal view with the slide pane in the center and the slide thumbnails pane at the left side of the screen.

What You Will Do Chris Greenbaum, production manager for Marquee Productions, has asked you to prepare slides for a movie production meeting. You decide to prepare the presentation using a design template offered by PowerPoint.

Tutorial
Opening a Blank Presentation

Tutorial
Applying a Design Theme

Tutorial
Inserting and Deleting Text in Slides

Tutorial
Inserting a New Slide

1 Open PowerPoint.

2 At the PowerPoint 2016 opening screen, click the *Blank Presentation* template.

3 At the PowerPoint window, click the Design tab.

4 Click the More Themes button ⏷ in the Themes group.

5 Click the *Wisp* option in the *Office* section of the drop-down gallery.

> When you click the More Themes button, a drop-down gallery displays. This gallery contains the live preview feature. When you hover your mouse pointer over one of the design themes, the slide in the slide pane displays with the design theme formatting applied. With the live preview feature, you can view a design theme before actually applying it to the presentation.

6 Click the second option from the left in the Variants group.

> This changes the tab at the left side of the slide to a dark gold color.

7 Click anywhere in the *Click to add title* placeholder that displays in the slide in the slide pane and then type Marquee Productions.

> A placeholder is a location on a slide that is marked with a border and holds text or an object.

8 Click anywhere in the *Click to add subtitle* placeholder that displays in the slide and then type Movie Production Meeting.

9 Click the Home tab and then click the New Slide button [icon] in the Slides group.

> When you click this button, a new slide displays in the slide pane with the Title and Content layout. You will learn more about slide layouts in Activity 1.3.

10 Click anywhere in the *Click to add title* placeholder that displays in the slide and then type Agenda.

11 Click anywhere in the *Click to add text* placeholder that displays in the slide and then type Production Team.

12 Press the Enter key and then type the following agenda items, pressing the Enter key after each item except the last one: Production Assignments, Production Schedule, Locations, and Summary.

> You can use keys on the keyboard to move the insertion point to various locations within a placeholder in a slide. Refer to Table 1.2 on the next page for a list of insertion point movement commands.

13 Click the New Slide button in the Slides group on the Home tab.

Table 1.2 Insertion Point Movement Commands

To move insertion point	Press
One character left	Left Arrow
One character right	Right Arrow
One line up	Up Arrow
One line down	Down Arrow
One word to the left	Ctrl + Left Arrow
One word to the right	Ctrl + Right Arrow
To end of a line of text	End
To beginning of a line of text	Home
To beginning of current paragraph in placeholder	Ctrl + Up Arrow
To beginning of previous paragraph in placeholder	Ctrl + Up Arrow two times
To beginning of next paragraph in placeholder	Ctrl + Down Arrow
To beginning of text in placeholder	Ctrl + Home
To end of text in placeholder	Ctrl + End

14 Click anywhere in the *Click to add title* placeholder that displays in the slide and then type Department Reports.

15 Click anywhere in the *Click to add text* placeholder that displays in the slide and then type the bulleted text as shown in the slide below. Press the Enter key after each item except the last one.

16 Click the New Slide button in the Slides group on the Home tab.

17 Click anywhere in the *Click to add title* placeholder that displays in the slide and then type Locations.

18 Click anywhere in the *Click to add text* placeholder that displays in the slide, type Studio Shoots, and then press the Enter key.

19 Press the Tab key, type Vancouver Studio, and then press the Enter key.

Pressing the Tab key demotes the insertion point to a second-level bullet, while pressing Shift + Tab promotes the insertion point back to the first level.

20 Type Los Angeles Studio and then press the Enter key.

In Brief

Choose Design Theme
1. Click Design tab.
2. Click More Themes button.
3. Click theme at drop-down gallery.

Insert New Slide
1. Click Home tab.
2. Click New Slide button.

21 Press Shift + Tab, type Location Shoots, and then press the Enter key.

22 Press the Tab key, type Stanley Park, and then press the Enter key.

23 Type Downtown Streets.

24 Click the Save button on the Quick Access Toolbar.

25 At the Save As backstage area, click the *Browse* option.

26 At the Save As dialog box, click the drive in the Navigation pane that contains your storage medium.

27 Double-click the *PowerPointS1* folder in the Content pane.

28 Click in the *File name* text box, type 1-MPProdMtg, and then press the Enter key (or click the Save button).

29 Close the presentation by clicking the File tab and then clicking the *Close* option.

Check Your Work Compare your work to the model answer to ensure that you have completed the activity correctly.

In Addition

Planning a Presentation

Consider the following basic guidelines when preparing content for a presentation:

- **Determine the main purpose.** Do not try to cover too many topics. Identifying the main point of the presentation will help you stay focused and convey a clear message to the audience.
- **Determine the output.** To help decide the type of output needed, consider the availability of equipment, the size of the room where you will make the presentation, and the number of people who will be attending the presentation.
- **Show one idea per slide.** Each slide in a presentation should convey only one main idea. Too many ideas on a slide may confuse the audience and cause you to stray from the purpose of the slide.

- **Maintain a consistent design.** A consistent design and color scheme for slides in a presentation will create continuity and cohesiveness. Do not use too much color or too many images or other graphic elements.
- **Keep slides uncluttered and easy to read.** Keep slides simple to make them easy for your audience to understand. Keep words and other items, such as bullets, to a minimum.
- **Determine printing needs.** Will you be providing audience members with handouts? If so, will these handouts consist of a printing of each slide? an outline of the presentation? a printing of each slide with space for taking notes?

Open an existing presentation by displaying the Open backstage area and then clicking the presentation in the *Recent* option list. You can also open a presentation at the Open dialog box. Display the Open dialog box by clicking the File tab and then clicking the *Open* option. At the Open backstage area, click the *Browse* option. Navigate through slides in a presentation with buttons on the vertical scroll bar, by clicking slide thumbnails in Normal view, or by using keys on the keyboard. Insert a new slide with a specific layout by clicking the New Slide button arrow in the Slides group on the Home tab or the Insert tab and then clicking the desired layout at the drop-down list. Choose the layout that matches the type of text or object you want to insert in the slide.

What You Will Do   Chris Greenbaum has asked you to add more information to the movie production meeting presentation. You will insert a new slide between the second and third slides in the presentation and another at the end of the presentation.

Tutorial
Opening from a
Removable Disk

Tutorial
Navigating to Slides

Tutorial
Choosing a Slide
Layout

Tutorial
Saving with the
Same Name

1 Click the File tab and then click the *Open* option.

2 At the Open backstage area, click the *Browse* option.

3 In the Navigation pane of the Open dialog box, click the drive where your USB flash drive is located (such as *Removable Disk (F:)*).

> You can also display the Open dialog box without displaying the Open backstage area by pressing Ctrl + F12.

4 Double-click the *PowerPointS1* folder in the Content pane.

5 Double-click *1-MPProdMtg.pptx* in the Content pane.

6 With **1-MPProdMtg.pptx** open, click the Next Slide button ⏬ at the bottom of the vertical scroll bar.

Step 6

> Clicking this button displays the next slide, Slide 2, in the presentation. Notice that *Slide 2 of 4* displays at the left side of the Status bar.

7 Click the Previous Slide button ⏫ above the Next Slide button to display Slide 1.

> When you click the Previous Slide button, Slide 1 displays in the slide pane and *Slide 1 of 4* displays at the left side of the Status bar.

Step 9

Step 8

8 Display Slide 2 in the slide pane by clicking the second slide in the slide thumbnails pane (the slide titled *Agenda*).

9 Insert a new slide between Slides 2 and 3 by clicking the New Slide button in the Slides group on the Home tab.

> When you select a slide in the slide thumbnails pane and then click the New Slide button, the new slide is inserted after the selected slide.

10 Click in the *Click to add title* placeholder in the slide in the slide pane and then type Production Schedule.

11 Click in the *Click to add text* placeholder in the slide and then type the bulleted text as shown at the right. Press the Enter key after typing each item except the last one.

12 Click below the last thumbnail in the slide thumbnails pane. (You may need to scroll down the slide thumbnails pane to display the last slide.)

> When you click below the slide thumbnail, an orange horizontal line displays below Slide 5.

13 Click the New Slide button arrow on the Home tab and then click the *Title Slide* layout that displays in the drop-down list.

14 Click in the *Click to add title* placeholder and then type Production Leader.

15 Click in the *Click to add subtitle* placeholder and then type Chris Greenbaum.

16 Click the Save button on the Quick Access Toolbar to save **1-MPProdMtg.pptx**.

> **Check Your Work** Compare your work to the model answer to ensure that you have completed the activity correctly.

In Addition

Opening a Presentation from the *Recent* Option List

At the Open backstage area with the *Recent* option selected, a list of the most recently opened presentations display. The presentations are grouped into categories such as *Today*, *Yesterday*, and possibly *This Week* and *Older*. To open a presentation from the *Recent* option list, open PowerPoint to display the opening screen or display the Open backstage area with the *Recent* option selected and then click the desired presentation in the list.

Activity 1.4 Changing Views

PowerPoint provides different viewing options for a presentation. Change the presentation view with buttons in the Presentation Views group on the View tab or with buttons in the view area on the Status bar. The Normal view is the default view, and you can change the view to Outline view, Slide Sorter view, Notes Page view, or Reading view. Choose the view based on the type of activity you are performing in the presentation. Another method for entering text in a slide is in Outline view. When Outline view is active, the slide thumbnails pane changes to an outline pane for entering text. Insert speaker's notes into a presentation using the notes pane, which can be displayed by clicking the Notes button on the Status bar.

Tutorial
Changing Views

Tutorial
Entering Text in the Outline Pane

Tutorial
Changing the Display of a Slide in the Slide Pane

What You Will Do After reviewing the movie production presentation, Chris Greenbaum has asked you to add a new slide and edit an existing slide.

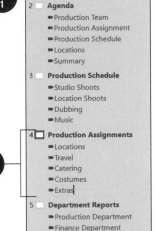

1 With **1-MPProdMtg.pptx** open, click the View tab and then click the Outline View button in the Presentation Views group.

2 Click immediately right of the text *Music* in the third slide (located toward the middle of the outline pane), press the Enter key, and then press Shift + Tab.

> This moves the insertion point back a level and inserts the number *4* followed by a slide icon.

3 Type Production Assignments, press the Enter key, and then press the Tab key. Type the remaining text for Slide 4 as shown at the right. Do not press the Enter key after typing *Extras*.

4 Click immediately right of the text *Location Shoots* in the third slide.

5 Press the Enter key and then type Editing.

> This inserts *Editing* between *Location Shoots* and *Dubbing*.

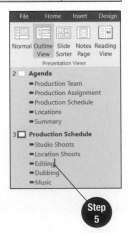

6 Make Slide 6 the active slide in the slide pane, click in the *Click to add notes* placeholder in the notes pane (if the text is not visible, click the Notes button on the Status bar to display the notes pane), and then type Camille Matsui will report on the park location.

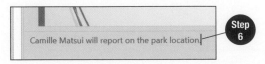

7 Display the slides in Notes Page view by clicking the Notes Page button in the Presentation Views group.

> In Notes Page view, an individual slide displays on a page with any added notes displayed below it. Notice that the note you created about Camille Matsui displays below the slide in the page.

8 Click the Previous Slide button on the vertical scroll bar until Slide 1 displays.

9 Increase the zoom by clicking the Zoom button in the Zoom group on the View tab, clicking *100%* at the Zoom dialog box, and then clicking OK.

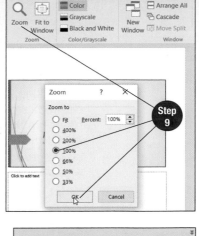

10 You can also change the zoom using the Zoom slider bar. Change the zoom by positioning the mouse pointer on the Zoom slider button at the right side of the Status bar. Hold down the left mouse button, drag to the right until the zoom percentage at the right side of the Zoom slider bar displays as approximately *138%*, and then release the mouse button.

11 Click the Zoom Out button at the left side of the Zoom slider bar until *70%* displays at the right side of the slider bar.

> Click the Zoom Out button to decrease the zoom display and click the Zoom In button to increase the display.

12 View all slides in the presentation as slide thumbnails by clicking the Slide Sorter button in the view area on the Status bar.

13 View the presentation in Reading view by clicking the Reading View button in the Presentation Views group.

> Use Reading view to show the presentation to someone viewing the presentation on his or her own computer. You can also use Reading view to view a presentation in a window with controls that make the presentation easy to view. In Reading view, navigation buttons display in the lower right corner of the screen immediately left of the view area on the Status bar.

14 View the slides in the presentation in Reading view by clicking the left mouse button on the slides until a black screen displays. At the black screen, click the mouse button again.

> This returns the presentation to the previous view—in this case, Slide Sorter view.

15 Return the presentation to Normal view by clicking the Normal button in the Presentation Views group.

16 If necessary, close the notes pane by clicking the Notes button on the Status bar.

17 Save **1-MPProdMtg.pptx**.

Check Your Work — Compare your work to the model answer to ensure that you have completed the activity correctly.

In Addition

Navigating Using the Keyboard

You can also use the keyboard to display slides in a presentation. In Normal view, press the Down Arrow or Page Down key to display the next slide or press the Up Arrow or Page Up key to display the previous slide in the presentation. Press the Home key to display the first slide in the presentation and press the End key to display the last slide in the presentation. Navigate in Outline view and Slide Sorter view by using the arrow keys on the keyboard. Navigate in Reading view by using the Right Arrow key to move to the next slide or the Left Arrow key to move to the previous slide.

So far, you have created slides based on a default slide layout. Change the slide layout by clicking the Layout button in the Slides group on the Home tab and then clicking the desired layout at the drop-down list. Objects in a slide, such as text, charts, tables, and other graphic elements, are generally positioned in placeholders. Click the text or object to select the placeholder and a dashed border will surround the placeholder. You can move, size, and/or delete a selected placeholder.

What You Will Do   You have decided to make a few changes to the layout of slides in the movie production presentation.

Tutorial
Modifying Placeholders

Tutorial
Changing Slide Layout

1   With **1-MPProdMtg.pptx** open, make Slide 7 active in the slide pane.

2   Click the Home tab, click the Layout button in the Slides group, and then click the *Title and Content* layout at the drop-down list.

3   Click immediately right of the *r* in *Leader* (this selects the placeholder), press the Backspace key until *Leader* is deleted, and then type Team.

Sizing handles display around the selected placeholder. Use these sizing handles to increase and/or decrease the size of the placeholder.

4   Click immediately right of the *m* in *Greenbaum*.

5   Type a comma (,), press the spacebar, and then type Production Manager.

6   Press the Enter key and then type the remaining names and titles shown in the slide at the right. (Do not press the Enter key after typing *Josh Hart, Locations Director*.)

7   Click the Previous Slide button on the vertical scroll bar until Slide 4 displays.

8   Change the slide layout by clicking the Layout button in the Slides group and then clicking the *Title Slide* layout at the drop-down list.

9   Click in the title *Production Assignments*.

This selects the placeholder.

10   Decrease the size of the placeholder by positioning the mouse pointer on the middle sizing handle at the top of the placeholder until the pointer turns into an up-and-down-pointing arrow. Hold down the left mouse button, drag down to the approximate location shown at the right, and then release the mouse button.

11 Move the title placeholder so it positions the title as shown in Figure 1.2. To do this, position the mouse pointer on the placeholder border until the mouse pointer displays with a four-headed arrow attached, hold down the left mouse button, drag to the approximate location shown in the figure, and then release the mouse button.

12 Increase the size of the subtitle placeholder (and the size of the text). Begin by clicking in the word *Locations*.

This selects the placeholder containing the text.

13 Position the mouse pointer on the middle sizing handle at the top of the placeholder until the pointer turns into an up-and-down-pointing arrow. Hold down the left mouse button, drag up approximately one inch, and then release the mouse button.

Increasing the size of the placeholder automatically increases the size of the text in the placeholder. This is because, by default, PowerPoint automatically sizes the contents to fit the placeholder. Read the In Addition at the bottom of this page for information on the AutoFit Options button.

14 Move the content placeholder so it positions the text as shown in Figure 1.2. To do this, position the mouse pointer on the placeholder border until the mouse pointer displays with a four-headed arrow attached, hold down the left mouse button, drag to the approximate location shown in the figure, and then release the mouse button.

Figure 1.2 Slide 4

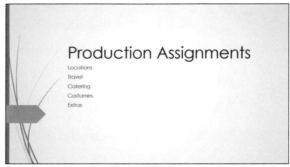

15 Click outside the placeholder to deselect it.

If you are not satisfied with the changes you make to a placeholder, click the Reset button in the Slides group on the Home tab. This resets the placeholder's position, size, and formatting to the default settings.

16 Save **1-MPProdMtg.pptx**.

Check Your Work ▷ Compare your work to the model answer to ensure that you have completed the activity correctly.

In Addition

Using the AutoFit Options Button

If you decrease the size of a placeholder so the existing text does not fit within it, PowerPoint will automatically decrease the size of the text so it fits in the placeholder. If you click anywhere in the text that has been decreased in size, an AutoFit Options button displays at the left side of the placeholder. Click the AutoFit Options button and a list of choices displays for positioning objects in the placeholder, as shown at the right. The *AutoFit Text to Placeholder* option is selected by default and tells PowerPoint to fit text within the boundaries of the placeholder. Click the middle choice, *Stop Fitting Text to This Placeholder*, and PowerPoint will not automatically

fit the text or object within the placeholder. Choose the last option, *Control AutoCorrect Options*, to display the AutoCorrect dialog box with the AutoFormat As You Type tab selected. Additional options may display depending upon the placeholder and the type of data it contains.

Activity 1.6　Rearranging, Deleting, and Hiding Slides

As you edit a presentation, you may need to rearrange, delete, or hide specific slides. PowerPoint provides various views for creating and managing a presentation. Manage slides in the slide thumbnails pane or in Slide Sorter view. Switch to Slide Sorter view by clicking the Slide Sorter button in the view area on the Status bar or by clicking the View tab and then clicking the Slide Sorter button in the Presentation Views group.

Tutorial
Rearranging Slides

Tutorial
Deleting Slides

Tutorial
Hiding and Unhiding Slides

What You Will Do　Chris Greenbaum has asked you to make some changes to the presentation, including rearranging the slides, deleting a slide, and hiding a slide.

1 With **1-MPProdMtg.pptx** open, click Slide 5 in the slide thumbnails pane and then press the Delete key on the keyboard.

> You can also delete a slide by right-clicking the slide in the slide thumbnails pane and then clicking *Delete Slide* at the shortcut menu.

2 Click the Slide Sorter button in the view area on the Status bar.

3 Click Slide 6 to make it active.

> A selected slide displays with an orange border.

4 Position the mouse pointer on Slide 6, hold down the left mouse button, drag the slide (the arrow pointer will display with a square attached) to the left of Slide 3, and then release the mouse button.

5 Click the Normal button in the view area on the Status bar.

6 Position the mouse pointer on the Slide 5 thumbnail in the slide thumbnails pane, hold down the left mouse button, drag up until the slide displays immediately below the Slide 3 thumbnail, and then release the mouse button.

In Brief

Delete Slide
1. Right-click slide thumbnails.
2. Click *Delete Slide*.
OR
1. Click slide in slide thumbnails pane.
2. Press Delete key.

Move Slide
1. Click Slide Sorter button on Status bar.
2. Click slide.
3. Drag slide to position.
OR
1. Click slide in slide thumbnails pane.
2. Drag slide to new position.

Hide Slide
1. Click slide thumbnail.
2. Click Slide Show tab.
3. Click Hide Slide button.

7 With the Slide 4 thumbnail selected in the slide thumbnails pane (thumbnail displays with an orange border), hide the slide by clicking the Slide Show tab and then clicking the Hide Slide button in the Set Up group.

When a slide is hidden, the slide thumbnail displays dimmed and the slide number displays with a diagonal line across the number.

8 Run the slide show by clicking the From Beginning button in the Start Slide Show group. Click the left mouse button to advance each slide until a black screen displays. At the black screen, click the left mouse button again.

9 After running the slide show, you decide to redisplay the hidden slide. To do this, make sure the Slide 4 thumbnail is selected in the slide thumbnails pane and then click the Hide Slide button in the Set Up group.

10 Save **1-MPProdMtg.pptx**.

Check Your Work Compare your work to the model answer to ensure that you have completed the activity correctly.

In Addition

Copying Slides within a Presentation

Copying a slide within a presentation is similar to moving a slide. To copy a slide, position the arrow pointer on the desired slide and hold down the Ctrl key and the left mouse button. Drag to the location where you want the slide copied, release the left mouse button, and then release the Ctrl key. When you drag with the mouse, the mouse pointer displays with a square and a plus symbol attached.

PowerPoint includes the Tell Me feature, which provides information as well as guidance on how to complete a function. To use Tell Me, click in the *Tell Me* text box that displays on the ribbon to the right of the View tab and then type the function for which you want help. As you type, a drop-down list displays with options for completing the function, displaying information on the function from sources on the web, or for displaying information on the function in the Word Help window. The Word Help window can also be opened by pressing the F1 function key on the keyboard.

What You Will Do   To enhance the visual appeal of Slide 1 in the presentation, you will change the font size of the subtitle *Movie Production Meeting*, using the Tell Me feature to complete the task. You will also use the Tell Me feature to access the PowerPoint Help window and locate articles about slide masters.

Tutorial
Using the Tell Me Feature

Tutorial
Using the Help Feature

1 With 1-MPProdMtg.pptx open, make Slide 1 the active slide, click in the subtitle *Movie Production Meeting*, and then click the border of the placeholder to select it.

2 Click in the *Tell Me* text box.

The *Tell Me* text box is located on the ribbon to the right of the View tab and contains the text *Tell me what you want to do*. When you click in the text box, the last five functions entered will display in a drop-down list.

3 Type font size in the *Tell Me* text box.

A drop-down list displays with options such as *Font Size, Decrease Font Size, Increase Font Size, Font Settings*, and *Font*.

4 Position the mouse pointer on the *Font Size* option at the drop-down list.

When you position the mouse pointer on the *Font Size* option, a side menu displays.

5 At the side menu that displays, click *28*.

The 28-point font size is applied to the selected title. The Tell Me feature guided you through the process of changing font size without you having to learn how to change font size using a button on the ribbon or an option at a dialog box.

6 The Tell Me feature also includes access to the PowerPoint Help window. To display the PowerPoint Help window with information on slide masters, click in the *Tell Me* text box and then type slide master.

7 Click *Get Help on "slide master"* option at the drop-down list.

The PowerPoint Help window opens with articles on slide masters. You can also display the Help window by pressing the F1 function key.

8 At the PowerPoint Help window, click the first article hyperlink that displays in the list box.

> Clicking the hyperlink opens the article in the PowerPoint Help window.

9 The PowerPoint Help window contains five buttons for navigating and managing the window. Click the Back button (contains a left-pointing arrow) in the PowerPoint Help window to display the previous window.

10 Click the Use Large Text button to increase the display of text in the window.

11 Click the Home button to return to the opening PowerPoint Help window.

12 Close the PowerPoint Help window by clicking the Close button in the upper right corner of the window.

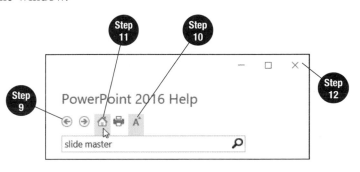

Check Your Work — Compare your work to the model answer to ensure that you have completed the activity correctly.

In Addition

Accessing Smart Lookup

Using the Smart Lookup feature, you can access information on a function from a variety of sources on the web such as Wikipedia, Bing, and the Oxford Dictionary. The Tell Me feature is one way to access Smart Lookup. To use Tell Me for Smart Lookup, click in the *Tell Me* text box, type the function on which you want to display information, and then click the *Smart Lookup* option that displays in the drop-down list. Clicking the *Smart Lookup* option displays the Smart Lookup task pane at the right side of the screen with information on the function from a variety of locations on the Internet. Smart Lookup can also be accessed with the Smart Lookup button on the Review tab or by selecting text on which you want additional information, right-clicking the selected text, and then clicking *Smart Lookup* at the shortcut menu.

Getting Help on Specific Functions

Some dialog boxes and backstage areas contain a help button you can click to display the PowerPoint Help window with specific information about the functions in the dialog box or backstage area. If you hover your mouse over some buttons, the ScreenTip that displays may include a Help icon and the text *Tell me more*. Click this hyperlinked text and the PowerPoint Help window opens with information about the button feature. You can also hover the mouse pointer over a button and then press F1 to display the Word Help window with information about the button feature.

Use PowerPoint's spelling checker to find and correct misspelled words and duplicated words (such as *and and*). The spelling checker compares words in your slides with words in its dictionary. If a match is found, the word is passed over. If no match is found, the spelling checker stops, selects the word, and offers replacements. Use the Thesaurus to find synonyms, antonyms, and related words for a particular word. To use the Thesaurus, click the word for which you want to display synonyms and antonyms, click the Review tab, and then click the Thesaurus button in the Proofing group. This displays the Thesaurus task pane with information about the word in which the insertion point is positioned.

What You Will Do   You have decided to create a new slide in the movie production presentation. Because several changes have been made to the presentation, you know that checking the spelling of all the slide text is important. Complete a spelling check of all slides and then use the Thesaurus to replace a couple of words with synonyms.

Tutorial
Checking Spelling

Tutorial
Using the Thesaurus

1 With **1-MPProdMtg.pptx** open, position the mouse pointer on the scroll box on the vertical scroll bar at the right side of the screen. Hold down the left mouse button, drag the scroll box to the bottom of the scroll bar, and then release the mouse button.

> This displays Slide 6 in the slide pane. As you drag the scroll box on the vertical scroll bar, a box displays indicating the slide number and slide title (if the slide contains a title).

2 Click the Home tab and then click the New Slide button in the Slides group.

> This inserts a new slide at the end of the presentation.

3 Click in the *Click to add title* placeholder and then type Summary.

4 Click in the *Click to add text* placeholder and then type the text shown in the slide at the right.

> Type the words exactly as shown. You will check the spelling in the next steps.

5 Complete a spelling check by moving the insertion point to the beginning of the word *Timetable*, clicking the Review tab, and then clicking the Spelling button in the Proofing group.

6 When the spelling checker selects *Asignments* in Slide 7 and displays *Assignments* in the list box in the Spelling task pane, click the Change button.

> Refer to the In Addition for a description of the Spelling task pane buttons.

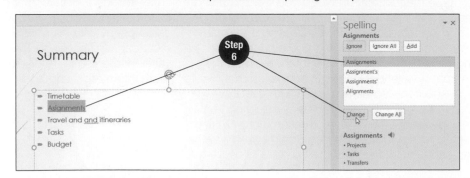

7 When the spelling checker selects the second *and* in the slide, click the Delete button.

8 When the spelling checker selects *Greenbaum* in Slide 3, click the Ignore button.

> Greenbaum is a proper name and is spelled correctly. Clicking the Ignore button tells the spelling checker to leave the name as spelled.

9 When the spelling checker selects *Almonzo* in Slide 3, click the Ignore button.

10 At the message telling you that the spelling check is complete, click OK.

11 Display Slide 7 in the slide pane and then click in the word *Timetable*.

12 Look up synonyms for *Timetable* by clicking the Thesaurus button [icon] in the Proofing group.

> The Thesaurus task pane displays at the right side of the screen and contains lists of synonyms for *Timetable*. Depending on the word you are looking up, the words in the Thesaurus task pane list box may display followed by *(n.)* for *noun*, *(adj.)* for *adjective*, or *(adv.)* for *adverb*. Antonyms may display in the list of related synonyms, usually toward the end and followed by *(Antonym)*.

13 Position the mouse pointer on the word *Schedule* in the Thesaurus task pane, click the down-pointing arrow at the right of the word, and then click *Insert* at the drop-down list.

> This replaces *Timetable* with *Schedule*.

14 Close the Thesaurus task pane by clicking the Close button in the upper right corner of the task pane.

15 Right-click in the word *Tasks*, point to *Synonyms*, and then click *Responsibilities*.

> The shortcut menu offers another method for displaying synonyms for words.

16 Save **1-MPProdMtg.pptx**.

Check Your Work — Compare your work to the model answer to ensure that you have completed the activity correctly.

In Addition

Using Spelling Task Pane Buttons

This table displays descriptions of the Spelling task pane buttons.

Button	Function
Ignore	skips that occurrence of the word and leaves currently selected text as written
Ignore All	skips that occurrence of the word and all other occurrences of the word in the presentation
Delete	deletes the currently selected word(s)
Change	replaces the selected word with the selected word in the suggestions list box
Change All	replaces the selected word and all other occurrences of the word in the presentation with the selected word in the suggestions list box
Add	adds the selected word to the main spelling check dictionary

Activity 1.9 — Running a Slide Show; Using Ink Tools; Using the Pen Tool during a Slide Show

You can run a slide show in PowerPoint manually, advance the slides automatically, or set up a slide show to run continuously for demonstration purposes. In addition to the Start From Beginning button on the Quick Access Toolbar, you can run a slide show with the From Beginning button on the Slide Show tab or the Slide Show button on the Status bar. Run the slide show beginning with the currently active slide by clicking the From Current Slide button in the Start Slide Show group or clicking the Slide Show button in the view area. Use the mouse or keyboard to advance through the slides. You can also use buttons on the Slide Show toolbar that displays when you move the mouse pointer while running a slide show. Use the pen tool to emphasize major points or draw the attention of the audience to specific items in a slide during a presentation. To use the pen tool on a slide, run the slide show, and when the desired slide displays, move the mouse to display the Slide Show toolbar. Click the Pen button on the toolbar and then click *Pen*. Use the mouse to draw in the slide to underline, circle, or otherwise emphasize specific text. Options at the Pen button drop-down list also include a laser pointer, highlighter, and eraser. You can also write and highlight on a slide in Normal view with options on the Ink Tools Pens tab. Display this tab by clicking the Start Inking button in the Ink group on the Review tab. This feature is useful when using a pen, stylus, or finger to draw on a tablet.

What You Will Do   You are now ready to run the movie production meeting slide show. You will use the mouse to perform various actions while running the slide show and use the pen tool and ink tools to emphasize points in slides.

Tutorial
Running a Slide Show

Tutorial
Changing the Display when Running a Slide Show

Tutorial
Displaying Slide Show Help and Hiding Slides during a Slide Show

Tutorial
Using the Pen Tool during a Slide Show

Tutorial
Using Ink Tools

1 With **1-MPProdMtg.pptx** open, click the Slide Show tab and then click the From Beginning button in the Start Slide Show group.

Clicking this button begins the slide show, and Slide 1 fills the entire screen.

2 After viewing Slide 1, click the left mouse button to advance to the next slide.

3 At Slide 2, move the mouse pointer until the Slide Show toolbar displays dimmed in the lower left corner of the slide and then click the Previous button (displays with a left arrow) on the toolbar to display the previous slide (Slide 1).

With buttons on the Slide Show toolbar, you can display the next slide, the previous slide, or a specific slide; use the pen, laser pointer, and highlighter to emphasize text on the slide; display slide thumbnails; and zoom in on elements of a slide. You can also display the Slide Show Help dialog box, shown in Figure 1.3, which describes all the navigation options available while running a slide show. Display this dialog box by clicking the More slide show options button on the Slide Show toolbar and then clicking *Help*.

4 Click the Next button (displays with a right arrow) on the Slide Show toolbar to display the next slide (Slide 2).

5 Display the previous slide (Slide 1) by right-clicking anywhere in the slide and then clicking *Previous* at the shortcut menu.

Right-clicking displays the shortcut menu with a variety of options including options to display the previous or next slide.

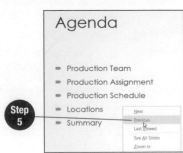

Figure 1.3 Slide Show Help Dialog Box

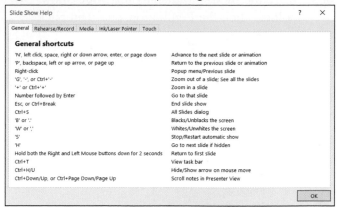

6 Display Slide 4 by pressing the number 4 key and then pressing the Enter key.

Move to any slide in a presentation by typing the slide number and then pressing the Enter key.

7 Change to a black screen by pressing the letter B key.

When you press the letter B key, the slide is removed from the screen and the screen displays black. This might be useful in a situation where you want to discuss something with your audience that is unrelated to the slide.

8 Return to Slide 4 by pressing the letter B key.

Pressing the letter B key switches between the slide and a black screen. Press the letter W key if you want to switch between the slide and a white screen.

9 Zoom in on the bulleted items in Slide 4 by clicking the Zoom into the slide button (displays as a magnifying glass) on the Slide Show toolbar, hovering the magnification area over the bulleted items, and then clicking the left mouse button.

10 Right-click anywhere on the screen to display Slide 4 without magnification.

11 Display thumbnails of all the slides in the presentation while viewing the slide show by clicking the See all slides button on the Slide Show toolbar.

12 Click the Slide 3 thumbnail on the screen.

This displays Slide 3 in the slide show.

13 Click the left mouse button to display Slide 4. Continue clicking the left mouse button until a black screen displays. At the black screen, click the left mouse button again.

This returns the presentation to the Normal view.

14 Make Slide 1 active.

15 Display Slide 2 by clicking the Next Slide button at the bottom of the vertical scroll bar.

16 Click the From Current Slide button 🖳 in the Start Slide Show group on the Slide Show tab.

Clicking this button begins the slide show with the active slide.

17 Run the slide show by clicking the left mouse button at each slide until Slide 5 is active (contains the title *Production Schedule*).

18 Move the mouse to display the Slide Show toolbar, click the Pen button, and then click *Laser Pointer*.

> This turns the mouse pointer into a red, hollow, glowing circle.

19 Practice moving the laser pointer around the screen.

20 Click the Pen button on the Slide Show toolbar and then click *Pen*.

> This turns the mouse pointer into a small circle.

21 Using the mouse, draw a circle around the text *Location Shoots*.

22 Using the mouse, draw a line below *Dubbing*.

23 Erase the pen markings by clicking the Pen button on the Slide Show toolbar and then clicking *Erase All Ink on Slide*.

24 Change the color of the ink by clicking the Pen button and then clicking the *Blue* color (ninth color option).

25 Draw a blue line below the word *Music*.

26 Return the mouse pointer back to an arrow by pressing the Esc key.

27 Click the left mouse button to advance to Slide 6.

28 Click the Pen button and then click *Highlighter*.

29 Using the mouse, drag through the words *Studio Shoots*.

30 Using the mouse, drag through the words *Location Shoots*.

31 Return the mouse pointer back to an arrow by pressing the Esc key.

32 Press the Esc key on the keyboard to end the slide show without viewing the remaining slides. At the message asking if you want to keep your ink annotations, click the Discard button.

In Brief

Run a Slide Show
Click Start From Beginning button on Quick Access Toolbar.
OR
1. Click Slide Show tab.
2. Click From Beginning button or From Current Slide button.
OR
Click Slide Show button on Status bar.

Use Pen Tool When Running a Slide Show
1. Run slide show.
2. Move mouse.
3. Click Pen button on Slide Show toolbar.
4. Click Pen option.
5. Draw in slide with pen.

Use Ink Tools
1. Click Review tab.
2. Click Start Inking button.
3. Draw or highlight on slide using pen or highlighter options.
4. Click Stop Inking button.

33 With Slide 6 displayed in Normal view, draw a circle around text to display when running a slide show. Begin by clicking the Review tab and then clicking the Start Inking button 🖉 in the Ink group.

> The Ink Tools Pens tab will display with options for writing or highlighting on a slide. This feature is particularly useful for tablets. The mouse pointer will display as a small circle.

34 Click the Convert to Shapes button 🖻 in the Ink Art group.

35 Click the *Red Pen (0.35 mm)* option in the Pens gallery (second column, first row).

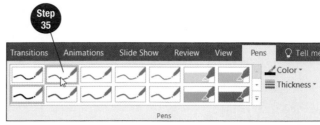

36 Using the mouse, draw a rectangle around the text *Studio Shoots*.

> Notice that PowerPoint automatically converted the drawn rectangle into a more precise rectangle. If you are not satisfied with the appearance of the rectangle, click the Undo button on the Quick Access Toolbar two times, click the Pen button 🖉 in the Write group, and then draw the rectangle again.

37 Click the *Aqua Highlighter (4.0 mm)* option in the Pens gallery (seventh column, first row).

38 Using the mouse, drag through the words *Los Angeles Studio*.

39 Click the Stop Inking button ⊠ in the Close group to turn off the inking feature.

40 Click the Slide Show button in the view area on the Status bar.

41 Notice that the red rectangle and aqua highlighting display on the slide and then press the Esc key to return the presentation to Normal view.

42 Save **1-MPProdMtg.pptx**.

> **Check Your Work** ▷ Compare your work to the model answer to ensure that you have completed the activity correctly.

In Addition

Hiding and Displaying the Mouse Pointer
When running a slide show, the mouse pointer is set, by default, to be hidden after three seconds of inactivity. The mouse pointer will appear again when you move the mouse. Change this default setting by clicking the More slide show options button on the Slide Show toolbar, clicking *Arrow Options*, and then clicking *Visible* if you want the mouse pointer always visible or *Hidden* if you do not want the mouse pointer to display at all as you run the slide show. The *Automatic* option is the default setting.

Viewing in Presenter View
If you are running a slide show using two monitors, you can display the presentation in Presenter view on one of the monitors. Use this view to control the slide show. For example, in Presenter view you can see your speaker notes, you have all the Slide Show toolbar options available, and you can advance slides and set slide timings. Press Alt + F5 to display the presentation in Presenter view.

Adding Transitions and Transition Sounds

You can apply a variety of transitions and transition sounds to a presentation. A transition is how one slide is removed from the screen during a slide show and the next slide is displayed. Interesting transitions such as fades, dissolves, push, cover, wipes, stripes, and bar can add interest to your presentation. You can also insert a sound that you want to play as one slide is removed from the screen and the next slide is displayed. Add transitions and sounds with options on the Transitions tab.

What You Will Do   You have decided to enhance the movie production meeting presentation by adding transitions and sound to the slides.

Tutorial
Adding Transitions

Tutorial
Adding Sound to Slide Transitions

1 With **1-MPProdMtg.pptx** open, click Slide 1 in the slide thumbnails pane and then click the Transitions tab.

2 Click the More Transitions button in the gallery in the Transition to This Slide group.

3 Click the *Ripple* option in the *Exciting* section at the drop-down list.

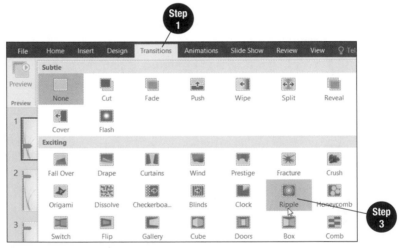

4 Click the Effect Options button [icon] in the Transition to This Slide group and then click *From Top-Left* at the drop-down list.

  The effect options change depending on the transition selected.

5 Click the *Sound* option box arrow in the Timing group.

6 Click the *Breeze* option at the drop-down list.

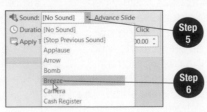

7 Apply three seconds to each slide transition by clicking in the *Duration* measurement box, typing 3, and then pressing the Enter key.

8 Click the Apply To All button in the Timing group.

> Notice that Play Animations star icons display below the slide numbers in the slide thumbnails pane.

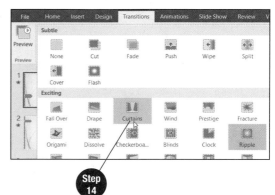

9 Click the Slide 1 thumbnail in the slide thumbnails pane.

10 Run the slide show by clicking the Slide Show button in the view area on the Status bar.

11 Click the left mouse button to advance each slide.

12 At the black screen that displays after the last slide, click the left mouse button again to return the presentation to the Normal view.

13 Click the More Transitions button in the gallery in the Transition to This Slide group.

14 Click the *Curtains* option in the *Exciting* section of the drop-down list.

15 Click the *Sound* option box arrow and then click *Whoosh* at the drop-down list.

16 Click the *Duration* measurement box down arrow until *02.50* displays.

17 Click the Apply To All button in the Timing group.

18 With Slide 1 active, run the slide show.

19 Save **1-MPProdMtg.pptx**.

In Addition

Running a Slide Show Automatically

Slides in a slide show can be advanced automatically after a specific number of seconds by inserting a check mark in the *After* check box in the Timing group and removing the check mark from the *On Mouse Click* check box. Change the time in the *After* measurement box by clicking the *After* measurement box up or down arrow or by selecting the number in the measurement box and then typing the specific time. If you want the transition time to affect all slides in the presentation, click the Apply To All button. In Slide Sorter view, the transition time displays below each affected slide. Click the Slide Show button to run the slide show. The first slide displays for the specified amount of time and then the next slide automatically displays.

Activity 1.11 Previewing Slides and Printing

You can print each slide on a separate piece of paper; print each slide at the top of the page, leaving the bottom of the page for notes; print up to nine slides or a specific number of slides on a single piece of paper; or print the slide titles and topics in outline form. Before printing a presentation, consider previewing it. Choose print options and display a preview of the presentation in the Print backstage area. Display this view by clicking the File tab and then clicking the *Print* option. Click the Back button or press the Esc key to exit the backstage area without clicking an option.

Previewing Slides
and Printing

What You Will Do Staff members need the movie production meeting slides printed as handouts and as an outline. You will preview and print the presentation in various formats.

1 With **1-MPProdMtg.pptx** open, display Slide 1 in the slide pane.

2 Click the File tab and then click the *Print* option.

> Slide 1 of the presentation displays at the right side of the screen as it will when printed. Use the Next Page button (right-pointing arrow) located below and to the left of the slide to view the next slide in the presentation, click the Previous Page button (left-pointing arrow) to display the previous slide in the presentation, use the Zoom slider bar to increase or decrease the size of the slide, and click the Zoom to Page button to fit the slide in the preview area in the Print backstage area. The left side of the Print backstage area displays three categories—*Print*, *Printer*, and *Settings*. Galleries display below each category name. For example, the *Printer* category has one gallery that displays the name of the currently selected printer. The *Settings* category has a number of galleries that describe how the slides will print.

3 Click the Next Page button below and to the left of the preview slide to display the next slide in the presentation.

> This displays Slide 2 in the preview area.

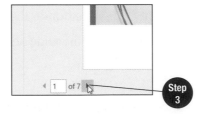

4 Click the Zoom In button ➕ at the right side of the Zoom slider bar two times.

> Click the Zoom In button to increase the size of the slide or click the Zoom Out button (displays with a minus symbol) to decrease the size of the slide.

5 Click the Zoom to Page button 🔲 at the right side of the Zoom slider bar.

> Click the Zoom to Page button to fit the entire slide in the viewing area in the Print backstage area.

6 You decide to print the slides on two pages and you want to preview how the slides will display on the pages. To do this, click the second gallery in the *Settings* category (contains the text *Full Page Slides*) and then click *4 Slides Horizontal* in the *Handouts* section.

> Notice how four slides display on the preview page.

7 Click the Print button at the top of the Print backstage area.

8 You want to print all slide text on one page to use as a reference during your presentation. To do this, click the File tab and then click the *Print* option.

9 At the Print backstage area, click the second gallery in the *Settings* category (contains the text *4 Slides Horizontal*) and then click *Outline* in the *Print Layout* section.

10 Click the Print button at the top of the Print backstage area.

> With the *Outline* option selected, the presentation prints on one page with slide numbers, slide icons, and slide text in outline form.

11 You want to print only Slide 6. To do this, click the File tab and then click the *Print* option.

12 At the Print backstage area, click the second gallery in the *Settings* category (contains the text *Outline*) and then click *Full Page Slides* in the *Print Layout* section.

13 Click in the *Slides* text box below the first gallery in the *Settings* category, type 6, and then click the Print button.

14 Save **1-MPProdMtg.pptx**.

15 Close the presentation by clicking the File tab and then clicking the *Close* option.

> **Check Your Work** Compare your work to the model answer to ensure that you have completed the activity correctly.

In Addition

Using Options at the Slide Size Dialog Box

You can change orientation with options at the Slide Size dialog box, shown at the right. Display this dialog box by clicking the Design tab, clicking the Slide Size button in the Customize group, and then clicking *Customize*

Slide Size at the drop-down list. With options at this dialog box you can specify how you want slides sized; page width and height; orientation for slides; and orientation for notes, hand-outs, and outlines.

Features Summary

Feature	Ribbon Tab, Group	Button/Option	File Tab Option	Keyboard Shortcut
apply transitions and sound to all slides	Transitions, Timing	▣		
close a presentation			*Close*	Ctrl + F4
close PowerPoint		✕		
display Presenter view				Alt + F5
Help				F1
ink tools	Review, Ink	▨		
layout	Home, Slides	▤		
new slide	Home, Slides OR Insert, Slides	▤		Ctrl + M
Normal view	View, Presentation Views	▤		
Notes Page view	View, Presentation Views	▤		
Open backstage area			*Open*	Ctrl + O
open blank presentation				Ctrl + N
Outline view	View, Presentation Views	▤		
Print backstage area			*Print*	Ctrl + P
run slide show from current slide	Slide Show, Start Slide Show	▣		Shift + F5
run slide show from Slide 1	Slide Show, Start Slide Show	▣		F5
save		💾	*Save*	Ctrl + S
Save As backstage area			*Save As*	
Slide Sorter view	View, Presentation Views	▦		
spelling checker	Review, Proofing	✓ABC		F7
themes	Design, Themes			
Thesaurus	Review, Proofing	▤		Shift + F7
transitions	Transitions, Transition to This Slide			
transition duration	Transitions, Timing	🕐		
transition sound	Transitions, Timing	🔊		
Zoom dialog box	View, Zoom	🔍		

Workbook Section study tools and assessment activities are available in the *Workbook* ebook. These resources are designed to help you further develop and demonstrate mastery of the skills learned in this section.

PowerPoint

Editing and Enhancing Slides

Data Files Before beginning section work, copy the PowerPointS2 folder to your storage medium and then make PowerPointS2 the active folder.

Skills

- Increase and decrease the indent of text
- Select, cut, copy, and paste text
- Apply font and font effects
- Find and replace fonts
- Apply formatting with Format Painter
- Change alignment and line and paragraph spacing

- Change the slide size and format design themes and slide background
- Insert, size, move, and format images
- Insert and format a screen clipping
- Insert and format a SmartArt graphic
- Apply animation to objects and text in a slide

Precheck Check your current skills to help focus your study of the skills taught in this section.

Projects Overview

Open an existing project presentation, save the presentation with a new name, and then edit and format the presentation. Open an existing annual meeting presentation for Marquee Productions and then save, edit, and format the presentation.

Prepare and format a presentation on the services offered by The Waterfront Bistro.

Prepare and format a presentation on company structure, policies, and benefits.

Open an existing presentation for the Theatre Arts Division and then save, edit, and format the presentation.

Prepare and format a presentation for a planning meeting of the distribution department.

Open an existing presentation on vacation specials and then save, edit, and format the presentation.

 SNAP If you are a SNAP user, launch the Precheck and Tutorials from your Assignments page.

Model Answers Preview the model answers for an overview of the projects you will complete in the section activities.

31

Activity 2.1 — Increasing and Decreasing Indent; Cutting, Copying, and Pasting Text

Text that is formatted as a bulleted list in a slide can have multiple levels. Click the Decrease List Level button in the Paragraph group on the Home tab or press Shift + Tab to promote text to the previous level. Click the Increase List Level button or press the Tab key to demote text to the next level. You can also promote text levels (decrease the text indent) and/or demote text levels (increase text indent) in the slide in Outline view. Select text in a slide and then delete the text from the slide, cut text from one location and paste it into another, or copy and paste the text. Use buttons in the Clipboard group on the Home tab to cut, copy, and paste text.

What You Will Do   Chris Greenbaum, production manager for Marquee Productions, has prepared a documentary project presentation and has asked you to edit the presentation by increasing and decreasing text levels and selecting, deleting, moving, copying, and pasting text in slides.

Tutorial
Increasing and Decreasing Indent

Tutorial
Selecting Text

Tutorial
Cutting, Copying, and Pasting Text

1 Open **MPProj.pptx** from the PowerPointS2 folder on your storage medium and then save the presentation with the name **2-MPProj.pptx**.

2 Display Slide 5 in the slide pane.

3 You decide to promote the names below *Script Authors* so that they display as second-level bullets. To do this, position the mouse pointer immediately left of the *D* in *Dana*, click the left mouse button, and then click the Decrease List Level button in the Paragraph group on the Home tab.

> Clicking the Decrease List Level button will promote text to the previous tab position, while clicking the Increase List Level button will demote text to the next tab position.

4 Position the insertion point immediately left of the *K* in *Karl* in Slide 5 and then promote the text to the previous level by pressing Shift + Tab.

5 Demote two of the names below *Script Consultants*. Begin by clicking immediately left of the *J* in *Jaime* and then clicking the Increase List Level button in the Paragraph group on the Home tab.

6 Position the insertion point immediately left of the *G* in *Genaro* and then press the Tab key.

7 Display Slide 6 in the slide pane.

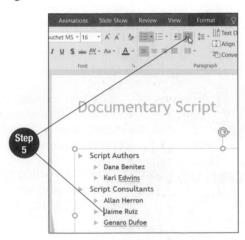

Decrease Text Level Indent
Click Decrease List Level button or press Shift + Tab.

Increase Text Level Indent
Click Increase List Level button or press Tab.

Cut and Paste Text
1. Select text.
2. Click Cut button.
3. Position insertion point.
4. Click Paste button.

Copy and Paste Text
1. Select text.
2. Click Copy button.
3. Position insertion point.
4. Click Paste button.

8 Position the mouse pointer on the bullet that displays before *Script Rewriting* until the mouse pointer turns into a four-headed arrow and then click the left mouse button.

> This selects the text *Script Rewriting* and displays the Mini toolbar, which provides easy access to formatting options and buttons. Refer to the In Addition for additional information on selecting text.

9 Press the Delete key.

> This deletes the selected text.

10 Display Slide 5 in the slide pane.

11 Position the mouse pointer on the bullet that displays before *Genaro Dufoe* until the mouse pointer turns into a four-headed arrow and then click the left mouse button.

12 Click the Cut button ✂ in the Clipboard group on the Home tab.

> The keyboard shortcut to cut text is Ctrl + X.

13 Position the mouse pointer immediately left of the *A* in *Allan Herron*, click the left mouse button, and then click the Paste button 📋 in the Clipboard group.

> The keyboard shortcut to paste text is Ctrl + V.

14 Using the mouse, drag to select the text *Script Authors* and then click the Copy button 📋 in the Clipboard group.

> The keyboard shortcut to copy text is Ctrl + C.

15 Make Slide 2 active, position the insertion point immediately left of the *S* in *Scouting*, and then click the Paste button in the Clipboard group.

> If *Script Authors* and *Scouting* display on the same line, press the Enter key.

16 Save **2-MPProj.pptx**.

Check Your Work — Compare your work to the model answer to ensure that you have completed the activity correctly.

In Addition

Selecting Text

To select	Perform this action
entire word	Double-click word.
entire paragraph	Triple-click anywhere in paragraph.
text mouse pointer passes through	Click and drag with mouse.
all text in selected object box	Click Select button in Editing group and then click Select All; or press Ctrl + A.

Applying Font Formatting and Font Effects

The Font group on the Home tab contains two rows of options and buttons. The top row contains options and buttons for changing the font and font size and a button for clearing formatting. The bottom row contains buttons for applying font effects such as bold, italics, underlining, text shadow, strikethrough, and character spacing, as well as buttons for changing the case and/or font color of selected text.

What You Will Do   Certain text elements on slides in the documentary project presentation need to be highlighted to make them stand out. You decide to apply font effects to and change the font size of specific text.

Tutorial

Applying Font Formatting

1 With **2-MPProj.pptx** open, display Slide 1 in the slide pane.

2 Select the title *Marquee Productions* and then click the Italic button I in the Font group on the Home tab.

3 Select the subtitle *Documentary Project*, click the Increase Font Size button $\text{A}^{\hat{}}$, and then click the Bold button **B** in the Font group.

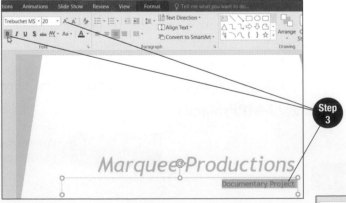

4 Make Slide 6 active in the slide pane, select the text *Phase 1*, and then click the Underline button **U** in the Font group.

5 Select and then underline the text *Phase 2*.

6 Select and then underline the text *Phase 3*.

7 Make Slide 1 active.

In Brief

Apply Font Effects with Font Group
1. Select text.
2. Click appropriate button in Font group.

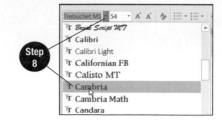

8 Select the title *Marquee Productions*, click the *Font* option box arrow in the Font group, scroll down the drop-down gallery (fonts display in alphabetical order), and then click *Cambria*.

9 Select the subtitle *Documentary Project*, click the *Font* option box arrow, and then click *Cambria* at the drop-down gallery.

> The drop-down gallery displays the most recently used fonts toward the top of the gallery.

10 Make Slide 6 active, select the text *Phase 1*, click the Underline button to remove underlining, and then click the Bold button to apply bold formatting.

11 With *Phase 1* still selected, click *Trebuchet MS* in the *Font* option box, type cam, and then press the Enter key.

> An alternative method for selecting a font is to type the first few letters of the font name in the *Font* option box until the entire font name displays and then press the Enter key.

12 Click the *Font Size* option box arrow and then click *28*.

13 Select the text *Phase 2*, remove the underlining, apply bold formatting, change the font to Cambria, and then change the font size to 28 points.

14 Select the text *Phase 3*, remove the underlining, apply bold formatting, change the font to Cambria, and then change the font size to 28 points.

15 Print Slides 1 and 6. Begin by clicking the File tab and then clicking the *Print* option.

16 At the Print backstage area, click in the *Slides* text box (located below the first gallery in the *Settings* category) and then type 1,6.

17 Click the second gallery in the *Settings* category (contains the text *Full Page Slides*) and then click *2 Slides* in the *Handouts* section of the drop-down list.

18 Click the Print button.

> The two slides print on the same page.

19 Save **2-MPProj.pptx**.

> **Check Your Work** Compare your work to the model answer to ensure that you have completed the activity correctly.

In Addition

Choosing Fonts

A typeface is a set of characters with a common design and shape. PowerPoint refers to a typeface as a *font*. Fonts can be decorative or plain and are either mono-spaced or proportional. A monospaced font allots the same amount of horizontal space for each character, while a proportional font allots a different amount of space for each character. Proportional fonts are divided into two main categories: serif and sans serif. A serif is a small line at the end of a character stroke. Consider using a serif font for text-intensive slides, because the serifs can help move the reader's eyes across the text. Use a sans serif font for titles, subtitles, headings, and short lines of text.

In addition to options and buttons in the Font group on the Home tab, you can apply font formatting with options at the Font dialog box. Use options at this dialog box to change the font, as well as its style and size; change the font color; and apply formatting effects such as underline, strikethrough, superscript, subscript, small caps, and all caps. If you decide to change the font for all slides in a presentation, use the Replace Font dialog box to replace all occurrences of a specific font in the presentation.

What You Will Do You are still not satisfied with the fonts in the documentary project presentation, so you decide to change the font for the title and subtitle and replace the Verdana font on the remaining slides.

Tutorial
Applying Font
Formatting at the
Font Dialog Box

Tutorial
Replacing Fonts

1 With **2-MPProj.pptx** open, make Slide 1 active.

2 Select the title *Marquee Productions*.

3 Display the Font dialog box by clicking the Font group dialog box launcher 🔲 on the Home tab.

4 At the Font dialog box, click the *Latin text font* option box arrow and then click *Candara* at the drop-down list.

5 Select the current measurement in the *Size* measurement box and then type 60.

6 Click the Font color button in the *All text* section and then click the *Blue, Accent 2, Darker 25%* option (sixth column, fifth row in the *Theme Colors* section).

7 Click OK to close the Font dialog box.

8 Select the subtitle *Documentary Project*.

9 Click the Font group dialog box launcher.

10 At the Font dialog box, click the *Latin text font* option box arrow and then click *Candara* at the drop-down list.

11 Click the *Font style* option box arrow and then click *Bold Italic* at the drop-down list.

12 Select the current measurement in the *Size* measurement box and then type 30.

13 Click the Font color button in the *All text* section and then click the *Turquoise, Accent 1* color option (fifth column, first row in the *Theme Colors* section).

14 Click OK to close the Font dialog box.

15 Make Slide 2 active.

16 You decide to replace all occurrences of the Trebuchet MS font in the presentation with the Cambria font. To begin, click the Replace button arrow in the Editing group on the Home tab and then click *Replace Fonts* at the drop-down list.

17 At the Replace Font dialog box, click the *Replace* option box arrow and then click *Trebuchet MS* at the drop-down list.

18 Click the *With* option box arrow, scroll down the drop-down list to display Cambria, and then click *Cambria* at the drop-down list.

19 Click the Replace button and then click the Close button.

20 Save **2-MPProj.pptx**.

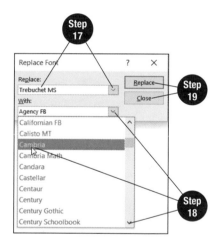

Check Your Work — Compare your work to the model answer to ensure that you have completed the activity correctly.

In Addition

Choosing Fonts

Choose a font for a presentation based on the tone and message you want the presentation to convey. For example, choose a more serious font such as Constantia or Cambria for a conservative audience and choose a less formal font such as Comic Sans MS, Lucida Handwriting, or Mistral for a more informal or lighthearted audience. For text-intensive slides, choose a serif font such as Cambria, Constantia, Garamond, or Bookman Old Style. For titles, subtitles, headings, and short text items, consider a sans serif font such as Calibri, Candara, Arial, or Trebuchet MS. Use no more than two or three different fonts in each presentation. To ensure text readability in a slide, choose a font color that contrasts with the slide background.

Activity 2.4 Formatting with Format Painter

Use the Format Painter feature to apply the same formatting in more than one location in a slide or slides. To use the Format Painter, apply formatting to text, position the insertion point anywhere in the formatted text, and then double-click the Format Painter button in the Clipboard group on the Home tab. Using the mouse, select the additional text to which you want the formatting applied. After applying the formatting in the desired locations, click the Format Painter button to deactivate it. If you only need to apply formatting in one other location, click the Format Painter button just once. The first time you click or select text, the formatting will be applied and the Format Painter button will be deactivated.

What You Will Do   Improve the appearance of slides in the documentary project presentation by applying a font and then using the Format Painter to apply the formatting to other text.

Formatting with
Format Painter

1 With **2-MPProj.pptx** open, make sure Slide 2 is active.

2 Select the title *Project Development*.

3 Click the Font group dialog box launcher.

4 At the Font dialog box, click in the *Latin text font* option box, type can, and then press the Tab key.

> As you type letters, fonts that match the letters display in the list box.

5 Click the *Font style* option box arrow and then click *Bold Italic* at the drop-down list.

6 Select the current measurement in the *Size* measurement box and then type 40.

7 Click the Font color button in the *All text* section and then click the *Blue, Accent 2, Darker 25%* color option (sixth column, fifth row in the *Theme Colors* section).

8 Click OK to close the Font dialog box.

9 Deselect the text by clicking in the slide in the slide pane.

10 Click in the title *Project Development*.

11 Double-click the Format Painter button in the Clipboard group on the Home tab.

12 Click the Next Slide button to display Slide 3.

13 Triple-click *Team Meetings* to select the title.

> The mouse pointer displays with a paintbrush attached. This indicates that the Format Painter is active. You can also apply the formatting by clicking individual words in the title, but doing so will not format the spaces within titles that consist of more than one word. If the paintbrush is no longer attached to the mouse pointer, Format Painter has been turned off. Turn it back on by clicking in a slide title with the desired formatting and then double-clicking the Format Painter button.

14 Click the Next Slide button to display Slide 4.

15 Using the mouse, select the title *Preproduction Team*.

16 Apply formatting to the titles in the remaining three slides.

17 When formatting has been applied to all slide titles, click the Format Painter button in the Clipboard group on the Home tab.

> Clicking the Format Painter button turns off the feature.

18 Save **2-MPProj.pptx**.

Check Your Work Compare your work to the model answer to ensure that you have completed the activity correctly.

In Addition

Choosing a Custom Color

Click the Font color button at the Font dialog box and a palette of color choices displays. Click the *More Colors* option and the Colors dialog box displays with the Standard tab selected, showing a honeycomb of color options. Click the Custom tab and the dialog box displays as shown at the right. Use options on this tab to mix your own color. Click the desired color in the *Colors* palette or enter the values for the color in the *Red*, *Green*, and *Blue* text boxes. Adjust the luminosity of the current color by dragging the slider at the right side of the color palette.

The slide design theme generally determines the horizontal and vertical alignment of text in placeholders. Text may be left-aligned, center-aligned, right-aligned, or justified in a placeholder as well as aligned at the top, middle, or bottom of the placeholder. Change alignment for specific text with buttons in the Paragraph group on the Home tab or with options from the Align Text button drop-down gallery. Use options at the Line Spacing button drop-down gallery or the *Line Spacing* option at the Paragraph dialog box to change line spacing. The Paragraph dialog box also contains options for changing text alignment and indentation as well as spacing before and after text.

What You Will Do   Change the alignment and improve the appearance of specific text in slides by adjusting the vertical alignment and paragraph spacing of text.

Tutorial
Changing Alignment

Tutorial
Changing Line Spacing

Tutorial
Changing Paragraph Spacing

1   With **2-MPProj.pptx** open, make Slide 1 active.

2   Click in the text *Marquee Productions* and then click the Center button ≡ in the Paragraph group on the Home tab.

>   You can also change text alignment with the keyboard shortcuts shown in Table 2.1.

Step 2

3   Click in the text *Documentary Project* and then click the Center button.

4   Make Slide 3 active (contains the title *Team Meetings*), click in the bulleted text, and then press Ctrl + A to select all of the bulleted text.

>   Ctrl + A is the keyboard shortcut for selecting all text in a placeholder.

5   Justify the text by clicking the Justify button ≡ in the Paragraph group.

6   Click the Align Text button ⬍ in the Paragraph group and then click *Middle* at the drop-down gallery.

>   This aligns the bulleted text vertically in the middle of the placeholder.

Step 5

Step 6

7   With the bulleted text still selected, click the Line Spacing button ‡≡ ▾ and then click *Line Spacing Options* at the drop-down gallery.

8 At the Paragraph dialog box, click the *After* measurement box up arrow two times.

> This inserts *12 pt* in the *After* measurement box.

9 Click OK to close the dialog box.

10 Make Slide 4 active (contains the title *Preproduction Team*).

11 Click in the bulleted text and then select all of the bulleted text by clicking the Select button in the Editing group on the Home tab and then clicking *Select All* at the drop-down list.

12 Click the Line Spacing button and then click *1.5* at the drop-down gallery.

13 Make Slide 7 active (contains the title *Preproduction Assignments*).

14 Click in the bulleted text and then press Ctrl + A.

15 Click the Line Spacing button in the Paragraph group and then click *Line Spacing Options* at the drop-down gallery.

16 At the Paragraph dialog box, click the *After* measurement box up arrow two times.

> This inserts *12 pt* in the *After* measurement box.

17 Click OK to close the dialog box.

18 Print only Slide 1 of the presentation as a handout.

19 Save **2-MPProj.pptx**.

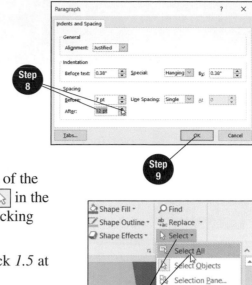

Table 2.1 Alignment Keyboard Shortcuts

Alignment	Keyboard Shortcut
left	Ctrl + L
center	Ctrl + E
right	Ctrl + R
justify	Ctrl + J

Check Your Work Compare your work to the model answer to ensure that you have completed the activity correctly.

In Addition

Inserting a New Line

When creating bulleted text in a slide, pressing the Enter key causes the insertion point to move to the next line, inserting another bullet. Situations may occur wherein you want to create a blank line between bulleted items without creating another bullet. One method for doing this is to use the New Line command, Shift + Enter. Pressing Shift + Enter inserts a new line that is considered part of the previous paragraph.

By default, the slide size in PowerPoint 2016 is Widescreen (16:9), but you can change the slide size with options in the Slide Size button drop-down list in the Customize group on the Design tab. Change the design theme applied to slides in a presentation or change the color, font, or effects of a theme with options on the Design tab. Format the slide background with options in the Format Background task pane. Display this task pane by clicking the Format Background button in the Customize group on the Design tab.

What You Will Do You are not pleased with the design theme for the documentary project presentation and decide to apply a different theme and then change the colors and fonts for the theme.

Tutorial
Changing Slide Size

Tutorial
Changing and Modifying Design Themes

Tutorial
Formatting the Slide Background

1 With **2-MPProj.pptx** open, click the Design tab.

2 Click the Slide Size button ▢ in the Customize group and then click *Standard (4:3)* at the drop-down list.

3 At the Microsoft PowerPoint dialog box, click the Ensure Fit button.

Click the Ensure Fit button to scale down the contents of the slide to fit on the new slide. Click the Maximize button to maximize the size of the content on the new slide.

4 Run the slide show beginning with Slide 1 and notice any changes to the layout of the slides.

5 Click the Slide Size button and then click *Custom Slide Size* at the drop-down list.

6 At the Slide Size dialog box, click the *Slide sized for* option box arrow and then click *Widescreen* at the drop-down list.

7 Click OK.

8 Click the More Themes button in the Themes group.

9 Click *Dividend* at the drop-down gallery.

10 Click the More Variants button in the Variants group.

11 Click *Colors*, and then click *Yellow Orange* at the side menu.

12 Make Slide 2 active.

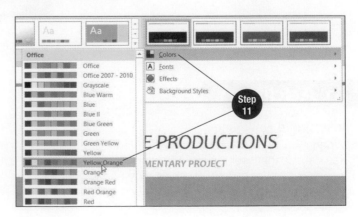

Change Slide Size
1. Click Design tab.
2. Click Slide Size button.
3. Click slide size.

Change Design Theme
1. Click Design tab.
2. Click More Themes button.
3. Click theme.

Change Theme Colors
1. Click Design tab.
2. Click More Variants button.
3. Point to *Colors*.
4. Click option.

Change Theme Fonts
1. Click Design tab.
2. Click More Variants button.
3. Point to *Fonts*.
4. Click option at side menu.

Format Slide Background
1. Click Design tab.
2. Click Format Background button.
3. Make changes in task pane.

13 Click the More Variants button in the Variants group.

14 Click *Fonts*, scroll down the side menu, and then click *Cambria*.

15 Apply a background style by clicking the More Variants button in the Variants group, pointing to *Background Styles*, and then clicking *Style 9* at the side menu (first column, third row).

16 Run the slide show beginning with Slide 1.

17 Customize the background by clicking the Format Background button 🖼 in the Customize group on the Design tab.

> This displays the Format Background task pane with a number of options for customizing slide backgrounds.

18 At the Format Background task pane, if necessary, click *Fill* to display fill options.

19 Click the *Solid fill* option, click the Color button, and then click the *Light Yellow, Background 2* color option (third column, first row in the *Theme Colors* section).

20 Click the Apply to All button toward the bottom of the task pane.

21 Close the task pane by clicking the close button in the upper right corner.

22 Save **2-MPProj.pptx** and then print Slide 1 of the presentation.

Check Your Work — Compare your work to the model answer to ensure that you have completed the activity correctly.

In Addition

Inserting an Image as a Slide Background

Insert an image as the background of an entire slide by clicking the Design tab and then clicking the Format Background button in the Customize group. At the Format Background task pane, click *Fill* to display fill options, and then click the *Picture or texture fill* option.

Click the File button in the *Insert picture from* section, navigate to the folder containing the image, and then double-click the image. The image will automatically be inserted as the current slide's background.

Add visual interest to a presentation by inserting an image such as a logo, picture, or clip art in a slide. Insert an image from a drive or folder with the Insert Picture dialog box. Display the Insert Picture dialog box by clicking the Pictures button on the Insert tab or clicking the picture image in the content placeholder. At this dialog box, navigate to the desired drive or folder and then double-click the image. Click the Online Pictures button on the Insert tab and the Insert Pictures window displays. Use options in this window to search for images using Bing. At the window, type a category in the search text box to the right of the *Bing Image Search* option and then press the Enter key. In the list of images that displays, double-click the desired image. The image is inserted in the slide and the Picture Tools Format tab is selected. Use buttons on the Picture Tools Format tab to recolor the image, apply a picture style, arrange the image in the slide, and size the image. You can also size an image using the sizing handles that display around the selected image and move the image using the mouse.

What You Will Do   Chris Greenbaum has asked you to insert the company logo on the first slide of the presentation and insert and format an image on a new slide at the end of the presentation.

Tutorial
Inserting, Sizing, and Moving an Image

Tutorial
Formatting an Image

1. With **2-MPProj.pptx** open, make sure Slide 1 is active.

2. Click in the title *Marquee Productions*, click the title placeholder border (border turns into a solid line when selected), and then press the Delete key.

   The title text will be deleted but the placeholder will not.

3. Click the title placeholder border again and then press the Delete key.

4. Complete steps similar to those in Steps 2 and 3 to delete the subtitle text and placeholder.

5. Insert the company logo in the slide as shown in Figure 2.1 on the next page. To begin, click the Insert tab and then click the Pictures button in the Images group.

6. At the Insert Picture dialog box, navigate to the PowerPointS2 folder on your storage medium and then double-click *MPLogo.jpg*.

   The image is inserted in the slide, selection handles display around the image, and the Picture Tools Format tab is selected.

7. Increase the size of the logo by clicking in the *Shape Width* measurement box in the Size group, typing 6.5, and then pressing the Enter key.

   When you change the width of the logo, the height automatically adjusts to maintain the proportions of the logo. You can also size an image using the sizing handles that display around the selected image. Use the middle sizing handles to change the width of an image. Use the top and bottom handles to change the height, and use the corner sizing handles to adjust both the width and height of the image at the same time.

8 Move the logo so it is positioned as shown in Figure 2.1. To do this, position the mouse pointer on the image until the pointer displays with a four-headed arrow attached, click and hold down the left mouse button, drag the image to the position shown in the figure, and then release the mouse button.

9 With the image selected, click the Color button in the Adjust group and then click the *Saturation 200%* option (fifth option in the *Color Saturation* section).

10 Click the Corrections button in the Adjust group and then click the *Brightness: +20% Contrast: -40%* option (fourth column, first row in the *Brightness/Contrast* section).

11 Click the *Drop Shadow Rectangle* option in the Picture Styles gallery (fourth option).

12 Click the Picture Effects button in the Picture Styles group, point to *Glow*, and then click the *Orange, 5 pt glow, Accent color 1* option (first column, first row in the *Glow Variations* section).

13 Click outside the logo to deselect it.

Figure 2.1 Slide 1

14 Make Slide 7 active.

15 Insert a new slide by clicking the New Slide button in the Slides group on the Home tab.

16 Click in the *CLICK TO ADD TITLE* placeholder and then type Travel Arrangements.

17 Click in the *Click to add text* placeholder and then type the bulleted text shown in Figure 2.2.

18 Click the Insert tab and then click the Online Pictures button in the Images group.

19 At the Insert Pictures window, click in the search text box at the right of *Bing Image Search*, type airport, symbol, and then press the Enter key.

20 Double-click the image shown below.

> If the image is not available, insert the **Airport.png** image from the PS2 folder on your storage medium.

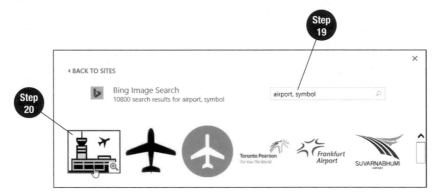

21 Click in the *Shape Height* measurement box in the Size group on the Picture Tools Format tab, type 3.5, and then press the Enter key.

> When you change the height measurement, the width measurement changes automatically to maintain the proportions of the image.

22 Using the mouse, drag the image so it is positioned as shown in Figure 2.2.

23 Click the Color button in the Adjust group on the Picture Tools Format tab and then click the *Brown, Accent color 2 Light* option (third column, third row in the *Recolor* section).

24 Click the Corrections button in the Adjust group and then click the *Brightness: 0% (Normal) Contrast: +40%* option (third column, fifth row in the *Brightness/Contrast* section).

In Brief

Insert Image
1. Click Insert tab.
2. Click Pictures button.
3. At Insert Picture dialog box, navigate to folder.
4. Double-click image file.

Insert Online Image
1. Click Insert tab.
2. Click Online Pictures button.
3. At Insert Pictures window, type category, press Enter.
4. Double-click image.

25 Click the Picture Effects button in the Picture Styles group, point to *Shadow*, and then click the *Offset Diagonal Top Right* option (first column, third row in the *Outer* section).

26 Click the Rotate button in the Arrange group and then click *Flip Horizontal* at the drop-down gallery.

27 Make Slide 7 active and then click the Home tab.

28 Click in the title *PREPRODUCTION ASSIGNMENTS* and then click the Format Painter button in the Clipboard group.

29 Make Slide 8 active and then select the entire title *TRAVEL ARRANGEMENTS*.

This applies 40-point Candara bold italic formatting in a brown accent color.

30 Save **2-MPProj.pptx**.

Figure 2.2 Slide 8

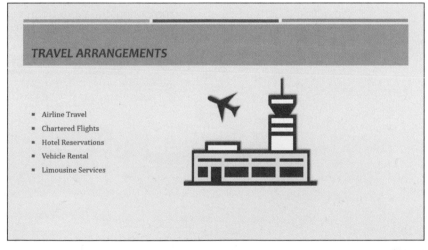

Check Your Work Compare your work to the model answer to ensure that you have completed the activity correctly.

In Addition

Formatting with Buttons on the Picture Tools Format Tab

Format images in a slide with buttons and options on the Picture Tools Format tab. Use buttons in the Adjust group to adjust the brightness and contrast of the image; change the image color or change to a different image; reset the image to its original size, position, and color; and compress the image. (Compress an image to reduce the resolution or discard extra information to save room on a hard drive or to reduce download time.) Use buttons in the Picture Styles group to apply a pre-designed style, insert a picture border, or apply a picture effect. The Arrange group contains buttons for positioning the image and aligning and rotating the image. Use options in the Size group to crop the image and specify the height and width of the image.

Inserting and Formatting a Screen Clipping

The Images group on the Insert tab contains the Screenshot button, which you can use to capture all or part of the contents of a screen as an image. Format a screenshot with options on the Picture Tools Format tab.

What You Will Do   Chris Greenbaum has asked you to include a screen clipping of the title page of a script document in a slide.

Tutorial

Inserting and Formatting Screenshot and Screen Clipping Images

1   With **2-MPProj.pptx** open, make Slide 6 active.

2   Insert a screenshot image from a Word document into the slide. Begin by opening Word and then opening **MPScript.docx**.

> Make sure 2-MPProj.pptx and MPScript.docx are the only open files.

3   Click the Zoom Out button at the left side of the Zoom slider bar until *40%* displays at the right side of the slider bar.

4   Click the button on the taskbar representing the PowerPoint presentation **2-MPProj.pptx**.

5   Click the Insert tab, click the Screenshot button 🖼 in the Images group, and then click *Screen Clipping* at the drop-down list.

> When you click the *Screen Clipping* option, the Word document will automatically display in a dimmed manner and the insertion point will display as crosshairs.

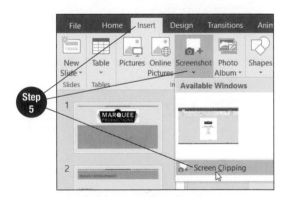

6   With the Word document displayed in a dimmed manner, position the crosshairs in the top left corner of the Word document and then drag down and to the right to select the entire document.

> Once you have created a screenshot of the Word document, the image will automatically be inserted into Slide 6 of 2-MPProj.pptx.

7   With the screenshot selected, click in the *Shape Height* measurement box in the Size group on the Picture Tools Format tab, type 5, and then press the Enter key.

8 Click the Picture Border button arrow in the Picture Styles group and then click the *Orange, Accent 1* option at the drop-down list (fifth column, first row in the *Theme Colors* section).

Step 8

9 Position the screenshot in the slide as shown in Figure 2.3.

10 Click the Word button on the taskbar, close the document, and then close Word.

If a message displays asking if you want to save changes made in the document, click the Don't Save button.

11 Save **2-MPProj.pptx**.

Figure 2.3 Slide 6

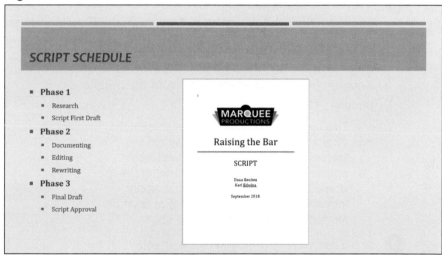

Check Your Work Compare your work to the model answer to ensure that you have completed the activity correctly.

In Addition

Inserting a Screenshot

If you want to capture the entire screen, open the desired file, click the Insert tab, click the Screenshot button in the Images group, and then click the screen thumbnail at the drop-down list. The currently active file does not display as a thumbnail at the drop-down list— only any other files that you have open.

Use the SmartArt feature to create a variety of graphic diagrams, including process, cycle, relationship, matrix, and pyramid diagrams. You can also use SmartArt to visually illustrate hierarchical data. To display a menu of SmartArt choices, click the Insert tab and then click the SmartArt button in the Illustrations group. This displays the Choose a SmartArt Graphic dialog box. At this dialog box, click the type of organization chart or graphic in the left panel and then double-click the graphic in the middle panel. This inserts the chart or graphic in the slide. Some SmartArt graphics are designed to include text. Type text in a graphic shape by selecting the shape and then typing text in the shape. Use buttons on the SmartArt Tools Design tab and the SmartArt Tools Format tab to customize a graphic.

What You Will Do   Chris Greenbaum has asked you to create a slide containing an organizational chart that illustrates the hierarchy of the people involved in production and a slide containing a SmartArt graphic of travel expenses.

Tutorial
Inserting, Sizing, and Moving SmartArt

Tutorial
Formatting SmartArt

1   With **2-MPProj.pptx** open, make Slide 2 active and then click the New Slide button in the Slides group on the Insert tab.

2   Create the organizational chart shown in Figure 2.4. To begin, click the Insert tab and then click the SmartArt button in the Illustrations group.

3   At the Choose a SmartArt Graphic dialog box, click *Hierarchy* in the left panel and then double-click the *Hierarchy* option in the middle panel.

> This displays the organizational chart in the slide with the SmartArt Tools Design tab selected. Use buttons on this tab to add additional boxes, change the order of the shapes, choose a different layout, apply formatting with a SmartArt style, or reset the formatting of the organizational chart.

4   If a *Type your text here* window displays at the left side of the organizational chart, close it by clicking the Text Pane button in the Create Graphic group.

> You can also close the window by clicking the Close button in the upper right corner of the window.

5   Delete one of the boxes in the organizational chart. Begin by clicking the border of the second text box from the top at the left side of the chart.

> Make sure *[Text]* displays in the box.

6   Press the Delete key.

7   With the second box from the top at the right side selected, click the Add Shape button in the Create Graphic group.

> This inserts a box to the right of the selected box. Your organizational chart should contain the same boxes shown in Figure 2.4. (The new box does not contain a *[Text]* placeholder, but you can still type text in the box.)

8 Click the *[Text]* placeholder in the top box, type Chris Greenbaum, press the Enter key, and then type Production Manager. Click in each of the remaining boxes and type the text as shown in Figure 2.4.

9 Click the Change Colors button in the SmartArt Styles group on the SmartArt Tools Design tab and then click the *Colorful Range - Accent Colors 4 to 5* option (fourth option in the *Colorful* section).

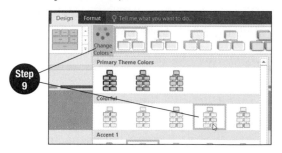

10 Click the More SmartArt Styles button at the right side of the gallery in the SmartArt Styles group.

11 Click the *Inset* option at the drop-down gallery (second column, first row in the *3-D* section).

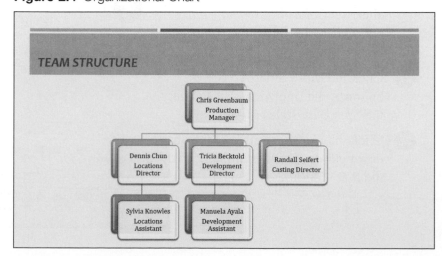

12 Click the SmartArt Tools Format tab.

13 Click inside the SmartArt graphic border but outside any shape.

14 Click in the *Shape Height* measurement box in the Size group, type 5, click in the *Shape Width* measurement box, type 10, and then press the Enter key.

15 Move the graphic so it is positioned in the slide as shown in Figure 2.4. Do this by positioning the mouse pointer on the graphic border until the pointer displays with a four-headed arrow attached, clicking and holding down the left mouse button, dragging the graphic to the desired location, and then releasing the mouse button.

Figure 2.4 Organizational Chart

16 Click in the *CLICK TO ADD TITLE* placeholder and then type Team Structure.

17 Make Slide 2 active, click in the title *Project Development*, click the Home tab, and then click the Format Painter button in the Clipboard group.

18 Make Slide 3 active and then select the entire title *Team Structure*.

19 Make Slide 9 active.

20 Click the New Slide button arrow in the Slides group on the Home tab and then click the *Blank* layout at the drop-down list.

21 Create the SmartArt graphic shown in Figure 2.5. To begin, click the Insert tab and then click the SmartArt button in the Illustrations group.

22 At the Choose a SmartArt Graphic dialog box, click *Relationship* in the left panel and then double-click the *Converging Radial* option. (This option may be the first option from the right in the sixth row or the first option from the left in the seventh row.)

23 If necessary, close the *Type your text here* window by clicking the Close button in the upper right corner of the window.

24 Click the Add Shape button in the Create Graphic group.

25 Click in each of the shapes and insert the text shown in Figure 2.5.

26 Click the Change Colors button in the SmartArt Styles group and then click the *Colorful - Accent Colors* option (first option in the *Colorful* section).

27 Click the More SmartArt Styles button at the right side of the gallery in the SmartArt Styles group.

28 Click the *Cartoon* option at the drop-down gallery (third column, first row in the *3-D* section).

29 Click the SmartArt Tools Format tab.

30 Click inside the SmartArt graphic border but outside any shape.

This deselects the shapes but keeps the graphic selected.

31 Click the More WordArt button at the right side of the gallery in the WordArt Styles group and then click the *Fill - White, Outline - Accent 1, Glow - Accent 1* option (fourth column, second row).

32 Click in the *Shape Width* measurement box in the Size group, type 9.5, and then press the Enter key.

33 Click the Align button in the Arrange group and then click *Align Center* at the drop-down list.

34 Save **2-MPProj.pptx**

Figure 2.5 SmartArt Graphic

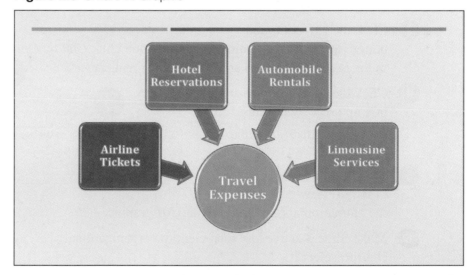

Check Your Work Compare your work to the model answer to ensure that you have completed the activity correctly.

In Addition

Inserting Text in the Text Pane

Enter text in a SmartArt shape by clicking in the shape and then typing the text. You can also insert text in a SmartArt shape by typing text in SmartArt's text pane. Display the text pane by clicking the Text Pane button in the Create Graphic group on the SmartArt Tools Design tab.

Animate individual objects and text in a slide with options on the Animations tab. Click the Animations tab and the tab displays with a variety of animation styles and options for customizing and applying times to animations in a presentation. Click the More Animations button at the right side of the gallery in the Animation group and a drop-down gallery of animation styles displays that you can apply to objects and text as they enter a slide, exit a slide, and/or follow a motion path. You can also apply animations to emphasize objects in a slide. If you want the same animation applied to other objects in a presentation, use the Animation Painter button in the Advanced Animation group on the Animations tab.

What You Will Do   To finalize the presentation, Chris Greenbaum has asked you to apply animation to objects and text in the presentation.

Tutorial
Applying and
Removing Animations

Tutorial
Modifying Animations

1 With **2-MPProj.pptx** open, make sure Slide 10 is active and the SmartArt graphic is selected.

2 Click the Animations tab and then click the *Fly In* option in the Animation gallery in the Animation group.

3 Click the Effect Options button 🔼 in the Animation group and then click *One by One* in the *Sequence* section at the drop-down gallery.

4 Click the *Duration* measurement box up arrow two times.

> This inserts *01.00* in the measurement box.

5 Click the Preview button ⭐ in the Preview group to view the animation applied to the SmartArt graphic.

6 Make Slide 3 active and then click the organizational chart to select it.

7 Click the More Animations button at the right of the Animation gallery and then click the *Zoom* option in the *Entrance* section at the drop-down gallery.

8 Click the Effect Options button in the Animation group and then click *One by One* in the *Sequence* section at the drop-down gallery.

9 Click Slide 2 to make it active and then click in the bulleted text to select the placeholder.

10 Click the *Fly In* option in the gallery in the Animation group.

> Applying this animation creates a *build* for the bulleted items. A build displays important points in a slide one point at a time and is useful for keeping the audience's attention focused on the point being presented rather than reading ahead.

11 Click the *Duration* measurement box up arrow in the Timing group two times.

> This inserts *01.00* in the measurement box.

12 Apply the same animation to the bulleted text in Slides 4 through 9. To begin, click in the bulleted text to select the placeholder and then double-click the Animation Painter button ⭐ in the Advanced Animation group.

13 Make Slide 4 active and then click in the bulleted text. (This selects the placeholder and applies the Fly In animation and the duration time.)

14 Make Slide 5 active and then click in the bulleted text.

15 Make Slide 6 active and then click in the bulleted text. Repeat this action for Slides 7–9.

16 Click the Animation Painter button to turn off the feature.

17 Make Slide 1 active and then run the slide show. Click the mouse button to advance slides and to display the individual organizational chart boxes, bulleted items, and SmartArt graphic boxes.

18 Print the presentation as handouts with six slides displayed horizontally on one page. To do this, click the File tab and then click the *Print* option.

19 At the Print backstage area, click the second gallery (contains the text *Full Page Slides*) in the *Settings* category and then click *6 Slides Horizontal* at the drop-down list.

20 Click the Print button.

21 Save and then close **2-MPProj.pptx**.

> **Check Your Work** ▸ Compare your work to the model answer to ensure that you have completed the activity correctly.

In Addition

Applying Custom Animation

Apply custom animation to selected objects in a slide by clicking the Animation Pane button in the Advanced Animation group on the Animations tab. This displays the Animation task pane at the right side of the screen. Use options in this task pane to control the order in which objects appear on a slide, choose animation direction and speed, and specify how objects will appear in the slide.

Features Summary

Feature	Ribbon Tab, Group	Button	Keyboard Shortcut
align left	Home, Paragraph		Ctrl + L
align right	Home, Paragraph		Ctrl + R
align vertically	Home, Paragraph		
animation effect options	Animations, Animation		
bold	Home, Font		Ctrl + B
center	Home, Paragraph		Ctrl + E
copy selected text	Home, Clipboard		Ctrl + C
cut selected text	Home, Clipboard		Ctrl + X
decrease font size	Home, Font		Ctrl + Shift + <
decrease list level	Home, Paragraph		Shift + Tab
font	Home, Font		
font color	Home, Font		
Font dialog box	Home, Font		Ctrl + Shift + F
font size	Home, Font		
format background	Design, Customize		
Format Painter	Home, Clipboard		
increase font size	Home, Font		Ctrl + Shift + >
increase list level	Home, Paragraph		Tab
insert image	Insert, Images		
insert online image	Insert, Images		
insert screenshot	Insert, Images		
insert SmartArt	Insert, Illustrations		
italic	Home, Font		Ctrl + I
justify	Home, Paragraph		Ctrl + J
line spacing	Home, Paragraph		
paste selected text	Home, Clipboard		Ctrl + V
preview animation	Animations, Preview		
slide size	Design, Customize		
underline	Home, Font		Ctrl + U

Workbook ▶ Section study tools and assessment activities are available in the *Workbook* ebook. These resources are designed to help you further develop and demonstrate mastery of the skills learned in this section.

PowerPoint

SECTION 3

Customizing a Presentation

Skills

- Copy and paste items using the Clipboard task pane
- Find and replace text
- Insert and format WordArt
- Draw and customize objects
- Display gridlines
- Insert a text box
- Copy and rotate shapes

Data Files — Before beginning section work, copy the PowerPointS3 folder to your storage medium and then make PowerPointS3 the active folder.

- Create and format a table
- Insert action buttons
- Insert a hyperlink
- Format with a slide master
- Insert headers and footers
- Add audio and video
- Set and rehearse timings for a slide show

Precheck — Check your current skills to help focus your study of the skills taught in this section.

Projects Overview

 Add visual appeal to a presentation on filming in Toronto by inserting WordArt, shapes, text boxes, and a table. Improve a presentation on a biography project by inserting WordArt, shapes, text boxes, an image, a logo, and a footer. Update a presentation on the annual meeting by applying a design theme, theme colors, and theme fonts and formatting using a slide master. Prepare and format a project schedule presentation.

 Format a presentation on costume designs for Marquee Productions and add visual appeal by inserting a logo, WordArt, shapes, text boxes, a table, and a footer.

 Add a video clip and audio file to a presentation on eco-tour adventures. Format a presentation about a vacation cruise and add visual appeal by inserting a logo and audio clip, setting and rehearsing timings, and setting up the slide show to run continuously. Enhance a presentation on tours in Australia and New Zealand by inserting WordArt, a footer, and an audio clip; setting and rehearsing timings; and setting up the slide show to run continuously. Prepare a presentation on a Moroccan tour.

SNAP — If you are a SNAP user, launch the Precheck and Tutorials from your Assignments page.

Model Answers — Preview the model answers for an overview of the projects you will complete in the section activities.

57

Using the Clipboard task pane, you can collect up to 24 different items and then paste them in various locations in slides. To display the Clipboard task pane, click the Clipboard group task pane launcher in the Clipboard group on the Home tab. The Clipboard task pane displays at the left side of the screen. Select text or an object you want to copy and then click the Copy button in the Clipboard group. Continue selecting text or items and clicking the Copy button. To paste an item into a slide in a presentation, position the insertion point in the desired location and then click the item in the Clipboard task pane. (If the copied item is text, the first 50 characters display in the Clipboard task pane.) After inserting all items into the presentation, click the Clear All button to remove any remaining items from the Clipboard task pane.

What You Will Do   In preparation for a meeting about the Toronto location shoot, you will open the Toronto presentation and then copy and paste multiple items into the appropriate slides.

Tutorial
Using the Clipboard
Task Pane

1. Open **MPToronto.pptx** and then save it with the name **3-MPToronto**.

2. Display the Clipboard task pane by clicking the Clipboard group task pane launcher ⬜. If items display in the Clipboard task pane, click the Clear All button in the upper right corner of the task pane.

3. Make Slide 2 active and then select the name *Chris Greenbaum*. (Do not include the space after the name.)

4. With *Chris Greenbaum* selected, click the Copy button in the Clipboard group.

    When you click the Copy button, the name *Chris Greenbaum* is inserted as an item in the Clipboard task pane.

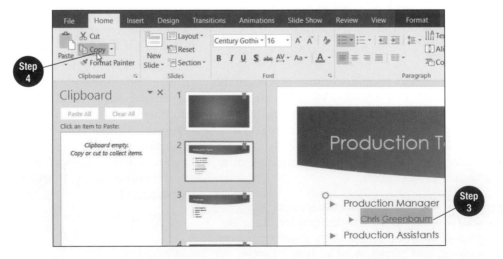

5. Select the name *Camille Matsui* (do not include the space after the name) and then click the Copy button. Select the name *Dennis Chun* (without the space after) and then click the Copy button. Select the name *Josh Hart* (without the space after) and then click the Copy button.

6. Make Slide 3 active, position the insertion point immediately to the right of *Location Expenses*, press the Enter key, and then press the Tab key.

Use Clipboard Task Pane
1. Click Clipboard group task pane launcher.
2. Select text, click Copy button.
3. Continue selecting text and clicking Copy button.
4. Position insertion point.
5. Click item in Clipboard task pane.
6. Insert additional items.
7. Click Clear All button.
8. Close Clipboard task pane.

7 Click *Chris Greenbaum* in the Clipboard task pane.

8 Position the insertion point immediately right of *Production*, press the Enter key, press the Tab key, and then click *Camille Matsui* in the Clipboard task pane.

9 Make Slide 4 active, position the insertion point immediately right of *Royal Ontario Museum*, press the Enter key, press the Tab key, and then click *Dennis Chun* in the Clipboard task pane.

10 Position the insertion point immediately right of *Island Airport*, press the Enter key, press the Tab key, and then click *Dennis Chun* in the Clipboard task pane.

11 Position the insertion point immediately right of *King Street*, press the Enter key, press the Tab key, and then click *Josh Hart* in the Clipboard task pane.

12 Click the Clear All button in the Clipboard task pane and then click the Close button ⊠ in the upper right corner of the task pane.

13 Make Slide 1 active and then insert the **MPLogo.jpg** file. To begin, click the Insert tab and then click the Pictures button in the Images group. Make the PowerPointS3 folder active and then double-click *MPLogo.jpg*.

14 Size and move the logo so it better fills the slide.

15 Save **3-MPToronto.pptx**.

> **Check Your Work** Compare your work to the model answer to ensure that you have completed the activity correctly.

In Addition

Using Clipboard Task Pane Options

Click the Options button at the bottom of the Clipboard task pane and a drop-down list displays with five options, as shown at the right. Click to insert a check mark before those options you want active. For example, you can choose to display the Clipboard task pane automatically when you cut or copy text, cut and copy text without displaying the Clipboard task pane, display the Clipboard task pane by pressing Ctrl + C twice, display the Office Clipboard icon on the taskbar when the Clipboard is active, and display the item message near the taskbar when copying items to the Clipboard.

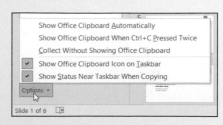

Use the Find and Replace feature to search for specific text or formatting in slides in a presentation and replace it with other text or formatting. Display the Find dialog box if you want to find something specific in a presentation. Display the Replace dialog box if you want to find something in a presentation and replace it with another item.

What You Will Do   A couple of people have been replaced on the Toronto location shoot. Use the Replace feature to find names and replace them with new names in the Toronto presentation.

Tutorial

Finding and Replacing Text

1 With **3-MPToronto.pptx** open, make sure Slide 1 is active.

2 Camille Matsui has been replaced by Jennie Almonzo. Begin the find and replace by clicking the Replace button ⓐ in the Editing group on the Home tab.

> This displays the Replace dialog box with the insertion point positioned in the *Find what* text box.

3 Type Camille Matsui in the *Find what* text box.

4 Press the Tab key and then type Jennie Almonzo in the *Replace with* text box.

5 Click the Replace All button.

> Clicking the Replace All button replaces all occurrences of the *Find what* text in the presentation. If you want control over which occurrences are replaced in a presentation, click the Find Next button to move to the next occurrence of the text. Click the Replace button if you want to replace the text, or click the Find Next button if you want to leave the text as written and move to the next occurrence.

6 At the message telling you that two replacements were made, click OK.

> The Replace dialog box remains on the screen.

7 Josh Hart had to leave the project and is being replaced by Jaime Ruiz. At the Replace dialog box, type Josh Hart in the *Find what* text box.

> When you begin typing the name *Josh Hart*, the previous name, *Camille Matsui*, is deleted.

8 Press the Tab key, type Jaime Ruiz in the *Replace with* text box, and then click the Replace All button.

9 At the message telling you that two replacements were made, click OK.

> The Replace dialog box remains on the screen.

10 The title *Manager* has been changed to *Director*. At the Replace dialog box, type Manager in the *Find what* text box.

11 Press the Tab key, type Director in the *Replace with* text box, and then click the Replace All button.

12 At the message telling you that one replacement was made, click OK.

13 Close the Replace dialog box by clicking the Close button in the upper right corner of the dialog box.

14 Save **3-MPToronto.pptx**.

Check Your Work ▷ Compare your work to the model answer to ensure that you have completed the activity correctly.

In Addition

Using Replace Dialog Box Options

The Replace dialog box, shown at the right, contains two options for completing a find and replace. Choose the *Match case* option if you want to exactly match the case of the find text. For example, if you look for *Company*, PowerPoint will stop at *Company* but not *company* or *COMPANY*. Choose the *Find whole words only* option if you want to find a whole word, not a part of a word. For example, if you search for *his* and do not select *Find whole words only*, PowerPoint will stop at *this*, *his*tory, c*his*el, and so on.

Activity 3.3   Inserting and Formatting WordArt

Use the WordArt feature to create text with special formatting that makes it stand out. You can format WordArt in a variety of ways, including conforming it to a shape. To insert WordArt, click the Insert tab, click the WordArt button in the Text group, and then click a WordArt style at the drop-down list. When WordArt is selected, the Drawing Tools Format tab displays. Use options and buttons on this tab to modify and customize WordArt.

What You Will Do   You want to improve the appearance of the slide containing information on exterior shots by changing text to WordArt. You also want to insert a new slide with the title of the film formatted as WordArt.

Tutorial

Inserting and Formatting WordArt

1 With **3-MPToronto.pptx** open, make sure Slide 1 is active.

2 Click the New Slide button arrow in the Slides group on the Home tab and then click the *Blank* layout (first column, third row).

3 Insert WordArt by clicking the Insert tab, clicking the WordArt button [A] in the Text group, and then clicking the *Fill - Tan, Accent 1, Outline - Background 1, Hard Shadow - Accent 1* option (third column, third row).

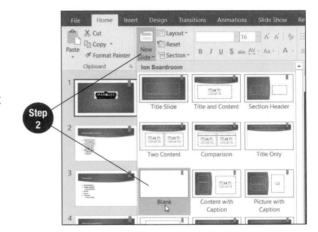

> This inserts a text box with *Your text here* inside and makes the Drawing Tools Format tab active.

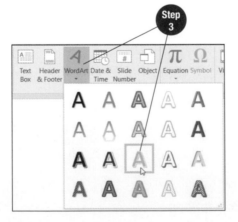

4 Type Ring of Roses.

5 Click in the *Shape Height* measurement box in the Size group, type 4, and then press the Enter key.

6 Click in the *Shape Width* measurement box in the Size group, type 9, and then press the Enter key.

In Brief

Insert WordArt
1. Click Insert tab.
2. Click WordArt button.
3. Click WordArt option.
4. Type WordArt text.
5. Apply formatting.

7 Click the Text Effects button ⒜ in the WordArt Styles group, point to *Transform* at the drop-down list, scroll down the side menu, and then click *Deflate* (second column, sixth row in the *Warp* section).

8 Click the border of the WordArt (border will display as a solid line), click the Text Outline button arrow ⒜, and then click the *Orange, Accent 1* color option at the drop-down gallery (fifth column, first row in *Theme Colors* section).

9 Position the WordArt in the middle of the slide as shown in Figure 3.1 by clicking the Align button ⊞ in the Arrange group and then clicking *Distribute Horizontally* at the drop-down list. Click the Align button again and then click *Distribute Vertically* at the drop-down list.

10 Make Slide 4 active and then insert the **DollarSymbol.png** from the PowerPointS3 folder. You determine the size, position, and color of the image.

11 Save **3-MPToronto.pptx**.

Figure 3.1 Slide 2

Check Your Work ▸ Compare your work to the model answer to ensure that you have completed the activity correctly.

In Addition

Using the Drawing Tools Format Tab

When WordArt is selected in a slide, the Drawing Tools Format tab displays as shown below. You can draw a shape or text box with buttons in the Insert Shapes group. Apply a style, fill, outline, and/or effects to the WordArt text box with options in the Shape Styles group. Change the style of the WordArt text with options in the WordArt Styles group, specify the layering of the WordArt text with options in the Arrange group, and identify the height and width of the WordArt text box with measurement boxes in the Size group.

Activity 3.4 Drawing and Customizing Shapes

Use the shape options in the Drawing group on the Home tab or the Shapes button on the Insert tab to draw shapes in a slide, including lines, rectangles, basic shapes, block arrows, equation shapes, flowchart shapes, stars, banners, and callout shapes. Click a shape and the mouse pointer displays as crosshairs (plus sign). Click in the slide to insert the shape or position the crosshairs where you want the image to begin, click and hold down the left mouse button, drag to create the shape, and then release the mouse button. This inserts the shape in the slide and also displays the Drawing Tools Format tab. Use buttons on this tab to change the shape, apply a style to the shape, arrange the shape, and change the size of the shape. You can type text directly into a shape or you can use the Text Box button in the Text group on the Insert tab to draw a text box inside a shape and then type text in the box. The Drawing Tools Format tab also provides a Text Box button you can use to draw a text box in a slide.

Tutorial
Inserting, Sizing, and
Positioning Shapes

Tutorial
Formatting Shapes

What You Will Do You will create a new slide for the Toronto site presentation that includes the Toronto office address inside a shape.

1 With **3-MPToronto.pptx** open, make Slide 2 active.

2 Click the New Slide button in the Slides group on the Home tab. (Make sure the slide layout is *Blank*.)

3 Click the More Shapes button in the Drawing group on the Home tab.

4 Click *Horizontal Scroll* at the drop-down list (sixth column, bottom row in the *Stars and Banners* section).

5 Position the mouse pointer in the slide, click and hold down the left mouse button, drag to create the shape as shown below, and then release the mouse button.

> If you are not satisfied with the size and shape of the image, press the Delete key to remove the image, select the desired shape, and then draw the image again.

Step 4

Step 5

6 With the image selected, click the Drawing Tools Format tab and then change the shape style by clicking the More Shape Styles button in the Shape Styles group and then clicking the *Subtle Effect - Green, Accent 6* option at the drop-down gallery (seventh column, fourth row in the Theme Styles section).

7 Click the Shape Effects button in the Shape Styles group, point to *Glow*, and then click the *Orange, 18 pt glow, Accent color 1* option (first column, fourth row in the *Glow Variations* section).

8 Click the Home tab.

9 Click the *Font Size* option box arrow and then click *24* at the drop-down gallery.

10 Click the Bold button in the Font group.

11 Click the Font Color button in the Font group and then click the *Orange, Accent 1, Darker 25%* color option (fifth column, fifth row in the *Theme Colors* section).

12 If the paragraph alignment is not set to center, click the Center button in the Paragraph group.

13 Type the following text in the text box:

MARQUEE PRODUCTIONS
Toronto Office
905 Bathurst Street
Toronto, ON M4P 4E5

14 Distribute the shape horizontally and vertically on the slide using options in the Arrange button drop-down list in the Drawing group on the Home tab.

15 Save **3-MPToronto.pptx**.

Check Your Work Compare your work to the model answer to ensure that you have completed the activity correctly.

In Addition

Displaying the Selection Task Pane

If you want to select an object or multiple objects in a slide, consider turning on the display of the Selection task pane. Turn on the display of this task pane by clicking the Selection Pane button in the Arrange group on the Drawing Tools Format tab. Select an object by clicking the object name in the Selection task pane (see example at right). Select multiple objects by holding down the Ctrl key as you click objects. Click the button that displays at the right side of the object name to turn on/off the display of the object.

To help position elements such as shapes and images on a slide, consider displaying gridlines. Gridlines are intersecting horizontal and vertical dashed lines that display on the slide in the slide pane. Display gridlines by clicking the View tab and then clicking the *Gridlines* check box in the Show group to insert a check mark. Create a text box in a slide by clicking the Text Box button in the Text group on the Insert tab. Click or drag in the slide to create the text box. Draw a shape in a slide and the selected shape displays with sizing handles and a rotation handle. Rotate a shape with the rotation handle or with the Rotate button in the Arrange group on the Drawing Tools Format tab. If you draw more than one object in a slide, you can select multiple objects at once so you can work with them as if they were a single object. You can format, size, move, flip, and/or rotate selected objects as a single unit.

What You Will Do   You need to create a new slide for the Toronto presentation that displays the date for the last day of filming in Toronto. To highlight this important information, you will insert an arrow shape and then copy and rotate the shape.

Tutorial
Displaying Rulers, Gridlines, and Guides; Copying and Rotating Shapes

Tutorial
Inserting and Formatting Text Boxes

1 With **3-MPToronto.pptx** open, make Slide 8 active and then click the Insert tab.

2 Click the New Slide button arrow and then click *Title Only* at the drop-down list.

3 Click in the *Click to add title* placeholder and then type Last Day of Filming.

4 Turn on the display of gridlines by clicking the View tab and then clicking the *Gridlines* check box in the Show group to insert a check mark.

Step 4

5 Click the Insert tab and then click the Text Box button in the Text group.

6 Position the mouse pointer in the slide and then draw a text box similar to what you see below. Use the gridlines to help you position the mouse when drawing the text box.

Step 6

7 Change the font size to 24 points, apply bold formatting, apply the Orange, Accent 1, Darker 25% font color (fifth column, fifth row in *Theme Colors* section), change to center alignment, and then type August 28. Click outside the text box to deselect it.

8 Click the Insert tab, click the Shapes button in the Illustrations group, and then click the *Notched Right Arrow* shape (sixth column, second row in the *Block Arrows* section).

9 Position the mouse pointer at the left side of the slide, click and hold down the left mouse button, drag to create the arrow shape as shown at the right, and then release the mouse button.

Use the gridlines to help position the arrow.

10 With the arrow shape selected, copy the arrow by positioning the mouse pointer inside the shape until the mouse pointer displays with a four-headed arrow attached. Press and hold down the Ctrl key and then click and hold down the left mouse button. Drag the arrow to the right side of the date, release the left mouse button, and then release the Ctrl key.

11 Click the Drawing Tools Format tab and then flip the copied arrow by clicking the Rotate button in the Arrange group and then clicking *Flip Horizontal* at the drop-down list.

12 Using the mouse pointer, draw a border around the three objects.

When you release the mouse button, the three objects are selected.

13 With the Drawing Tools Format tab active, center-align the three grouped objects by clicking the Align button in the Arrange group and then clicking *Align Middle* at the drop-down list.

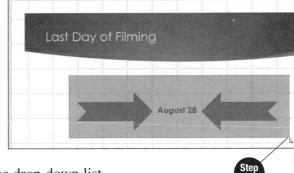

14 With the three objects still selected, horizontally distribute them by clicking the Align button and then clicking *Distribute Horizontally* at the drop-down list.

15 Turn off the display of gridlines by clicking the View tab and then clicking the *Gridlines* check box to remove the check mark.

16 Click outside the objects to deselect them.

17 Save **3-MPToronto.pptx**.

Check Your Work > Compare your work to the model answer to ensure that you have completed the activity correctly.

In Addition

Rotating Objects

Use the rotation handle that displays near a selected object to rotate the object. Position the mouse pointer on the rotation handle until the pointer displays as a circular arrow, as shown at the right. Click and hold down the left mouse button, drag in the desired direction, and then release the mouse button.

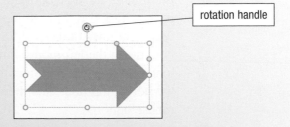

PowerPoint includes a Table feature you can use for displaying columns and rows of data. Insert a table in a slide with the Table button on the Insert tab or with the Insert Table button in a content placeholder. When you insert a table in a slide, the Table Tools Design tab is selected. Use buttons on this tab to enhance the appearance of the table. With options in the Table Styles group, apply predesigned colors and border lines to a table. Maintain further control over the predesigned style formatting applied to columns and rows with options in the Table Style Options group. Apply additional design formatting to cells in a table with the Shading and Borders buttons in the Table Styles group. Draw a table or draw additional rows and/or columns in a table with options in the Draw Borders group. Click the Table Tools Layout tab and display options and buttons for inserting and deleting columns and rows; changing cell size, alignment, direction, and margins; changing the table size; and arranging the table in the slide.

What You Will Do   After reviewing the slides, you decide to include additional information on the location timeline. To do this, you will insert a new slide and then create a table with specific dates.

Tutorial
Creating a Table

Tutorial
Changing the Table Design

Tutorial
Changing the Table Layout

1 With **3-MPToronto.pptx** open, make Slide 8 active and then click the Insert tab.

2 Click the New Slide button arrow and then click the *Title and Content* layout at the drop-down list.

3 Click the *Click to add title* placeholder in the new slide and then type Timeline.

4 Click the Insert Table button ⊞ in the content placeholder.

5 At the Insert Table dialog box, press the Delete key and then type 2 in the *Number of columns* measurement box.

6 Press the Tab key and then type 9 in the *Number of rows* measurement box.

7 Click OK to close the Insert Table dialog box.

8 Turn on the display of the horizontal and vertical rulers. To do this, click the View tab and then click the *Ruler* check box in the Show group to insert a check mark.

9 Column 1 needs to be widened to accommodate the project tasks. To do this, position the mouse pointer on the middle gridline in the table until the pointer turns into a left-and-right-pointing arrow with two short lines in the middle. Click and hold down the left mouse button, drag to approximately the 6-inch mark on the horizontal ruler, and then release the mouse button.

10 Starting with the insertion point positioned in the first cell, type all of the text shown in Figure 3.2. Press the Tab key to move the insertion point to the next cell. Press Shift + Tab to move the insertion point to the previous cell.

11 Click the More Table Styles button in the gallery in the Table Styles group on the Table Tools Design tab.

12 Click the *Medium Style 1 - Accent 1* option in the drop-down gallery (second column, first row in the *Medium* section).

13 Click the Table Tools Layout tab.

14 Select the first row in the table by positioning the mouse pointer at the left side of the first row in the table until the pointer turns into a black, right-pointing arrow and then clicking the left mouse button.

15 Click the Center button in the Alignment group.

16 Click in the *Height* measurement box in the Table Size group, type 4, and then press the Enter key.

17 Distribute the table horizontally on the slide.

18 Save **3-MPToronto.pptx**.

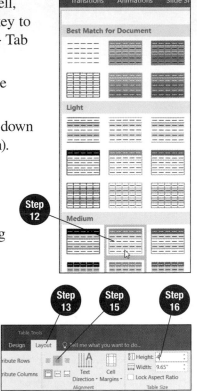

Figure 3.2 Slide 9 Table

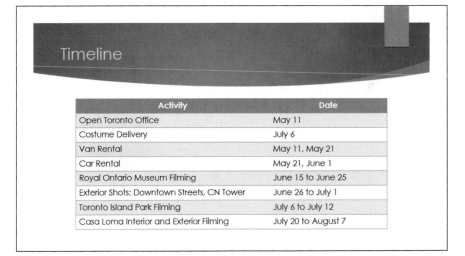

Activity	Date
Open Toronto Office	May 11
Costume Delivery	July 6
Van Rental	May 11, May 21
Car Rental	May 21, June 1
Royal Ontario Museum Filming	June 15 to June 25
Exterior Shots: Downtown Streets, CN Tower	June 26 to July 1
Toronto Island Park Filming	July 6 to July 12
Casa Loma Interior and Exterior Filming	July 20 to August 7

Check Your Work Compare your work to the model answer to ensure that you have completed the activity correctly.

In Addition

Moving and Sizing a Table

Increase or decrease the size of a table by typing the measurements in the *Height* and *Width* measurement boxes in the Table Size group on the Table Tools Layout tab. You can also drag the sizing handles that display around a table border to increase or decrease the size. When the insertion point is positioned in a table, a border containing sizing handles that display as small white circles surrounds the table. Position the mouse pointer on one of the sizing handles until the pointer displays as a two-headed arrow, click and hold down the left mouse button, and then drag to increase or decrease the size. Drag a corner sizing handle to change the size of the table proportionally. To move the table, position the mouse pointer on the table border until the pointer displays with a four-headed arrow attached and then drag to the desired position.

Action buttons are drawn objects on a slide that have a routine attached to them. The routine is activated when the presenter clicks the action button. For example, you can insert an action button that displays a specific web page, a file in another program, or the next slide in the presentation. Creating an action button is a two-step process. The first step is to draw the button in the slide, and the second step is to define the action that will take place using options in the Action Settings dialog box. You can customize an action button in the same way you would customize a drawn shape. You can also insert a hyperlink in a slide that, when clicked, will display a website or open another slide show or file. Insert a hyperlink with the Hyperlink button on the Insert tab.

What You Will Do To facilitate the running of the slide show, you decide to insert an action button at the bottom of each slide that will link to the next slide or the first slide. You also decide to insert a hyperlink to a website.

Tutorial
Inserting Action Buttons

Tutorial
Applying an Action to an Object

Tutorial
Inserting Hyperlinks

1 With **3-MPToronto.pptx** open, make Slide 1 active.

2 Insert an action button that, when clicked, will display the next slide. To begin, click the Insert tab, click the Shapes button, and then click the *Action Button: Forward or Next* option (second button in the *Action Buttons* section).

3 Position the mouse pointer (displays as crosshairs) in the lower right corner of Slide 1, click and hold down the left mouse button, drag to create a button that is approximately one-half inch square, and then release the mouse button.

4 At the Action Settings dialog box that displays, click OK. (The default setting is *Hyperlink to Next Slide.*)

5 With the button selected, if necessary, click the Drawing Tools Format tab.

6 Select the current measurement in the *Shape Height* measurement box, type 0.5, and then press the Enter key. Select the current measurement in the *Shape Width* measurement box, type 0.5, and then press the Enter key.

7 Instead of drawing the button on each slide, you decide to copy it and then paste it in the other slides. To do this, make sure the button is selected, click the Home tab, and then click the Copy button in the Clipboard group.

8 Make Slide 2 active and then click the Paste button in the Clipboard group. Continue pasting the button in Slides 3 through 9. (Do not paste the button on the last slide, Slide 10.)

9 Make Slide 10 active and then insert an action button that will display the first slide. To begin, click the Insert tab, click the Shapes button, and then click *Action Button: Home* (fifth option in the *Action Buttons* section).

In Brief

Insert Action Button
1. Click Insert tab.
2. Click Shapes button.
3. Click action button.
4. Click or drag in slide to create button.
5. At Action Settings dialog box, click OK.

10 Position the mouse pointer in the lower right corner of Slide 10 and then click the left mouse button.

> When you click in the slide, a small square shape with a home icon in the center is inserted in the slide.

11 At the Action Settings dialog box that displays, click OK. (The default setting is *Hyperlink to First Slide*.)

12 With the button selected, click in the *Shape Height* measurement box on the Drawing Tools Format tab, type 0.5, and then press the Enter key. Click in the *Shape Width* measurement box, type 0.5, and then press the Enter key.

13 Make Slide 6 active and then create a hyperlink to the museum website. To begin, select *Royal Ontario Museum*, click the Insert tab, and then click the Hyperlink button 🌐 in the Links group.

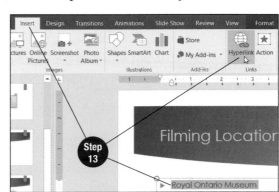

14 At the Insert Hyperlink dialog box, type www.rom.on.ca in the *Address* text box and then press the Enter key.

> PowerPoint automatically inserts *http://* at the beginning of the web address. The hyperlink text displays underlined and in a different color in the slide.

15 Run the slide show, beginning with Slide 1. Navigate through the slide show by clicking the action buttons. When Slide 6 (*Filming Locations*) displays, click the Royal Ontario Museum hyperlink.

16 After viewing the museum website, close the browser. Continue running the slide show. After viewing the slide show at least twice, press the Esc key to end the slide show.

17 Print the presentation as handouts with six slides displayed horizontally per page.

18 Save and then close **3-MPToronto.pptx**.

Check Your Work Compare your work to the model answer to ensure that you have completed the activity correctly.

In Addition

Linking with Action Buttons

You can set an action button to link to a website during a slide show. To do this, draw an Action button. At the Action Settings dialog box, click the *Hyperlink to* option, click the *Hyperlink to* option box arrow, and then click *URL* at the drop-down list. At the Hyperlink to URL dialog box, type the web address in the *URL* text box and then click OK. Click OK to close the Action Settings dialog box. Other actions you can link to using the *Hyperlink to* drop-down list include: *Next Slide, Previous Slide, First Slide, Last Slide, Last Slide Viewed, End Show, Custom Show, Slide, URL, Other PowerPoint Presentation,* and *Other File*. The Action Settings dialog box can also be used to run another program when the action button is selected, to run a macro, or to activate an embedded object.

Activity 3.8 Formatting with a Slide Master

If you use a PowerPoint design theme, you may choose to use the formatting provided by the theme or you may want to customize the formatting. If you customize formatting in a presentation, PowerPoint's slide master can be very helpful in reducing the steps needed to format slides. A presentation contains a slide master for each of the various slide layouts. To display slide masters, click the View tab and then click the Slide Master button in the Master Views group. The available slide masters display in the slide thumbnails pane at the left side of the screen. Apply formatting to the slide masters and then click the Close Master View button in the Close group to return to the Normal view.

What You Will Do   Melissa Gehring, manager at First Choice Travel, has asked you to complete a presentation on upcoming eco-tours offered by First Choice Travel. You decide to change the theme colors and fonts of the presentation, as well as insert the company's logo in the upper right corner of all slides except the title slide.

Tutorial

Formatting with a Slide Master

1 Open **FCTEcoTours.pptx** and then save it with the name **3-FCTEcoTours**.

2 Click the View tab and then click the Slide Master button ☐ in the Master Views group.

> Hover the mouse pointer over a slide master in the slide thumbnails pane at the left side of the screen to display a ScreenTip with information about the slide layout and the number of slides in the presentation that use the layout.

3 Click the Theme Colors button ☐ in the Background group and then click *Blue* at the drop-down gallery.

4 Click the Theme Fonts button [A] in the Background group, scroll down the drop-down gallery, and then click *Calibri Light-Constantia*.

5 Select the *Click to edit Master title style* placeholder text in the slide in the slide pane, click the Home tab, click the Font Color button arrow, and then click the *Blue* color option (eighth option in the *Standard Colors* section).

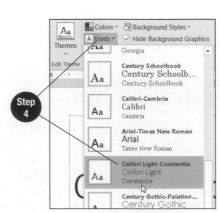

6 Click the top slide master in the slide thumbnails pane at the left side of the screen.

7 Select the *Click to edit Master title style* placeholder text, click the Home tab, and then click the Font Color button.

> This applies the Blue font color.

Step 6

8 Insert the First Choice Travel logo in the slide master (so it prints on all slides except the first one). Begin by clicking the Insert tab and then clicking the Pictures button in the Images group.

9 Navigate to the PowerPointS3 folder on your storage medium and then double-click *FCTLogo.jpg*.

10 Make sure the logo is selected.

11 Click in the *Shape Height* measurement box, type 0.5, and then press the Enter key.

12 Click the Align button in the Arrange group and then click the *Align Right* option at the drop-down list.

Step 12

13 Click the Align button and then click the *Align Top* option.

14 Click the Slide Master tab.

15 Click the Close Master View button in the Close group on the Slide Master tab.

16 Save **3-FCTEcoTours.pptx**.

Check Your Work — Compare your work to the model answer to ensure that you have completed the activity correctly.

In Addition

Applying More Than One Slide Design Theme

Each design theme applies specific formatting to slides. You can apply more than one design theme to slides in a presentation. To do this, select the specific slides and then choose the desired design theme. The design theme is applied only to the selected slides. If you apply more than one design theme to a presentation, multiple slide masters will display in Slide Master view.

Formatting Changes in Slide Master View

If you edit the formatting of text in a slide in Normal view, the link to the slide master is broken. Changes you make to a slide master in Slide Master view will not affect the individually formatted slide. For this reason, make formatting changes in Slide Master view before editing individual slides in a presentation.

Insert information you want to appear at the top or bottom of individual slides or at the top and bottom of individual printed notes and handouts pages using options at the Header and Footer dialog box. If you want the same types of information to appear on all slides, display the Header and Footer dialog box with the Slide tab selected. With options at this dialog box, you can insert the date and time, insert the slide number, and create a footer. To insert header or footer elements you want to print on all notes or handouts pages, choose options at the Header and Footer dialog box with the Notes and Handouts tab selected.

What You Will Do   Melissa Gehring has asked you to insert the current date and slide numbers in the slides and to create a header for notes pages.

Tutorial

Inserting Headers and Footers

1   With **3-FCTEcoTours.pptx** open, insert a footer that prints at the bottom of each slide. To begin, click the Insert tab and then click the Header & Footer button ⬚ in the Text group.

Step 1

2   At the Header and Footer dialog box with the Slide tab selected, click the *Date and time* check box to insert a check mark. If necessary, click the *Update automatically* option to select it.

Step 2

Step 3

3   Click the *Slide number* check box to insert a check mark.

Step 4

4   Click the *Footer* check box to insert a check mark and then type First Choice Travel Eco-Tours in the *Footer* text box.

Step 5

5   Click the Apply to All button.

6   Make Slide 7 active.

7   Display the notes pane by clicking the Notes button on the Status bar.

8   Click in the notes pane and then type Include additional costs for airfare, local transportation, and daily tours.

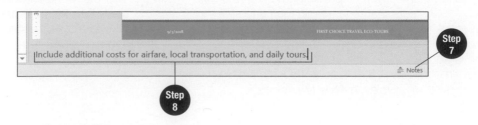

Step 7

Step 8

Insert Header/Footer on Slide
1. Click Insert tab.
2. Click Header & Footer button.
3. At Header and Footer dialog box with Slide tab selected, choose options.
4. Click Apply to All button.

Insert Header/Footer in Notes and Handouts
1. Click Insert tab.
2. Click Header & Footer button.
3. At Header and Footer dialog box, click Notes and Handouts tab.
4. Choose options.
5. Click Apply to All button.

9 Insert a header that will display on notes and handouts pages by clicking the Header & Footer button on the Insert tab.

10 At the Header and Footer dialog box, click the Notes and Handouts tab.

11 Make sure a check mark does not display in the *Date and time* check box. If a check mark does display, click the check box to remove the check mark.

12 Click the *Header* check box to insert a check mark and then type First Choice Travel in the *Header* text box.

13 Click the *Footer* check box to insert a check mark and then type Eco-Tours in the *Footer* text box.

14 Click the Apply to All button.

15 Print the presentation as handouts with nine slides displayed horizontally per page.

16 Print Slide 7 as a notes page. To do this, click the File tab, click the *Print* option, click the second gallery (contains the text *9 Slides Horizontal*) in the *Settings* category, and then click *Notes Pages* in the *Print Layout* section.

17 Click in the *Slides* text box (located below the first gallery in the *Settings* category) and then type 7.

18 Click the Print button.

19 Click the Notes button on the Status bar to close the notes pane.

20 Save **3-FCTEcoTours.pptx**.

Check Your Work   Compare your work to the model answer to ensure that you have completed the activity correctly.

In Addition

Using the Package for CD Feature

The safest way to transport a PowerPoint presentation to another computer is to use the Package for CD feature. With this feature, you can copy a presentation onto a CD or to a folder or network location and include all of the linked files and fonts, as well as the PowerPoint Viewer program in case the destination computer does not have PowerPoint installed on it. To use the Package for CD feature, click the File tab, click the *Export* option, click the *Package Presentation for CD* option, and then click the Package for CD button. At the Package for CD dialog box, type a name for the CD and then click the Copy to CD button.

Activity 3.10 Adding Audio and Video

Adding audio and/or video effects to a presentation will turn a slide show into a true multi-media experience for your audience. Including a variety of elements in a presentation will stimulate interest in your slide show and keep the audience motivated. You can insert an audio file or video file from a folder or from the Insert Video window.

FIRST CHOICE
TRAVEL

What You Will Do   To add interest, you decide to experiment with adding a video file and an audio file to the presentation. The last slide of the slide show will display the video file and play an audio file. This will allow the presenter time to answer questions from the audience while the video and audio files play.

Tutorial
Inserting and
Modifying an Audio
File

Tutorial
Inserting and
Modifying a Video File

1 With **3-FCTEcoTours.pptx** open, make Slide 7 active, click the Insert tab, and then click the New Slide button.

2 Click in the title placeholder and then type Let the adventure begin!

3 Click the Insert Video button ⬚ in the content placeholder.

4 At the Insert Video window, click the Browse button to the right of the *From a file* option.

You can also display the Insert Video dialog box by clicking the Insert tab, clicking the Video button in the Media group, and then clicking *Video on My PC*.

5 At the Insert Video dialog box, navigate to the PowerPointS3 folder on your storage medium and then double-click **Wildlife.wmv**.

This inserts the video file in a window in the slide with the Video Tools Format tab selected. Use options and buttons on this tab to preview the video file, change the brightness, contrast, and color of the video, apply a formatting style to the video window, and arrange and size the video in the slide.

6 Click the Play button ▶ in the Preview group (left side of Video Tools Format tab) to preview the video file.

The video plays for approximately 30 seconds.

7 After viewing the video, click the Video Tools Playback tab.

8 Click the *Fade In* measurement box up arrow in the Editing group until *01.00* displays and then click the *Fade Out* measurement box up arrow until *01.00* displays.

9 Click the Volume button 🔊 in the Video Options group and then click *Low* at the drop-down list.

10 Click the *Loop until Stopped* check box in the Video Options group to insert a check mark.

In Brief

Insert Video Clip
1. Click Insert Video button in placeholder.
2. Navigate to folder.
3. Double-click video file.
OR
1. Click Insert tab.
2. Click Video button arrow.
3. Click *Video on My PC*.
4. Navigate to folder.
5. Double-click video file.

Insert Audio Clip
1. Click Insert tab.
2. Click Audio button.
3. Click *Audio on My PC*.
4. Navigate to folder.
5. Double-click audio file.

11 Make Slide 1 active and then run the slide show. When the slide containing the video file displays, move the mouse pointer over the video file window and then click the Play button at the bottom left side of the window.

12 After viewing the video a couple of times, press the Esc key two times.

13 You decide that you want the video window to fill the slide, start automatically when the slide displays, and play only once. To do this, make sure Slide 8 is active, click the video file window, and then click the Video Tools Playback tab.

14 Click the *Play Full Screen* check box in the Video Options group to insert a check mark and then click the *Loop until Stopped* check box to remove the check mark.

15 Click the *Start* option box arrow in the Video Options group and then click *Automatically* at the drop-down list.

16 Make Slide 1 active and then run the slide show. When the slide containing the video displays, the video will automatically begin. When the video is finished playing, press the Esc key to return to Normal view.

17 You decide that you want music to play after the presentation. Begin by making sure Slide 8 is the active slide, clicking the Insert tab, clicking the Audio button 🔊 in the Media group, and then clicking *Audio on My PC* at the drop-down list.

18 At the Insert Audio dialog box, navigate to the PowerPointS3 folder on your storage medium and then double-click the file named *FCTAudioClip-01.mid*.

This inserts the audio file in the slide with the Audio Tools Playback tab selected.

19 If necessary, click the Audio Tools Playback tab.

20 Click the *Start* option box down arrow in the Audio Options group and then click *Automatically* at the drop-down list.

21 Click the *Hide During Show* check box in the Audio Options group to insert a check mark and then click the *Loop until Stopped* check box to insert a check mark.

22 Make Slide 1 active and then run the slide show. When the last slide displays, watch the video, listen to the audio file for about a minute or two, and then press the Esc key to return to the Normal view.

23 Save **3-FCTEcoTours.pptx**.

Check Your Work Compare your work to the model answer to ensure that you have completed the activity correctly.

In Addition

Changing the Video Color

With the Color button in the Adjust group on the Video Tools Format tab, you can change the video color. If you want the video to play in black and white, click the Color button and then click the *Grayscale* option at the drop-down gallery. Click the *Sepia* option if you want the video to have an old-fashioned appearance when played.

Setting and Rehearsing Timings for a Slide Show

If you want a slide show to run automatically and each slide to display for a specific number of seconds, use the Rehearse Timings feature to help set the times for slides as you practice delivering the slide show. To set times for slides, click the Slide Show tab and then click the Rehearse Timings button in the Set Up group. The first slide displays in Slide Show view and the Recording toolbar displays. Use buttons on this toolbar to specify times for each slide. Use options at the Set Up Show dialog box to control the slide show. Display this dialog box by clicking the Set Up Slide Show button in the Set Up group. Use options in the *Show type* section to specify the type of slide show you want to display. If you want the slide show to be totally automatic and run continuously until you end the show, click the *Loop continuously until 'Esc'* check box to insert a check mark. In the *Advance slides* section, the *Using timings, if present* option should be selected by default. Select *Manually* if you want to advance the slides using the mouse instead of your preset times.

What You Will Do   Melissa Gehring has asked you to automate the slide show so it can be run continuously at the upcoming travel conference.

Tutorial
Setting Timings for a Slide Show

Tutorial
Looping a Slide Show Continuously

1 With **3-FCTEcoTours.pptx** open, save it with the name **3-FCTEcoTours-Rehearsed**.

2 Make Slide 8 active, click the audio icon to select it, and then press the Delete key. Click the video window to select it and then press the Delete key.

3 Type the following information in the content placeholder:

> Call today to schedule your exciting eco-tour adventure:
>> ○ 1-888-555-1330
> Or visit our website:
>> ○ www.emcp.net/fc-travel

4 Select the content placeholder (make sure the border is a solid line) and then click the Bold button in the Font group on the Home tab.

5 Make Slide 1 active, click the Slide Show tab, and then click the Rehearse Timings button 🕒 in the Set Up group.

Step 5

The first slide displays in Slide Show view, the Recording toolbar displays as well. The timing for the first slide begins automatically. Refer to Figure 3.3 for the names of the Recording toolbar buttons.

6 Wait until the time displayed for the current slide reaches four seconds and then click the Next button →.

Step 6

If you miss the time, click the Repeat button ↺ to reset the clock back to zero for the current slide.

7 Set the following times for the remaining slides:

Slide 2: 5 seconds	Slide 6: 8 seconds
Slide 3: 5 seconds	Slide 7: 7 seconds
Slide 4: 4 seconds	Slide 8: 8 seconds
Slide 5: 6 seconds	

8 After the last slide has displayed with the total slide show time, click Yes at the message asking if you want to keep the new slide timings.

9 Click the Slide Sorter button on the Status bar. Notice the slides display with the times listed below. The times that display may be off by one second.

> You can adjust the timings manually with options in the Timing group on the Transitions tab. See the In Addition below.

10 Double-click Slide 1 to change to Normal view.

11 Set up the slide show to run continuously by clicking the Set Up Slide Show button in the Set Up group on the Slide Show tab.

12 At the Set Up Show dialog box, click the *Loop continuously until 'Esc'* check box.

13 Click OK to close the dialog box.

14 Insert an audio file that will play continuously throughout the slide show. To begin, click the Insert tab, click the Audio button in the Media group, and then click the *Audio on My PC* option.

15 At the Insert Audio dialog box, navigate to the PowerPointS3 folder on your storage medium and then double-click the file named ***FCTAudioClip-02.mid***.

16 If necessary, click the Audio Tools Playback tab. Click the *Start* option box arrow in the Audio Options group and then click *Automatically* at the drop-down list.

17 Click the *Play Across Slides* check box in the Audio Options group to insert a check mark, click the *Loop until Stopped* check box to insert a check mark, and then click the *Hide During Show* check box to insert a check mark.

18 Drag the audio icon to the bottom center of the slide.

19 Run the slide show, beginning with Slide 1. The slide show will start and run continuously. Watch the presentation until it starts for the second time and then end the show by pressing the Esc key.

20 Print the presentation as handouts with nine slides displayed horizontally per page.

21 Save and then close **3-FCTEcoTours-Rehearsed.pptx**.

Figure 3.3 Recording Toolbar Buttons

Check Your Work Compare your work to the model answer to ensure that you have completed the activity correctly.

In Addition

Setting Times Manually

The time a slide remains on the screen during a slide show can be manually set using options in the Timing group on the Transitions tab. To set manual times for slides, click the *On Mouse Click* check box to remove the check mark and then click the *After* check box to insert a check mark. Click in the *After* text box, type the desired number of seconds you want the slide to display on the screen when running the slide show, and then press the Enter key. Click the Apply To All button to apply the time to each slide in the presentation.

Features Summary

Feature	Ribbon Tab, Group	Button	Keyboard Shortcut
action button	Insert, Illustrations		
audio file	Insert, Media		
Clipboard task pane	Home, Clipboard		
draw shape	Insert, Illustrations OR Home, Drawing		
gridlines	View, Show		Shift + F9
header and footer	Insert, Text		
hyperlink	Insert, Links		Ctrl + K
rehearse timings	Slide Show, Set Up		
replace	Home, Editing		Ctrl + H
table	Insert, Tables		
text box	Insert, Text		
video file	Insert, Media		
WordArt	Insert, Text		

Workbook — Section study tools and assessment activities are available in the *Workbook* ebook. These resources are designed to help you further develop and demonstrate mastery of the skills learned in this section.

Word, Excel, and PowerPoint

Data Files ▶ Before beginning section work, copy the Integrating3 folder to your storage medium and then make Integrating3 the active folder.

Skills

- Export a PowerPoint presentation to a Word document
- Export a Word outline document to a PowerPoint presentation
- Link an Excel chart with a Word document and a PowerPoint presentation
- Edit a linked object
- Embed a Word table in a PowerPoint presentation
- Edit an embedded object

Precheck ▶ Check your current skills to help focus your study of the skills taught in this section.

Projects Overview

Create presentation handouts in Word for use in an annual meeting PowerPoint presentation.

Prepare a PowerPoint presentation for the Distribution Department of Worldwide Enterprises using a Word outline. Copy an Excel chart and link it to the Distribution Department meeting presentation and to a Word document and then edit the linked chart. Copy a Word table containing data on preview distribution dates, embed it in a PowerPoint slide, and then update the table.

Export a PowerPoint presentation containing information on vacation specials offered by First Choice Travel to a Word document.

Link an Excel chart containing information on department enrollments to a PowerPoint slide and then update the chart in Excel. Embed a Word table in a PowerPoint slide and then edit the table in the slide.

 SNAP If you are a SNAP user, launch the Precheck and Tutorials from your Assignments page.

Model Answers ▶ Preview the model answers for an overview of the projects you will complete in the section activities.

One of the benefits of a suite like Microsoft Office is that you can send data in one program to another program. For example, send Word content to a PowerPoint presentation and PowerPoint content to a Word document. To send presentation content to a document, click the File tab, click the *Export* option, click the *Create Handouts* option, and then click the Create Handouts button. At the Send to Microsoft Word dialog box, specify the layout of the content in the Word document and whether you want to paste or paste link the content and then click OK. One of the advantages to sending PowerPoint presentation content to a Word document is that you can have greater control over the formatting of the content in Word.

NIAGARA
PENINSULA
COLLEGE

What You Will Do   Create a Word document handout that contains slides from a PowerPoint presentation on the Theatre Arts Division at Niagara Peninsula College.

1 Open PowerPoint and then open **NPCDivPres.pptx**.

2 Save the presentation with the name **3-NPCDivPres**.

3 Click the File tab, click the *Export* option, click the *Create Handouts* option, and then click the Create Handouts button.

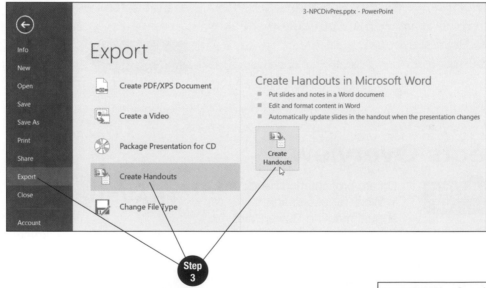

4 At the Send to Microsoft Word dialog box, click the *Blank lines next to slides* option.

5 Click the *Paste link* option in the *Add slides to Microsoft Word document* section and then click OK.

6 If necessary, click the Word button on the taskbar.

  The slides display in a Word document as thumbnails followed by blank lines.

7 Save the Word document on your storage medium and name it **3-NPCDivPresHandout**.

8 Print and then close **3-NPCDivPresHandout.docx**.

9 Click the PowerPoint button on the taskbar.

10 Make Slide 3 active and then change *$750* to *$850*, *$350* to *$450*, and *$250* to *$300*.

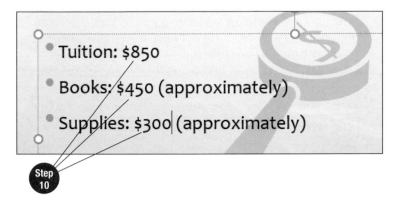

Step 10

11 Save **3-NPCDivPres.pptx**.

12 Click the Word button on the taskbar and then open **3-NPCDivPresHandout.docx**. At the message asking if you want to update the document with the data from the linked files, click the Yes button.

13 Scroll through the document and notice that the dollar amounts in Slide 3 reflect the changes you made to Slide 3 in the PowerPoint presentation.

14 Save, print, and then close **3-NPCDivPresHandout.docx**.

15 Make PowerPoint active and then close **3-NPCDivPres.pptx**.

Check Your Work ▸ Compare your work to the model answer to ensure that you have completed the activity correctly.

In Addition

Pasting and Linking Data

The *Paste* option at the Send to Microsoft Word dialog box is selected by default and is available for all of the page layout options. With this option selected, the data inserted in Word is not connected or linked to the original data in the PowerPoint presentation. If you plan to update the data in the presentation and want the data to be updated in the Word document as well, select the *Paste link* option at the Send to Microsoft Word dialog box. This option is available for all of the page layout options except the *Outline only* option.

As you learned in the previous activity, the Microsoft Office suite allows you to send content in one program to another program. For example, you can send Word content to a PowerPoint presentation and content in a PowerPoint presentation to a Word document. You can create text for slides in a Word outline and then export that outline to PowerPoint. PowerPoint creates new slides based on the heading styles used in the Word outline. Text formatted with a Heading 1 style become slide titles. Heading 2 text becomes first-level bulleted text, Heading 3 text becomes second-level bulleted text, and so on. If styles are not applied to outline text in Word, PowerPoint uses tabs or indents to place text on slides. To export a Word document to a PowerPoint presentation, you need to insert the Send to Microsoft PowerPoint button on the Quick Access Toolbar.

Worldwide Enterprises

What You Will Do   Prepare a presentation for the Distribution Department of Worldwide Enterprises using a Word outline.

1 Make sure both Word and PowerPoint are open.

2 With Word active, open **WEOutline.docx**.

> Text in this document has been formatted with the Heading 1 and Heading 2 styles.

3 Insert a Send to Microsoft PowerPoint button on the Quick Access Toolbar. Begin by clicking the Customize Quick Access Toolbar button ⏷ at the right side of the Quick Access Toolbar.

4 Click *More Commands* at the drop-down list.

5 Click the *Choose commands from* option box arrow and then click *All Commands* at the drop-down list.

6 Scroll down the list box below the *Choose commands from* option box and then double-click *Send to Microsoft PowerPoint*.

> Items in the list box display in alphabetical order.

7 Click OK to close the Word Options dialog box.

> Notice that the Send to Microsoft PowerPoint button has been added to the Quick Access Toolbar.

8 Send the outline to PowerPoint by clicking the Send to Microsoft PowerPoint button 📇 on the Quick Access Toolbar.

9 When the presentation displays on the screen, make sure Slide 1 is active. (If the presentation does not display, click the PowerPoint button on the taskbar.)

> The presentation is created with a blank design template.

10 With Slide 1 active, change the layout by clicking the Layout button in the Slides group on the Home tab and then clicking the *Title Slide* option at the drop-down list.

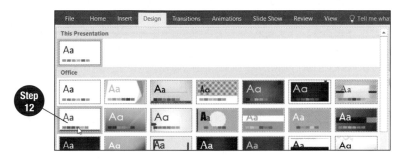

11 Make Slide 4 active and then apply the Title Only layout. Apply the Title Only layout to Slides 5 and 6 as well.

12 Apply a design theme by clicking the Design tab, clicking the More Themes button in the Themes group, and then clicking the *Retrospect* option (shown below).

13 Click the second variant option in the Variants group (white with green).

14 Save the presentation and name it **3-WEDistDeptMtg**.

15 Close **3-WEDistDeptMtg.pptx**.

16 Click the Word button on the taskbar.

17 Right-click the Send to Microsoft PowerPoint button on the Quick Access Toolbar and then click *Remove from Quick Access Toolbar* at the shortcut menu.

18 Close **WEOutline.docx** without saving the changes.

> **Check Your Work**   Compare your work to the model answer to ensure that you have completed the activity correctly.

In Addition

Applying a Style in Word

Heading styles were already applied to the text in **WEOutline.docx**. If you create an outline in Word that you want to export to PowerPoint, apply styles using options in the Styles group on the Home tab. A Word document contains a number of predesigned formats grouped into style sets. Click the Design tab to display the available style sets in the Document Formatting group. Choose a style set and the styles visible in the

Styles group on the Home tab change to reflect your selection. To display additional available styles, click the More Styles button (contains a horizontal line and a down-pointing triangle) at the right side of the gallery in the Styles group on the Home tab. To apply a heading style, position the insertion point in the desired text, click the More Styles button, and then click the specific style at the drop-down gallery.

You can copy and link an object such as a table or chart to files created in other programs. For example, you can copy an Excel chart and link it to a Word document and/or a PowerPoint presentation. The advantage to copying and linking over copying and pasting is that when you edit the object in the originating program, called the *source program*, the object is automatically updated in the linked file in the other program, called the *destination program*. When an object is linked, it exists in the source program but not as a separate object in the destination program. Since the object is located only in the source program, changes made to the object in the source program will be reflected in the destination program. An object can be linked to more than one destination program or file.

Worldwide Enterprises

What You Will Do   In preparation for a company meeting, you will copy an Excel chart and then link it to both the Worldwide Enterprises Distribution Department meeting presentation and to a Word document.

1 Make sure PowerPoint and Word are open and then open Excel.

2 Make Word active and then open **WERevDoc.docx**. Save the document with the name **3-WERevDoc**.

3 Make PowerPoint active, open **3-WEDistDeptMtg.pptx**, and then make Slide 6 active.

4 Make Excel active and then open **WERevChart.xlsx**. Save the workbook with the name **3-WERevChart**.

5 Copy and link the chart to the Word document and the PowerPoint presentation. Start by clicking in the chart to select it.

> Make sure you select the entire chart and not a specific chart element. To do so, try clicking just inside the chart border.

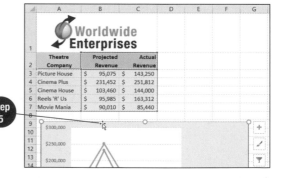

Step 5

6 With the chart selected, click the Copy button in the Clipboard group on the Home tab.

7 Click the Word button on the taskbar.

8 Press Ctrl + End to move the insertion point to the end of the document.

9 Click the Paste button arrow and then click *Paste Special* at the drop-down list.

10 At the Paste Special dialog box, click the *Paste link* option, click the *Microsoft Excel Chart Object* option in the *As* list box, and then click OK.

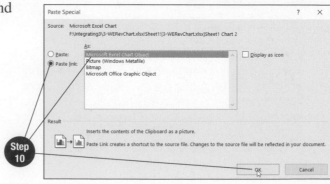

Step 10

In Brief

Link Object between Programs
1. Open source program, open file containing object.
2. Select object, click Copy button.
3. Open destination program, open file into which object will be linked.
4. Click Paste button arrow, click *Paste Special*.
5. At Paste Special dialog box, click *Paste link*.
6. Click OK.

11 Select the chart and then center it by clicking the Center button in the Paragraph group on the Home tab.

12 Save, print, and then close **3-WERevDoc.docx**.

13 Click the PowerPoint button on the taskbar.

14 With Slide 6 active, make sure the Home tab is selected, click the Paste button arrow, and then click *Paste Special* at the drop-down list.

15 At the Paste Special dialog box, click the *Paste link* option, make sure *Microsoft Excel Chart Object* is selected in the *As* list box, and then click OK.

Step 15

16 Increase the size of the chart so it better fills the slide and then center it on the slide, as shown in Figure 3.1.

17 Click outside the chart to deselect it.

18 Save the presentation, print only Slide 6, and then close **3-WEDistDeptMtg.pptx**.

19 Click the Excel button on the taskbar.

20 Click outside the chart to deselect it.

21 Save, print, and then close **3-WERevChart.xlsx**.

Figure 3.1 Step 16

Check Your Work Compare your work to the model answer to ensure that you have completed the activity correctly.

In Addition

Linking Data or an Object within a Program

In this section, you learned to link an object between programs using the Paste Special dialog box. You can also link an object in Word using options at the Object dialog box. To do this, click the Insert tab and then click the Object button in the Text group. At the Object dialog box, click the Create from File tab. At the dialog box, type the file name in the *File name* text box or click the Browse button and then select the file from the appropriate folder. Click the *Link to file* check box to insert a check mark and then click OK.

The advantage to linking an object over simply copying it is that editing the object in the source program will automatically update the object in the destination program(s) as well. To edit a linked object, open the file containing the object in the source program, make edits, and then save the file. The next time the document, workbook, or presentation is opened in the destination program, the object will be updated.

Worldwide Enterprises

What You Will Do   Edit the actual and projected revenue numbers in the Worldwide Enterprises Excel worksheet and then open and print the Word document and the PowerPoint presentation that contain the linked chart.

1 Make sure Word, Excel, and PowerPoint are open.

2 Make Excel active and then open **3-WERevChart.xlsx**.

3 You discover that one theatre company was left out of the revenues chart. Add a row to the worksheet by clicking in cell A6 to make it active. Click the Insert button arrow in the Cells group on the Home tab and then click *Insert Sheet Rows* at the drop-down list.

4 Type the following data in the specified cells:

    A6: Regal Theatres
    B6: 69550
    C6: 50320

5 Click in cell A3.

6 Save, print, and close **3-WERevChart.xlsx** and then close Excel.

7 Make Word active and then open **3-WERevDoc.docx**. At the message asking if you want to update the linked file, click the Yes button.

8 Notice how the linked chart is automatically updated to reflect the changes you made to it in Excel.

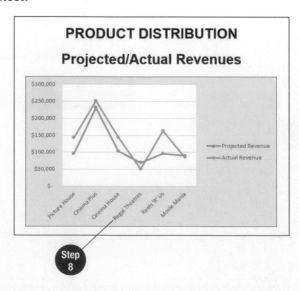

9 Save, print, and then close **3-WERevDoc.docx**.

10 Make PowerPoint active and then open **3-WEDistDeptMtg.pptx**.

11 At the message telling you that the presentation contains links, click the Update Links button.

12 Make Slide 6 active and then notice how the linked chart has been automatically updated to reflect the changes you made to it in Excel.

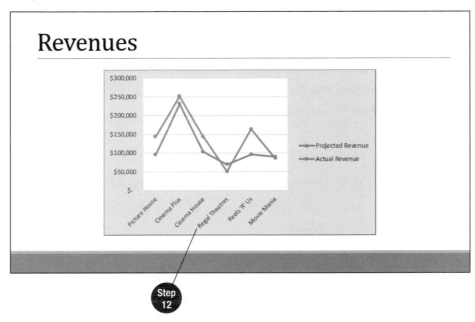

13 Save the presentation and then print only Slide 6.

14 Close **3-WEDistDeptMtg.pptx**.

Check Your Work Compare your work to the model answer to ensure that you have completed the activity correctly.

In Addition

Updating a Link Manually

You can choose to update a link manually in the destination program. To do this, open a Word document containing a linked object. Right-click the object, point to *Linked (type of object) Object*, and then click *Links*. At the Links dialog box, click the *Manual update* option and then click OK. With *Manual update* selected, the link will only be updated when you right-click the linked object and then click *Update Link* or when you display the Links dialog box, click the link in the list box, and then click the Update Now button.

Copy and paste, copy and link, or copy and embed an object from one file into another. A linked object resides in the source program but not as a separate object in the destination program. An embedded object resides in the source program as well as in the destination program. If a change is made to an embedded object in the source program, the change will not be made to the object in the destination program. The main advantage to embedding rather than simply copying and pasting is that you can edit an embedded object in the destination program using the tools of the source program.

What You Will Do   Copy a Word table containing data on preview distribution dates for Worldwide Enterprises and then embed the table in a slide in a PowerPoint presentation. Update the distribution dates for the two embedded tables.

1 Make sure both Word and PowerPoint are open.

2 Make PowerPoint active and then open **3-WEDistDeptMtg.pptx**.

3 At the message telling you that the presentation contains links, click the Update Links button.

4 Make Slide 4 active.

5 Make Word active and then open **WEPrevDistTable.docx**.

6 Click in a cell in the table and then select the table. To do this, click the Table Tools Layout tab, click the Select button in the Table group, and then click *Select Table* at the drop-down list.

7 With the table selected, click the Home tab and then click the Copy button in the Clipboard group.

8 Click the PowerPoint button on the taskbar.

9 With Slide 4 active, click the Paste button arrow and then click *Paste Special* at the drop-down list.

10 At the Paste Special dialog box, click *Microsoft Word Document Object* in the *As* list box and then click OK.

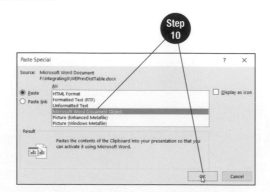

11 With the table selected in the slide, use the sizing handles to increase the size and change the position of the table as shown in Figure 3.2.

12 Click outside the table to deselect it.

Figure 3.2 Step 11

Preview Distribution

Theatre Company	Location	Date
Cinema House	Montreal, Toronto	May 18
Cinema House	Vancouver	May 11
Cinema Plus	Los Angeles, San Diego	May 4
Cinema Plus	New York, Newark	May 11
Movie Mania	Wichita	May 25
Picture House	St. Louis	May 25
Picture House	Denver	May 18
Picture House	Salt Lake City	May 25

13 Save the presentation and then print only Slide 4.

14 Click the Word button on the taskbar and then close the document.

15 Click the PowerPoint button on the taskbar and then make Slide 5 active.

16 Make Word active and then open **WEGenDistTable.docx**.

17 Click in a cell in the table and then select the table. To do this, click the Table Tools Layout tab, click the Select button in the Table group, and then click *Select Table* at the drop-down list.

18 Click the Home tab and then click the Copy button in the Clipboard group.

19 Click the PowerPoint button on the taskbar.

20 With Slide 5 active, click the Paste button arrow and then click *Paste Special* at the drop-down list.

21 At the Paste Special dialog box, click *Microsoft Word Document Object* in the *As* list box and then click OK.

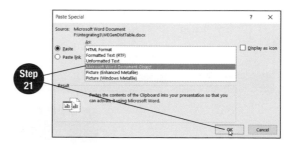

22 Increase the size and position of the table in the slide so it displays as shown in Figure 3.3 on the next page.

23 The distribution date to Cinema Plus in Sacramento and Oakland has been delayed until June 1. Edit the date by double-clicking the table in the slide.

Double-clicking the table displays the Word tabs and ribbon at the top of the screen. Horizontal and vertical rulers also display around the table.

24 Using the mouse, select *May 25* in the *Sacramento, Oakland* row and then type June 1.

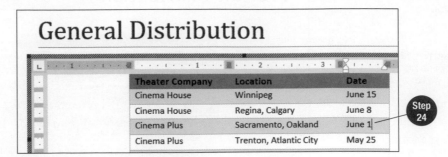

25 Click outside the table to deselect it.

Notice that the Word tabs disappear.

26 Print Slide 5 of the presentation.

27 Apply a transition and transition sound of your choosing to all slides in the presentation and then run the slide show.

28 Save and close **3-WEDistDeptMtg.pptx** and then close PowerPoint.

29 Click the Word button on the taskbar, close the document, and then close Word.

Figure 3.3 Step 22

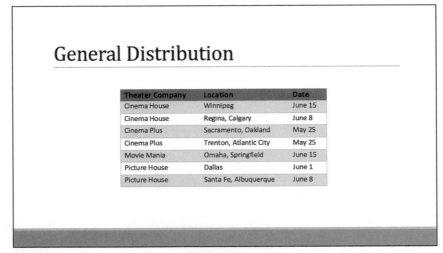

Check Your Work Compare your work to the model answer to ensure that you have completed the activity correctly.

In Addition

Working with a Cropped Object

Some embedded or linked objects may appear cropped on the right or bottom side even if enough room is available to fit the image on the page or slide. A large embedded or linked object may appear cropped because Word converts the object into a Windows metafile (.wmf), which has a maximum height and width. If the embedded or linked object exceeds this maximum size, it appears cropped. To prevent an object from appearing cropped, consider reducing the size of the data by reducing the font size, column size, line spacing, and so on.

Workbook Section assessment activities are available in the *Workbook* ebook. These activities are designed to help you demonstrate mastery of the skills learned in this section.

INDEX

Complicated Kris Northern

"This image illustrates some of the best qualities of fractals—infinity, reiteration, and self similarity."– **Kris Northern**

Investigations
IN NUMBER, DATA, AND SPACE®

Glenview, Illinois • Boston, Massachusetts
Chandler, Arizona • Upper Saddle River, New Jersey

The Investigations curriculum was developed by TERC, Cambridge, MA.

This material is based on work supported by the National Science Foundation ("NSF") under Grant No. ESI-0095450. Any opinions, findings, and conclusions or recommendations expressed in this material are those of the author(s) and do not necessarily reflect the views of the National Science Foundation.

ISBN-13: 978-0-328-60012-0

ISBN-10: 0-328-60012-1

Co-Principal Investigators

Susan Jo Russell

Karen Economopoulos

Authors

Lucy Wittenberg
Director Grades 3–5

Karen Economopoulos
Director Grades K–2

Virginia Bastable
(SummerMath for Teachers,
Mt. Holyoke College)

Katie Hickey Bloomfield

Keith Cochran

Darrell Earnest

Arusha Hollister

Nancy Horowitz

Erin Leidl

Megan Murray

Young Oh

Beth W. Perry

Susan Jo Russell

Deborah Schifter
(Education
Development Center)

Kathy Sillman

Note: Unless otherwise noted, all contributors listed above were staff of the Education Research Collaborative at TERC during their work on the curriculum. Other affiliations during the time of development are listed.

Administrative Staff

Amy Taber
Project Manager

Beth Bergeron

Lorraine Brooks

Emi Fujiwara

Contributing Authors

Denise Baumann

Jennifer DiBrienza

Hollee Freeman

Paula Hooper

Jan Mokros

Stephen Monk
(University of Washington)

Mary Beth O'Connor

Judy Storeygard

Cornelia Tierney

Elizabeth Van Cleef

Carol Wright

Technology

Jim Hammerman

Classroom Field Work

Amy Appell

Rachel E. Davis

Traci Higgins

Julia Thompson

Collaborating Teachers

This group of dedicated teachers carried out extensive field testing in their classrooms, met regularly to discuss issues of teaching and learning mathematics, provided feedback to staff, welcomed staff into their classrooms to document students' work, and contributed both suggestions and written material that has been incorporated into the curriculum.

Bethany Altchek

Linda Amaral

Kimberly Beauregard

Barbara Bernard

Nancy Buell

Rose Christiansen

Chris Colbath-Hess

Lisette Colon

Kim Cook

Frances Cooper

Kathleen Drew

Rebeka Eston Salemi

Thomas Fisher

Michael Flynn

Holly Ghazey

Susan Gillis

Danielle Harrington

Elaine Herzog

Francine Hiller

Kirsten Lee Howard

Liliana Klass

Leslie Kramer

Melissa Lee Andrichak

Kelley Lee Sadowski

Jennifer Levitan

Mary Lou LoVecchio

Kristen McEnaney

Maura McGrail

Kathe Millett

Florence Molyneaux

Amy Monkiewicz

Elizabeth Monopoli

Carol Murray

Robyn Musser

Christine Norrman

Deborah O'Brien

Timothy O'Connor

Anne Marie O'Reilly

Mark Paige

Margaret Riddle

Karen Schweitzer

Elisabeth Seyferth

Susan Smith

Debra Sorvillo

Shoshanah Starr

Janice Szymaszek

Karen Tobin

JoAnn Trauschke

Ana Vaisenstein

Yvonne Watson

Michelle Woods

Mary Wright

Advisors

Deborah Lowenberg Ball,
University of Michigan

Hyman Bass, Professor of Mathematics and Mathematics Education
University of Michigan

Mary Canner, Principal, Natick Public Schools

Thomas Carpenter, Professor of Curriculum and Instruction,
University of Wisconsin-Madison

Janis Freckmann, Elementary Mathematics Coordinator,
Milwaukee Public Schools

Lynne Godfrey, Mathematics Coach,
Cambridge Public Schools

Ginger Hanlon, Instructional Specialist in Mathematics,
New York City Public Schools

DeAnn Huinker, Director, Center for Mathematics and
Science Education Research, University of Wisconsin-Milwaukee

James Kaput, Professor of Mathematics, University of
Massachusetts-Dartmouth

Kate Kline, Associate Professor, Department of Mathematics
and Statistics, Western Michigan University

Jim Lewis, Professor of Mathematics,
University of Nebraska-Lincoln

William McCallum, Professor of Mathematics,
University of Arizona

Harriet Pollatsek, Professor of Mathematics,
Mount Holyoke College

Debra Shein-Gerson, Elementary Mathematics Specialist,
Weston Public Schools

Gary Shevell, Assistant Principal,
New York City Public Schools

Liz Sweeney, Elementary Math Department,
Boston Public Schools

Lucy West, Consultant, Metamorphosis:
Teaching Learning Communities, Inc.

This revision of the curriculum was built on the work of the many
authors who contributed to the first edition (published between
1994 and 1998). We acknowledge the critical contributions of
these authors in developing the content and pedagogy of
Investigations:

Authors

Joan Akers

Michael T. Battista

Douglas H. Clements

Karen Economopoulos

Marlene Kliman

Jan Mokros

Megan Murray

Ricardo Nemirovsky

Andee Rubin

Susan Jo Russell

Cornelia Tierney

Contributing Authors

Mary Berle-Carman

Rebecca B. Corwin

Rebeka Eston

Claryce Evans

Anne Goodrow

Cliff Konold

Chris Mainhart

Sue McMillen

Jerrie Moffet

Tracy Noble

Kim O'Neil

Mark Ogonowski

Julie Sarama

Amy Shulman Weinberg

Margie Singer

Virginia Woolley

Tracey Wright

Contents

Investigations

CURRICULUM

Overview of Program Components

The **Curriculum Units** are the teaching guides. (See far right.)

Implementing Investigations in Grade 2 offers suggestions for implementing the curriculum. It also contains a comprehensive index.

The **Differentiation and Intervention Guide** offers additional activities for each Investigation to support the range of learners.

Investigations for the Interactive Whiteboard provides whole-class instructional support to enhance each session.

The **Resource Masters and Transparencies CD** contains all reproducible materials that support instruction. The **Shapes CD** provides an environment in which students investigate a variety of geometric ideas.

The **Student Activity Book** contains the consumable student pages (Recording Sheets, Homework, Practice, and so on).

The **Student Math Handbook** contains Math Words and Ideas pages and Games directions.

The *Investigations* Curriculum

Investigations in Number, Data, and Space® is a K–5 mathematics curriculum designed to engage students in making sense of mathematical ideas. Six major goals guided the development of the *Investigations in Number, Data, and Space®* curriculum. The curriculum is designed to:

- Support students to make sense of mathematics and learn that they can be mathematical thinkers

- Focus on computational fluency with whole numbers as a major goal of the elementary grades

- Provide substantive work in important areas of mathematics—rational numbers, geometry, measurement, data, and early algebra—and connections among them

- Emphasize reasoning about mathematical ideas

- Communicate mathematics content and pedagogy to teachers

- Engage the range of learners in understanding mathematics

Underlying these goals are three guiding principles that are touchstones for the *Investigations* team as we approach both students and teachers as agents of their own learning:

1. *Students have mathematical ideas.* Students come to school with ideas about numbers, shapes, measurements, patterns, and data. If given the opportunity to learn in an environment that stresses making sense of mathematics, students build on the ideas they already have and learn about new mathematics they have never encountered. Students learn that they are capable of having mathematical ideas, applying what they know to new situations, and thinking and reasoning about unfamiliar problems.

2. *Teachers are engaged in ongoing learning* about mathematics content, pedagogy, and student learning. The curriculum provides material for professional development, to be used by teachers individually or in groups, that supports teachers' continued learning as they use the curriculum over several years. The *Investigations* curriculum materials are designed as much to be a dialogue with teachers as to be a core of content for students.

3. *Teachers collaborate with the students and curriculum materials* to create the curriculum as enacted in the classroom. The only way for a good curriculum to be used well is for teachers to be active participants in implementing it. Teachers use the curriculum to maintain a clear, focused, and coherent agenda for mathematics teaching. At the same time, they observe and listen carefully to students, try to understand how they are thinking, and make teaching decisions based on these observations.

Investigations is based on experience from research and practice, including field testing that involved documentation of thousands of hours in classrooms, observations of students, input from teachers, and analysis of student work. As a result, the curriculum addresses the learning needs of real students in a wide range of classrooms and communities. The investigations are carefully designed to invite all students into mathematics—girls and boys; members of diverse cultural, ethnic, and language groups; and students with a wide variety of strengths, needs, and interests.

Based on this extensive classroom testing, the curriculum takes seriously the time students need to develop a strong conceptual foundation and skills based on that foundation. Each curriculum unit focuses on an area of content in depth, providing time for students to develop and practice ideas across a variety of activities and contexts that build on each other. Daily guidelines for time spent on class sessions, Classroom Routines (K–3), and Ten-Minute Math (3–5) reflect the commitment to devoting adequate time to mathematics in each school day.

About This Curriculum Unit

This **Curriculum Unit** is one of nine teaching guides in Grade 2. The second unit in Grade 2 is *Shapes, Blocks, and Symmetry.*

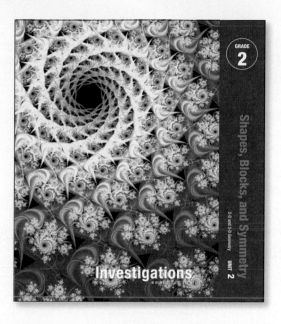

- The **Introduction and Overview** section organizes and presents the instructional materials, provides background information, and highlights important features specific to this unit.

- Each Curriculum Unit contains several **Investigations.** Each Investigation focuses on a set of related mathematical ideas.

- Investigations are divided into one-hour **Sessions,** or lessons.

- Sessions have a combination of these parts: **Activity, Discussion, Math Workshop, Assessment Activity,** and **Session Follow-Up.**

- Each session also has one or more **Classroom Routines** that are done outside of math time.

- At the back of the book is a collection of **Teacher Notes** and **Dialogue Boxes** that provide professional development related to the unit.

- Also included at the back of the book are the **Student Math Handbook** pages for this unit.

- The **Index** provides a way to look up important words or terms.

Overview

Investigation	Session	Day	
INVESTIGATION 1 **Features of 2-Dimensional and 3-Dimensional Shapes** Students study the features of 2-D shapes by describing and sorting Shape Cards (a set of 24 polygons). They study the features of 3-D shapes by describing, sorting, and matching the faces of Geoblocks. They use pattern blocks to compose larger 2-D shapes and use Geoblocks to make larger 3-D shapes. Students also add the doubles combinations to their set of Addition Combination Cards.	**1.1** Geoblock Faces	1	
	1.2 Working with Geoblocks	2	
	1.3 Sorting Geoblocks	3	
	1.4 Addition Combinations and Ways to Fill	4	
	1.5 Combining Shapes	5	
INVESTIGATION 2 **What Is a Rectangle?** Students continue to work with Shape Cards to learn about the polygon attributes and ways that polygons are categorized. They use Geoboards and square tiles to explore the properties of rectangles and the concept of area. Students make rectangular prisms using rectangles as faces.	**2.1** Assessment: Sorting Shapes by Number of Sides	6	
	2.2 Sorting Quadrilaterals	7	
	2.3 Ordering Rectangles	8	
	2.4 Building Rectangles	9	
	2.5 Drawing Rectangles	10	
	2.6 How Many Rectangles?	11	
	2.7 Assessment: Is It a Rectangle?	12	
	2.8 Making Boxes from Rectangles	13	
	2.9 Assessment: Faces of a Geoblock	14	
INVESTIGATION 3 **Symmetry** Students investigate symmetry using pattern blocks and mirrors. They complete symmetrical designs made with color tiles. Students also explore symmetry by folding and cutting out shapes.	**3.1** Mirror Symmetry	15	
	3.2 Copy Tiles	16	
	3.3 Paper Folding and Cutting	17	
	3.4 Is It Symmetrical?	18	
	3.5 End-of-Unit Assessment	19	

Each *Investigations* session has some combination of these five parts: **Activity, Discussion, Math Workshop, Assessment Activity,** and **Session Follow-Up.** These session parts are indicated in the chart below. Each session also has one **Classroom Routine** that is done outside of math time.

 (W) Interactive Whiteboard

Activity	Discussion	Math Workshop	Assessment Activity	Session Follow-Up
(W) ● ●				●
(W) ●		●		●
● ●		●		●
● (W)	(W)			●
(W) ●		●		●
(W)	(W)		●	●
●	(W) ●			●
● ●	(W) (W)			●
(W) ●		●		●
(W)		●		●
(W)		●		●
●			(W)	●
● (W)				●
●	●		(W)	●
(W) ●		●		●
(W) ●		●		●
● ●		●		●
(W)	●			●
			(W)	●

Classroom Routines

Quick Images	What Time Is It?	Today's Number	How Many Pockets?
		(W)	
		(W)	
			(W)
	(W)		
(W)			
	(W)		
	(W)		
(W)			
		(W)	
	(W)		
(W)			
	(W)		
			(W)
	(W)		
(W)			
		(W)	
	(W)		
		(W)	
(W)			

Mathematics

Shapes, Blocks, and Symmetry is the second of nine units in the Grade 2 sequence. This unit is part of the geometry strand of *Investigations.* These units develop students' ideas about 2-dimensional (2-D) and 3-dimensional (3-D) shapes and their characteristics and attributes. Students work on how to compose and decompose the shapes in different ways, and how to sort, categorize, name, and think about the relationships between them. The mathematical focus of this unit is attending to features of 2-D and 3-D shapes as a way of distinguishing them. Students do in-depth work with rectangles and rectangular prisms and also investigate symmetry. They use a variety of tools, including pattern blocks, Geoblocks, Geoboards, and the *Shapes* software.

LOOKING BACK

Geometry is a part of mathematics that students experience every day. Shapes, angles, and symmetry are everywhere in the child's world. Part of young students' work in developing mathematical understanding is to begin to observe, describe, compare, and represent the shapes they see around them.

The geometry units in Grade 1 emphasized careful observation and description of geometric shapes. Students looked for shapes in their environment, and they worked with several sets of 2-dimensional and 3-dimensional objects. They described, compared, and sorted these objects, and they explored how shapes can go together and be taken apart to make other shapes. Students focused specifically on attributes of triangles. Finally, they investigated the relationship between 3-D shapes and 2-D representations by matching 3-D objects to their outlines, and then drawing their own pictures of 3-D blocks and buildings. Students should be familiar with a variety of geometric materials, including pattern blocks, Geoblocks, Geoboards, and the *Shapes* software from their work in Kindergarten and Grade 1.

This unit focuses on 5 Mathematical Emphases:

1 Features of Shape Composing and decomposing 2-dimensional and 3-dimensional shapes

Math Focus Points

- Combining shapes to make a new shape

- Covering a region, without gaps or overlaps, with a single shape or multiple shapes

- Covering a region, without gaps or overlaps, using different shapes

- Combining 3-D shapes to make a 3-D whole

- Drawing 3-D shapes

A major idea of geometry is that shapes can be combined or decomposed to make other shapes. As students use pattern blocks and Geoblocks, they explore relationships within each of these sets. For example, they notice that three pattern-block triangles can be combined to make a trapezoid, or that two Geoblock cubes can be combined to make a different rectangular prism. When solving numerical problems, students compose and decompose numbers to make them more manageable. In the same way, solving geometric problems often involves understanding how to pull shapes apart and put them together so that they can be viewed in new ways. Much of what we understand about geometric shapes is based on our knowledge of how shapes are related. When second graders see how a regular hexagon can be constructed from six equilateral triangles, they are developing a foundation that will help them investigate the properties of the hexagon's angles, sides, and area.

The *Shapes* software offers students a powerful tool to further experiment with ideas about composing and decomposing shapes. They solve puzzles using a variety of shape sets, including pattern blocks, Power Polygons™, and tangrams.

2 Features of Shape Describing, identifying, comparing, and sorting 2-dimensional and 3-dimensional shapes

Math Focus Points

◆ Describing attributes of and sorting 2-D and 3-D shapes

◆ Identifying names and attributes of 2-D and 3-D shapes

◆ Attending to features of 3-D shapes, particularly the number and shape of faces

◆ Identifying categories for 2-D shapes

◆ Identifying a 3-D shape by touch

◆ Sorting polygons by the number of sides

◆ Sorting quadrilaterals by angle

◆ Identifying quadrilaterals as shapes with 4 sides

◆ Identifying rectangles as 4-sided shapes with 4 right angles

◆ Identifying important features of a rectangle

◆ Defining *biggest* in different ways

◆ Ordering rectangles from biggest to smallest

◆ Recognizing that rectangular prisms have rectangular faces

◆ Recognizing which faces of a rectangular prism are the same size and shape

◆ Constructing a rectangular prism from rectangles

◆ Visualizing and describing rectangular prisms

◆ Comparing rectangular prisms

As students explore 2- and 3-dimensional shapes, they begin to think about their similarities and differences. This focus leads to classification and definition of basic shapes—important processes in geometry. For example:

• What makes a triangle a triangle?

• What are the characteristics of a cube?

• What distinguishes a prism from a pyramid?

As students use 2-dimensional shapes in this unit, they engage in activities that require them to take a closer look at shapes. They describe them, sort them, compare them, and think about what makes a rectangle a rectangle and how rectangles are different from squares. Developing visual images of shapes, as well as drawing 2-dimensional shapes, are some of the ways that students come to know about the important features of shapes.

When students use the *Shapes* software, they are looking at familiar shapes in a new way. As students use computers to precisely manipulate shapes, the visual images become even more powerful. The "on-computer" activities support and deepen the work that students are doing throughout this unit.

This unit provides students with an opportunity to explore rectangles in-depth and to consider which properties are important and which are not. For example, is a rectangle still a rectangle if it is oriented so that one of its angles is pointed toward the bottom of the page?

Is it a rectangle if a "bite" is taken out of one corner?

Students have opportunities to sort shapes, build rectangles from tiles, and draw rectangles on dot paper to see that they are four-sided figures with four right angles.

Through building boxes from a set of rectangular pieces, students also explore more deeply the properties of rectangular prisms—3-dimensional objects with rectangular faces and congruent opposite faces.

3 Area Measurement Visualizing the structure of arrays

Math Focus Points

◆ Covering rectangles with arrays of tiles

◆ Arranging square tiles in rectangular arrays

◆ Constructing and describing rectangular arrays of tiles

◆ Making different rectangular arrays using the same number of tiles

◆ Drawing rectangles by attending to the lengths of the sides

The task of ordering a set of rectangles by size raises the issue that there are different ways to think about size. There are different answers to the question, "Which is the biggest rectangle?" They depend on whether you are considering height, width, or the number of tiles it takes to cover it (the area).

As students create rectangles with square tiles, they see how rectangular surfaces can be covered with many of the same unit. They also begin to learn about the structure of an array. Although the array structure may be obvious to an adult, it requires significant work for a child to see how a row is made up of squares and how that same row is repeated to make up the rectangle.

In their study of arrays, students' explorations in geometry are closely linked with their work with number and operations. Students use a variety of numerical strategies that are based on addition and multiplication to calculate— from the size of a row and the number of rows—the total number of tiles in an array.

4 Features of Shape Exploring mirror symmetry

Math Focus Points

◆ Describing and identifying objects and designs that have mirror symmetry

◆ Constructing 2-D and 3-D symmetrical designs with mirror symmetry

◆ Reflecting a shape across a line of symmetry

◆ Exploring symmetry by folding and cutting paper patterns

◆ Identifying lines of symmetry

◆ Orienting shapes so that a line of symmetry aligns with a mirror (*Shapes* software)

◆ Determining what makes a design symmetrical

While many students intuitively recognize that many things are symmetrical, they need the opportunity to explore symmetry and think about it in more depth. As they create or investigate symmetric shapes, they develop clearer language and ideas about what symmetry is and how it behaves. Students develop an understanding of mirror symmetry as they identify objects that have it. They create patterns and designs, fold and cut paper, and build 3-dimensional structures—all with mirror symmetry.

The *Shapes* software supports students to investigate and deepen their ideas about symmetry, offering them computer tools for reflecting shapes in a vertical or horizontal mirror, and for flipping shapes over their vertical or horizontal midline. In addition, the *Lines of Symmetry Puzzles* and *Reflection Puzzles* challenge students to identify and create symmetrical pictures in more sophisticated ways.

5 Computational Fluency Knowing addition combinations to 10 + 10

Math Focus Points

- Reviewing known addition combinations (combinations of 10, Plus 1, Plus 2)

- Developing fluency with the doubles combinations up to 10 + 10

- Achieving fluency with the doubles combinations

Classroom Routines focus on

- Generating equivalent expressions for a number

- Developing fluency with addition and subtraction

- Using standard notation (+, −, =) to record expressions and write equations

- Using clocks as tools for keeping track of and measuring time

- Naming, notating, and telling time to the hour, half hour, and quarter hour on digital and analog clocks

- Associating times on the hour and half hour with daily events

- Developing and analyzing visual images for quantities

- Identifying names and attributes of 2-D shapes

- Developing fluency with the doubles combinations up to 10 + 10

- Using arrays and standard notation (+, =) to represent doubles up to 10 + 10

- Making predictions about data

- Collecting, counting, representing, discussing, interpreting, and comparing data

- Counting by groups

- Counting a quantity in more than one way

LOOKING FORWARD In Grades 3 through 5 students will continue to study the attributes of 2-dimensional and 3-dimensional shapes, and how these attributes determine their classification (e.g., that a shape is classified as a triangle or a quadrilateral on the basis of the number of its sides). In Grades 3 and 4, the work will focus especially on the characteristics of triangles and rectangles, and in Grade 5 the work expands to many different polygons. Students will continue their work with rectangular arrays in their study of multiplication and division in Grade 3. Rectangular arrays are an important representation for multiplication and division in both Grades 4 and 5. Students in Grades 3 through 5 continue to develop their visualization skills and their understanding of the relationship between 2-D pictures and the 3-D objects they represent. Students determine the volume of "boxes" (rectangular prisms) made from 2-D patterns and create patterns for boxes to hold a certain number of cubes. They develop strategies for determining the number of cubes in 3-D arrays by mentally organizing the cubes—for example, as a stack of three rectangular layers, each three by four cubes. Students deepen their understanding of the relationship between volume and the linear dimensions of length, width, and height.

Technology Note

Introducing the Software The *Shapes* software is introduced to students in this unit. If you are planning to use the software, you will need to familiarize yourself with it. For information about *Shapes* software, refer to the *Software Support Reference Guide* found on the CD. To prepare to integrate this work into your classroom and to manage the computer environment, see **Teacher Note:** Introducing and Managing the *Shapes* software, page 152, and **Teacher Note:** About the Math in *Shapes* software, page 155.

Assessment

IN THIS UNIT

ONGOING ASSESSMENT: Observing Students at Work

The following sessions provide **Ongoing Assessment: Observing Students at Work** opportunities:

- **Session 1.1, pp. 29 and 30**
- **Session 1.2, pp. 35, 37, 38, and 39**
- **Session 1.3, pp. 42 and 44**
- **Session 1.4, pp. 46 and 48**
- **Session 1.5, pp. 53, 54, and 55**
- **Session 2.1, pp. 64 and 68**
- **Session 2.2, p. 73**

- **Session 2.3, pp. 78–79 and 81**
- **Session 2.4, pp. 87, 89, and 90**
- **Session 2.5, p. 95**
- **Session 2.6, pp. 98 and 100**
- **Session 2.7, pp. 104 and 105**
- **Session 2.8, pp. 107 and 109**

- **Session 2.9, pp. 111 and 113**
- **Session 3.1, pp. 123, 125, and 126**
- **Session 3.2, pp. 130 and 131**
- **Session 3.3, pp. 135 and 136**
- **Session 3.4, p. 141**
- **Session 3.5, pp. 143 and 144**

WRITING OPPORTUNITIES

The following sessions have **writing** opportunities for students to explain their mathematical thinking:

- **Session 2.3, p. 81**
  Student Activity Book, p. 17

- **Session 2.4, p. 89**
  Student Activity Book, p. 20

- **Session 3.4, p. 140**
  Student Activity Book, pp. 38–39

- **Session 3.5, p. 143**
  M42, End-of-Unit Assessment

PORTFOLIO OPPORTUNITIES

The following sessions have work appropriate for a **portfolio:**

- **Session 1.5, p. 54**
  Student Activity Book, pp. 9–10

- **Session 2.3, p. 81**
  Student Activity Book, p. 17

- **Session 2.4, p. 89**
  Student Activity Book, pp. 19–20

- **Session 2.7, p. 104**
  M30, Assessment: Is It a Rectangle?

- **Session 2.9, p. 113**
  M31, Assessment: Faces of
  a Geoblock

- **Session 3.4, p. 140**
  Student Activity Book, pp. 38–39

- **Session 3.5, p. 143**
  M42–M43, End-of-Unit Assessment

Assessing the Benchmarks

Observing students as they engage in conversation about their ideas is a primary means to assess their mathematical understanding. Consider all of your students' work, not just the written assessments. See the chart below for suggestions about key activities to observe.

See the **Differentiation and Intervention Guide** for quizzes that can be used after each Investigation.

Benchmarks in This Unit	Key Activities to Observe	Assessment
1. Identify the number of sides of a polygon.	**Session 1.1:** *Quick Images: Shapes*	**Session 2.1:** Assessment Checklist: Sorting Shapes by Number of Sides ☑
2. Identify the number of rows and the number of squares in each row in an array.	**Session 2.4:** Describing Rectangles, Rectangle Riddles **Session 2.6:** How Many Rectangles?	**Session 3.5:** End-of-Unit Assessment: Make a Rectangle
3. Identify rectangles as four-sided shapes with four right angles.	**Session 2.2:** What's a Rectangle? **Session 2.5:** Rectangles on the Geoboard	**Session 2.7:** Assessment Activity: Is It a Rectangle?
4. Identify the number of faces on a rectangular prism and show which faces are congruent.	**Session 1.2:** Find the Block **Session 2.9:** Making Boxes	**Session 2.9:** Assessment Activity: Faces of a Geoblock
5. Make a symmetrical picture based on an image provided.	**Session 3.1** Mirror Designs, Symmetrical Geoblock Buildings **Session 3.4:** Doubling with Pattern Block Designs	**Session 3.5:** End-of-Unit Assessment: Complete the Shape
6. Demonstrate fluency with addition combinations: doubles combinations to 10 + 10.	**Session 1.4:** Addition Combinations: Doubles **Session 3.4:** Doubling with Pattern Block Designs	**Session 3.5:** Assessment Checklist: Doubles Combinations ☑

 Checklist Available

Relating the Mathematical Emphases to the Benchmarks

Mathematical Emphases	Benchmarks
Features of Shape Composing and decomposing 2-dimensional and 3-dimensional shapes	2, 4
Features of Shape Describing, identifying, comparing, and sorting 2-dimensional and 3-dimensional shapes	1, 3, and 4
Area Measurement Visualizing the structure of arrays	2
Features of Shape Exploring mirror symmetry	5
Computational Fluency Knowing addition combinations to 10 + 10	6

Classroom Routines

Classroom Routines offer practice and review of key concepts for this grade level. These daily activities, to be done in ten minutes outside of math class, occur in a regular rotation every 4–5 days. Specific directions for the day's routine are provided in each session. For the full description and variations of each classroom routine see *Implementing Investigations in Grade 2.*

Today's Number

Students use addition and subtraction, double combinations and combinations of 10 to make Today's Number.

Math Focus Points

- Generating equivalent expressions for a number

- Developing fluency with addition and subtraction

- Using standard notation ($+$, $-$, $=$) to record expressions and write equations

What Time Is It?

Students are introduced to telling and notating time to the half hour and explore the length of half hours by keeping track of what time it is and what the class is doing every half hour on the half hour. They also continue to practice naming, notating, and telling time to the hour.

Math Focus Points

- Using clocks as tools for keeping track of and measuring time

- Naming, notating, and telling time to the hour, half hour, and quarter hour on digital and analog clocks

- Associating times on the hour and half hour with daily events

Quick Images

Students draw and compare various shapes. They also view and write equations to represent double arrays.

Math Focus Points

- Developing and analyzing visual images for quantities

- Identifying names and attributes of 2-D shapes

- Developing fluency with the doubles combinations up to $10 + 10$

- Using arrays and standard notation ($+$, $=$) to represent doubles to $10 + 10$

How Many Pockets?

The class estimates how many pockets students are wearing. Students then determine the total number of pockets in the class and record the data.

Math Focus Points

- Making predictions about data

- Collecting, counting, representing, discussing, interpreting, and comparing data

- Counting by groups

- Counting a quantity in more than one way

Practice and Review

Practice and review play a critical role in the *Investigations* program. The following components and features are available to provide regular reinforcement of key mathematical concepts and procedures.

Books	Features	In This Unit ...
Curriculum Unit	**Classroom Routines** offer practice and review of key concepts for this grade level. These daily activities, to be done in ten minutes outside of math class, occur in a regular rotation every 4–5 days. Specific directions for the day's routine are provided in each session. For the full description and variations of each classroom routine see *Implementing Investigations in Grade* 2.	• **All sessions**
Student Activity Book	**Daily Practice** pages in the *Student Activity Book* provide one of three types of written practice: **reinforcement** of the content of the unit, **ongoing review,** or **enrichment** opportunities. Some Daily Practice pages will also have Ongoing Review items with multiple-choice problems similar to those on standardized tests.	• **All sessions**
	Homework pages in the *Student Activity Book* are an extension of the work done in class. At times they help students prepare for upcoming activities.	• **Session 1.1** • **Session 2.1** • **Session 2.2** • **Session 2.6** • **Session 3.1**
Student Math Handbook	**Math Words and Ideas** in the *Student Math Handbook* are pages that summarize key words and ideas. Most Words and Ideas pages have at least one exercise.	• **Student Math Handbook, pp. 43, 47, 112, 114, 116, 118–129**
	Games pages are found in a section of the *Student Math Handbook*.	• **No games are introduced in this unit.**

Supporting the Range of Learners

The **Differentiation and Intervention Guide** provides Intervention, Extension, and Practice activities for use within each Investigation.

Sessions	1.1	1.2	1.3	1.4	1.5	2.1	2.3	2.4	2.6	2.8	2.9	3.1	3.2	3.3
Intervention		•		•	•	•		•	•		•	•	•	•
Extension		•							•	•	•	•	•	•
ELL	•	•	•				•	•						

Intervention

Suggestions are made to support and engage students who are having difficulty with a particular idea, activity, or problem.

Extension

Suggestions are made to support and engage students who finish early or may be ready for additional challenge.

English Language Learners (ELL)

To take part in many of this unit's activities, students must be familiar with both the names of shapes and words that are commonly used to describe them. You can support English Language Learners by helping them develop this vocabulary. Before starting this unit, meet with a small group of English Language Learners. Examine a set of Geoblocks together, and encourage students to say what they notice about them. Record the words they use on a vocabulary poster (e.g., *square, point, corner, flat, side, big, small, skinny,* and *wide*). Draw pictures to illustrate the words. As students share descriptions, have them look for other Geoblocks that can be described with the same terms. If students do not mention the shape of the faces (*squares, rectangles, triangles*), bring these up yourself. For example, hold up a Geoblock and ask a student to choose a face of the Geoblock to trace on the vocabulary poster. Ask questions about the shape (e.g., How many sides?; How many corners?; etc.) Identify the name of each shape and write it on the

chart. Continue with other faces and other Geoblocks until triangles, squares, and rectangles of different sizes appear on the poster.

Keep the chart posted and encourage students to refer to the chart during class discussions and other activities. Students can add new shapes, as well as relevant vocabulary (*face, vertex, angle*) to the poster as these words come up in class. In addition, remind students to refer to the Math Words and Ideas pages about geometry in the *Student Math Handbook.*

Working with the Range of Learners is a set of episodes written by teachers that focuses on meeting the needs of the range of learners in the classroom. In the first section, *Setting up the Mathematical Community,* teachers write about how they create a supportive and productive learning environment in their classrooms. In the next section, *Accommodations for Learning,* teachers focus on specific modifications they make to meet the needs of some of their learners. In the last section, *Language and Representation,* teachers share how they help students use representations and develop language to investigate and express mathematical ideas. The questions at the end of each case provide a starting point for your own reflection or for discussion with colleagues. See *Implementing Investigations in Grade 2* for this set of episodes.

Mathematical Emphases

Features of Shape Composing and decomposing
2-dimensional and 3-dimensional shapes

Math Focus Points

◆ Drawing 3-D shapes

◆ Covering a region, without gaps or overlaps, using different shapes

◆ Combining shapes to make a new shape

◆ Combining 3-D shapes to make a 3-D whole

◆ Covering a region, without gaps or overlaps, with a single shape or multiple shapes

Features of Shape Describing, identifying, comparing, and sorting 2-dimensional and 3-dimensional shapes

Math Focus Points

◆ Identifying names and attributes of 2-D and 3-D shapes

◆ Attending to features of 3-D shapes, particularly the number and shape of faces

◆ Describing attributes of and sorting 3-D shapes

◆ Identifying a 3-D shape by touch

Computational Fluency Knowing addition combinations to $10 + 10$

Math Focus Points

◆ Developing fluency with the doubles combinations to $10 + 10$

◆ Reviewing known addition combinations (combinations of 10, Plus 1, Plus 2)

Features of 2-Dimensional and 3-Dimensional Shapes

	Student Activity Book	Student Math Handbook	Professional Development: Read Ahead of Time
SESSION 1.1 p. 24			
Geoblock Faces Students are introduced to a variation of *Quick Images*; they draw and describe the attributes of 2-D shapes. Students use the Geoblocks to focus on two attributes of 3-D shapes—the number of faces and their shape—as they describe and draw their own blocks.	1–2	112, 116, 122, 123, 124–125	• **Mathematics in This Unit,** p. 10 • **Teacher Notes:** 2-Dimensional Materials in This Unit, p. 147; Identifying Types of 2-Dimensional Shapes, p. 148; Identifying Types of 3-Dimensional Shapes, p. 150
SESSION 1.2 p. 31			
Working with Geoblocks Students are introduced to the Find the Block activity where they match a 3-D shape (a Geoblock) to its 2-D representation. The *Shapes* software is introduced in this session. The Math Workshop includes Geoblock activities, plus a doubling numbers activity from the previous unit.	3	47, 116, 122, 123, 124–125	• **Teacher Notes:** Introducing and Managing the *Shapes* Software, p. 152; About the Math in the *Shapes* Software, p. 155
SESSION 1.3 p. 40			
Sorting Geoblocks Students sort Geoblocks based on attributes that they identify. They are introduced to Mystery Block, a new Math Workshop activity that involves describing the attributes of 3-D shapes.	4	116, 124–125	

Classroom Routines See page 16 for an overview.

Today's Number	Quick Images
• Chart paper	• T15–T18, Shape Cards 🖳 Cut out the cards and store in envelope.
How Many Pockets?	
• Connecting cubes (class set)	
What Time Is It?	
• T20, Analog and Digital: 2:30 🖳	
• Student clocks (1 per pair)	

Materials to Gather	Materials to Prepare
• Geoblock K	• **M5–M6, Family Letter** Make copies. (1 per student) • **T15–T18, Shape Cards** 🖳 Cut out the cards and store in an envelope. • **Chart paper** Title 1 sheet of chart paper, "Describing Geoblocks." • **Geoblocks** Divide 2 sets of Geoblocks into 2 or 3 subsets.
• **5 Geoblocks, including Geoblock D** • **Geoblocks** (3 subsets; from Session 1.1) • **Primary Number Cards** (1 deck per pair; If you are not using the manufactured cards, use the cards you prepared from Unit 1, *Counting, Coins, and Combinations*)	• **M7–M12, Find the Block Task Cards** Make two copies of each page on cardstock or heavy paper. Cut out cards to make two sets. Divide each set in half to create two decks of Task Cards 1–6 and two decks of Task Cards 7–12. Store in separate envelopes or resealable plastic bags. (1 deck per pair) • **M13, Drawing Geoblocks** Make copies. (1 per student, plus extras as needed) • **M14, Double Arrays** Make copies. (1 per student, plus extras as needed) • **M15, Inch Grid Paper** (as needed for intervention) • **T19, Find the Block Task Cards** 🖳 Cut apart the images to create Task Card 1 and Task Card 2. • **Find the Block stations** Set up 2 separate stations that each include 1 subset of Geoblocks, 1 deck of Task Card 1–6, and 1 deck of Task Cards 7–12. • **Computers with *Shapes* software installed** Install the *Shapes* software on the computers that your students will be using. (optional)
• **Materials for Find the Block** See Session 1.2. • **Materials for Drawing Geoblocks** See Sessions 1.1 and 1.2. • **Materials for Double Arrays** See Session 1.2. • **Geoblocks** • **Chart paper** • **Self-stick notes** (as needed) • **Paper bags, cloth bags, or socks** (3 or 4) • **Computers with *Shapes* software installed** See Session 1.2. (optional)	• **11″ x 17″ paper** Two sheets; one labeled "Match" and one labeled "Don't Match"

🖳 Overhead Transparency

Features of 2-Dimensional and 3-Dimensional Shapes, *continued*

SESSION 1.4 p. 45	Student Activity Book	Student Math Handbook	Professional Development: Read Ahead of Time	
Addition Combinations and Ways to Fill The class reviews addition combinations from the previous unit. Students add the doubles combinations to their set of Addition Combination Cards. The class works with pattern blocks using different combinations of shapes to cover a region.	5	43, 47, 114		

SESSION 1.5 p. 50				
Combining Shapes Students are introduced to the Build the Geoblock activity and a new *Shapes* software activity, *Puzzles*. These activities, along with Ways to Fill from the previous session, are part of a Math Workshop that focuses on combining 2-D and 3-D shapes to make other shapes.	6–11	114, 122, 124–125		

Materials to Gather	Materials to Prepare
• **T21–T22, Ways to Fill: Pattern 1** • **"Combinations I Know" and "Combinations I'm Still Working On" envelopes** (from Unit 1) • **Overhead pattern blocks** (optional) • **Pattern blocks** (1 set per every 6–8 students)	• **M19, Addition Cards Set 2: Doubles Combinations** Make copies on cardstock or heavy paper and cut out cards. (1 set per student) • **M20–M21, Ways to Fill: Pattern 1** Make copies. (1 per student)
• **Materials for Ways to Fill** See Session 1.4. • **Geoblock K** • **Class set of Geoblocks** (divided into 2 subsets) • **Computers with *Shapes* software installed** See Session 1.2. (optional) • **Paper bags, cloth bags, or socks** (3 or 4)	• **M17–M18, Family Letter** Make copies. (1 per student)

Overhead Transparency

Geoblock Faces

Math Focus Points

◆ Identifying names and attributes of 2-D and 3-D shapes

◆ Attending to features of 3-D shapes, particularly the number and shape of faces

◆ Drawing 3-D shapes

Vocabulary

polygon
geometry
two-dimensional shape
three-dimensional shape
face

Today's Plan		Materials
ACTIVITY ① **Introducing** *Quick Images: Shapes*	15 MIN · INDIVIDUALS · CLASS	• T15–T18*
ACTIVITY ② **Looking Closely at Geoblocks**	30 MIN · CLASS	• Chart: "Describing Geoblocks"*; Geoblock K; Geoblocks*
ACTIVITY ③ **Drawing Geoblocks**	15 MIN · INDIVIDUALS · CLASS	
SESSION FOLLOW-UP ④ **Daily Practice and Homework**		• *Student Activity Book,* pp. 1–2 • M5–M6*, Family Letter • *Student Math Handbook,* pp. 112, 116, 122, 123, 124–125

*See *Materials to Prepare,* p. 21.

Classroom Routines

Today's Number: 14 As a whole class, students generate numerical expressions for the number 14 using addition and/or subtraction. These expressions are recorded on a class chart. Students can add to the chart throughout the day.

ACTIVITY

Introducing *Quick Images: Shapes*

15 MIN INDIVIDUALS CLASS

In the previous unit, students were introduced to the *Quick Images* routine using Ten-frames.❶ In this session, they will be looking at and drawing shapes.

From the set of transparent Shape Cards (T15–T18), select the square (Shape F), the triangle (Shape B), the trapezoid (Shape E), and the right triangle (Shape R). Each student will need blank paper.❷

Today we are going to look at some *Quick Images,* but instead of looking at dot patterns and Ten-frames like we did in our last unit, we are going to look at some shapes. I'd like you to watch carefully because I'm going to show you a shape for just a few seconds. Then I'll hide it, and you will try to draw the shape you just saw.

Show a square (Shape F) for about five seconds and then turn off the projector to hide the shape. Ask students to quickly sketch what they saw. After students have put their pencils down, show them the shape for another five seconds and ask them to look carefully again. They can then revise their shapes based on their second look. Finally, turn on the projector and leave the image visible while students make any final revisions.

Students identify attributes of 2-D shapes by viewing Quick Images.

What did you notice about the shape? [Holly] says it's a square. Who can say more about that? How would you describe this shape?❸

Teaching Note

❶ **Showing** *Quick Images* *Quick Images* is designed for use with an overhead projector. However, if none is available, you can sketch the shape on the board or on chart paper and then cover it or flip the paper over to hide the image.

Professional Development

❷ **Teacher Note:** 2-Dimensional Materials in This Unit, p. 147

❸ **Teacher Note:** Identifying Types of 2-Dimensional Shapes, p. 148

▲ **Resource Masters, M1–M4; T15–T18**

Math Note

❹ Types of Angles Geometric shapes can have three types of angles: acute, obtuse, and right. In this unit, students are introduced to right angles. Students are not formally introduced to the terminology for obtuse and acute angles until Grades 4 and 5, but they should be beginning to notice that the angles are an important feature of a geometric shape. Second graders are likely to refer to the different types of angles in the following ways: pointy (acute), like an L (a right angle), or open wide (obtuse).

After students describe the shape, ask them about its number of sides (if they have not discussed that yet). If they have not discussed the angles —or "corners" as students typically call them—ask about that.❹

Repeat the same procedure with a triangle (Shape B). When students have finished drawing, ask the same questions again.

Next, try a somewhat more difficult shape, perhaps the trapezoid (Shape E) or the right triangle (Shape R). Then ask some more detailed questions.

What did you notice the first time you saw the shape? Could you remember the whole shape? What happened when you saw the shape the second time? Did that help you add anything or change anything?

Before going on to the next activity, display a few more shapes on the overhead and ask students what they know about them. Do not do *Quick Images;* just show the shapes individually. This will give you a chance to assess which shapes students recognize and which shape names they know. It will also give you an opportunity to talk about the number of sides and the size of angles.

Ask students what is similar about all the shapes they have seen so far.

Students might say that they all have straight sides or they all have corners or angles. If no one mentions it, point out that they are all closed; they do not have any openings.

All of the shapes we have been looking at are closed shapes with straight sides, and they all have corners or angles. Mathematicians have a name for these types of shapes. They are called polygons. *Polygon means "a shape with many sides."*

DIFFERENTIATION: Supporting the Range of Learners

ELL To help English Language Learners follow and participate in these whole-class discussions, you can meet with a small group ahead of time to preview vocabulary such as *shape, rectangle, square, triangle, trapezoid, corner, angle, side, prism, cube,* and *face.* (See Differentiation in This Unit on page 18.)

ACTIVITY

② Looking Closely at Geoblocks

Post the "Describing Geoblocks" chart. Draw a rectangle on the board.

For the next few weeks, we are going to be working on geometry. Does anyone have an idea about what geometry is? What types of activities might we be doing? What kinds of materials do you think we might use?

Point to the rectangle that you just drew and hold up the large rectangular prism, Geoblock K.

I have drawn a rectangle on the board. This block that I'm holding is called a prism. How are the rectangle and the prism different?

Students might say:

 "The rectangle is flat."

 "The prism pops up, and you can hold it."

Sometimes we will be working with flat shapes like the rectangle. They are called two-dimensional shapes. Other times we will be using solid objects like the Geoblocks. They are called three-dimensional shapes.

Pass around a set of Geoblocks and have each student take out one block and examine it carefully. Ask students to describe one attribute of their block. List these on the "Describing Geoblocks" chart.

Professional Development

⑤ **Teacher Note:** Identifying Types of 3-Dimensional Shapes, p. 150

Describing Geoblocks
Made of wood

Cube

Pyramid

Smooth

When mathematicians talk about a three-dimensional object, such as a Geoblock, they call the side of the block a face.⑤ When you put your block down on the floor or a table, it sits on one of its faces. What do you notice about a face of your Geoblock? When you touch a face of a block with the palm of your hand, what does it feel like?

Students are likely to notice that the faces of the blocks are flat or smooth. If you have not listed this attribute on the chart paper, add it now.

The shape of a face is an important feature of a block. What shapes are the faces on your block?

The shapes of the faces of all the Geoblocks are triangles and rectangles (of which some are squares). The Geoblock shapes have either five or six faces.

In our work with geometry, we are going to be thinking a lot about the shapes of the faces of Geoblocks and the number of faces that the different Geoblocks have. Count the faces on your block. How many faces does it have?

Record the different numbers on the board. Some students might have difficulty keeping track of the number of faces on their block, so ask a couple of students to share their strategies for keeping track as they count.

Sort the blocks by the number of faces. Ask students whose blocks have the same number of faces to stand together. Have them look at other blocks in their group to make sure that the blocks all have the same number of faces.

Besides having the same number of faces, is there anything else that you notice about the blocks that are in your group? Compare the shapes of the faces of your blocks. What do you notice?

Students are likely to notice that all of the blocks with five faces have two triangular faces. They might notice that the remaining three faces are rectangular. All of these students will be holding triangular prisms. Use this opportunity to introduce the term *triangular prism* to students and record this on the chart.

Those of you who are holding shapes with six faces noticed that the faces of your blocks are squares or rectangles. These blocks are called rectangular prisms. Does anyone have a rectangular prism with only square faces? Does anyone know the special name of this shape? It is called a cube. A cube is a special kind of rectangular prism. All of its faces are squares. If you have a cube, hold it up so that everyone can see it.❻

Ask students to return to their tables or seats for the final activity of this session. They should keep the Geoblock that they have been working with.

ONGOING ASSESSMENT: Observing Students at Work

Students explore and describe the features of 3-D shapes.

- **How do students describe the Geoblocks?** Do they comment on important features of the shape, such as the shape of the faces and the number of sides and vertices?

- **Are students able to identify other blocks with similar and different features?**

ACTIVITY

③ Drawing Geoblocks

15 MIN INDIVIDUALS CLASS

Give each student a sheet of blank paper.

You have been looking very closely at your Geoblock. For this final activity, you are going to try to draw your block so that it doesn't look flat. Try to make it look like a 3-D shape. See whether you can draw it in a way that helps us see more than just one face. Then we'll look at some of the pictures and see whether we get some ideas about how to make our drawings look more realistic.

Reassure students that this kind of drawing is rather difficult and that you are all going to be experimenting to see how to make a picture of a 3-D block not look flat. Students will have other opportunities to draw Geoblocks during Math Workshop in subsequent sessions.❼

Teaching Notes

❻ **Names of 3-D Shapes** While the names for these 3-D shapes can seem cumbersome at first, it is important for students to begin to hear them in natural ways as they relate to the tasks they are working on. It is not expected that students will be able to define these 3-D shapes. However, through their work in this unit, they will attend to the important features of these shapes as they draw, sort, and construct them.

❼ **Drawing Shapes** Many factors affect how well students can represent their Geoblocks on paper. Students' fine motor skills are developing in different ways, and some are simply more skilled at or more interested in drawing than others. Another factor is students' care in observing the characteristics of the three-dimensional blocks. The mathematics work in these sessions focuses on observing, describing, and comparing three-dimensional shapes. As you work with students, keep the emphasis on this careful observation and description, rather than on drawing skill.

▲ Student Activity Book, p. 1

▲ Student Activity Book, p. 2

When most students have a completed picture of their Geoblock, ask them to share their work and say what was easy or hard for them while drawing the block. Ask them to describe what it means to make something look three-dimensional on paper. Students often offer comments that to make something look three-dimensional on paper means that it pops out at you, it doesn't look flat, or it looks like something you can hold.

Encourage them to describe what it is like to draw something that is three-dimensional on a flat surface and what they did to try to make it look three-dimensional.

What did you notice about your block that helped you draw it?

You will find a wide range in students' drawings and explanations. The goal here is not to improve drawing skills—although that will happen for some students—but to observe and describe three-dimensional objects.

ONGOING ASSESSMENT: Observing Students at Work

Students attend to important features of shape while making a two-dimensional representation of a three-dimensional block construction.

- **Do students' drawings contain the two-dimensional shapes of each of the faces of the block?**

- **Is there any attempt to draw the block from different angles?**

- **Are you—or another student—able to identify the block by looking at the drawing?**

SESSION FOLLOW-UP

4 Daily Practice and Homework

 Daily Practice: For ongoing review, have students complete *Student Activity Book* page 1.

 Homework: Students find and record objects in their surroundings that have a face that matches one of the shapes on *Student Activity Book* page 2.

 Student Math Handbook: Students and families may use *Student Math Handbook* pages 112, 116, 122, 123, 124–125 for reference and review. See pages 178–182 in the back of this unit.

 Family Letter: Send home copies of the Family Letter (M5–M6).

Working with Geoblocks

Math Focus Points

◆ Attending to features of 3-D shapes, particularly the number and shape of faces

◆ Drawing 3-D shapes

◆ Developing fluency with the doubles combinations to 10 + 10

Today's Plan			Materials
ACTIVITY **❶ Introducing Find the Block**	🕐 10 MIN	👥 CLASS	• M7–M12*; T19*, Card 1 🖥 • Five Geoblocks, including Geoblock D; Find the Block stations*
ACTIVITY **❷ Introducing the *Shapes* Software: *Free Explore* (optional)**	👥 PAIRS	👥 CLASS	• Computers with *Shapes* software installed (optional)*
MATH WORKSHOP **❸ Blocks and Doubles** **❸A Find the Block** **❸B Drawing Geoblocks** **❸C Double Arrays** **❸D *Shapes* Software: *Free Explore* (optional)**	🕐 50 MIN		**3A** • Find the Block Task Cards • Geoblocks from Session 1.1; Find the Block stations **3B** • M13* • Geoblocks from Session 1.1 **3C** • M14*; M15* (as needed) • Primary Number Cards **3D** • Computers with *Shapes* software installed (optional)
SESSION FOLLOW-UP **❹ Daily Practice**			• *Student Activity Book,* p. 3 • *Student Math Handbook,* pp. 47, 116, 122, 123, 124–125

*See *Materials to Prepare,* p. 21.

Classroom Routines

Today's Number: 10 Using Subtraction Students write numerical expressions for the number 10 using only subtraction. Depending on the expressions generated, students may notice and use certain patterns that are apparent in expressions such as 20 — 10, 30 — 20, and so on, or 13 — 3, 17 — 7, 25 — 15, and so on.

▲ **Resource Masters, M7; T19**

1 Introducing Find the Block

10 MIN CLASS

In Find the Block, students match a Geoblock to its 2-D image.

Display five Geoblocks—including Geoblock D, the large cube—so that everyone can see them. Then hold up Task Card 1 from Find the Block Task Cards (M7) or display its transparency (T19).

Yesterday, we looked very closely at the faces of the Geoblocks. Take a look at this card. This card shows all the faces of one Geoblock, and was made by tracing around each face. Can you figure out by looking at this card how many faces or sides the Geoblock had?

In addition to noticing the number of sides, ask students to describe the shape of the faces on the block. Then, using this information, ask them to select the Geoblock that Task Card 1 represents.

Once the correct block has been chosen, show students how every face of the block can be matched to one of the outlines on the card. Show students some of the Task Cards for this activity. Clarify for students that each card represents only one block.

This activity is called Find the Block. In Math Workshop, you will work with a partner to Find the Block.

There can be four students at each station. Each station has Geoblocks and two decks of Task Cards. One pair will work with Task Cards 1–6 (M7–M9) and the other will work with Task Cards 7–12 (M10–M12).

Decide with your partner which card to work on and try to find the block that matches that card. Once you have each found a block, compare them and then prove to each other that yours is the correct block by showing how each side matches the outlines on the card.

Students find the block that matches a set of faces.

Each pair of students should find the blocks for at least one deck of six Task Cards. Be sure to emphasize that one block matches all the face outlines on a card.

DIFFERENTIATION: Supporting the Range of Learners

ELL To participate in the following activity and to complete the homework assignment, students need to understand the word *face* as used in relation to three-dimensional shapes. English Language Learners might or might not know other meanings of the word (e.g., a human face, the face of a clock). It would be helpful to review each of the meanings, so English Language Learners will not be confused when they hear the word used in other contexts.

ACTIVITY

PAIRS   CLASS

2 Introducing the *Shapes* Software: *Free Explore* (optional)

One of the math tools that we will be using during our geometry unit is the computer. How many of you have ever used a computer before? What types of activities do you do on the computer?

▲ **Resource Masters, M8–M9**

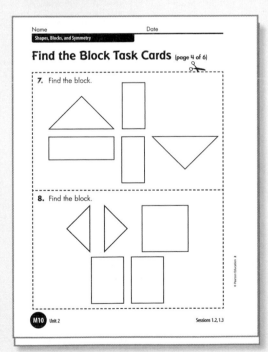

▲ **Resource Masters, M10–M12**

❶ Working with the *Shapes* Software. For a complete description and instructions about the *Shapes* software, see the *Software Support Reference Guide* contained in your curriculum unit package. Some students may have worked with the *Shapes* software in previous years. If so, they may be able to help their peers learn how to use the software.

❷ Assisting Students with Computer Tasks Many students who are using computers and the *Shapes* software for the first time will need assistance. Most of their questions can be handled with short answers or simple demonstrations. For example, some students may not be aware of how to use the mouse. Often students who are more familiar with computers can assist those who need help. Encourage students to experiment to see whether they can figure out what they need to do, and then encourage them to share what they have found out with one another and with you. It is not unusual for students to discover things about the software that the teacher does not know.

❺ Sets of Geoblocks If you have divided the set of Geoblocks into three subsets, there should be enough in each subset for four students. Find the Block will use two subsets and Drawing Geoblocks will use one subset. You may want to identify separate work areas that are not too close together so that the sets do not get mixed.

❸ Teacher Note: Introducing and Managing the *Shapes* Software, p. 152

❹ Teacher Note: About the Math in the *Shapes* Software, p. 155

To introduce the *Shapes* program, tell them that they work with a partner and will build pictures and designs with *Shapes* just the way they did with pattern blocks in the previous unit. For this introduction, demonstrate each of the following on the computer:

- How to open *Shapes* by double-clicking on the icon (CD-ROM version) or going to the Web site and logging in (Web version).

- How to open the *Free Explore* activity by clicking on it once.

- How to get Pattern Block shapes from the *Shapes* palette and place them in the drawing window. If students want to use the Power Polygons™ or Tangrams shape sets, they can press the arrow to the right of the palette and select another shape set.

- How to slide shapes by dragging them. Point out that they snap into position when their corners are close if the Magnet tool is "on."

- How to turn shapes with the two Turn tools. Point out that you can change the size of the turn with the pull-down palette.

- How to use the Eraser tool to erase one shape at a time and the Broom tool to erase all of the shapes.

Immediately following your introduction, give students time to use *Free Explore* in the *Shapes* software ❶ to make their own pictures or designs.❷ You can introduce more of the tools available in *Shapes* as students indicate the need for them.❸ ❹

MATH WORKSHOP

③ Blocks and Doubles

50 MIN

Students are familiar with the Find the Block activity and the Drawing Geoblocks activity.❺ They will also work on Double Arrays—introduced in the previous unit—to extend their work with doubling numbers and in preparation for the doubles addition combinations, which will be assessed at the end of this unit. In the next session, students will receive a set of Doubles Combination Cards to add to their Addition Combination Cards.

③A Find the Block

PAIRS

Students work in pairs to match a Geoblock to the face outlines on a Task Card. For complete details, see Activity 1 in this session.

ONGOING ASSESSMENT: Observing Students at Work

Students use features of a three-dimensional shape to match a Geoblock to a two-dimensional representation.

- **Can students identify one block that has faces that match the outlines on the card?** Do students understand that each card represents one block?

- **Do students use a trial and error approach or do they identify the shapes of faces and then look for blocks that match that information?**

DIFFERENTIATION: Supporting the Range of Learners

Intervention Some students may need help in understanding that each card represents one block. Initially, some students may benefit from working with an even smaller subset of blocks.

Intervention If students are having difficulty understanding the task, consider selecting the blocks that match Task Cards 1–6 (M7–M9) and seeing whether the student can match the correct block to each card.

Extension Some students may be adept at "seeing" the block by just looking at its two-dimensional image. Show these students a Task Card and see whether they can describe what features the block will have.

Students might say:

"It has five faces. Three are rectangles and two are triangles."

⑥ **Drawing in 3-D** When students first try to draw block constructions, most will draw a picture that looks two-dimensional. Many students draw the faces of blocks they can see in one view of the building. Students vary in their ability to draw the shapes of the block faces they see. Some are very careful to draw squares, rectangles, and triangles that are very close in shape to the faces of the blocks, but others have some difficulty drawing these shapes or showing how the blocks go together. Some may even show the outline of the whole construction without showing individual blocks.

Encourage these students to carefully identify the shapes of the faces on the individual blocks, as well as how the blocks come together. Although these drawing tasks can be challenging for some, students do become more aware of the different-shaped faces of three-dimensional objects, and how these faces are connected to make a solid object.

▲ **Resource Masters, M13**

3B Drawing Geoblocks

INDIVIDUALS

Students build small constructions with two–three Geoblocks and then draw what they have built as accurately as they can on Drawing Geoblocks (M13).⑥ Encourage students to draw their construction from more than one angle.

Sample Student Work

Sample Student Work

Sample Student Work

Name _____ Date _____
Shapes, Blocks, and Symmetry

Double Arrays
Pick a card. Double the number. Color that many
squares. Write an equation.

I picked a 3.   3 + 3 = 6

M14 Unit 2   Sessions 1.2, 1.3, 2.4, 2.5

▲ **Resource Masters, M14**

ONGOING ASSESSMENT: Observing Students at Work

Students attend to important features of the shape while making a two-dimensional representation of a three-dimensional block construction.

- **Do students' drawings contain the two-dimensional shapes of each block face they used?**

- **Is there any attempt to draw the construction from different angles?**

- **Are you (or another student) able to reconstruct the block construction by looking at the drawing?**

DIFFERENTIATION: Supporting the Range of Learners

Intervention If some students are having difficulty drawing in 3-D, you might want to ask them about the shapes of the faces and where they see them. For instance, does the student see that there is a triangle in front and a rectangle on the side?

3C Double Arrays

PAIRS

Students draw a Primary Number Card from the pile and color in that number of squares in one row on the Double Arrays (M14) grid. They then double that number and color in the same number of squares in a second row directly underneath. They record an equation that illustrates the double (e.g., $4 + 4 = 8$).

⑦ Saving Pictures Saving pictures is only possible when you use the CD-ROM version of *Shapes* and have room on a hard drive. Printing is only possible when you are connected to a working printer. Test these features on your own before trying to use them with students.

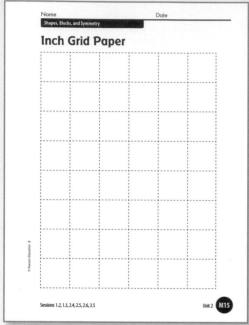

Name _____ Date _____
Shapes, Blocks, and Symmetry

Inch Grid Paper

Sessions 1.2, 1.3, 2.4, 2.5, 2.6, 3.5   Unit 2 **M15**

▲ **Resource Masters, M15**

ONGOING ASSESSMENT: Observing Students at Work

Students practice doubling numbers. This activity also provides a first experience with seeing doubling as an array of two equal groups (multiplication).

- **Are students able to accurately draw an array with double the number of squares that are on the card?**

- **How do students calculate the double of a number?** Do they count all? Count on? Use combinations they know? Do they "just know" some or all of the doubles combinations? Are they accurate?

- **Can students write an equation that represents the array they have drawn?**

DIFFERENTIATION: Supporting the Range of Learners

Intervention Some students will need larger-sized grids or Inch Grid Paper (M15). Others will benefit from building the doubles with cubes or tiles, rather than coloring them.

Extension Challenge students who are ready to name the double after they pick the card, but before they color the grid paper.

③ᴰ *Shapes* Software: *Free Explore* (optional) 👥 **PAIRS**

Students use the *Free Explore* option of the *Shapes* software to create pattern block designs on the computer screen. As you observe, ask students to describe what they are doing. Talk to them about the way they are moving the shapes—sliding them and using the Turn, and possibly, the Flip tools. This will help them become more aware of these geometric motions. And, equally important, it will help them become familiar with seeing shapes in different orientations and realize that changing the orientation of a shape does not affect its name or attributes.

If students do not have time to complete their design in one session, show them how to save their pictures. You might have students walk around to view one another's work so they can see a range of possibilities. Students who complete their work may want to print their final design.⑦

ONGOING ASSESSMENT: Observing Students at Work

Students experiment with geometric motions (moving, turning, and flipping), to see how shapes fit together, and to gain experience with the idea that changing a shape's orientation does not change the shape's name or attributes.

- **How do students decide what shapes to select?** Do they select shapes randomly? Do they begin to plan what shapes they need for their design and select these deliberately?

- **Once a shape has been moved onto the screen, can students figure out how to move it into position?** When a shape is in the right position but has the wrong orientation, can they see that it needs to be turned? Do they begin to visualize how they will have to move and turn a shape to add it to their design in the way they want?

SESSION FOLLOW-UP

Daily Practice

 Daily Practice: For reinforcement of this unit's content, have students complete *Student Activity Book* page 3.

 Student Math Handbook: Students and families may use *Student Math Handbook* pages 47, 116, 122, 123, 124–125 for reference and review. See pages 178–182 in the back of this unit.

Name _____ Date _____
Shapes, Blocks, and Symmetry   Daily Practice

The Match Game
Match the 3-D block to the 2-D face.

NOTE Students practice identifying the 2-D faces of 3-D shapes.
SMH 122

1.
2.
3.
4.

Ongoing Review

5. How many sides does a cube have?
   (A) 4   (B) 5   (C) 6   (D) 8

Session 1.2   Unit 2 3

▲ **Student Activity Book, p. 3**

Sorting Geoblocks

Math Focus Points

◆ Describing attributes of and sorting 3-D shapes

◆ Identifying a 3-D shape by touch

Today's Plan		Materials
ACTIVITY **① Sorting Geoblocks**	20 MIN PAIRS CLASS	• Set of Geoblocks; 11" x 17" paper; self-stick notes ; chart paper
ACTIVITY **② Introducing Mystery Block**	5 MIN CLASS	• Paper bag, cloth bag, or sock; Geoblocks
MATH WORKSHOP **③ Blocks and Doubles** 3A Mystery Block 3B Find the Block 3C Drawing Geoblocks 3D Double Arrays 3E *Shapes* Software: *Free Explore* (optional)	35 MIN	3A • Materials from Activity 2 3B • Materials from Session 1.2, p. 31 3C • Materials from Session 1.1, p. 24 3D • Materials from Session 1.2, p. 31 3E • Computers with *Shapes* software installed
SESSION FOLLOW-UP **④ Daily Practice**		• *Student Activity Book*, p. 4 • *Student Math Handbook*, pp. 116, 124–125

Classroom Routines

How Many Pockets? At some point outside of math time, collect Pocket Data. Remind students of the data collected previously. Ask them to predict whether the class is wearing more, fewer, or about the same number of pockets today. Then each student takes as many cubes as they have pockets. Discuss different ways to count the cubes (e.g., by 5s or 10s). Use one suggestion to count the cubes, and another to double-check the count. Record the data on your class chart.

Professional Development

❶ **Teacher Note:** Identifying Types of 3-Dimensional Shapes, p. 150

ACTIVITY

① Sorting Geoblocks

20 MIN   PAIRS   CLASS

Call the class together in a circle. Pass a set of Geoblocks around and have each student take one block.

Look at your block. Describe your block to the person sitting next to you, and then listen while your partner tells you about his or her block. How are your blocks alike? How are they different?

Provide time for students to describe their blocks and then call the class together. Ask one student to stand, hold up his or her block, and describe one of its attributes. Other students should hold up their blocks if the statement is also true for theirs.

[Jeffrey], tell us one thing about your block. Now, everyone else look at your block. Is the statement [Jeffrey] made about his block also true for your block? If so, hold up your block.

Students may describe their blocks in imprecise ways. Comments from second graders include:

"My block is smooth"; "My block is pointy"; and "My block is a square."

Students at this age have not developed much vocabulary for describing three-dimensional geometric shapes. The purpose of this activity is for them to begin to examine the blocks and look at different attributes of the set, rather than to learn the correct terminology. Students will begin to use the correct terminology over a long period of time as they use shapes and see a need for more precise language.❶

Place one $8\frac{1}{2}'' \times 11''$ sheet of paper and two $11'' \times 17''$ sheets in the center of the circle. Label one $11'' \times 17''$ sheet, "Match" and the other, "Don't Match."

I would like a volunteer to put his or her block on the small paper and then tell us one thing that you notice about your block.

Students might say:

"My block has square faces."

"My block has six corners."

If necessary, ask the student to clarify the description. On a self-stick note, write the word that describes the attribute and place it on the small paper next to the block.

The rest of the students determine whether the statement also applies to their blocks. They then place their blocks on either the "Match" or "Don't Match" sheet. Students examine both sets to see whether the blocks are correctly placed and then take back their blocks.

Have different students try this several more times. Notice the attributes students suggest and know that there will be times when everyone's block will match the attribute; for example, "My block has corners" or "My block is smooth."

At the end of the activity, attach the notes to chart paper to begin a list of descriptive words. You can add more attributes as students continue to use Geoblocks.

ONGOING ASSESSMENT: Observing Students at Work

Students sort three-dimensional shapes by different attributes.

- **Do students suggest geometric attributes, such as the number or shape of faces or do they focus on such attributes as "made of wood"?**

- **Do students suggest attributes that differentiate the blocks, such as the number or shape of faces?**

ACTIVITY

2 Introducing Mystery Block

5 MIN   CLASS

In Math Workshop, students will work with a partner and take turns choosing, hiding, and identifying a mystery block. Introduce this activity by asking two volunteers to demonstrate.

While one partner's back is turned, the other chooses a block and puts it in a bag. The first partner then reaches in the bag without looking, feels the block, and describes at least three of its attributes. Then he or she finds an identical block in the set.

Students name block attributes in the activity
Mystery Block.

DIFFERENTIATION: Supporting the Range of Learners

ELL The language-based nature of this activity may be challenging for English Language Learners. Meet with a small group during Math Workshop to preview the activity. Begin by modeling the activity yourself. Ask a student to place a block in the bag. Reach in and describe how the block feels. *This block feels small. It has a lot of corners. Let me see if I can count them . . . one, two, three . . . I wonder how many faces it has . . . one, two, three . . .* Write the attributes on a piece of chart paper and repeat them aloud as you look for the matching block. *Hmm . . . I'm looking for a small block with eight corners and six faces. Can anyone help me find it?* When you find the matching cube, point to the relevant features as you review the attributes again. Then have English Language Learners play the game in pairs, providing them with English-language vocabulary as needed.

MATH WORKSHOP

3 Blocks and Doubles

35 MIN

Students spend the remainder of the session on Math Workshop activities. Students who are working on the Mystery Block activity can borrow blocks from one of the other two Geoblock activities.

If students have not worked with the Find the Block Task Cards, they should do so by the end of today's session.

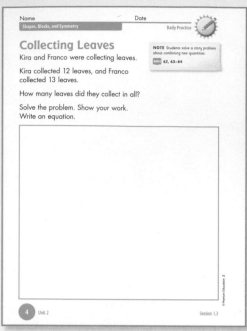

Name _____ Date _____
Shapes, Blocks, and Symmetry   Daily Practice

Collecting Leaves
Kira and Franco were collecting leaves.

Kira collected 12 leaves, and Franco
collected 13 leaves.

How many leaves did they collect in all?

Solve the problem. Show your work.
Write an equation.

NOTE Students solve a story problem
about combining two quantities.
Steps 62, 63–64

4 Unit 2   Session 1.3

▲ **Student Activity Book, p. 4**

3A Mystery Block

For complete details about Mystery Block, see Activity 2 and consider the following notes.

ONGOING ASSESSMENT: Observing Students at Work

Students identify a three-dimensional shape by touch.

- **Are students able to find a matching block without looking at the block in the bag?**

- **Do they need to confirm their match by looking at the blocks?** Does this seem easy or difficult?

- **Which geometric attributes do students name?** Do students suggest the number or shape of faces?

3B Find the Block

For complete details about this activity, see Session 1.2, page 32.

3C Drawing Geoblocks

For complete details about this activity, see Session 1.1, page 29.

3D Double Arrays

For complete details about this activity, see Session 1.2, page 37.

3E *Shapes* Software: *Free Explore* (optional)

For complete details about this activity, see Session 1.2, pages 33–34.

SESSION FOLLOW-UP
4 Daily Practice

Daily Practice: For ongoing review, have students complete *Student Activity Book* page 4.

Student Math Handbook: Students and families may use *Student Math Handbook* pages 116, 124–125 for reference and review. See pages 178–182 in the back of this unit.

Addition Combinations and Ways to Fill

Math Focus Points

◆ Reviewing known addition combinations (combinations of 10, Plus 1, Plus 2)

◆ Developing fluency with the doubles combinations to 10 + 10

◆ Covering a region, without gaps or overlaps, using different shapes

◆ Combining shapes to make a new shape

Today's Plan		Materials
ACTIVITY ❶ **Addition Combinations: Doubles**	20 MIN INDIVIDUALS	• M19* • "Combinations I Know" and "Combinations I'm Still Working" envelopes (from Unit 1)
ACTIVITY ❷ **Ways to Fill**	25 MIN INDIVIDUALS GROUPS	• M20*; T21–T22 • Overhead pattern blocks (optional); pattern blocks
DISCUSSION ❸ **Combining Shapes**	15 MIN CLASS	• M20; T21–T22 • Overhead pattern blocks (optional); pattern blocks; chart paper
SESSION FOLLOW-UP ❹ **Daily Practice**		• *Student Activity Book*, p. 5 • *Student Math Handbook*, pp. 43, 47, 114

*See *Materials to Prepare*, p. 23.

Classroom Routines

What Time Is It? Write 2:00 on the board and ask pairs to set their clocks to that time.

Introduce students to the half hour by asking:

• What would the clock look like if the minute hand went half way around the clock or 30 minutes past 2:00?

Write 2:30 on the board.

Show students Analog and Digital: 2:30 (T20). Briefly discuss the representation of 2:30 on both clocks. Repeat with 1:30, 6:30, and 12:30. In pairs, students set their clocks to 30 minutes past the hour and look at the the hands' arrangement.

Teaching Note

❶ Practicing Doubles Combinations In the previous unit, students were assessed on their fluency with the Combinations of 10, Plus 1, and Plus 2 Addition Combinations. At the end of this unit, students should be fluent with the Doubles Combinations as well. In addition to this practice session, students play Double Arrays during Math Workshop and work with doubles in several Classroom Routines. In Investigation 3, they will also work with doubling as they investigate symmetry. Students should practice all of their Addition Combinations for short periods of time throughout this unit.

Shapes, Blocks, and Symmetry

Analog and Digital: 2:30

▲ Transparencies, T20

20 MIN INDIVIDUALS

❶ Addition Combinations: Doubles

Hand out one set of Addition Cards Set 2: Doubles Combinations (M19) to each student.❶ Students should write their initials on the back of each card, but remind them *not* to write the answers on the cards.

I'd like you to get out your envelopes that have the Addition Combination Cards that we've been working on. Take a few minutes to go through each envelope. Start with the "Combinations I Know" group. Review them to make sure you still know them. Then look through the "Combinations I'm Still Working On" group and see whether you now know any of those.

Students are likely to recognize and know many of these combinations from the doubling games that they have been playing in this and the previous unit.

ONGOING ASSESSMENT: Observing Students at Work

Observe and informally check in with students as they go through the cards in their "Combinations I Know" and "Combinations I'm Still Working On" envelopes.

- **Have students retained fluency with the combinations in the "Combinations I Know" envelope?**

- **Are students familiar with any of the doubles facts?**

DIFFERENTIATION: Supporting the Range of Learners

Intervention If students are still having difficulty with the combinations of 10 and the Plus 1 and Plus 2 facts, they may benefit from playing games such as *Make 10, Tens Go Fish,* or *Plus 1* and *Plus 2 Bingo* that were introduced in the previous unit.

Additionally, try to find time to work with small groups of students on adding clues to their Combination Cards. For example, a clue for a Plus 2 fact such as 9 + 2 might be, "9, 10, 11." Explain to the students that when they add 1 or 2, they are counting up from one number.

ACTIVITY
② Ways to Fill

25 MIN INDIVIDUALS GROUPS

Distribute a set of pattern blocks to each table or group.❷ Give each student a copy of Ways to Fill: Pattern 1 (M20–M21) and place the transparencies (T21–T22) on the overhead.

Look at the outline at the top of the page. How many sides does this shape have?

Do not spend a long time on this question, but see whether students are able to count the number of sides of this shape *(ten)*.

Try to fill in this shape using one type of pattern-block shape. For example, try to fill it with only triangles or only trapezoids. After you have filled it with only one type of block, record how many blocks you used and their type in the space labeled "Use 1 type of pattern block." Since you will be filling in the shape again using a different type of block, make sure you leave space to write in more information.❸

Students fill in the outline several ways—using only one type of pattern block at a time—and record the ways that work. They then move on to using two shapes to fill the outline and again record the number and type of shapes they use. They will continue to work on this and another similar sheet during the next session. After most students have finished filling the outline with one shape, call the class together for a discussion.

Students fill an outline with pattern blocks.

Professional Development

❷ **Teacher Note:** 2-Dimensional Materials in This Unit, p. 147

Math Note

❸ **Ways to Fill** The outlines on these *Student Activity Book* pages can be filled using the hexagon, the trapezoid, the triangle, and the blue rhombus. They cannot be filled using the square or the tan rhombus.

Name _____ Date _____

Shapes, Blocks, and Symmetry

Addition Cards Set 2: Doubles Combinations

3 + 3 =	7 + 7 =
Clue: _____	Clue: _____
4 + 4 =	8 + 8 =
Clue: _____	Clue: _____
5 + 5 =	9 + 9 =
Clue: _____	Clue: _____
6 + 6 =	10 + 10 =
Clue: _____	Clue: _____

Session 1.4   Unit 2 M19

▲ **Resource Masters, M19**

Math Note

❹ Relationships Among Shapes Students are likely to notice the relationship among some of the pattern block shapes, such as two trapezoids making one hexagon. They will continue to work with this relationship in Unit 5, *How Many Floors? How Many Rooms?*, later in the year.

Name _____ Date _____

Shapes, Blocks, and Symmetry

Ways to Fill: Pattern 1 (page 1 of 2)

Use different types of pattern blocks to fill the shape. Record your work.

Use 1 type of pattern block.

Use 2 types of pattern blocks.

M20 Unit 2   Sessions 1.4, 1.5

▲ **Resource Masters, M20; T21**

ONGOING ASSESSMENT: Observing Students at Work

Students fill an outline in different ways as they begin to notice how combinations of shapes make other shapes and how pattern-block shapes are related.

- **Do students notice relationships among the various blocks?** For example, do they see that they can replace one hexagon with two trapezoids, or with a trapezoid and three triangles?

- **Do students see that some shapes (the square and thin rhombus) will not fit on the patterns no matter how they are arranged?**

- **Do students have a recording method that is accurate and easy to understand?**

DIFFERENTIATION: Supporting the Range of Learners

Intervention Some students may need clarification about what it means to "use two types of blocks" to fill the specified outline. Demonstrate by selecting two shapes—a triangle and rhombus. Ask students to fill the outline using only those shapes.

DISCUSSION

3 Combining Shapes

15 MIN   CLASS

Math Focus Points for Discussion

◆ Combining shapes to make a new shape

Begin the discussion by asking students to share the ways that they filled Pattern 1 (M20) with only one type of pattern block. Record these on the board or on the Pattern 1 transparency (T21) using the names of the shapes, such as two hexagons, four trapezoids, etc.

Once students think that they have shared all the ways, ask them to explain why they think these combinations are possible.

*You all seem to agree that we can fill the outline only four ways when we use one type of pattern block. That's with two yellow hexagons, four red trapezoids, six blue rhombuses, or 12 green triangles. Are you certain there are no other possibilities? Why or why not?*❹

Next, focus on how students recorded their combinations. On chart paper, list the various ways. Some students may have

- Drawn pictures of the blocks and written the amount next to or inside of the shape

- Used a number and the name of the shape, such as two hexagons

- Used abbreviations, such as, "12 T" for 12 triangles or "12 G" for 12 green

Explain to students that in the next session they will continue to work on this activity and that everyone will have a chance to fill the outline using more than one type of block.

SESSION FOLLOW-UP

Daily Practice

 Daily Practice: For reinforcement of this unit's content, have students complete *Student Activity Book* page 5.

 Student Math Handbook: Students and families may use *Student Math Handbook* pages 43, 47, 114 for reference and review. See pages 180–184 in the back of this unit.

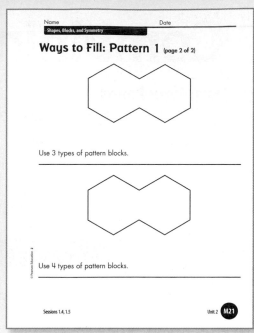

▲ **Resource Masters, M21; T22**

▲ **Student Activity Book, p. 5**

Combining Shapes

Math Focus Points

◆ Combining 3-D shapes to make a 3-D whole

◆ Identifying a 3-D shape by touch

◆ Covering a region, without gaps or overlaps, with a single shape or multiple shapes

◆ Developing fluency with the doubles combinations to 10 + 10

Today's Plan		Materials
ACTIVITY ❶ **Introducing Build the Geoblock** 10 MIN CLASS		• *Student Activity Book,* pp. 6–8 • Geoblock K; Geoblocks
ACTIVITY ❷ *Shapes* **Software: Introducing** *Puzzles* **(optional)** PAIRS CLASS		• Computers with *Shapes* software installed
MATH WORKSHOP ❸ **Combining and Covering** ❸ⓐ **Build the Geoblock** ❸ⓑ **Ways to Fill** ❸ⓒ **Mystery Block** ❸ⓓ *Shapes* Software: *Puzzles* 50 MIN		❸ⓐ • Materials from Activity 1 ❸ⓑ • *Student Activity Book,* pp. 9–10 • Materials from Session 1.4, p. 45 ❸ⓒ • Materials from Session 1.3, p. 40 ❸ⓓ • Computers with *Shapes* software installed
SESSION FOLLOW-UP ❹ **Daily Practice**		• *Student Activity Book,* p. 11 • *Student Math Handbook,* pp. 114, 122, 124–125 • M17–M18*, Family Letter

*See *Materials to Prepare,* p. 23.

Classroom Routines

Quick Images: Drawing Shapes Using the transparent Shape Cards (T15–T18), display Shape D. Follow the basic *Quick Images* activity. Display the shape as students discuss what they saw and describe the attributes of the shape. Repeat with the Shape I and then, Shape T. If time allows, have students compare and contrast the three shape cards.

ACTIVITY

1 Introducing Build the Geoblock

10 MIN   CLASS

Yesterday, when we worked on Ways to Fill, you combined pattern blocks to fill a region. Many of you found that you could combine certain shapes to make other shapes, such as combining two red trapezoids to make a hexagon shape. In the Math Workshop today, you will continue with that activity, but you will also work on combining shapes to make other shapes. This activity is called Build the Geoblock.

Hold up, or place on a table where everyone can see, the rectangular prism, Geoblock K, which is 8 x 4 x 4 cm.

If I could glue Geoblocks together, how could I build a block that is the same size and shape as this one? One way would be to glue these two blocks together.

Hold up two 4 cm cubes (Geoblock D) to show that they could be glued together to make a block the same size and shape as Geoblock K.

Use *Student Activity Book* pages 6–8 to demonstrate how to find the Geoblocks that match the ones shown on the sheets. (The front faces of the Geoblocks fit the drawings.) Explain that students should find the Geoblock that fits each of the three illustrated blocks. They should then determine how many different ways they can combine other Geoblocks to make a block of the same size and shape.

You should try to find at least two ways to make each block. When you find a combination of blocks that works, try to draw the blocks you used. You might trace around one of the faces and then try to make the block look three-dimensional.

Encourage students to use their experience from the Drawing Geoblocks activity to record their work.

ACTIVITY

PAIRS   CLASS

2 *Shapes* Software: Introducing *Puzzles* (optional)

For the *Puzzles* activity in *Shapes,* students are given multiple outlines to fill in different ways, just as they do with the actual pattern blocks. However, on the computer, they need to think more deliberately about how to move, turn, and flip the shapes in order to put them where they want them. The highest two or three levels of *Puzzles* using pattern blocks, Power Polygons™, or tangrams are intended for use in Grade 2. However, students should be encouraged to use any of the puzzles in the sets. Some students may have completed some *Shapes* puzzles during earlier grades.❶

Students who have used *Free Explore* will already be familiar with the tools needed for this activity. In addition to what students learned about the software using *Free Explore,* introduce students to the following:

• How to select *Puzzles* by clicking on it once from the screen of activity choices.

• How to select a shape set, level, and puzzle by clicking on options in the puzzle selection screens.

• How to read the directions, and then click on [OK] or press RETURN.

• How to use the visual and text Hints that are available to help them think of new ways when they are stuck.

• How to select another puzzle when they finish one.

Teaching Note

❶ **Different Block Sets** The *Puzzles* activity in *Shapes* lets students solve puzzles with three different types of blocks: pattern blocks, Power Polygons™, and tangrams. Students should begin the activity using pattern blocks, but feel free to explore the other block sets as they become familiar with the software.

▲ **Student Activity Book, p. 6**

Puzzles do not need to be solved in any order and Puzzles can be solved several ways. If students complete a puzzle one way, they can try the same puzzle again in a new way, or go on to a new puzzle. If your computers are connected to a printer, students could print out their solutions before trying again. Ask students to compare their solutions. How many different ways can they find to solve the same puzzle? Which pieces can substitute for one another to fill a section of the puzzle?

MATH WORKSHOP

3 Combining and Covering

⏱ **50 MIN**

Students can select from the following activities.

3A Build the Geoblock

INDIVIDUALS

For complete details about Build the Geoblock, see Activity 1 in this session and consider the following notes.

ONGOING ASSESSMENT: Observing Students at Work

Observe how students put the blocks together to gain insight into how they perceive three-dimensional shapes.

- **Do students randomly choose smaller blocks and try to build a larger one?**

- **Do they seem to "see" blocks that are half of a block, and put two of them together?**

- **Do they use smaller cubes to build the larger cube?**

- **Are students comfortable with their attempts to draw the blocks they used?** Is it clear from their drawings which blocks they used?

DIFFERENTIATION: Supporting the Range of Learners

Intervention If students are finding it difficult to draw their block combinations, suggest that they put together as many combinations as possible and then show you their work. For some students, drawing the blocks may be such a difficult task that they may be less willing to work on the task of combining them.

▲ **Student Activity Book, p. 7**

▲ **Student Activity Book, p. 8**

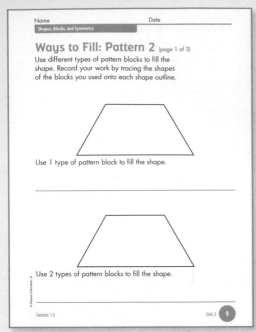

▲ Student Activity Book, p. 9 [PORTFOLIO]

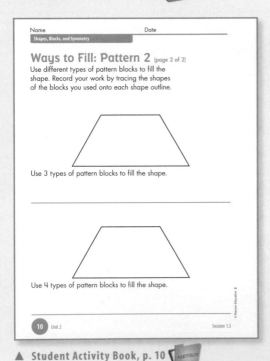

▲ Student Activity Book, p. 10 [PORTFOLIO]

3B Ways to Fill

GROUPS INDIVIDUALS

Students continue filling in the outlines on Ways to Fill: Pattern 1 (M20–M21). When they have finished, students can move on to Ways to Fill: Pattern 2 on *Student Activity Book* pages 9–10. After students find all of the ways to fill a pattern using one type of block, they should try two, three, and four different types.

For complete details about this activity, see Session 1.4, page 47.

Students show ways to fill outlines with pattern blocks.

ONGOING ASSESSMENT: Observing Students at Work

Students use a specified number of blocks to cover a region without gaps or overlaps.

- **Do students notice relationships among the various blocks?** For example, do they see that they can replace one hexagon with two trapezoids, or with a trapezoid and three triangles?

- **Do students see that some shapes (the square and thin rhombus) will not fit on the patterns no matter how they are arranged?**

- **Do students have a recording method that is easy to understand?**

3C Mystery Block

PAIRS

For complete details about this activity, see Session 1.3, pages 42–43.

3D Shapes Software: *Puzzles*

PAIRS

Puzzles on the computer is a variation of the off-computer activity, Ways to Fill. Students are given an outline that they fill with pattern block shapes.

ONGOING ASSESSMENT: Observing Students at Work

As students work with the software, they will become better at thinking about and imagining spatial relationships and transformations.

- **Do students notice relationships among the various shapes?** For example, when working with pattern blocks, do they see that they can replace one hexagon with two trapezoids or with a trapezoid and three triangles?

- **Do students see that some shapes will not fill a region no matter how they are arranged?**

SESSION FOLLOW-UP

4 Daily Practice

 Daily Practice: For reinforcement of this unit's content, have students complete *Student Activity Book* page 11.

 Student Math Handbook: Students and families may use *Student Math Handbook* pages 114, 122, 124–125 for reference and review. See pages 178–182 in the back of this unit.

 Family Letter: Send home copies of the Family Letter (M17–M18).

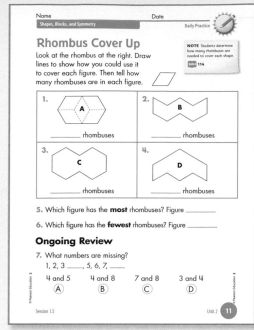

▲ **Student Activity Book, p. 11**

Mathematical Emphases

Features of Shape Describing, identifying, comparing, and sorting 2-dimensional and 3-dimensional shapes

Math Focus Points

◆ Describing attributes of and sorting 2-D shapes

◆ Identifying categories for 2-D shapes

◆ Sorting polygons by the number of sides

◆ Sorting quadrilaterals by angle

◆ Identifying quadrilaterals as shapes with 4 sides

◆ Identifying rectangles as 4-sided shapes with 4 right angles

◆ Defining *biggest* in different ways

◆ Ordering rectangles from biggest to smallest

◆ Identifying important features of a rectangle

◆ Recognizing that rectangular prisms have rectangular faces

◆ Recognizing which faces of a rectangular prism are the same size and shape

◆ Constructing a rectangular prism from rectangles

◆ Comparing rectangular prisms

◆ Visualizing and describing rectangular prisms

Area Measurement Visualizing the structure of arrays

Math Focus Points

◆ Covering rectangles with arrays of tiles

◆ Arranging square tiles in rectangular arrays

◆ Constructing and describing rectangular arrays of tiles

◆ Drawing rectangles by attending to the lengths of the sides

◆ Making different rectangular arrays using the same number of tiles

Computational Fluency Knowing addition combinations to $10 + 10$

Math Focus Points

◆ Developing fluency with the doubles combinations to $10 + 10$

What Is a Rectangle?

SESSION 2.1 p. 62	Student Activity Book	Student Math Handbook	Professional Development: Read Ahead of Time
Assessment: Sorting Shapes by Number of Sides Students describe shapes from a set of Shape Cards and group shapes that have the same attributes. They sort the cards in different ways and discuss their categories, and then sort them by the number of sides. The teacher assesses whether students can identify the number of sides of the polygons.	12–13	116, 117, 118	• **Dialogue Box:** Categorizing Shape Cards, p. 172
SESSION 2.2 p. 69			
Sorting Quadrilaterals Students examine the angles of quadrilaterals and sort these shapes into two categories—shapes with 4 sides and 4 right angles and shapes with 4 sides, but not 4 right angles. The class creates a poster of shapes sorted into these categories and discusses names for them.	15–16	118, 119, 120, 121	• **Teacher Note:** What's a Rectangle?, p. 156
SESSION 2.3 p. 77			
Ordering Rectangles Students cut out and arrange rectangles from biggest to smallest and discuss whether the rectangles can be ordered a different way. Students cover the rectangles with color tiles to determine which has the largest area.	17–18	121, 127	• **Teacher Note:** Area and Arrays, p. 157
SESSION 2.4 p. 84			
Building Rectangles Students build rectangles from color tiles and describe and draw what they have made. They continue this and two other activities in Math Workshop and are introduced to a new *Shapes* software activity, *Quick Images*.	19–21	126, 128	

Today's Number	Quick Images
• Chart paper	• T15–T18, Shape Cards
What Time Is It?	• T24, Rectangular Arrays
• Student clocks (1 per pair)	Cut out the images of Rectangular Arrays
• Large demonstration clock	**How Many Pockets?**
	• Connecting cubes

Materials to Gather	Materials to Prepare
• **11″ x 17″ paper** (1 sheet; optional) • **Envelopes** (1 per every 2 to 4 students)	• **M1–M4, Shape Cards** Make copies on cardstock if available. Cut apart the cards. Put each set of cards in an envelope with 3 paper clips. (1 demonstration set and 1 set per every 2 to 4 students) • **M22, Assessment Checklist: Sorting Shapes by Number of Sides** ☑ Make copies. (2 or 3 sheets)
• **M1–M4, Shape Cards** (1 set per every 3 or 4 students; from Session 2.1) • **Color tiles** (1 per student) • **Tape**	• **Chart paper** To set up the chart "Quadrilateral," divide a piece of chart paper into two sections. Label the first section, "4 Sides and 4 Right Angles." Label the second section, "4 Sides, but not 4 Right Angles." Leave enough space at the top for 2 additional labels and the title.
• **Scissors** (1 per student) • **11″ x 17″ paper** (1 sheet; optional) • **Color tiles** (1 set per every 6 to 8 students)	• **M23–M25, Which Is Biggest?** Make copies. (1 of each per pair)
• **M14, Double Arrays** (1 per student, plus extras as needed) See Session 1.2. • **Primary Number Cards** (1 deck per pair; from Unit 1) • **Color tiles** (36 per student) • **Overhead color tiles** (optional) • **Chart paper** (1 sheet) • **Computers with *Shapes* software installed** (optional)	• **M15, Inch Grid Paper** Make copies. (1 per student)

Overhead Transparency   ☑ Checklist Available

What Is a Rectangle?, *continued*

	Student Activity Book	Student Math Handbook	Professional Development: Read Ahead of Time
SESSION 2.5 p. 92			
Drawing Rectangles After a demonstration of how to create and count the length of a rectangle's sides on a Geoboard and on dot paper, students create and count their own rectangles. The Math Workshop continues with a focus on constructing and describing rectangles.	19–20, 22	118, 119, 121, 126	
SESSION 2.6 p. 97			
How Many Rectangles? The class investigates how many different rectangles can be made from a given number of tiles. This activity is now included in the Math Workshop, which continues for the rest of the session.	19–20, 23–26	126	• **Dialogue Boxes:** Strategies for Building Rectangles, p. 174; Is It the Same Rectangle?, p. 176
SESSION 2.7 p. 102			
Assessment: Is It a Rectangle? Students build rectangles from color tiles to match each other's descriptions and then discuss what makes a good description of a rectangle. As an assessment, students identify whether or not each of 4 shapes is a rectangle and explain why or why not.	27	118, 119, 121, 126	• **Teacher Note:** Assessment: Is It a Rectangle?, p. 159
SESSION 2.8 p. 106			
Making Boxes from Rectangles Students examine a rectangular prism and discuss the properties of its faces. Then they construct their own boxes using index/cardstock rectangles.	28	124–125, 128	• **Teacher Notes:** Identifying Types of 3-Dimensional Shapes, p. 150; Students Make Their Own Boxes, p. 145
SESSION 2.9 p. 110			
Assessment: Faces of a Geoblock Students continue constructing their own boxes out of cardboard rectangles and then compare their sizes and shapes. At the end of the session, students complete an assessment in which they identify the number of faces on a rectangular prism and show which ones are congruent.	29	122, 124–125	• **Teacher Note:** Assessment: Faces of a Geoblock, p. 162

Materials to Gather	Materials to Prepare
• **Materials for Double Arrays** See Session 1.2 p. 31. • **Materials for Describing Rectangles** See Session 2.4. • **T23, Geoboard Dot Paper** • **Geoboards with rubber bands** (1 per pair) • **Computers with** *Shapes* **software installed**	• **M26, Geoboard Dot Paper** Make copies. (2 per student)
• **Overhead projector and overhead color tiles** (optional) • **Color tiles** (several sets); **chart paper** (optional); **construction paper; tape; gluesticks** • **Materials for Rectangles on the Geoboards** See Session 2.5. • **Materials for Describing Rectangle**s See Session 2.4. • **Materials for Rectangle Riddles** See Session 2.4. • **Computers with** *Shapes* **software installed**	• **M15, Inch Grid Paper** Make copies. (1–2 per student, plus extras) • **M27, Only One Rectangle** Make copies. (1 of each per student) • **M29, Centimeter Grid Paper** Make copies. (as needed; optional)
• **Color tiles** (2 sets) • **Students' written descriptions and drawings of rectangles** (from Sessions 2.4–2.6) • **Chart paper** (optional)	• **M30, Assessment: Is It a Rectangle?** Make copies. (1 per student)
• **Geoblocks** (class set) • **Clear or masking tape** (several rolls) • **Scissors** (1 pair per every 3 or 4 students) • **Index cards** (seven 3″ x 5″ cards and four 5″ x 8″ cards per pair)	• **A box that's approximately 9″ x 5″ x 3″** Choose a box, such as a shoe box, cereal box or another box without square faces. • **Box pieces in envelopes** Use index cards to make box pieces. Each set should contain four 3″ x 5″ cards, two 5″ x 8″ cards, two 3″ x 8″ pieces, two 2″ x 3″ pieces, and two 2″ x 5″ pieces. Make the pieces by cutting up three 3″ x 5″ index cards and two 5″ x 8″ index cards per set. Place each set in an envelope. (1 set per pair) See p. 108.
• **Students' boxes-in-progress** (from Session 2.8) • **Clear or masking tape** (several rolls); **index cards** (optional) • **Scissors** (1 per every 3 or 4 students) • **Rectangular prisms from a set of Geoblocks** (1 per student)	• **M31, Assessment: Faces of a Geoblock** Make copies. (1 per student)

Overhead Transparency

Assessment: Sorting Shapes by Number of Sides

Math Focus Points

- Describing attributes of and sorting 2-dimensional shapes
- Identifying categories for 2-dimensional shapes
- Sorting polygons by the number of sides

Today's Plan		Materials
ACTIVITY ➊ **Sorting Shape Cards**	20 MIN · CLASS · GROUPS	• M1–M4* • 11" x 17" paper (optional)
DISCUSSION ➋ **Different Ways to Sort**	20 MIN · CLASS	• Materials from Activity 1
ASSESSMENT ACTIVITY ➌ **Sorting Shapes by Number of Sides**	✔ · 20 MIN · GROUPS · CLASS	• M1–M4; M22*☑ • Envelopes
SESSION FOLLOW-UP ➍ **Daily Practice and Homework**		• *Student Activity Book*, pp. 12–13 • *Student Math Handbook*, pp. 116, 117, 118

*See *Materials to Prepare*, p. 59.

Classroom Routines

Today's Number: 18 Using Double Combinations Sometime during the day (outside of math class), do *Today's Number* with 18 using double combinations. Students generate expressions for the number 18 using double combinations such as $2 + 2$, $5 + 5$, etc. For example: $6 + 6 + 3 + 3, 8 + 8 + 1 + 1$, or $9 + 9$.

ACTIVITY

1 Sorting Shape Cards

20 MIN CLASS GROUPS

Gather students in a circle so that they can all see your set of Shape Cards (M1–M4).

The cards in this envelope have different shapes. As I come around, I would like you to reach in, take out one card, and place it in front of you. Look at your shape and think about how you can describe it.

When all students have a card, ask a volunteer to place his or her Shape Card in the center of the circle and share one thing about it.

Students might say:

"My shape [Shape Card L] has one long side."

Write the sorting rule [One Long Side] on the board or on a large sheet of paper. Students with shapes that match this rule should place their cards in the center of the circle. These might include Shapes D, E, I, J, P, and R. Students with shapes that do not match should place their cards in front of them so that everyone can see.

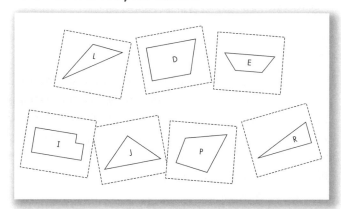

Look at all the shapes in the center. Do they all have [one long side]? Look at all the shapes that are not in the center. Do they all not have [one long side]?

Based on the discussion, students may want to adjust where they placed their shapes. When everyone agrees that the shapes are sorted correctly, students retrieve their Shape Cards and place them in front of them. Repeat the activity two times. Each time, a student must describe an attribute of his or her shape that has not been mentioned before.

Professional Development

❶ **Dialogue Box:** Categorizing Shape Cards, p. 172

Teaching Note

❷ **Think Ahead** As you observe students, decide which ways of sorting you particularly want to bring up in the following discussion.

Collect the demonstration set of Shape Cards to use later in Session 2.2. Distribute an envelope containing a set of Shape Cards to each group of two to four students.

Sort your Shape Cards in at least two different ways. Each time, sort them into two, three, or four groups so that every card has a place. Pick one of the ways you sorted the Shape Cards and write down the labels of your groups. Later we will have a discussion about how you sorted your shapes.

Walk around and observe students while they work. Encourage students to place all the cards in the set into categories. Some students may choose to sort into two groups as in the previous activity, with one group following a rule and the other not. Others will make several categories.❶

ONGOING ASSESSMENT: Observing Students at Work

Students identify an attribute or set of attributes of a geometric shape and sort shapes accordingly.❷

- **Do students' categories allow them to sort all of the shapes?**

- **Do students' categories allow each shape to be placed unambiguously?**

- **Are students able to come up with different ways to sort the shapes?** Do their categories relate to size? Number of sides? Angles?

DIFFERENTIATION: Supporting the Range of Learners

Intervention If students have difficulty organizing their shapes into groups, suggest that they begin with two or three shapes that they think are the same in some way. Ask them to explain how they are the same. You may need to verbalize the rule for them at first. Once they have placed all of the relevant shape cards, have them focus on the remaining set of cards. Ask questions, such as:

- Which shapes seem to go together?

- If you're sorting this way, where does this shape go?

- What do you call this group of shapes?

- Why did you place this shape in this group instead of that one?

Intervention If students are having difficulty following a rule that they have made, ask them first to sort the cards using rules that you have previously defined. This will allow you to observe whether they are able to identify the attribute and sort the cards appropriately.

DISCUSSION

② Different Ways to Sort

20 MIN CLASS

Math Focus Points for Discussion

◆ Describing attributes of and sorting 2-D shapes

◆ Identifying categories for 2-D shapes

In this discussion, students share the categories they used to sort their shapes. Some students may have sorted their shapes by size into categories, such as "long and skinny" and "big and fat." Others will focus more on the number of sides and corners that a shape has. Discuss how students know which shape goes into which group.

Some students' categories might touch on the idea of angles. They may use descriptive words, such as "pointy" or "sharp." To draw their attention to the angles of a shape, encourage students to talk about what it means to be "pointy." Use the language that students use.

How would I know if something is pointy? Could Shape Q (a rectangle) go in a "long and pointy" category? What part of the shape is pointy?

Since Shape Q isn't pointy, how would you describe it? What are some other shapes that are like Shape Q and not pointy?

As students are discussing these shapes, listen to see whether anyone is using the term *angle* to describe the shapes in their categories. Students are likely to have heard this word, but may not yet be using it to describe geometric shapes.

Look at Shape Q. I want you to pay particular attention to the corners of these shapes. Mathematicians have a special name to describe the place where two sides of a polygon come together. It's called a vertex. When the two lines meet, they make an angle.❸

Math Note

❸ **Vertices and Angles** A vertex is the place where two lines meet. Sometimes students refer to this as a point or a corner. When two lines meet, they make an angle. A triangle has three vertices and three angles. A quadrilateral has four vertices and four angles. While second graders are not expected to use this language, it is important that they begin to focus on these important features of polygons. To model this language, you could say, "You noticed that the triangle has three corners or vertices."

❹ Completing the Assessment Sorting Shapes is an observable assessment. Use Assessment Checklist: Sorting Shapes by Number of Sides (M22) to keep track of each student's ability to count the sides of a polygon. You can get a sense of this by observing how students sort their Shape Cards, and also by selecting one or two cards from the "more than four sides group" and asking students to identify the number of sides.

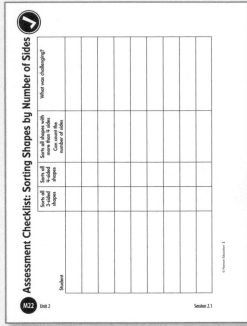

▲ **Resource Masters, M22** ☑

Ask students to think about the number of angles that the shapes in their groups have. In the next session, students will continue to work with these polygons, focusing on the number of angles and sides they have.

ASSESSMENT ACTIVITY

③ Sorting Shapes by Number of Sides

20 MIN   GROUPS   CLASS

During this activity you can observe students as they sort a set of Shape Cards by the number of sides each shape has. This activity will give you the information needed to assess Benchmark 1. You can record your observations on Assessment Checklist: Sorting Shapes by Number of Sides (M22).❹

Assessment Checklist: Sorting Shapes by Number of Sides

Student	Sorts all 3-sided shapes	Sorts all 4-sided shapes	Sorts all shapes with more than 4 sides Can count the number of sides	What was challenging?
Katrina	✓	✓	shape I - 6 sides shape X - 8 sides	∅
Jacy	✓	✓	sorts correctly but has some trouble counting + keeping track of	counting and keeping track of sides
Chen	✓	✓	shape I - 6 sides shape X - 8 sides	∅
Nadia	✓	✓	counts # of sides as she sorts	∅
Leo	but misses ✓ one - moves from 4 to 3 group	✓	counts sides on shape I, X, and V correctly	misplaced one shape shape K- but fixed mistake when asked how many sides
Henry	✓	✓	counts shape S, T, X, and V	∅
Carla	✓	✓	shape I - 6 sides shape X - 8 sides shape V - 6 sides	∅
Travis	✓	✓	counts I- 6 sides counts X-8 sides	∅
Tia	✓	✓	counts as she sorts cards into this group	∅

For this assessment, it is important to use the following language:

• Shapes with three sides (rather than *triangles*)

• Shapes with four sides

• Shapes with more than four sides

Although students will agree that Shape L, for example, has three sides, they may not all agree that Shape L is a triangle. During this lesson, students work with categories they can all agree on.

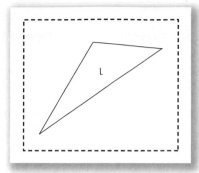

Introduce the activity by following up on the previous discussion.

Did anybody count the number of sides to sort the shapes? Let's look at Shape R (a triangle). How many sides does it have? (three) Do all the shapes have three sides? What shape doesn't have three sides?

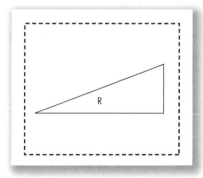

Now, you will sort shapes by the number of their sides. With your partners, you will make three groups: shapes with three sides, shapes with four sides, and shapes with more than four sides.

As students are working, check in with each small group to see whether they are in agreement about the category that each shape belongs in.❺

❺ **Save the Cards** Before the end of the session, ask students to write their names on their group's envelope, clip together the Shape Cards in the three categories, and put them in the envelope for use in Session 2.2.

▲ Student Activity Book, p. 12

▲ Student Activity Book, p. 13

ONGOING ASSESSMENT: Observing Students at Work

Students sort Shape Cards into three groups: three sides, four sides, and more than four sides.

- **Do students correctly sort the shapes according to the number of sides?**

- **How do students identify the number of sides?**

- **How do students know whether a side has already been counted?**

SESSION FOLLOW-UP

4 Daily Practice and Homework

 Daily Practice: For ongoing review, have students complete *Student Activity Book* page 12.

 Homework: Students look around at home to find at least five examples of different shapes. On *Student Activity Book* page 13, they draw a picture of what they found and write the name of the shape.

 Student Math Handbook: Students and families may use *Student Math Handbook* pages 116–118 for reference and review. See pages 178–182 in the back of this unit.

Sorting Quadrilaterals

Math Focus Points

◆ Sorting quadrilaterals by angle

◆ Identifying quadrilaterals as shapes with 4 sides

◆ Identifying rectangles as 4-sided shapes with 4 right angles

Vocabulary

angle
right angle
rectangle
quadrilateral

Today's Plan

		Materials
DISCUSSION ① **Looking at Angles**	15 MIN GROUPS CLASS	• Shape Cards (from Session 2.1) • Color tiles
ACTIVITY ② **Creating a Quadrilateral Chart**	30 MIN GROUPS CLASS	• Shape Cards (from Session 2.1) • Chart: "Quadrilateral"*; tape
DISCUSSION ③ **What's a Rectangle?**	15 MIN CLASS	• Chart: "Quadrilateral"*
SESSION FOLLOW-UP ④ **Daily Practice and Homework**		• *Student Activity Book,* pp. 15–16 • *Student Math Handbook,* pp. 118–121

*See *Materials to Prepare,* p. 59.

Classroom Routines

What Time Is It? Students work together with a partner to practice setting their individual clocks to the half hour. One student suggests a time and the other one sets the clock. They take turns with these two roles.

DISCUSSION

Looking at Angles

Math Focus Points for Discussion

◆ Sorting quadrilaterals by angle

Distribute a set of Shape Cards and one color tile per student to each small group. Ask students to make a group of shapes that have four sides (Shape Cards A, D, E, F, G, H, K, M, N, P, and Q).

Look at your shapes with four sides. What do you notice about these shapes?

Some students might comment on the number of sides, the number of corners or angles, or they might identify a shape as a rectangle. Once students have offered their observations, draw their attention to the angles of the shapes.

Look at Shape Card A. I'd like you to point to the place where two sides of this polygon come together. Does anyone know what this is called? Mathematicians call this an angle. Sometimes students, and even adults, call this a corner. How many angles or corners does Shape A have?

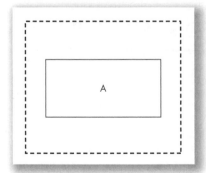

Ask students what they notice about the angles of a rectangle. Students may say that all the corners are the same. They may describe them as shaped like an L or a square.

This kind of corner is very special and so it has a special name. Does anyone know what its name is?

If nobody knows the name, tell the class that these corners are called right angles.

Let's look at the square tiles that I gave to each of you. Pick your tile up and feel the corners. What do you notice about the angles, or corners, of the square tile?

The square tile has four right angles. Explain to students that sometimes people use the term *square corner* to refer to a right angle. Show students how the square tile can fit into the corner, or right angle, of Shape Card A.

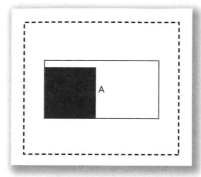

Now let's look at Shape N. Does Shape N have right angles? How can we tell?

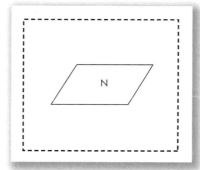

Shape N does not have right angles, and students might have different ways of explaining how they know this. If nobody mentions seeing whether the square tile fits in the corner, suggest it. Have students try to fit the tile in the corners of Shape A and then in the corners of Shape N. Shape N has two angles that are larger than a right angle and two angles that are smaller.

Now let's look at Shape Q. Does Shape Q have right angles? How can we tell?

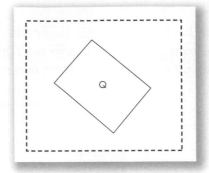

Since the sides of Shape Q are not horizontal and vertical, students may not recognize that it has right angles. Elicit different points of view about whether or not Shape Q has right angles.

Point out to students that they can rotate Shape Q so that its sides do look horizontal and vertical or side-to-side and up-and-down. Also, the square tile can be rotated so that its sides are *not* horizontal and vertical. The angle, or the shape of the corner, does not change when the shape is rotated. Shape Q does have four right angles.

ACTIVITY

2 Creating a Quadrilateral Chart

30 MIN GROUPS CLASS

Now we're going to sort all the shapes with four sides. One group will be "4 Sides and 4 Right Angles." The second group will be "4 Sides, but not 4 Right Angles."

Students work in small groups to sort shapes with four sides.

Shapes G, M, and Q all have four right angles, but these might be harder to see because of their orientation on the card. Shape G might also be difficult to see because two of its sides are shorter than the side of a tile. Note that Shape D has two right angles and two angles that are not right; it belongs in the "4 Sides, but not 4 Right Angles" category.

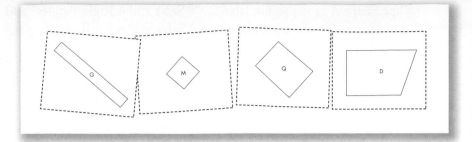

ONGOING ASSESSMENT: Observing Students at Work

Students sort four-sided shapes into two categories—those that have four right angles and those that do not.

- **Can students identify the shapes that have right angles?**

- **Do students recognize right angles that are not oriented with horizontal and vertical sides?** Can they see that they can turn the square tile to determine whether it fits into a shape's angle?

- **Can students recognize a right angle even if the sides of the shape are shorter than the sides of the square tile?**

When groups are done sorting their shapes, bring the whole class together. Show students the chart that you have prepared.

4 Sides and 4 Right Angles	4 Sides, but not 4 Right Angles

❶ Teacher Note: What's a Rectangle?, p. 156

Tape Shape A in the region labeled, "4 Sides and 4 Right Angles" and tape Shape N in the region labeled, "4 Sides, but not 4 Right Angles."

We are going to make a class chart of these two categories of shapes with four sides. We already discussed Shape A and decided it has four sides and four right angles, and we decided Shape N has four sides, but not four right angles.

Ask a student to choose a four-sided shape and say which category it belongs in.

[Anita] says that Shape H has four sides, but not four right angles. Do you agree?

If students agree, add that shape to the chart accordingly. Where there is disagreement, have students explain how they determine whether an angle is right or not and show how they measured the angles of the shape.

Ask a different student to choose another four-sided shape and to say which category it belongs in. Continue until all the four-sided shapes appear on the chart. Shapes A, F, G, M, and Q should go under "4 Sides and 4 Right Angles." Shapes D, E, H, K, N, and P will go under "4 Sides, but not 4 Right Angles."

15 MIN   CLASS

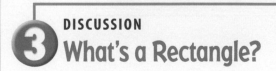

DISCUSSION

③ What's a Rectangle?

Math Focus Points for Discussion

◆ Identifying quadrilaterals as shapes with 4 sides

◆ Identifying rectangles as 4-sided shapes with 4 right angles.

Introduce vocabulary for the categories of shapes on the chart.❶

We're going to talk about the names mathematicians use for the shapes on our chart. You might be surprised by some of them. Does anyone know the name for all the shapes in our category, "4 Sides and 4 Right Angles"?

Some students might talk about individual shapes.

Students might say:

"Shape F is a square."

"Shape M is a diamond."

"Shape A is a rectangle."

Ask whether there is a name for all the shapes in this category. If some students say that all the shapes are called *rectangles,* let them explain why that is so. Allow students to debate this question for several minutes.

I know this might be surprising to many of you, but mathematicians say that rectangles are shapes with four sides and four right angles. All of the shapes in our first category have four sides and four right angles, so they are all rectangles. Did you know that a square is a special kind of rectangle?

Write "Rectangle" under the label, "4 Sides and 4 Right Angles." Then allow students to respond. Some students may reject the idea that a square is a special kind of rectangle. At this time, listen to students and allow them to object. The chart will remain on the wall for the rest of the unit so students can ponder this. They will return to the idea in later grades.

The word that mathematicians use for all four-sided shapes is quadrilateral. Has anyone heard the word *quadrilateral* before?

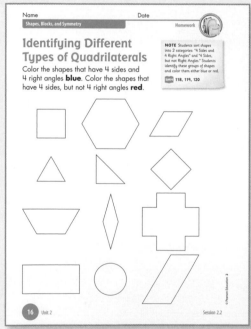

Write "Quadrilateral" at the top of the chart. Then write "Other Quadrilaterals" under the label, "4 Sides, but not 4 Right Angles."

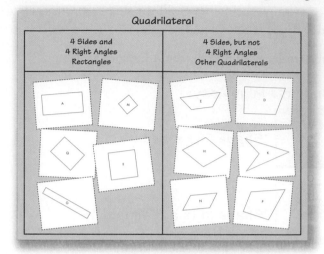

Ask students whether they know any other names of shapes on the chart. They might offer trapezoid, parallelogram, or rhombus.

Hang the chart in a place in the room where students will be able to see it for the rest of the unit.

Ask students to put away their four-sided Shape Cards and to take out the remaining cards—the ones with three sides and more than four sides.

What do you notice about the angles, or corners, of these shapes? Do any of these shapes have right angles?

Shapes I and S have only right angles, but also have more than four sides. Shape T has three right angles and five sides. Shapes J and R are right triangles; each has one right angle.

SESSION FOLLOW-UP

4 Daily Practice and Homework

 Daily Practice: For ongoing review, have students complete *Student Activity Book* page 15.

 Homework: Students identify and color specific types of quadrilaterals red or blue on *Student Activity Book* page 16.

 Student Math Handbook: Students and families may use *Student Math Handbook* pages 118–121 for reference and review. See pages 178–182 in the back of this unit.

Ordering Rectangles

Math Focus Points

◆ Defining *biggest* in different ways

◆ Ordering rectangles from biggest to smallest

◆ Covering rectangles with arrays of tiles

Vocabulary

area

Today's Plan		Materials
ACTIVITY ❶ **Ordering Rectangles**	20 MIN · PAIRS · CLASS	• M23–M25* • Scissors
DISCUSSION ❷ **Which Is Biggest?**	10 MIN · PAIRS · CLASS	• Which Is Biggest? cutouts; 11″ × 17″ paper (optional)
ACTIVITY ❸ **Covering Rectangles**	20 MIN · INDIVIDUALS PAIRS · CLASS	• *Student Activity Book,* p. 17 • Which Is Biggest? cutouts; color tiles
DISCUSSION ❹ **Which Rectangle Has the Biggest Area?**	10 MIN · CLASS	• *Student Activity Book,* p. 17 • Which Is Biggest? cutouts; color tiles
SESSION FOLLOW-UP ❺ **Daily Practice**		• *Student Activity Book,* p. 18 • *Student Math Handbook,* pp. 121, 127

*See *Materials to Prepare,* p. 59.

Classroom Routines

Quick Images: Drawing Shapes Using the transparent Shape Cards (T15–T18), display Shape A. Follow the basic *Quick Images* activity. Display the shape as students discuss what they saw and describe the attributes of the shape. Repeat with Shape H and then Shape P. Have students compare and contrast the three shape cards, if time allows.

Teaching Note

❶ Cutting Rectangles Some students may be extremely slow at cutting out the rectangles. You may want to ask others to help them so that everyone has enough time to complete the activity.

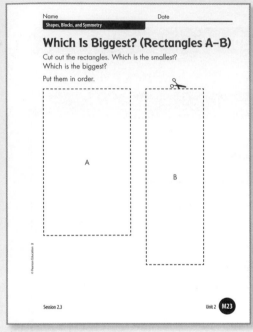

▲ Resource Masters, M23

ACTIVITY

20 MIN   PAIRS   CLASS

① Ordering Rectangles

There are different ways to think about which rectangle is the biggest in a set of rectangles. One might be taller than the rest, another might be wider, and yet another might have the largest area. In this activity, students will order a set of rectangles and learn about different ways to think about size.

Distribute scissors and have students work in pairs to cut apart the rectangles on Which Is Biggest? (M23–M25). Provide each student with blank paper.

Ask students about the name of the shapes on these pages and ask how they know that these are rectangles. If they do not mention that rectangles have four sides *and* four right angles, point to the chart that you made in the previous session and remind them.

If some students insist that shape G is not a rectangle because it is a square, say that shape G is a square, but it is also a special kind of rectangle. Point to the squares in the "Rectangles: 4 Sides and 4 Right Angles" category of the chart. If students are still reluctant to consider that shape G is a rectangle, ask them to compare shape G to the rest of the shapes anyway.

When you are finished cutting out your rectangles, work with your partner to decide how to put your rectangles in order. Start with the rectangle that you think is biggest, and then order them from the next biggest to the smallest. Then, on your paper, write the order. When everyone has finished, we'll discuss what you've done.

Students may use any materials they want to determine the order of the rectangles. Observe what they do to compare the rectangles and if there is any discussion or disagreement among them about how to determine the size of the rectangles.❶

ONGOING ASSESSMENT: Observing Students at Work

Students decide on an attribute for ordering a set of rectangles and record that order. This task will offer some insight into how students are thinking of biggest and which attributes they focus on while ordering their rectangles.

• **Do pairs of students agree on the attribute they are using to compare rectangles?**

- Do students consistently apply the same attribute to order the set of rectangles?

- Do students recognize that, when considering a different attribute, the rectangles may be ordered differently?

DIFFERENTIATION: Reaching the Range of Learners

 ELL Students need to understand comparatives, such as *smaller* and *bigger* and superlatives, such as *smallest* and *biggest* to follow the instructions for this activity. Meet with a small group of English Language Learners and begin by showing students three squares of three different sizes. Here are three squares. They're all the same shape, but they're different sizes. I'm going to put them in order from *biggest* to *smallest*. Let's see . . . Which one is *bigger*, this square or that square? Which one is the *smallest* square? Add two more squares of different sizes to the group, and ask students to put all five squares in order from *biggest* to *smallest*. Students can then apply this knowledge to the Ordering Rectangles and Covering Rectangles activities.

DISCUSSION

2 Which Is Biggest?

10 MIN   PAIRS   CLASS

Math Focus Points for Discussion

◆ Defining *biggest* in different ways

When all pairs of students have ordered their rectangles, call the class together. You may want to seat students in a circle so that everyone can see. Students should bring their rectangles and recording sheets with the way they ordered the rectangles.

Ask each pair to share their order, putting the rectangles in the center. As each pair shares, record their work on the board or on a piece of chart paper.

Why did you order the rectangles this way? Does anyone else have the same order, but for a different reason? Does anyone have a different order?

Most second graders will arrange the rectangles by height. When two rectangles are the same height, they usually put the wider one first. A common order is C, F, B, A, D, G, E, with each rectangle "standing up."

▲ **Resource Masters, M24**

▲ **Resource Masters, M25**

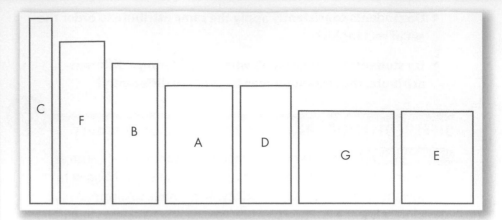

A few students may have arranged the rectangles differently, for example, "lying down," or by area. Emphasize that there are different ways to define *biggest*.

In order to push their thinking about *biggest*, take the longest rectangle (C) and turn it so that it is lying on its longest side.

Many people have said that Rectangle C is the biggest because it is the tallest. If I turn it this way [turn so the long direction is horizontal], is it still the biggest rectangle? Why or why not?

As students discuss this question, it is likely that they will bring up the issue of *biggest* being dependent on which attribute you are focusing on. The next activity will offer students an opportunity to consider *biggest* by looking at the area of these rectangles.

ACTIVITY

3 Covering Rectangles

20 MIN INDIVIDUALS PAIRS CLASS

Each pair of students will need access to a set of color tiles. With rectangles still visible from the previous activity, pose the following question:

Suppose these rectangles are chocolate bars. Which one would have the most chocolate? Which would have the least? How could you find out?

Some students may suggest measuring the rectangles in some way. If no one mentions it, suggest covering the rectangles with color tiles. When comparing rectangles by the number of tiles it takes to cover them, students are essentially comparing the rectangles by area.②

Demonstrate by having one student cover a rectangle with tiles. Record the total on the board. Even if area was one of the attributes used to order the rectangles in the previous activity, it is important that all students practice covering the rectangles with square tiles.

A student finds the area of a rectangle by covering it with square tiles.

 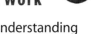
▲ **Student Activity Book, p. 17**

Now, order your rectangles from biggest to smallest by figuring out how many square tiles it takes to cover them.

Working in pairs, students order the rectangles by covering them with tiles. On *Student Activity Book* page 17, they each record their work and answer the questions.

ONGOING ASSESSMENT: Observing Students at Work

Students cover rectangles with tiles. This is a step toward understanding rectangular arrays.

- **Are students able to cover the rectangles without gaps or overlaps?**

- **Do students use a system to cover the rectangles?** Do they, for example, fill out the rectangle row by row or column by column?

- **Are students able to order the rectangles using area as the attribute?**

- **Do students see that all the rows in a rectangle are the same length?**

DISCUSSION

4

10 MIN   CLASS

Which Rectangle Has the Biggest Area?

Math Focus Points for Discussion

◆ Defining *biggest* in different ways

Call students together to share the results they recorded on *Student Activity Book* page 17. Do they all agree on the number of tiles it takes to cover each rectangle? Where there is disagreement, work together to cover the rectangle with tiles.

Discuss with the class the number of rows and the size of the rows of a rectangle.

Let's look at Rectangle A. How many tiles do you think are in the first row?

Some students may remember and some may guess. Fill in the first row so that everyone can see that there are three tiles in it.

How many tiles are in the second row?

Some students may be sure that it is the same number as the first row, but others may not. Keep adding rows and counting the tiles in each row. Then count the number of rows.

Do you think the other rectangles also have the same number of tiles in each row? Let's try it with another rectangle.

Fill in the first row of rectangle D. It takes five tiles. Then fill the second row. It also has five tiles.

Then, discuss those rectangles that take the same number of tiles to be covered.

Look at Rectangles B and E. Which one has more chocolate? Is one bigger than the other?

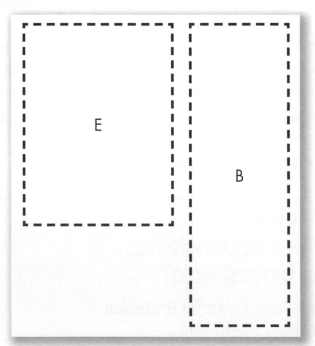

Encourage students to discuss whether they think these two shapes are the same size or different sizes. Some students may be sure that the tallest rectangle is biggest. Others may change what they consider *biggest* to mean, depending on the attribute. This is fine, since the meaning of *biggest* depends on the attribute that is being compared and the context of the situation.

We can use different words to explain the way in which we are thinking about *biggest*. For example, we can talk about which rectangle is tallest. Everyone agrees that Rectangle C is the tallest. The word we use when we're thinking about the number of tiles to cover a rectangle is *area*. We see that Rectangle G has the biggest area.

As a way of reinforcing the concept of area as an attribute to determine size, ask students to look at their rectangles and decide whether there are two rectangles that have the same area, and which rectangle has the smallest area. Students will build on this work in subsequent sessions.

SESSION FOLLOW-UP

⑤ Daily Practice

 Daily Practice: For reinforcement of this unit's content, have students complete *Student Activity Book* page 18.

Student Math Handbook: Students and families may use *Student Math Handbook* pages 121, 127 for reference and review. See pages 178–182 in the back of this unit.

Teaching Note

❸ **Different Words** When comparing pencils or fishing poles, we focus on the attribute of length, so in this context, *biggest* means longest. To find which of several rooms will use the most carpeting, we are interested in which floor has the largest area. Point out to students that we sometimes use different words to be clear about the context in which we are thinking about *biggest*.

▲ Student Activity Book, p. 18

Building Rectangles

Math Focus Points

◆ Arranging square tiles in rectangular arrays

◆ Describing rectangular arrays of tiles

◆ Developing fluency with the doubles combinations to $10 + 10$

Vocabulary

congruent

column

Today's Plan		Materials
ACTIVITY ❶ **Describing Rectangles** — 15 MIN, CLASS		• Color tiles; overhead color tiles (optional); chart paper
ACTIVITY ❷ ***Shapes* Software: Introducing *Quick Images* (optional)** — CLASS, PAIRS		• Computers with *Shapes* software installed
MATH WORKSHOP ❸ **Rectangles** — 45 MIN ❸Ⓐ Describing Rectangles ❸Ⓑ Rectangle Riddles ❸Ⓒ Double Arrays ❸Ⓓ *Shapes* Software: *Quick Images* (optional)		**3A** • M15* • Color tiles **3B** • *Student Activity Book,* pp. 19–20 • Color tiles **3C** • Materials from Session 1.2, p. 31 **3D** • Computers with *Shapes* software installed
SESSION FOLLOW-UP ❹ **Daily Practice**		• *Student Activity Book,* p. 21 • *Student Math Handook,* pp. 126, 128

*See *Materials to Prepare,* p. 59.

Classroom Routines

Today's Number: 15 As a whole class, students generate numerical expressions for the number 15 using addition and/or subtraction. These expressions are recorded on a class chart. Students can add to the chart throughout the day.

ACTIVITY

1 Describing Rectangles

Distribute color tiles and two sheets of blank paper to each student.

We are going to put color tiles together to make our own rectangles. Take six tiles and make a rectangle with them. Then cover the rectangle with a sheet of paper.

When everyone has built a rectangle and covered it, give the next direction.

Take a quick peek at your rectangle and cover it up again. Then draw a picture of it on the other sheet of paper. Show all six tiles in your drawing.

Now take the cover off your tiles. Compare your drawing to the tiles. If you need to make changes, draw a new picture beside your first one. This time, you don't need to cover your tiles.

Who can describe the rectangle they made so others can tell whether they made the same one?

As a volunteer describes a rectangle, build it on the overhead projector or draw it on the board. If the description is not clear, encourage the student to tell you more about the rectangle.

Do you all think this is the rectangle [Darren] made? Why or why not? Did anyone make the same rectangle? Can anyone describe the rectangle in a different way?

As students describe the same rectangle in different ways, record their descriptions on chart paper. Save this chart for students to refer to in the first Math Workshop activity and in Sessions 2.5 and 2.6. You may refer to it again in Session 2.7.

Darren's Rectangle

1. 1st row—2 tiles
   2nd row—2 tiles
   3rd row—2 tiles

2. 3 rows, each row has 2 tiles

3. 3 + 3

4. 2 + 2 + 2

Use this opportunity to introduce the word *column* (the tiles going down). Darren's rectangle has two columns.

Many of you made the same rectangle as [Darren]. Did anyone make a different rectangle? Can you describe the rectangle you made?

Again, construct the rectangle from the student's description on the overhead using the overhead tiles or draw it on the board. Then discuss whether this rectangle is different from the first. Encourage students who made a different rectangle to describe their work.

Students can make two rectangles using six tiles, a 1 × 6 rectangle and a 2 × 3 rectangle. It is common for students to see two rectangles with the same dimensions as different, if one of them is rotated 90°.

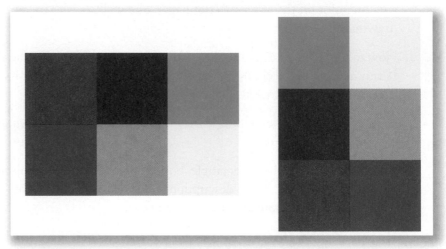

If students do not recognize these as the same rectangle, but do say they are turned in different directions, ask whether the rectangles would be the same if one were turned around. Introduce the term *congruent*, but do not expect students to memorize the word.

When two shapes are the same size and shape, we say they are congruent. It doesn't matter whether they are turned in different directions. They are congruent if one shape could fit exactly on top of the other one.

Some students may make other shapes that are not rectangles, but have rectangular parts. If they do, ask them to point out the rectangles in the shapes they make.

Yes, I can see that rectangle in your shape. But for this activity, the whole shape made with the tiles must be a rectangle.

Remind the students that to build rectangles from tiles, all the rows should be lined up and have the same number of tiles.

Some might say that a rectangle that is one tile wide is "a line," not a rectangle.

Ask them:

What shape would it be if we drew around the outside edges and then took away the tiles?

ONGOING ASSESSMENT: Observing Students at Work

Students build rectangles from tiles and describe them. This activity allows them to examine the structure of an array.

- **Do students recognize that a rectangular arrangement of tiles must have equal rows lined up to make equal columns?**

- **Do students describe their rectangles in terms of the number of tiles in a row and the number of rows and/or in terms of the number of tiles in a column and the number of columns?**

- **Do students recognize that rectangles may have the same dimensions but different orientations?**

ACTIVITY

CLASS PAIRS

2 Shapes Software: Introducing Quick Images (optional)

Tell students that they will work individually or with a partner to solve *Quick Images Puzzles* that the computer displays. You will need to introduce them to how to pick a *Quick Images Puzzle* and get clues using the software. ❶ ❷

Specifically, show them how to:

- Choose the *Quick Images* activity from the Activity menu

- Choose a shape set (pattern blocks, Power Polygons, or tangrams)

- Choose a level and a specific puzzle

Technology Notes

❶ *Quick Images* **on the Computer** In the *Shapes* software *Quick Images* activity, students can work on a wide variety of *Quick Images Puzzles* presented by the computer. The *Quick Images* format should already feel familiar to them. With the software, they can choose when to display the quick image and they can use the regular *Free Explore* tools to recreate the image. Some students may already be familiar with the *Shapes* software *Quick Images* activity from previous grades.

❷ **Making** *Quick Images Puzzles* The CD-ROM version of the *Shapes* software also allows users— students or the teacher—to create their own *Quick Images Puzzles* and save them to disk. Use this feature to customize puzzles for your class, or allow students to challenge one another. See the *Software Support Reference Guide* for details on how to make your own *Quick Images Puzzles*.

- Press the eyes on the right-hand side to see the *Quick Images Puzzle*. The puzzle is displayed for one second. Their task is to recreate the puzzle on the left-hand side of the screen. If they want to see the *Quick Images Puzzle* again, they can press the eyes. Each time the eyes are pressed, the puzzle is displayed for one additional second. After nine times, the puzzle is displayed continuously.

- Select a new puzzle by using the arrows in the menu bar or the up arrow.

Students may want to begin with the pattern block shape set, but can also try Power Polygons™ and tangrams for an additional challenge.

MATH WORKSHOP

③ Rectangles

45 MIN

Introduce and post a list of the following Math Workshop activities.

Double Arrays is included in this session and subsequent sessions to provide students with additional practice with the doubles combinations. Students will be familiar with this activity from the previous investigation.

③A Describing Rectangles

INDIVIDUALS

Students use color tiles to make several rectangles. They choose one and draw it on the bottom half of Inch Grid Paper (M15), staying on the dotted lines. They fold the top half of the paper over their drawing and write a description of their rectangle on the top flap so that someone else can reproduce it without looking at the drawing. Point out to students that if they need help describing their rectangles, they can use the chart they made in the first activity. ❸

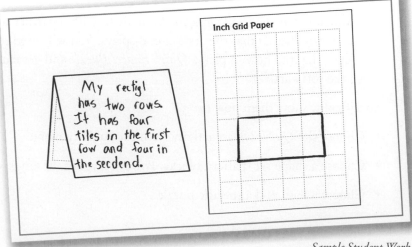

Inch Grid Paper

My rectigl has two rows. It has four tiles in the first row and four in the secdend.

Sample Student Work

ONGOING ASSESSMENT: Observing Students at Work

Students practice building and describing rectangular arrays.

- **Are students able to make rectangular arrays (arrangements with equal rows and columns)?**

- **How do students build rectangles?** Do they place one tile at a time until they form a rectangle, do they grab a handful of tiles and try to arrange them into a rectangle, or do they start with a specific number of tiles? Do they frame the outside first and fill in or do they go by rows or columns?

- **Are students able to reproduce their rectangles on grid paper?**

- **Do students give enough information in their descriptions to allow someone else to reproduce their rectangles?**

DIFFERENTIATION: Supporting the Range of Learners

Intervention If students have difficulty copying their rectangles, suggest that they place the tiles on the graph paper and trace around them.

If students have trouble writing descriptions, suggest that they first tell you how to build their rectangles. If they still have difficulty, structure the writing for them. For example, "My rectangle has _____ rows. There are _____ tiles in each row."

ELL Some English Language Learners may have difficulty writing descriptions of their rectangles. Some of these students may be able to give oral descriptions which they can then write with your guidance. Refer students to the vocabulary poster and the pages on rectangular arrays in the *Student Math Handbook*. Some English Language Learners may not yet be able to describe their rectangles orally or in writing, but will be able to respond to questions such as, How many rows does your rectangle have? How many tiles are in each row? They can then be provided with writing templates like those mentioned above: "My rectangle has _____ rows. There are _____ tiles in each row."

3B Rectangle Riddles

INDIVIDUALS

Students use color tiles to make a rectangle for each riddle on *Student Activity Book* pages 19–20. They draw the rectangular array below the riddle. When they have finished, they write their own rectangle riddles.

▲ Student Activity Book, p. 19

▲ Student Activity Book, p. 20

Professional Development

④ **Teacher Note:** Area and Arrays, p. 157

Technology Note

⑤ **Choosing Puzzles** *Shapes* software provides *Quick Images Puzzles* across a wide range of levels of difficulty. Students should feel free to select puzzles at a level that they find challenging but not too frustrating. If the puzzles seem easy, encourage them to try more difficult puzzles. If the puzzles are too hard, suggest that they try easier ones. Students can also select puzzles using any of the three shape sets.

ONGOING ASSESSMENT: Observing Students at Work

Students draw arrays on unlined paper. This activity provides another context for students to work on the array structure of a rectangle. This will give you more information about how students visualize the array.④

- **How do students use the clues in the riddles?** Do they build first and then check the number of rows and columns? Do they use the clues independently or together? Do students realize that in Riddle 3, just one piece of information is sufficient to build a rectangle? Do they have difficulty with others, such as Riddle 4, "This rectangle has 3 columns and 3 rows"?

- **How do students draw their array?** Do they draw individual squares?

- **How do students write their own riddles?** Do they build a rectangle first? Do they provide sufficient information so someone else could build it?

3C Double Arrays

For complete details about this activity, see Session 1.2, page 37.

3D *Shapes* Software: *Quick Images* (optional)

Students use the *Quick Images* activity in *Shapes* to solve *Quick Images Puzzles* on the computer. They press the "eyes" to briefly show the image. They recreate the image using a shape from the shape set. This activity is similar to the Classroom Routine *Quick Images: Shapes* introduced in Session 1.1.⑤

ONGOING ASSESSMENT: Observing Students at Work

Students use visual images to recreate shapes.

- **Are students able to recreate the image they have seen?**

- **What strategies do students use to visualize the shape?** Do they divide the shape into component parts? Do they think of an object that the shape resembles? Do they count sides? Do they look at the size of the angles?

- **Some students may have trouble when shapes need to be turned or flipped to get into the right position—they may know both that something is right (the shape) and something is wrong (the way it is oriented).** Ask them to describe what they would have to do to the shape to make it right, and then encourage them to use the Turn and Flip tools to do so.

Intervention The *Quick Images* activity is designed to give students several opportunities to recreate the image. Each time they press the "eyes" they see the image for one second longer. After the ninth time, the image no longer disappears. If students are having difficulty, ask them to find one more piece to add each time they press the "eyes." Students can add pieces to the image progressively, or try to recreate as much of the image as they can, and then look again to adjust and continue.

SESSION FOLLOW-UP

4 Daily Practice

 Daily Practice: For ongoing review, have students complete *Student Activity Book* page 21.

 Student Math Handbook: Students and families may use *Student Math Handbook* pages 126, 128 for reference and review. See pages 180–184 in the back of this unit.

Name _____ Date _____

Shapes, Blocks, and Symmetry   Daily Practice

Stickers for the Class

There are 23 students in Mr. Z's class.
Mr. Z has 19 stickers.

NOTE Students determine whether there are enough items for each child. They then figure out how many are left over or how many more are needed.

SMH 71–72

Mr. Z wants to give 1 sticker to each student.

1. Are there enough for the class?   YES   NO

2. Are there any extra stickers?   YES   NO

   How many? _____

3. Does Mr. Z need more stickers?   YES   NO

   How many? _____

4. How did you figure it out? Show your work.

Session 2.4   Unit 2 21

▲ **Student Activity Book, p. 21**

Drawing Rectangles

Math Focus Points

◆ Drawing rectangles by attending to the lengths of the sides

◆ Making different rectangular arrays using the same number of tiles

◆ Describing rectangular arrays of tiles

Today's Plan		Materials
ACTIVITY **① Rectangles on the Geoboard**	20 MIN INDIVIDUALS PAIRS CLASS	• Geoboards with rubber bands • M26*; T23
MATH WORKSHOP **② Making Rectangles** **2A** Rectangles on the Geoboard **2B** Describing Rectangles **2C** Rectangle Riddles **2D** Double Arrays **2E** *Shapes* Software: *Quick Images* (optional)	40 MIN	**2A** • Materials from Activity 1 **2B** • Materials from Session 2.4, p. 84 **2C** • Materials from Session 2.4, p. 84 **2D** • Materials from Session 1.2, p. 31 **2E** • Computers with *Shapes* software installed
SESSION FOLLOW-UP **③ Daily Practice**		• *Student Activity Book,* p. 22 • *Student Math Handbook,* pp. 118, 119, 121, 126

*See *Materials to Prepare,* p. 61.

Classroom Routines

What Time Is It? During the course of the school day, stop and take note of what the class is doing every half hour. Set a timer so that it will ring every half hour. Ask students to note what time it is, describe the position of the hands on the clock and then set the large demonstration clock. Record on the board what time it is and what activity the students are involved in.

ACTIVITY

1 Rectangles on the Geoboard

20 MIN INDIVIDUALS PAIRS CLASS

Up until now, students have been building rectangles from squares. In this activity, they create rectangles on Geoboards and then draw the outline on dot paper.

Put students in pairs. Give each pair a Geoboard and each student a sheet of Geoboard Dot Paper (M26). Students who used *Investigations* in Grade 1 will be familiar with these materials. Give students time to explore their Geoboards. Encourage them to make rectangles.

After about five minutes, bring the class together. Place a transparency of Geoboard Dot Paper (T23) on the overhead and draw a 2 × 4 rectangle.

Yesterday we built rectangles from squares and drew rectangles by paying attention to the rows of squares. Today, we are going to draw just the outlines of rectangles. To start, let's look at the rectangle I've drawn on my dot paper. To figure out how long a side is, I count the number of spaces between dots.

Demonstrate how to count the number of spaces along each side of the rectangle.❶ Count and label the length of all four sides.

Build the same rectangle on your Geoboards. Make it so that two opposite sides are four spaces and the other two sides are two spaces.

Teaching Note

❶ **Counting Spaces** It is important that students get in the habit of counting the spaces between dots or pegs—the units of length—rather than counting pegs.

Name _____ Date _____

Shapes, Blocks, and Symmetry

Geoboard Dot Paper

Draw the rectangles that you made on your Geoboard.

M26 Unit 2   Sessions 2.5, 2.6

▲ **Resource Masters, M26; T23**

After students have built the rectangle on Geoboards, ask them about the angles of their rectangles. Create a parallelogram that is not a rectangle on a Geoboard and show the class.

Nobody created a shape like this. What's the difference between your shapes and this one?

Students are likely to notice that the sides of the parallelogram are slanted. Ask why this is. If no one mentions it, point out the different angles of each shape; a rectangle has four right angles and this parallelogram does not have any right angles.

Then ask students to reproduce their rectangles on Geoboard Dot Paper (M26). Have students count the spaces of each side and write that number next to the side.

Lead the class through two more examples: a 1 × 3 rectangle and a 3 × 5 rectangle.

Now create a rectangle that you choose.

As pairs finish making their rectangles, ask them to identify the length of each side by counting the number of spaces.

Look at the side across the top of the rectangle. How many spaces long is it? Now look at the side down the left of the rectangle. How many spaces long is it?

Ask about the length of the bottom and right side of the rectangle, too. Have each pair report the lengths of the four sides of their rectangle so they notice that—in each case—the top and bottom sides are the same length and the right and left sides are the same length.

Now, I want directions to draw a rectangle on dot paper.

Place a clean sheet of dot paper on the overhead, and mark the spot where you will start drawing. Select one pair of students, and have them give each step of the drawing. For each side, make sure they tell you where to start, in what direction to draw the line, and how far to draw the line. Label the length of each side, and point out that the sides make right angles.

Once you have drawn the rectangle, have the other pairs take a new rubber band and represent that rectangle on their Geoboards. Then, have students draw the same rectangle on their own sheet of dot paper.

Choose another pair of students to give you directions for drawing their rectangle on the overhead. Again, have pairs represent that rectangle on their Geoboards and have each student draw the rectangle on dot paper.

Explain that this is what they will be doing in the first Math Workshop activity and reiterate the steps.

ONGOING ASSESSMENT: Observing Students at Work

Students focus on the rectangle's outline (as opposed to its array structure).

- **Are students able to create rectangles on Geoboards?**

- **Are they able to reproduce rectangles on dot paper?**

- **Do students count the number of spaces between pegs or dots to determine the length of a side?**

- **Do students recognize that opposite sides of rectangles have equal lengths?**

- **Do students identify the angles of a rectangle as right angles?**

MATH WORKSHOP

40 MIN

2 Making Rectangles

For the remainder of Session 2.5, students will work on the following activities.

2A Rectangles on the Geoboard

INDIVIDUALS

Students make a rectangle on the Geoboard, draw the rectangle on Geoboard Dot Paper (M26), and identify the length of each of its sides. For complete details, see Activity 1 in this session.

Name _____ Date _____

Shapes, Blocks, and Symmetry | Daily Practice

The Rectangle Riddler
Draw the rectangle that solves
the riddle.

NOTE Students practice drawing
rectangles based on given information
about dimensions and area.
SMH 126, 127

1. I have 4 rows
and 6 columns.

2. I have 15 squares
and 3 rows.

3. I have 6 rows
and 5 columns.

4. I have 18 squares
and 6 columns.

5. In the problems above, which rectangle is the largest? _____

22 Unit 2   Session 2.5

▲ **Student Activity Book, p. 22**

*By using Geoboard Dot Paper (M26) students
continue to make rectangles of certain
dimensions.*

2B Describing Rectangles
INDIVIDUALS

For complete details about this activity, see Session 2.4, page 88.

2C Rectangle Riddles
INDIVIDUALS

For complete details about this activity, see Session 2.4, page 89.

2D Double Arrays
PAIRS

For complete details about this activity, see Session 1.2, page 37.

2E *Shapes* Software: *Quick Images* (optional)
PAIRS

For complete details about this activity, see Session 2.4, pages 87 and 88.

SESSION FOLLOW-UP
3 Daily Practice

Daily Practice: For reinforcement of this unit's content, have
students complete *Student Activity Book* page 22.

Student Math Handbook: Students and families may use
Student Math Handbook pages 118, 119, 121, 126 for reference
and review. See pages 178–182 in the back of this unit.

How Many Rectangles?

Math Focus Points

◆ Drawing rectangles by attending to the lengths of the sides

◆ Making different rectangular arrays using the same number of tiles

◆ Describing rectangular arrays of tiles

Today's Plan	Materials
ACTIVITY ➊ **How Many Rectangles?** 10 MIN INDIVIDUALS PAIRS CLASS	• Color tiles; overhead projector and overhead color tiles or chart paper
MATH WORKSHOP ➋ **Rectangles** 50 MIN **2A** How Many Rectangles? **2B** Rectangles on the Geoboard **2C** Describing Rectangles **2D** Rectangle Riddles **2E** *Shapes* Software: *Quick Images* (optional)	**2A** • M15*; M29* (optional); color tiles; tape; construction paper; glue sticks **2B** • Materials from Session 2.5, p. 92 **2C** • Materials from Session 2.4, p. 84 **2D** • Materials from Session 2.4, p. 84 **2E** • Computers with *Shapes* software installed
SESSION FOLLOW-UP ➌ **Daily Practice and Homework**	• *Student Activity Book,* p. 23–26 • M27* • *Student Math Handbook,* p. 126

*See *Materials to Prepare,* p. 61.

Classroom Routines

Quick Images: Double Arrays Using the transparent double arrays from Rectangular Arrays (T24) display the 2 × 3 array. Follow the basic *Quick Images* activity. Students determine the total number of squares and share how they determined the amount. Record an equation using addition (e.g., $3 + 3 = 6$) that represents the array. Repeat with 2 × 5 and then 2 × 6.

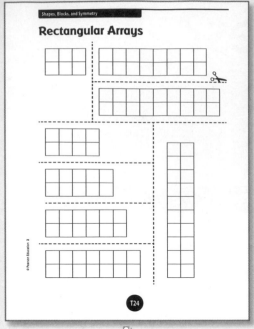

Shapes, Blocks, and Symmetry

Rectangular Arrays

© Pearson Education 2

T24

▲ Transparencies, T24

ACTIVITY

① How Many Rectangles?

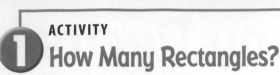

10 MIN INDIVIDUALS PAIRS CLASS

Each student takes 12 tiles of the same color.

How many different rectangles do you think can be made from 12 tiles? Make as many rectangles as you can. When you make one, take 12 more tiles of the same color and see whether you can make another. Then, compare your work with a partner to see whether either of you made any different ones.

After a few minutes, have the class discuss the rectangles that everyone has made. As students describe a rectangle, draw the array on the overhead or on chart paper. Next to each one, record students' descriptions.

You've made one rectangle that has two tiles in each of six rows, and another that is three rows with four tiles in each row. Do you think you've made all the possible rectangles using 12 tiles? See whether you can make a different rectangle.

Ask students to share their findings. If they do not suggest a 1×12 rectangle, ask them whether they can make a rectangle that uses 12 tiles and is only one tile wide.

Suppose these rectangles were chocolate bars. Which one would have the most chocolate?

When students point out that they would have the same amount of chocolate because they are all made of 12 tiles, point out that all three rectangles have the same area.

You've just made three different rectangles using 12 tiles. In Math Workshop, you'll be able to investigate the different rectangles that you can make using different numbers of tiles. There are some numbers of tiles that will make only one rectangle. And others—like 12—will make many rectangles.

ONGOING ASSESSMENT: Observing Students at Work

Students create different rectangles using a fixed number of color tiles.

- **Do students create rectangular arrangements of tiles: equal rows and equal columns?**

- **Do students recognize that rectangles made of one row of tiles are rectangles?**

- **Do students see that different rectangles can be made from the same number of tiles?**

MATH WORKSHOP

2 Rectangles

50 MIN

Post the following activities. Students will work on them for the remainder of the session.

2A How Many Rectangles?

PAIRS

Students investigate the number of rectangles they can make for one or two of the following numbers of color tiles: 16, 18, 24, 36. When they think they have found all the rectangles for one of the numbers, students draw or trace around them on Inch Grid Paper (M15), cut them out, and paste them on construction paper.❶

Students may need to tape two sheets of grid paper—as well as two sheets of construction paper—together to record and glue their rectangles.

Students make different rectangles with 16 tiles each.

Teaching Note

❶ **Centimeter Grid Paper** Students may choose to record their rectangles on Centimeter Grid Paper (M29), which allows larger rectangles to be recorded in a smaller space.

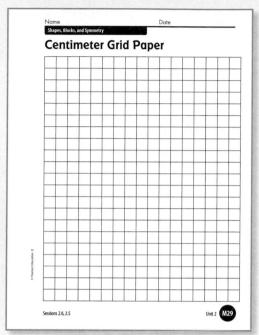

Name _____ Date _____

Shapes, Blocks, and Symmetry

Centimeter Grid Paper

Sessions 2.6, 3.5   Unit 2 **M29**

▲ **Resource Masters, M29**

2 Dialogue Box: Strategies for Building Rectangles, p. 174

3 Dialogue Box: Is it the Same Rectangle?, p. 176

Teaching Note

4 Collect the Descriptions At the end of the session, collect students' written descriptions and drawings from Describing Rectangles so you can see how students are doing. But do not make any corrections. Students will be using these descriptions in Session 2.7.

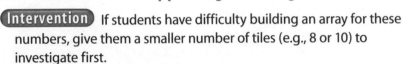

▲ Student Activity Book, p. 23

ONGOING ASSESSMENT: Observing Students at Work

Students investigate the different arrays that can be made with a specific number of tiles.

- **Are students able to make rectangular arrays (arrangements with equal rows and equal columns)?**

- **How do students try to construct rectangles from a given number of tiles?** Do they randomly try to arrange them or do they structure them as an array in rows and columns?**2**

- **Do students see pairs of rectangles (e.g., 6 × 3 and 3 × 6) as the same rectangle or as different rectangles?**3**

- **Do students have a strategy for finding different rectangles for the same number or do they randomly try to form rectangles?**4**

DIFFERENTIATION: Supporting the Range of Learners

Intervention If students have difficulty building an array for these numbers, give them a smaller number of tiles (e.g., 8 or 10) to investigate first.

Extension If students have made rectangles for one or two of the larger numbers, they can choose a number of their own—from 8 to 36—to see how many different rectangles they can make. Challenge them to think about whether they have found all the possible arrays for a number and how they know when they have found them.

2B Rectangles on the Geoboard

INDIVIDUALS

For complete details about this activity, see Session 2.5, pages 93–95.

2C Describing Rectangles

INDIVIDUALS

For complete details about this activity, see Session 2.4, page 88.**4**

2D Rectangle Riddles

INDIVIDUALS

For complete details about this activity, see Session 2.4, page 89.

2E *Shapes* Software: *Quick Images* (optional)

PAIRS

For complete details about this activity, see Session 2.4, pages 87–88.

3 Daily Practice and Homework

 Daily Practice: For ongoing review, have students complete *Student Activity Book* page 23.

 Homework: Students cut out the paper squares on Only One Rectangle (M27) and use them to create rectangles for specified numbers of tiles. They then draw the rectangles on *Student Activity Book* pages 24–26.

Student Math Handbook: Students and families may use *Student Math Handbook* pages 118, 119, 126 for reference and review. See pages 178–182 in the back of this unit.

▲ Resource Masters, M27

▲ Student Activity Book, pp. 24–25

▲ Student Activity Book, p. 26

Assessment:
Is It a Rectangle?

Math Focus Points

◆ Constructing and describing rectangular arrays of tiles

◆ Drawing rectangles by attending to the lengths of the sides

◆ Identifying important features of a rectangle

Today's Plan		Materials
ACTIVITY **① Describing Rectangles**	40 MIN CLASS	• Color tiles; students' written descriptions and drawings of rectangles (from Sessions 2.4–2.6); chart paper (optional)
ASSESSMENT ACTIVITY **② Is It a Rectangle?**	20 MIN INDIVIDUALS	• M30*
SESSION FOLLOW-UP **③ Daily Practice**		• *Student Activity Book*, p. 27 • *Student Math Handbook*, pp. 118, 119, 121, 126

*See *Materials to Prepare*, p. 61.

Classroom Routines

Today's Number: 19 Using Combinations of 10 Sometime during the day outside of math class do *Today's Number* with 19. Students generate expressions for the number 19 using combinations of 10 such as $7 + 3, 8 + 2, 5 + 5$. For example: $2 + 8 + 9 = 19, 5 + 5 + 3 + 6 = 19$.

ACTIVITY

Describing Rectangles

40 MIN   CLASS

Students will need their written descriptions and drawings of rectangles that they have been working on in the previous Math Workshops. They will also need access to color tiles, and enough space to build the rectangles as they are described.

Today we're going to think about what makes a good description of a rectangle. We want to know whether the descriptions you wrote are clear enough so that someone else can build the rectangle.

Some of you will read the description you wrote to the class without showing the picture. Then everyone will try to build your rectangle with color tiles. We'll compare the ones we've made with one another's and then with your original drawing.

Choose several students to read their descriptions. Students should compare their rectangles with one another before the reader shows his or her drawing. If students have made different rectangles than the reader, encourage them to share why they think the rectangle they have made is the one that was described. Do this several times and then gather as a class for a discussion.

Who can share with the rest of the class a description you got that you thought was so clear that you found it easy to build the rectangle? What makes a good description?

When a student shares his or her description, write it on the board or chart paper. Ask what makes the description so clear.

Students might say:

 "I knew how many tiles to use."

 "It told me how many tiles to put in each row."

Professional Development

1 Teacher Note: Assessment: Is It a Rectangle?, p. 159

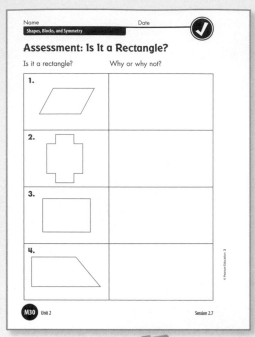

▲ **Resource Masters, M30** PORTFOLIO

ONGOING ASSESSMENT: Observing Students at Work

Students reproduce rectangular arrays from descriptions, and then discuss what makes a good description.

- **Do students' descriptions include at least two of the following: the number of tiles in a row, the number of rows, or the number of tiles in the rectangle?**

- **Are students able to reproduce the rectangle when given a clear description?**

- **Are students able to identify what makes a clear description?**

ASSESSMENT ACTIVITY

2 Is It a Rectangle?

20 MIN INDIVIDUALS

Distribute Assessment: Is It a Rectangle? (M30). Explain to students that you are interested in learning more about how they are thinking about rectangles and other polygon shapes.**1**

For each shape on the sheet, explain to students that they should say whether it is a rectangle and explain why or why not. Remind students to write as complete an answer as possible.

Students explain why a shape is or is not a rectangle.

ONGOING ASSESSMENT: Observing Students at Work

This assessment provides information about Benchmark 3: Identify rectangles as four-sided shapes with four right angles.

- **Are students able to identify shapes that are rectangles?**

- **Do their written explanations indicate their understanding that a rectangle has four straight sides and four right angles?**

SESSION FOLLOW-UP

3 Daily Practice

Daily Practice: For ongoing review, have students complete *Student Activity Book* page 27.

Student Math Handbook: Students and families may use *Student Math Handbook* pages 118, 119, 121, 126 for reference and review. See pages 178–182 in the back of this unit.

▲ **Student Activity Book, p. 27**

The Student Activity Book page shown reads:

Name _____ Date _____

Shapes, Blocks, and Symmetry — Daily Practice

Double Trouble

Look at each problem. If the answer is wrong, cross it out and write the correct answer.

NOTE Students practice the doubles combinations. 47

For example:
2 + 2 = ~~3~~ 4

1. 4 + 4 = 10	2. 5 + 5 = 10
3. 6 + 6 = 11	4. 9 + 9 = 16
5. 7 + 7 = 15	6. 3 + 3 = 5
7. 8 + 8 = 14	8. 10 + 10 = 20

Ongoing Review

9. Which answer could **not** be correct?

Shannon has 12 pets. Some of them are cats, and some of them are dogs. How many of Shannon's 12 pets might be cats?

Ⓐ 12   Ⓑ 11   Ⓒ 6   Ⓓ 1

Session 2.7   Unit 2   27

Making Boxes from Rectangles

Math Focus Points

◆ Recognizing that rectangular prisms have rectangular faces

◆ Recognizing which faces of a rectangular prism are the same size and shape

◆ Constructing a rectangular prism from rectangles

◆ Comparing rectangular prisms

Vocabulary

congruent

Today's Plan		Materials
ACTIVITY ❶ **Examining Rectangular Prisms**	🕐 10 MIN 👥 CLASS	• A box that is approximately 9″ × 5″ × 3″*; Geoblocks
ACTIVITY ❷ **Making Boxes**	🕐 50 MIN 👥 PAIRS	• Box pieces in envelopes*; clear or masking tape; scissors
SESSION FOLLOW-UP ❸ **Daily Practice**		• *Student Activity Book,* p. 28 • *Student Math Handbook,* pp. 124–125, 128

*See *Materials to Prepare,* p. 61.

Classroom Routines

How Many Pockets? At some point outside of math time, collect Pocket Data. Remind students of the data collected previously. Ask them to predict whether the class is wearing more, fewer, or about the same number of pockets today. Then each student takes as many cubes as they have pockets. Discuss different ways to count the cubes (e.g., by 5s or 10s). Use one suggestion to count the cubes and another to double-check the count. Record the data on your class chart.

ACTIVITY

1 Examining Rectangular Prisms

10 MIN CLASS

Professional Development

❶ **Teacher Note:** Identifying Types of 3-Dimensional Shapes, p. 150

❷ **Teacher Note:** Students Make Their Own Boxes, p. 145

Show a box that is approximately 9″ × 5″ × 3″, such as a shoe box, a cereal box, or another box without square faces. Hold it up or place it where all can see.

Take a look at this box. In some ways it resembles some of the Geoblocks we examined in the last investigation.

Ask a student to go to the box of Geoblocks and find a block that resembles the box.

Let's compare our box to the Geoblock. In what ways are they the same and in what ways are they different?

Students might say that the block is made of wood and the box is made of cardboard or that the box is larger than the block.

If students do not mention that the faces are all rectangles, point to a face and ask what the shape is. Bring up that both the box and the block have six rectangular faces.

Let's just look at this box. What can you say about the sizes of the faces? Are they all the same? Are some bigger than others?

Students may see that each face has another face that is the same size and shape, or congruent. They may also see that two adjacent faces have at least one pair of sides that are the same length.❶ ❷

ONGOING ASSESSMENT: Observing Students at Work

Students compare two rectangular prisms.

- **Can students count the six faces of a rectangular prism?**

- **Do students recognize that opposite faces of a rectangular prism have the same size and shape and that they are rectangles?**

Math Note

3 Making Boxes in Grade 1 Students who worked with Investigations in Grade 1 may have already made boxes from rectangular pieces. Revisiting this challenging activity allows them to solidify the idea of how rectangles can be used to create rectangular prisms and to further develop their sense of the structure of rectangular prisms.

Teaching Notes

4 Preparing Tape Many teachers precut a lot of small pieces of tape and put them on the edge of the tables where students are working. Students can just take a piece when they are ready. This helps supply students with reasonably-sized pieces.

5 Storing Boxes Decide ahead of time where students can keep their boxes-in-progress. They will continue working on them during the next session. Before they set them aside, students should be sure to write their names or initials on them.

ACTIVITY

2 Making Boxes

50 MIN   PAIRS

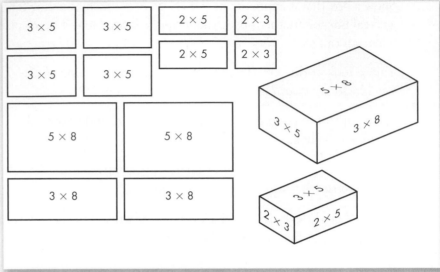

Hold up some of the rectangles from the prepared sets.**3**

You're going to make your own box with rectangles and tape. Here's what the flat rectangles look like. You're going to figure out how to put them together.

Each pair of students works with one envelope of box pieces. This gives students the pieces they need to make two different boxes: one that is 3″ × 5″ × 8″ and another that is 3″ × 5″ × 2″.

You and your partner will get a set of rectangles of different sizes. These pieces won't all fit together. It's like a puzzle. You have to figure out which pieces you can put together to make a box. The box should have sides, a bottom, and a top.

Ask for volunteers to suggest how you might start by choosing two rectangles that could be taped together. Demonstrate how to do it.**4**

Before they start taping, encourage students to do some planning by holding pieces next to each other to see how they want to put them together. If they want to separate pieces that they have already taped, they can just cut through the tape.**5**

ONGOING ASSESSMENT: Observing Students at Work

Students build boxes out of rectangular pieces and develop their sense of the structure of rectangular prisms.

- **Do students make use of the information that opposite faces of a rectangular prism are the same size and shape?** Do they choose adjacent faces with edges of equal lengths?

- **Do students lay out the pieces on the table and see how they can "fold" them into a box?**

- **When students begin a box that does not work, do they seem stuck or do they try a different combination of pieces?** Do they refer to a Geoblock prism and consider the structure of that shape? Do they learn how to make better choices from what does not work or do they start again, choosing pieces randomly?

- **When students run into a problem, can they figure out a way to overcome it to finish their box—even if the result is not a conventional box?**

DIFFERENTIATION: Supporting the Range of Learners

Extension If some students complete the two boxes, ask them to open the top of the larger box—by cutting through the tape on the top face—and figure out how many smaller boxes could fit inside without going over the top. (If the smaller box is oriented with a 3″ × 5″ face against the 3″ × 5″ face of the larger box, four of them would fit.)

SESSION FOLLOW-UP

3 Daily Practice

Daily Practice: For ongoing review, have students complete *Student Activity Book* page 28.

Student Math Handbook: Students and families may use *Student Math Handbook* pages 124–125 and 128 for reference and review. See pages 178–182 in the back of this unit.

▲ **Student Activity Book, p. 28**

Assessment:
Faces of a Geoblock

Math Focus Points

◆ Constructing a rectangular prism from rectangles

◆ Recognizing which faces of a rectangular prism are the same size and shape

◆ Visualizing and describing rectangular prisms

◆ Comparing rectangular prisms

Vocabulary
rectangular prism

Today's Plan		Materials
ACTIVITY ❶ **Making Boxes**	🕐 25 MIN 👥 PAIRS	• Students' boxes-in-progress (from Session 2.8); clear or masking tape; scissors; extra index cards (optional)
DISCUSSION ❷ **Comparing Boxes**	🕐 20 MIN 👥 CLASS	• Students' boxes (from Activity 1)
ASSESSMENT ACTIVITY ❸ **Faces of a Geoblock**	✔ 🕐 15 MIN 👤 INDIVIDUALS	• M31* • Various rectangular prisms from a set of Geoblocks
SESSION FOLLOW-UP ❹ **Daily Practice**		• *Student Activity Book,* p. 29 • *Student Math Handbook,* pp. 122, 124–125

*See *Materials to Prepare,* p. 61.

Classroom Routines

What Time Is It? Using the large demonstration clock, set the hands to a half hour time such as 4:30. Students record the time in digital format (e.g., 4:30) on a piece of paper. Repeat several times so that you can get a sense of how comfortable students are reading the clock to the half hour.

ACTIVITY

1 Making Boxes

25 MIN PAIRS

Students continue their work making boxes. For complete details about this activity, see Session 2.8, page 108.

ONGOING ASSESSMENT: Observing Students at Work

For complete information about what to observe, see Session 2.8, page 109.

DIFFERENTIATION: Supporting the Range of Learners

Intervention Some students may complete their boxes while others are still working. Have them return to the How Many Rectangles? activity from Session 2.6, page 99.

Extension Students who want more of a challenge can try to cut their own pieces—instead of starting with a prepared set—to make boxes in shapes and sizes of their own choosing.

DISCUSSION

2 Comparing Boxes

20 MIN CLASS

Math Focus Points for Discussion

◆ Visualizing and describing rectangular prisms

◆ Comparing rectangular prisms

Gather students together to discuss the boxes they have made. Ask pairs to sit together with their boxes.

❶ What Is the Same? Some students may not see boxes that are the same size and shape, but turned differently, as the same. For example, if the 3″ × 5″ × 8″ box is placed with the 3″ × 5″ card on the bottom, it looks tall and not very wide. With the 5″ × 8″ card on the bottom, it looks long and wide, but not very tall. These different-looking shapes do have the same dimensions. Engage students in conversations about why they think boxes are, or are not, the same. You might display three or four boxes and then show another box that is the same as one of them, but in a different position. Ask which box it matches.

Begin by taking a box from one pair of students. Ask everyone who has made the same box to hold it up. Once the class agrees that everyone is holding up the same box, pairs put that box aside.❶

Now hold up another box from a different pair of students. Again, ask students who made the same box to hold it up and then put it aside. If any students have used new cards to make different boxes (see Extension page 111), have them share their boxes, too. In this way, create a collection that includes one example of the two different boxes that students have made using the box pieces along with any boxes made from other pieces.

What were some of the things that you needed to pay attention to as you began to make a box out of the pieces?

Students might say:

"I knew I needed six sides and I knew that opposite sides had to be the same."

"I looked at some of the Geoblocks and I tried to match up some of the cardboard pieces, like I needed two squares for my end pieces."

"First I tried to find pieces that I thought went together. They were either the same or they each had a side that was the same—like the square piece and one of the long rectangle pieces. Then I tried to match those up and see what it looked like before I added another piece."

So, you are giving some important hints about how to make a box, but you are also giving us some important information about what makes a box be a box or as mathematicians call it, a rectangular prism.

Mathematical Emphases

Area Measurement Visualizing the structure of arrays

Math Focus Points

◆ Constructing and describing rectangular arrays of tiles

Features of Shape Exploring mirror symmetry

Math Focus Points

◆ Describing and identifying objects and designs that have mirror symmetry

◆ Constructing 2-D and 3-D symmetrical designs with mirror symmetry

◆ Reflecting a shape across a line of symmetry

◆ Orienting shapes so that a line of symmetry aligns with a mirror (*Shapes* software)

◆ Exploring symmetry by folding and cutting paper patterns

◆ Identifying lines of symmetry

◆ Determining what makes a design symmetrical

Computational Fluency Knowing addition combinations to $10 + 10$

Math Focus Points

◆ Developing fluency with the doubles combinations to $10 + 10$

◆ Achieving fluency with the doubles combinations

Symmetry

	Student Activity Book	Student Math Handbook	Professional Development: Read Ahead of Time	
SESSION 3.1 p. 120				
Mirror Symmetry The class talks about what symmetry means by looking at a symmetrical design and by looking around their classroom for symmetrical objects. They then investigate mirror images. During the Math Workshop, students build symmetrical designs and constructions with pattern blocks and Geoblocks.	30–32	47, 129	• **Teacher Note:** Making Symmetrical Designs, p. 164 • **Dialogue Box:** Discussing Symmetry, p. 177	
SESSION 3.2 p. 127				
Copy Tiles Students learn a new activity, Copy Tiles, in which partners build and copy a design, piece by piece, along a line of symmetry. Students are also introduced to two *Shapes* software activities. The Math Workshop continues to focus on symmetry.	30, 33–34	47, 129		
SESSION 3.3 p. 132				
Paper Folding and Cutting Students cut symmetrical shapes from folded paper. The Math Workshop continues to focus on symmetry.	30, 33, 35	47, 129		

Classroom Routines See page 16 for an overview.

Quick Images	What Time Is It?
• T24, Rectangular Arrays 🖨	• Student clocks (1 per pair)
Today's Number	
• Chart paper	

Materials to Gather	Materials to Prepare
• **Overhead pattern blocks** (optional) • **Pattern blocks** (1 bucket per every 6–8 students) • **Geoblocks in subsets** (as needed) • **Mirrors** (1 per pair) • **Glue sticks** (as needed; optional) • **Crayons or markers** (as needed)	• **M32, Symmetrical Pattern Block Design** Make 1 copy and color in the shapes to make a symmetrical design. • **T26, Symmetrical Pattern Block Design** 🖨 Fill in the design on the transparency with overhead pattern blocks. (optional) • **M33–M38, Paper Pattern Blocks** Make a copy of each sheet on the assigned colored paper. Cut out the shapes. (3 or 4 sets; plus extras as needed; optional) • **M40, Double It Recording Sheet** Make copies. (1 per pair)
• **T27, Copy Tiles Grid Paper** 🖨 • **M33–M38, Paper Pattern Blocks** (3 or 4 sets; plus extras as needed; from Session 3.1; optional) • **M40, Double It Recording Sheet** (as needed; from Session 3.1) • **Color tiles** (1 bucket per every 4–6 students) • **Computers with *Shapes* software installed** • **Materials for Mirror Design** See Session 3.1. • **Materials for Symmetrical Geoblock Buildings** See Session 3.1. • **Materials for Double It** See Session 3.1.	• **M39, Copy Tiles Grid Paper** Make copies. (as needed)
• **Materials for Copy Tiles** See Session 3.2. • **Materials for Double It** See Session 3.1. • **Construction paper** (about 2 per student) • **Scissors** (1 per student) • **Glue sticks** (1 per student) • **Computers with *Shapes* software installed**	• $8\frac{1}{2}'' \times 5\frac{1}{2}''$ **paper** Cut $8\frac{1}{2}'' \times 11''$ paper in half. (4 per student; plus extras as needed)

🖨 Overhead Transparency

Symmetry, *continued*

SESSION 3.4 p. 137	Student Activity Book	Student Math Handbook	Professional Development: Read Ahead of Time	
Is It Symmetrical? Students share the symmetrical designs they have made with different materials. They use the fold-and-pinch procedure as another way to check whether their designs are symmetrical. Students then construct half of a design out of pattern blocks along a line of symmetry, predict the total number of blocks, complete the design, and count the total number.	36–40	47, 129		
SESSION 3.5 p. 142				
End-of-Unit Assessment Students complete assessment tasks that focus on rectangles, symmetry, and the doubles combinations.	41	47, 126, 129	• **Teacher Note:** End-of-Unit Assessment, p. 166	

Materials to Gather	Materials to Prepare
• **Students' symmetry examples** See Sessions 3.1, 3.2, and 3.3. • **Mirrors** (as needed; optional) • **Chart paper** (1 sheet; optional) • **Glue sticks** (1 per pair) • **Crayons or markers** (as needed) • **Pattern blocks** (1 bucket per 4–6 students; optional)	• **M33–M38, Paper Pattern Blocks** Make copies. (as needed; from Session 3.1) Decide whether students will use the cut-outs or blocks to record their work. If you choose cut-outs, gather glue sticks. If you choose blocks, gather crayons or markers. • **M41, Half and Half** Make copies. (as needed)
• **Doubles Combinations Cards** (1 blank set; from Session 1.4; optional) • **Color tiles** (18 per student) • **Tape** (as needed)	• **M15, Inch Grid Paper** Make copies. (1 per student; plus extras as needed) • **M29, Centimeter Grid Paper** Make copies. (optional) • **M42–M44, End-of-Unit Assessment** Make copies. (1 per student) • **M45, Assessment Checklist: Doubles Combinations** ☑ Make copies. (2 or 3 sheets)

☑ Checklist Available

Mirror Symmetry

Math Focus Points

◆ Describing and identifying objects and designs that have mirror symmetry

◆ Constructing 2-D and 3-D symmetrical designs with mirror symmetry

◆ Developing fluency with the doubles combinations to $10 + 10$

Vocabulary

symmetry

Today's Plan | Materials

		Materials
ACTIVITY ① **Mirror Designs**	25 MIN · CLASS · PAIRS	• M32*; T26 (optional)* • Overhead pattern blocks (optional); pattern blocks; mirrors
ACTIVITY ② **Introducing Symmetrical Geoblock Buildings**	5 MIN · CLASS	• Geoblocks
MATH WORKSHOP ③ **Symmetry and Doubling** ③A Mirror Designs ③B Symmetrical Geoblock Buildings ③C Double It	30 MIN	③A • M33–M38* (as needed; optional) • Pattern blocks; blank paper; mirrors; glue sticks; crayons or markers ③B • Geoblocks in subsets ③C • *Student Activity Book*, p. 30 • M40* • Primary Number Cards
SESSION FOLLOW-UP ④ **Daily Practice and Homework**		• *Student Activity Book*, pp. 31–32 • *Student Math Handbook*, pp. 47, 129

*See *Materials to Prepare,* p. 117.

Classroom Routines

Quick Images: Double Arrays Using the transparent double arrays from Rectangular Arrays (T24), display the 2 × 4 array. Follow the basic *Quick Images* activity. Students determine the total number of squares and share how they determined the amount. Record an equation using addition (e.g., $4 + 4 = 8$) that represents the array. Repeat with 2 × 7 and then 2 × 9.

ACTIVITY

25 MIN   CLASS   PAIRS

Mirror Designs

Hold up the design that you prepared on Symmetrical Pattern Block Design (M32) or display its transparency (T26) on the overhead.

Take a look at this design. What do you notice?

It is likely that students will comment on the arrangement of the blocks by noting either that the left and right sides are similar because they use the same blocks, or that the design appears "balanced." Depending on the experiences of your students, someone may comment that the design is symmetrical. If no one mentions the word symmetry, you will need to introduce it.❶

Some people would say that this design has symmetry or is symmetrical. Has anyone heard that word before? How might you describe what it means for something to be symmetrical?❷

Lots of things in the world are symmetrical. Look around. What are some that you see?

After a few students have shared, let them know that in this next set of geometry activities, they will be investigating the idea of symmetry and creating designs and pictures that are symmetrical.

Distribute a blank piece of paper, a small set of pattern blocks, and a small mirror to each pair of students. Explain that this will be one of the activities that they can work on during the Math Workshop.

I'd like you to fold your paper in half and then open it up. We are going to call the fold the "mirror line."

Next, have students choose two of the same pattern blocks. They should choose any block except the yellow hexagon for this activity.

Place one of the pattern blocks on one side of the fold. What do you think you'll see in the reflection when you place your mirror on the mirror line facing the block?

Professional Development

❶ **Teacher Note:** Making Symmetrical Designs, p. 164

❷ **Dialogue Box:** Discussing Symmetry, p. 177

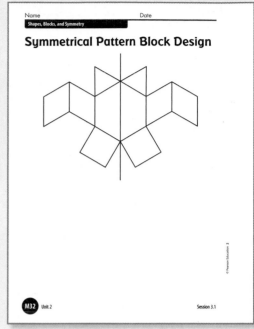

Name   Date

Shapes, Blocks, and Symmetry

Symmetrical Pattern Block Design

M32   Unit 2   Session 3.1

▲ **Resource Masters, M32; T26**

Place your mirror on the folded line facing the block, look into the mirror, and describe to your partner what you see.

Students use mirrors to begin to explore symmetry.

Ask a few pairs to share their observations.

What do you see in the mirror? What do you notice about the direction of the block, or the way it's faced?

Not only do you want students to notice a duplicate of the block, but also the orientation of the block in its reflection. Next, direct students to remove the mirror and place the other pattern block on the other side of the fold (where the reflection was). Check the placement by putting back the mirror. Pairs can add another block or two to one side of their designs and again use the mirror to check how the reflected or symmetrical design will look once they build it on the other side.

This type of symmetry—when half of a design, a picture, or an object is a reflection of the other—is called mirror symmetry. When a design has mirror symmetry, you can imagine folding the design or object in half—along the mirror line—and having each side match up exactly.

Demonstrate how to do this with the Symmetrical Pattern Block Design (M32). Show students how you can fold the paper in half and how the blocks on the left side match up with the blocks on the right side.

ONGOING ASSESSMENT: Observing Students at Work

Students use mirror reflections to identify the line of symmetry.

- **Are students familiar with symmetry?**

- **Are they able to place blocks on either side of the mirror line?**

- **Do they seem to understand that the mirror reflects the opposite or symmetrical half of their block design?**

5 MIN   CLASS

ACTIVITY

2 Introducing Symmetrical Geoblock Buildings

Many buildings are symmetrical. They have parts that match. Let's build a symmetrical building with Geoblocks.

Start building a simple symmetrical building.

What block should I add to make it symmetrical? Which direction should the block be placed?

Have a student place the block on the building. You might have the student place it so it first slopes one way and then the other. Ask others to tell which way makes the building symmetrical.

❸ **Symmetry Display** Start a bulletin board for students to post symmetrical objects, pictures, and their own drawings of symmetrical things.

▲ Resource Masters, M33–M35

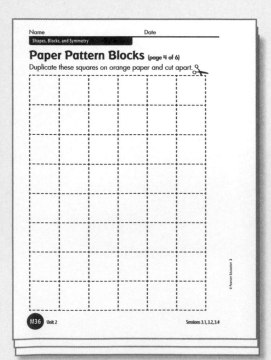

▲ Resource Masters, M36–M38

MATH WORKSHOP

③ Symmetry and Doubling

30 MIN

The following activities give students the opportunity to practice creating symmetrical designs, buildings in both two and three dimensions, and to practice the doubles combinations.❸

During the next three Math Workshops, students will participate in Double It, an activity they engaged in during *Counting, Coins, and Combinations* (Unit 1). In this activity, students draw a number card, double the result, and record the sum on *Student Activity Book* page 30.

③A Mirror Designs

INDIVIDUALS PAIRS

Students work individually or with partners to build a symmetrical design with pattern blocks using a mirror. When finished, they show their design to someone else and see whether the person agrees that it is symmetrical. Students record at least one of their designs, using Paper Pattern Blocks (M33–M38) or by tracing blocks and coloring in the shapes. They will use this design in the discussion in Session 3.4.

Students build a symmetrical design with pattern blocks.

ONGOING ASSESSMENT: Observing Students at Work

Students create and record symmetrical designs with pattern blocks and mirrors.

- **Are students' designs symmetrical?**

- **Are students able to identify and change blocks that are placed incorrectly either with or without use of the mirror?**

- **Are students' designs simple or elaborate?** Do any have more than one line of symmetry? If so, can students identify this?

DIFFERENTIATION: Supporting the Range of Learners

Intervention Some students may benefit from having a line drawn down the center of their folded paper to accentuate the line of symmetry.

Extension Suggest that some students try building larger symmetrical designs. Ask them whether they can cover a desk or table. This kind of challenge often turns into a cooperative venture among many students.

3B Symmetrical Geoblock Buildings

INDIVIDUALS

Students build symmetrical buildings with Geoblocks. When they finish, students share their buildings with you and tell you how they know the buildings are symmetrical.

ONGOING ASSESSMENT: Observing Students at Work

Students build three-dimensional symmetrical buildings.

- **Are students able to construct a building that is symmetrical?**

- **Are they able to describe to you why their building is symmetrical?**

DIFFERENTIATION: Supporting the Range of Learners

Intervention If a student has difficulty understanding how to build a symmetrical building, build one together. Have the student place one block at a time while you add the corresponding blocks.

Extension Some students may build Geoblock buildings that are symmetrical on four sides. If they do so, encourage them to continue.

▲ **Student Activity Book, p. 30; Resource Masters, M40**

▲ Student Activity Book, p. 31

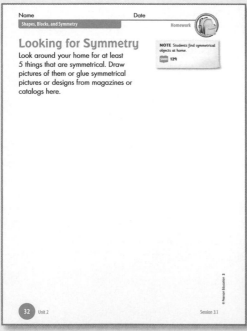

▲ Student Activity Book, p. 32

PAIRS INDIVIDUALS

3C Double It

Students practice the doubles combinations by drawing a number card, doubling the result, and recording the sum on the Double It Recording Sheet (*Student Activity Book* page 30, or M40).

ONGOING ASSESSMENT: Observing Students at Work

Students practice doubling numbers and writing the numbers up to 20.

- **How do students calculate the double of a number?** Do they count all? Count on? Use combinations they know? Do they just know some or all of the doubles combinations? Are they accurate?

- **How accurate and legible are students' written numbers?**

DIFFERENTIATION: Supporting the Range of Learners

Extension Some students will notice and become excited about the pattern they see as they record their work (every other column on the Student Sheet will be empty). Encourage students to think about why this pattern appears, but know that a formal investigation of even and odd numbers will take place in Unit 3, *Stickers, Number Strings, and Story Problems.*

SESSION FOLLOW-UP

4 Daily Practice and Homework

 Daily Practice: For ongoing review, have students complete *Student Activity Book* page 31.

 Homework: Ask students to look around their homes or in magazines to find things that are symmetrical. They can paste and draw these objects on *Student Activity Book* page 32.

 Student Math Handbook: Students and families may use *Student Math Handbook* pages 47, 129 for reference and review. See pages 178–182 in the back of this unit.

Copy Tiles

Math Focus Points

◆ Constructing 2-D and 3-D symmetrical designs with mirror symmetry

◆ Reflecting a shape across a line of symmetry

◆ Orienting shapes so that a line of symmetry aligns with a mirror (*Shapes* software)

Today's Plan		Materials
ACTIVITY ❶ **Introducing Copy Tiles**	10 MIN　CLASS	• T27 • Color tiles
ACTIVITY ❷ ***Shapes* Software: *Reflection Puzzles* (optional)**	CLASS　PAIRS	• Computers with *Shapes* software installed
MATH WORKSHOP ❸ **Symmetry** ❸A **Copy Tiles** ❸B **Mirror Designs** ❸C **Symmetrical Geoblock Buildings** ❸D ***Shapes* Software: *Reflection Puzzles* (optional)** ❸E **Double It**	50 MIN	❸A • *Student Activity Book,* p. 33 • M39* • Color tiles; crayons or markers (as needed) ❸B • Materials from Session 3.1, p. 120 ❸C • Geoblocks in subsets ❸D • Computers with *Shapes* software installed ❸E • *Student Activity Book,* p. 30 • Materials from Session 3.1, p. 120
SESSION FOLLOW-UP ❹ **Daily Practice**		• *Student Activity Book,* p. 34 • *Student Math Handbook,* pp. 47, 129

*See *Materials to Prepare,* p. 117.

Classroom Routines

Today's Number: 20 Using Double Combinations　Sometime during the day outside of math class do *Today's Number* with 20. Students generate expressions for the number 20 using doubles combinations such as $2 + 2$, $5 + 5$, etc. For example: $6 + 6 + 3 + 3 + 1 + 1$, $8 + 8 + 2 + 2$, $5 + 5 + 5 + 5$.

Name _____ Date _____

Shapes, Blocks, and Symmetry

Copy Tiles Grid Paper

Sessions 3.2, 3.3   Unit 2 **33**

▲ **Student Activity Book, p. 33;
Resource Masters, M39; T27**

ACTIVITY

10 MIN   CLASS

1 Introducing Copy Tiles

Place Copy Tiles Grid Paper (T27) on the overhead.

Today you are going to work with a partner to make symmetrical designs on grid paper using square tiles.

Ask for a volunteer to be your partner to demonstrate Copy Tiles on the overhead. Place one color tile in a square along the center line and ask a volunteer to copy you by placing a matching color tile in a corresponding (reflected) square on the other side of the line. Continue to add tiles to make a symmetrical design.

Make a few designs and take turns being the leader and the copier.

Choose one or two of your designs to record by coloring in the design on the grid paper.

The teacher and a volunteer model a round of Copy Tiles.

ACTIVITY

2 *Shapes* Software: Reflection Puzzles (optional)

CLASS PAIRS

Introduce students to the *Reflection Puzzles* activity of the *Shapes* software.❶ ❷ Specifically, show students how to:

- Choose the *Reflection Puzzles* activity from the Activity menu

- Choose a shape set (pattern blocks, Power Polygons, or tangrams)

- Choose a level and a specific puzzle

The *Reflection Puzzles* outline appears with a mirror and the grid showing. Place a shape on the opposite side of the mirror so its reflection lands near the puzzle outline and ask,

How can we make the reflection of the puzzle piece fit inside the puzzle outline? What happens to the reflection if we move the shape to the right or left? What happens to the reflection if we move the shape up or down?

What happens to the reflection if we turn the shape to the left? To the right?

You may also want to show students how to:

- Turn the mirrors off and on, and how to turn the grid off and back on

- Get a text or visual hint

- Pick another puzzle when they are done

Students may want to begin with the pattern block shape set, but can also try Power Polygons and tangrams.

MATH WORKSHOP

3 Symmetry

50 MIN

The following activities give students the opportunity to practice building symmetrical designs and buildings in both two and three dimensions, to think about how designs are reflected across a line of symmetry, and to practice the doubles combinations.❸

❶ **Using *Shapes* All Year Long** *Shapes* software offers students a variety of opportunities to work with the geometric ideas in this unit. Depending on the number of computers in your classroom, it is likely that most students have had only limited experience with the software. Plan to make it available throughout the year. Students' understanding of each activity will deepen over time with each experience.

❷ **Mirror Images** The *Shapes* software has several tools for exploring mirror images. In addition to the Flip tools, which reflect shapes or groups of shapes across their horizontal or vertical midlines, there is a horizontal and a vertical mirror that can be turned on separately or together; a grid to help measure distances from the mirror; and a variety of built-in *Reflection Puzzles*. Like regular *Puzzles*, the goal of *Reflection Puzzles* is to fill an outline, but this time with the *reflections* of shapes rather than the shapes themselves. Students place shapes on the opposite side of the mirror from the outline they want to fill. They place shapes and orient them so their *reflections* fill the outline.

Teaching Note

❸ **Save Five Minutes** Consider saving five minutes at the end of this session for students to share the work they have been doing in the Symmetrical Geoblock Buildings activity. The class can then discuss why the buildings are or are not symmetrical.

Teaching Notes

❹ Copy Tile Variation Partners make a design with several color tiles on one side of the fold, color in the squares, exchange papers, and then complete each other's designs by building the reflection with color tiles. You can collect these papers and start a class set of Copy Tile Task Cards for students to choose during Math Workshop.

❺ Photograph the Geoblock Buildings Consider photographing the students' buildings to create a permanent record of their work. You can post the photos and/or keep them in their math folders.

Explain that today is the last chance that students will have to work on the Mirror Design and Symmetrical Geoblock Buildings activities. Students who have not worked on these yet should choose to do them first.

3A Copy Tiles

PAIRS

Partners build their own symmetrical designs with color tiles on *Student Activity Book* page 33. One student places a tile on one side of the center line and the other "copies" by placing the same-color tile in the corresponding (reflected) square on the other side.❹

When partners finish one design, they switch roles so that each has a turn being the leader and the copier. Students then choose one or two of their designs to color in on the grid paper. Save the recorded color-tile designs for the discussion in Session 3.4.

ONGOING ASSESSMENT: Observing Students at Work

Pairs of students use color tiles to make symmetrical designs.

- **Do they take turns making and copying the pattern?**

- **How do they resolve disagreements about where a "copied" tile should be placed?**

- **How do they talk about their designs to convince others that each side is a mirror image?**

DIFFERENTIATION: Supporting the Range of Learners

Extension Suggest that some students try building larger symmetrical designs. Ask them whether they can cover a desk or table. This kind of challenge often turns into a cooperative venture among many students.

3B Mirror Designs

INDIVIDUALS   PAIRS   GROUPS

For complete details about this activity, see Session 3.1, pages 121 and 122.

3C Symmetrical Geoblock Buildings

INDIVIDUALS

For complete details about this activity, see Session 3.1, page 123.❺

3D *Shapes* Software: *Reflection Puzzles* (optional)

PAIRS

Students work in pairs on the computer to solve *Reflection Puzzles.* They place shapes on the side of the mirror opposite the puzzle outline so that the reflection of these shapes fills the outline. *Reflection Puzzles* can be difficult at first, as students learn about the relationship between the motions of a shape and its reflection. Encourage students to use trial and error to experiment with moving and turning shapes until their reflections land in the puzzle outlines.

ONGOING ASSESSMENT: Observing Students at Work

- **Can students describe what happens to the reflection when they move a shape in different directions?**

- **Can they begin to predict how to turn a shape so the reflection will be oriented the right way to fill the outline?**

DIFFERENTIATION: Supporting the Range of Learners

Intervention If students are having difficulty, ask them to *watch the reflection* as they move or turn the shape. Focusing separately on the position of the reflections, and then on their orientation, may also help.

Extension If students have mastered *Reflection Puzzles* and need an additional challenge, they can turn the mirror off before placing shapes, and then turn it on again to see all their pieces reflected at once and where those land compared to the puzzle outline.

3E Double It

PAIRS   INDIVIDUALS

For complete details about this activity, see Session 3.1, page 126.

SESSION FOLLOW-UP
4 Daily Practice

 Daily Practice: For reinforcement of this unit's content, have students complete *Student Activity Book* page 34.

 Student Math Handbook: Students and families may use *Student Math Handbook* pages 47, 129 for reference and review. See pages 178–182 in the back of this unit.

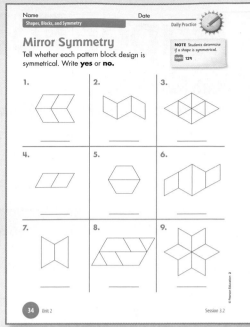

▲ Student Activity Book, p. 34

Paper Folding and Cutting

Math Focus Points

◆ Exploring symmetry by folding and cutting paper patterns

◆ Reflecting a shape across a line of symmetry

◆ Orienting shapes so that a line of symmetry aligns with a mirror (*Shapes* software)

Vocabulary

line of symmetry

Today's Plan		Materials
ACTIVITY ① **Introducing Fold and Cut** 🕐 10 MIN CLASS		• $8\frac{1}{2}"$ x $5\frac{1}{2}"$ paper*; scissors
ACTIVITY ② *Shapes* Software: Introducing *Line of Symmetry* (optional) 🕐 10 MIN PAIRS		• Computers with *Shapes* software installed
MATH WORKSHOP ③ **Fold and Copy** 🕐 40 MIN ③A Fold and Cut ③B Copy Tiles ③C *Shapes* Software: *Reflection Puzzles* (optional) ③D *Shapes* Software: *Line of Symmetry* (optional) ③E Double It		③A • $8\frac{1}{2}"$ x $5\frac{1}{2}"$ paper*; construction paper; scissors; paste or glue sticks ③B • *Student Activity Book,* p. 33 • Materials from Session 3.2, p. 127 ③C • Computers with *Shapes* software installed ③D • Computers with *Shapes* software installed ③E • Materials from Session 3.1, p. 120
SESSION FOLLOW-UP ④ **Daily Practice**		• *Student Activity Book,* p. 35 • *Student Math Handbook,* pp. 47, 129

*See *Materials to Prepare,* p. 117.

Classroom Routines

What Time Is It? On the board or overhead, write down the hour in digital format (4:30) and have students set their individual clocks to the appropriate time. Repeat several times so that you can get a sense of how comfortable students are with interpreting and setting times to the half hour.

10 MIN   CLASS

ACTIVITY

Introducing Fold and Cut

Fold a sheet of paper in half and draw half a pine tree, turtle, or other symmetrical design on it.

I am going to cut along this outline. What will I have when the paper is unfolded?

Students will probably recognize that you will have a tree or turtle. Cut out the shape, unfold it, and show it to the students.

I just folded a paper and cut out a symmetrical tree. The tree is symmetrical; the folding line, or line of symmetry, divides the tree into two halves that are alike. In a new Math Workshop activity, you will be cutting symmetrical objects from paper. Who has an idea for some symmetrical shapes or objects you could try to cut from folded paper?

List students' suggestions on the board. Some possibilities may include: heart, butterfly, diamond, rectangle, square, and tree.

Explain that if students need to make modifications to their design, they should refold the paper before they cut so that their design remains symmetrical.

When you have a shape or an object that you really like, you should glue it—and the paper that it was cut from—onto a sheet of construction paper.

❶ Reflection and Symmetry *Line of Symmetry Puzzles* in the *Shapes* software provides another way for students to explore ideas of reflection and symmetry. In these puzzles, students are presented with a glued group of shapes and a mirror. The task is to rotate the shape so that its line of symmetry is in the same direction as the mirror. They test to see if they've been successful by moving the shape to the mirror and matching the shape with its own reflection. Puzzles can have one, more than one, or sometimes no lines of symmetry.

❷ Customized Puzzles The CD-ROM version of the *Shapes* software also allows users—students or the teacher—to design their own *Reflection Puzzles* and *Line of Symmetry Puzzles* and to save them to a disk. Use this feature to customize puzzles for your class, or allow students to challenge one another. See the *Software Support Reference Guide* for details on how to do *Make Your Own Puzzles*.

ACTIVITY

10 MIN   PAIRS

② *Shapes* Software: Introducing *Line of Symmetry Puzzles* (optional)

Introduce students to the *Line of Symmetry Puzzles* activity of the *Shapes* software.❶ Specifically, show students how to:

- Choose the *Line of Symmetry Puzzles* activity from the Activity menu.

- Choose a shape set (pattern blocks, Power Polygons, or tangrams).

- Choose a level and a specific puzzle.

The puzzle—a glued group of shapes—appears with a mirror showing.

If we move this group of shapes to the mirror, do you think it will exactly match its reflection? Why or why not? If not, is there something we could do to the group of shapes to make it match its reflection?

Take suggestions about what to do to make the puzzle match its reflection until, as a group, students find a way to make the puzzle match. Tell students that when the shape matches its reflection, the mirror is marking a "line of symmetry" for the shape. Then ask:

Is there another way we could turn the puzzle and make it match its reflection? That is, is there another line of symmetry?

Tell students they will be exploring other *Line of Symmetry Puzzles* in Math Workshop. Also tell them that some puzzles have one line of symmetry, some puzzles have several lines of symmetry, and some puzzles have no lines of symmetry.❷

MATH WORKSHOP

40 MIN

③ Fold and Copy

The following activities give students the opportunity to practice creating symmetrical designs and buildings in both two and three dimensions and the opportunity to practice the doubles combinations.

In the next session, students will share the symmetric designs they made from different materials. Watch during Math Workshop for Copy Tiles examples that you can use to inform that discussion.

If you use one or both of the computer activities, you may choose to eliminate one of the other Workshop activities.

3A Fold and Cut

INDIVIDUALS

Students fold their paper in half, draw a shape or an object, and cut it out. When students have cut a shape they like, they glue the shape—and the paper from which it was cut—on construction paper. Students may make several tries if they are not satisfied with their first attempts.

Students make a symmetrical design by folding and cutting paper.

ONGOING ASSESSMENT: Observing Students at Work

Students explore symmetry by folding and cutting out shapes. Encourage them to talk about both parts of the paper having the same shape. Some may bring up symmetry or balance—how a cut on one side of the paper also appears on the other.

- **Do students start by cutting or do they draw a pattern first?**

- **If their results do not match their expectations, are they able to use their results to modify their next attempt?**

DIFFERENTIATION: Supporting the Range of Learners

Intervention Have handy some models that you have already cut out, such as your original tree or turtle. Help students who are having trouble getting started trace around your model and then cut it out.

Extension Suggest that students investigate which geometric shapes (e.g., squares, rectangles, some triangles) have more than one line of symmetry. They can do this by folding each shape after they cut it out.

Teaching Note

❸ **Using *Shapes* Software After This Unit** Students may continue to work on the *Shapes* software activities after the unit is over to continue to develop their understanding of symmetry.

▲ **Student Activity Book, p. 35**

3B Copy Tiles

PAIRS

For complete details about this activity, see Session 3.2, page 128.

3C *Shapes* Software: *Reflection Puzzles* (optional)

PAIRS

For complete details about this activity, see Session 3.2, page 129.

3D *Shapes* Software: *Line of Symmetry Puzzles* (optional)

PAIRS

On the computer, students reorient a "glued" set of shapes so that a line of symmetry aligns with a mirror. Students can work with existing *Line of Symmetry Puzzles* or make their own symmetric designs. ❸

ONGOING ASSESSMENT: Observing Students at Work

Students reorient a design so that its line of symmetry aligns with a mirror.

- **Can students identify a line of symmetry of their design?** If designs have more than one line of symmetry, can students identify them both (or all)? If designs have no line of symmetry, can students explain how they know that?

- **Can they reorient their design so that the line of symmetry aligns with the mirror?**

3E Double It

PAIRS

For complete details about this activity, see Session 3.1, page 126.

SESSION FOLLOW-UP

4 Daily Practice

 Daily Practice: For ongoing review, have students complete *Student Activity Book* page 35.

 Student Math Handbook: Students and families may use *Student Math Handbook* pages 47, 129 for reference and review. See pages 178–182 in the back of this unit.

Is It Symmetrical?

Math Focus Points

◆ Identifying lines of symmetry

◆ Developing fluency with the doubles combinations to 10 + 10

◆ Determining what makes a design symmetrical

Today's Plan		Materials
DISCUSSION ① **Is It Symmetrical?**	30 MIN · CLASS	• Students' symmetry examples (from Sessions 3.1, 3.2, and 3.3); mirrors (optional)
ACTIVITY ② **Doubling with Pattern Block Designs**	30 MIN · CLASS · PAIRS	• *Student Activity Book,* pp. 36–39 • M33–M38 (from Session 3.1) or pattern blocks*; M41* • Chart paper; glue sticks or crayons or markers
SESSION FOLLOW-UP ③ **Daily Practice**		• *Student Activity Book,* p. 40 • *Student Math Handbook,* pp. 47, 129

*See *Materials to Prepare,* p. 119.

Classroom Routines

Today's Number: 29 Students individually generate numerical expressions for the number 29 using addition and/or subtraction. They record these expressions on blank paper, which they have labeled with the date and heading *Today's Number: 29*. This work will give you some information on how students are understanding and working with *Today's Number*. Additionally this is the second in a series of work samples for *Today's Number* that will be collected throughout the year.

DISCUSSION

Is It Symmetrical?

30 MIN   CLASS

Math Focus Points for Discussion

◆ Determining what makes a design symmetrical

Begin this session by having students share the designs that they have made using pattern blocks (Sessions 3.1 and 3.2) and color tiles (Sessions 3.2 and 3.3). As students show a design, ask them to explain how they planned it and made it and why they think the design is symmetrical. Encourage them to use their own language to explain their thinking. Listen to the language they use to describe symmetry and list the words you hear on the board.

How could you prove this shape is symmetrical? What are some other ways you found for showing symmetry?

Choose one student's recorded color-tile design that has mirror symmetry and show it to the class. As students watch, fold the design along the line of symmetry so the colors are on the outside—rather than on the inside—of the paper.

Another way to see whether this design is symmetrical is to pinch a colored square.

Hold the paper so only the top side is visible to students and ask someone to pinch one of the colored squares.

Demonstrate how to pinch, bringing forefinger and thumb together in the same place on opposite sides of the paper. Students may want to try pinching their fingers together in the air a few times.

Student pinches one of the colored squares.

[Juan], pinch one of the colored squares on this folded paper. What color did you pinch under your top finger? What color do you think is under your thumb on the bottom side of the paper?

Have students check their color-tile designs by folding and pinching colors or by using a mirror.

Students may describe or mention other types of symmetry or share an example. For instance, a design may not have mirror symmetry, but it may have rotational symmetry.❶

ACTIVITY

② Doubling with Pattern Block Designs

30 MIN　PAIRS　CLASS

To introduce this activity, make a large copy of Half and Half (M41) or sketch it on the board or chart paper.

Each Half and Half sheet has a mirror line, or line of symmetry, down the middle of it. Just as we did with Mirror Designs, you are going to begin by making a pattern block design on Side A.

Professional Development

❶ **Teacher Note:** Making Symmetrical Designs, p. 164

Name _____ Date _____

Shapes, Blocks, and Symmetry

Half and Half (page 1 of 2)

Side B

Side A

36　Unit 2　　　Session 3.4

▲ **Student Activity Book, pp. 36–37; Resource Masters, M41**

How Many Blocks? (page 1 of 2)
Use this sheet with the Half and Half sheet and
your pattern blocks.

Pattern Block Design 1

1. Build Side A of your design.

2. Number of blocks in Side A: _____

3. I think there will be _____ blocks in the
   whole design because:

   _____
   _____
   _____
   _____

4. Build Side B to finish your design.

5. How many blocks are in your finished design? _____

▲ Student Activity Book, p. 38

How Many Blocks? (page 2 of 2)
Use this sheet with the Half and Half sheet and
your pattern blocks.

Pattern Block Design 2

1. Build Side A of your design.

2. Number of blocks in Side A: _____

3. I think there will be _____ blocks in the
   whole design because:

   _____
   _____
   _____
   _____

4. Build Side B to finish your design.

5. How many blocks are in your finished design? _____

▲ Student Activity Book, p. 39

Illustrate by placing pattern blocks on the overhead or by drawing a very
simple example on the board.

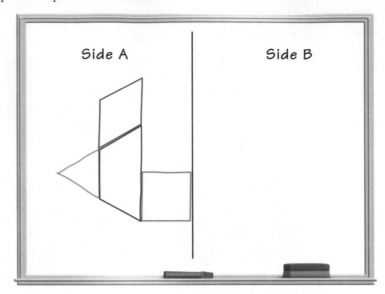

How many blocks do I have on this side of my design? How many
blocks will I have in the whole design when I make the other half?
How do you know? What equation represents this problem?

At this point in the unit, students should easily recognize the doubles
combination,

$$4 + 4 = 8.$$

Explain that they should create and record two designs on *Student Activity
Book* pages 36–37 and complete *Student Activity Book* pages 38–39. You
may want to write the following instructions on the board as a reference:

• Build half of a design out of pattern blocks along the line of symmetry.

• Predict the total number of blocks.

• Complete the design.

• Count the total number of blocks.

When students make their predictions about how many blocks will be in
the whole design, make sure they describe how they figured out the total.

ONGOING ASSESSMENT: Observing Students at Work

Students follow the steps to construct and record two symmetrical designs and complete the student sheet.

- **Are the students' designs symmetrical?**

- **How do students figure out the total number of blocks in the whole picture?** Do they know the total amount will be double the amount on Side A? Do they count to figure the total or do they use doubles combinations?

Students work on doubling with pattern blocks.

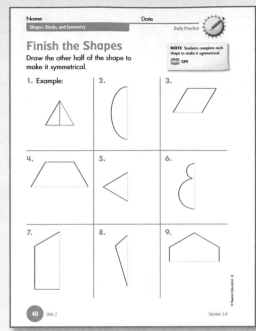

Finish the Shapes
Draw the other half of the shape to make it symmetrical.

NOTE Students complete each shape to make it symmetrical. SMH 129

▲ Student Activity Book, p. 40

SESSION FOLLOW-UP
3 Daily Practice

 Daily Practice: For reinforcement of this unit's content, have students complete *Student Activity Book* page 40.

 Student Math Handbook: Students and families may use *Student Math Handbook* pages 47, 129 for reference and review. See pages 178–182 in the back of this unit.

End-of-Unit Assessment

Math Focus Points

◆ Constructing and describing rectangular arrays of tiles

◆ Constructing 2-D symmetrical designs

◆ Achieving fluency with the doubles combinations

Today's Plan	Materials
① ASSESSMENT ACTIVITY **End-of-Unit Assessment Problems** ✔ ⏱ 👤 60 MIN INDIVIDUALS	• M15*; M29* (optional); M42–M44*; M45* ☑ • Doubles Combinations Cards (from Session 1.4; optional); color tiles; tape
② SESSION FOLLOW-UP **Daily Practice**	• *Student Activity Book,* p. 41 • *Student Math Handbook,* pp. 47, 126, 129

*See *Materials to Prepare,* p. 119.

Classroom Routines

Quick Images: Double Arrays Using the transparent double arrays from Rectangular Arrays (T24), display the 2 × 6 array. Follow the basic *Quick Images* activity. Students determine the total number of squares and share how they determined the amount. Record an equation using addition (e.g., 6 + 6 = 12) that represents the array. Repeat with 2 × 8 and then, 2 × 10.

ASSESSMENT ACTIVITY

1 End-of-Unit Assessment

60 MIN INDIVIDUALS

This End-of-Unit Assessment focuses on three of the unit's benchmarks.❶

There are three parts to the End-of-Unit Assessment. Each student works independently to solve the problem Make a Rectangle (M42) that assesses Benchmark 2: Identify the number of rows and the number of squares in each row in an array. Students also solve the problem Complete the Shape (M43) that assesses Benchmark 5: Make a symmetrical picture based on an image provided. Students complete Doubles Combinations (M44) that assess Benchmark 6: Demonstrate fluency with addition combinations: doubles combinations to 10 + 10.

Students make and describe a rectangle composed of 18 tiles and complete a symmetrical design. They are also assessed on their fluency with the double combinations.

As students are working on the assessment have individuals or small groups of students cycle through a station with you to complete the Doubles Combinations assessment.

Part 1: Make a Rectangle
On End-of-Unit-Assessment: Make a Rectangle (M42), students make a rectangle using 18 tiles, draw it on Inch Grid Paper (M15), cut it out, and attach it to the Student Sheet. Then students describe the rectangle.

Students may need to tape together two sheets of inch grid paper to make their rectangle, or students may choose to draw their rectangle on Centimeter Grid Paper (M29).

ONGOING ASSESSMENT: Observing Students at Work

Students make a rectangular array and describe it.

- **Do students make a rectangular array with 18 tiles?**

- **Do students identify the number of rows and number of tiles in each row?**

Part 2: Complete the Shape
On End-of-Unit-Assessment: Complete the Shape (M43), students are shown half of a symmetrical design on a folded sheet of paper. They draw what the paper will look like when it is unfolded.

Professional Development

❶ **Teacher Note:** End-of-Unit Assessment, p. 166

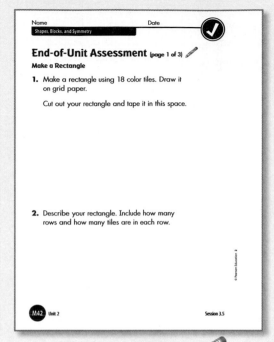

▲ **Resource Masters, M42** PORTFOLIO WRITING M

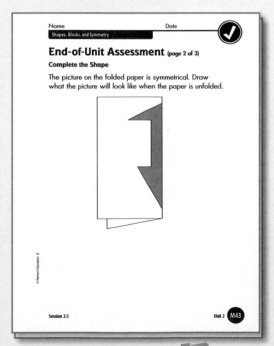

▲ **Resource Masters, M43–M44** PORTFOLIO

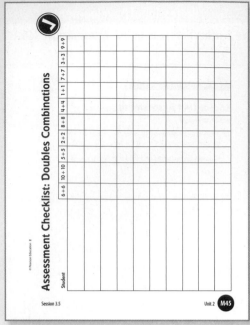

▲ Resource Masters, M45 ✓

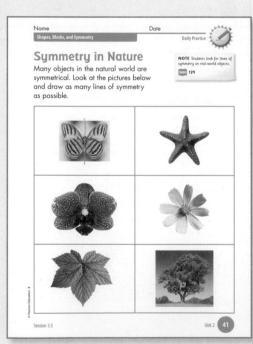

▲ Student Activity Book, p. 41

ONGOING ASSESSMENT: Observing Students at Work

Students draw the second half of a symmetrical design.

- **Have students drawn a symmetrical picture?**

- **Is their picture based on the image that was provided?**

Part 3: Double Combinations

The Doubles Combinations assessment can be done in one of two ways. Both involve observation. If you choose to use End-of-Unit Assessment: Doubles Combinations (M44), observe students as they complete the sheet to see how fluent they are in their responses.

Alternately you can interview students, using a blank set of the Addition Cards Set 2: Doubles Combinations (M19) and they can respond orally. Since there are only ten combinations, you can complete this assessment within the math session. Keep track of student responses on the Assessment Checklist: Doubles Combinations (M45).

ONGOING ASSESSMENT: Observing Students at Work

Students solve doubles combination problems.

- **Do students accurately solve all the problems in a reasonable amount of time?**

SESSION FOLLOW-UP

2 Daily Practice

 Daily Practice: For enrichment, have students complete *Student Activity Book* page 41.

 Student Math Handbook: Students and families may use *Student Math Handbook* pages 47, 126, 129 for reference and review. See pages 178–182 in the back of this unit.

Professional Development

UNIT 2

Shapes, Blocks, and Symmetry

In Part 6 of *Implementing Investigations in Grade 2,* you will find a set of Teacher Notes that addresses topics and issues applicable to the curriculum as a whole rather than to specific curriculum units. They include the following:

Computational Fluency and Place Value

Computational Algorithms and Methods

Representations and Contexts for Mathematical Work

Foundations of Algebra in the Elementary Grades

Discussing Mathematical Ideas

Racial and Linguistic Diversity in the Classroom:
    What Does Equity Mean in Today's Math Classroom?

Students Make Their Own Boxes

Materials to Prepare:

Prepare one set of box pieces per pair of students.

One set has 12 box pieces in five sizes.

For each set use seven 3 x 5 cards and four 5 x 8 cards.

Cut three 3 x 5 cards and two 5 x 8 cards as shown, discarding the leftover strips.

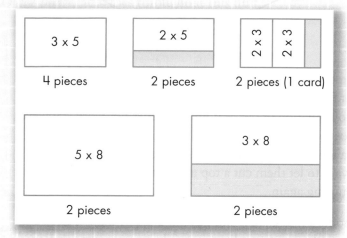

Put the pieces for each set in an envelope, one per pair of students.

Students at this age level have a variety of approaches to making boxes out of flat pieces. Making a box requires visualizing how 2-D pieces can go together to make a 3-D shape, selecting pieces that fit together in the right way, and enough manual dexterity to actually put the pieces together. Some students carefully lay out pieces flat on the table and can see how they will "fold up" once they are taped together to make a box. They put on the top after the rest is taped.

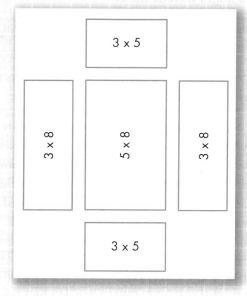

Some students who use this approach have difficulty finding the pieces that make a box. In the following example, these students have placed five sides in relationship to each other to make the bottom and sides of the box, but not all the opposite sides match in size and shape. When they tape these pieces, they will find that one side is larger than the opposite side.

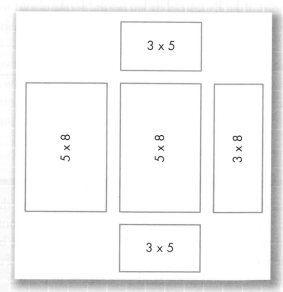

Identifying Types of 3-Dimensional Shapes

Like the 2-dimensional shapes, the 3-dimensional shapes are divided into two major categories: polyhedra and shapes that are not polyhedra. *Polyhedra* is the name given to 3-dimensional closed shapes with flat surfaces. The term *polyhedron* comes from Greek roots; *poly* means "many," and *hedron* means "face." Each surface or side of a polyhedron is called a *face*. Each face is a polygon. The intersections of the faces—which are the sides of the polygonal faces—are called *edges*. Edges intersect at a vertex. (The plural of *vertex* is *vertices*.)

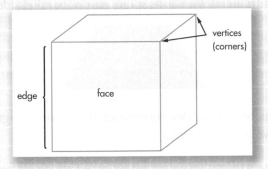

You can use the correct names for 3-dimensional shapes and their parts so that students hear the terms, but you do not need to insist that they use them. It is more important that they focus on describing and comparing these shapes.

Students will also encounter—in their environment and in other building sets—shapes that are not polyhedra, such as spheres, cylinders, cones, etc.

Polyhedra are sometimes classified by their number of faces. For example, a four-faced polyhedron is called a *tetrahedron,* and an eight-faced polyhedron is an *octahedron*. However, polyhedra are also classified another way, as they are in the Geoblock set. Most of the blocks in the set—and many of the common 3-dimensional shapes you and your students see in everyday life—are prisms.

In this unit, students work with Geoblocks. There are 25 different types of blocks in a set. All of the Geoblocks are polyhedra. Most of them are prisms.

Prisms are 3-dimensional shapes that have two congruent faces connected by faces that are parallelograms.

A prism is named by the two congruent faces. All of the shapes shown above are right prisms because the congruent faces are connected by faces that are rectangles. The first shape above is called a *triangular prism* because it has two faces that are triangles. These triangles are connected by faces that are rectangles. The second shape is called a *rectangular prism;* all of its faces are rectangles. The third shape is a *hexagonal prism*. The fourth is an *octagonal prism*.

The Geoblock set includes a variety of rectangular prisms, including cubes (rectangular prisms in which all of the faces are squares). The set also includes a variety of triangular prisms. See the chart on the next page for examples. Some students enjoy learning the names *triangular prism* and *rectangular prism*.

One shape in the Geoblock set is not a prism—the pyramid. A pyramid may have any polygon as its base. All the other faces are triangles that connect at a single vertex. Like prisms, pyramids are named by the shapes of their bases. Here are a triangular pyramid, two square pyramids, and a pentagonal pyramid.

The third pyramid is like the one in the Geoblock set. A chart depicting all 25 different types of Geoblocks, and their quantities, appears on page 151.

Cube A
1 cm × 1 cm × 1 cm
Quantity: 128

Rectangular prism H
2 cm × 4 cm × 4 cm
Quantity: 12

Triangular prism O
4 cm × 4 cm × 2 cm
Quantity: 12

Triangular prism U
4 cm × 8 cm × 1 cm
Quantity: 6

Cube B
2 cm × 2 cm × 2 cm
Quantity: 32

Rectangular prism I
1 cm × 8 cm × 4 cm
Quantity: 8

Triangular prism P
3 cm × 3 cm × 4 cm
Quantity: 8

Triangular prism V
2 cm × 4 cm × 2 cm
Quantity: 7

Cube C
3 cm × 3 cm × 3 cm
Quantity: 12

Rectangular prism J
2 cm × 8 cm × 4 cm
Quantity: 4

Triangular prism Q
2 cm × 4 cm × 4 cm
Quantity: 2

Triangular prism W
4 cm × 3.5 cm × 2 cm
Quantity: 6

Cube D
4 cm × 4 cm × 4 cm
Quantity: 8

Rectangular prism K
4 cm × 8 cm × 4 cm
Quantity: 2

Triangular prism R
4 cm × 8 cm × 2 cm
Quantity: 6

Triangular prism X
2 cm × 8 cm × 2 cm
Quantity: 6

Rectangular prism E
2 cm × 4 cm × 2 cm
Quantity: 8

Triangular prism L
2 cm × 2 cm × 2 cm
Quantity: 32

Triangular prism S
2 cm × 8 cm × 4 cm
Quantity: 6

Square pyramid Y
4 cm × 4 cm × 4 cm
Quantity: 6

Rectangular prism F
2 cm × 6 cm × 2 cm
Quantity: 4

Triangular prism M
4 cm × 4 cm × 4 cm
Quantity: 6

Triangular prism T
2 cm × 4 cm × 8 cm
Quantity: 6

Rectangular prism G
2 cm × 8 cm × 2 cm
Quantity: 4

Triangular prism N
4 cm × 8 cm × 4 cm
Quantity: 2

Introducing and Managing the *Shapes* Software

The use of computer activities is optional in this unit. However, if you have computers available, it is recommended that you use the software. The geometry software activities are integrated into Math Workshop activities. The software activities extend and deepen the mathematical ideas that are emphasized in this unit. In some cases, the software activities allow students to work with geometric shapes in ways that they are not able to in the off-computer activities.

In this unit, activities with the *Shapes* software are suggested throughout each Investigation. How you introduce and incorporate these computer activities into your curriculum depends on the number of computers and the computer technology that you have available. First you will need to consider how you will introduce your students to the *Shapes* software. Then you will need to consider how students will have access to the software. Possible options are to introduce each new software activity to the whole class if you have access to a large-screen projection setup. Or if you have access to a computer lab, consider introducing each new activity to the whole class in this environment. In this unit, the activities are included as Math Workshop activities so once students are introduced to an activity they can then access the activity during Math Workshops.

Regardless of the number of computers you have, we suggest that students always work in pairs. This not only maximizes computer resources, but also encourages students to consult, monitor, and teach one another. Generally, more than two students at one computer find it difficult to share. You may need to monitor computer use more closely than the other choices, to ensure that all students get sufficient computer time. Each pair should spend at least 15–20 minutes at the computer for each activity.

Introducing the *Shapes* Software

Computer Lab If you have a computer laboratory with one computer for each pair of students, all your students can be introduced to and can become familiar with the computer activities at the same time. In this situation you will not need to devote time during math class for introducing students to the new software activity. Students will access the activity during Math Workshop.

Large Screen Monitor or Projection Screen If you have access to either of these devices, you can introduce the software activities to the whole class during the math session immediately before Math Workshop or at another time of the day.

Small Groups of Students You can introduce the software activities to small groups of students either before or during Math Workshop. These students can then be paired with other students and become "teachers" of the software.

Managing the Computer Environment

Math Workshop Students should have access to the *Shapes* software consistently throughout the unit. If you have daily access to a computer lab, you might choose to add this experience into your day in addition to your regular math class. A more typical computer situation is that classrooms have a small number of computers. While three to five computers is ideal, students can have a successful computer experience with only one to two computers. In the case of fewer computers, you will need to incorporate additional computer time for students throughout the day. If you have computers available in your classroom, pairs of students can cycle through the computer activities, just as they cycle through the other Math Workshop activities.

Using *Shapes* All Year This is the only unit in the Grade 2 sequence that explicitly uses the *Shapes* software. However, we recommend that students continue using it for the remainder of the school year. With more experience, they become more fluent in the mechanics of the software itself and can better focus on the designs they want to make and how to select and arrange shapes for those designs. They can explore the tangram shapes as well as the pattern block and Power Polygon™ shapes. They can also spend time solving the many different kinds of puzzles that come with the software, or even making their own puzzles.

Introducing the *Shapes* Software

In your first introduction of the *Free Explore* activity show students the following:

- How to open *Shapes* by double-clicking on the icon or accessing the Web site

- How to open the *Free Explore* activity by clicking on it once

- How to get shapes from the shapes palette

- How to slide shapes by dragging them. (Point out that they snap into position when their corners are close if the Magnet tool is on.)

- How to turn shapes with the two Turn tools ⟳ ⟲. (Point out that they can change the amount of turning using the pull down palettes ▾.)

- How to use the Erase tool 🖉 to erase one shape at a time and the Broom tool 🧹 to erase all the shapes. (Point out that the Broom tool can be found in the pull down palette ▾.)

You can introduce more of the tools available in *Shapes* as students indicate a need for them. Some of these tools allow students to do things they cannot do with the physical blocks:

- The two Flip tools flip, or reflect, shapes over a vertical or horizontal midline. For example, if you select the first "Flip Vertical" tool ⬛ and then click on a shape, the shape flips over a horizontal line though the center of the shape so that the top becomes the bottom and the bottom becomes the top. The "Flip Horizontal" tool ⬛ switches right and left sides of the shape.

- The Duplicate tool 🗐 makes copies of shapes. This is especially useful if you have already turned or flipped a shape so it is in the orientation that you want. Use Duplicate to get another copy of that shape in the same orientation, rather than having to get and turn or flip a new shape. You can also use the Duplicate tool to make copies of groups of shapes that have been glued (see below).

- The Arrow tool ⬚ selects shapes. This is useful if students want to apply a tool or command such as Duplicate or Glue to several shapes at the same time.

- The Glue tool 🖉 glues several shapes together into a "group," a new composite shape that can be slid, turned, and flipped as a unit.

- The Hammer tool 🔨 breaks apart a glued group with one click. (The Hammer tool can be found in the pull down palette under the Glue tool ▾.)

- The Pattern tool 🖐 allows students to record a "duplicate, move, and turn" combination and apply it repeatedly to the same or different shapes. Students can use this tool to tile the workspace or to make other patterns. Press the Record pattern button ⏺ to begin recording a pattern. Select a shape or group of shapes to duplicate, and then move and/or turn the duplicate in relation to the original. Press the Stop pattern button ⏹ to end recording. The pattern is the combination of moves and turns needed to move the original into the position of the duplicate. Choose the Apply pattern tool 🖐 and click on a shape or group of shapes to move and turn the shape(s) according to the pattern.

- The Color tool 🖌 allows students to change the colors of shapes in their drawings.

- Settings: By default the Magnet 🧲 is on, so that shapes snap together at their corners. Students can turn this setting on or off. Students can also turn on or off a background Grid tool to help them measure distances. Students will use the horizontal and/or vertical Mirrors when doing *Reflection Puzzles* and *Line of Symmetry Puzzles*.

- Saving or Printing Work: If you want to discuss students' work later, they should save their pictures on disk or print out copies of their pictures. For information about saving to a disk or printing, refer to the *Software Support Resource Guide* found on the *Shapes* CD-ROM.

Teacher Note

About the Math in the *Shapes* Software

The *Shapes* software is a computer environment designed for students to explore a variety of geometric ideas—how different shapes go together; geometric transformations such as rotation (turns), translation (slides), and reflection (flips); patterning and tiling; and symmetry. Students can choose a variety of activities and puzzles using three different shape sets: pattern blocks, Power Polygons, and tangrams.

On the most basic level, the software provides another context in which students can do some things that they can also do with real blocks—including moving shapes around and combining them to make patterns and pictures; finding ways to fill in puzzle outlines; overlapping shapes to see how their angles and sides compare; and recreating *Quick Images* puzzles. Students explore how to compose and decompose pictures, and which shapes can be substituted for other shapes (e.g., three green triangles for one red trapezoid).

Yet, even when they are doing "the same" thing with the *Shapes* software as with real blocks, the software requires students to be more intentional and precise about their actions, which helps them learn. Instead of intuitively turning their hand to make a block fit into place, students must select a tool to turn it or flip it, and decide how much of a turn is needed. This helps students realize that thinking about the orientation of an object is another important step.

Some issues with managing the blocks and displaying student work are more easily dealt with in the software environment. Shapes can snap together to form neater pictures; they can be glued together to form larger groups that can be moved, turned, or flipped together; and software blocks cannot be knocked off the table. The software also allows students to more easily save their work either by printing it so they can display and discuss it or, in the CD-ROM version, saving it to disk so they can come back to work on it more later.

Certain kinds of mathematical exploration are much better suited for work with the software than with real blocks. By using the vertical and horizontal mirrors, students can see how a shape's reflection switches right for left (vertical mirror) or top for bottom (horizontal mirror), and can explore issues of symmetry. By using the grid along with the mirror, students can see how shapes are reflected an equal distance on the opposite side of the mirror.

Students can explore how repetition of geometric shapes creates patterns. In the Quilt Squares environment, they can see how the patterns they make in one square are repeated and extended across the three-by-three quilt, sometimes with surprising results. The pattern tool allows students to define a set of motions—translation and/or rotation—and apply it repeatedly to the same shape, or even a different shape or group of shapes. By doing so, they can explore ways to tile the plane, can see how repeated rotation, even with a translation, eventually comes back to the original position, and can start to think of this set of motions as a rule that has its own mathematical properties.

Some of these ideas can be quite complex, but *Shapes* gives students an environment in which they can naturally explore and begin to understand them.

The *Shapes* software offers students two challenging activities, *Reflection Puzzles* and *Line of Symmetry Puzzles*, to explore and work with mirror symmetry. In *Line of Symmetry Puzzles*, when the shape matches its reflection, the mirror is marking a "line of symmetry." If students want to use the *Shapes* software to test for rotational symmetry, they can use the Duplicate tool to copy the shape and try turning it to see whether the rotated copy matches the original.

Although the *Shapes* software is introduced in this unit, it is suggested that students have the opportunity to work with the software throughout the year.

What's a Rectangle?

What is so hard about understanding what a rectangle is? The definition of a rectangle seems very clear to us as adults: It is a 4-sided polygon with four right angles. If we just show rectangles to students and describe what they are, will they not understand?

Research with students throughout the elementary grades makes it clear that understanding what a geometric object is, and how it is classified, does not come from learning a definition. Although students hear the definitions of rectangle and triangle all through the elementary grades—and can even repeat those definitions accurately—they still may not agree that an unusual rectangle (e.g., a square) or an unusual triangle (e.g., a scalene triangle with three unequal sides) fits the definition. Definitions of everyday objects often depend on the perception of a typical representation.

For example, some fourth- and fifth-grade students do not believe that a square is still a square if it is rotated 45°.

They have an implicit definition—based on seeing many squares presented—that a square must be "sitting" on a side to be a square. Similarly, students will argue that a square is not a rectangle—even though they know the definition of a rectangle—because their image of a rectangle is that one of its dimensions must be longer than the other.

For students to develop an understanding of a definition, they must examine many examples and counterexamples of the thing they are defining. They must describe, compare, and argue about what is similar and what is different. To develop definitions, students must develop the habit of paying careful attention to characteristics. Careful observation and description are what we want students to begin to do in this unit.

Area and Arrays

In this investigation, students come to recognize that they can use different, specific attributes of objects to compare sizes. They might compare height or width, for example. Or they might compare area—the space inside a 2-dimensional shape. Measuring area requires counting a space-filling unit that can cover an object without gaps or overlaps. Although squares are most commonly used as the unit to measure area, it is possible to use units of other shapes, such as triangles or non-square rectangles.

In the activity Ordering Rectangles in Session 2.3, students use square tiles—thought of as squares of chocolate—to cover a rectangle. By finding the number of square tiles it takes to cover a rectangle, students are, in effect, finding the area of the rectangle.

Covering their rectangles, students arrange their tiles into arrays: an arrangement of objects in equal rows and equal columns. The rectangular array is a powerful representation that students will use to explore various mathematical topics. In addition to measuring area, arrays are used to explore multiplication, division, fractions, and volume.

Seeing the structure of an array—equal rows and columns—requires significant cognitive work on the part of the child. Students began to develop the idea when they created arrays with two rows in the Double Arrays activity in Investigation 1. In Investigation 2, students have many more opportunities to build and describe arrays.

You will find a wide variety of sophistication in students' structuring or organization of the rectangular arrays of squares.

- Some will not have the correct number of squares in their drawings.

- Some will have different numbers of squares in the rows or columns.

- Some will have the number of squares in rows and columns correct, but will not have the squares properly aligned.

Many students will draw square blocks one at a time. Others will draw the squares using full-length vertical and horizontal lines to make the rows and columns.

Looking at students' drawings will help you understand how they are thinking about the structure of arrays. In particular, it will help you understand whether students are seeing the array as a series of individual squares or whether they are beginning to organize these individual squares into larger chunks. You will be able to see some aspects of students' thinking from the finished products, but you will get even more information about their ideas as you watch them draw their arrays.

Here are samples of students' work from a second-grade classroom. Students worked on Rectangle Riddle 2 on *Students Activity Book* page 19, "This rectangle has 3 rows. There are 7 tiles in each row."

Sample Student Work

This student constructed the array by using a series of single tiles. He first draws three squares in a column, and then he draws six more squares going across the top—one square at a time. He has a sense of the overall shape of a rectangle and tries to make his squares fit into that shape, but he does not work with larger units, such as a column of three or a row of seven.

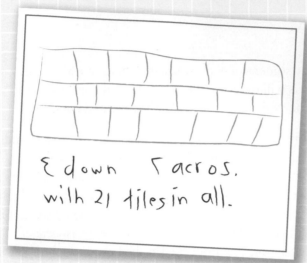

Sample Student Work

This student sees that there are three tiles going one way and seven tiles going another way, but she has trouble coordinating the two. She builds a "frame" of three tiles going down and seven tiles going across, and then fills in that frame. She has a sense of the shape of a rectangle, knows that a rectangular array is made up of rows and columns, and draws her rows and columns so that they have the same number.

Several students seemed to view the array as a whole. They do not need to draw individual squares. They divide up the rectangle using parallel lines.

Sample Student Work

This student draws a rectangle first, and then divides it into rows and columns using parallel lines. She labels the array in a way that shows that she sees the coordination of rows and columns to make the whole array.

The work with arrays in this unit lays the foundation for the extensive work that students will do in Grades 3–5. They will use arrays as a tool for representing and modeling multiplication.

Assessment: Is It a Rectangle?

Benchmark addressed:

Benchmark 3: Identify rectangles as 4-sided shapes with four right angles.

In order to meet the benchmark, students' work should show that they can:

• Correctly identify which shapes are rectangles and which are not;

• Explain that rectangles are shapes with four sides and four right angles.

Meeting the Benchmark

Students in this category correctly identify which shapes are and are not rectangles. Their explanations also refer to the fact that rectangles have four sides and four right angles. Many of these students also use this information about what a rectangle *is* to explain why a shape *is not* a rectangle.

▲ Resource Masters, M30

Sample Student Work

Sample Student Work

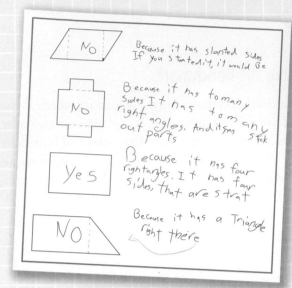

Sample Student Work

Partially Meeting the Benchmark

Some students correctly identify which shapes are and are not rectangles, but their explanations are not specific enough or are incomplete. For example, Tia uses right angles to explain her answer, but does not mention anything about the number of sides.

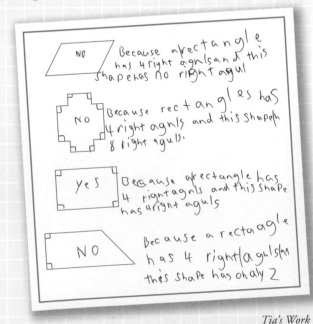

Tia's Work

While Rochelle correctly identifies the shapes and gives explanations that are accurate, she says that a rectangle has four corners without specifying the size or type of those corners. Many second graders use the word *corner* to describe angles. Ask students who respond like Rochelle to explain what they mean. Listen for evidence that they are distinguishing between the types of corners in the third shape and the first shape.

Rochelle's Work

Not Meeting the Benchmark

Students in this group do not have a coherent understanding of what a rectangle is. For example, Luis correctly rules out shapes 2 and 4 based on the number and length of the sides, but incorrectly identifies the first shape as a rectangle. While he has noticed something important about shapes that are rectangles (the opposite sides are equal), he appears to think that any shape with opposite sides that are equal are rectangles. The size or shape of the angles does not factor into his explanations. In addition, his writing about the rectangle suggests that he is basing his response on an overall visual image—or what the shape looks like. While this student has, and can articulate, some important beginning ideas about rectangles, there is not enough evidence to say that he partially meets the benchmark.

Many students who do not meet the benchmark base their responses on what the shapes look like, attending to one or two features of the shapes that resemble rectangles.

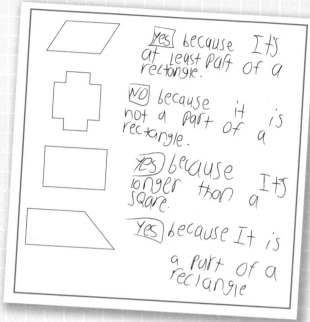

Nate's Work

Other students offer little or no explanation.

Students who do not meet the benchmark need continued experience working with rectangles and other shapes. The *Shapes* software is one place where such continued practice can happen. The focus of this work should be on attending to features of shapes—specifically the number of sides and what the angles look like. Describing shapes in terms of how they are the same and different can help highlight what makes a rectangle a rectangle and a triangle a triangle. Keep in mind that students will work with rectangles and rectangular arrays again in Unit 5, *How Many Floors? How Many Rooms?*

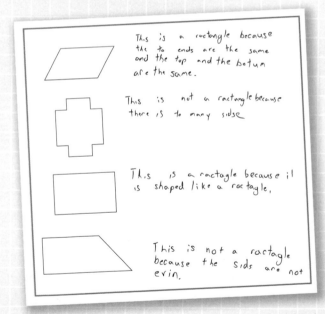

Luis's Work

Assessment: Faces of a Geoblock

Benchmark addressed:

Benchmark 4: Identify the number of faces on a rectangular prism and show which faces are congruent.

In order to meet the benchmark, students' work should show that they can:

- Correctly identify that a rectangular prism has six faces;

- Draw the six rectangular faces;

- Show which faces are congruent.

▲ **Resource Masters, M31**

Meeting the Benchmark

Many students will be able to complete this task and meet the benchmark by the end of this unit.

Amaya states that there are six faces, draws six rectangles, and clearly identifies the three pairs of congruent rectangles.

Amaya's Work

Alberto has also stated that there are six faces. Since this student's Geoblock is a *square* prism, there is one pair of congruent faces and a set of four congruent faces.

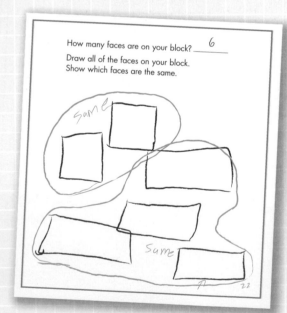

Alberto's Work

Partially Meeting the Benchmark

Students who partially meet the benchmark state that there are six faces, but leave something out of their drawing of the faces. For example, Yama has drawn only four faces, showing two congruent pairs.

Yama's Work

Point out to these students that they stated there are six faces, but did not draw all six. Then have them complete their drawings.

If students draw six faces, but do not indicate which are congruent, ask them whether any of the faces are the same.

Not Meeting the Benchmark

Travis stated that there are four faces on the block, but drew eight faces.

Travis's Work

Ask these students to show you how they counted the faces. As they count each face, mark it with a piece of tape to help them count it only once.

We recommend that students in Grade 2 have continued access to the Geoblocks. Students who do not yet meet the benchmark may need more experience working with these and other 3-dimensional shapes. These students in particular may benefit from more experience in somewhat structured activities. For example, students can combine smaller Geoblocks to make a rectangular prism, a small group experience with a teacher that is focused on examining different rectangular prisms, or revisit the Making Boxes activity from Session 2.8, page 108.

Teacher Note

Making Symmetrical Designs

Investigation 3, Symmetry, builds on students' intuitive recognition of symmetry. Students are aware of symmetry in butterflies, hearts, designs, and pictures. They seem to know when something is in balance. They frequently draw or make designs or pictures that are symmetrical.

Designs or patterns that can be flipped or folded over along a line so that one half is on top of the other half have *mirror symmetry*. The two halves are reflections of each other. (Some shapes have more than one line of symmetry or folding lines.)

Designs that revolve around a central point have *rotational symmetry* or *circular symmetry*. As a design is rotated, at some point(s) it will fit upon itself before it is completely rotated.

Some designs have both mirror and rotational symmetry.

Many shapes are symmetrical. Shapes such as a circle, a regular hexagon (like the yellow pattern block), and any even-sided regular polygon have both mirror and rotational symmetry. Other shapes, such as the trapezoid or a heart, have only mirror symmetry.

Mirror Symmetry Only	Rotational Symmetry Only	Both Mirror and Rotational Symmetry

In this unit, we focus on mirror or reflective symmetry. You may observe, however, that some students will make pattern-block designs that have rotational symmetry and not mirror symmetry. It is common for students to start pattern-block designs with a central hexagon and with the design radiating out like a sunburst. Some of these designs might also have mirror symmetry, others may not.

Ask students to describe how the designs do or do not have mirror symmetry. You can point out that some designs have another kind of symmetry, even though you cannot fold or flip them to show mirror symmetry.

The *Shapes* software offers students two challenging activities, *Reflection Puzzles* and *Lines of Symmetry,* to explore and work with mirror symmetry. While the *Shapes* software is introduced in this unit, we suggest that students have the opportunity to work with it throughout the year.

Teacher Note

End-of-Unit Assessment

Make a Rectangle

Benchmark addressed:

Benchmark 2: Identify the number of rows and the number of squares in each row in an array.

In order to meet the benchmark, students' work should show that they can:

- Make an array of 18 tiles;

- Indicate, in some way, the dimensions of their array in their description.

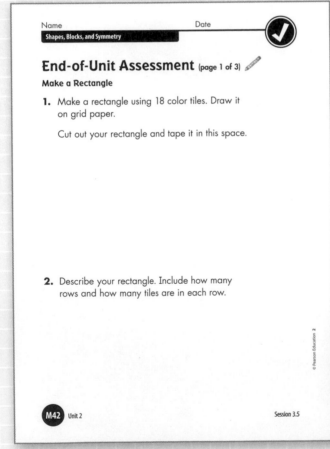

Name _____ Date _____

Shapes, Blocks, and Symmetry

✓

End-of-Unit Assessment (page 1 of 3)

Make a Rectangle

1. Make a rectangle using 18 color tiles. Draw it on grid paper.

   Cut out your rectangle and tape it in this space.

2. Describe your rectangle. Include how many rows and how many tiles are in each row.

M42 Unit 2   Session 3.5

▲ **Resource Masters, M42**

Meeting the Benchmark

Many second graders will be able to build an array with 18 tiles. The way that they communicate the dimensions of their array will vary.

2. Describe your rectangle. Include how many rows and how many tiles are in each row.

My rectangle has 2 rows whith 9 tiles in each row. It has 18 tiles in all.

Simon's Work

Simon has identified that the array has two rows with nine tiles in each row.

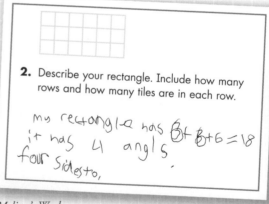

2. Describe your rectangle. Include how many rows and how many tiles are in each row.

My rectangle has 6+6+6=18 it has 4 angls. four sidesto,

Melissa's Work

Melissa has described the rectangle as $6 + 6 + 6 = 18$, indicating that it has three rows with six tiles in each row. She also indicates that her array "has four angles and four sides too."

Students might also describe a rectangle as:

- 9 across and 2 down
- 3 columns and 6 rows
- 3 rows of 6

Partially Meeting the Benchmark

Some students make an array of 18 tiles, but their description does not identify the two dimensions of the array.

Roshaun says that the array has three columns and three rows. Ask this student to show you the columns to see what he thinks they are, and then ask how many tiles are in each row.

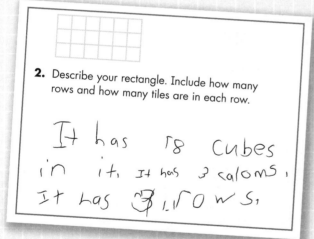

Roshaun's Work

Nadia has given a more general description of the rectangle. Ask this student to say how many rows there are and give the number of tiles in each row.

Nadia's Work

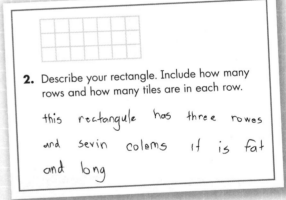

Gregory's Work

Gregory has made a rectangular array and has correctly described it (3 rows and 7 columns), but it is composed of 21, not 18, squares. Ask this student to count the number of tiles in his array and ask him to make an array with 18 tiles. Depending on the student's response, he may not meet the benchmark.

Not Meeting the Benchmark

Students who do not make an array, or those who cannot identify the number of rows and columns in an array, do not meet the benchmark. Students will have further opportunities to work with rectangular arrays in Unit 5, *How Many Floors? How Many Rooms?*

Complete the Shape

Benchmark addressed:

Benchmark 5: Make a symmetrical picture based on an image provided.

In order to meet the benchmark, students' work should show that they can:

- Draw a double-headed arrow.

▲ **Resource Masters, M43**

Meeting the Benchmark

Malcolm has completed the half arrow.

Malcolm's Work

Paige drew the unfolded page with the double-headed arrow in the middle.

Paige's Work

Partially Meeting the Benchmark

Some students draw parts of the picture symmetrically, but not others.

Monisha's Work

Lonzell's Work

Suggest to these students that they draw the picture by completing the half that is already shown. Then ask them what is the same about the two pictures and what is different.

Nate sees the lines that indicate the page as the symmetrical object.

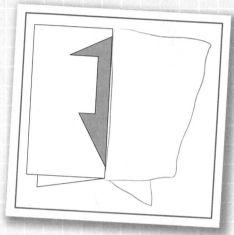

Nate's Work

Leo sees the folded page itself as the symmetrical object. This student explained, "When it's unfolded, the rectangle will be wider."

Leo's Work

Point out to these students that the picture shaded black is symmetrical and ask them to draw what that picture will look like when it is unfolded.

Not Meeting the Benchmark

If students do not draw a symmetrical object, like Leigh, give them another copy of the assessment sheet to fold along the line of symmetry and have them cut out the shape. Ask them to compare the cutout shape to the shape they have drawn.

Leigh's Work

Students who do not meet the benchmark may, in fact, be able to identify and also construct a symmetrical design in other contexts. For example, consider whether you have observed these students—in other activities during this investigation—constructing a symmetrical design with pattern blocks or symmetrical building with Geoblocks. Your observations may indicate that a student partially meets or fully meets the benchmark.

Encourage students to make symmetrical designs throughout Grade 2. Additionally, encourage them to use the *Reflection Puzzles* and *Lines of Symmetry* activities that are part of the *Shapes* software.

Double Combinations

Benchmark addressed:

Benchmark 6: Demonstrate fluency with addition combinations: doubles combinations to $10 + 10$.

▲ **Resource Masters, M44**

Students are likely to fall into the following three categories:

Fluent Students who are fluent with all of the doubles combinations can hear or read a problem, think for a moment, and then say the answer. Most second graders should be in this category at this point in the year.

Nearly Fluent Students in this category are fluent with most of these combinations, but pause to figure out the answer to one or two. Note which combinations still cause trouble and check that these match the cards in students' "Combinations I'm Still Working On" envelopes. Continued practice with one or several of the activities described below will help these students become fluent. You might also assign two particular combinations per week for students to work on until they know them all.

Not Yet Fluent These students need to figure out many of these combinations by using their fingers to count up or by using cubes to model the problem. There should be very few students in this category. They need more intensive practice with activities, such as:

- Double Arrays (Session 1.2)

- Doubling with Pattern Block Designs (Session 3.4)

- Double It (Session 3.1)

All students should continue to review and practice their addition combinations throughout the year.

Categorizing Shape Cards

The students are working in small groups to sort their Shape Cards into categories. In a discussion during the activity Sorting Shape Cards, the teacher checks in with each group and talks with them about the characteristics of each of their categories.

Rochelle and Nadia group one or two shapes at a time, define a category that describes them, and then move on to another small group of shapes, until all the shapes are categorized. So far they have five categories: Squares, Triangles, Diamonds, Big, and Small.

Teacher: Could any of the diamonds go in big or in small?

Rochelle: We want them to be diamonds.

Teacher: How would I know which group to put this one in? [points to Shape M, the small square rotated 90 degrees]

Nadia: Well, it is small, but it's a diamond, too.

Rochelle: Small can be just anything, but diamonds have to go in diamonds.

Nadia: We can put arrows between small and diamonds so people would know it can go in both.

The teacher moves to Simon and Chen, who have used two characteristics for each of their categories. They have labeled their groups: Long and Pointy Pile, Big and Fat Pile, Long and Skinny Pile and Different Pile: The Different Pile seems to have everything they could not fit into another category.

Sample Student Work

Another pair, Malcolm and Carla, have two categories so far, Pointy and Big.

Teacher: How would I know if something is Pointy?

Carla: Like this. [Carla holds up a triangle and points to an angle.]

Teacher: Could a rectangle go in this category?

Carla: No. Points aren't like that. They don't go straight. They have to go up.

Malcolm holds up two rectangles.

Malcolm: What do you call these?

Teacher: Which ones?

Malcolm: The kind with the long and short sides.

Carla: Rectangles. If we said three sides and four sides, we'd be all done. [Carla shows how she could sort the shapes into two big piles of 3-sided and 4-sided shapes.]

Malcolm: [picks up Shape I, the rectangle with the corner cut out, which Carla has placed in the 4-sided pile] I don't think this one goes.

Carla: Well, it can't go in the threes.

Teacher: How many sides does it have?

Carla: Four, except it has a bite out of it. It can go with these. [indicates the four-sided group] It is close enough.

Teacher: What do you think Malcolm?

Malcolm: It doesn't go there either. Look. It has 1, 2, 3, 4, 5, 6 sides. [traces with his finger]

Carla: But it's really just like these. It's just like you ripped out the corner.

Students at this age may often choose categories that are not mutually exclusive, so that some of the shapes they are using will fit into more than one category. While an adult might sort either into big and small or into triangle and quadrilateral, choosing to focus on either size or shape, students often mix categories. For example, Rochelle and Nadia use Big, Small, Triangle, and Square in the same sort. However, as students make decisions and describe their categories, they begin to make important distinctions, as Carla does when she describes the difference between right angles that go "straight" and acute angles that "go up."

Some students will focus more on their impression of the whole shape, as Simon, Chen, and Carla do. For Carla, the rectangle with the missing corner still looks basically like a rectangle. From a certain point of view, she is correct about its overall similarity to a rectangle. Malcolm can focus on the number of sides—a separate and important characteristic of this rectangle-like shape. Throughout these activities, what is important is that students are challenged to articulate as clearly as they can what criteria they are using to make their category decisions.

Dialogue Box

Strategies for Building Rectangles

In this conversation during the Math Workshop activity How Many Rectangles?, students are sharing their strategies for finding all the rectangles for numbers they have chosen. Leo uses his knowledge of numbers to find rectangles for 30. This motivates some students to consider what happens when you split an array to make a new array. Travis uses a spatial model to do his splitting, while Rochelle uses a numerical one.

Teacher: What strategies did you use to find all the rectangles for a number?

Leo: I started with one column of 30. Since 30 is an even number, you can split it. Since two of the same number gives you an even number.

Monisha: Since 30 is even, you can split it in two to get another way of making it.

Teacher: What did you get when you split it?

Monisha: It was 15 down and 2 across.

Teacher: Can you split that again?

Rochelle: Yes, but it's odd.

Monisha: Right, 15 is odd.

Travis: You can split that into 5s. You have two columns. Take 2 of the 5s off and then put them together to make 10 and you'll have 3 tens. [He comes to the board.] I took these off to make their own column.

Travis took these top two groups of five off and moved them down next to the others to make another rectangle.

Teacher: So this is ten tiles high and how many across?

Travis: Three.

Teacher: Can we break it down more?

Rochelle: You can make 15 using $7\frac{1}{2}$s.

Teacher: Let's stick with whole numbers for now.

Luis: That's the limit.

Travis: Yes! Yes! Six 5s.

Travis took these top 3 groups of 5 and moved them down next to the bottom 3 groups of 5 going from a 3 × 5 to a 6 × 5.

Travis: I did it a different way from the way we did it before. We'd broken the 5s off, so we had 3s. I took the 5s off and put them down here.

Rochelle: Well 5 + 5 = 10.   5 + 5 = 10. 10 + 10 = 20. And then the other 5 + 5 = 10 is 30.

In this discussion, the use of colored tiles allowed students to model and represent their strategies for making different sized rectangles using the same number of tiles.

Dialogue Box

Is It the Same Rectangle?

During the Math Workshop activity, How Many Rectangles?, Juan and Henry are building rectangles with 18 tiles—trying to find all possibilities. As they build, the issue of congruence comes up: Is a rectangle built "the 9 way" (9 across by 2 down) the same as a rectangle built "the 2 way" (2 across by 9 down)? As the dialogue opens, Henry is describing the rectangles to his teacher—who is circulating among the students—when Juan announces he has found another way to make a rectangle with 18 tiles.

Henry: This one's long; it's from 1s. This one's 2s. It's nine long. And we made 1 from 3s, and it's six long. And we're going to make one more.

Juan: I found another one! Do it the nine way!

Henry: We already did it the two way.

Juan: But if you do it the nine way, it will make a different rectangle.

Henry demonstrates with a 3 × 6 rectangle, displayed so that it is three across.

Juan: So now we change this one this way, 6 + 6 + 6.

Henry: We already did that, though.

Juan: But this is the six way.

Juan colors the 6 × 3 rectangle as he talks.

Henry: But it's six on *this* side.

Juan: But that's the three way.

Franco brings his new 6 × 3 rectangle to the display.

Teacher: What will happen if you put it on top of this rectangle (the 3 × 6)? Why don't you try it?

Juan: It's the same. But if I turn it . . .

Teacher: Does it make a difference if you turn it?

Juan: No, but that's the three way and this is the six way.

This discussion illustrates a common mathematical issue: When are mathematical objects mathematically equivalent and in what ways? For example, we agree that 3 × 5 = 5 × 3. However, a game played with three teams of five people will not be the same as a game played with five teams of three people. A triangle and a rectangle are the same in that they are both closed straight-sided shapes; they are both polygons. However, they are quite distinct in other respects. What is the "same" depends on what attributes we consider. Through discussions like these, students develop experience with making these kinds of distinctions. The 3 × 6 and 6 × 3 arrays are congruent; they are the same size and shape. But they can be different if we consider position and orientation. Henry and Juan are thinking about this distinction.

Discussing Symmetry

With the class gathered in the meeting area, the teacher introduces symmetry by building her own design with pattern blocks. She builds a symmetrical design that has one line of symmetry. She continues to place blocks one by one until there are eight blocks in her design. In the discussion that follows, students share their knowledge of symmetry and use their own language to describe it.

Teacher: What do you notice about this design? Amaya?

Amaya: It's symmetrical.

Teacher: Say more about that.

Amaya: It's the same on both sides. If you cut it, it's the same on both sides.

Amaya points out where the two trapezoids meet and draws an imaginary vertical line of symmetry with her finger.

Paige: If you add a green triangle and a blue block to each side, then it's the same this way too.

Paige shows how to place two more rhombuses and two more triangles so that the design has a horizontal line of symmetry, as well as a vertical line.

Jeffery: I know another way too. You can trade the two red trapezoids for a hexagon. Like this.

He draws an imaginary vertical line down the middle of the hexagon with his finger.

Teacher: Jeffery's saying that if I put these blocks here [replaces the trapezoids with a hexagon], it still looks the same on both sides, but you'd have to cut the block.

The teacher then goes back to the original design.

Teacher: Let's look at this design. What else can you say about symmetry?

Leigh: It's symmetrical with each side like a mirror.

Chen: First you put a trapezoid down, then another trapezoid, and then the hexagons. If you just put a bunch of shapes down, it wouldn't work. You have to plan it.

Monisha: If the two sides were twins and this was the middle [points to the line of symmetry], the twins could look through and see themselves.

Teacher: Those are good ways to explain it; ways I hadn't thought of.

In this discussion, the teacher builds on the students' own language to describe symmetry and symmetrical designs. This brief discussion also provides her with an initial assessment of what her students are bringing to this next set of activities.

Student Math Handbook

The *Student Math Handbook* pages related to this unit are pictured on the following pages. This book is designed to be used flexibly: as a resource for students doing classwork, as a book students can take home for reference while doing homework and playing math games with their families, and as a reference for families to better understand the work their children are doing in class.

When students take the *Student Math Handbook* home, they and their families can discuss these pages together to reinforce or enhance students' understanding of the mathematical concepts and games in this unit.

Addition Combinations

One of your goals in math class this year is to practice and review all the addition combinations up to 10 + 10.

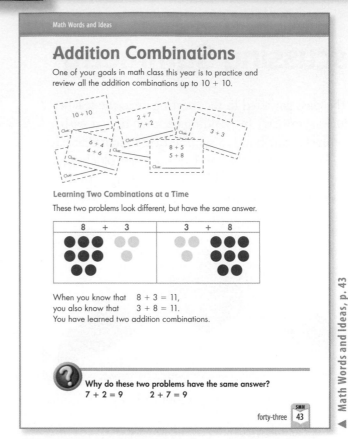

Learning Two Combinations at a Time

These two problems look different, but have the same answer.

8 + 3	3 + 8

When you know that   8 + 3 = 11,
you also know that   3 + 8 = 11.
You have learned two addition combinations.

? Why do these two problems have the same answer?
7 + 2 = 9   2 + 7 = 9

forty-three   **SMH 43**

▲ Math Words and Ideas, p. 43

Doubles

Any number plus itself is a double.
Here are the doubles from 1 to 10.

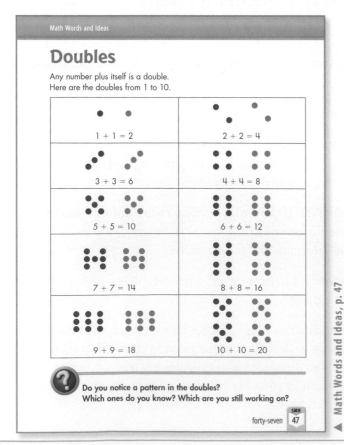

1 + 1 = 2	2 + 2 = 4
3 + 3 = 6	4 + 4 = 8
5 + 5 = 10	6 + 6 = 12
7 + 7 = 14	8 + 8 = 16
9 + 9 = 18	10 + 10 = 20

? Do you notice a pattern in the doubles?
Which ones do you know? Which are you still working on?

forty-seven   **SMH 47**

▲ Math Words and Ideas, p. 47

Geometry

Geometry is the study of shapes.

There are shapes everywhere. We can find shapes in our classroom, at home, on the street, and in the world around us.

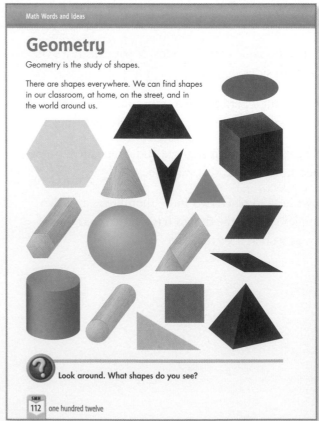

? Look around. What shapes do you see?

SMH 112   one hundred twelve

▲ Math Words and Ideas, p. 112

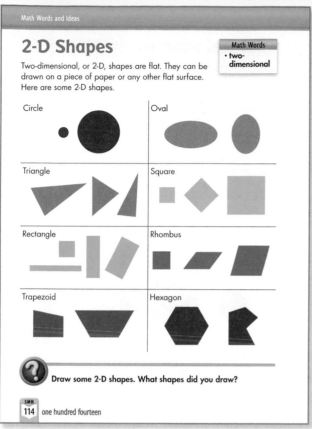

Math Words and Ideas

2-D Shapes

Math Words
• two-dimensional

Two-dimensional, or 2-D, shapes are flat. They can be drawn on a piece of paper or any other flat surface. Here are some 2-D shapes.

Circle	Oval
Triangle	Square
Rectangle	Rhombus
Trapezoid	Hexagon

? Draw some 2-D shapes. What shapes did you draw?

SMH 114 one hundred fourteen

◀ Math Words and Ideas, p. 114

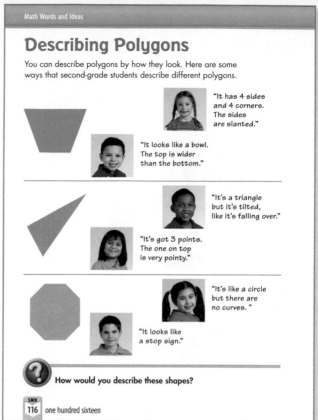

Math Words and Ideas

Describing Polygons

You can describe polygons by how they look. Here are some ways that second-grade students describe different polygons.

"It has 4 sides and 4 corners. The sides are slanted."

"It looks like a bowl. The top is wider than the bottom."

"It's a triangle but it's tilted, like it's falling over."

"It's got 3 points. The one on top is very pointy."

"It's like a circle but there are no curves."

"It looks like a stop sign."

? How would you describe these shapes?

SMH 116 one hundred sixteen

◀ Math Words and Ideas, p. 116

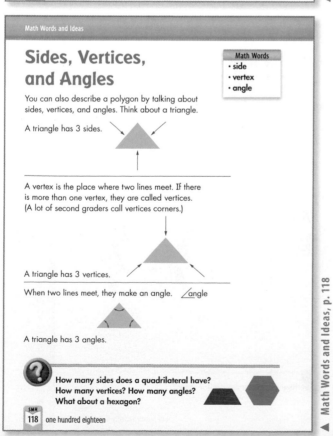

Math Words and Ideas

Sides, Vertices, and Angles

Math Words
• side
• vertex
• angle

You can also describe a polygon by talking about sides, vertices, and angles. Think about a triangle.

A triangle has 3 sides.

A vertex is the place where two lines meet. If there is more than one vertex, they are called vertices. (A lot of second graders call vertices corners.)

A triangle has 3 vertices.

When two lines meet, they make an angle. ∠angle

A triangle has 3 angles.

? How many sides does a quadrilateral have? How many vertices? How many angles? What about a hexagon?

SMH 118 one hundred eighteen

◀ Math Words and Ideas, p. 118

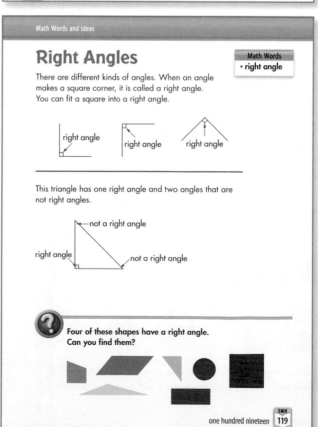

Math Words and Ideas

Right Angles

Math Words
• right angle

There are different kinds of angles. When an angle makes a square corner, it is called a right angle. You can fit a square into a right angle.

right angle   right angle   right angle

This triangle has one right angle and two angles that are not right angles.

not a right angle

right angle   not a right angle

? Four of these shapes have a right angle. Can you find them?

one hundred nineteen **SMH 119**

◀ Math Words and Ideas, p. 119

Quadrilaterals

Math Words
• quadrilateral

A quadrilateral is a polygon that has 4 sides.

There are quadrilaterals in the world all around you. Do you see anything shaped like a quadrilateral near you right now?

These shapes are quadrilaterals.

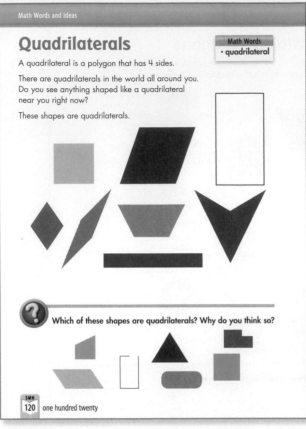

? Which of these shapes are quadrilaterals? Why do you think so?

120 one hundred twenty

▲ Math Words and Ideas, p. 120

Rectangles and Squares

Math Words
• rectangle
• square

A rectangle is a special kind of quadrilateral. Rectangles have 4 sides and 4 right angles. Here are some rectangles.

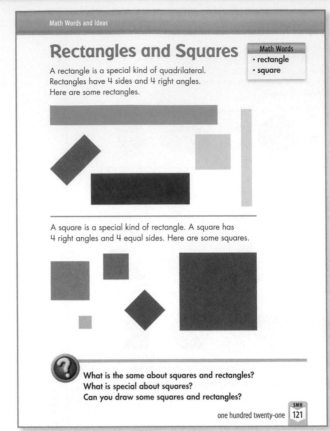

A square is a special kind of rectangle. A square has 4 right angles and 4 equal sides. Here are some squares.

? What is the same about squares and rectangles?
What is special about squares?
Can you draw some squares and rectangles?

one hundred twenty-one **121**

▲ Math Words and Ideas, p. 121

3-D Shapes

Math Words
• three-dimensional

Three-dimensional, or 3-D, shapes are solid objects. If they are small, you can pick them up and hold them. Here are some 3-D shapes.

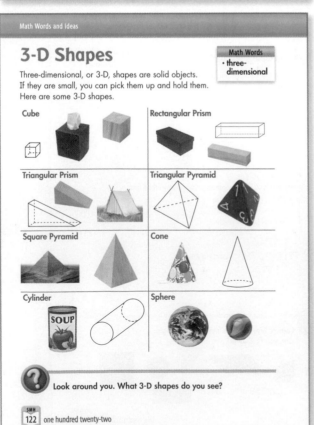

Cube | Rectangular Prism
Triangular Prism | Triangular Pyramid
Square Pyramid | Cone
Cylinder | Sphere

? Look around you. What 3-D shapes do you see?

122 one hundred twenty-two

▲ Math Words and Ideas, p. 122

Drawing 3-D Shapes

It is hard to draw 3-D shapes on paper.

Here are some examples of how to draw 3-D shapes.

Here are some second-grade drawings of 3-D shapes.

? How would you draw a 3-D shape?

one hundred twenty-three **123**

▲ Math Words and Ideas, p. 123

Describing 3-D Shapes

(page 1 of 2)

You can describe a 3-D shape by how it looks.
Here are some ways to describe 3-D shapes.

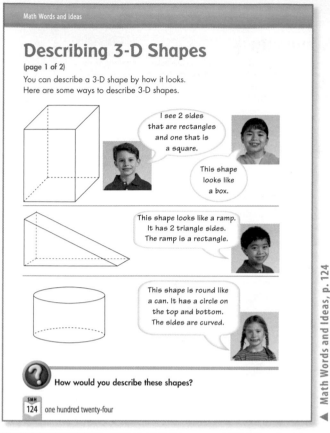

I see 2 sides that are rectangles and one that is a square.

This shape looks like a box.

This shape looks like a ramp. It has 2 triangle sides. The ramp is a rectangle.

This shape is round like a can. It has a circle on the top and bottom. The sides are curved.

How would you describe these shapes?

SMH
124   one hundred twenty-four

▲ Math Words and Ideas, p. 124

Describing 3-D Shapes

Math Words
- faces
- edges
- vertices

(page 2 of 2)

3-D shapes have faces, edges, and vertices or corners. Think about a cube.

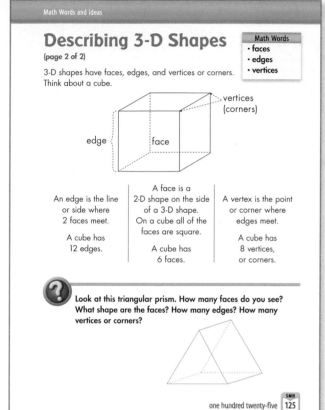

vertices (corners)

edge

face

An edge is the line or side where 2 faces meet. A cube has 12 edges.	A face is a 2-D shape on the side of a 3-D shape. On a cube all of the faces are square. A cube has 6 faces.	A vertex is the point or corner where edges meet. A cube has 8 vertices, or corners.

Look at this triangular prism. How many faces do you see? What shape are the faces? How many edges? How many vertices or corners?

one hundred twenty-five   SMH 125

▲ Math Words and Ideas, p. 125

Rectangular Arrays

Math Words
- array
- row
- column

Rectangular arrays are arrangements of objects that are in equal rows and equal columns. Here are some arrays you may see in the world around you.

The same number of objects can form different arrays. Here are 16 oranges arranged in different ways.

column

row

How many rows are in these arrays? How many columns? Can you find another way to arrange 16 oranges in an array?

SMH
126   one hundred twenty-six

▲ Math Words and Ideas, p. 126

Area of Rectangles

Math Words
- area

One way to measure and compare the size of different rectangles is to see how many square tiles it takes to cover them. The number of tiles used to cover a rectangle is called the area.

It takes 6 tiles to cover this rectangle. It has an area of 6 square tiles.

6 square tiles

Rectangles that look different can have the same area. For example, both of these rectangles have an area of 12 tiles.

This rectangle has 3 rows and 4 columns.

This rectangle has 2 rows and 6 columns.

What is the area of each rectangle? Which has the biggest area? The smallest?

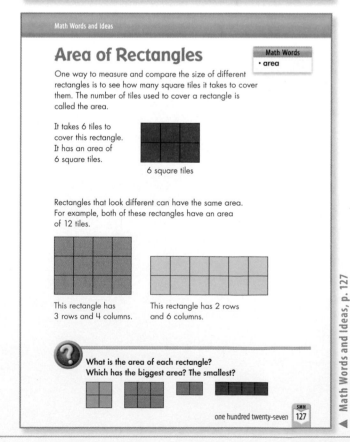

one hundred twenty-seven   SMH 127

▲ Math Words and Ideas, p. 127

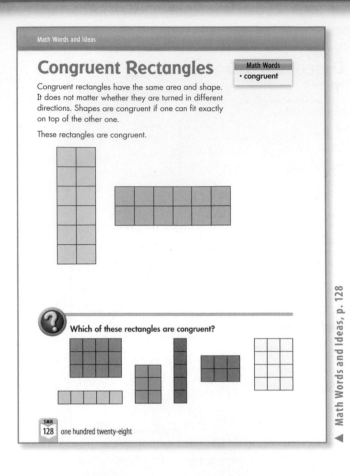

Math Words and Ideas

Congruent Rectangles

Math Words
• congruent

Congruent rectangles have the same area and shape. It does not matter whether they are turned in different directions. Shapes are congruent if one can fit exactly on top of the other one.

These rectangles are congruent.

? Which of these rectangles are congruent?

▲ Math Words and Ideas, p. 128

SMH
128 one hundred twenty-eight

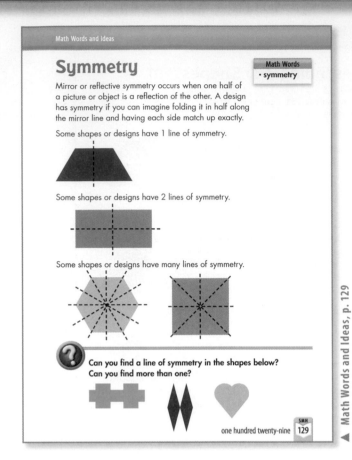

Math Words and Ideas

Symmetry

Math Words
• symmetry

Mirror or reflective symmetry occurs when one half of a picture or object is a reflection of the other. A design has symmetry if you can imagine folding it in half along the mirror line and having each side match up exactly.

Some shapes or designs have 1 line of symmetry.

Some shapes or designs have 2 lines of symmetry.

Some shapes or designs have many lines of symmetry.

? Can you find a line of symmetry in the shapes below? Can you find more than one?

one hundred twenty-nine SMH
129

▲ Math Words and Ideas, p. 129

Index

IN THIS UNIT